The Red Flag

First published in 2009 in Great Britain by Allen Lane
an imprint of the Penguin Group, London

Published simultaneously in Canada
Printed in the United States of America

ISBN-13: 978-0-8021-1924-7

Grove Press
an imprint of Grove/Atlantic, Inc.
841 Broadway
New York, NY 10003
Distributed by Publishers Group West
www.groveatlantic.com

09 10 11 12   10 9 8 7 6 5 4 3 2 1

In memory of my mother

Contents

List of Illustrations

Photographic acknowledgements are given in parentheses.

1. Eugene Delacroix, *July 28: Liberty Leading the People*, 1830, Musée du Louvre, Paris (copyright © akg-images/Erich Lessing)
2. Cartoon from the 1898 German elections, from *Der Wahre Jacob*, 7 June 1898 (copyright © akg-images/Coll. Archiv f.Kunst & Geschichte)
3. Vladimir Lenin speaks at the opening of a monument to Marx and Engels, 7 November 1918 (copyright © RIA Novosti/TopFoto)
4. A still from Sergei Eisenstein's *October* (Ronald Grant Archive, London)
5. Russian civil war poster, 1919 (Musée d'Histoire Contemporaine, Paris)
6. Starvation in the Ukraine, 1921 (copyright © Mary Evans Picture Library/Rue des Archives)
7. 'A Spectre Haunts Europe, the Spectre of Communism'; lithograph published by Mospoligraf, 1917–24 (The Hoover Institution Archives, Stanford University RU/SU 524)
8. D. S. Moor, *Death to World Imperialism*, 1919 (private collection)
9. Vladimir Tatlin, model of the Monument to the Third International, 1920, Museum of Modern Art (MoMA), New York (PA76. Digital image copyright © 2009 The Museum of Modern Art, New York/ Scala, Florence)
10. Ho Chi Minh speaking at the opening session of the Socialist Congress in France, 25 December 1920 (copyright © Mary Evans Picture Library/Rue des Archives)
11. Poster of the International Red Aid, 1930s (copyright © Mary Evans Picture Library/Rue des Archives)

Acknowledgements

Writing global history is a challenge, but I have benefited from the enormous amount of exciting new scholarship published in the last twenty years, much of it based on newly available archival sources. I am also extemely grateful to a number of friends and colleagues who have given me advice and helped me avoid errors. Tom Buchanan, Martin Conway, Mary McAuley, Rory Macleod, Rana Mitter, Mark Pittaway and Stephen Whitefield all read substantial parts of the manuscript; Steve Smith was especially generous with his time and read nearly all of it. Ron Suny has shown me unpublished work on Stalin, Steve Heder shared material on the Khmer Rouge and Laurence Whitehead gave me advice on Cuba. The Cambridge History of the Cold War project, led by Mel Leffler and Arne Westad, was an ideal group in which to discuss the international role of Communism.

The fellows of St Edmund Hall and the History Faculty of Oxford University have provided me with a stimulating and congenial working environment and granted me periods of study leave to work on the book. I am also grateful to the British Academy and the Chinese Academy of Social Sciences (both in Shanghai and the Institute of Marxism-Leninism and Mao Zedong Thought in Beijing) for arranging a fruitful study trip to China; to Shio Yun Kan for his brilliant Chinese-language teaching; and to the archivists and librarians at the Russian State Archive for Socio-Political History in Moscow, the Bodleian Library, Oxford, the British Library, and the Russian State Library in Moscow.

Gill Coleridge was an ideal agent, and played a major role in the project from the very beginning; I am very grateful to her for her encouragement and advice. I have also been very fortunate in my publishers. Simon Winder at Penguin was an extremely incisive and impressively knowledgeable editor. Morgan Entrekin at Grove Atlantic was also very supportive, as was Stuart Proffitt at Penguin, and both gave me invaluable comments on the text. I would also like to thank Jofie Ferrari-Adler and Amy Hundley at Grove Atlantic. Thomass Rathnow at Siedler, and Alice Dawson, Richard Duguid and Mari Yamazaki at Penguin. Charlotte Ridings was an extremely effective and patient copy-editor and Amanda Russell's extensive knowledge of the visual sources was a great help with the illustrations.

My greatest thanks go to Maria Misra, who made an enormous contribution to the book. Her knowledge of Asian and African history helped me to range far more widely than I otherwise would have done, and she read the whole manuscript, saving the reader from a good deal of clumsy prose.

NOTE ON TRANSLATION

Russian transliteration accords with the Library of Congress system (while suppressing soft and hard signs) except for a few well-known proper names (such as 'Trotsky' and 'Yeltsin'); similarly, Chinese transliteration generally follows the pinyin system, except for a few well-known names (such as 'Chiang Kaishek').

Introduction

1789–1889–1989

I

In November 1989 the Berlin Wall – the concrete and graffiti-daubed symbol of division between the Communist East and the capitalist West – was breached; joyful demonstrators from both sides danced and clambered on the wreckage of Europe's ideological wars. Earlier that year Communism had been dealt another blow by popular protests (though on that occasion brutally suppressed) in Beijing's Tiananmen Square. And so, exactly a century after the ascendancy of organized international Communism was marked by the foundation of the 'Second International' of Communist parties, and two hundred years after the Parisian populace had stormed another symbol of authoritarian order – the Bastille – revolution had again erupted in the world's capitals. These new revolutions, however, were aimed not at toppling the bastions of traditional wealth and aristocratic privilege, but at destroying states supposedly dedicated to the cause of the poor and oppressed. The dramatic, and largely unpredicted, fall of Communism in 1989 was, then, much more than the collapse of an empire: it was the end of a two-century-long epoch, in which first European and then world politics was powerfully affected by a visionary conception of modern society, in which the wretched of the earth would create a society founded on harmony and equality.

For many, Communism could now be consigned to Trotsky's 'rubbish-heap of history' – a hopeless detour into a cul-de-sac, an awful mistake. The American academic Francis Fukuyama's claim that 'history', or the struggle between ideological systems, had 'ended' with the victory of liberal capitalism was greeted with much scepticism, but deep down, many believed it.[1] Liberalism, not class struggle, was the only way to resolve social conflict, and capitalism was the only economic system that worked. And for some time, the world seemed to lose interest in Communism. It seemed to be a fading set of sadly fossilized attitudes surviving amongst a generation that would soon be crushed by the forces of 'reform'. It was a phenomenon best left to dry scholarship, an ancient civilization akin perhaps to the Ancient Persians, with its own Ozymandian wreckage reminding us of past delusions. In the mid-1980s, when I began to research Communism, at the height of Cold War tensions, it seemed an exciting subject, but within a decade it seemed irrelevant in a new world of triumphant liberal capitalism.

However, two events in this decade have brought Communism back to the foreground of public attention. The first – the destruction of New York's twin towers on 11 September 2001 – had no direct connection with Communism at all. Indeed, the Islamist terrorists responsible were militantly anti-Marxist. Nevertheless, the Islamists, like the Communists, were a group of angry radicals who believed they were fighting against 'Western imperialism', and parallels were soon being drawn, by politicians, journalists and historians. Though the term 'Islamofascism' was more commonly used than 'Islamocommunism', Islamism has been widely depicted as the latest manifestation of 'totalitarianism' – a violent, anti-liberal and fanatical family of ideologies that includes both fascism and Communism. For American neo-conservatives, these threats demanded an ideological and military struggle every bit as determined as the one Ronald Reagan waged against Communism in the Third World.[2] In 2004 the European Parliament's centre-right parties sought to condemn Communism as a movement on a par with fascism, whilst in June 2007 President George W. Bush dedicated a memorial to the victims of Communism in Washington DC.

If the 11 September attacks showed that the post-1989 political order had not resolved serious conflicts in the Middle East, the fall of the American bank Lehman Brothers on 15 September 2008 and the financial crisis it triggered demonstrated that the post-1989 economic order had failed to create stable, sustainable and enduring prosperity. The lessons drawn from these latter events, however, have differed from those learnt after 2001. Whilst nobody is calling for the return of the rigid Soviet economic model, Marx's critique of the inequality and instability brought by unfettered global capital has seemed prescient; sales of *Capital*, his masterwork, have soared in his German homeland.

The history of Communism therefore seems to be more relevant to today's concerns than it was in the early 1990s. However, we have found it difficult to grasp the nature of Communism – much more so than other aspects of our recent history; whilst many warned of the Nazis' aggression and their persecution of the Jews, very few predicted the Bolshevik Revolution, Stalin's Terror, Khrushchev's 'de-Stalinization', the Cultural Revolution, Pol Pot's 'killing fields', or the collapse of the USSR. In part, the obsessive secrecy of Communist regimes accounts for this, but more important has been the enormous gap between the out-look of historians and commentators today, and Communist views of the world at the time. Explaining Communism demands that we en-ter a very different mental world – that of Lenin, Stalin, Mao, Ho Chi Minh, Che Guevara and Gorbachev, as well as those who supported or tolerated them.

II

This book is the product of many years of thinking about Commun-ism. I had my first glimpse of the Communist world in the summer of that Orwellian year, 1984. I was then a nineteen-year-old student and had taken the cheapest route to Russia – a Russian-language course run by sovietophile 'friendship societies' throughout Europe, in a dingy Moscow institute for civil engineers. I knew little about either Russia or Communism, but they seemed to me, as to many people in that era, to be the most important issue of the time. That year was, in retrospect, an unusually turbulent one. I was visiting the capital of Reagan's 'evil empire' at the height of what is now known as the 'second Cold War', as relations between East and West deteriorated after the brief détente of the 1970s. Debate was raging over NATO's decision to deploy cruise missiles in Western Europe, and the previous autumn West Germany experienced its largest demonstrations of the post-World War II era. I went to Russia, at least in part, so that I could answer for myself some of the questions that obsessed Western opin-ion at the time: what was Communism, and what was the Soviet leadership trying to do? Was the USSR really an evil empire run by Leninist fanatics who, having broken their own people, were now intent on imposing their repressive system on the West? Or was it a regime which, regardless of its many shortcomings, enjoyed genuine popular support?

I arrived in the sinister gloom of Moscow's Sheremetyevo airport burdened with teenage intellectual as well as physical baggage – an ill-thought-out jumble of preconceptions and prejudices. Though I was sceptical of Reagan's rhetoric, I was also apprehensive of finding the grim and fearful dystopia of Orwell's *Nineteen Eighty-Four* or John le Carré's spy novels. From childhood I had been aware of the moral objections to nuclear weapons; my mother had joined the Aldermaston marches in the early 1960s. But at the same time I found the triumphalist demonstrations of military hardware in Red Square, shown proudly on Soviet TV, frightening enough to justify a defensive response.

My sojourn in Moscow merely increased my confusion. Orwell had, in some ways, been right. I did encounter fear. Some of the Russians I met smuggled me into their apartments, terrified lest their neighbours hear my foreign accent; the atmosphere in Moscow was drab – under Gorbachev these years were to be dubbed the 'period of stagnation'. I also encountered cynicism about the regime, and criticisms of its hypocrisy and corruption. Nevertheless in many ways Russia could not have been more different to the world portrayed by Orwell. Everyday life for most people was relatively relaxed, if devoid of creature comforts. I also sensed a genuine nationalist pride in Russia's strength and achievements under Communism, and a real emotional commitment to world peace and global harmony.

My first visit to Moscow answered few of the questions that bothered me, and on my return to Britain I read all that I could find about Russia and Communism. A few years later, it seemed that I would have a real chance of understanding this enigmatic society. I was a graduate student at Moscow State University for the year 1987–8, studying (in secret) that most mysterious event of Soviet history, Stalin's Terror fifty years before, with a room high up in Stalin's massive 'wedding-cake' skyscraper on the Lenin Hills. I lived at the ideological centre of a curious Communist civilization: my neighbours had come from all corners of the Communist world – from Cuba to Afghanistan, from East Germany to Mozambique, from Ethiopia to North Korea – to take degrees in science or history, but also to study 'Scientific Communism' and 'Atheism', the better to propagate Communist ideology back home. Moreover this was an extraordinary period in Russian history.

Gorbachev's *glasnost'* (openness), whilst still limited, was encouraging debate and the expression of a wide range of opinions. If there was a time to discover the attitudes that underlay Communism, at least in its mature phase, this seemed to be it. The system was unravelling and revealing its secrets, but it was still Communist.

Again, what I saw left me confused. Russians' reactions to the idealistic Gorbachev and his reforming policy of *perestroika* ('restructuring') were myriad. Some of my Russian friends believed that Communism was fundamentally flawed and they could hardly wait to join the capitalist world. Yet I found others far from ready to hold a wake for an alien ideology, but optimistic that Russia had finally found a path to a reformed 'Communism' and a better and more just society. Communism, some seemed to believe, was a positive, moral force which, though sadly corrupted by bureaucrats, could yet be reformed and harmonized in some obscure way with liberal democracy. It seemed that a version of the Communist ideal had established real roots in Russian life.

Now traditional Communism is all but dead. Mao Zedong still gazes serenely over Tian'anmen Square, but the Chinese Communist Party has jettisoned most of its Marxist principles, and Vietnam and Laos have followed its example. Yet the sudden demise of Communism merely added to the mystery. Which impression of Communism was the right one? Was it the nationalism I saw in 1984, the socialist idealism of 1987, or just the conservative authoritarianism of an ageing generation, manifest in the dwindling band of pensioners we see demonstrating in Moscow on the anniversary of the October Revolution?

III

A great deal has been written about Communism, addressing these and other questions, but efforts to understand it have sometimes been hindered by the highly politicized nature of the literature and the large number of contradictory interpretations this has yielded. At root, though, the various approaches may be reduced to three powerful, competing narratives.

The first – derived from Marx's writings – became the official credo of all Communist regimes: in one country after another, the story went, heroic workers and peasants, led by visionary Marxist thinkers, overthrew an evil and exploitative bourgeoisie, and embarked on the path to 'Communism'. Communism itself was an earthly paradise where humankind would not merely luxuriate in material plenty, but would also live in the most perfect democracy, harmonious, self-regulating and with no man subordinate to another. It was also a rational system, and would come about as the result of the laws of historical development. This story, the centrepiece of Marxist-Leninist ideology, remained inscribed in the dogma of all Communist states right up to their sudden demise. As late as 1961, for instance, the Soviet leader Nikita Khrushchev predicted that the Soviet Union would reach the promised land of 'Communism' by 1980.[3]

Since the beginning of the Cold War, few outside the Communist bloc or Communist parties have been convinced by this story, and Western commentators have preferred, in its stead, one of two alternatives. The first, most popular amongst the centre-left, might be dubbed the 'modernization' story, in which the Communists were not so much heroic liberators as rational, technically minded modernizers, committed to developing their poor and backward countries. Though undoubtedly and regrettably violent in their early stages (as was inevitable given the resistance they faced and the enormous economic and social changes that they proposed), they swiftly abjured extreme repression. Indeed, Khrushchev's foreswearing of terror following Stalin's death proved that Communism could reform. And in the 1960s and 1970s some even talked of the gradual 'convergence' between the now modernized Communist East and the Social Democratic West around a common set of values based on welfare states and state-regulated markets.[4]

The second account might, perhaps, be called the 'repression' narrative, and is popular amongst harsher critics of Communism.[5] For them, Communism was a dark horror story of extreme violence, followed by continuing repression, inflicted by an unrepresentative minority on a cowed majority. Within the 'repression' story there was some disagreement over the nature of the Communist minority. For some, they were essentially non-ideological political bosses who sought to recreate a version of the conservative bureaucracies and tyrannies of old under the guise of 'modern' Communism. Stalin's butchering of his opponents in the party, is seen, therefore, not so much as the work of a Marxist ideologue as that of a new tsar.[6] A version of this account became especially popular on the anti-Stalinist left. It was most fully developed by

Trotsky in his famous denunciation of Stalinism, *The Revolution Betrayed*, and was most successfully popularized in Orwell's fable *Animal Farm*.[7] For others more hostile to socialism, however, the Communists were not reincarnations of the strongmen of the past, but were genuinely driven by Marxist-Leninist ideology.[8] They were imposing an unnatural order on their populations, seeking to indoctrinate 'new socialist men and women' and establish totalitarian control. Violent repression of anybody who refused to submit was the inevitable result of this utopianism.[9]

The modernization account is justly unfashionable, and many today stress the role of ideology. Some Communist parties did genuinely seek to develop their countries and, at times, attracted significant support. But few won an electoral majority, and Communist regimes often desired the total transformation and control of their societies; they could also resort to extreme violence to further their ends. However, ideology does not explain everything. It is clear that many Communists were not the cool-headed technocrats of the modernization story: the archives show that some lived and breathed Marxist-Leninist ideology, and many of their more disastrous policies were driven by a real commitment to it, not by pragmatic calculation. But, as will be seen, Marx's ideas could be used to justify a number of widely divergent programmes, and Communists adapted Marxism to the specific conditions and cultures of their own societies. Also, we need to understand the specific contexts in which Communism emerged. War, sharp international competition and the emergence of modern nation states were especially important. We therefore require an approach that understands both the power of utopian ideas and the violent and stratified world in which the Communists lived.

Paradoxically, perhaps, the most helpful inspiration for new insights into Communism lies not in the contemporary but in the ancient world, and in the drama of fifth-century BCE Athens. Greek tragedies dramatized a set of fundamental transitions in human society – from a hierarchical order of fathers and sons, to an egalitarian community of brothers; from an aristocratic polity of kingly warriors, to a more 'democratic' one, in which all male citizens took part in politics and fought as equals in people's armies; and from a fragmented society of clans and feuds, to one more integrated and governed by law.[10]

Aeschylus' *Prometheus* trilogy offers an especially striking dramatization of this journey from paternal to fraternal politics, and also from 'backwardness' to knowledge. According to Greek mythology, Prometheus, one of the old 'Titan' gods, stole fire from Zeus and the newly powerful 'Olympian' gods, as a gift to mankind. In so doing, he brought knowledge and progress to humanity, but at the cost of angering Zeus, who was intent on keeping men in their place and preserving the old order. Prometheus is harshly punished for breaching the hierarchy to help mankind: he is shackled to a rock in the Caucasus mountains where daily an eagle feasts on his ever-regenerating liver. In *Prometheus Bound*, the first and only surviving part of Aeschylus' trilogy, four characters dominate the play: Power and Force, the servants of the tyrannical father-god, Zeus; Hermes, the messenger (and god of communication, merchants, tricksters and thieves); and Prometheus (literally 'Foresight'), who is both a rational thinker and an angry rebel. Prometheus is presented sympathetically, transformed by Zeus' intransigence and Hermes' cowardice from a humanitarian into a furious rebel. He is determined to resist Zeus, even at the cost of unleashing terrible violence:

> So let fire's sharp tendril be hurled
> At me. Let thunder agitate
> The heavens, and spasms
> Of wild winds. Let blasts shake
> The earth to its very roots . . .
> Me will he in no way kill.[11]

Prometheus and Zeus are still confronting each other as the play ends, although in the final part of the trilogy (which does not survive) Aeschylus probably showed his disapproval of Prometheus' anger. It is likely that Prometheus made his peace with Zeus, and that both admitted their extreme behaviour.

In *Prometheus Bound*, then, we have a brilliant dramatization of the seemingly insoluble tensions between hierarchy and tradition on the one hand, and equality and modernity on the other. The play recognizes the appeal, and the dangers, of the Promethean message, especially to intellectuals in a repressive, archaic world; for whilst Prometheus does desire to help mankind, when opposed his anger can also 'shake the earth to its very roots'.

The Communists can be seen as the heirs of Prometheus, but there were several elements to his legacy. 'Communism' literally means a political system in which men live cooperatively and hold property in common, and it was originally a broad and diverse movement. Some Communists placed most value on Prometheus' commitment to liberation. Coming from a more 'Romantic' Marxist tradition, they were more interested in human authenticity and creativity than in taking political power and building modern states. However, this outlook became increasingly marginal to the Communist tradition; it was Prometheus' hostility to inequality and his commitment to modernity that came to characterize the mainstream of the Communist movement.[12] But there was one aspect of Prometheus' legacy Aeschylus did not explore: his anger at those ordinary men and women who rejected the 'fire' of knowledge and Enlightenment. Communists could be as angry at – and violent towards – the 'backward' peasants and religious believers who rejected their vision as they were towards lords and merchants.

It is not surprising that it is Aeschylus' heroic but angry Prometheus who should have emerged as a key symbol of emancipation amongst the poet-critics of Europe's monarchies – from Goethe to Shelley. But it was Karl Marx who embraced the Promethean metaphor most fully. For Marx, Prometheus was 'the most eminent saint and martyr in the philosophical calendar'. He quoted his hero in the preface to his dissertation: 'In sooth all gods I hate. I shall never exchange my fetters for slavish servility. 'Tis better to be chained to a rock than bound to the service of Zeus.'[13] Marx went on to forge from Prometheus' belief in reason, freedom and love of rebellion a powerful new synthesis that would be both 'scientific' and revolutionary.

Marx's Prometheanism appealed to many critics of inequality, but it was especially compelling to the opponents of *ancien régimes* such as that of tsarist Russia. This paternalistic order presided over not only economic, but also political and legal inequalities, granting privileges to aristocratic elites and discriminating against the lower orders. It was also ideologically conservative and suspicious of modern ideas. By the nineteenth century it was increasingly evident that such stratified societies had created weak, divided states, which struggled to maintain their status in a world dominated by more unified powers. So, for some of the Tsar's educated critics, the Promethean synthesis of liberation, modernity and equality promised to solve all problems at once: it would bring equality in the household, overcoming the patriarchal subjugation of women and the young; it would achieve social equality within the nation state, creating citizens in place of lords and servants; and it would level international hierarchies as the revivified regimes developed sufficiently to hold their own abroad. At the same time, it would bring the latest discoveries of science to mankind and fortify the nation.

Russian conditions, and especially political repression, also helped to create the institution that would further the Promethean project: the conspiratorial vanguard party. Designed to seize power and forge 'new socialist men and women', the party's culture encouraged the more repressive and violent elements of the old Prometheanism. The Bolshevik party's quasi-religious desire to transform its members, and its Manichean division of the world into friends and enemies, combined with conditions of war to create a politics very different from that envisaged by Karl Marx.

It was this project, and the means of achieving it, that was to become so appealing over the course of the twentieth century, especially in the colonized and semi-colonized world, for it promised an end to the humiliating subjugation brought by European imperialism, whilst modernizing divided, agrarian societies. Revolution alone, many Communists believed, could destroy the imperialists and their local collaborators who were holding their nations back; planned economies would then propel them into modernity, finally giving them dignity on the world stage.

Once Communists were in power, Romantic ambitions were rapidly overshadowed by technocracy and revolutionary fervour, though in practice even these proved difficult to reconcile, and Communists tended to stress one or the other. 'Modernist' Marxism was an ideology of technocratic economic development – of the educated expert, the central plan and discipline. It offered a vision that appealed to the scores of technicians and bureaucrats educated by the new institutes and universities. 'Radical' Marxism, in contrast, was a Marxism of the mobilized masses, of rapid 'leaps forward' to modernity, of revolutionary enthusiasm, mass-meeting 'democracy' and a rough-and-ready equality. It could also be a Marxism of extreme violence – of struggles against 'enemies', whether the capitalists, the so-called 'kulaks' (rich peasants), the intellectuals, or the party 'bureaucrats'. Radical Marxism came into its own during war or fears of war, and suited a military style of socialism, similar to the workers' militias of the Russian revolutionary period, or the partisans and guerrillas of the post-war world.[14]

Each form of Marxism had its particular advantages and disadvantages for Communists. Radical Marxism could call forth deeds of self-sacrifice, inspiring heroic feats of productivity in the absence of the market and money incentives. However, by encouraging persecution of 'class enemies', it could bring division, chaos and violence. It encouraged the persecution of the educated and expert, and its militant commitment to 'Enlightenment' alienated the religious and the traditional, particularly in the countryside. Modernist Marxism, in contrast, established the stability necessary to embark on 'rational' and 'planned' economic modernization. But it could also be uninspiring and, more worryingly for an ostensibly revolutionary regime, it created rigid bureaucracies ruled by experts.

Both of these approaches to politics had little purchase in the societies they sought to transform, and it was difficult to sustain them for long periods of time. Communists therefore soon began to seek compromises with broader society.[15] Some became more pragmatic, seeking to combine central planning with the market, abjuring violence and embracing greater liberalism. This kind of Marxism became dominant in Western Europe in the later nineteenth century and, from the 1960s, was increasingly influential in Soviet-controlled Central and Eastern Europe. Others adopted a more 'humane', Romantic socialism. Still other Marxists, however, particularly in poor agrarian societies, took a very different course and inadvertently adapted Communism to the old patriarchal cultures of the past, whilst using versions of nationalism to mobilize the population. This form of Communism, developed by Stalin from the mid-1930s, began to resemble in some ways the hierarchical states the Communists had once rebelled against. As Cold War tensions lessened, the system became less military in style and more concerned with social welfare, but its paternalism and repressiveness remained. It was this system that Gorbachev sought to reform, and ultimately destroyed.

IV

This book follows the history of Communism in its four main phases, as the centre of its influence shifted from the West to the East and the South: from France to Germany and Russia, thence further East to China and South-East Asia after World War II, and then to the global 'South' – Latin America, Africa, the Middle East and South and Central

Asia in the 1960s and 1970s. It finally returns to Europe to trace the story of *perestroika* and Communism's collapse.

The book concentrates on the ideas, attitudes and behaviour of the Communists themselves, although it also explores the experience of those over whom they ruled. I have organized it broadly chronologically, but not strictly so, as chapters are also devoted to specific regions. I have also devoted more attention to some parties and regimes than others – partly because their influence varied, and partly because I have tried to achieve a balance between breadth of coverage and depth. The book starts with the French Revolution, for it is here that we can identify, for the first time, the main elements of Communist politics, though they were yet to be successfully combined. It was, however, Karl Marx and his friend Friedrich Engels who showed the true power of a form of socialism that melded rebellion with reason and modernity. They also tore socialism from its nationalist, Jacobin moorings and, one hundred years after the French Revolution, announced its global ambitions with the foundation of the Second International of Marxist parties. And whilst its inaugural congress was in Paris, the real capital of Communism had moved to Berlin, the home of the International's largest member – the German Social Democratic Party.

The second phase of Communism's history – the Soviet age – began in 1917. Once the self-proclaimed 'Third Rome' of Christianity, Moscow was now to be the 'First Rome' of the new Communist world. But despite its universalist pretensions, Soviet Communism acquired an increasingly nationalistic, 'patriotic' complexion, and was yoked to a project of state-building and economic development – features that made it attractive to colonized peoples as Western empires crumbled. It was in this period that the totalitarian objectives of Soviet Communism – the ambition for the total transformation of individuals and societies – became so dominant, even if that goal was by no means achieved.

In its third phase Communism, now firmly allied with nationalism, spread outside Europe as European and Japanese empires collapsed in the years following World War II, and the United States tried to ensure that pro-Western elites took their place. Meanwhile, within Europe, Communism ossified into Stalin's imperial order. Radical Communists throughout the world soon rebelled against both Stalinism and the West. The Trotskyists were the first, but after the War new Communist capitals began to rival Moscow – Mao's Beijing and Castro's Havana – and proselytized alternative rural Communisms in Asia, Latin America and Africa in the 1960s and 1970s. But by the mid-1970s guerrilla rebellion was being eclipsed by a much more urban, Stalinist Communism, especially in Africa.

Meanwhile, it was becoming clear that Communism was entering its final phase, as it lost ground to other forms of radicalism: the new militant liberalism of Ronald Reagan and Margaret Thatcher, and political Islam. By the mid-1980s, the Kremlin was forced to respond, and Gorbachev sought to bring a renewed energy to Communism. It was these efforts to revive popular enthusiasm for Communism in the Soviet Union that were to lead to the system's final dissolution.

Communism tended to follow cycles, through periods of radical revolutionary 'advance', followed by 'retreat' – whether towards technocratic Modernism, a more patriarchal Communism, or a pragmatic accommodation with liberalism. The revolutionary impulse renewed itself for various reasons, but the non-Communist world played its part. Capitalism, unrestrained, frequently discredited itself, as financial crises led to economic suffering, most spectacularly following the Wall Street Crash of 1929. As important, though, were sharp international inequalities. The widespread attraction of the extreme right contributed to Germany's and Japan's bloody attempts to create new empires of ethnic privilege; and the Western powers' desire to maintain empire in the developing world, before and after World War II, fuelled nationalistic anger in the Third World. Communism also seemed to be a recipe for rapid economic development, narrowing the gap between the poor South and the rich West. Domestically, too, social tensions – especially in the countryside – created fertile ground for revolutionary parties.

Communism in its old form has been discredited, and will not return as a powerful movement. But now that globalized capitalism is in crisis, this is an ideal time to revisit Communists' efforts to create an alternative system, and the reasons why they failed. And to understand the origins of Communism, we need to start with Communism's stirrings amidst the first Promethean challenge to the rule of Zeus of the modern era – the French Revolution.

Prologue

Classical Crucible

I

In August 1793, the beginning of the most radical period of the French Revolution, Jacques-Louis David, the artist and propagandist for the new regime, designed one of the many political festivals staged throughout France. The Festival of the Unity and Indivisibility of the Republic celebrated the first anniversary of the end of the monarchy, and David erected five allegorical scenes to represent the various stages of the revolution so far, the most notable of which was the fourth. A huge figure of the Greek hero Hercules bestrode a model mountain in Paris's Place des Invalides, holding in his left hand the fasces – the bundle of rods that symbolized power and unity. In his right hand he wielded a club, with which he beat the Hydra, shown as a creature with a woman's head and serpent's tail. The scene was intended to illustrate the alliance of the militant French people with the radical 'Mountain' faction of the Jacobins and their spokesman Maximilien Robespierre.[1]

Aeschylus had seen Hercules as the protector of the oppressed, and David's interpretation was not dissimilar. When he proposed the construction of a permanent 46-foot-tall statue of Hercules after the festival, he described him as a figure 'of force and simplicity', an embodiment of the French people whose 'liberating energy' would destroy the 'double tyranny of kings and priests'.[2] His virtues, lest anybody be in doubt, would be quite literally carved into his body: 'force' and 'courage' along his arms, 'work' on his hands, and 'nature' and 'truth' across his chest. He represented, therefore, a very particular section of the French people: the people who laboured with their hands. These were the *sans-culottes* – the radical city-dwelling artisans 'without breeches' who were not afraid to use violence in pursuit of their ends. The editor of the journal *Révolutions de Paris* certainly saw David's statue in this light: 'We will see the people standing, carrying the liberty that it conquered and a club to defend its conquest. No doubt, amongst the models entered in the competition, we will prefer the one which best projects the character of a *sans-culotte* with its figure of the people.'[3] However, Hercules was not merely a figure of popular strength, but also of reason, as the inscription of the word 'light' across his brow showed. David had created a symbol merging the *sans-culotte* with the man of reason and Enlightenment, which embodied a powerful new view of politics.[4] No longer was it sufficient merely to strike down tyrants and disperse their power, as liberals argued. The state had to be of a fundamentally new type, at once radical, energetic and intelligent, capable not only of integrating ordinary people but also of mobilizing them against the state's enemies.

It is to David's Hercules and its underlying intellectual inspiration – the quasi-classical Spartan vision of the Jacobins – that we must look for the sources of modern Communist politics. Of course, Communism as an idea had much earlier origins. The inhabitants of Plato's ideal 'Republic' held property in common, and the early Church provided a model for fraternity and the sharing of wealth. This Christian tradition, combined with traditional peasant communities' cultivation of 'common land', was the foundation for the Communist experiments and utopias of the early modern period – whether the 'Utopia' of sixteenth-century English thinker Thomas More, or the community established by the 'Digger' Gerrard Winstanley on common land in Cobham, Surrey, during the English Civil War in 1649–50.

But all of these projects were founded on the desire to return to an agrarian 'golden age' of economic equality, whereas future Communists also claimed they were creating modern states based on principles of political equality.[5] And it is under the Jacobins that we can see this second, political ambition. The Jacobins did not redistribute property, nor did they oppose the market; indeed they persecuted those who did. Nor did they advocate 'class struggle'. But they did argue, like later Communists, that only a united band of fraternal citizens, free of privilege, hierarchy and division, could create a strong nation that was dignified and effective in the wider world. Jacobinism was, then, in some respects the prelude to the modern Communist drama, and it is in the Jacobin crucible that many of the elemental tendencies of Communist politics and behaviour appeared in rough, unalloyed form. It is also no accident that the first revolutionary Communist of the modern era – François-Noël (Gracchus) Babeuf – emerged from the ranks of the Jacobins.

The Jacobin approach to politics achieved some successes, for a time. The French, after years of defeats, actually began to win wars, and it seemed as if they had finally overcome the debilitating weaknesses of the Bourbon *Ancien Régime*. And yet there were tensions within the new type of politics, tensions that would become all too familiar in future Communist regimes. The revolutionary elite, seeking to build and consolidate an effective state, often found that their relations with the more radical masses were less confraternal than confrontational. Meanwhile, the Jacobins themselves split, between those for whom Hercules' 'courage', or emotional revolt, was paramount, and those who emphasized order, reason and 'light'. Ultimately these conflicts were to destroy the Jacobins, amidst much violence and turmoil.

II

With the end of the *Ancien Régime* in 1789, a social order founded on legally entrenched and inherited hierarchy collapsed. The estates system was abolished, and with it the notion that men were born into particular and tiered stations of society ordained by God. No longer were the first two estates – the clergy and the aristocracy – to be privileged over the rest of society – the 'third estate'. All men were declared to be legally equal, 'citizens' of a single, coherent 'nation' rather than members of separate estates, corporations and guilds. In part, these demands for legal equality arose from third-estate anger at the superciliousness of the aristocracy; ordinary people also resented having to pay taxes from which their 'superiors' were exempt. But the attack on the estates system was also a much more profound critique of French society. Royal power and social distinctions, it was commonly argued, had weakened France and rendered it feeble (even effete) against its enemies – and especially against its great rival Britain.[6] 'Despotism' and 'feudalism' not only created divisions between people but also engendered a servile and unmanly character. As Abbé Charles Chaisneau explained in 1792, the French had been naturally virtuous, but 'despotism ruined everything with its impure breath; this monster infected the truest feelings at the source'.[7] It was no wonder that the French had become impotent.

All the revolutionaries had initially agreed that they had to create a wholly new culture, and efforts were made to remove all traces of the

Ancien Régime from everyday life; indeed nothing less than a 'new man' was required, free of the habits of the past. As one revolutionary declared:

> A revolution is never made by halves; it must either be total or it will abort. All the revolutions which history has conserved for memory as well as those that have been attempted in our time have failed because people wanted to square new laws with old customs and rule new institutions with old men.[8]

At the centre of the new culture were political equality and 'reason', or the break with tradition. Old distinctions of dress became unfashionable, and costume became much plainer. Those keen to advertise their revolutionary sympathies wore cockades and red liberty bonnets, modelled on the Ancient Greek Phrygian cap, which was worn by freed slaves as a symbol of liberty. Meanwhile, the traditional was replaced with the 'rational'. Names of the days and months of the year were 'rationalized': a ten-day 'decade' took the place of a seven-day week, and the ten new months were to describe the changing natural world; the spring months, for instance, became 'Germinal' (from 'germination'), Floréal ('flowering') and Prairial ('pasture'). New rituals, such as David's Festival of the Unity and Indivisibility of the Republic, were designed to create a set of rites for the new citizens, replacing the old Christian traditions.

However, differences soon emerged between the revolutionaries over the content of the new culture, and two distinct visions can be discerned. The first, which prevailed for the first two years of the revolution, was fundamentally a liberal capitalist one.[9] *Ancien Régime* privileges, as well as traditional protections from the market granted to artisans and peasants, were all swept away in favour of individual property rights and free commerce. But the second vision proffered a much more politically collectivist idea of society, one which looked back to an austere classical republicanism for inspiration. It was this worldview that was to be the foundation of the radical Jacobins' ideology.

A vivid insight into this classical vision is to be found again in the work of David, this time his extraordinarily popular painting *The Oath of the Horatii*, completed in 1784. The picture showed three Roman heroes swearing an oath to their father before a battle: they would die, if necessary, for their fatherland; meanwhile the women of the family sit by, anxious but powerless. The episode, a tragic scene from the Roman historian Livy via the French dramatist Corneille, was intended to celebrate the triumph of patriotism over personal and familial attachments. Horatius and his two brothers had been chosen to fight for Rome against three warriors from the neighbouring town, Alba Longa. All except Horatius are killed, and when his sister grieves for one of the slain enemy, to whom she had been betrothed, Horatius, enraged, kills her. His crime is then pardoned by the senate. This was a drama in praise of masculine, military virtues, and David's austere neo-classical style was designed to reinforce the tough and high-minded message. His images of 'heroism' and 'civic virtues', he hoped, would 'electrify the soul' and 'cause to germinate in it all the passions of glory, of devotion to the welfare of the fatherland'.[10] And his wish was granted: a German observer wrote: 'At parties, at coffee-houses, and in the streets . . . nothing else is spoken of but David and the *Oath of the Horatii*. No affair of state of ancient Rome, no papal election of recent Rome ever stirred feelings more strongly.'[11]

The *Oath of the Horatii* was merely giving graphic form to a set of ideas already well-established, largely thanks to the intellectual who most influenced the revolutionary generation, Jean-Jacques Rousseau. At the root of Rousseau's philosophy was a critique of inequality. He condemned the old aristocratic patriarchy and the servility it bred, but he did not approve of the liberal alternative either – the high road, he believed, to greed, materialism, envy and unhappiness. For Rousseau, the ideal society was either a benign paternalism, or a fraternity: a citizenry of brothers modelled on the classical, self-sacrificing heroes portrayed by David so vividly. Heroism then, once exclusively an aristocratic quality, was to be democratized; a republic had to have 'heroes for citizens'.[12]

Rousseau described his ideal community in his work *The Social Contract* of 1762: it would combine the merits of his native puritanical Geneva and ancient Sparta. Sparta appealed to Rousseau because at one point in its history it had been a city-state in which everybody had seemed to submerge selfish desires to communal goals and lived an austere life of heroic endeavour. In Rousseau's utopia, the people as a whole would meet regularly in assemblies; abjuring individualism, they would act according to the 'General Will', a will that outlawed all inequality and privilege.[13] This would also be a society in which every citizen owed military service, for Rousseau's ideal was, at root, a quasi-military order – not because he was interested in expansionary wars, but because he saw armies as the ideal fusion of public service and self-sacrifice.[14]

However, Rousseau's ambitions went far beyond the remodelling of the political order: he urged that all spheres of human relationships be transformed, social, personal and cultural. The discipline of traditional, patriarchal family life had to yield to a benign paternalism. His most popular work, *Julie, or the New Héloïse*, told the story of an aristocratic young woman who falls in love with her bourgeois tutor, Saint-Preux, much to the horror of her harsh and status-obsessed father. Rather than abandon family ties and follow her immature passions, she embarks on the creation of a new, non-despotic community. She marries a wise father-figure, Wolmar, and they both live in a chaste *ménage à trois* with Saint-Preux and their servants, on a model estate. Wolmar is shown as a moral guide and educator, who persuades his 'children' – his wife and servants – to do what is right.[15]

Rousseau's vision of the state bears some resemblance to later Marxist ideals. However, there was one major difference. Rousseau, unlike most Communists, hated modernity, complexity and industry. Virtue, he believed, was more likely to flourish in small-scale, agrarian societies.

Even so, French revolutionaries believed that Rousseau's Spartan ideal had a great deal to teach a large, modern state like France, because it showed how its unity and strength could be restored. As Guillaume-Joseph Saige, one of Rousseau's disciples enthused, writing in 1770:

> The constitution of Sparta seems to me the *chef d'oeuvre* of the human spirit ... The reason why our modern institutions are eternally bad is that they are based on principles totally opposed to those of Lycurgus [Sparta's ancient legislator], that they are an aggregate of discordant interests and particular associations opposed to one another, and that it would be necessary to destroy them in their entirety in order to recover that simplicity which creates the force and duration of the social body.[16]

Rousseau's cult of Sparta and classical heroism appealed to many during the revolutionary period, but it was especially popular amongst those radicals who were particularly sensitive to the plight of the poor. No enemy of property, nonetheless he still maintained, unlike most of his contemporary *philosophes*, that virtue – 'the sublime science of simple souls' – was more likely to be found amongst the poor than the rich.[17] One of those radicals was a young lawyer from Arras, Maximilien Robespierre, the strongest critic of the liberal vision. In his *Dedication to Rousseau*, written in 1788–9, he declared: 'Divine man, you have taught me to know myself. As a young man you showed me how to appreciate the dignity of my nature and to reflect on the great principles of the social order.'[18] It was Robespierre and the Jacobins who transformed Rousseau's Romantic ideas of moral regeneration and small-scale communities into a political project for transforming the state.

Robespierre was elected to the Estates General in 1789, and soon became a member of the revolutionary Jacobin Club. From the very beginning he was on the radical wing of the Jacobins – the 'Mountain' group – more suspicious of the aristocracy and more sympathetic to the poor than the moderate majority. And as internal opposition to the revolution became stronger from late 1790, Robespierre became more radical, as did many other Jacobins. Fearful of conspiracies and attacks by royalists (both aristocrats within and their foreign allies) Robespierre and the Jacobins became increasingly obsessed with 'enemies' amongst the aristocracy and the bourgeoisie. Suspicious of the loyalty of the old aristocratic military officers, the republic had for some time recruited third-estate volunteers to fight alongside the regular army, explicitly following the model of classical citizen-armies. But the revolutionaries were now forced to look to a wider public – including the *sans-culottes*. As Robespierre explained, 'Internally the dangers come from the bourgeois. In order to convince the bourgeois, it is necessary to rally the people.'[19] It was, then, the needs of war that made a closer alliance with the poor a necessity. And in June 1793 a coup against the moderate Girondins mounted by the *sans-culottes* helped the more radical Robespierre and the Mountain faction into power.

III

In October 1793 a new play was performed in Paris, *The Last Judgement of Kings*, written by Sylvain Maréchal, a radical Jacobin intellectual and comrade of the proto-communist François-Noël Babeuf. Intended for a broad popular audience, the play combined spectacle with audience participation and clear, if not crude, political messages. The action takes place on a desert island, complete with erupting volcano. The players included the Pope and the kings of Europe, alongside a number of allegorical figures: a group of Rousseauian primitives, representing human contentment before the coming of evil civilization; an old French exile, standing for the dissidents of the past; and *sans-culottes* from all over Europe, the people of the future. The *sans-culottes* loudly list the crimes committed by the monarchs, whilst the monarchs themselves greedily squabble over bread. The old exile, the *sans-culottes* and the 'primitives' show how the new people, living simply, can work together. The play then loudly exhorts the audience to renounce monarchy for ever.[20]

In a rather crude way, the play encapsulated the Jacobins' outlook. The *sans-culottes* are moral; the 'enemies' are specifically monarchs (not the rich in general). However, *The Last Judgement of Kings* was in sharp contrast to other plays of the period, which adopted the restrained, classical style favoured by the Jacobins. This was burlesque, a garish pantomime. Whilst not written by a *sans-culotte*, it evoked their cultural world far more closely than the neo-classical festivals and plays of David and his lofty-minded colleagues. It suggested that Robespierre may have forged an alliance of sorts between the Jacobins and the *sans-culottes*, but it was a potentially fragile one.

The *sans-culottes* were not a 'working class' in the Marxist sense. Though most worked, or had worked, with their hands they were a mixed group, including some who were quite comfortably off alongside very poor artisans. The *sans-culottes*' politics was radical and collectivist, their loyalties attached to the 'people', an entity that excluded the rich. The main demands of their local councils (*sections*) focused on material matters, especially the state regulation of the economy. Food prices, they insisted, had to be controlled, so that everybody, including the poor, could survive. And though they did not want the end of property, they did want it to be more widely spread. Their vision of society was therefore a levelling one. Fundamentally, they were partisans of 'class struggle' *avant la lettre*. In their world, the rich and the speculators were just as much the 'vampires of the fatherland' as the aristocrats.

The *sans-culottes* did not develop a coherent political philosophy, but one of their most thoughtful sympathizers, François-Noël Babeuf, did. Babeuf had been a '*feudiste*', an agent who researched feudal archives and tried to maximize nobles' income by enforcing their ancient rights. He was ambitious, and even employed the latest bureaucratic methods, all the better to exploit the peasantry. However, he had become disillusioned even before the Revolution of 1789. He was moved by the plight of poorer peasants, victims of both feudal dues and intense competition from wealthier peasants, who benefited from a developing capitalism. As he explained later:

> I was a *feudiste* under the old regime, and that is the reason I was perhaps the most formidable scourge of feudalism in the new. In the dust of the seigneurial archives I uncovered the horrifying mysteries of the usurpation of the noble caste.[21]

He read what he could of the new Enlightenment literature, and looked back to the classical past, renaming himself 'Gracchus', after the brothers who, as Roman tribunes, redistributed land to the poor.

The revolution may have destroyed Babeuf's business, but it gave him the opportunity to put his ideals into practice. He helped to organize peasant resistance to taxes, and from 1791 he became committed to the 'agrarian law' – the land redistribution which the Gracchus brothers had introduced into ancient Rome. Babeuf joined the Jacobins and became a secretary to the Food Administration of the Paris Commune. The job entailed finding supplies to feed Paris, enforcing the Jacobins' price controls and punishing speculators. Babeuf saw his work in visionary terms, writing enthusiastically to his wife:

> This is exciting me to the point of madness. The *sans-culottes* want to be happy, and I don't think that it is impossible that within a year, if we carry out our measures aright and act with all the necessary prudence, we shall succeed in ensuring general happiness on earth.[22]

Although Babeuf was working for the Jacobins, his vision was closer to the levelling paradise of the *sans-culottes*. His utopia was a society in which everybody would be fed, and the immoral rich would be brought under strict control.

The fact that the Jacobins were employing people like Babeuf showed how radical Parisian politics had become. The army was particularly affected. Authority was democratized and the harsh discipline of the past was replaced by judgement by peers; meanwhile officers were appointed on the basis of ideological commitment rather than expertise.

The revolutionary general Charles Dumouriez argued that this was the best way to motivate the troops: 'a nation as spiritual as ours ought not and cannot be reduced to automatons, especially when liberty has just increased all its faculties'.[23] The War Ministry, under the control of the radical Jean-Baptiste Bouchotte, distributed *Le père Duchesne*, a newspaper published by the journalist Jacques Hébert, written in the voice of a crude, violent *sans-culotte*. Hundreds of thousands of soldiers read it or heard it read.

Conflict between the Jacobins and the *sans-culottes* seemed inevitable. Whilst the Robespierrists envisaged France as a classical city-state populated with high-minded, self-sacrificing citizens, the *sans-culottes* wanted a land of good-cheer, bawdy fun and violent class retribution. But the Jacobins needed the *sans-culottes* to fight for them, and so compromise was necessary. Various *sans-culotte* demands were conceded: price controls were imposed, and the death penalty for hoarders of grain introduced. Meanwhile 'revolutionary armies' of militant *sans-culottes* were sent to the countryside to seize food from recalcitrant peasants, thus supplying the towns. The new *levée en masse*, the universal military draft, which included all males, of whatever social background, also satisfied the *sans-culottes*' desire for equality.

However, whilst willing to make concessions, the Jacobins had no intention of being *led* by the untutored masses. Their goal was to mobilize and channel mass energies behind an increasingly centralized state. This was the meaning of the Festival of the Unity and Indivisibility of the Republic held in August 1793, when the figure of Hercules became the dominant allegorical figure. During the festival, pikes, the *sans-culottes*' weapon, were brought from every locality and bound together into a giant fasces. Ordinary people were to be players in the drama of politics, but the state was going to bind and discipline them. To this end, the Jacobins limited the powers of the Revolutionary Armies and constrained the powers of the *sans-culotte sections*.

The Jacobins were also intent on reducing the power of the *sans-culottes* because they were convinced that they needed people with expertise to help them win the war against their European enemies. Lazare Nicolas Carnot, a former engineer, reorganized the army along more professional lines. He protected aristocratic officers who had the right skills and brought back some of the old-style discipline of the *Ancien Régime* army. It was no longer enough that officers were

enthusiastic republicans; they had to be literate and have some knowledge of military science.

This technocratic approach was also applied to the economy. Carnot's ally, Claude-Antoine Prieur de la Côte-d'Or, was put in charge of
the Manufacture of Paris, a huge (for the time) collection of arms workshops built up by the state in an extraordinarily short space of time. By
the spring of 1794, about 5,000 workers were labouring in workshops
of 200–300 men, many of them housed in old monasteries or the houses
of expelled aristocrats, and they were producing most of France's munitions. They were organized by Prieur and a small group of engineers and
technicians – the 'techno-Jacobins' as they have been called.[24]

Even so, the Jacobins still tried to combine this technocratic approach
with popular enthusiasm, and there is some evidence it had an effect.
Soldiers were aware that they were fighting in an army that was much
more democratic than any other in Europe; as one song of the period
went:

> No coldness, no haughtiness,
> Good nature makes for happiness;
> Yes, without fraternity.
> There is no gaiety.
> Let us eat together in the mess.[25]

The Jacobins' mass army brought success abroad, at least for a time.
The French defeat of the Prussians at the Battle of Valmy in September
1792 had demonstrated the power of citizen armies and the disadvantages of the old aristocratic way of war. As Goethe, present at Valmy,
famously declared, 'From this place, and from this day forth begins a
new era in the history of the world, and you can all say that you were
present at its birth.'[26] By the end of 1793, the Jacobins' reforms had
strengthened the army further, and brought new victories. The regime
was now supplying an army of almost one million soldiers with food
and weapons, whilst inspiring its soldiers with its egalitarian principles.
Pierre Cohin, fighting in the Armée du Nord, sent letters back to his
family which were full of the Jacobins' messianic message of revolutionary internationalism:

The war which we are fighting is not a war between king and king or
nation and nation. It is a war of liberty against despotism. There can be

no doubt that we shall be victorious. A nation that is just and free is invincible.[27]

By May 1794 the French were no longer fighting a defensive war, but were spreading the revolution to their neighbours. Europe was riven by a new type of ideological struggle – an earlier, hotter version of the Cold War.

IV

Success abroad, however, was not matched by stability at home. In France itself the Jacobins found it much more difficult to reconcile revolutionary enthusiasm with discipline. The Revolutionary Armies, charged with collecting taxes and suppressing the Revolution's opponents in the provinces, were a particular source of disorder.[28] Collaborating with radical representatives of the National Convention they often used violence against the rich and the peasantry, and brought chaos to the regions. In many places the wealthy were arrested, their wealth confiscated and chateaux demolished, to the severe detriment of the local economy.

Robespierre and the Jacobins, anxious that the 'ultra' radicals were alienating vast swathes of the population, especially in the countryside, soon decided to restore order and rein in the sans-culottes. In December 1793 the governing Convention abolished the Revolutionary Armies, and established more centralized control over the regions. However, Robespierre also remained apprehensive that without the 'ultra' left, the revolution would lose momentum. He mistrusted the technocrat Carnot and his ally Danton, convinced that they were not real revolutionaries, but were planning to return to some form of the old order.

In March 1794, caught between the desire to keep the momentum of the revolution going, whilst saving it from the radicals and class division, Robespierre moved against both left and right. Both the ultra Hébert and the less radical Danton were arrested and guillotined. Having outlawed both ultras and moderates, Robespierre was left with an ever-shrinking base of support. In his efforts to continue the revolution without mass support, he turned to methods that had echoes in later Communist regimes: the persecution of those suspected of being 'counter-revolutionaries' and propaganda, or, in Jacobin language, 'Terror' and the promotion of virtue. As Robespierre famously put it:

> If the basis of popular government in peacetime is virtue, its basis in the time of revolution is both virtue and terror – virtue, without which terror is disastrous, and terror, without which virtue has no power ... Terror is merely justice, prompt, severe, and inflexible. It is therefore an emanation of virtue, and results from the application of democracy to the most pressing needs of the country.[29]

Robespierre energetically set about establishing his new reign of virtue. He set up a Commission for Public Instruction, designed to take control of all propaganda and moral education. As Claude Payan, the brother of its boss Joseph, said, the state had hitherto only centralized 'physical government, material government'; the task was now to centralize 'moral government'.[30] The Commission produced revolutionary songs, censored plays, and staged political festivals. It also promoted one of Robespierre's most ambitious projects: the founding of a new, non-Christian state religion – the 'Cult of the Supreme Being'.

Robespierre also spent a great deal of his time checking up on officials' ideological purity. Those with 'patriotic virtue' were promoted; 'enemies' – vaguely defined – removed and arrested. On 10 June the famous draconian law of 22 Prairial began what became known as the 'Great Terror'. Repression was now directed not only against actual conspirators, but anybody with 'counter-revolutionary' attitudes. The law created a new criminal category, one which was to be revived in the future: the 'enemy of the people'. Anybody who might threaten the Revolution – whether by conspiring with foreigners or behaving immorally – could be arrested, and the law had a marked effect on the use of political repression. From the beginning of the Terror in March 1794 to the law of 10 June, 1,251 people were guillotined on the orders of the Revolutionary Tribunal, whilst in the much shorter period between 10 June and Robespierre's fall on 27 July, 1,376 were killed.[31]

Robespierre saw this moralistic purging as a permanent method of rule. Other Jacobins, however, saw it as a wartime expedient, unnecessary now that the French armies were victorious. They were also becoming increasingly anxious about its arbitrariness, for Robespierre alone had the power to decide on the measure of virtue and vice. The deputies understandably became worried that they could be the next targets, and began to plot his removal. When Robespierre was finally arrested on the orders of the Convention on 9 Thermidor (27 July), he had little support. By abandoning the *sans-culotte* left, Robespierre had left himself vulnerable to the moderates in the National Convention. When Robespierre died, the victim of the guillotine, so too did the radical phase of the French Revolution. The subsequent 'Thermidorian' regime ended arrest on suspicion, and many of those formerly denounced as nobles and counter-revolutionaries were rehabilitated.

V

Looking at engravings of David's elaborate political festivals, one might be forgiven for assuming that he was the propagandist for a backward-looking, conservative regime. The classical style and static, allegorical scenes suggest a love of order and stability. But the events which David's festivals were celebrating were revolutionary: they involved heroism, social conflict and assaults on tradition. The contrast between David's images and the reality of the revolution shows how unprepared the Jacobins were for the politics they ultimately practised.[32] At first they had planned to transpose the unity and archaic simplicity of ancient Sparta to eighteenth-century France: David even designed a range of pseudo-classical costumes for the new revolutionary nation.[33] Instead they found themselves involved in war and class conflict, and in order to fight effectively, they sought to build a modern state, army and defence industry. In trying to reconcile their ideal of classical republicanism with the demands of modern warfare, they brought together many of the elements that were eventually to make up the Communist amalgam.

For a time, the very contradictions within the Jacobins' project were an advantage. They could use the language of classical virtue and morality to mobilize the *sans-culottes*, whilst employing technically efficient methods in the army and industry. Also, as a strategy for building a strong state and military, Jacobinism's combination of central authority and mass participation had its advantages. Indeed, it was under the Jacobins that revolutionary France recovered its military élan after a long decline. The Jacobins showed how effective equality could be in forging a modern nation in arms.

Ultimately, however, the Jacobins failed to deal with these conflicting forces. They could not reconcile the demands of the *sans-culottes* with the interests of the propertied, nor could they marry the rule of virtue (or ideological purity) with the power of the educated and expert. Confronted with these difficulties, the Jacobins split, and then split again and again, until Robespierre was left with a pitifully small network of the loyal and the trusted. His solution was the inculcation of 'virtue' combined with Terror.

As will be seen, the Communists of the future had to deal with similar contradictions: they often sought to satisfy or exploit a populist egalitarianism and anger towards the upper classes and an urban rage against the peasantry, whilst at the same time they sought unity and stability; and they tried to build effective modern, technologically sophisticated economies whilst also believing that emotional inspiration was the best way of mobilizing the masses. At times they, like Robespierre, tried to solve these contradictions by trying to impose strict discipline, or by imposing a reign of virtue with propaganda and violence against unbelievers. Yet the Communists had no qualms about destroying property rights, and so could, for a time, secure the support of the poor. They could also learn from the history of the revolutionary movement, and of the French Revolution itself. The Jacobins had nothing to look back to, except a classical past that was of dubious value.

Robespierre remained unloved for some time, spurned by the left as well as the right; it was only in the 1830s, as socialist ideas became more fashionable, that his rehabilitation began. But the ideas and forces he and the Jacobins had unleashed were enormously influential on the Communism of the future. For the next half-century, the example of the French Revolution and its failures loomed large over the left. And the events of 1793–4 exerted a particular pull over the imagination of one young radical, born in a Rhineland that had only recently been occupied by revolutionary France. For Karl Marx, the Jacobins had made serious mistakes, but the Jacobin era was still 'the lighthouse of all revolutionary epochs', a beacon that showed the way to the future.[34] Marx, like many other nineteenth-century socialists, was to construct his theory of revolution by learning the lessons of the Jacobins and their bloody history.

I

A German Prometheus

In 1831 Eugène Delacroix exhibited his extraordinary painting of the 1830 revolution, *July 28: Liberty Leading the People*. His representation of the first major uprising in Europe since 1789 has now become an iconic image of revolution; indeed it is often mistaken for an image of its more famous predecessor. This is understandable, as the painting, in some respects, showed the 1830 revolution – which toppled the restored post-Napoleonic Bourbon monarchy – as a reprise of 1789. The bare-breasted female figure of Liberty, wearing a Phrygian cap and holding a *tricolore* and a bayonet, is a semi-allegorical figure, echoing the classical heroes of the late eighteenth century. The painting was also designed to show the alliance of bourgeois and the poor that had existed in 1789: Liberty leads a rag-bag of revolutionaries, from the top-hatted young bourgeois intellectual to the bare-chested workman and a street child, clambering over the dead bodies of the revolutionary martyrs.

However, the painting also showed how views of revolution had changed since David's day. The workers and the poor figure more prominently than the bourgeois, and unsurprisingly, given the prevalent fear of the poor, hostile critics complained that lawyers, doctors and merchants had been omitted in favour of 'urchins and workers'. Moreover, the figure of Liberty was not entirely allegorical, but clearly a woman of the people; the *Journal des artistes* found her dirty, ugly and 'ignoble'.[1] In 1832 the painting was hidden from view for many years, for fear that it would incite disorder, only to re-emerge from the attics during the revolutions of 1848. For Delacroix, at the heart of revolution were not the bourgeoisie in togas but the workers in rags.

Delacroix's painting strikingly illustrates how far the imagination of revolution had moved from David's ordered and hieratic tableaux. Delacroix's Liberty may have included the odd classical feature, but his canvas exulted in its high Romanticism. There is a wildness and an elemental energy to the figures, far removed from David's classical restraint. However, Delacroix also inserted into his revolutionary ensemble a uniformed student from the École Polytechnique – the institution established by Carnot, Robespierre's 'techno-Jacobin' rival. The Romanticism of revolution was tempered, even if only mildly, by respect for science.

Delacroix, though, was only briefly enthused by the revolution of 1830. He was no political radical, and he soon became disillusioned. Indeed, many have seen in his famous painting a highly ambivalent attitude towards revolutionary violence: the figures closest to the viewer are corpses, and despite the title, it is not Liberty who leads the people but a pistol-brandishing child. Karl Marx, by contrast, did not oppose revolutionary violence, though like Delacroix he sought to apply the experience of 1789 to a newly powerful socialist politics. In the later 1830s and 1840s the German-born Marx was as obsessed with the legacy of 1789 as any French intellectual, and he even planned to write the revolution's history.[2] And like Delacroix, Marx was updating the revolutionary tradition, 'declassicizing' it and placing workers at the forefront of the *mise en scène*. The failure of the Jacobins, he insisted, arose precisely from their excessive admiration for the classical city-state. Their nostalgia for ancient Sparta and Rome had led them to oppose the *sans-culottes*. The *political* equality they espoused, giving all men full citizenship, was no longer enough; in a modern society true equality and harmony would be realized only with full *economic* equality, and without support from society, they had been forced to use violence.[3] Marx also made even greater efforts than Delacroix to temper his revolutionary Romanticism with an appreciation of science and economic modernity. The Jacobins, he argued, had exaggerated the power of morality and political will to transform society, underestimating the importance of economic forces.

It is in this remoulding of the French revolutionary tradition that Marx's originality lies. Marx was forging a new left-wing ideology fit for the new industrializing societies of the nineteenth century, with their belief in technological progress and their increasingly large industrial working classes. It was also suited to an era when social conflict –

between workers and employers supported by the state – was sharpening. Moreover, Marx sought to relocate the centre of socialism from the 'backward' France of the late eighteenth century to a new home – the new 'backward' nation, Germany.

II

After the guillotining of Robespierre in 1794, the gaols of France disgorged thousands of prisoners imprisoned by the revolutionary regime. Amongst them were three radical thinkers: François-Noël Babeuf, Comte Henri de Saint-Simon, and Charles Fourier. All three had been traumatized by the preceding Terror, and had tried to learn from it, though their conclusions about what had gone wrong and how to re-animate the radical tradition were very different. Babeuf condemned Robespierre for betraying the artisans and peasants of France, and became the leader of one of the first Communist movements. Saint-Simon, by contrast, was heir to the techno-Jacobins; for him it was Robespierre's neglect of the needs of production and modernity that was most culpable. Fourier differed from both in envisaging a future where the priority was neither equality nor productivity but creativity and pleasure. Each, then, founded a particular strain of socialism – egalitarian Communism, 'scientific' socialism and a more Romantic socialism – all three of which would be incorporated by Marx into a grand, if never wholly coherent, synthesis.

Babeuf's 'Communism' became more fully egalitarian during his second spell in prison after Robespierre's fall. He now developed a more radical condemnation of property than he had under the Jacobins.[4] He no longer thought that the agrarian law and the end of more obvious forms of inequality were enough; a radical form of 'absolute equality' had to be pursued. In the new society, money would no longer exist; everybody would send the products of their labour to the 'common storehouse', and then they would receive an equal proportion of the national product in exchange for their labour. Work would not be a chore because men would want to work out of patriotism and love of the community. In essence, his was an egalitarian version of the *sans-culotte* utopia of hard work and strict social justice, implemented by recourse to a super-efficient version of the Jacobin food supply administration.

On his release from prison in October 1795 he decided to take a revolutionary course. He helped to organize an 'Insurrectionary Committee of Public Safety', which issued a 'Manifesto of the Equals'. Babeuf and his comrades were planning an insurrection for May 1796, but the authorities discovered the conspiracy and he and several others were arrested and executed. Yet their strain of revolutionary politics and puritanical egalitarianism lived on. Filippo Buonarroti, who took part in the original conspiracy, wrote a history of the Equals in 1828, a time far more receptive to Babeuf's ideas than previous decades. Buonarroti ensured that Babeuf's broader ideas reached a wider public, and they became the core of what became known as 'Communism': communal ownership, egalitarianism and redistribution to the poor, and the use of militant, revolutionary tactics to seize power.

It was to this revolutionary egalitarian tradition that one of the best-known Communist figures of the 1840s belonged, the German itinerant tailor Wilhelm Weitling. Weitling was a highly accomplished autodidact, who taught himself Latin and Greek and was able to quote Aristotle and Homer, as well as the Bible – from which he extracted much of his social theory. Weitling arrived in Paris in 1835, and whilst there joined the League of Outlaws, a republican secret society which followed the teachings of Babeuf and Buonarroti but infused this Communism with a Christian apocalyptic vision. For Weitling, the ideal society, the outcome of a violent revolution, would be a return to the Christian community of goods. Like Babeuf, his principal concern was equality (though he was prepared to concede the odd luxury to those who did extra work). He did try to solve the problem of monotony, but his main proposal was that workers had to be taught to enjoy work by doing three years of compulsory service in a quasi-military industrial army. Weitling was probably the most influential socialist in Germany, and his ideas influenced a generation of German workers living in exile in London, Brussels, Paris and Geneva. The League of the Just, one of the largest of these German radicals' secret societies, adopted Weitling's ideas in its official manifesto in 1839, and members of the group took part in an insurrection in Paris in the same year, led by the conspiratorial, Jacobin-influenced August Blanqui.

However, not all Communists, including some within the League of the Just, were enthused by the hair-shirt socialism of the Babouvians and Weitling. Schapper, one of the leaders of the London branch of the

League, condemned Weitling's Communism as joyless and despotic: 'just like soldiers in a barracks ... In Weitling's system there is no freedom.'[5] But particularly hostile to this aspect of Communism were the Romantic, or 'utopian', socialists, and their most eccentric representative, Charles Fourier.

The term *'utopian* socialism' was used by Marx and Engels as a way of dismissing a large number of their rivals, and denigrating their ideas in comparison with their own *'scientific* socialism'. Despite this, it does describe one strain of socialism in the early nineteenth century.[6] Unlike the Communists, the utopians were generally not workers and initially did not have a close connection to working-class movements. They were also considerably less interested in seizing the central state. Instead, they focused their efforts on fashioning small, experimental communities, and presented a vision of the ideal society that was more appealing to many than the Spartan egalitarianism of the Babouvists. And rather than enforcing Weitling's Christian morality, they sought to challenge what they saw as the oppressive doctrine of original sin on which Christianity was founded. Mankind, they argued, was naturally altruistic and cooperative, and right-minded education would permit these qualities to predominate. They were particularly hostile to what they saw as the grim work ethic of the new industrial capitalism, which was so closely associated with Christian, and particularly Protestant, ideas of the time. The factory system and the division of labour transformed men into machines and life into joyless drudgery. Society had to be organized so that everybody in the community could be creative and develop their individuality. Their vision was therefore Romantic in spirit. Though unlike the Jacobins, whose Romanticism was one of the self-sacrificing heroism of the soldier, theirs extolled the self-expression and self-realization of the artist.

François Marie Charles Fourier was one of the principal theorists of this utopia of pleasure and creativity. Scarred by the experience of Jacobinism, he rejected all forms of violent revolution, and of economic equality. Instead he started from the notion that modern civilization, which suppressed the natural desire for pleasure, was responsible for human misery. In its stead he proposed new model communities – 'phalansteries' – in which social responsibility and passions would coexist.[7] Each of these communities would include 1,620 people. Work would be pleasurable and tasks would be allocated according to the character of each individual. People also needed variety, and the working day would be divided up into two-hour periods, in each of which workers would do something different. Fourier solved the problem of who would do the unpleasant work with the bizarrely original proposal that children – the 'Little Hordes' as he called them – who apparently enjoyed playing in dirt, would perform such tasks as cleaning latrines. He also mooted the idea that in the future a new type of animal would evolve, the 'anti-lion' and the 'anti-whale', who would befriend mankind and perform laborious work. Some of his suggestions may not have been seriously meant, but it is not surprising that the twentieth-century poet and critic André Breton should have regarded this dreamer as a forerunner of surrealism. However, in his desire to reconcile work with the self-fulfilment of mankind, and his hope that men could be made 'whole' by avoiding the narrowness imposed by the modern division of labour, Fourier represented the Romantic side of socialism, and had a significant influence on Marx and Engels.

A more influential socialist enemy of Babouvian Communism was Pierre Joseph Proudhon, a printer who outdid Weitling in his auto-didactic efforts, teaching himself not only Latin and Greek but also Hebrew. In 1840 he published *What is Property?*, which, with its powerful declaration 'property is theft', became the talk of the salons of France. However, Proudhon did not want to abolish private property – he merely wanted to spread it more evenly. Proudhon therefore objected to the Babouvian vision of an equal community, for the 'moral torture it inflicts on the conscience, the pious and stupid uniformity it enforces'.[8] For Proudhon, socialism had to allow people to control their own lives. He envisaged a form of industrial democracy, in which workers would no longer be slaves of their machines, but would manage their workplaces; his ideal was a highly decentralized society, a federation of workplaces and communities run by workers. Unsurprisingly, he came to be regarded as one of the main theorists of the anarchist movement.

Much closer to the Communist tradition was the socialism of Étienne Cabet, whose imagined utopia, 'Icaria', organized property in common and was governed by an elected government with complete control over the economy. His followers – who were numerous amongst French workers – were amongst the first to be called 'Communist'. But most typical of the Romantic utopian socialists was the British thinker Robert Owen, whose ideas were taken seriously by both radicals and more establishment figures, and whose plans for socialist communities were put into practice. The son of a businessman, he became a successful entrepreneur himself and bought a number of spinning mills on the Clyde in New Lanark. He found that the workforce was unreliable, and he set about motivating them by providing better conditions for workers and offering education for their children. But how could work and pleasure be reconciled? Owen's solution had much in common with Fourier's: people between the ages of fifteen and twenty would work, and with the help of children would be able to produce all that the community needed; those aged between twenty and twenty-five would supervise; and those aged between twenty-five and thirty would organize storage and distribution, but that would only take two hours of their day; the remaining time could be devoted to 'pleasure and gratification'.[9]

The utopian socialists, then, broadened the goals of Communism from mere equality to the achievement of human happiness. They also transferred the Romantic spirit from military heroism and patriotism to the new industrial age, by valuing man's creativity in work. But they had their own peculiar weaknesses: their plans often looked eccentric and absurd; their connections with workers were far more fragile than those of the Communists; and they seemed to be wishful thinkers – they had little to offer in terms of a strategy by which the ideal society might come to be realized. They merely exhorted the moral transformation of mankind which, whilst doubtless highly desirable, was hard to enact. At least the Babouvian Communists had a political programme founded on a proletarian revolutionary insurrection, which, given the worker unrest of the 1830s and 1840s, seemed plausible.

However, there was one weakness both the Babouvian and the utopian traditions shared: they rarely showed convincingly how Communism or socialism could solve the problem of economic security and productivity. It was liberal thinkers, the defenders of the market – amongst them Adam Smith and, later, Herbert Spencer – who seemed to have cornered the market in sound economic theory. But there was one variety of socialism that did address this criticism – Henri de Saint-Simon's 'scientific socialism'.

Count Claude Henri de Saint-Simon, born in 1760, was an aristocrat from an ancient ducal family but had originally welcomed the French Revolution. He fell foul of Robespierre, and was imprisoned, but his response to his persecution differed sharply from Fourier's and Babeuf's: he looked to science to rescue France. Saint-Simon was the prophet of the Plan. The goal of society was production, as 'the production of useful things is the only reasonable and positive aim that political societies can set themselves.'[10] Scientists, industrialists, or a combination of the two, therefore had to be in power. Democracy – the rule of the ignorant masses – was only dangerous and damaging, as the Jacobin experience had vividly illustrated. Indeed, ideally politics could be dispensed with altogether, in favour of rational decision-making.

Saint-Simon was condemned by Marx and Engels as a 'utopian socialist' because he was not 'scientific' enough for them, but this label is misleading. Saint-Simon was the heir of the anti-Romantic strain of Enlightenment thinking, and his ideas proved enormously appealing to later socialists who tried to reconcile equality with economic prosperity. And it was the combination of his ideas, together with those of Babouvian Communism and (to a lesser extent) Romantic 'utopian' socialism, that was to be the hallmark of the system created by Marx and Engels. Just as the left in the 1990s sought a 'third way' between visions of social justice and the 'rationality' of the global market, so too Marx and Engels tried to show how a much more radical social model, Communism, could be wedded to economic prosperity.

III

Karl Marx was born in 1818 in the Rhineland town of Trier. During the French occupation after the Revolution, Trier was governed according to the relatively liberal Napoleonic laws, which had benefited Marx's father, Heinrich, a respected lawyer and the son of the rabbi. However, the absorption of the town into the more hierarchical and conservative state of Prussia was a disaster for Heinrich; under Prussian law Jews were denied all positions in state service, unless they had a special dispensation. Heinrich was forced to convert to Protestantism, and was baptized in 1817, the year before his son Karl was born.

Marx, therefore, grew up in a region resting on a historical and political fault-line: between modern, revolutionary France, with its principles of equality of all citizens before the law, and *ancien régime* Prussia, founded on autocracy, hierarchy and aristocratic privilege. Unsurprisingly Marx, whose own family had briefly bathed in the rays of Enlightenment before being cast back into *ancien régime* darkness, was keenly interested in how the forces of history might be accelerated to bring 'progressive' politics to a 'backward' country. In his youth Marx, like the French revolutionary generation of the 1770s and 1780s, was obsessed with his country's backwardness. The German middle class, he complained, was weak and in thrall to the aristocracy, and, unlike its French counterpart, could not be relied on to challenge the old order.

The Rhineland in the early nineteenth century did not lie only on a political fault-line between French liberalism and German conservatism, but also on an intellectual one: between French Enlightenment and German Romanticism. Marx's father, according to Marx's daughter Eleanor, was a man of reason and the Enlightenment, 'a real Frenchman of the eighteenth century who knew his Voltaire and Rousseau by heart'.[11] Yet Marx also came under the influence of a rival mentor, Baron von Westphalen, father of his future wife, Jenny, who introduced him to the Romantic worldview. As Eleanor wrote, the baron 'filled Karl Marx with enthusiasm for the Romantic school, and whereas his father read Voltaire and Racine with him, the Baron read him Homer and Shakespeare – who remained his favourite authors all his life.'[12]

The tension between the Enlightenment devotion to reason, order and science, and a Romantic disdain for routine and passion for heroic struggle, was a fissure within Marx's own thinking. His personality certainly had more in common with the brilliant and extraordinary Romantic genius than the worldly and sociable Voltairean man of science. One of his father's letters to him at university captures the tension between the civilized, Enlightened father and the Romantic son:

> God help us! Disorderliness, stupefying dabbling in all the sciences . . . Unruly barbarism, running wild with unkempt hair in a learned dressing-gown . . . Shirking all social contacts, disregarding all conventions . . . your intercourse with the world limited to your sordid room, where perhaps lie strewn in classical disorder the love letters of a Jy [Jenny] and the well-meant, tear-stained exhortations of your father.[13]

As a student in Bonn in the mid-1830s, Marx attended courses on the philosophy of art, some delivered by the famous Romantic theorist August von Schlegel. He also planned to publish a work on Romanticism, and penned poetry infused with Romantic themes. Nevertheless, his worldview was far from the early Romanticism of Rousseau, with its elevated regard for virtue. Marx's was a high Romanticism, with the hero figured as the artist-as-rebel. In one poem, 'Human Life', he wrote of the dreary self-interestedness, or 'philistinism' as he often called it, of everyday life: 'Life is death / An eternal death; / Distress dominates / Human striving. / . . . / Greedy striving / And miserable goal / That is its life, / The play of breezes.'[14] Marx, however, was determined not to succumb to conventional life. He would rebel. As he explained in his poem 'Feelings':

> Never can I carry out in peace,
> What has seized my soul so intensely,
> Never remain comfortably quiet,
> And I storm without rest.[15]

And as has been seen, he identified with that great rebel of ancient myth – Prometheus, struggling against the tyrant Zeus.

Marx's sentiments did not change markedly as an adult. Intense, pugnacious and sensitive, he declared that his idea of happiness was 'to fight', and his idea of misery was 'submission'. He described his main characteristic as 'singleness of purpose', and this quality certainly put him at an advantage over his contemporaries. Although he was less original than many other socialist thinkers of the time, he was infinitely more energetic and painstaking in synthesizing ideas and forging them into a coherent whole, and he put this rigour at the service of rebellion rather than the forces of order.

Given Marx's self-image as a rebel, challenging authority to bring Enlightenment to humanity, it is not surprising that he became interested in radical ideas. Initially this radicalism emerged in debates on philosophy, when he was a member of the 'Young Hegelian' group of thinkers. Georg Hegel, the German philosopher, had developed a theory of world history by which history was seen as the unfolding story of the progress of mankind's spirit towards increasing freedom. The process was 'dialectical', that is, it moved forward through struggles between competing ideas and social systems, in which the clash between a principle ('thesis') and its opposite ('antithesis') resulted in 'synthesis', incorporating the positive aspects of both. Christianity, the Reformation, the French Revolution and modern constitutional monarchy were all syntheses, stages in the movement of humanity towards the ideal society. After Hegel's death,

Hegelians disagreed over what constituted that ideal society. The establishment saw it as the contemporary Prussian Protestant monarchy, arguing that the existing order represented the 'end of history'. The Young Hegelians, however, condemned the monarchy as reactionary and saw the ideal as a parliamentary system, which allowed freedom of the press and religion, though they decried the economic liberalism which, they argued, gave excessive power to private property.

On becoming editor of the Cologne-based liberal newspaper *Rhenische Zeitung* in 1842, Marx espoused these causes with energy. He showed a particular interest in social issues, protesting on behalf of peasants who were losing their old communal rights (to forest land) to individual ownership in the name of liberal ideas of private property. In 1843 the *Rhenische Zeitung* was closed down by the authorities, and this setback encouraged Marx to adopt an even more radical position. His hopes that a free press would be a force for reform now dashed, he argued instead that political change was not enough; a fundamental social and economic transformation was needed. Moreover he had also lost faith in the German middle classes, who had been cowardly in the face of the monarchy's assault on press liberties. Unlike the French bourgeoisie, which had led the French revolution of 1789 and had defended liberal freedoms in the 1830 revolution, the German bourgeoisie, he argued, was hopelessly backward.

Marx, along with several of his radical friends, decided to emigrate from a repressive Germany to the more open atmosphere of Paris, and it was here in 1843 and 1844 that he developed what was to be the core of his future ideas. Marx had always been interested in French socialism and in this period he increasingly fell under the influence of French socialist writers, their hostility to constitutional democracy becoming more evident in his own writings. Marx also became more aware of English intellectual currents through his life-long collaboration with Friedrich Engels. Engels, the son of a prosperous, Calvinist lace manufacturer from Barmen, Westphalia, had, like Marx, been a radical in his youth, dabbled in Romantic versification, and was a member of the Young Hegelians. But there were also significant differences between the two. Most marked was the contrast between their temperaments. Engels, more sociable and less combative than Marx, fitted well into conventional bourgeois society. He fenced and rode, enjoying music and the company of women, and drinking fine wines. Yet he was also well-organized and business-like, unlike the chaotic Marx, which was fortunate for Marx as Engels was able to bankroll his frequently impoverished friend. But most importantly, Engels brought an English perspective to Marx's thought. He had been sent by his father to work in the Manchester branch of the family firm, and it was here, in the city at the frontier of the modern economy, that Engels became aware of the nature and mechanisms of capitalism, and its socialist critics. Engels was close to the Owenite movement, and despite his later criticisms of its 'utopianism', he remained highly sympathetic to its goals. At this crucial time in the development of Marx's thought, therefore, Engels encouraged his interest in 'utopian' socialism, whilst also providing Marx with a more detailed, practical knowledge of how modern capitalism worked.[16]

In the next few years, on the basis of this fruitful partnership, the foundations of Marxism were built – in the *Paris Manuscripts* and a number of other works. It may seem strange, given later developments, that Marx's primary interest was freedom. But this was 'freedom' in a Rousseauian sense – the end of dependence on other people and material things.[17] In modern societies, Marx argued, man was losing his autonomy, his ability to express himself and the opportunities to develop his creative capabilities. In Marx's Hegelian philosophical language, man was being controlled by 'alienated' forces outside himself. Autocracies deprived the individual of freedom, but liberal democracy was no solution, because it merely allowed people to vote periodically for a government over which they then had little influence. Only when all citizens took part in running the state all the time – as had been the case in ancient Athens – would they end this political 'alienation'. The same was true in the economic sphere. Man was a naturally creative being who, collaborating with others, realized his full potential through labour, whilst also changing the world around him. But in modern, capitalist societies, men had become slaves to 'alien' forces, money, the market and the material things they themselves produced.[18] They worked not to express their creativity, but merely to eat, drink and acquire material things; they frequently worked for other people; they were cogs in a machine, forced to perform particular, narrow tasks, according to the modern division of labour; moreover, they were increasingly 'alienated' from other people, unable to establish true human relationships.

For Marx, the solution to this grim state of affairs was the abolition of the market and private property, that is, the establishment of 'Communism'. All men would govern the state directly, participating in government rather than electing parliamentary representatives. This, then, was not modern liberal democracy, which is based on the assumption that there will always be conflicts of interest between citizens. Marx's vision of Communism assumed that once class division was overcome, complete consensus could be achieved. Liberal rights and freedoms, which protect the minority against the majority, would be wholly unnecessary. This critique of liberalism was to become central to the ideologies of Communist regimes.

Under Communism, economic life would also be transformed: people would not work for money, the market would be abolished, work would become a creative activity, and people would express themselves through their labour. As Marx put it, 'our products would be like so many mirrors, each one reflecting our essence ... My work would be a free expression of my life, and therefore a free enjoyment of my life.'[19] And economic well-being would not suffer, because if men worked for enjoyment they would be much more energetic and enthusiastic than if they were downtrodden and exploited. The division of labour would end, and men would be 'whole'. In an extraordinarily utopian vision of Communist society, each person would be able to 'do one thing today and another tomorrow, to hunt in the morning, fish in the afternoon, rear cattle in the evening, criticize after dinner, without ever becoming hunter, fisherman, shepherd or critic.'[20]

In these early political writings, therefore, Marx's 'Communism' bore little resemblance to Babouvian equality, the 'crude Communism' which was merely 'universal envy setting itself up as a power'.[21] It was much closer to Fourier's vision, founded on a Romantic, fundamentally artistic view of life, which identified the philistinism and materialism of modern culture as the main evil. The German Romantic poet Heinrich Heine, with whom Marx spent a good deal of time in Paris, may have been an influence here. He strongly defended a 'sensualist' vision of a future society in which all could fulfil themselves, whatever their rank in society; his enemies were the socialist puritans, who would 'mercilessly smash the marble statues of beauty'.[22]

Yet Marx's Communism was also founded to some degree on his view of pre-capitalist societies, and a Rousseauian love of ancient 'wholeness'.[23] Marx explained that amongst primitive peoples there had been very little division of labour, except within the family; men produced for themselves or relatives, rather than employers or the market. Therefore they were not 'alienated' but had full control over their economic lives, in contrast to those who lived under capitalism, in which people were producing for a larger market. They also had power over their political lives, running their own affairs in small-scale communities.

However, crucially, Marx did not want his Communism to be 'backward'; he saw it as similar in some ways to pre-capitalist society, but operating at a higher level of economic development. Unlike most Communists and utopian socialists, he accepted that capitalism and markets had brought benefits which had to be built on, not destroyed. He praised the way in which capitalism had integrated the world and destroyed 'backward' institutions and old, primitive ways of life. Here we see the influence of Saint-Simon, an author whom Marx had admired as a youth, and of whom Engels wrote that almost all of the ideas of later socialists were contained in embryo in his theories. Marx, therefore, had little sympathy for the decentralized utopianism of a Proudhon or Owen. Indeed, in some places *The Communist Manifesto* might be taken for a paean of praise for capitalism and globalization, and even its progenitors, the bourgeoisie. The bourgeoisie of the *Manifesto* was a revolutionary class, in many ways to be admired. It had 'accomplished wonders far surpassing the Egyptian pyramids, Roman aqueducts, and Gothic cathedrals': by 'subject[ing] the countryside to the rule of towns', it had rescued 'a considerable part of the population from the idiocy of rural life'; by creating more 'massive and colossal productive forces than have all preceding generations together', and centralizing production in huge factories; it was forging nation states out of fragmented communities; and it was even replacing 'national seclusion' with 'universal interdependence of nations', a process which benefited the proletariat because, unlike the bourgeoisie, it had no fatherland.[24] Marx's Communism was therefore unmistakeably a modern society; it would follow capitalism but build upon it. It could not, he insisted, emerge in a backward country dominated by a feudal aristocracy and lacking a powerful industrial base and a large modern proletariat. A 'bourgeois revolution' against the feudal aristocracy, like the French Revolution, was therefore the essential precondition for the future proletarian revolution. Social development followed a series of stages, from feudalism, to capitalism, to socialism, and then on to Communism.

Yet, whilst Marx and Engels praised the bourgeoisie for shaping nation states and the global economic system, they also maintained that it could not control the dynamic world it had created. Indeed, the bourgeoisie was unwittingly fashioning the tools of its own destruction: using the Romantic, poetic language he loved so much, Marx described it as 'like the sorcerer, who is no longer able to control the powers of the nether world whom he has called up by his spells'.[25] Industrialization was destroying small-scale, artisanal production, and creating an enormous industrial working class, which would ultimately destroy the bourgeoisie. The bourgeoisie's nemesis would take the form of the new industrial proletariat. Proletarians, Marx insisted, would be much more collectivist and better organized than artisans, learning how to cooperate from their work together in large factories. They would also become increasingly dissatisfied, as the logic of capitalism inevitably led to their increasing exploitation. Competition between capitalists would force them to invest more and more in new labour-saving machinery, which would inevitably reduce their profits and compel them to exploit workers even more brutally. But it would also compel capitalists to produce too much for the market to absorb, leading to periodic economic crises, putting many small capitalists out of business, and concentrating ownership in ever fewer hands. The instability and irrationality of capitalism would thus prepare the ground for Communism: the workers, an increasingly revolutionary force, would be ready to seize control of a mechanized production process now ideally suited to rational management by central planning. The social and economic system, like a ripe fruit, would readily drop into the laps of the waiting workers. As the *Manifesto* declared, 'The proletariat will use its political supremacy to wrest, by degrees, all capital from the bourgeoisie, to centralize all instruments of production in the hands of the State, i.e. of the proletariat organized as the ruling class.' The state would improve the economy 'in accordance with a common plan', and all workers would be mobilized in 'industrial armies'.[26]

This image of society, then, was one of centralization and planning, and even military discipline. So how could it be married to the vision of work as joyful creativity? And how could either form of socialism be reconciled with revolutionary insurrection and violence? Marx and Engels struggled to resolve these tensions, but despite their best efforts a foundational flaw ran through the edifice of Marxism, reflecting its original three major constituent elements: the utopian Romanticism of people like Rousseau or Fourier, Babouvian revolution, and Saint-Simon's technocracy. Three rather different visions can therefore be found in Marx's and Engels' works from the 1840s: a 'Romantic' one, in which people work for the love of it and govern themselves, without the need for authority imposed from above; a 'Radical', revolutionary and egalitarian one, in which the heroic working class unite on the barricades to fight the bourgeoisie and establish a new modern revolutionary state; and a 'Modernist' one, in which the economy was run according to a central plan, administered, at least in the early stages, by some kind of bureaucracy. These different visions also affected Marx's and Engels' response to another question: how was Communism to be achieved? For a more Radical Marx, the proletariat was ready for Communist society. Just as it could be trusted to work diligently, without direction from above, so its heroism and self-sacrifice would lead it to stage a Communist revolution in the very near future. But for the Modernist Marx, the revolution would only arrive when economic conditions were ripe, when industry was highly developed and when capitalism was on the brink of an often hard-to-define crisis. Those who simply had faith in the heroism of the working class to deliver Communism and demanded an immediate end to capitalism were ignoring economic realities and committing the deadly sin of utopian thinking.[27]

The weight of the three elements after 1848, however, was unequal. Utopian Romanticism remained in the ultimate dream of 'Communism', but its prominence declined. Marxism was increasingly becoming a philosophy of both revolution and science, and the tension between the two created a fault-line within Marxism that persisted throughout its history. Marx and Engels struggled heroically to obscure it, yet paradoxically, this imperfection was not without its advantages. Whilst it offended their love of consistency, it also provided them with flexibility, allowing them to tilt towards Radicalism or Modernism depending on the particular situation. This balancing act was to prove vital for Marxism's survival during the violent upheavals and sudden changes of political fortune in nineteenth-century Western Europe.

IV

Norbert Truquin, a poor, frequently unemployed labourer, went to Paris in 1848 in search of work, and found it turning a grinding wheel for two francs a day. Though well aware of socialist ideas, he was ambivalent about them. His autobiography records that he felt 'anticommunist' because 'it seemed to me that community required an iron discipline, before which all individual will would be erased'. This would interfere with his 'desire to roam the world'. However, he also saw the advantages of Communism: 'If goods were held in common, we would not have to travel three leagues a day to get to work . . . we would not be reduced to eating nothing but broth, and children would not be forced to work so young.'[28] And when revolution actually broke out in February 1848, Truquin joined the barricades. Reminiscing about the joyful atmosphere, as both bourgeois and worker denounced the Orleanist monarchy, he also detected tensions beneath the surface: 'from the physical appearance of the bourgeois, you could tell that there was something false in their effusive gestures and that they were experiencing a poorly-disguised aversion for their comrades-in-arms.'[29] Truquin had indeed sensed the beginning of the end of the bourgeois–worker alliance that had typified French revolutionary history. By June the split had become permanent.

In fact the first signs of the split had emerged much earlier, in the aftermath of the 1830 revolution. The revolution had brought to power a regime that favoured laissez-faire economics, and the government of the Orleanist Louis-Philippe was unsympathetic to the demands of artisans and labourers who were suffering from the newly emerging capitalist economy. As cities grew, markets expanded and new technologies encouraged larger-scale 'industrial' factory production, small-scale artisans found themselves under pressure. Craft guilds, where they still existed, were damaged by the cheap goods churned out by capitalist entrepreneurs and their factories of less-skilled workers – Marx's 'proletarians'. Rebellion was the result, and the Lyon silk-workers' uprising of 1831 can be seen as one of the first modern workers' revolts.[30] Workers had protested before of course – the *sans-culottes* of 1793–4 amongst them – but they had generally done so as hard-hit consumers, not as producers. Now, as their slogan 'Live Working or Die Fighting!' (*Vivre en travaillant ou mourir en combattant!*) showed, popular rebels saw themselves primarily as workers fighting against the propertied. And unlike the 1789 and 1830 revolutions, when an alliance of the poor, middling artisans and relatively well-off masters came together to protest at an aristocratic order, these rebels were largely manual workers, protesting against a liberal government. Indeed, some called themselves 'proletarians' even though they were not Marx's new industrial workers and despite the fact that some owned their own businesses. Observers at the time understood that something new was happening. Eighteen thirty-one was the year that the term 'socialism' was coined by Henri Leroux, and the 'social question' became a fashionable topic of discussion.

The year after the Lyon strike, Parisian workers tried to follow their example, in events which Victor Hugo portrayed so dramatically in *Les Misérables*. Socialist movements and thinking flourished in 1830s and 1840s France, but it was in Britain, where modern industry was already becoming dominant, that workers' protest was most dramatic, as the Chartist movement united artisans and modern industrial workers in the demand for the vote. The events of the 1840s, in France and Britain, convinced many on both the right and the left that revolution was a real possibility; they certainly fuelled Marx's and Engels' optimism. As Marx wrote of one meeting with Parisian workers back in 1843:

> when Communist artisans form associations, teaching and propaganda are their first aims. But their association itself creates a new need – the need for society – and what appeared to be a means has become an end ... The brotherhood of man is no mere phrase with them, but a fact of life, and the nobility of man shines upon us from their work-hardened bodies.[31]

Yet, as is clear from these observations, Marx's profession of faith in the collectivism and revolutionary energies of workers was based largely on the experience of artisans, not in fact the industrial proletarians whom he assumed would be the creators of Communism. Artisans were indeed often very radical, though largely in defence of their old way of life against capitalism, not as heralds of the industrial future. Moreover, they lacked the power of numbers, coherence and organization. Production on the Continent was still largely artisanal, and where the proletariat did exist in large numbers – in England – it boasted few revolutionaries. Even so, whilst the *Communist Manifesto*, published in early 1848, was hardly noticed beyond a select circle of Communists, it appeared to be uncannily prescient, and the spread of revolution across Europe reinforced Marx's belief in the imminent collapse of capitalism at the hands of the proletariat.

The revolutionary events had begun in Switzerland in 1847, and early the following year spread to Sicily, Naples, Paris, Munich, Vienna, Budapest, Venice, Krakow, Milan and Berlin. In the vanguard were affluent liberal professionals who demanded freedom of speech and expansion of the franchise; sometimes, as in the Austrian empire, they called for national independence. The weaknesses of the old regimes, became rapidly evident, and monarchs were toppled, or were forced to grant liberal freedoms. The new authorities introduced moderate, liberal reforms, destroying autocratic government and the serfdom typical of the *ancien régime* where they still existed, especially in Germany and Austria-Hungary.

Marx had great hopes for these uprisings, seeing in them a prelude to his proletarian revolution. Together with his family and Engels, he left Paris for Cologne and set up a radical newspaper, the *Neue Rhenische Zeitung*, whilst working as a political activist. His attitude towards revolution depended on each country's particular situation. In France, he believed that the revolution would follow the pattern of 1789: the bourgeois revolution would inevitably be radicalized and class struggle would then erupt between workers and the bourgeoisie. Germany, however, he thought too backward for this scenario; a bourgeois revolution had not yet happened. Even so, by the end of 1848 he argued that the prospects for Communist revolution were particularly favourable in Germany, because of its uneven development. Although German states were ruled by the old feudal aristocracy, the bourgeois revolution would take place with the help of a 'developed proletariat'. Marx therefore urged his fellow Communists to support the bourgeoisie and fight for liberal political reforms, but then to carry on struggling for the proletarian revolution which would follow immediately after as the proletariat used its 'political supremacy' to centralize and increase production.[32] This was the first enunciation, in embryo, of the theory of 'permanent revolution', the idea that even in a backward country the proletariat should support a bourgeois revolution and then immediately prepare for a second proletarian revolution. It was this theory that Leon Trotsky enunciated, and was then used to justify the Bolshevik revolution in Russia.

For Marx and Engels the outcome of the proletarian revolution was to be a temporary 'dictatorship of the proletariat'. By this, they did not mean the rule of a revolutionary party over the majority, in the Jacobin or Blanquist tradition. Rather, they favoured a democracy in which the proletariat would rule through popular assemblies, and use emergency powers, violent if necessary, to break the old state.[33]

In the first half of 1848, Marx's predictions for revolution in France did not look too implausible, and whilst the revolution, like its predecessors, united the middle classes and workers, the latter were determined to learn the lesson of 1830 and not to allow their revolution to be 'stolen'.[34] The right-liberal government of François Guizot, working under King Louis-Philippe, had alienated both the middle classes and the workers: it retained a highly restricted franchise and manipulated elections, whilst taking a harsh line with the poor. On the night of 22 February, over a million paving stones were torn up and over 4,000 trees felled, and by the morning more than 1,500 barricades had been built. The authorities were unable to persuade the National Guard to take action, and by the following day Guizot had resigned. The day after, Louis-Philippe fled to England, where he lived quietly in Surrey until his death two years later.

The new French government was dominated by moderate republicans, leavened by a minority of radicals, amongst them the famous socialist Louis Blanc and a solitary worker by the name of Albert. But the radicals were reinforced by a huge crowd of workers who put direct pressure on the government by assembling menacingly outside the Hôtel de Ville. The Provisional Government rapidly met many of their demands: a republic was declared, universal male suffrage introduced, and reforms specifically designed to help workers enacted. Subcontracting – a method used by employers to reduce wages – was banned, and the working day was restricted to ten hours (the first time a government had tried to regulate work in this way).

However, it was the Provisional Government's commitment, under pressure from Louis Blanc, 'to guarantee labour to all citizens' that caused the most conflict with the bourgeois members of the government. 'National Workshops' were set up to employ the indigent, largely on public works schemes. The workshops were financed by a land tax, which fell on the mass of peasant farmers. But the elections of April, which were won by rural notables, showed how unrepresentative the Parisian radicals were and how sharply Paris and the countryside were split. The newly elected Assembly promptly proposed that the work-shops be closed, and workers fought back. In June they returned to the barricades – this time rather more sturdily built – and over 15,000 of them staged one of the most impressive of all worker insurrections. Some of the insurgents were members of the workshops, but most were artisans protesting against the new factory-based economy.[35] The rebel-lion was brutally crushed; the government was forced to recruit about 100,000 national guards from the provinces, and fighting was bitter and lasted for several days. Thousands of workers were killed, impris-oned, or sent to Algeria. It was clear that the artisanal workers were not numerous or powerful enough to impose a socialist settlement on France.

If Marx's predictions of a proletarian revolution had fared poorly in France, it was less likely that they would come to fruition in Germany. There the workers' movement was smaller and more divided, and the middle classes more conservative – though parts of the peasantry were radical. Marx himself initially favoured the pursuit of constitutional, democratic objectives, rather than socialist ones. But by September, as it became clear that the middle classes were not going to play a revolu-tionary role, he and Engels called for a 'red' republic that would adopt socialist policies. Marx also favoured revolutionary insurrections where he thought they might work, though he insisted they be mass revolu-tions – involving both workers and peasants – not 'Blanquist' conspir-acies.[36] Engels was especially militant, and personally took part in uprisings in Elberfeld and the Rhineland-Palatinate in May 1849. The previous September he wrote enthusiastically of the armed rebellions, 'Is there a revolutionary centre anywhere in the world where the red flag, the emblem of the militant, united proletariat of Europe, has not been found flying on the barricades during the last five months?'[37] In 1848–9, therefore, Marx and Engels were setting an example for so many future Communist revolutionaries, fomenting popular revolution in undevel-oped, agrarian societies.[38]

Throughout Western and Central Europe, artisans demonstrated against unemployment and competition, sometimes joined by rebellious peasants, as the loss of common land provoked enormous anger. The view of radicals like Marx, that 1789 could be repeated, was therefore understandable. But moderates and conservatives had also learnt the lessons of 1789, and were determined to suppress popular unrest, and

the authorities fought back.[39] By November 1848 the Prussian revolution had been defeated, and thousands of workers were deported from
Berlin and other cities. Meanwhile, Napoleon's nephew, Louis-Napoleon,
was elected president of France, trading on the Bonaparte name and
garnering support from opponents of revolution in the countryside, the
'party of order', and workers resentful at the violence used against
them by the liberal republicans. Once in power Louis-Napoleon's politics became increasingly conservative, and by mid-1849 his troops had
contributed to the defeats of the last revolutionary governments in
Italy.

For some time after, however, Marx and Engels refused to accept that
all was lost, and they continued to predict that revolution of the 1789
or 1848 type was about to break out. Their revolutionary hopes waxed
and waned, but it was clear by the late 1850s that revolution was not
on the horizon.

Socialists, however, could find solace in one revolutionary episode in
an otherwise distinctly unrevolutionary period: the Paris Commune of
1871. Paris had been surrounded by the Prussians in one of the longest
sieges of modern times (second only to Stalingrad), and when the government signed an armistice, Parisians were outraged. They held elections,
and about a third of the elected deputies were craftsmen, making it the
most worker-dominated government to appear in Europe thus far.
Thirty-two of the eighty-one members of the assembly were members of
the First International of socialist parties, which Marx had helped to
found, but they were not his disciples.[40] Most deputies were influenced
more by the decentralized socialism of Proudhon, or by Blanqui's insurrectionary Jacobinism.[41] However, the Commune's real significance lay
in its legacy. It was the first government to be connected with Marx, and
for the first time the red flag, not the Republic's tricolour, flew above a
seat of government, the Hôtel de Ville. Marx and Engels also described
it as the model of their 'proletarian dictatorship'.[42] For them, the
Commune had proved that the old state bureaucracy could be smashed,
and all areas of government democratized. Elected deputies ruled
directly, both legislators and executives, while all officials received
workers' wages and were subject to dismissal by the people.

V

In 1871 few places seemed further from the revolutionary turbulence of the Parisian Hôtel de Ville than the hushed neo-classical splendour of London's British Museum Library. Seated in his comfortable blue leather-upholstered chair at desk number G7, beneath the massive dome painted in cool Georgian azure and picked out in gold, Karl Marx immersed himself in tomes of economics and history. Despite the calm surroundings, it could be tough going; at one particularly low moment he told one of his daughters that he had been transformed into 'a machine condemned to devour books and then throw them, in a changed form, on the dunghill of history' (a sentiment many academics will recognize).[43]

Marx had decided to forsake politics for the library, and had shifted the focus of his struggles from the barricades to the realm of theory. Now that he was losing his earlier faith in proletarian heroism, he sought to show that another force would drive the world to Communism – economics. The result was his monumental, if little-read, work of synthesis: *Capital*.

As the title suggests, *Capital* was largely an analysis of the mechanisms, weaknesses and supposedly ultimate demise of capitalism, and said little about Communism. But as Marx became more interested in the realities of the modern economy his views of Communism and how to achieve it began to change. Both he and Engels now insisted that a Communist society had to be a more economically rational society than one based on capitalism, fully embracing the realities of industrial society. His earlier opinion that labour could be self-motivated, creative and enjoyable yielded to the much more pessimistic view that work would have to be directed from above, by technicians and bosses. Promises of workers' control over their factories were quietly dropped, and Marx made it clear that proletarian heroism and creativity were not enough. As he explained in *Capital*, 'all combined labour on a large scale requires . . . a directing authority'.[44] Self-realization and individual development could only happen after the end of the work-day, during leisure time.[45] Moreover, Marx increasingly implied that he no longer hoped for the Romantic dream of the 'complete' man as morning hunter, afternoon fisherman and evening critic; even under Communism, he suggested, the modern division of labour was the only efficient way of producing things. For Marx now, the main advantage of Communism over capitalism lay in efficiency: rational planning and its ability to end the chaotic booms and busts brought by the free market.

Marx and Engels were decisively tilting Marxism in a Modernist direction. Their Communism now increasingly resembled the mechanized and orderly modern factory rather than a Romantic idyll of self-fulfilment, whilst the heroism of the barricades was postponed. And given this view of Communism, it is not surprising that Marx insisted that it could only come about when the economic preconditions – large-scale industry and a dominant proletariat – had emerged. Marx had ceased to view the revolutionary heroism of the proletariat as the main driving-force of history. Rather, the objective, 'scientific' laws of social and economic development would deliver Communism, and the best people to accomplish this task were both proletarians and expert Marxists who understood the 'science' of history.[46] Revolution could not be premature; the proletariat would have to wait until the time was ripe.

This 'scientific' approach to Marxism was, in part, a response to the intellectual currents of the 1860s. Darwinian social theorists like Herbert Spencer were now in the ascendant; it was now fashionable to argue that mankind was on the verge of discovering general laws which would apply both to human societies and to the natural world. Marx and Engels were anxious to keep abreast of the latest scientific thinking. As Engels declared at Marx's funeral in 1883, 'Just as Darwin discovered the law of development of organic nature, so Marx discovered the law of development of human history.'[47] It was Engels who was particularly interested in transforming Marxism into a science, and thus proving the objective necessity of Communism. He spent a great deal of time trying to graft Hegel's ideas of the dialectical pattern of history onto the natural sciences. The result was a body of rather eccentric theories that came to be known as 'Dialectical Materialism'.[48] One of these dialectical 'laws' was the theory that the natural world, like human societies, advanced through periods of evolutionary change, followed by revolutionary 'leaps'; so, for instance, when heated, water changes gradually until it suddenly undergoes a 'revolutionary' transformation into steam.[49] As will be seen, in later years, under Communist regimes these theories were used to justify efforts to promote extraordinary, and usually disastrous, economic 'leaps forward'. Yet Engels himself tended not to take his ideas in this revolutionary direction. His attempt to recast Marxism as a science led inexorably to gradualist conclusions: if the laws of nature ensured that Communism was coming anyway, why try to force history?[50]

Nevertheless, the revolutionary Radicalism of 1848 and the Romanticism of the youthful Marx were never entirely purged from an increasingly Modernist Marxism. Instead, Marx himself tried to reconcile the three elements, sketching what was essentially a route-map, showing the way to Communism, but delaying its more egalitarian elements to the distant future. The map was not consistent, as Marx was notoriously resistant to speculating about the future, and his followers had to piece it together from his and Engels' often contradictory statements. But a broad outline was generally accepted by Marxists: Communist parties would organize the working class in preparation for the proletarian revolution, but during the initial stages of the revolution the working class could not entirely be trusted. Communists, 'the most advanced and resolute section of the working-class parties', would therefore have to take the lead.[51] Similarly, in the early stages of Communism immediately after the revolution, though the market and private property would be abolished, the state would persist. A new state, the 'Dictatorship of the Proletariat', would be established, which would suppress bourgeois opposition, and gradually 'centralize all instruments of production in the hands of the State'.[52] There would then follow a longer phase, the 'lower' stage of Communism (which the Bolsheviks later called 'socialism'), when workers, who still could not yet be trusted to work simply for the love of it, would be paid according to the amount they did. Only later, during the 'higher' stage of Communism (which the Bolsheviks described as 'Communism'), would workers become so collectivist and public-spirited that they could be relied on to work without recourse to either coercive discipline or monetary bribes; only then would society be governed by the principle, 'from each according to his ability, to each according to his needs'; and only then would the whole of the people be able to govern themselves, allowing the state finally to 'wither away'.[53]

This route-map dominated Marxist thinking, and all Marxists were obliged to follow it. But it could obviously be interpreted in many different ways. For example, the timetable could vary: the road to Communism might be very swift or rather gradual, it could be a journey accompanied by revolutionary violence or one of largely peaceful economic development. Marxists could and did disagree about who was to be in the driving seat – the revolutionary working class, or a group of wise Marxist experts on the laws of history. They also took different views of the role of the state, and how quickly it could be replaced by a Paris Commune-style democracy.

Marxism therefore still had its Romantic, Radical and Modernist elements, but from the 1860s until World War I a new equilibrium had been established, with its centre of gravity decisively shifted towards Modernism. The main Romantic Marxist texts of the 1840s were not published until the 1930s, and Engels, who became the leading theoretician after Marx's death in 1883, set about popularizing a Modernist form of Marxism in seminal works such as *Socialism, Utopian and Scientific*. According to this Marxism, the journey to Communism would be a gradual one, workers would have to wait until economic conditions were ripe, and the Communist ideal was to be founded on modern industry and a powerful bureaucracy (under the control of workers). In the meantime, Communists, or 'Social Democrats' as they were now called, were to establish well-organized, centralized political parties. They were to fight for workers' interests as far as they could within the existing 'bourgeois' political system, participate in elections, and were not to push for premature revolutions. However, they were to maintain their independence; they were not to slip too far to the right and collaborate with bourgeois parties. This Marxism was far from the revolutionary egalitarianism of the barricades.

After a long period in the 1850s when repression made any socialist politics very difficult, Marx and Engels returned to political activism in the 1860s, helping to found the 'First International', a grouping of national socialist parties, in 1864. The results were mixed. They failed to persuade the pragmatic British trade unionists to break from the Liberal party, and the International's influence in Britain never recovered. But the left, if anything, was even more of a threat to Marx and Engels. Their main opponents were the anarchists Proudhon and Mikhail Bakunin, for whom Marxism seemed authoritarian and who favoured a decentralized form of socialism. For Bakunin, the charismatic son of a Russian count, Marx was 'head to foot an authoritarian', and his 'scientific' socialism was designed to give power to 'a numerically small aristocracy of genuine or sham scientists'.[54] Marx responded in kind: Bakunin was a 'Monster. Perfect blockhead. Stupid. Aspiring dictator of Europe's workers.'[55]

Bakunin, however, enjoyed a great deal of support in the International, and the conflict between Marxism and anarchism was to contribute to the institution's destruction. The final meeting took place in The Hague in 1872. Marx, who had become associated in the public mind with the Paris Commune of the previous year, was now a notorious figure (the 'Red-Terror-Doctor'), and crowds followed the delegates from the station to their hotel, though according to one journalist, children were warned against going into the streets with valuables in case the evil International stole them.[56] Yet Marx was unable to bring the leverage of his street-level reputation as the leader of socialism into the conference hall; he antagonized many of the delegates by his harsh treatment of both Bakunin and the British trade unionists. He was only able to impose control by moving the General Council from London to New York, leaving the Italian, Spanish and Swiss socialist parties to Bakunin's rival, anti-Marxist international. The transfer to the United States was hardly practical, and soon afterwards the First International was dissolved.

Yet in the longer term, Marx's and Engels' Modernist version of socialism proved to be more enduring in Western Europe than its anarchist rival. The so-called 'Second Industrial Revolution' of the 1880s and 1890s led to the development of what we think of as the modern industrial economy.[57] Factories became bigger, as the metal, chemical, mining and transport industries came to the fore; machinery became increasingly complex and expensive; international competition became harsher; and the modern corporation emerged, employing hierarchies of managers to create efficient businesses and to police workers. All of this had an enormous effect on workers. The urban labour force became larger, and employers tried to increase productivity by cutting wages and using machinery to 'de-skill' workers, paying them less to perform routine mechanized tasks. At the same time, national economies were becoming more integrated, and workers became more aware of their fellow labourers.

Many of Marx's predictions were therefore being fulfilled by the time of his death in 1883. De-skilling and globalization were precisely what Marx had foretold, and the enlarged working classes provided a reservoir of recruits for Marxist parties. However, these new industrial workers were limited to a minority of the population in the more modern sectors of the economy, and they often had little in common with the mass of less organized, casual workers. Also, their reactions to economic change varied. De-skilling could anger workers and provoke militancy. But workers were often less radical than they had been in the early stages of industrialization. The labour unrest of early industrialization was fuelled by an ambivalence towards modern industry, and sometimes by a complete rejection of it. But now many workers had become part of the factory system, and had learnt to work within it. Employers often had a great deal of power over them and workers were more likely to accept the realities of the industrial world than rebel against it.[58]

The evolution of European politics also contributed to this mixture of conflict and compromise. Workers and trade unionists continued to be the victims of state repression in many parts of Europe. However, the violent social 'civil wars' of the 1830s and 1840s had become muted by the 1860s. States were granting the liberal reforms demanded and refused in 1848, and they were gradually extending them from the middle classes to workers. Marxism, therefore, benefited from some of the social and political changes of the late nineteenth century, but not others. The poor of the Western world had a number of paths available to them, and they by no means all chose the Marxist one.

VI

The year after Marx's death, in 1884, the French writer Émile Zola began his great 'socialist novel', determined to draw middle-class attention to what he regarded as the central issue of the time: the imminence of bloody revolution:

> The subject of the novel is the revolt of the workers, the jolt given to society, which for a moment cracks: in a word the struggle between capital and labour. There lies the importance of the book, which I want to show predicting the future, putting the question that will be the most important question of the twentieth century.[59]

Zola initially planned to call the novel *The Gathering Storm*, but finally decided on the title *Germinal*, in deliberate evocation of the Jacobins who had given the name to their new springtime month. Zola believed he needed to force his complacent readers to acknowledge the shaky foundations of the bourgeois order as capital and labour struggled, quite literally, beneath their feet. In the immense coalmine, 'Le Voreux' ('a voracious beast'), 'an army was growing, a future crop of citizens, germinating like seeds that would burst through the earth's crust one day into the bright sunshine'.[60]

Zola's main characters stand for four rather different socialist visions: Souvarine is a Russian émigré anarchist; Étienne Lantier a Marxist of sorts, an 'intransigent collectivist, authoritarian, Jacobin'; Rasseneur, a 'Possibilist', or moderate socialist (based on Émile Basly, the former miner and future parliamentary deputy); and the abbé Ranvier, a Christian socialist. Étienne, the Jacobin, is the hero of the novel, but, like Rasseneur, is also shown to be egotistical and ambitious. Meanwhile Souvarine, though idealistic, is destructive, and Ranvier is ineffectual. Ultimately, Zola believes that none of the socialists can control the masses – a violent, almost animalistic force of nature. Zola terrifies his readers with his accounts of the uncontrollably violent strikes and demonstrations. His bourgeois characters saw

> a scarlet vision of the revolution that would inevitably carry them all away, on some blood-soaked *fin de siècle* evening ... these same rags and the same thunder of clogs, the same terrifying pack of animals with dirty skins and foul breath, would sweep away the old world, as their barbarian hordes overflowed and surged through the land.[61]

Zola himself had little sympathy with revolutionary politics, and ultimately Étienne, the leader of a disastrous strike, is shown to have 'outgrown his immature resentment', in favour of a future when workers would abjure violence and form a 'peaceful army'. Organized trade unions would fight for their rights and bring about the demise of Capital by legal means. Then 'the crouching, sated god, that monstrous idol who lay hidden in the depths of his tabernacle untold leagues away, bloated with the flesh of miserable wretches who never even saw him, would instantly give up the ghost.'[62]

Zola's prediction, that leftist politics would become less revolutionary and more law-abiding, was true for some countries but not for others. Where existing 'bourgeois' political parties were willing to accommodate workers in the political order and concede trade union representation, as was the case with the British Liberal Party and its 'Lib-Lab' politics, workers tended to jettison revolutionary goals; why confront an established order that gave workers what they wanted?[63] In these more liberal conditions, the Étiennes did poorly, and the Rasseneurs were in the ascendant. Yet Marxists did not prosper in societies that were too illiberal either. In repressive countries with underdeveloped industries, such as Russia, the Balkans and much of Austria-Hungary, it was difficult for Marxists to organize parties and trade unions. In parts of Italy and Iberia, in contrast, anarchistic Souvarines and more radical Marxists who demanded immediate revolution seemed to have a more compelling case. There it was easier to organize politically, but the state often used harsh repression against popular demands, most strikingly during the violence of 'Tragic Week' in Catalonia in 1909. Anarchists also did well where poor peasants were demanding land redistribution, whilst Marxists often saw peasants as 'backward', and peasants them-selves were often hostile to Marxist plans for centralized states. France was a hybrid case, and the Étiennes, Souvarines, Rasseneurs and Ranviers all found a constituency. Because sporadic state repression continued, Marxist parties enjoyed some success, but anarchists contin-ued to thrive amongst artisans (who were still an important economic group), whilst relatively liberal governments made the lure of reform-ism irresistible to many potential Marxist recruits. Churches were also powerful opponents of Marxist parties. Marxists, following Marx, usually saw Christianity as a reactionary ideology that justified the old social structure, and the churches usually responded with equal hostil-ity. The Catholic Church was especially antagonistic to Marxism, and it was particularly effective in resisting Marxist influence through its political parties and social organizations.

In the United States, Marxists and other socialists were also con-fronted with a mixture of repression and liberal democracy, but they were less successful in establishing a foothold than in most industrial-ized countries in Europe. Trade unions and socialist movements attracted a large following until the early twentieth century: the medievally named Knights of Labour had about 10 per cent of the non-agricultural labour force as members by 1886. But this left was later undermined by a combination of forces: ethnic divisions; a dominant liberal ideology; male suffrage as an alternative way of seeking change; and high levels of repression.

The ideal home for the Étienne Lantiers was to be found in Northern and Central Europe. The largest and most successful party was the Social Democratic Party of Germany (the 'SPD'), but Marxist parties were also successful in Scandinavia and some parts of the Austro-Hungarian Empire. It is not surprising that the centre of the Marxist hopes moved from France, where they had been in the middle of the century, towards the East. Germany now had a large industrial working class, and many of these workers were attracted by the Marxists' commitment to modern heavy industry and their promise that the proletariat would inherit the earth. But political conditions were as important, if not more so, than economic structure. In 1878, following an attempt on the life of the Kaiser (for which the socialists were not responsible) Bismarck demanded that the Reichstag pass anti-socialist laws, banning the SPD and repressing workers' organizations more generally. Nevertheless, the party and unions maintained an underground existence, and Social Democrats were still able to stand for parliament as individuals, thus providing a focus for working-class politics. But discrimination continued, even after the anti-socialist laws lapsed in 1890. The SPD was subject to police harassment, and employers were often harsh in dealing with strikes; workers were often treated as second-class citizens, patronized by the middle class and excluded from their clubs and associations. This state schizophrenia, its combination of freedom and repression, helped the Modernist Marxism of Marx and Engels to flourish. Repression kept the SPD outside established politics and ensured that it did not become a reformist party; the party adopted a Marxist programme at Erfurt in 1891, which promised the revolutionary overthrow of capitalism at some point in the future. But at the same time, the SPD had deputies in parliament, and its representation and strength grew after 1890, allowing the party to achieve a great deal through the existing order. It was therefore only to be expected that pressure for revolution was weak. As a result of these complex circumstances, the SPD was to embody the ideal Marx and Engels pursued in the First International: an independent Marxist party that fought for workers' interests within the current system without collaborating with the bourgeoisie.

VII

Nikolaus Osterroth, born in 1875, was a devout Catholic and a clay miner in Bavaria. On his return from military service in the mid-1890s, he found the mine-owners determined to reduce wages by introducing a new piecework system (paying workers according to how much they produced). Initially, he and the other miners turned for support to the local priest, but they received little sympathy. The priest declared that the employers were appointed by God, and had to be obeyed. Osterroth, in his autobiography, written thirty years later, recalled this incident as provoking a 'crisis of conscience', after which he left the church with 'an empty head and a dying heart'. It was in this low mood that he read a Social Democratic leaflet, thrown through his window by a group of 'Red Cyclists' who were passing through the village. 'The leaflet,' he remembered, 'affected me like a revelation':

> Suddenly I saw the world from the other side, from a side that until now had been dark for me. I was especially aroused by the criticism of the tariff system and the indirect taxes. I'd never heard a word about them before! In all the [Catholic] Centre Party speeches they kept completely quiet about them. And why? Wasn't their silence an admission that they'd committed an injustice, a clear sign of a guilty conscience? I didn't believe my eyes – a six-pfennig tax on a pound of salt! I was seized by a feeling of wild fury about the obvious injustice of a tax system that spared the ones who could best pay and plundered those who already despaired of life in their bitter misery.[64]

This Damascene moment of almost religious revelation, followed by 'conversion' to socialism, can be found in several socialist autobiographies of the period. Conflict with bosses could trigger a more general questioning of their old value system, particularly amongst those who had been Christian believers. Once Osterroth began to think about his economic predicament, he found that there was a whole alternative worldview available to him – one founded on the notion that workers had power and dignity:

> God, how clear and simple it all was! This new world of thought that gave the worker the weapons of self-awareness and self-consciousness was very

different to the old world of priestly and economic authority where the worker was merely an object of domination and exploitation![65]

He became a Social Democratic activist, and ultimately a politician, replacing the old 'dark, vengeful and punishing' Mosaic God, with a 'new trinity' – one that included a new, charitable God, together with Faust and Prometheus, 'god-men who embody the deepest yearnings of our race'.[66]

The Red Cyclists continued to woo Osterroth, giving him a copy of the party's Marxist Erfurt programme to read. But Osterroth was typical of many German workers in showing little interest in the details of Marxist economics or in the notion that workers would take control of production. Most workers joined the SPD not out of a profound interest in Marxist economic ideas, but because they were angry about wages and conditions and, commonly, out of a sense of humiliation at the hands of bosses. Some felt that they were being treated 'like dogs', sworn at and humiliated;[67] others resented bosses' control over their lives. The cigar-maker Felix Pauk, for instance, became sympathetic to the Social Democratic cause when a fellow worker was sacked for suggesting to his boss that sales would improve if the picture of the Kaiser on the cigars were replaced with one of the Marxist leader August Bebel.[68]

However unschooled in Marxist theory, it is probable that many members of the party, even at its lower levels, had at least a rudimentary idea of its fundamental principles, learnt from popularizations of the ideology. These included the idea of Marxism as a science, the centrality of economic forces in historical development, the class struggle, the proletariat's status as the progressive class emancipating the whole of mankind, and the ultimate crisis of capitalism. But workers had little interest in studying the details of Marxist theory, however much Social Democratic intellectuals encouraged them. A survey of Social Democratic workers' libraries between 1906 and 1914 shows that 63.1 per cent of books borrowed were imaginative literature, and only 4.3 per cent were in the social sciences, including Marxist texts. Zola was number one or two on most library lists, much to the irritation of socialist intellectuals who regarded him as a pessimist, with too little faith in human reason.[69]

But there was much the SPD could offer beyond theory, or even political radicalism: it provided an alternative world to that of the factory, where workers were accorded dignity and could improve themselves. For Otto Krille, an unskilled factory worker from Dresden, this was its main attraction. He despaired of the 'general stupor' in his factory, and felt 'completely isolated' amidst his fellow workers' parochialism and 'erotic banter'; for him, Social Democracy provided an escape from this grim world. He observed that 'only a tiny fraction [of party members] are socialists from scientific conviction; most come to socialism from a vast internal and external wasteland like the people of Israel out of the wilderness. They have to believe in order not to despair.'[70] Krille's attitude was typical of the average Social Democratic Party member: a young, urban, male and Protestant worker, with ambitions to better himself.[71]

In place of Krille's 'wasteland', the Social Democratic Party provided a world of culture, self-improvement and orderly recreation.[72] Educational societies promised a socialist version of *Bildung*, or cultivation and learning – precisely what gave the bourgeoisie its status in German society – through lectures and classes. The subjects covered included 'socialist' and 'scientific' topics, like political economy and hygiene, as well as the study of conventional 'bourgeois' culture – art, literature and music. Even more popular were the leisure societies. A whole range of activities and societies were on offer under the party's auspices, from shooting and cycling clubs to choral societies (which had 200,000 members), and even smoking clubs. The ideological content of the clubs' activities varied. Some had their own club languages: members of gymnastic clubs used the greeting '*Frei Heil!*' ('Hail to Freedom!') from the late 1890s.

The most visible aspect of Social Democratic culture was the parade – especially the May Day parade. Despite the threat of harassment by the police, thousands attended and watched processions celebrating socialism and workers' trades. Some of the symbolism came from the socialist past, stretching back to the classicism of the French Revolution. A central place in the 1910 Nuremberg Social Democratic choral festival was taken by the 'Goddess of Freedom' – a figure in a white Grecian gown, a Phrygian cap on her head, a 'Freedom banner' in her right hand, surrounded with busts of Marx, the German socialist leader Lassalle, and a lion, symbolizing power.[73] Other festivals, however, had a more explicitly military style, complete with uniforms, marching bands, standards and flags. Many Social Democratic songs reveal the martial culture:

What moves down there along the valley?
A troop in white uniform!
How courageous sounds their vigorous song!
Those tones are known to me.
They sing of Freedom and the Fatherland.
I know this troop in their white uniform:
Freedom Hail! Freedom Hail! Freedom Hail!
The gymnasts are moving out.[74]

The appeal of military types of organization was not, of course, new, and Marx himself had used military metaphors when discussing socialism. Indeed Marxism was committed to a strong, disciplined socialist state, unlike anarchists to the left and reformists to the right. But Marx's and Engels' vision was more commonly an industrial one, and the military style of German Social Democracy probably owed much to the political culture of Imperial Germany – even though the party's ideology favoured internationalism.[75] Whilst the party – like other Social Democratic parties – in theory championed the equality of women, in practice party members frequently saw women as apolitical and 'backward', and the party culture was highly masculine. A high value was also placed on discipline and even hierarchy. Gymnastic exercises were regimented, and teams were organized in military fashion: an elected overseer presided over a number of squad leaders, who, in turn, organized the teams. As the 'gymnastic code' ruled: 'Ranks must be strictly held in each team. No one may move from the team without special permission.'[76]

It was discipline and organization that appealed to Otto Krille – a man educated in a military school but expelled as 'unfit'. As he remembered:

> I slowly became familiar with Social Democratic ideas. In the past, the idea of the state had seemed to me to have a kind of medieval crudity that was embodied in barracks and prisons. This attitude changed imperceptibly, because I learned to see myself as a citizen of this state who, though oppressed, still had an interest in it because I hoped to take it over for my own class. And the strangest thing was . . . that I, the despiser of unconditional military discipline, willingly submitted to party discipline. As contradictory as it may seem, socialist ideology reconciled me to a certain extent with my proletarian existence, and taught me to respect manual labour. I no longer shied away from the name 'worker'.[77]

For Krille and many others, the SPD provided a parallel state in which workers could achieve some dignity, and which had the organization necessary to defend the working class against a fundamentally hostile German Empire.

The Social Democratic culture could therefore have a martial flavour, as was captured by 'The Red Flag' – the song written by the Irish journalist James Connell in 1889, inspired by a London meeting of the Social Democratic Federation:

> The people's flag is deepest red,
> It shrouded oft our martyr'd dead
> And 'ere their limbs grew stiff and cold,
> Their hearts' blood dyed its ev'ry fold.
> Then raise the scarlet standard high,
> Within its shade we'll live and die,
> Though cowards flinch and traitors sneer,
> We'll keep the red flag flying here.

Connell's second verse was designed to underscore the international appeal of Social Democracy's red flag:

> Look round, the Frenchman loves its blaze,
> The sturdy German chants its praise,
> In Moscow's vaults its hymns are sung,
> Chicago swells the surging throng.

Yet references to the 'sturdy German' were distinctly patronizing, given how central the Germans were to the movement. In 1914, seven Social Democratic parties had at least a quarter of the national vote: the Austrian, the Czech, the Danish, the Finnish, the German, the Norwegian and the Swedish.[78] But the German party was by far the most successful of all. On the eve of World War I it had over 1 million paid-up members and in the 1912 elections attracted over 4 million votes – about a third of the electorate, though the skewed franchise deprived it of a majority of seats in the Reichstag. The trade unions associated with the SPD – the Free Trade Unions – also had a membership of about 2.6 million. This was the largest Marxist party in the world, and became a model for socialists throughout Europe.

Even so, there were real limits to Social Democratic influence. Whilst some parties, like the French SFIO and the Swedish, forged alliances with peasants, the SPD was committed to the rigid view that peasant agriculture was an outmoded form of production.[79] But even in Europe's proletarian heartlands, such as the mines of the Ruhr, Social Democrats could only attract a third of the vote, and they faced stiff competition from Catholicism and liberalism.[80] They were also unable to integrate Polish migrant workers, revealing Social Democracy's difficult relationship with nationalism. The Austrian party faced some of the greatest problems, as it hoped to preserve the boundaries of the Austro-Hungarian Empire. The Austrians' solution was to create a federal party of the Empire's constituent peoples, but they were still seen as overbearing big brothers by the Czech Social Democrats and other smaller parties.[81] Women were another group Social Democracy could have done more to attract, although women did constitute 16 per cent of the German Party's membership, and their organization remained one of the most radical groups in the SPD.[82]

However, despite such failures, the youthful Marx's ambition to move the centre of socialist politics from France to the German lands had been achieved. The somewhat chauvinistic leader August Bebel declared: 'It is not by chance that it was Germans who discovered the laws of modern society . . . It is furthermore not by chance that Germans are the pioneers who bring the socialist idea to the workers of the various peoples of the world.'[83]

VIII

The Germans' hegemony in the international socialist movement was clear even as it paid obeisance to the French revolutionary tradition. On 14 July 1889, the hundredth anniversary of the storming of the Bastille, the Second International held its inaugural meeting in the Rue Petrelle, Paris. Its initial prospects did not look good. A group of moderate socialists – the French 'Possibilists' – held a rival congress at the same time, and there were rumours that they were plotting to accost naïve foreign delegates at the railway station and lure them away from the Social Democrats. But these fears proved groundless. The Rue Petrelle Congress was an enormous success: 391 delegates attended from twenty countries, including the USA.[84] British representatives included the poet and Romantic medieval nostalgist William Morris, and the Independent

Labour Party MP Keir Hardie.[85] The French delegation was the largest, as was to be expected given the location. The foreign delegates could visit the newly built monument to industrial modernity and the French Revolution – the Eiffel Tower, and for a time Paris indeed seemed to be the centre of the progressive world. But the most cohesive and dominant group at the Congress was the German SPD. The Second International, which met every two to four years, was by no means a rigid, doctrinaire organization, but it did demonstrate the dominance of the Marxist tradition, and of the elder-brother party, the SPD.

Engels could take much of the credit for this success. On Marx's death, few countries had popular Marxist workers' parties. Engels was determined to remedy this weakness and establish Marxism as a powerful political force, unlike Marx, who took little interest in Marxist political organization. Engels' easy-going nature, sociability and patience proved to be good assets, and he acted as a mentor to European socialist politicians, engaging in lengthy correspondence and writing hundreds of letters of advice and criticism from his base in London. Marxists throughout Europe, in turn, treated him as the voice of orthodoxy. But Engels did not only use letters to bind his virtual community of Marxists together; he also sent Christmas puddings, cooked in his own kitchen, to favoured revolutionaries every December. They even reached distant Russia – Petr Lavrov, the non-Marxist 'Populist' socialist, was a regular recipient of this annual internationalist gift.[86]

If Engels founded the Marxist 'church', then the first 'pope' of socialism, as he was called at the time, was Karl Kautsky. Kautsky was born in Prague to a theatrical family, and his mother was a well-known writer of Romantic socialist novels. However, he was not as 'bohemian' as one might have expected, and he was commonly regarded as a pedant.[87] Engels found him a pleasant drinking companion, but commented that he was 'thoroughly cocky' with a superficial and unserious approach to politics, made worse by the fact that he wrote a great deal for money. Kautsky was indeed an autodidact. Yet his wide interests, and his willingness to pronounce confidently on a range of subjects, were ideal qualities for the task which Kautsky set himself: creating and popularizing a single, coherent, 'orthodox' Marxist worldview, based on the Modernist version of Marxism. Discussion of Kautsky has often been couched in religious terms: he was the socialist 'pope', his commentary on the Erfurt programme, The Class Struggle, was the 'catechism of

Social Democracy', and his version of Marxism was the 'orthodoxy'. However, Kautsky's own intellectual interests lay in science, in particular in Darwinism, and he sought to build on Engels' modern, 'scientific' Marxism.

He certainly proved highly effective in defending the Modernist Marxism of Engels against its opponents, and propagating it in the parties of the Second International. He even had success in Russia, where one might expect an oppressive regime to have produced a more Radical Marxism, and Georgii Plekhanov, the 'father of Russian Marxism', broadly followed the Kautskian line. For Kautsky, using a scholastically fine distinction, the SPD was a 'revolutionary' but not a 'revolution-making' party. Marxists were not to participate in bourgeois governments and were to keep their place outside the political establishment. They had to believe that ultimately the capitalist system would be destroyed in a revolution, by which Kautsky meant a conscious seizure of power by the proletariat, but this would not necessarily involve violence. At the same time, however, Marxists were to press for reforms to help the working class, including the expansion of liberal democratic rights, and the organization of parliamentary campaigns. These two positions were rather awkwardly conjoined in a policy of 'revolutionary waiting'. The revolution would only take place when economic conditions were right, and until then the Social Democrats had to wait. But even after the revolution removed the German Reich, the party's goal would be the perfection of parliamentary democracy, not a Paris Commune-style state.

Although the German SPD never joined a government, in practice it became increasingly willing to work for reform within the existing system. Even though Social Democrats continued to be subject to petty harassment in many areas – in Prussia in 1911 police even banned the use of the colour red on the first letters of banners in demonstrations – they increasingly acted as a reformist party within the system, controlling local governments and proposing legislation in the Reichstag to improve working conditions.[88] This reformist effort was particularly effective from the 1890s, as the party and the unions enjoyed more success. The internal organization of the party became highly complex, and full-time party officials tended to be politically cautious. Kautsky himself complained about the ossification of the party in 1905: the party executive was 'a collegium of old men' who had become 'absorbed in bureaucracy and parliamentarism'.[89] But the Germans were not the only ones who proved susceptible to the discreet charms of the bourgeoisie. In more liberal countries, such as France, it was even more difficult to maintain a principled distance from bourgeois politics, and the head of the Social Democratic SFIO, Jean Jaurès, was willing to collaborate with the Third Republic over some issues;[90] in Italy, too, the Italian Socialist Party (PSI) cooperated with Giolitti's Liberal government for a time, although much of the party objected.[91]

Kautsky's Modernist orthodoxy was therefore difficult to sustain, and it came under increasing attack from a reformist 'right' within the party, which agitated for the abandonment of the revolution completely, and from a Radical left which believed that Social Democracy was undergoing a debilitating process of *embourgeoisement*. From the 1890s, even as Marxism appeared to be at the height of its power in Western Europe, it was increasingly divided, both amongst the party elite and the mass membership. Whilst war and the Bolshevik revolution ultimately destroyed the unity which Engels and Kautsky had forged in the 1880s and 1890s, the conflicts had become evident long before then, and the balancing act between right and left became very difficult to maintain.[92]

The first major challenge to Kautskian orthodoxy came from the reformists. In 1899 Alexandre Millerand became the first socialist to become a minister in a liberal government – that of the French Prime Minister Pierre Waldeck-Rousseau. Although he achieved significant social reforms, his decision to serve in the government ultimately split the Socialist party into reformists, under Jean Jaurès, and hardliners under Jules Guesde. At the same time, in Germany, Kautskian orthodoxy was being challenged in a more fundamental way by a major figure in the SPD, Eduard Bernstein.

Bernstein's heresy came as a shock to party elders, because he was close to Marx and Engels and was thought to be their natural successor. The son of a plumber turned railway engineer, he was brought up in poverty, but had been bright enough to attend the *Gymnasium*, and became a bank clerk. Yet despite this semi-proletarian background, his behaviour and tastes were conventionally bourgeois. His early politics developed at the time of the Franco-Prussian war, and were nationalistic, but from 1872 he became an adherent of a broadly Marxist line. After the promulgation of the anti-socialist laws, Bernstein left Germany for exile in Switzerland, where he edited the party journal *Der Sozial-demokrat* between 1880 and 1890. Deported from Switzerland in 1888 he left for London, where, unable to return to Germany for legal reasons, he was forced to stay until 1901.

It is probable that Bernstein's views were changed by his enforced sojourn in England. Governments there were relatively responsive to working-class demands, the socialist movement was highly reformist, and it seemed difficult to believe that a crisis of capitalism was imminent. And from 1896 he plucked up courage to tackle orthodox Marxism head on in a number of articles for *Neue Zeit*. Marx, he claimed, had been too willing to accept revolutionary violence as the way to reach socialism. He was also wrong in predicting the crisis of capitalism and the increasing poverty of the proletariat. Neither, Bernstein argued with some justification, was happening; as he stated baldly: 'Peasants do not sink; middle class does not disappear; crises do not grow ever larger; misery and serfdom do not increase.'[93]

Social Democrats, he insisted, could peacefully reform capitalism through parliament, and public ownership would gradually emerge from private property because it was more rational. As he famously declared, full Communism was less important than social reform: 'What is generally called the ultimate goal of socialism is nothing to me; the movement is everything.'[94]

Just as Bernstein argued for workers to become full members of the 'bourgeois' nation state, so he appealed for Social Democrats to accept the nationalist and imperialist projects of those states.[95] He rejected Marx's view that the working man had no fatherland, and insisted that proletarians had to show loyalty to their nations. He was also prepared to accept empire, as long as it acted as a force of civilization.

Bernstein's ideas were met with a torrent of criticism from the leading figures of the Second International. He was charged, justly, with destroying the identity of Marxism and transforming it into a form of left-wing liberalism. Yet ultimately his 'revisionism' had a good deal of support within the Social Democratic movement – whether from the French Jean Jaurès, the Swedish Hjalmar Branting, or the Italian Francesco Merlino. It also proved attractive to many ordinary socialist supporters, though there was enormous regional variation. In Italy, revisionism, together with orthodoxy, was more popular in the North than in the more repressive South, where a more revolutionary Marxism flourished. Similarly, in Germany it was more common in the liberal South-West. Revisionist sentiments also seem to have been popular amongst ordinary German workers, and especially within the trade unions. As one explained, 'There will always be rich and poor. We would not dream of altering that. But we want a better and just organization at the factory and in the state.'[96]

Despite this support, Bernstein and revisionism were denounced as heretical in a number of Social Democratic congresses. At the Amsterdam Congress of the International in 1904, Kautsky and the SPD attracted a majority for their motion opposing participation in bourgeois governments. Even so, substantial opposition to the anti-revisionist line was expressed, largely by parties in countries where liberal democracy was strong and socialists had a chance of power – in Britain, France, Scandinavia, Belgium and Switzerland. Representatives from parties in more authoritarian countries, in contrast, opposed revisionism. Amongst them were the representative from Japan, the Bulgarian and future Bolshevik Christian Rakovsky, and a young radical from Russia, Vladimir Lenin. They were joined by the brilliant polemicist Rosa Luxemburg, a Polish Communist active in the German SPD.

The influence of these radicals presaged a new challenge to Kautsky's orthodoxy from the authoritarian East. In January 1905 revolution broke out in Russia, which seemed to suggest that popular action could push history forward towards Communism and that Kautsky's strategy of 'revolutionary waiting' was flawed. The Russian workers' deployment of the weapon of the General Strike in October 1905 also encouraged a working-class radicalism in the West that had been brewing for some time.[97] There is a good deal of evidence that many workers were becoming more radical in the decade before World War I. Trade-union membership swelled throughout Europe, and strikes became much more common in this period, especially between 1910 and 1914 as inflation eroded workers' living standards. But this renewed labour militancy was in some ways the rebirth of the old artisanal radicalism amongst skilled factory workers. Technological change was mechanizing areas of production that had previously been dominated by skilled craftsmen. In the metal-working industry, for instance, the use of more effective lathes and mechanical drills allowed employers to replace more skilled workers with cheaper, unskilled labour. And these skilled, often literate workers were precisely those who were most likely to defend themselves.

Metal-workers were to become some of the most radical sections of the working class in the next few decades.

Initially, this militancy fuelled the syndicalist movement, which was in some ways an updating of Proudhon's anarchism. Emerging in the French trade unions in the 1890s, syndicalists condemned Social Democrat parties for taking part in elections and parliaments, and called for direct working-class action in mass strikes and acts of sabotage. They also condemned Marxists' love of organization and centralization.

Syndicalists had a good deal of support in France, Italy and Spain. They even flourished in the United States, under the banner of the Industrial Workers of the World – the 'Wobblies'. In Germany they had very little influence, though their views were not too far from a group of radical Marxists in the SPD surrounding Rosa Luxemburg. Luxemburg, like the old Radical Marx, had faith in the revolutionary capabilities of the proletariat, and accused Kautsky and the SPD leadership of neglecting them in favour of reforms that merely buttressed the capitalist system. Eager for revolutionary politics, she travelled illegally to Warsaw (then part of the Russian empire) at the end of 1905 to take part in the revolution, and was arrested and imprisoned for several months. On her return to Germany, she urged that the SPD follow the Russian example and use mass strikes to mobilize the working class. Predictably, her ideas were opposed by Kautsky, who feared that mass action would threaten his sacrosanct party organization.

However, it was foreign, not internal affairs that would ultimately destroy the unity of Marxism, as Marxists found that they had to respond to the increasing power of imperialism and nationalism. Marxists prided themselves on their internationalism, and their leaders were part of a transnational community. Wars abroad, empires and mass armies were anathema. They therefore tried to stress the overriding importance of domestic inequality between classes. Some also tried to adapt Marxism to explain a new international inequality: between Europe and the colonized world. Marxist theorists like Rudolf Hilferding and Rosa Luxemburg developed a new view of an 'imperialist' capitalism. If in the 1840s the main forces of history had been capital and labour, half a century later the nation state and empire had joined them. Aggressive monopoly capitalists, they argued, had forged an alliance with states, and together they waged wars to dominate the colonized world.

Internationalists had some support from industrial workers who did not identify with the nation state. The international community of workers, united under the slogan 'Workers of All Lands Unite', seemed much more comfortable a home for many workers than an 'imagined community', as they saw it, created by aristocrats, liberal middle classes and generals.

The International's Stuttgart Congress of 1907 therefore denounced imperialism and nationalism. But orthodox internationalism came under pressure from revisionists – people like Bernstein and the British Labour Party's Ramsay MacDonald. They saw the advantages of empire for jobs, and believed that support for imperialist foreign policies was a price that had to be paid if workers were to be integrated into the nation state; some also sympathized with imperialist claims that they were bringing civilization to the colonial world.

But even orthodox Marxists found it difficult to resist the pressure to support the war effort as peace broke down in 1914, partly because many had implicitly nationalistic attitudes, and partly because they were afraid of the alternative.[98] If they opposed the war, there was always the risk that trade unions and Marxist parties would be banned in the name of national security. Also, the French feared a German regime that might be repressive towards workers, whilst the Germans and Austrians feared the even more reactionary Russians; and whilst the French socialist party largely saw the war as a defensive one against German aggression, the German party saw it as resistance to Russian barbarism and autocracy. As the SPD leader Hugo Haase told a French socialist, 'what the Prussian boot means to you the Russian knout means to us'.[99]

When war came in August 1914 Marxist leaders were wholly unpre-pared. But it was no surprise that all socialist parties bar two decided to vote for war credits. Some leaders, including Kautsky, tried to stand against the nationalistic tide, but they soon sacrificed principle to prag-matism and the desire for unity. Victor Adler, the head of the Austrian party, summed up the dilemma of international Social Democracy:

> I know we must vote for it [war credits]. I just don't know how I opened my mouth to say so. An incomprehensible German to have done any-thing else. An incomprehensible Social Democrat to have done it without being racked with pain, without a hard struggle with himself and with his feelings.[100]

It looked as if the International, and Marx's dream, was dead. Most Marxists in Europe had signed up to what they had previously denounced as 'bourgeois nationalism' and 'imperialism'. They were now part of a war effort in alliance with national elites.

Having emerged from an amalgam of Romantic socialisms, Marxism became a movement of revolutionary radicalism, before evolving into a Modernist Marxism, which then increasingly yielded to a more Pragmatic, reformist socialism. But a new cycle was soon to begin, as the revolutionaries once again seized the initiative in the international Communist movement. Although it appeared that elites and capitalists were in the ascendant in 1914, they were to be virtually destroyed by war, their nationalism discredited. Only three years later it looked as if the majority of Marxist parties had made the wrong call and lost the moral high ground.

The beneficiaries of this error were the parties within the International that had stood firm against the nationalist current: the Russian Social Democratic Workers' Party (both the Bolshevik and Menshevik factions), their allies, the small Serbian party, and the Italian socialists (PSI). Bernstein might have been right to insist, contra Marx, that the German working classes did have a fatherland, but the situation in Russia was very different. There many ordinary people felt deeply alienated from the national project, and war was to strain relations between them and the state to breaking point. Marx had been mistaken to think that he could transfer the banner of revolution from Paris to Berlin. Berlin was merely a transit point on its journey eastwards: to St Petersburg.

2

Bronze Horsemen

I

In November 1927, Soviet citizens were treated to a number of films made for the tenth anniversary of the October revolution. This was a golden era of film-making, and the Bolsheviks could call on several talented directors to tell the story of the revolution and explain its meaning, including the already famous Sergei Eisenstein. But it was Vsevolod Pudovkin's *End of St Petersburg* that elicited the greatest acclaim among the party elite. Pudovkin's film presented revolution as a resolutely modernizing force. It tells the story of 1917 through the life of a peasant – 'the Lad' – who is forced by poverty to move from the countryside to St Petersburg. In a classic Soviet 'socialist realist' plot-line, the Lad makes a journey from ignorance to political 'consciousness'. He finds work by joining a group of strike-breakers. But he soon learns to despise the tsarist secret police, and sees how cruel the bosses are towards their workers. He turns against the regime, is briefly imprisoned, and is then released to fight the Germans; whilst in the army he becomes a Bolshevik, and ultimately joins the assault on the Winter Palace.[1]

Pudovkin, then, insists that the peasant masses had become both modern and revolutionary. He also shows how the revolution took up the baton of modernization, dropped by the *ancien régime*, using the motif of the famous St Petersburg equestrian statue, the 'Bronze Horseman'. Ever since Alexander Pushkin wrote his famous poem on the subject in 1833, this monument to Peter the Great – the ruler who founded St Petersburg as a European-style city in 1703 – had become a symbol of the tsars' occasional harsh efforts to modernize Russia. Pudovkin followed Pushkin in presenting the Bronze Horseman as a symbol of the state's brutality, as well as of its modernizing ambitions.

During his scenes of the storming of the Winter Palace, he intercuts images of the Bronze Horseman with frames of the classical statues surmounting the Palace, as they are destroyed by the guns of the invading Bolsheviks. Pudovkin is suggesting that the Bolsheviks will end tsarist arrogance. But he makes it clear that they will not destroy the modernity brought by Peter. Soaring cranes replace the elegant classical statues, and an anonymous worker holds up his hand commandingly, evoking the Bronze Horseman's masterful gesture. Pudovkin tells his audience that the revolution will continue the work of Peter. But the new bronze horsemen bringing modernity will be the workers, not their erstwhile lords.

Pudovkin's drama showed how far the image of revolution had altered since the days of Delacroix, and how influential Modernist Marxism had become. His was a violent revolution, but it was also much more modern and scientific even than Delacroix's. Machines and metal had taken the place of billowing robes and blood-stained flags. Yet in many ways Pudovkin's story departed from the conventional Modernist Marxism of Kautsky and the German Social Democrats. The hero was not a solid worker, but a peasant who had only recently entered proletarian ranks. Also, Pudovkin's revolution was not only going to bring social justice; it would inherit a state-building project from a failing regime, and bring modernity to a poor, peasant country.

Pudovkin's film was well received by the members of the Bolshevik elite who watched it at its first showing in Moscow's Bolshoi Theatre, largely because he had captured the essence of Lenin's revolution.[2] Lenin was trying to forge a new combination of Radical and Modernist Marxism, suitable for a society that orthodox Marxists thought much too backward to experience a revolution. As the French Jacobins had found, it was precisely weak and failing states, with their repressive regimes, angry intelligentsias, urban workers and peasantries, which provided the most fertile ground for revolutions. Lenin was yoking a popular desire for equality with a plan to overcome backwardness, but by the 1920s he and the Bolsheviks had also added a crucial ingredient to the Marxist tradition. A specifically Russian organization, the militant, vanguard 'party of a new type' was to become the bearer of revolution and modernity.

In retrospect, though, Pudovkin's story was unconvincing. The idea that peasants and workers would move rapidly from a populist socialism, angry at injustices perpetrated by an elite, to become loyal Bolsheviks and dutiful citizens in a modern, planned economy, was a fanciful one. Soon after Lenin had seized power, he understood how much wishful thinking there had been in 1917. As the Jacobins discovered, it was impossible to marry ordinary people's demands for equality with a project to create a powerful state. The chaos of revolution led many of the Bolsheviks to abandon their temporary flirtation with Radical Marxism. They now embraced a more Modernist Marxism: workers and peasants would have to be subjected to strict discipline. But soon they even realized that this order was unsustainable, and they retreated further, from a revolutionary Radicalism, to Modernist faith in science, to a Pragmatism that appealed to larger groups of the population.

II

In May 1896 the coronation of Tsar Nicholas II was celebrated in Moscow with extraordinary pomp – 'Versailles relived', according to one contemporary. The Tsar entered the city on a 'pure white horse', followed by representatives of subject peoples, each in national costume. The procession also included delegates of the social estates and the local governments (*zemstva*), as well as foreigners.[3] Despite the profusion of social and ethnic groups, though, the procession was designed to stress the empire's unity. The newspaper *Moskovskie Vedomosti* declared:

> No one lived his own personal life. Everything fused into one whole, into one soul, pulsing with life, sensing and aware that it was the Russian people. Tsar and people created a great historical deed and, as long as the unity of people and Tsar exists, Rus' will be great and invincible, unfearing of external and internal enemies.[4]

The correspondent was mistaking propaganda for reality. As part of the government's paternalistic attempts to involve the ordinary people in the coronation events, it had become customary to hold a 'people's feast' on Khodynka Field, featuring plays and games for the entertainment of all. This year, however, more numbers than expected came and too few Cossack troops were deployed to control the crowds. As the festival began, there was panic, and between 1,350 and 2,000 were killed in the crush. The public, domestic and international, were horrified by reports in the press. It was clear that for all his claims to be the head of the invincible Rus', the Tsar's government was a poorly managed shambles. Nor was the much-vaunted unity of Tsar and people in evidence. Though Nicholas expressed his regret at the events, the festivities were not cancelled, and that same evening he attended a lavish ball given by the French Ambassador. An English observer wrote, 'Nero fiddled while Rome was burning, and Nicholas II danced at the French ball on the night of the Khodynskoe massacre.'[5] The future Bolshevik worker Semén Kanatchikov, arriving at the festival shortly after the disaster, similarly railed at the 'irresponsibility' and 'impunity' of the authorities.[6] The Khodynka affair was a bad omen for the Tsar – his grandiose pretensions at the coronation had been humiliatingly exposed, and he had responded with insouciant arrogance. There could be no clearer display of despotic decadence.

As the coronation rituals made clear, the Russian empire at the end of the nineteenth century was proud to be an *ancien régime*. Indeed, it consciously overtook pre-1789 France as the embodiment of reactionary principles. Paradoxically, its *ancien régime* was of relatively recent vintage. Just as Enlightenment *philosophes* were condemning hierarchy and difference, the tsars were entrenching them, and after its defeat of revolutionary France in the Napoleonic wars, the regime self-consciously styled itself the bastion of tradition and autocracy against enlightenment and revolution. Russia continued to be made up of a series of unequal estates, status groups and nationalities, each with their own specific legal privileges and obligations.[7] The peasants were notoriously disadvantaged, and before 1861 they were unfree – the last serfs in Europe.

As the French monarchy discovered in 1789, such a system could persist only so long as the state did not make too many demands of its subjects. But once it sought to compete with rival states – to the West and the East – which could mobilize large, well-trained armies, raise high levels of taxation, and build modern munitions, it had to do the same. Inevitably the peasants, and later the industrial workers and ethnic minorities in the Russian empire, who were expected to make these sacrifices, demanded something in return. If they were to contribute money or their lives to the state, they wanted to be treated with dignity, as valued participants in a common enterprise, not as cannon-fodder or milch-cows.

A series of military defeats – by the British and Ottoman Empire in the Crimean War (1853–6), by the Japanese (1904–5) and by the Germans in the Great War – forced some of the Tsar's officials to recognize that the *ancien régime* was not working; reformers realized that the empire had to become something like a unified nation state, with modern industry and agriculture. The divisions within society had to be overcome and an emotional bond forged between people and the state. Against them, however, were ranged conservatives who feared reform would undermine the monarchy and the hierarchies which were its foundation. The result was a series of unstable compromises, which only partially integrated the population into the political system, and increased popular resentment. Alexander II introduced a series of reforms in the 1850s and 1860s, the most important of which, the emancipation of the serfs, legally freed the peasants. But they still had an inferior legal status, and they did not receive the land they believed was their due. They also continued to be tied to the ancient village 'commune' (*obshchina*) – an ancient institution of local self-regulation – the better to control and tax them. The peasants' anger at the inequitable settlement, expressed as a populist, almost anarchistic resentment against the state, continued to simmer until the Bolsheviks gave them land in 1917.[8]

If the peasantry, a separate estate, remained isolated and discriminated against, the working class was completely excluded from the estate structure, despite its growing size during Russia's belated industrialization in the 1880s and 1890s. Pudovkin's 'Lad' was typical of the millions who left the increasingly overpopulated countryside for industry in the towns. In the fifty years before 1917 the urban population of Russia quadrupled from 7 to 28 million; and whilst the industrial working class was still a relatively small 3.6 million, it was highly concentrated in the politically important cities. On arriving in the city, workers sometimes joined informal communities, or 'artels'. The worker Kanatchikov remembered his group of fifteen men, who rented an apartment and ate cabbage soup every day together from a common bowl with wooden spoons, celebrating their twice-monthly pay-cheque with 'wild carousing'.[9] But workers were not allowed to organize themselves into trade unions or any larger bodies, at least before 1905, and so the rich culture of the German unions and SPD was completely lacking. However, resentment at poor conditions and treatment remained; indeed the workers' impotence fuelled it. The worker A. I. Shapovalov recalled in his memoirs his attitude towards his boss:

> At the sight of his fat belly and healthy red face I not only did not take off my hat, but in my eyes, against my will, there flared up a terrible fire of hatred when I saw him. I had the mindless idea of grabbing him by the throat, throwing him to the ground, and stamping on his fat belly with my feet.[10]

Eventually, Kanatchikov and Shapovalov, and many other so-called 'conscious' workers, decided to act on their anger by joining a larger organization. But it was to the radical intelligentsia that they looked for leadership – another group excluded from the estate system, and determined to overcome Russia's divisions and accelerate its modernization.

III

From the middle of the 1860s, the Russian authorities became worried about a new fashion amongst young educated people: women were escaping their highly restrictive families by contracting fictitious marriages; the newly-weds would then separate after the wedding, or live together without consummating the relationship. The police were also concerned with what they saw as a related phenomenon: the popularity of the *ménage à trois*. They located the roots of this subversive behaviour in an extraordinarily influential, though poorly written, novel published in 1863, *What is to be Done? From Tales of New People*, by the Russian socialist intellectual Nikolai Chernyshevskii.[11]

The impact of Chernyshevskii's novel amongst young educated people was comparable to the influence of Rousseau's novels before the French Revolution; this was not accidental, for Chernyshevskii set out to produce a Russified, socialist version of Rousseau's *La Nouvelle Héloïse*.[12] Chernyshevskii told the story of a woman, Vera, whose authoritarian parents, like Julie's, want her to accept a loveless, arranged marriage. Vera is rescued by Lopukhov, a Saint-Preux-like tutor, who lives with her in a chaste quasi-marriage, but she subsequently marries his friend, Kirsanov. After a short period when they live together as a *ménage à trois*, Lopukhov leaves, to return later and live, now married to another, with Vera and Kirsanov in a harmonious joint family.

The novel also presents several Romantic socialist utopias. In one Vera and Lopukhov set up a cooperative workshop and a commune of seamstresses. In another, Vera dreams of a society of rationally organized, communal labour; men and women live in a huge iron and glass palace full of technological wonders including, prophetically, air-conditioning and light-bulbs, modelled on London's Crystal Palace which Chernyshevskii had once seen from a distance. His characters work joyously in the fields by day, happy because most of the work is done by machines; and in the evenings they have lavish balls, dressed in Greek robes of 'the refined Athenian period'.[13]

We do not know how seriously Chernyshevskii wanted his readers to take these socialist and revolutionary ideas.[14] The novel was written in an obscure style to evade the censors. Yet *What is to be Done?*, like Rousseau's writings, had an enormous effect on young men and women because it showed an alternative to their everyday experience of hierarchy, subordination and social division; just as Robespierre thanked Rousseau for revealing his innate dignity to him, so Russian youths praised Chernyshevskii for showing them how to live their lives as 'new people' – in equality, standing up to supercilious aristocrats, escaping their controlling families and devoting themselves to the common good. The appeal of the 'new man' is shown in the story told of Lopukhov, when he finds himself sharing a St Petersburg pavement with an arrogant dignitary. Rather than giving way to him, he picks him up bodily and, whilst maintaining absolute self-discipline and formal politeness, deposits him in the gutter, cheered on by two passing peasants.

Chernyshevskii, like most Russian socialists of the time, was deeply hostile to Russian nationalism. But his view that the *ancien régime* was an affront to ordinary men and women's dignity resonated deeply at a time when Russia itself was being humiliated by foreign rivals, just as Rousseau's ideas had appealed to youths desperate to revive French power. Chernyshevskii was convinced that Russia was weak because its hierarchies made men servile. Everybody had to adopt an obsequious, sycophantic manner, and social solidarity was impossible. These 'Asiatic values' (*aziatchina*) had corrupted Russians' personalities and behaviour.[15]

Chernyshevskii, however, departed from Rousseau in insisting that Russia could only escape its humiliation by becoming more modern, and more like the West. He therefore combined a Rousseauian interest in egalitarian utopias with a Marx-like interest in a modern socialism and revolution. For alongside Vera and her fellow 'new people', *What is to be Done?* introduced a 'special person', committed to focused, purposeful political action – the ascetic revolutionary Rakhmetov.

The novel suggests that Chernyshevskii did not entirely approve of Rakhmetov, but his readers found him an exciting figure.[16] He hails from an ancient aristocratic family, and significantly he is of mixed Eastern and Western – Tartar and Russian – blood. He also has the dual virtues of both the intellectual and the man of the people. Though well-read in French and German literature, he is also a self-strengthener. At seventeen he resolves to transform his physique, following a diet involving raw beefsteak, and even becomes a boat-hauler on the Volga. He then goes to university, where he meets Kirsanov, but he continues to lead an austere life, eating the diet of the common people – apples rather than apricots (though he does allow himself oranges in St Petersburg). He abstains from drink, and even subjects himself to self-inflicted tortures, lying on a bed of nails so that he can know what he is capable of. His whole life is dedicated to the service of the people. He reads only books that will be useful, spurning frivolous works such as Macaulay's *History of England*. His utilitarianism also extends to personal relations. He only speaks to people who have authority with others, bidding a dismissive 'Excuse me, I have no time' to anyone less weighty.[17]

Rakhmetov deploys these single-minded qualities to foment revolution in Russia, and understandably many readers saw *What is to be Done?* as an appeal to emulate him. 'Great is the mass of good and honest men, but Rakhmetovs are rare,' the novel declares. 'They are few in number, but they put others in a position to breathe, who without them would have been suffocated.'[18] Chernyshevskii seemed to have been calling for an elite organization of modern, rational people, who also had an affinity with the common folk. They alone could overthrow the old weak and unequal order.

Chernyshevskii's characters were viciously satirized in Dostoyevsky's *Notes from the Underground*, published in 1864. His 'Underground Man' emulates Lopukhov's assertion of dignity by refusing to give way to an officer in the street. But after days of planning the confrontation, his attempts end in comic failure; when he finally does brush against the baffled officer, it is not clear that the arrogant grandee has even noticed his revolutionary gesture.[19]

Dostoyevsky's cynical response, however, was unusual, at least among the young, and Chernyshevskii's work became a holy book for generations of radical Russian students. Alexander II's reforms liberalized and expanded the universities, opening the way for non-nobles to become students. The government hoped that they would make their way up the ranks of the imperial bureaucracy and bring new talent to government. In practice a new radical student culture emerged, intolerant of the tsarist regime's obscurantism, committed to science, and determined to liberate the people. Radicalism in the 1860s and 1870s became a lifestyle, much as it did in Western universities in the 1960s and 1970s. Students challenged authority by using direct, disrespectful speech, and wearing shabby, 'poor' clothes. One remembered that the medical students were the most political group, and expressed their opinions openly: 'Blue glasses, long hair, red shirts not tucked in but belted with sashes – these were surely medical students.' Radical women students, meanwhile, wore puritanical black dresses and short cropped hair. This counter-uniform helped to forge a moral community, a group of 'apostles of knowledge', committed to using their privileged education to help the benighted people.[20]

However, sharp disagreements over how best to bring socialism emerged amongst the students. One remembered the two views competing for the students' loyalty:

> It is a debt of honour before the people we want to serve that we receive a solid, scientific, well-rounded, and serious education; only then can we assume with a clear conscience the spiritual leadership of the revolution.
>
> 'Continue to study!' others jeered. [That means] to remove yourself from the revolutionary cause ... It is not in the university or from books but in immediate interaction with the people and the workers where you can receive the knowledge useful to the revolutionary cause.[21]

Chernyshevskii had favoured the first argument, but he was imprisoned and exiled for his political views between 1862 and 1883, and it was his heir, the agrarian socialist Petr Lavrov, who became its main proponent. Students, the Westernizing Lavrov urged, had to master science to prepare for the new order, not engage in destructive revolution. As has been seen, Lavrov, whilst not a Marxist himself, was the Russian socialist who maintained most contact with West European Marxists, and was on Engels' Christmas pudding list. Mikhail Bakunin defended the second view: Western culture was bourgeois and philistine, and students had to merge with the peasantry, absorbing their inherently collectivist culture – embodied in the traditional peasant 'commune'.[22] Ultimately, in Bakunin's view, peasant revolution, with its roots in Russian brigandage, would destroy the fundamentally alien, 'German' Russian state:

> The brigand is always the hero, the defender, the avenger of the people, the irreconcilable enemy of the entire state regime, both in its civil and social aspects, the life and death fighter against our statist-aristocratic, official-clerical civilization.[23]

The debate between Lavrov and Bakunin carried distinct echoes of the conflict between Modernist and Radical Marxism. But unlike Marx, both believed in the revolutionary potential of the peasantry – happily so, as there was not yet much of a proletariat in Russia. Yet neither Lavrov's nor Bakunin's strategies altered the fundamental conservatism of the regime, and official repression encouraged a turn towards revolutionary violence. Crucial was the failure of the Lavrovite 'Going to the People' movement of 1874, when over a thousand young people abandoned their lives in the towns and went to live with the peasantry. Dressing as peasants, the men in red shirts and baggy trousers, and women in white blouses and skirts, they hoped to educate them, enlighten them and encourage them to rise up and demand a redistribution of land. The youths and the peasantry did not always have much in common, but it was official repression, not peasant hostility, that led to the movement's failure. Large numbers of the youthful idealists were arrested and sentenced in large open trials in 1877–8.[24]

The lessons seemed clear: the radical movement had to become more organized, secretive and conspiratorial. In 1879 one wing of the Russian socialist movement, the 'People's Will' (*Narodnaia Volia*), created the model for all terrorist organizations in the modern world: it was pyramidal in structure, and was made up of discrete cells, which, for reasons of security, were supposed to be ignorant of the activities of the others. The People's Will was also the first organization to use the innovative explosive technology recently developed by the businessman Alfred Nobel. That year it passed a death sentence on Alexander II, which was enacted in 1881 when two hand-held bombs were thrown at the Tsar's carriage.

The harsh repression that followed the assassination only strengthened the terrorists and their most prominent theorist, Petr Tkachev. The son of a petty nobleman, he argued that only action by a small 'revolutionary minority' would bring socialism to the country. It was in the 1880s that Rakhmetov eclipsed Vera and Kirsanov as the role model of choice for Russian youth. Osipanov, one of the members of the terrorist organization that made an assassination attempt on Alexander III in 1887, the 'Group of March 1', emulated his hero by sleeping on nails. *What is to be Done?* was also the favourite book of another member of the Group of March 1, Aleksandr Ulianov, and, after his execution, that of his brother, Vladimir – later known as 'Lenin'.

Russian socialist terrorists continued to operate throughout the 1890s, killing thousands of officials, including several ministers – one author has estimated that over 17,000 people died as a result of terrorism in the twenty years before 1917.[25] Meanwhile the *okhrana* (secret police) fought back, often very effectively. In 1908 it emerged that one of the terrorist leaders was none other than an undercover police agent – Evno Azef.

The temper of politics changed, however, with the devastating famine of 1891. The tsarist state's failure to deal with the crisis encouraged educated society to take its place and organize famine relief. It now seemed imperative that socialists become involved in peaceful reform. However, it proved impossible to return to the politics of Lavrov and the 1870s. Russia was industrializing rapidly, and the famine had destroyed any lingering idealism about the countryside. The old agrarian socialist consensus that the peasant commune was Russia's gift to world socialism, and that suitably modernized it would become the germ of the ideal society, was damaged beyond repair; agriculture and the peasantry appeared now to be irremediably backward, the embodiment of Russia's *aziatchina*, and a new revolutionary class would have to be found. It was this lacuna that explains the attractiveness of Marxism. The principles of Marxism provided an alternative to the tsarist hierarchy, but also promised a new vanguard – the working class – and a path out of backwardness. Moreover they appeared to be 'scientific' and Western. As the revolutionary and friend of Lenin, Nikolai Valentinov, remembered:

> We seized on Marxism because we were attracted by its sociological and economic *optimism*, its strong belief, buttressed by facts and figures, that the development of the economy, the development of capitalism, by

demoralizing and eroding the foundations of the old society, was creating new forces (including us) which would certainly sweep away the autocratic regime together with its abominations ... We were also attracted by its *European* nature. Marxism came from Europe. It did not smell and taste of home-grown mould and provincialism, but was new, fresh and exciting. Marxism held out the promise that we would not stay a semi-Asiatic country, but would become part of the West with its culture, institutions and attributes of a free political system. The West was our guiding light.[26]

The 'Marxism' adopted by the Russian socialists was firmly of the Modernist variety: a backward Russia would have to endure capitalist development first and as such socialism was a long way away. This was not immediately apparent when Marx was first translated into Russian. When *Capital* was delivered to Skuratov, one of the two tsarist censors deputed to read half of it in 1872, he reported: 'it is possible to state with certainty that very few people in Russia will read it, and even fewer will understand it'.[27] He concluded that it could be published, arguably the most important mistake made by the censors since *What is to be Done?* appeared nine years before. The Russian edition of the work – the first translation from its original German – was an extraordinary hit among the Russian reading public, massively outselling its Hamburg predecessor. But Skuratov was right that not all would understand it, at least initially. Both agrarian socialists and official, pro-regime newspapers welcomed it, as a warning of the capitalist nightmare of child labour and satanic mills. Yet even though Marx himself seems to have been persuaded in the 1880s that Russia could avoid capitalism and preserve the commune, the message of *Capital* was the exact opposite: capitalism was inevitable. And in 1883, this became the doctrine of the first Marxist organization in Russia, 'The Liberation of Labour', founded by the exiled revolutionary Georgii Plekhanov. Plekhanov abandoned the old Russian agrarian socialist faith in the peasantry and declared firmly that Russia would not be ready for socialism until it had been through the travails of capitalism and liberalism. The working class, led by intellectuals in the Social Democratic party, would stage a revolution against the autocracy, but this would bring only liberal democracy, and only at a much later stage socialism. Plekhanov's doctrine became the orthodoxy amongst Russian Marxists, as did the socialism of Kautsky and the Second International.

Yet the relevance of Kautskian Marxism to Russia was highly debatable. It had been developed in semi-democratic, maturing industrial societies, in which workers were being gradually integrated into the political system, and where liberal democracy, suitably broadened, seemed to be in the interests of the working masses. In Russia, in contrast, much more repressive circumstances contributed to a very different culture. Like the Bavarian worker Nikolaus Osterroth, Russian radical students in the 1890s and 1900s saw their lives as a journey from 'darkness' to 'light'; they were becoming 'new', 'conscious' people, embracing both the modern city and a socialist identity. However, in Russia they were a much more embattled community, infiltrated by the police. Their culture was a highly moralistic and Manichaean one, in which 'honourable', heroic students confronted evil spies. 'Courts of honour' were held to expose and 'purge' suspected enemies from the student community, their accusers judging them by their public and private lives – practices rather similar to those found in the later Bolshevik party. In these threatening conditions, it is no surprise that a more radical, sectarian vision of politics was to challenge the more inclusive Kautskian tradition.[28]

I V

Vladimir Ulianov (Lenin) was the figure who adapted Chernyshevskii's socialism to the modern world, and the Second International's Modernist Marxism to the conditions of Russia. Both Lenin's background and personality suited him to the role of Westernizer and modernizer. Although his father was formally an aristocrat – a nobleman who could expect to be addressed as 'your excellency' – it would be misleading to think of the Ulianovs as a family with aristocratic values. Lenin's father was a professional educationalist and had earned his title when he became Director of Schools for Simbirsk Province. Both Lenin's parents were from mixed ethnic background, his father probably of Russian and indigenous Volga background, and his mother was a Lutheran of mixed German, Swedish and Jewish ancestry. They could, therefore, be seen as ambitious outsiders, eager to succeed and assimilate, and they implanted their socially aspirational self-discipline in their children.[29] They were typical of many professionals of the time who devoted themselves to improving Russia and her people whilst remaining loyal to the tsar. The Ulianovs were reformist progressives, interested in the latest enlightened ideas, whilst the Lutheranism and German background of Maria, Lenin's mother, gave the family a particularly Westernizing cast of mind, which Lenin betrayed in later life when he compared Russian laziness unfavourably with Jewish and German discipline.[30] In many ways, then, Lenin's background was not unlike Marx's – a professional family of a successful minority ethnicity, willing to assimilate to the dominant ethnicity in an *ancien régime*, but remaining faithful to enlightened ideas and committed to eliminating backwardness and obscurantism. As in other cases, it was the children of these first-generation assimilators who rebelled, convinced that their parents had been too accommodating to the powers that be.

However, whilst Lenin's background bore some similarity to Marx's, his character was very different. Lenin was never a Romantic utopian socialist, nor was he a rebel as a child; he enjoyed good relations with his father, and he was a model pupil at school: in his end-of-school report his headmaster stated that 'The guiding principles of his upbringing were religion and rational discipline' (a judgement delivered by none other than Fedor Kerenskii, the father of Aleksandr, the head of the liberal Provisional Government whom Lenin overthrew in October 1917).[31] Throughout his life, Lenin observed the practices of bourgeois 'rational discipline'. His desk was spotlessly tidy, he was careful about money (even cutting any scrap of blank paper from letters he received for re-use), and he evinced nothing but contempt for his more bohemian co-editors on the Marxist newspaper *Iskra* (*Spark*).[32]

It is not surprising that Lenin should have found efficient Germanic cultures appealing – especially their post offices. According to his wife, Nadezhda Krupskaia, when, exiled from Russia and in an Alpine village, he had 'nothing but praise' for Swiss culture and its postmen, who delivered his precious books to him so he could work on his pamphlets.[33] In 1917 it was only semi-humorously that he described the German postal service as a model of the future socialist state.[34]

Yet Lenin was to channel his bourgeois discipline in the service of a revolution against the bourgeoisie. The execution of his brother, Aleksandr, for involvement in revolutionary terrorism doubtless explains a great deal. Vladimir was discriminated against as a member of a suspect family, and he was left not only Aleksandr's example but also his books, including *What is to be Done?* Lenin later declared that this work had 'ploughed him over again and again'. 'It completely reshaped me.' 'This is a book that changes one for one's whole lifetime.'

> Chernyshevskii not only showed that every right-thinking and really honest man must be a revolutionary, but he also showed – and this is his greatest merit – what a revolutionary must be like, what his principles must be, how he must approach his aim, and what methods he must use to achieve it.[35]

It may also be that the book provided the model for the romantic triangle involving his wife, Krupskaia, and the future theorist of socialism and love, Inessa Armand.[36] And there is much of the Rakhmetov about Lenin's puritanical commitment to revolution and utilitarian rejection of anything that might distract him. Although he did not consume a raw-beef diet or sleep on nails (his health was poor), unusually amongst his fellow revolutionaries, he kept himself fit with gymnastics.

Following his brother's death in 1887, Lenin entered university in Kazan, but was expelled after a year for his involvement in demonstrations. He joined agrarian socialist groups for a time, but it is no surprise that he was attracted by the Modernist Marxism of Plekhanov, and in 1893 he went to St Petersburg with ambitions to become a Marxist revolutionary and theorist. He became known in revolutionary circles as a particularly hard-line opponent of agrarian socialism. But Lenin also differed from most Russian Marxists of his time in significant ways. He appreciated the difficulties confronting Marxists in Russian circumstances where capitalism was only just emerging: they would effectively condemn Russia to a very long journey to the socialist paradise, and in the meantime radicals would have to tolerate the top-hatted speculators and satanic mills. This was something he found very difficult, for he hated the bourgeoisie as a class more viscerally than many other Marxists, and was especially hostile to 'bourgeois' ideas like liberal democracy and the rule of law. According to his wife, his view of the liberal bourgeoisie was poisoned early in his life when local society shunned his mother after the arrest of Aleksandr, and she could not find anybody to accompany her in her carriage on the first stage of her journey to visit him in gaol.[37] His personal experience only strengthened the view, common among Russian Marxists, that the Russian bourgeoisie had a particularly craven attitude towards the aristocracy and the tsarist state. Lenin strongly approved of the sentiments stated in the first Russian

Social Democratic Party programme: 'The further east in Europe one proceeds, the weaker, more cowardly, and baser in the political sense becomes the bourgeoisie and the greater are the cultural and political tasks that devolve on the proletariat.'[38] His hatred of the existing order was doubtless strengthened by his imprisonment in 1895 and his subsequent exile to Siberia in 1897.

Lenin was therefore always looking for reasons to push the revolutionary process forward – he was in more of a hurry than most of his fellow Modernist Marxists, who were happy to contemplate living under a temporary bourgeois hegemony. But his view of the forces that would 'accelerate' history towards socialism varied depending on circumstances. Most frequently, he looked to a conspiratorial elite of modernizers to take on this accelerator role, in a manner reminiscent of Chernyshevskii or Tkachev. But whilst this elitism was his default position, he did not always put his faith in a revolutionary elite. His Marxism was always flexible, and he adapted it to the conditions of Russia, with its occasionally radical workers and peasants. When it looked as if the people were in insurrectionary mood, Lenin could be more populist than other Marxists, and veered towards a Radical Marxist line. From 1902, he was also more willing to see the peasantry as a potentially revolutionary class than his fellow Russian Marxists (and certainly more than the German Marxists), although Bolshevism remained fundamentally suspicious of the 'backward' peasantry.

Freed from his Siberian exile in 1900, Lenin decided it was too risky to stay in Russia, and he began several years' sojourn abroad, in Zurich, Munich and London. But he still lived and breathed revolutionary politics amongst the small communities of revolutionary exiles. He also continued to argue for the imminence of revolution, most famously in his pamphlet 'What is to be Done?' of 1902. A group of Russian Marxists (the so-called 'Economists') had in effect adopted Eduard Bernstein's revisionism, insisting that as the revolution was so far off, Marxists should just help workers to improve their working conditions and wages. Lenin reacted angrily to this heresy. Marxists had to have ambition and inspire workers with Communist ideas. By themselves workers would only develop 'trade-union' consciousness – the desire for better conditions. 'Social Democratic' consciousness – the desire for fundamental political change – had to be brought to workers 'from without', by a revolutionary intelligentsia versed in Marxist ideology. But this intelligentsia would not be a group of Marxist theorists, as Kautsky assumed.[39] They were to be 'professional' revolutionaries, ideologically 'conscious' and acting conspiratorially and in secret, bringing Western efficiency to Russian radicalism at a time when the police was becoming more repressive.[40] The party, he argued, needed to be centralized, like a 'large factory'.[41] Such revolutionaries, both modern and conspiratorial, were, of course, reminiscent of Chernyshevskii's Rakhmetov, to whom he paid obeisance in the work's title.[42]

Initially Lenin's idea of a centralized, vanguard party was not controversial amongst Marxists, and in strictly ideological terms it may not have been that new.[43] But Lenin's idea of the ideal party culture was very different from the assumptions of Kautsky (and indeed Marx). Lenin's approach to politics was militant, sectarian and hostile to compromise. He was convinced that his colleagues were refusing to prepare seriously for the revolution he believed was imminent; they, by contrast, saw him as over-optimistic about the end of the old order, authoritarian and excessively hostile towards the bourgeoisie. The first major row, which split the party in 1903, took place over the party's membership rules. Lenin demanded that the party be made up of party activists only; Iulii Martov, his fellow *Iskra* editor, wanted a broader membership of supporters. Lenin was in a minority, but because a number of his opponents walked out before the vote, his faction won and became known as the Bolsheviks (from the Russian word *bolshinstvo* – 'majority'), whilst Martov's group was labelled the Mensheviks (from *menshinstvo* – 'minority'). Lenin then escalated the conflict, acting in an aggressive and high-handed way – even he admitted that he 'often behaved in a state of frightful irritation, frenziedly'.[44] He also alienated most of international Marxism's leading figures, including Plekhanov, Kautsky and Rosa Luxemburg.

Lenin turned out to be more prescient than his Menshevik rivals, for revolution did break out in Russia two years later. The fall of the naval base of Port Arthur (Lüshunkou) in the then Russian Far East to the Japanese in December 1904 was even more humiliating for the tsarist regime than its previous major defeat, by the British in the Crimea. For the first time a European power had been defeated by Asians fighting alone. It is therefore not surprising that at this juncture the many subterranean tensions in Russia should burst into open conflict. An orthodox priest, Father Gapon, used the opportunity to press the demands of

urban workers. On what became known as 'Bloody Sunday', he organized a demonstration of 50,000–100,000 people, which assumed the
form of a religious procession of icon-bearing loyal subjects presenting a
humble petition to the Tsar. The petition resounded with the Tsar's own
paternalistic rhetoric. However, the demands were radical, and included
democratic suffrage, the legalization of trade unions and civil rights for
all citizens. The police declared the march illegal, and when it failed to
disperse, troops fired indiscriminately on the peaceful, unarmed crowd.

In the midst of the shooting, Gapon is said to have declared, 'There is
no God any longer! There is no Tsar!'[45] Certainly, this unprovoked violence damaged the image of Tsar Nicholas as benevolent father beyond
repair. It was now absolutely clear that his familial model of politics
would not give workers and peasants what they wanted. Workers
responded by setting up a new type of body – the council, or 'soviet', of
workers' deputies – to coordinate strikes. These soviets were organized
on the basis of direct democracy, rather like the Paris Commune; in
theory, constituents could recall their deputies. Some of those elected
were socialists – Lev Trotsky was the chairman of the St Petersburg
Soviet – and they helped to organize the general strike which forced the
regime to grant the 'October Manifesto', a promise of elections to a
legislative assembly and civil liberties. The Social Democrats, though,
had a modest role in the revolution. It was a genuinely cross-class and
cross-party affair. As in the 1830 and early 1848 revolutions, liberals,
workers and the small number of socialists were united against a hide-
bound autocracy.

Lenin was enthusiastic about the revolution, and the October Manifesto convinced him that it would be safe to return to Russia from
exile. He was now allied with some of the most left-wing Marxists in
the Russian movement – Aleksandr Bogdanov's 'Forward' group – who
had the utmost faith in the proletariat's ability to build socialism in the
near future.[46] Neither, though, went as far as Trotsky, who argued that
Russia was ready for a one-stage 'permanent revolution' that would
rapidly lead from the bourgeois democratic stage to socialism.[47] Lenin
argued for a 'revolutionary-democratic dictatorship of the proletariat
and the peasantry' to bring in the bourgeois revolution – unlike the
moderate Mensheviks, who urged an alliance between workers and the
middle classes.[48]

In the event, the 1905 revolution broadly followed the course of its failed European predecessors of 1848. The liberals, satisfied with the concessions of October and fearing the radicalism of workers and peasants, abandoned the revolutionary movement. Meanwhile the regime managed to regroup, bringing troops back from the Far East to suppress the peasant unrest. In December some Moscow workers staged a final, doomed resistance in the Presnia district where they threw up barricades and set up a local form of workers' government. But they were no match for the regime's artillery; carnage ensued and much of Presnia was reduced to rubble.

Prospects again looked bleak for socialists, and in December 1907 Lenin was forced again into exile, travelling to Switzerland. He devoted himself to reading and writing: he began with philosophy, but as war approached he immersed himself in the latest works on capitalism and imperialism, by people like Luxemburg, the up-and-coming Russian Marxist Nikolai Bukharin, and especially by the influential Austrian Marxist Rudolf Hilferding. Hilferding convinced him that the old competition between small entrepreneurs had given way to a vicious struggle between nation states for markets, leading to imperialist expansion and war between the great powers.[49] Capitalism's fundamental immorality had been exposed. No longer did capitalists even pretend to be liberal humanitarians; they were open racists and Social Darwinists, justifying their interests with war-mongering nationalism. At the same time, though, modern capitalism had become highly centralized, and had prepared the ground for socialist planning.

Lenin, always on the lookout for signs of capitalism's imminent demise, seized on Hilferding's insights. In his *Imperialism, the Highest Stage of Capitalism*, written in 1915 and published in 1917, he berated both capitalists and Kautsky's Second International for supporting war.[50] He also followed other, more radical, theorists of imperialism in arguing that just as capitalism was becoming globalized, so would revolution. Because imperial states were exploiting states on the colonial periphery, socialist revolution could occur even in semi-'backward' countries. The struggle against capitalism could begin in Russia, although he accepted it would have to be supported by socialist revolutions in other more advanced countries. Lenin also argued that Marxists in colonial societies could lead revolutions for political independence against imperialists, even if capitalism had barely taken hold and socialism was far away. Lenin's text laid the foundations for the merging of Marxism and anti-colonial nationalism. As will be seen, his *Imperialism* was crucial in bringing Communism to the non-European world.

Few Russians read Lenin's *Imperialism*, but its main function was to explain to himself and his fellow revolutionaries why history was on their side. When, in 1917, the tsarist regime collapsed, workers and peasants behaved as they had done in 1905, establishing soviets, revolutionary committees and other forms of self-government. Lenin and the Bolsheviks were now in a position to offer a confident and seemingly coherent alternative.

V

Between 1913 and 1916, the avant-garde symbolist novelist Andrei Bely (born in 1880) published his great modernist novel, *Petersburg*. The city had featured as a major character in previous novels, but Bely's Petersburg was a very different place to that of Chernyshevskii's and Dostoyevsky's novels. Set in 1905, it was a city in ferment, surrounded by a 'ring of many-chimneyed factories' from which the menacing sound of the revolutionary proletariat emanated, 'oooo-oooo-oooo'.[51] The tsarist official in the novel, Apollon Apollonovich Beleukhov, is no longer an aristocratic reactionary but the embodiment of rational modernization (in the popular Nietzschean imagery of the time, Apollo was the god of reason). The cold Apollon enjoys looking at the perfect cubes and straight lines of Petersburg's planned streets, and surrounds himself with neo-classical art, including a painting by David. But his command of reason is insufficient to control his own radicalized son, let alone Russia, and he is terrified of the revolutionary forces surrounding him.[52] The other embodiments of reason in the novel are equally ineffectual, though more violent. The revolutionary Dudkin and his mentor, the Azef figure Lippachenko, impose dogmatic and violent schemes on others. Dudkin is even visited by the Bronze Horseman, who pours metal into his veins and hails him as 'my son'.[53] Yet the Bronze Horseman and the spirit of modernity solve nothing, merely setting off a cycle of revenge and violence.[54]

For Bely, as for Pushkin, the Bronze Horseman, with two legs on Russian soil and two rearing into the air, was a symbol of Russia's division into two – the native traditions of ordinary Russians and the cruel rationalism of Peter the Great.[55] But Bely denied that either officials or revolutionaries could reconcile these halves. For him, only the apocalypse, which he identified with the 'eastern' revolutionary forces from below, would allow Russia to escape its predicament and 'leap across history'.[56] Ultimately Bely was wrong. The revolution did not bind Russia's fragmented society together. But he was prescient about the events of 1917. Forces from below were to overwhelm Russia's bronze horsemen, whether tsarist, liberal or Bolshevik.

The outbreak of war in 1914 brought the third and final crisis for Russia's post-1815 regime. As Savenko, the leader of the Nationalist Party, declared in 1915, 'War is an exam, a great exam', and it was a tougher one than any the tsarist regime had sat in the past.[57] Russia's main enemy, Germany, was aiming at a 'total' mobilization of all resources – men, food, industrial production – for war. And Russia, as a semi-reformed *ancien régime*, was at a severe disadvantage in the contest. Mistrustful of involvement from society as a whole – both elites and ordinary people – the state found it difficult to engage their support for the war effort. Its factories could not produce enough munitions, and it could not raise the troops needed. These structural weaknesses, combined with poor trench technology, led to massive defeats in Galicia and Poland, and by August 1915 over 4 million soldiers had been killed, wounded or captured.

The crisis forced the Tsar to give in to the reforming Apollon Apollonoviches of his regime, and to allow elements of 'society' – members of educated society committed to modernization – a role in the war effort. In some ways this was successful, and by early 1917 Russia had destroyed the Habsburg army and was producing more munitions than the Germans.[58] Yet the Russian monarchy's partial attempts to transform itself from an *ancien régime* into a mobilized nation state, along the lines of Germany's, only hastened its end. Its efforts to reform the food supply system were especially disruptive. A peculiar alliance of modernizing ministers and experts, including a future planner under the Bolsheviks, the Menshevik economist V. Groman, tried to replace the market in grain with state-led grain procurement. But the regime could not cope with the organization and transport of supplies, and the peasantry refused to sell grain for the low prices offered.[59]

Educated society blamed the Tsar for the economic and military disasters, and accusations of inefficiency became intertwined with the poisonous charge of treason. It was commonly believed that Tsarina Alexandra, English in culture though German by birth, was at the centre of a conspiracy centred in Berlin to sabotage the war effort. Tsardom, a branch of the international European aristocracy, lacked the patriotic charisma to unite Russia against its enemies. And when, on 23 February 1917, protests against bread shortages by St Petersburg women developed into a general strike and soldiers' mutinies, few were willing to defend the regime.

For a brief time Russians were united in favour of 'freedom' and 'democracy'. Russia seemed to have experienced its 1789, and everybody was aware of the parallel. The 'Marseillaise' (or '*Marsiliuza*') became the new regime's national anthem, played at every opportunity, and forms of address based on the old hierarchy were abolished in favour of the terms 'citizen' (*grazhdanin*) and 'citizeness' (*grazhdanka*).[60] Even French revolutionary festivals were imitated, with plans for a 'grandiose-carnival spectacle' in the Summer Garden in Petersburg, involving a cardboard city representing eighteenth-century Paris.[61] Yet, even though socialist party organizations had a minimal role in the February revolution, the new symbolism showed how much more radical the new dispensation was than its French predecessor. The socialist red flag, not a Russian tricolour, was flown over the Winter Palace and effectively became the national flag. It was at this time that the symbols of the urban and rural masses – the hammer and the sickle – first appeared, appended to the Marinskii Palace, the seat of the Provisional Government.[62]

Yet despite this apparent unity, signs of division between educated, liberal groups on the one side, and workers and peasants on the other, were soon evident. The word 'comrade' (*tovarishch*) – a socialist form of address – could be heard alongside 'citizen'. And competing with the conventional 'Marseillaise', a hymn of praise to nationalist unity translated into a Russian context, was a 'workers' Marseillaise', a socialist version. This exhorted its listeners to 'kill and destroy' 'the parasites', 'the dogs' and 'the rich'. It also had another competitor, much preferred by all Marxist parties – the anti-nationalist 'Internationale', whose words had been written in 1871 by a member of the Paris Commune to the tune of the 'Marseillaise', but which had been given new music in 1888.[63] Conflicts over symbols and songs were institutionalized from the very beginning of the February revolution in the existence of 'dual power'. The Provisional Government, dominated by the propertied and professional classes, ruled alongside the Petrograd (formerly Petersburg) Soviet, elected by the lower classes.

The Provisional Government was initially made up of liberals. But from March it included Menshevik and Socialist Revolutionary (SR) members of the Soviet, and from July was led by the moderate socialist Aleksandr Kerenskii. The government was committed to liberal democracy and the rule of law, and declared itself a provisional body until one-man-one-vote elections could be held to a Constituent Assembly. It also sought to continue the war, though from the spring only a defensive one, against the Germans.

However, the Provisional Government found it no easier to enlist the support of workers and peasants into its vision of Russia than the Tsar's reformist ministers. The political and cultural gap between the propertied and educated elites and the mass of the population was too great. The government tried to achieve a compromise on the war, continuing to fight but abandoning the Tsar's old expansionist war aims. Yet following the failure of the offensive in June, it could not maintain discipline within the army, and elected soldiers' committees believed it was their right to discuss whether to obey officers' orders.[64] In the countryside, the Provisional Government tried to end food shortages by creating an even tighter state grain monopoly, but peasants were no more willing to grow and sell than before. It made a start on addressing the peasants' demands for land, but it was slow and cautious. It soon lost control of the countryside as peasants seized landlords' property, with little fear of retribution.

The Provisional Government also granted concessions to workers, on wages and conditions, but again these were not enough. Conflicts between factory-owners and workers became more acrimonious. Managers who laid workers off were accused of 'sabotage', and workers' factory committees demanded the right to supervise management, or 'workers' control' over their factories.[65] A massive wave of strikes ensued in September.

By the summer of 1917 the language of class struggle had permeated popular culture. Demands for the rule of the masses, operating through the soviets, and the overthrow of the 'bourgeois' Provisional Government – which, it was claimed, could not be a representative 'people's government' – became common.[66] As a resolution of the soldiers' committee of the 92nd Transport Battalion declared in September:

Comrades! It is time for us to wake up! . . . It is time to shake off the spell of the bourgeoisie; it is time to discard it like an oozing scab, so that it doesn't do any more damage to the revolution . . . The people can rely only on itself and must not extend a comradely hand to the hated enemy. It is time to shake off these 'saviours of the revolution', who have stuck to the body of the country like leeches.[67]

In some cases, this type of language reflected an interest in socialism and Marxism. Anna Litveiko, a Ukrainian factory worker and future Communist Youth (Komsomol) member, remembered her idealism as a young woman:

We thought that Communism would begin as soon as the soviets assumed power. Money was not even mentioned; it was clear to us that money would disappear right away . . . On clothing, however, our opinions were divided: some of us rejected this form of property as well. And anyway, how were the members of the new society supposed to dress? . . . I could not part with my own ribbon or braids. Did that mean I was not a true Bolshevik? But I was prepared to give my life for the revolution![68]

Much more common among ordinary people, though, was not Marxism but a deep-rooted populist worldview. The socialist word 'bourgeois' (*boorzhui*) was a common insult, but underlying the revolutionary mood was less a Marxist economic critique of exploitation than a moral outrage at the remnants of *ancien régime* privilege. An officer, writing from the front, recognized the deep-seated resentment which his men displayed towards the socially privileged:

Whatever their personal attitudes toward individual officers might be, we remain in their eyes only masters . . . In their view, what has taken place is not a political but a social revolution, in which, according to them, we are the losers and they the winners . . . Previously, we ruled; now they themselves want to rule. In them speak the unavenged insults of centuries past. A common language between us cannot be found. This is the cursed legacy of the old order.[69]

His observation was a perceptive one. The demand for dignity, so evident among Chernyshevskii's students and clerks of the 1860s, had been passed on to workers from the 1890s, and many of the complaints of workers in 1917 were preoccupied with rudeness from superiors. The first act of the Petrograd Soviet, Order No. 1, concerning the army, included the demand that officers address soldiers by the respectful 'you' (*vy*) rather than its informal equivalent (*ty*).[70]

Workers, therefore, increasingly demanded that organizations of the ordinary people, such as the soviets and factory, soldiers' and village committees take power, whilst excluding the upper classes from politics. This did not mean they were necessarily opposed to the power of the state. In fact they commonly demanded that the state take harsh, dictatorial measures in the interests of the people against 'enemies'; as the delegates of the sixth army corps declared in October, 'the country needs a firm and democratic authority founded on and responsible to the popular masses'.[71] At a time of food shortages, collapsing transport and disorder, it is not surprising that people should have sought a stronger state and berated the Provisional Government for its weakness.

This popular worldview, that the 'people' should engage in a struggle against the privileged, and build a powerful, centralized people's state, may not have been Marxist in origin, but it seemed to coincide with Lenin's ideas, at least for a short time in mid-1917. He presented his political agenda most clearly in his powerful synthesis, *State and Revolution*, written during his temporary exile in Finland. In this crucial work, he reconciled the Modernist Marxism of planning and centralization with the Radical Marxism of proletarian democracy and class struggle. He first used Hilferding's ideas to claim that the war had forged the economy into a single, centralized machine.[72] At the same time, though, Lenin went back to the egalitarian Marx of 1848 and 1871. Workers, he claimed, would soon be able to run this simplified economy by themselves; in his famous phrase, any female cook could run the state. Granting special privileges to technical specialists was no longer justified. Marx's dream – the merging of 'mental and manual labour' – would soon become a reality.

Lenin's vision was therefore one of complete equality, not only economic and legal, but also social and political. Liberal democracy, where citizens elected deputies who in turn controlled officials, was not enough. Officials had to be directly elected by the masses, as had happened in the Paris Commune – the model for Lenin's new 'commune-state'. The state would then start to merge with the people, and all hierarchies would start to disappear. The vanguard party was barely mentioned.

Lenin, then, talked a great deal about 'democracy' in *State and Revolution*, but this was not a democracy of universal rights. Democracy for the proletariat was perfectly compatible with a violent repression of its enemies. Lenin's commune-state was rather like a group of vigilante volunteers: it could suppress the 'exploiters' 'as simply and readily as any crowd of civilized people . . . interferes to put a stop to a scuffle or prevent a woman from being assaulted'.[73] Lenin had no qualms about violence, and described the proletariat as the '"Jacobins" of the twentieth century'.[74] But he denied extensive repression would be necessary. Only a few demonstrative arrests, he insisted, would be required. Whilst the vigilante volunteers might initially be a minority, they would very soon expand into a 'militia embracing the whole people'.[75] This form of socialism, then, had a martial style, but it harked back to the barricades of 1848 and 1871; it had little in common with the conventional armies of World War I.

Did Lenin, a hard-nosed revolutionary, really take the utopian vision of *State and Revolution* seriously? Did he really believe that it would be so straightforward for workers to run the economy and the state? His language is ambiguous, and he may have planned a less egalitarian outcome. But as a Marxist ideologue, he was convinced that classes had single, coherent interests. If proletarians ran the state, there was no reason why it could not forge a consensus with the working class as a whole.

Of course, it soon became clear after the October Revolution that Lenin was wrong. Inevitably unity disintegrated into conflicts between the regime and society, within society, and amongst workers themselves. But in the radicalized Russia of 1917, the idea that a popular, revolutionary 'General Will' existed, and that it could rule through a state both 'democratic' and centralized, was not Lenin's alone. It seemed to make sense, not only to him, but to large sections of the Russian working class.[76]

Lenin returned to Russia from exile in April 1917 determined to impose his uncompromising vision of class struggle on his party. Against the doubts of many of his fellow Bolsheviks Lenin insisted that power be transferred from the Provisional Government to the soviets. The time was not yet ripe for the end of the market, but the workers and peasants, not the bourgeoisie, had to lead and build the 'commune-state'; meanwhile the soviets had to supervise the production and distribution of goods.

The Bolsheviks, therefore, were the only major party outside the government, and they were calling for rule by the lower classes and an end to the war. The Menshevik high command continued to argue that a proletarian revolution would fail in a backward country like Russia, as did Kautsky and the Second International. In July, when the Provisional Government cracked down on the Bolsheviks and Lenin was again forced into exile, it looked as if he had miscalculated. But conditions were more similar to the France of 1789 than that of 1848 or 1871, and the middle-class forces of order could not rely on a peasant army to resist urban revolution. The Commander-in-Chief of the army, Kornilov, tried to use the army to restore discipline, and believed that he had Kerenskii's support for the 'coup'. But many of his soldiers would not obey, Kerenskii denied he was involved, and the episode undermined the Provisional Government as a whole.

The Bolsheviks' popularity, conversely, increased. Even if most were unaware of the detailed policies of the party, it seemed to many that it was the only force that might save the revolution. It won formal majorities in both the Moscow and Petrograd soviets, and Lenin used this evidence of support to argue for the immediate seizure of power by the Bolsheviks. On 25 October the Petrograd Soviet's Military Revolutionary Committee, led by Trotsky and other Bolsheviks, readily took control of the poorly defended Winter Palace. This was, then, a coup of sorts. The famous scene in Eisenstein's film *October* of thousands swarming over the gates and invading the palace is pure fiction, but the Provisional Government's failure to rally forces to defend itself, and the ease with which the Bolsheviks took over the major cities, shows how far the Bolshevik approach to politics in 1917 was in tune with the radicalism of many of the urban population. The Bolsheviks never won an all-Russia election. They were an urban party in an overwhelmingly rural country. But in the elections to the Constituent Assembly towards the end of 1917 they gained a majority of workers' and 42 per cent of soldiers' votes, and took 10.9 million votes out of 48.4 million. They also shared much of the programme of the victors of the election – the Left Socialist Revolutionaries (Left SRs). So this was not, properly speaking, a 'Bolshevik revolution'. It was a Bolshevik insurrection amidst a radical populist revolution, whose values were partly endorsed, for a very short time, by the Bolsheviks. The liberal alternative – of class compromise and the rule of law – supported by most of propertied and

educated Russia, had little chance of victory, for the mass of the population was simply too wedded to the radical redistribution of property
and power. Lenin and the Bolsheviks were soon to retreat from their
populism towards a much more authoritarian politics, and ultimately
they only secured their power by force of arms in a civil war. The Bolshevik victory was therefore by no means inevitable, but some radical
socialist outcome was likely. And once the Bolsheviks had taken power,
however unpopular they might become, there was little desire for the
return of the old order.

VI

In 1923, the writer Isaak Babel published *Red Cavalry*, a series of stories
about his experiences as a Bolshevik political agitator with Budennyi's
Cossack cavalry in the Polish war of 1920. The book received instant
acclaim and was widely read. In one story, entitled 'A Letter', Babel told
of the civil war within one peasant family through a fictional letter from
the red cavalryman Vasilii Kordiukov to his mother. It is a peculiar
document, poorly written, bland and matter-of-fact, peppered with
banal descriptions of the places he has visited. But its subject matter is
horrific: the bloody struggle between Vasilii's father Timofei, a former
tsarist policeman fighting with General Denikin's anti-Bolshevik Whites,
and his brothers Fedor and Semen, fellow soldiers with the Bolsheviks.
His father, finding Fedor among Red prisoners of war, hacks him to
death, only to be pursued by his other sons, intent on revenge. They
finally find him. Semen, nicknamed 'the wild one', declares: 'Papa . . . if
I fell into your hands, I would find no mercy. So now, Papa, we will fin-
ish you off!', and proceeds to slaughter him. The story ends with Vasilii
showing the narrator a photograph of the whole family. Timofei, 'a
wide-shouldered police constable in a policeman's cap . . . was stiff,
with wide cheekbones and sparkling, colourless vacant eyes'; beside
him sat his wife, a 'tiny peasant woman . . . with small, bright, timid
features'.

And against this provincial photographer's pitiful backdrop, with its
flowers and doves, towered two boys, amazingly big, blunt, broad-faced,

goggle-eyed, and frozen as if standing to attention: the Kordiukov brothers, Fedor and Semen.[77]

Many of Babel's stories were about the gruesome violence he witnessed, and participated in, during the civil war, and his attempts to come to terms with it. As a Jewish intellectual among martial Cossack peasants, he was appalled by the casual brutality (and anti-Semitism) of men like the Kordiukov brothers. And yet he admired their bravery, and at times an unattractive Nietzschean power-worship creeps into his writing. The result is disconcerting – a deliberately distanced account of his cruel heroes, a firm refusal to judge.[78] He cannot understand them; they are opaque with 'vacant eyes', as in a photograph. They are forces of nature, Aeschylean furies, seeking revenge for past wrongs.

This was, of course, not the world Lenin had expected to inherit. Lenin, whilst not a Nietzschean revelling in violence, was perfectly pre- pared to use it, and from early on he embraced class revenge. But he soon found it difficult to control; he insisted that the 'masses' had to be both revolutionary *and* disciplined. It was clear from the beginning that the transition to the 'Dictatorship of the Proletariat' would not go as smoothly as Lenin hoped.

The first challenge came from moderate socialists who objected to soviet, class power as opposed to liberal parliamentary rule. The dele- gates to the Constituent Assembly, 85 per cent of whom were socialists, insisted that they represented the Russian people, but Lenin denounced them as an example of 'bourgeois parliamentarism'. Red Guards shot several supporters demonstrating in favour of the Assembly just before it convened in Petrograd's Tauride Palace – the first time since February 1917 that troops had fired at unarmed crowds – and the Assembly was later broken up. The Left SRs survived in coalition with the Bolsheviks for four months, but by March 1918 it was clear to everybody that all power was being transferred to the Bolsheviks, not the soviets.

Lenin had claimed that power was to be passed to the soviets as a whole, but he never pretended to be a pluralist democrat, and it was no surprise that he refused to work with rival parties. At the same time, how- ever, he seems to have taken his promises for some kind of 'democracy' within the working class seriously, and during the first months of Bolshe- vik rule, Lenin may have believed that the ambitious plans of *State and*

Revolution were realistic: popular initiative and centralization could coexist; or he may have merely been giving workers what they wanted when the party was weak. He continued to call for 'workers' democracy', knowing how popular it was in the factories, and in November 1917 issued a Decree on Workers' Control, which gave considerable powers to elected factory committees. The army also continued to be run in a 'democratic', or 'citizens' militia' style, with soldiers electing officers. Lenin's approach towards the peasantry was less Marxist, but it also gave in to the demands of the masses. Rather than creating large-scale, collective farms, as Marxist theory (and earlier Bolshevik policy) dictated, his Decree on Land gave the peasants what they wanted – they could keep their small plots and subsistence agriculture.

As Isaak Babel observed, for many ordinary people, the flip-side of 'democracy', or power to the masses, was 'class struggle', or revenge against the 'bourgeoisie' – as it had been for the *sans-culottes*. And in the first few months of the revolution Lenin was prepared to encourage this 'popular' terror. 'Loot the Looters' was the slogan of the moment, and in December 1917 Lenin declared a 'war to the death against the rich, the idlers, the parasites'.[79] However, he was happy to delegate the conduct of the struggle to local communities. Each town or village was to decide how to 'cleanse' Russia of these 'vermin': they might imprison them, put them to work cleaning latrines, give them special documents or 'yellow tickets' so that everybody could keep an eye on them (a treatment traditionally meted out to prostitutes), or shoot one in every ten.[80]

Lenin's principles were embraced enthusiastically by party activists in Russia's regions. Bolsheviks seized the goods of the rich, imposed special taxes on them, and took members of 'bourgeois' classes – the so-called 'former people' – as hostages. Anna Litveiko herself took part in a detachment to seize bourgeois property:

The slogan was 'Peace for the huts, war on the palaces!' It was important to demonstrate to the people right away what the revolution would bring to the huts . . .

We would enter the [rich] apartments and say: 'This building is being nationalized. You have twenty-four hours to move out.' Some obeyed immediately while others cursed us – the Bolsheviks in general or Soviet rule.[81]

The experience of the aristocracy and bourgeoisie was, of course, trau-matic, even for those who were not arrested or physically abused. Princess Sofia Volkonskaia remembered how the authorities forced her to accept lodgers to live in her flat:

> The couple thus forced on us – a young man and his wife – seemed quite nice, but ... they were Communists ... Nothing could be more disagree-able than this living in close contact (having to cook our dinners on the same stove, to use the bathroom devoid of hot water, etc.) with people who considered themselves a priori and in principle as our foes ... 'Take care', 'Shut the door', 'Do not talk so loud; the Communists may hear you.' Pin-pricks? Yes, of course. But in that nightmare life of ours every pin-prick took the proportion of a serious wound.[82]

In the early months, 'class struggle' permeated all aspects of life, includ-ing the symbolic world, and the Bolsheviks, like their Jacobin predeces-sors, were determined to create a new culture that would propagate their values. Petrograd, in particular, was the home to several mass theatrical events, echoing the plays and festivals of the Paris of 1793. One, 'The Mystery of Liberated Labour', was staged on May Day 1920. In front of the Petrograd Stock Exchange, a group of debauched kings and capitalists indulged in a drunken orgy, whilst toilers slaved to the sounds of 'moans, curses, sad songs, the scrape of chains'. Waves of revolutionaries, from Spartacus and his slaves to the *sans-culottes* in their Phrygian caps, mounted attacks on the potentates' banquet table, but were repulsed, until the star of the Red Army rose in the East. Finally the gates to the Kingdom of Peace, Freedom and Joyful Labour were destroyed, and within was revealed the liberty tree, around which the people danced, in the style of David. Huge numbers participated – 4,000 actors, workers and soldiers, merging at the end with 35,000 spectators.[83]

Lenin himself, however, had little interest in the carnivalesque theatre of class struggle. As Bely would have predicted, his view of the new revolutionary culture was much closer to Apollon Apollonovich's. Moscow, the new capital of the revolution, was to be filled with statues of the revolutionary heroes and plaques bearing the principles of Marxism. Yet the conservative neo-classical taste favoured by Lenin, and much of the Muscovite populace, clashed with the modernism of some of the sculptors. A cubo-futurist statue of Bakunin had to be hidden by wooden boards for fear of popular disapproval; when the partitions were stolen for firewood and the statue revealed, the authorities, fearing a riot, had to demolish it. The project, moreover, suffered from shortages of materials. In the end several temporary plaster and cement figures were erected, many of which were washed away by the rain.[84] One statue of Robespierre suffered a different fate – destruction by a terrorist bomb. Bizarrely, one of the few to have survived to this day was originally built by the *ancien régime*: a marble obelisk constructed outside the Kremlin to celebrate the three hundredth anniversary of the Romanovs in 1913, its inscription replaced with a remarkably eclectic list of Bolshevik 'forefathers', including Thomas More, Gerrard Winstanley, Fourier, Saint-Simon, Chernyshevskii and Marx.[85]

Given Lenin's love of order, it was perhaps predictable that he would eventually abandon his brief flirtation with Radical Marxism. But it was the near destruction of the regime at the beginning of 1918 that forced his *volte-face*. The Bolsheviks had expected that revolution in Russia would be accompanied by a world revolution, and Germany's proletariat would help the backward Russians to achieve socialism. Instead, however, German militarists were still in power, and were imposing humiliating peace terms. Lenin realized how weak his new state was and counselled acceptance, but he was outvoted on the Central Committee. As the Germans marched into Ukraine, the leaders continued to argue. At the last minute Trotsky changed his mind, and the treaty of Brest-Litovsk averted the almost certain fall of the regime. The hope that the revolution would be rescued by the expected revolution in Germany was clearly a dream.

It was at this point that Lenin realized that the promises of 1917 were incompatible with the preservation of the new regime. Allowing workers and peasants to control their factories and fields, and encouraging anti-bourgeois pogroms, was only fuelling economic chaos. Food supplies suffered from the expropriation of the gentry's lands and the break-up of large estates. Meanwhile workers used 'workers' control' to benefit their own factories, rather than the economy as a whole, and harassed the hated managers and engineers. Labour discipline collapsed, a problem only worsened by the food shortages. The ranks of the unemployed swelled and opposition to the Bolsheviks in the soviets grew rapidly.

It had become clear by early 1918, as it had in France at the end of 1793, that the goals of the popular and elite revolutions were diverging; Lenin's Marxist synthesis was disintegrating. But Lenin did not adopt Robespierre's course and launch a moral reformation or reign of virtue. Rather, he reverted to technocratic type, abandoning his short-lived Radical Marxism for a severe Modernist version. In March–April 1918 he announced his retreat from the 'commune-state' and the citizens' militia model of socialism. Lenin now declared that his earlier optimism about the working class had been misplaced. The Russian worker was a 'bad worker compared with people in advanced countries' and could not be trusted with workers' democracy. Lenin's solution was the creation of a 'harmonious', economic machine, run by experts – bourgeois if necessary – and based on the principles of the latest technology. If workers were 'mature' enough, this would only amount to the 'mild leadership of a conductor of an orchestra'; until then individual bosses and experts must exercise 'dictatorial power'.[86]

Lenin had learnt the lesson of Brest-Litovsk. As he wrote at the time: 'The war taught us much . . . that those who have the best technology, organization, discipline and the best machines emerge on top . . . It is necessary to master the highest technology or be crushed.'[87] He now turned from the example of the Paris Commune to the system of the American 'scientific management' theorist Frederick W. Taylor, used in Henry Ford's car plants in the United States. Taylor deployed experts with stop-watches, dividing workers' tasks up into precise movements, timing them to the second and paying them according to how much they had produced. Previously Lenin had condemned this system as typical of a brutalizing capitalism. But now there was no longer room for such radical notions; workers' enthusiasm and creativity would not revive the economy. They had to be encouraged by the carrot – money – and the stick – labour discipline.[88] The old hated bourgeois experts would have to be given back their power and higher wages; in the army that meant restoring the old imperial officers and disbanding soldiers' committees. The 'red guard' assault on the bourgeoisie, Lenin now declared, was over.

Lenin justified his 'retreat' from the promises of 1917 by recourse to Marxist theory. The Bolsheviks, he asserted, had been overambitious to talk about workers' democracy, especially in the absence of world revolution; the time was not yet ripe for the withering of the state, which would only arrive with full Communism.[89] Lenin's new vision, of a modern state with powers over the economy, was closer to Marx's lower stage of 'socialism' than to his higher stage of 'Communism'.[90] But Lenin had transformed Marx's vision in a crucial way: modernity would be brought by the elite vanguard party, which now had to transfer its attention from revolution to state-building.[91] Over the next few years, the party was to centralize power in its own hands, emasculating or destroying the elected soviets and committees that had made the revolution.

The Bolsheviks' vision of modernity was not only one of heavy industry and hard work. It included a commitment to mass education, welfare, the end of religion and the emancipation of women – though little progress was made on much of this programme, especially that relating to women's equality.[92] But Bolshevism's technocratic culture was unmistakeable, and some took it to extremes. Aleksei Gastev, a metal-worker before 1917 and a poet, the 'Ovid of engineers, miners and metal-workers', was one of the most committed propagandists of the Taylorist system. In his most popular poem published in 1914, 'We Grow out of Iron', he described a worker growing into a giant, merging with the factory with 'new iron blood' flowing into his veins, but after the revolution he sought to combine man and machine in more practical ways.[93] As a board member, alongside Lenin and Trotsky, of the 'League for the Scientific Organization of Labour' founded in 1921 – a vigilante body which sought to expose time-wasting and laziness in factories and offices[94] – Gastev embraced a new world in which workers would become anonymous cogs, 'permitting the classification of an individual proletarian unit as A, B, C, or 325, 0.075, 0, and so on'; 'Machines from being managed will become managers' and the movement of workers would become

> similar to the movement of things, in which there is no longer any individual face but only regular, uniform steps and faces devoid of expression, of a soul, of lyricism, of emotion, measured not by a shout or a smile but by a pressure gauge or a speed gauge.[95]

This horrifying utopia was satirized by the writer Evgenii Zamiatin in his science fiction novel We, written in 1920–1 (and first published outside the USSR in 1924), an important influence on Orwell's Nineteen Eighty-Four.[96] And yet it was not this vision that prevailed, much as Lenin may have wanted it to. The system that emerged after 1918 was less the factory-style socialism of Modernist Marxism than a union of Marx and Mars. This was the system that the Bolsheviks' detractors described as 'barracks communism', and they themselves came to describe as 'war communism' – a form of Communism that was to have an influence on the Soviet model well into the future. The pure, white horse of Nicholas II had been replaced by Babel's Red Cavalry, not by Lenin's bronze horsemen.

After a brief respite following the Brest-Litovsk peace of March 1918, a combination of SR rebels and former tsarist army officers (the 'Whites'), bolstered by British and other allied help, challenged the Reds. The Bolsheviks were faced with a full-scale civil war that erupted across the former Russian empire. They responded by embracing wartime methods with gusto, but they also moved away from the decentralized civilian militia style of military organization towards a new, more conventional military one, as had the Jacobins. Trotsky founded the 'Red Army'; he dissolved the soldiers' committees, banned the election of officers, and appointed 'military experts' – a euphemism for the former tsarist officers. By the end of the civil war, three quarters of officers were from the old officer corps. Meanwhile the harsh discipline, so unpopular in the hands of the old regime, returned.[97]

Many of the other practices of wartime also returned, reinforced by Marxist ideology. Spying and surveillance of popular opinion was one. During and after World War I many European powers, including the Russian Provisional Government and later the Whites, became anxious about the mood of the population. They both produced propaganda and employed officials to check up on its effectiveness. The Bolsheviks did the same, though unlike Western powers they maintained this spying even after war started to wind down – for they had broader ambitions to transform society and create 'new socialist people'. The Cheka – the new secret police – soon took over from the military in this role, and by 1920 the Bolsheviks employed 10,000 people to open letters and write reports on popular opinion.[98]

The Bolsheviks also used wartime methods to control the economy, though as Marxists they were even more hostile to the market than their predecessors. They imposed high grain quotas on the countryside and tried to ban private trade. The Cheka arrested 'baggers', who illegally sought to bring food to sell in the towns, and the authorities rationed much of the food in urban areas. Inflation and shortages had rendered money worthless. However, some hailed these developments as the achievement of a Marxist goal: the end of the market and money, and the state's control over the whole economy. Trotsky tried to show how this extreme manifestation of state power was compatible with the ultimate withering away of the state:

Just as a lamp, before going out, shoots up in a brilliant flame, so the state, before disappearing, assumes the form of the dictatorship of the proletariat, i.e. the most ruthless form of the state, which embraces the life of the citizen authoritatively in every direction.[99]

However, 'war communism' did not merely consist of brute discipline. When it came to their supporters, the Bolsheviks could be more populist. Trotsky's Red Army was not a mere copy of conventional Western armies but tried to combine discipline with at least some remnants of the populist spirit of the early revolutionary era. By 1919 the Bolsheviks had begun to solve the problem of military recruitment, which had bedevilled their tsarist and liberal predecessors, by giving a range of incentives to peasants, from guaranteed rations for their families, to education and land for themselves and their children. The Bolsheviks' continuing message of class struggle also appealed to many soldiers, and an elaborate propaganda and educational department was established to bring the Marxist worldview to the men.[100] Abstract language was translated into terms comprehensible to peasants. So, a cartoon in the peasant journal *Bednota* (*Poverty*) showed a peasant boy covered with spiders and leeches labelled 'landowner', 'priest' and 'interventionist'.[101] Soldiers were taught a Manichaean worldview with struggle and conflict at its centre. Even their biology lessons included a discussion of 'animals that are friends and animals that are enemies of humans'.[102]

By 1921, the Red Army numbered a massive 5 million men. It became a bulwark of the new regime, the germ of a new society within the old. The urban Bolsheviks, having come to power with a deep suspicion of the countryside, had created a new power-base amongst peasant army recruits, many of them young men at the bottom of the patriarchal village hierarchy.[103] After the civil war, many of these veterans went on to staff the party and state bureaucracies. The experience of war, and the militarized culture it produced, was to shape Soviet Communism, and the politics it projected around the world, for decades to come.

It was Trotsky (and, as will be seen, Stalin), rather than Lenin, who really revelled in this military culture. Lenin hoped to move from class revenge to a society of dutiful workers who had internalized 'real bourgeois culture', instilled by a modern and educated Communist party.[104] But this was unlikely to happen at a time of fratricidal conflict, and the Bolsheviks' own rhetoric was still full of revolutionary violence. From the summer of 1918 Lenin, like Robespierre towards the end of 1793, tried to control the terror, channelling it against the Bolsheviks' political opponents and discouraging its use as an attack on the whole bourgeoisie 'as a class'. However, local authorities continued to persecute indiscriminately.[105] During the civil war hundreds of thousands of people were executed by the Cheka and internal security troops, many of them described as 'rebellious' peasants.[106]

Whilst many Red Army soldiers may have been enthused by the Bolshevik message, other groups were deeply alienated. Peasants, whose main concern was local autonomy, were especially hostile to Bolshevik exactions.[107] Yet however brutal the Bolsheviks were, they could plausibly claim that they were merely fighting fire with fire. For the Whites also pursued campaigns of violent revenge against Jews, Communist sympathizers and peasants who refused to enrol in their armies. The Whites were distinctly ambiguous on the land question, and peasants were convinced that they would reverse what for them was the main gain of the revolution – the redistribution of the gentry's estates. So whilst many certainly believed that the Bolsheviks had betrayed the ideals of 1917, many also saw them as the main bulwark against a return of the aristocracy and the tsar.[108] As the famous Red Army marching song warned:

> White army, black baron,
> Again prepare for us the tsarist throne.
> But from the taiga to the British seas,
> The Red Army is strongest of all.[109]

As long as the Whites were a threat, the Reds seemed like a lesser evil. The Menshevik Martov certainly found this ambivalence when he tried to convert workers to Menshevism in early 1920: 'So long as we denounced Bolshevism, we were applauded; as soon as we went on to say that a changed regime was needed to fight Denikin successfully our audience turned cold or even hostile.'[110]

The real crisis for the Bolsheviks came when the Whites were finally defeated in the spring of 1920; military methods no longer seemed justified. Yet Trotsky, far from giving up his vision, argued that military methods had to be extended to society as a whole, in peacetime. He set demobilized soldiers to work on economic projects, and took over the railways, seeking to apply top-down military organization and discipline. The 'labour front' was to become yet another military campaign, the whole population mobilized into labour brigades. Men and women would work 'to the sound of socialist hymns and songs'.[111] At the same time, he called for the economy to be subjected to a single rational 'plan'.

Trotsky came under attack from the Radical Marxist wing of the Bolshevik party on the left, who disliked his use of tsarist officers and favoured a more egalitarian model of society. A number of groups on the left – the 'Left Communists', the 'Workers' Opposition' – condemned the party leadership for betraying its promises of 'workers' democracy' and anti-bourgeois struggle. Meanwhile Bogdanov and his allies – more interested in Romantic, utopian ideas of workers' cooperation and creativity than the conquest of political power – set up 'proletarian culture' organizations (Proletkults), which they believed would foster workers' naturally collectivist psychology.[112] Lenin banned Proletkults, seeing them as a rival to the party, and the political left was easily outvoted, but it remained a constant thorn in Lenin's side.

However, even Lenin resisted Trotsky's more ambitious projects. He was right to be sceptical. The Russian state was no more able to organize an efficient economic machine than it had been before the October revolution. Indeed, it was probably less able to. As it took over all areas of economic and social activity, it became a Hydra of proliferating, overlapping and competing organizations. At the same time, officials used their increased power for private gain, with corruption blackening the reputation of the regime. Everybody bemoaned the problem of careerist, amoral and uncontrollable bureaucrats. The Saratov Cheka described one party organization as a 'mob of drunks and card sharks', and Timofei Sapronov, a leftist Bolshevik, complained that 'in many places the word "communist" is a term of abuse' because officials lived in 'bourgeois' luxury.[113]

The hypocrisy of socialist officials living the high life only intensified popular dissatisfaction with the intrusive Bolshevik state. The harvest of

1920 was a poor one, and by the spring of 1921 much of rural Russia was starving. As in 1905 and 1917, shortages of food fuelled a potentially revolutionary insurgency. Peasants rebelled against state grain procurement throughout the Volga region, the Urals and Siberia. The most serious uprising was in Tambov, where the rebels called for a soviet power free of Bolshevik repression. They united behind a series of rather confused slogans: 'Long live Lenin, down with Trotsky!' and 'Long live the Bolsheviks, death to the Communists!'[114]

Unrest soon spread to the towns and, most dangerously for the Bolsheviks, to the Kronstadt naval base, on an island near Petrograd. The Kronstadters had for long been on the more radical wing of the revolution. They had been ruled until the summer of 1918 by a coalition of radical leftist parties, and now demanded a return to rule by a freely elected soviet. They did not call for the overthrow of the Bolsheviks, but for an end to 'war communism', the destruction of Taylorism, and a return to the old ideals of October 1917.[115] At the beginning of March 1921, the rebels organized new elections and for over two weeks created a mini commune-state. It looked as if a populist socialist revolution was brewing – a 'third revolution' – but this time the Bolsheviks would be its victims, not its beneficiaries.[116] At precisely this time the tenth party congress was meeting, and Lenin faced a challenge within the party, from the Bolshevik left.

Lenin was faced with a stark choice. It was clear that the divisive 'war communism' model, with its heavy reliance on state power and coercion, had failed. The idea that the Russian people would work as cogs in an efficient machine was a fantasy, as was Trotsky's dream of universal soldierly enthusiasm. Marx's 'socialist' lower stage of Communism – centralized state control without the market – which war communism most closely resembled, was clearly not suited to Russia in 1921. This left a dilemma for the Bolsheviks. They could either return to the 'commune-state' of 1917 – an 'advance' towards Communism in Marxist terms – and rely yet again on working-class mobilization. Or they could 'retreat' towards capitalism. Lenin's choice was never in doubt. The commune-state would only hasten disintegration and chaos, and was incompatible with the Bolsheviks' modernizing ambitions. It also would not solve the main economic crisis, the shortage of food. It had become clear that the market alone would give peasants the incentives to grow grain. Lenin, unwillingly, was forced to allow peasant demands to sell grain on the open market. Shortly after he announced the 'New Economic Policy' (NEP), Bolshevik troops brutally put down the Kronstadt rebellion; at the same time a 'ban on factions' suppressed the leftist groups within the party, and the leadership ordered the first party 'purge' (*chistka* – or 'cleansing') of the politically unreliable and the class 'impure'. In 1918 the Bolsheviks had responded to the regime's near-collapse by centralizing power in the hands of the party; in 1921 they reacted to a second crisis by disciplining the party itself.

Lenin conceded that he had 'retreated' from the economic ambitions of 1919–20. 'We made a mistake,' he admitted, in thinking that the regime could eliminate the market, and moved too rapidly towards Communism. The Bolsheviks, he argued, had to adopt 'state capitalism'.[117] Lenin was worried about the reaction within the party, and insisted that full-blown capitalism was not on the cards; the heavy industry at the 'commanding heights' of the economy would still be nationalized. But the free market in grain had a cascade of effects throughout the economy:[118] private traders – 'nepmen' – had to be permitted to operate, to supply grain to the towns; factories producing consumer goods, like textiles, had to be denationalized to produce goods peasants might want to buy in exchange for their grain. Subsidies to nationalized industries had to be cut, to control inflation – vital if peasants were to trust the currency. As a result, wages had to be cut, labour discipline tightened, and the power of managers and bourgeois specialists strengthened. The position of workers further deteriorated, and unemployment increased. For many workers and some Bolsheviks, this looked just like the old capitalist order. NEP had become the 'New Exploitation of the Proletariat'. What had happened to socialism?

NEP rescued the Communists by appeasing the peasantry. The Bolsheviks, a tiny sect within the revolutionary intelligentsia, had ridden to power on the back of a popular revolution, but they found the construction of their Marxist state much more challenging. Their early revolutionary methods proved too disruptive, the Modernist vision was impractical, and the martial politics of the civil war created too much opposition. The Bolsheviks did find supporters, not so much within the urban working class, as amongst the young peasants who made up the Red Army. Nevertheless, the regime's appeal was too narrow; and indeed, their economic system was unsustainable. Recognizing the need for greater support, the Bolsheviks moderated their old sectarianism and concessions were made to the mass of the rural population.

The Bolsheviks may have avoided becoming victims of a new social-ist revolution, but the crisis seems to have taken its toll on Lenin's health. From 1920 to 1921 his exhaustion was evident. In May 1922 he had his first stroke, and he remained seriously ill until his death in January 1924. It is tempting to link his deteriorating health with the failure of his revolutionary hopes. Lenin's unique contribution to Marxism in 1917 had lain in his ability to combine a hard-nosed com-mitment to modernization with a furious revolutionary impatience. In March 1921 this project was in ruins. Lenin was forced to accept that the semi-capitalism of NEP would last for a long time. Socialism would only be feasible once the working class had undergone a 'cultural revo-lution', by which Lenin seems to have meant education and the suc-cessful inculcation of the work ethic that he had himself learnt from his parents.[119] He never admitted the charge of the Second International and the Mensheviks, that his revolution had been premature. But in practice he had reverted to a Marxism that had distinct echoes of Kautsky's 'revolutionary waiting'.

In 1920 the painter and sculptor Vladimir Tatlin was commissioned to design a building for the Third 'Communist' International ('Comintern'), which Lenin had founded the previous year to rival the Second Inter-national of Social Democratic Parties. A 'productivist' artist, who sought to combine mathematical and geometrical forms with social usefulness, Tatlin did a good job of representing Modernist Marxism's hierarchical and technocratic vision of politics. The monument was to be a Com-munist successor to the Eiffel Tower: it would demonstrate that the capital of the world revolution had moved from Paris to Moscow. It was a cross between a spiral and a pyramid. There were to be three rooms on top of each other, which were designed to rotate at different speeds. The largest, on the bottom, was for legislative assemblies, and was to rotate once a year; the next storey, designed for executive bodies, would turn once a month; the smallest room at the top would rotate daily, and would be 'reserved for centres of an informative character: an information office, a newspaper, the issuing of proclamations, pam-phlets and manifestoes' by means of radio.[120]

The model became a classic of modern design, representing Soviet creativity to the avant-garde intelligentsia of the West. At a time of shortages and poverty it was a clearly utopian project. The model had to be made of wood, not the metal and glass planned for the actual building. And in place of the intended machinery, a small boy manipulated the ropes and pulleys that rotated the rooms. The avant-garde poet Maiakovskii welcomed it as an alternative to the pompous busts going up around Moscow – the 'first monument without a beard' – but it is unlikely that Lenin approved.[121] Even so, Lenin's mechanical state had much in common with Tatlin's tower. It was hollow and ramshackle. But it did provide a symbol of a modern, non-capitalist system, controlled by a disciplined 'vanguard party' issuing 'proclamations' to the workers of the world. It was this party that was to appeal to so many future Communists, eager to find some Promethean force capable of fomenting revolutions and forging modernity. And at a time when the old order was in crisis, many on the left saw Tatlin's tower as a beacon, showing the way to the future.

3

Under Western Eyes

In February 1919 one of the most prominent Communist-sympathizing intellectuals of the inter-war era, the German playwright Bertolt Brecht, wrote the play *Spartakus*. Later entitled *Drums in the Night*, it was published for the first time in 1922 and told the story of a soldier, Andreas Kragler, who has returned from the war to find a Germany full of venality and corruption. His girlfriend, Anna, encouraged by her grasping parents, is planning to marry a bourgeois war profiteer, Murk. Kragler wins Anna back, but in the meantime he has become a revolutionary, leading the denizens of Glubb's Gin Mill onto the streets in support of the insurgent Marxist 'Spartacists'. Anna, seeing him in the demonstrations, rushes out, and urges him to leave the revolution and choose love instead. Kragler gives in. He hands over responsibility for the revolution to the audience and decides on Anna.[1]

Brecht wrote *Spartakus* during the third, and most radical, revolutionary conflagration to engulf Europe, following those of 1789 and 1848. Much, though, had changed since the previous revolutionary eras. Now, for a vocal minority, government without the bourgeoisie seemed not only possible but necessary; Russia, and the Bolsheviks, had actually created a viable 'proletarian' government; and the imperialism and nationalism of Europe's elites – both aristocratic and bourgeois – had killed millions. Many believed the old order had forfeited its right to rule.

Intellectuals, writers and artists were at the forefront of revolution, and Brecht was one of them, but his attitude was ambivalent. He was sceptical about ideas of heroic self-sacrifice and *Spartakus* suggested that the German masses did not want a revolutionary, workers' government. Kragler defeats his bourgeois rival Murk, but then retreats to the comforts of private life. Brecht's view turned out to be realistic. The Communists did not take power in 1919 in Germany, and by 1921 it was clear that the revolutionary tide in the West had receded. Pro-Soviet Communist parties never captured the affections of the majority of the European working classes or peasants. By the mid-1920s the ruling elites had restored order and the edifice of authority and property.

Yet the hatreds unleashed by war and revolution had not entirely abated, and Communists remained significant minorities in several countries. But Communists were forced to change their style and approach. Lenin's 'retreat' from revolutionary Radicalism to a Marxism of discipline and hierarchy infused the international Communist movement. This gritty realism was much more in tune with Brecht's own sensibility. His leather-jacketed machismo, hatred of sentimentality, love of the modern, and disdain for romantic dreams all reflected the hard-nosed Communist sectarianism of Western Europe in the 1920s. The contrast with the idealism of 1918–19 could not have been greater.

II

In 1915, as Europe was consumed by violence, neutral Switzerland hosted two groups of intellectuals profoundly disgusted by the bloodshed. The first was the anti-war Social Democrats, who gathered in the holiday village of Zimmerwald in September 1915, and again in Kiental in April 1916. Attendance was sparse. Most representatives were from Russia and Eastern Europe, and included Lenin and Trotsky, although the Italian Socialists (PSI) and the Swiss Social Democrats were also important members. The large Western Social Democratic parties had supported the war and were therefore absent. Trotsky recalled bitterly that half a century following the founding of the First International Europe's internationalists could be comfortably accommodated in four charabancs.[2] It was in these inauspicious circumstances that the foundations for the international Communist movement were laid.

A couple of months before the meeting at Kiental, at a rather different type of venue – the newly opened Cabaret Voltaire in Zurich – another intellectual groupuscule expressed its horror at the war: the primitivist artistic movement, Dada. Hans Arp remembered how he and his fellow rebels thought:

In Zurich in 1915, losing interest in the slaughterhouses of the world war, we turned to the Fine Arts. While the thunder of the batteries rumbled in the distance, we pasted, we recited, we versified, we sang with all our soul. We searched for an elementary art that would, we thought, save mankind from the furious folly of those times.[3]

Dadaists therefore differed from the Marxists in cutting themselves off from politics, at least at first. But in other ways they had much in common. They wanted to outrage the bourgeoisie, with Dadaist performances at the Cabaret Voltaire designed directly to provoke violence and bring confrontations with the police.

In 1915 both radical Social Democrats and Dadaists seemed to be whistling in the wind. The war continued. Lenin could not even persuade his fellow anti-war Marxists to approve a split in the Second International. Yet within a year, everything had changed. As the bloodshed continued, the more the left became disillusioned with the war. By 1916 the executive of the French Social Democratic SFIO was seriously divided over war credits, and soon the German Social Democratic Party itself split. The majority continued to support the war, but significant figures such as Kautsky and Bernstein now opposed it. At the same time, however, a more radical left-wing minority, led by Rosa Luxemburg and the Marxist lawyer Karl Liebknecht, emerged, calling themselves the 'Spartacists' after the leader of the Roman slave revolt. By April 1917 the party had split, with the foundation of the new minority radical Independent Social Democratic Party (USPD).

In 1916, Lenin and the Dadaists would have had nothing but mutual contempt for each other. Lenin would have seen them as utopian Romantics. But by 1918 some Dadaists, especially the Germans, had embraced a radical Marxist politics, and the incongruously named 'Revolutionary Central Committee of Dada' had been formed. One of the most famous, the painter George Grosz, incorporated graffiti, children's drawings and other forms of popular art into angry caricatures of arrogant militarists and greedy capitalists. Grosz was to become a leading member of the German revolutionary movement, and was a founding member of the German Communist Party, the KPD.[4]

The war had also dented the faith of many ordinary people in the old pre-war elites. Governments demanded enormous sacrifices in the name of patriotism. But as the fighting dragged on, resentment increased.

Equal sacrifice did not seem to produce equal reward. On the home front, living standards and working conditions deteriorated, and food shortages were endemic. Meanwhile on the frontline what many believed was pointless carnage continued.

Unlike the tsarist regime, most combatant governments were willing to forge serious alliances with non-revolutionary socialists. The German Social Democrats continued to support war credits, and the French SFIO joined a 'sacred union' (*union sacrée*) with the government. In return they were given a role in running the industrial economy. As the war dragged on, however, the socialists of the Second International became increasingly compromised by their cooperation with the ruling elites. For many ordinary workers the socialists seemed little more than establishment stooges; conditions on the shop-floor were worsening as discipline tightened. A gulf soon emerged between rank-and-file workers on the one side, and moderate socialists and trade unionists on the other. The socialist establishment's hold over workers was further weakened by an influx of new workers – women, migrants from the countryside and, in the case of Germany, foreign conscripts from occupied lands.[5] These new arrivals had few links with established socialist parties and trade unions, and it was these semi-skilled workers, flooding into the new mass industries of the war, who formed the base of support for the post-war revolutions.[6]

Strikes reached a peak in the years 1918–25.[7] In Germany in 1917, over 500 strikes involved 1.5 million workers;[8] in Britain strikes remained at a high level throughout the war, and especially affected a few radical areas such as 'Red Clydeside'. Strikes also became increasingly politicized, with protesters obsessively attentive to the unequal wartime sacrifices made by different classes. In November 1916 railwaymen's wives in the town of Knittefeld, in the Austro-Hungarian Empire, complained that they were being deprived of sugar so that the bourgeois and officers could waste their time in coffee houses.[9] In the spring and summer of 1917 mass protests swept Europe and workers also began to demand an end to the war.

So even before the events in Petrograd, a popular backlash was brewing against the war, but the example of the Bolshevik revolution further strengthened the radical left, and in January 1918 massive strikes and demonstrations rocked Germany and the Austro-Hungarian Empire. But it was defeat in war, when it seemed that all the sacrifices had been for nothing, which was crucial in triggering the revolutions. For their radical critics, elites – aristocratic, bourgeois and moderate socialist – had led their countries along a disastrous and pointless path of aggression. As the art-nouveau artist Heinrich Vogeler declared, 'The war has made a Communist of me. After my war experiences, I could no longer countenance belonging to a class that had driven millions of people to their deaths.'[10] It was no surprise then that in October and November 1918 the old regimes should have collapsed amidst popular, often nationalist revolutions.

Superficially, German politics looked strikingly similar to Russia's after February 1917. Workers' and soldiers' councils sprang up alongside a new provisional government consisting of left-wing liberals, moderate socialists (the SPD) and a minority of radicals (the USPD), under the SPD's Friedrich Ebert. At the same time, Luxemburg and a small Spartacist group were demanding a Soviet-style revolution and the end of parliamentary democracy. In fact, most of the councils did not demand a soviet republic, and supported a liberal order; the radicals were a small minority.[11] The sharp division between 'people' and elites present in Russia did not exist in Germany – predictably given the profound differences between German and Russian politics before the war. But Ebert was convinced that he was under threat from a new Bolshevik revolution, and was determined not to become another Kerenskii. He therefore acted more decisively than his Russian predecessor, believing that only an alliance with the military and the old imperial elites would ward off the revolutionary danger and guarantee liberal democracy.

Ebert's willingness to ally his government with the right against the workers' councils has generated a great deal of debate, and in retrospect it seems to have been an overreaction that contributed to the damaging polarization of German politics between the wars.[12] But at the time, the prospects for European Bolshevik revolutions did not look far-fetched, either to the left or to the right. The Bolsheviks themselves were certainly full of optimism. In March 1919 the foundation of the Third 'Communist' International (Comintern) formalized the split within Marxism between Communists and Social Democrats and brought together the more radical, pro-Soviet parties. Soviet republics were declared in Hungary (in March), Bavaria (April) and Slovakia (June), and seemed to show that there was a real chance that Bolshevism would spread, although the Hungarian government of the pro-Moscow journalist Béla Kun was the only Communist regime fully to take power in the West. Strikes and radical protest continued throughout the period 1919–21. In the June 1920 elections in Germany, the radical left were at rough parity with the moderate socialists (20.3 per cent of the vote, compared with the Social Democrats' 21.6 per cent). The red wave also affected southern Europe, and the years 1918–20 were to be dubbed the 'Trieno Bolchevista' in Spain, whilst Italy experienced its 'biennio rosso' in 1919–20. In Northern Italy it briefly seemed as if the factory council movement and the 'occupation of the factories' would really bring about an Italian Communist revolution. Worker unrest, some inspired by the Wobblies and other leftists, was especially widespread in the United States, and 1919 and 1920 saw the most powerful strike wave in American history, as workers demanded improvements in conditions and more factory democracy.

Communist parties benefited from this grassroots radicalism. Their members were generally young, and often unskilled or semi-skilled: a majority of the participants in the Second Comintern Congress of July 1920 were under forty and few had played important roles in the pre-war Social Democratic movement.[13] Many had emerged from the workers' and soldiers' councils of wartime, rather than through organized parties or trade unions, and were reacting against what they saw as a middle-aged, stodgy and excessively compliant Social Democratic culture.[14]

Communists were in part driven by economic concerns, but several were also radicalized by their experience of the German and Austro-Hungarian armies, with their rigid hierarchies and harsh discipline. Walter Ulbricht was typical of these Communist activists. Born in Leipzig, his father a tailor and his mother a seamstress and Social Democrat, he was brought up within the all-embracing culture of Marxist socialism and Kautsky's party. But it was the outbreak of war that led him to embrace militant leftist socialism. His experience of the German army gave him a life-long hatred of 'the spirit of the Prussian military'. He certainly had a difficult four years, suffering both from disease (he caught malaria) and punishments for distributing Spartacist literature. He finally escaped military prison and returned to Leipzig, becoming active in KPD politics. He then swiftly rose in the Communist hierarchy, becoming party leader in Thuringia, and a delegate to the Fourth Comintern Congress in Moscow in 1921, where he met Lenin.[15] It was this generation of Communists – born into the proletarian, Marxist subculture of imperial Germany, and radicalized by war – that was to dominate the Communist East German regime after World War II; Ulbricht himself rose to be General Secretary of the ruling Communist party between 1950 and 1971.

The experience of war and defeat also pushed some intellectuals towards revolutionary Marxism. Much of the reason for this lay in their attitude to the 'bourgeoisie', but the bourgeois they railed against was of a particular type. He was not the narrow, hard-nosed Gradgrind of Marx's *Capital* but was best represented by Diederich Hessling, the anti-hero of Heinrich Mann in his popular novel *Man of Straw* (*Der Untertan*, literally *The Subject*) (1918). Hessling is a 'feudalized' bourgeois, a submissive Hermes to the Wilhelmine Zeus. He is, at root, a cynical opportunist but has learnt at school and university to venerate hierarchy. Pathetically he attempts to ingratiate himself with the aristocracy, joining duelling fraternities and even adopting a Kaiser-style moustache, and embraces the fashionable militarism and imperialism. Meanwhile he exploits the workers beneath him.[16]

Man of Straw dramatized the theories of imperialism of Marxists like Rosa Luxemburg. They suggested that capitalism had become intimately connected with imperialism and militarism. The old liberal defence of capitalism as the bearer of freedom and peace no longer seemed credible. This analysis made sense to many, even those who were not fully paid-up Marxists. Karl Kraus, the owner of the Viennese satirical magazine *Die Fackel* (*The Torch*) and a critic of nationalism (but by no means a Marxist), captured the appeal of Communism to angry intellectuals. Writing in November 1920 he explained:

> Communism is in reality nothing but the antithesis of a particular ideology that is both thoroughly harmful and corrosive. Thank God for the fact that Communism springs from a clean and clear ideal, which preserves its idealistic purpose even though, as an antidote, it is inclined to be somewhat harsh. To hell with its practical importance: but may God at least preserve it for us as a never-ending menace to those people who own big estates and who, in order to hang on to them, are prepared to despatch humanity into battle, to abandon it to starvation for the sake of patriotic honour. May God preserve Communism so that the evil brood of its enemies may be prevented from becoming more bare-faced still, so that the gang of profiteers ... shall have their sleep disturbed by a few pangs of anxiety.[17]

But whilst Kraus may have had his doubts about Communism's 'harshness', for others it now seemed normal; fire had to be fought with fire. Before the war, many of the avant-garde intelligentsia despaired of mundane, 'philistine', bourgeois life, with its enslavement to money and technology. They hoped for a politics of spirit, soul and enthusiasm. These Romantic anti-capitalists often welcomed the war as an opportunity to smash bourgeois complacency and create a new man, full of renewed vigour and spirit.[18] But the war affected radicals in different ways. For some, like the Futurist Marinetti, who ended up on the fascist right, it showed the need for even more intense, messianic nationalism. But a more common response was a profound disillusionment with nationalistic flag-waving. Many of the leftist intellectuals of the Weimar period were deeply affected by fighting at the front.

Yet whilst the war may have discredited nationalist militarism, it did not do the same for wartime Romanticism. Artists and intellectuals were more determined than ever to create the new man, free of the confines of bourgeois society. But now the new man was to be the ideal worker, not a nationalist warrior. Many champions of expressionism in the arts – a movement that prized intense feeling and extreme imagery – moved to the left. The playwright Ernst Toller, for instance, became a leader of the short-lived Bavarian Soviet Republic in April 1919.[19]

Given the temper of the time, it is no surprise that the major Marxist theorists of this wartime generation should have been in the Radical Marxist camp, and were closer to Aleksandr Bogdanov and the Bolshevik left than to Lenin. György Lukács, for instance, an intellectual born to a wealthy Jewish family in Budapest, had been a Romantic critic of capitalism before the war, but his interests were in utopian forms of mysticism, not the socialist left; socialism, for him, did not have the 'religious power capable of filling the entire soul'.[20] However, the war and ensuing Bolshevik revolution convinced him that Communism was the best way of creating a new society, free of the bourgeoisie's stifling rationality. His friend, Paul Ernst, attributed the following views of the Bolsheviks to him:

> The Russian Revolution ... is just taking its first steps to lead humanity beyond the bourgeois social order of mechanization and bureaucratization, militarism and imperialism, towards a free world in which the Spirit will once again rule and the Soul will at last be able to live.[21]

It took Lukács some time to overcome his mistrust of Communist violence, and it was only in December 1918 that he was finally converted to Communism by Béla Kun. When Kun formed the Hungarian Soviet government in March 1919, Lukács was appointed the Deputy People's Commissar for Public Education for the 133 days the regime survived, staging performances of George Bernard Shaw, Gogol and Ibsen for the workers of Budapest. In the final days of the Soviet government, this most cerebral of intellectuals became the political commissar for a division of the Hungarian Red Army, recklessly patrolling the trenches and braving the enemy's fire.[22] His Marxism was always more leftist and radical than Lenin's, and he even suggested that the Communist Party should be dissolved once it had taken power.[23] He became more orthodox in the years of his exile in Vienna, but his *History and Class Consciousness* of 1923 became one of the most important texts of 'Western Marxism' – a form of Marxism that stressed the power of culture and the subjective over science and the laws of history.[24] Lukács was famously, and rather unfairly, satirized by Thomas Mann in his novel of 1924, *The Magic Mountain*, as 'Naphta', a strange combination of Jew, Jesuit and Communist. In one of the lengthy debates within the novel, he declared:

> The proletariat has taken up [the medieval Pope] Gregory the Great's task, his godly zeal burns within it, and his hands can no more refrain from shedding blood than could his. Its work is terror, that the world may be saved and the ultimate goal of redemption be achieved: the children of God living in a world without classes or laws.[25]

A preoccupation with cultural power over economics was also characteristic of the Marxism of the influential Italian theorist Antonio Gramsci, even though his background was very different to that of the wealthy Lukács. The sickly son of a poor government clerk from Sardinia, where the landed aristocracy was still very dominant, Gramsci admitted to having had an 'instinct of rebellion against the rich' from a young age.[26] He was perhaps therefore a more natural socialist than Lukács, and once he had entered the University of Turin – an industrial town with a strong union movement – he threw himself into leftist politics. However, he shared Lukács's desire to reconcile Marxism with a politics of the spirit and cultural transformation. Communist intellectuals were not to be arid Kautskian scientists, agronomists and economists. Like the priests of the medieval Catholic Church, they had to be able to understand the passions of the masses. Influenced by the Russian Proletkult, Gramsci hoped that the factory council movement would create a new egalitarian proletarian culture, for socialism was 'an integral vision of life' with 'a philosophy, a mystique, a morality'.[27] He always remained true to this radical democratic tradition which placed its faith in elected workers' organizations, rather than a centralized party.[28] Even so, in the complex factional politics of the early 1920s he was recognized as head of the Italian Communist Party by Moscow in late 1923.

Lukács's and Gramsci's interest in the cultural and subjective aspects of Marxism was shared by many other Western intellectuals of their generation. The Marxist Institute for Social Research, or 'Frankfurt School', founded in Germany in 1923 (and which moved to New York in 1934 after Hitler came to power), included figures with few links to Communist politics, such as the Marxist cultural critics Walter Benjamin and Herbert Marcuse.[29] But all of these figures were less influential in the inter-war period than during the next flowering of Romantic Marxism in the West, in the 1960s. They were too young, although their most influential work was written in the 1930s – Gramsci's whilst he was in a Fascist prison. Their rejection of scientific, Modernist Marxism was also extreme. Yet there was one critic of the old Modernist Marxism who was both a major theorist and was active in Communist politics: 'Red Rosa' Luxemburg. A Radical Marxist and a strong supporter of revolutionary democracy, Luxemburg was a critic of Modernist Marxist 'waiting' and a Social Democratic leadership she saw as stolid and unimaginative. Her tastes were the opposite of Lenin's. She hated what she called the 'German mentality' for its routine and officiousness, admiring instead Russian revolutionary verve.[30] If Lenin saw his role as Westernizing Russia, Luxemburg saw hers as Russifying Germany. But in other ways she was close to Lenin – a Marxist, born in the Russian empire in the early 1870s, brought up in an orthodox Marxism, who insisted on a revolution whilst at the same time remaining convinced that capitalism was about to crumble anyway. She also shared Lenin's interest in economics – her main theoretical work, *The Accumulation of Capital*, tried to show, like Marx's *Capital*, why capitalism was doomed by its own internal economic contradictions. And like Lenin, a personal bourgeois fastidiousness in everyday life contrasted rather drastically with implacable criticism of the bourgeoisie.

Luxemburg also shared Lenin's attitudes towards revolutionary strategy in 1918 and 1919. A committed militant activist, she called for socialism, immediately, in Germany, and her Spartakus League became the core of the KPD, the German Communist party established on 30 December 1918. She was always a revolutionary democrat and critic of terror, and she condemned the authoritarianism of the Bolsheviks. Even so, Lenin retained his affection for her. After her death he compared her to the eagle, in the Russian fable of the eagle and the chicken. She could sometimes fly lower than the chicken – as when she disagreed with him on the question of violence and revolution – but she also soared to heights of Marxist virtue.[31]

In 1918 and early 1919 Lenin himself was prepared to accede to the revolutionary radicalism in the West which he had begun to abandon in Russia itself. Western workers, Lenin reasoned, were more mature than backward Russians. In the West revolutions might 'proceed more smoothly', and achieve power in more diverse ways, without the need for the iron discipline of a vanguard party. So, whilst Lenin was eager to establish a third, Communist International – the Comintern – to rival the second, Social Democratic one, he did not think it needed to impose centralized control. The first Comintern congress took place in a draughty Kremlin hall on a cold Sunday in March 1919, and was a chaotic affair. Very few of the foreign delegates had arrived, and those who did had to deal with the 'flimsy chairs at rickety tables obviously borrowed from some café', whilst 'the carpets strove, though in vain, to make up for the heaters that blew terrible gusts of frigid air at the delegates'.[32] The frosty temperature was soon countered by the heat of the rhetoric. Many delegates were convinced that world revolution was imminent, and that workers' councils were the seeds of the new state. Indeed, Trotsky's 'Manifesto to the Proletariat of the Entire World' did not even mention the rule of the vanguard, the Communist party; the model of the new order was that outlined in *State and Revolution*.[33]

III

For a time, Marxist theory and popular attitudes appeared to be moving in tandem, as Marxist Radicals tapped into the ideas of the more militant strains of the workers' movement. Communists did better in some countries than in others, though the pattern was not the one predicted by orthodox Marxism. Unified, cohesive working classes did not produce powerful Communist movements. Instead, they helped moderate socialists and trade unionists, who could use the power of organized labour to win concessions from the ruling classes. Rather, Communists did best in underdeveloped agrarian economies where industrialization was late and patchy, and the working class was poorly organized. In these countries, peasants tended to be angry at the remnants of an old agrarian order, and moderate socialists were weak.[34] Communists were also helped by defeat in war, which discredited aristocracies and the socialists who had cooperated with them.

Russia, of course, fulfilled these conditions most closely. But Hungary also partially fitted the template. Unlike Russia, it did not have a strong tradition of revolutionary Marxist politics; however, it was a predominantly agrarian society ruled by a narrowly based, conservative aristocratic regime, which had lost the war and refused to make concessions either to other classes, or to its minority nationalities. With the discrediting of elites and the threat of territorial disintegration, rural unrest and a bloodless revolution by Budapest workers brought the liberal Count Karolyi to power in October 1918, presiding over a Provisional Government of liberals and moderate socialists. Though it was supposedly preparing for elections to a Constituent Assembly, these were repeatedly postponed, on the grounds that they could not take place while Allied troops occupied Hungary. The government was also paralysed by divisions between liberals and socialists over land reform. The result was pressure from increasingly radical workers, peasants and demobilized soldiers.

Hungary seemed to be following a path similar to Russia's a year and a half earlier. It also had a Bolshevik party (strongly influenced by Russian socialists), that took advantage of the unfolding situation. However, that party had been germinated abroad, in Russia, not at home. On the outbreak of the February revolution, Russia hosted about half a million Hungarian prisoners of war, many of whom were highly sympathetic to the Bolsheviks. One of them, the charismatic journalist Béla Kun, became closely involved in the politics of the soviets and was transferred to Petrograd, where he organized a group of Hungarian prisoner-of-war Communists in Russia. This was one of the first Bolshevik attempts to export revolution. They believed that after Germany,

Hungary was the 'weakest link' in the capitalist chain. Revolutionary schools were established in Moscow and Omsk to train Hungarian ex-prisoners, and then to send them as revolutionaries into Hungary. In November 1918, the Hungarian Communist Party was formally established in the Hotel Dresden, Moscow, and from there Kun led a group home to convert the 'Hungarian Kerenshchina' (rule of Kerenskii) into the 'Hungarian October'.

Kun was an effective propagandist and beguiling rhetorician, as even his enemies admitted. One, a socialist, described one of his speeches:

> Yesterday I heard Kun speak ... it was an audacious, hateful, enthusiastic oratory. He was a hard-looking man with a head of a bull, thick hair and moustache, not so much Jewish, but peasant features, would best describe his face ... He knows his audience and rules over them ... Factory workers long at odds with the Social Democratic Party leaders, young intellectuals, teachers, doctors, lawyers, clerks who came to his room ... met Kun and Marxism.[35]

This energy, combined with Soviet financial help, was highly effective, but the Communists also benefited from the radicalization of the workers' councils, and the threats to Hungarian territorial integrity.[36] The Karolyi government soon became a victim of Allied support for Romanian, Czechoslovak and Yugoslav demands for chunks of Hungarian territory, whilst the Communists argued that an alliance with the USSR would deliver more than kow-towing to the perfidious Allies. In March the socialists merged with the Communists to create a joint government to resist them, and the Hungarian Soviet Republic was born.

The Hungarians were therefore amongst the first Communists explicitly to embrace nationalism *cum* revolutionary fervour, and initially they had some success in prevailing on the Allies to improve their terms. It looked as if rejecting Lenin's internationalist orthodoxy might unite a large number of Hungarians behind the Communist banner. But in other areas, Kun and the Hungarian Communists were much less pragmatic than Lenin. They derived their economic ideas from the Radical Marxism of *State and Revolution* and its model of 'proletarian democracy', which had been in the forefront of Bolshevik rhetoric in 1917 and early 1918.[37] For Kun, Hungarians were superior to Russians, and therefore more capable of the rapid transition to Communism than the Russians. Payment of workers by results – piece rates – was abolished, wages were increased and workers' rents reduced; factories were to be nationalized and the economy subjected to central control. Moreover, the army was declared a purely proletarian body, conscription was outlawed, and all non-worker soldiers were dismissed. At the same time, a 'Terror Squad of the Revolutionary Governing Council' nicknamed the 'Lenin boys', comprising leather-coated toughs, pursued the wealthy and the former leaders of the old regime.

Many of these Communist experiments caused chaos, and, under social-ist pressure, were reversed. But the regime failed to restore order to the urban economy, and, most importantly, it continued to rule in the narrow interests of the proletariat. It ordered that the land be nationalized and farmed collectively. Lenin urged the Hungarians not to attempt this fool-ishly ambitious step, but Kun's obstinacy was tinged with national pride: 'Let us carry out the revolution on the agrarian field as well. We should be able to do it better than the Russians . . .'[38] The Communists' use of forced requisitions to feed the army, and their anti-religion campaign, merely convinced the peasantry that the regime was at war with it.

The Hungarian Soviet government soon found itself with very little support. Peasants were particularly hostile, but workers too were angered by shortages and a worthless inflated currency. But it was the regime's ultimate failure to defend the nation from foreign aggression that really destroyed it. In the late spring of 1919 the Hungarian Red Army responded to a Czech incursion, and struck deep into Slovakia, establishing a Slovak Soviet Republic in June. Kun even planned a coup in Vienna, although this was easily foiled. However, when the French Prime Minister Clemenceau and the Allies demanded a Hungarian with-drawal, Kun complied, leading to a collapse in army morale and encour-aging Hungary's neighbours to counter-attack. In its final weeks the regime launched a 'red terror' against internal 'enemies' to consolidate their rule, leading to the deaths of 587 people. Kun desperately appealed to Lenin for military help but in vain. The Bolsheviks were too hard-pressed in Russia itself. On 1 August the Revolutionary Governing Council decided to hand over power to a trade-union government, and Kun and his allies fled to Austria. The Hungarian Soviet Republic was the victim of foreign pressure rather than popular uprising, but Kun realized that his regime had failed to gain the support of the Hungarian workers, let alone the population as a whole.

The Hungarian Communists were victims of their own dogmatism and their inability to deliver on nationalistic promises at a time when the state was fighting for its life. In comparison, conditions looked more favourable for Communists in Italy. The radical Italian Socialist Party (PSI) had a long history of effective organization and opposition to the war; Northern Italy, like Russia a late and uneven industrializer, had a concentrated working class in the Turin–Genoa–Milan triangle, with a radical peasantry in the nearby Po Valley; and the Communists were more willing than the Hungarians to appeal to peasants. In October 1919 the PSI declared that liberal reforms were not enough and the time had come for the creation of a new type of socialist state. The radical left gained local electoral support, and strikes and boycotts were reinforced by factory occupations in the spring and autumn of 1920. These were the factory councils Gramsci believed could be the foundations of the new state.[39]

Yet, as was the case in Russia, the radicals found it difficult to reconcile factory democracy with effective economic coordination. Factory councils narrowly pursued their own interests, and it was difficult to ensure that they delivered supplies to each other to keep the economy going.[40] Coordinating the revolutionary movement also posed difficulties. Radical socialists controlled some areas, but the army and old liberal parties were still masters of the state, and large sections of the population, especially in the countryside, were conservative. Meanwhile, there were profound divisions amongst the socialist workers themselves. The PSI's leadership, and most of its membership, were not committed to revolution, and in September 1920 a referendum within the trade unions rejected a proposal that the factory councils become the basis of an alternative revolutionary state – albeit narrowly, by 591,245 to 409,569 votes. Gramsci, like others who had placed their faith in the factory council movement, soon became convinced that a centralized, Leninist party was needed to lead the revolution. The PSI finally split in 1921 into Socialist and Communist parties, and this divided left was no match for the paramilitary right. From early in 1920, the Fascists – a coalition of ex-socialist nationalists like Mussolini, supporters of landowners in the countryside and anti-socialist groups, often young and middle class, fought what they saw as a Red tide. Convinced that class struggle was destroying the unity and power of Italy, they unleashed formidable violence against the left, and ultimately seized power in October 1922. In 1926 Gramsci himself was arrested and imprisoned.

Moscow had harboured great hopes for revolution in Italy, but its main ambitions were concentrated on Germany. The Communists' first attempt to seize power, however, was a failure. In January 1919 Ebert's new government began to root out enclaves of radical influence, and on 4 January 1919 dismissed the leftist president of the Berlin police authorities, Eichhorn. Unexpectedly large demonstrations erupted in his defence, and although Rosa Luxemburg was sceptical of the wisdom of challenging the government, she and the newly formed Communists (KPD) ultimately decided to support the mass uprising, in alliance with the leftist Independent Social Democratic Party (USPD). The Ebert government responded by sending in members of the Freikorps, right-wing paramilitary squads set up to oppose the revolution, and on 11 January they stormed the headquarters of the Social Democratic newspaper *Vorwärts*, which had been occupied by the revolutionaries. By 15 January the uprising was over and the Communist leaders went into hiding. The Freikorps discovered and subsequently killed them with the tacit support of the Social Democratic government.

The murders caused profound shock, and the 'martyrdom' of Luxemburg and Liebknecht transformed them into potent icons for the young Communist party. 'LLL' (Lenin–Luxemburg–Liebknecht) festivals became central to Communist culture throughout the Weimar period.[41] But the repression worked, at least for a time. As Brecht had shown in *Spartakus*, a majority favoured peace and order over revolution, and in the elections that followed, the Social Democrats won 37.9 per cent of the vote, compared with 7.6 per cent won by the USPD – the only far-left party standing.

This, however, was not the end of the revolutionary era. The repressiveness of the Social Democrat-led government and its military allies was counterproductive, and Wolfgang Kapp's failed right-wing coup convinced many workers that the Social Democrats could not be trusted to resist the return of the old elites. The factory council movement was revived, several areas were cleared of the army and the Freikorps, and in the June 1920 elections the radical left achieved its highest ever vote – 20 per cent for the USPD and Communists against the Social Democrats' 21.6 per cent. Strikes and unrest continued in the industrial regions of Germany, and the newly merged USPD and Communists continued to do well.

In July 1920 the Second Congress of the Comintern met amidst enormous optimism. The factory council movement in Italy seemed on the verge of success, and the Red Army was advancing on Warsaw, bringing Communism to the West, or so the Bolsheviks supposed. But by the autumn, the Communists were in retreat on all fronts. The persecution of the Wobblies and other American radicals that began during the war reached a high point during the 'Red Scare' of 1919–20. Thousands were arrested, and many deported.[42] In Europe, the failure of the Italian factory council movement in late 1920 and the retreat of the Red Army from Warsaw after August, following its defeat by the new Polish army, marked the beginning of the end. It became clear, however, that the revolutionary era was over with the catastrophic failure of the German Communists' so-called 'March Action' of 1921. The police and army had been deployed to crush strikes in Saxony, and Béla Kun, who materialized in Berlin as a Comintern leader, encouraged the Communist party to organize a proletarian revolution in response. The rebels were in a minority, and strikes were broken with the help of Social Democrat workers. They were inevitably defeated; thousands were imprisoned and 145 individuals killed.

Brecht had been proved prescient, and it may be that his analysis was right too: people were tired of struggle. Whilst many might have been profoundly disillusioned with the old regimes and their stubborn bellicosity, most did not want a horrific international conflagration to be followed by class war. But there were other reasons for the failures of the revolutions. Some Communists were too sectarian and ambitious, as in Hungary. Others were discredited by their lack of realism, unable to explain how decentralized factory councils could run a modern industrial economy. Repression from moderate left and far right was also effective. But crucial in undermining the revolutionary impulse was the power of democratic and welfare reforms. Throughout Western Europe, states extended the franchise and increased welfare benefits for workers – especially in Weimar Germany, where the Social Democrats retained considerable influence. The hope of peaceful improvement, combined with the end of the post-war booms that had given workers economic power, soon vanquished Communist insurgencies.

Even so, the social conflicts of the past had not been resolved. Governments and the middle classes wanted a return to the pre-1914 laissez-faire economic system and the gold standard, which inevitably restricted growth. But this was hard to reconcile with promises made after the war for improved welfare, and living standards were regularly sacrificed, nailed to the 'cross of gold' – the need to keep the currency stable. Workers protested against the resulting low wages and high unemployment, most famously when Winston Churchill returned sterling to the gold standard and the 1926 British General Strike was called against the resulting wage cuts. There was a boom of sorts at the end of the 1920s, but it proved to be fragile. Wages remained low as profits soared, and in the United States capital flooded into share and property speculation rather than production for an expanding market; in Central Europe the temporary prosperity was dependent on high levels of short-term loans from American banks. The developed world had failed to forge a sustainable capitalism that secured both prosperity and social harmony – as was soon to become clear.

For a time, then, the capitalist system had 'stabilized' itself, as Communists admitted. But the revolutionary tide left rock pools of radicalism as it retreated, and Communism found a home in many communities of workers and the unemployed throughout Europe. However, its real stronghold was in Germany, where the Communists continued to attract over 10 per cent of the vote. The old home of Marx and Engels remained the centre of Communism outside the USSR.

IV

In December 1930, Brecht, by now a serious Marxist and supporter of the KPD, produced what was probably his most controversial play: *The Measures Taken*. Staged with a 'control chorus' (adapted from the Greek chorus) made up of large numbers of workers, it told the story of three Communist activists on a secret mission to foment revolution in China. They find a young guide, and tell him that they must all keep their identities secret. If the authorities discover them, not only will they be killed, but the whole Communist movement will be in jeopardy. All four put on masks. Yet the guide, emotional and undisciplined, is so outraged by the sufferings of the Chinese people that he tries to help them, removing his mask and revealing his identity. The authorities pursue the young guide, and the three Communists realize that he is a liability. They cannot leave him and they cannot take him. So they decide they must kill him, and he himself agrees that this is the only solution. He is shot and his body is left in a lime pit to remove all traces of his identity. The chorus then chillingly declares that the comrades have made the right decision; the necessary 'measures have been taken' for the salvation of the revolution.[43]

The play caused a storm of controversy within the left. Ruth Fischer, a Communist and sister of Brecht's collaborator Hanns Eisler, later accused him of justifying Soviet brutality, as 'the minstrel of the GPU [the Soviet secret police]'.[44] Brecht protested that he was merely encouraging his audience to explore the problem of revolutionary tactics and the need for self-sacrifice at a time when Communists were under attack from fascism. Even so, the play was to damage him. During the McCarthyite campaign against Communists, the House Un-American Activities Committee saw The Measures Taken as evidence that Brecht was wedded to revolutionary violence, and their judgement precipitated his move from America to Communist East Germany in 1949.

However controversial and ambiguous Brecht's message on violence, the play does capture the austere character of European Communism outside the Soviet Union in the 1920s and early 1930s. Brecht's scepticism of revolutionary radicalism, already evident in 1919, was now widespread; the emotionalism of expressionist art and literature had given way to a sober 'new objectivity' (Neue Sachlichkeit). The failure of the post-war revolutions and the growth of an anti-Communist radical right both fed the sectarian and unsentimental culture that Brecht espoused in The Measures Taken. Revolution was still the goal, but emotionalism had to be replaced by discipline. European Communists became increasingly reliant on the Soviet Union, and subject to a new authoritarian ethos, worlds away from the council democracy of 1919. They also became more isolated, members of a persecuted sect.

The first sign of these changes in the international Communist movement came in the summer of 1919, and was precipitated by defeats. If the humiliating Treaty of Brest-Litovsk in March 1918 was the trigger for the end of 'proletarian democracy' within Russia, the collapse of the Hungarian Soviet Republic in August 1919 convinced Lenin that the Bolsheviks must radically revise their approach to world revolution. He now believed that his earlier hope that the Western revolutions could be more democratic than their Russian counterpart was misplaced. Lenin held Béla Kun responsible for the failure of the Budapest republic. He had mistakenly merged the Communist party with the socialists, had placed too little faith in the vanguard party, and needlessly alienated the peasantry.[45] As Lenin explained in his highly influential *Left-wing Communism: An Infantile Disorder* of April 1920, Russian lessons showed that 'absolute centralization and rigorous discipline in the proletariat' were essential in a 'long, stubborn and desperate life-and-death struggle' against the bourgeoisie.[46]

At the Second Comintern Congress of 1920, Lenin and the Bolsheviks seriously began the task of centralizing international Communism under tight Bolshevik control. The Congress decided that all parties had to fulfil 'Twenty-one Conditions', the most important being Communists' complete separation from the unified 'Social Democratic' parties. Furthermore, only 'tested Communists' could remain members; 'reformists' and 'opportunists' were to be expelled. The principles of the conspiratorial Bolshevik vanguard party were now being applied to the international movement. There was some opposition to this Communist purism, especially from the German Independent Social Democrats, but Grigorii Zinoviev, the Comintern boss, was adamant. Those who opposed the creation of separate Communist parties, he sneered, 'think of the Communist International as a good tavern, where representatives of various countries sing the "Internationale" and pay each other compliments, then go their separate ways and continue the same old practices. That is the damnable custom of the Second International and we will never tolerate it.'[47] All member parties had to be reconstituted as 'Communist parties', and were to be subordinate to an executive committee dominated by the Bolshevik party.

The result was the emergence of pure Communist parties, disentangled from the mixed-left parties of pre-war Europe. The division in the Russian party of 1903, between revolutionary Bolsheviks and gradualist Mensheviks, was being replicated in the international Communist movement. In some countries, the Communists benefited from the resulting splits. In Germany, the tiny Communist Party succeeded in attracting the majority of the Independent Social Democrats into the fold, and emerged as a mass party with 350,000 members. Meanwhile in France, the French Communist Party (PCF) took the majority of the members of the old Second International socialist party, the SFIO. But in Italy, the splitting of the old Socialist Party (PSI) left a smaller Italian

Communist Party with a mere 4.6 per cent of the vote. Significant parties also emerged in Bulgaria, Czechoslovakia and Finland. But elsewhere, in Iberia, the Low Countries, Britain, Ireland, the USA, Denmark and Sweden, Switzerland and much of Eastern Europe, Communist parties were minuscule. Apart from in Germany and Finland, they rarely secured more than 5 per cent of the popular vote, and the Communist Party of Great Britain won a mere 0.1–0.4 per cent of the vote (although it did win a single seat in Parliament in 1922).[48] Germany had by far the largest and most powerful Communist party outside the USSR.

It was clear that the revolutionary tide was ebbing, and in March 1921, the new situation faced the Bolshevik leaders starkly. The March Action in Germany had failed; economic collapse had forced Russia to introduce the New Economic Policy; and it was now glaringly obvious that the Soviet economy could only be built by exporting raw materials (especially grain) to the outside world. In the same month, the Soviets concluded their first trade agreement with a capitalist country – Great Britain. It was clear that full socialism lay over a very distant horizon; as Trotsky explained in June 1921, 'Only now do we see and feel that we are not immediately close to our final aim, to the conquest of power on a world scale . . . We told ourselves back in 1919 that it was a question of months, but now we say that it is perhaps a question of several years.'[49] The result was a new policy. Communist parties were to cease to agitate for immediate revolution, though they were still to prepare for it in the longer term; instead 'united fronts' had to be forged with the members – but not the leaders – of reformist socialist parties. As the icy relations between the USSR and the West thawed slightly (the Treaty of Rapallo was concluded with Germany in 1922, and the British Labour government extended diplomatic recognition to the Soviet Union in 1924), the new policy seemed to be justified.

In some parts of the world the new line had some real effects, most strikingly in China in the collaboration between the Chinese Communists and the Nationalist Guomindang, and in Britain, where the Communist Party established links with the trade unions through the Anglo-Russian Committee. Many Communists, especially in the smaller, more marginal parties, welcomed the opportunity to play a role in the broader left. But in most places the isolation of Communists continued. The 'united front' policy was bafflingly contradictory, banning contacts with Social Democratic parties, but calling for collaboration with reformist trade unions. Many Communists also resisted collaboration, especially in Germany, where they retained their hatred for the Social Democrats; their hostility was fully reciprocated.

The frequent zigzags in Moscow's policy compounded the difficulty of forging links with the moderate left, and isolated the Communists even further. A major turning point came with the humiliating failure of yet another attempt at a German revolution – the 'German October' of 1923. Following the French and Belgian occupation of the Ruhr in 1923, the left of the German Communist Party, with their allies in Moscow, Trotsky and Zinoviev, insisted that the Communists could create an alliance with nationalists, forging them into a revolutionary force. Moscow provided substantial funding for the insurrection, but the Communists had massively exaggerated working-class support, and the revolution had to be called off.[50]

The failure coincided with Lenin's terminal illness and the resultant power struggle within the Soviet party leadership. Trotsky's rivals, including Stalin, fully exploited the disaster, and the humiliation was used as an excuse to centralize power and curtail local radicalism. In 1924 the Kremlin launched the 'Bolshevization' of the Comintern, meaning that member parties had to become 'Bolshevik parties', all part of a 'homogeneous Bolshevik world party permeated with the ideas of Leninism'.[51] In practice, this meant that Communist parties were increasingly transformed into tools of Soviet foreign policy. Stalin did not pretend otherwise: 'An *internationalist* is one who is ready to defend the USSR without reservation, without wavering, unconditionally; for the USSR is the base of the world revolutionary movement, and this revolutionary movement cannot be defended and promoted without defending the USSR.'[52]

The actual degree and effect of Moscow's interventions in national Communist parties is a complex, and controversial, question.[53] The Comintern, a relatively small organization, clearly could not monitor and control the activities of all Communist parties at all levels. Also, in several places Communist subcultures emerged, founded on local radical left-wing traditions, which had little to do with Moscow.[54] However, the Comintern did try to establish control over the parties' leaderships, and it had several ways of exerting influence – by sending agents to 'fraternal' parties, by supporting party factions against opponents, and, at the other extreme, by expelling recalcitrants and closing parties down (as happened to the Polish Communist Party in 1938). Financial aid also played a role.[55] However, perhaps as important in sustaining Moscow's power was the USSR's prestige amongst Communists, and the national parties' weaknesses. Whilst there was resentment at Moscow's arrogance, the Western parties had to accept that the Bolsheviks had brought Communists to power whilst they had not. And defeat convinced many that strict discipline, imposed by Moscow, was even more crucial than in the past.[56]

One way the Bolsheviks controlled the movement was by summoning leading international Communists to report regularly to Moscow, and a close network was formed around the inappropriately named Hotel Lux.[57] A grand *fin-de-siècle* building on Moscow's central Tverskaia (later Gorkii) Street, it had, however, passed its prime and was now a notoriously shabby and spartan hostel. It was to be a temporary home to many Communist leaders, from the Bulgarian Dimitrov to the Vietnamese Ho Chi Minh, from the German Ulbricht to the Italian Togliatti. Communist activists ran into each other in the cold showers – the Yugoslav Tito first met the American party leader Earl Browder in these unpromising circumstances.[58]

Moscow's International Lenin School for Western Communists, founded in 1926, was another tool by which the Kremlin attempted to exert influence over the movement. Thousands of party members studied there between the wars, most of them young, male and working class. Compulsory courses included academic classes in Marxism and the 'History of the Workers' Movement', and the study of political tactics and how to organize strikes and insurrections. The wisdom of Lenin was supplemented by the insights of the classic German military theorist Clausewitz. Students also visited factories – a rather riskier event for the Comintern authorities: some visitors were shocked at the low living standards of Russian workers compared with their fellow proletarians in capitalist countries, and asked awkward questions.[59] But most important for the Comintern, especially after Stalin's rise to power, was the inculcation of a Bolshevik party culture of discipline and 'conspiracy', much like that described by Brecht. Students were given new names and were forbidden from telling friends or family where they were. One Welsh miner engaged in 'self-criticism' for neglecting these principles. His connections with the Labour party, he accepted, had left him with 'Social Democratic remnants I have brought with me from my own country. [I] ended up by committing this gross breach of Party discipline and conspiracy which is impermissible in our Party as a Party of a new type.'[60]

Life for the Comintern student was tough and intense. Wolfgang Leonhard, a German Communist who was at the school during World War II when it was evacuated eastwards to the Urals city of Ufa, remembered his rigorous lessons on Nazi ideology and how to refute it. He spent so much time learning about Nazism that when he returned to Germany after the war and met real Nazis he found he was better versed in their beliefs and mores than they were themselves.[61] Much of the rest of his time was taken up with either exercise or improving manual labour; students had to maintain their links with the working class:

> Our working time was so full up that the only free time we had was on Saturday afternoon and Sunday. At the weekends we were allowed to do whatever we wanted – except to drink, fall in love, leave the school compound, admit our real names, tell anything about our previous life, or write anything about our present life in our letters.[62]

Relaxation was rare and consisted largely of regimented folk singing. Some students, like the Yugoslav leader Tito's son, Zharko, who had an affair with an 'enchanting Spanish girl', refused to submit to the discipline and were expelled.[63] Most survived though, and several went on to be fully committed Leninists and Stalinists, becoming future leaders of European Communist parties.[64] Efforts were being made to 'forge' the young, radical and chaotic parties of the revolutionary period according to a new template issued in Moscow.

However, whilst Moscow did generally succeed in persuading or forcing national parties to follow the frequently changing party line, it was not always easy, for national Communists had their own agendas and could engage in passive, or even active, resistance. As has been seen, in Germany the party left objected to the united front with the socialists in the mid-1920s, whilst later in the decade, when the line moved to the left under Stalin, the right resisted. The British leadership also opposed the Kremlin from the right. In October 1927 the leader of the British Communists, blacksmith's son Harry Pollitt, initially opposed the new Comintern demand that a harsh struggle had to be fought against the Labour Party, realizing how unpopular it would be; it was only in 1929 that the British party leadership fully accepted the new line.[65]

Bolshevization therefore made life difficult for the national parties, partly because Moscow's line could be unpopular, and partly because the Comintern's culture could be alien. Party members not only had to learn heavy Marxist jargon (originally in German, the official Comintern language), but also new Russian Bolshevik argot ('agitprop', or 'party cell'). Party propaganda was often drafted in Moscow, without local consultation, and Communists struggled to make the clotted slogans sound appealing.[66] Even so, despite Bolshevization, local parties did try to blend local and Comintern cultures, and they had their distinct characteristics. In Germany, the militant culture fostered by Rosa Luxemburg and the Social Democratic left before 1914 survived, whilst in Britain, and elsewhere, the puritanical morality of Communism made sense to people brought up in a Christian socialist culture of temperance and earnestness.[67] Meanwhile, the Oxford-educated and half-Indian British Communist Rajani Palme Dutt persisted in referring to younger party members as 'freshers' – the Oxbridge slang term for first-year students.[68]

Several Communist parties saw a gradual decline in membership over the 1920s and early 1930s; the membership of the French party, for instance, fell continuously between 1921 (109,391) and 1933 (28,000). This was doubtless helped by the clumsy hand of the Kremlin: in countries like France and Britain, where moderate socialist political parties were well-established, the Comintern's sectarianism was clearly counter-productive. Yet for some party members, subject to harassment after the failure of the revolutions, Bolshevik 'discipline' and support could be welcomed. For activists suffering privations, the 'Soviet Union' represented the ideal they were fighting for, a land of milk and honey. Annie Kriegel, in her ethnographic study of French Communism, tried to capture their thinking:

> To the youth with empty hands who approached them, asking to join the movement, they [the Communists] responded by giving him a pile of pamphlets 'There you are, comrade'. Shortly thereafter, hounded by the police, his name inscribed on employers' blacklists, the neophyte found himself unemployed. From then on he had plenty of time – time to be hungry but also time to spread the good word (when he was able to eat thanks to the money he collected selling the pamphlets) . . . He knew with a certainty that there was one country in the world where the workers had

waged a revolution and made themselves the masters of that state, the bosses of the factories, the generals of the Red Army.[69]

Small, embattled Communist communities emerged throughout Europe, even where national parties were tiny. Britain had its 'little Moscows' in Fife, Stepney in East London and the South Wales coalfields – homogeneous working-class communities where Communists became involved in defending jobs and union rights, whilst also organizing leisure and cultural activities.[70] Communist activists reported back to Moscow, explaining why miners in South Wales were so receptive to a militant, sectarian Communism:

> Their conditions are bad, and obviously bad. They are largely free from the distracting influence of the cities. Their time is not so broken up, as it is with workers who live in the big cities, by the long journeys and the many varieties of amusement the big cities provide ... Their minds are more fallow. The factor of exploitation is very obvious to them ... [The] pits, themselves, provide opportunities for instant contact and the development of a sense of solidarity amongst them.[71]

The party where the culture of sectarian struggle and loyalty to the USSR was most fully established was the German one. Here party membership and its popular vote remained high throughout the 1920s and early 1930s. The KPD was often divided over strategy, and the culture of the party also varied by region, but under Ernst Thälmann, its leader from 1925, it combined revolutionary activism with adherence to hierarchy and loyalty to the Kremlin. It soon became the Bolsheviks' favourite little brother, and much of its intransigent hostility to any compromise with social democracy survived the revolutionary era of 1918–19. The separation between the Communists and Social Democrats was not an absolute one: they shared the same trade unions until 1928 and sometimes attended the same festivals;[72] and both Communists and Social Democrats addressed their fellows as 'comrades', and marched beneath the red flag. Even so, the Social Democrats' participation in suppressing Communism had left a legacy of bitterness, as did their identification with the political status quo. In some factories in the Halle-Merseburg region, the mutual hatred was so great that Social Democratic and Communist workers even went to work on different train carriages and ate in separate parts of the company cafeteria.[73] Communists tended to see

Social Democrats as the bosses' lackeys, and certainly the latter were better represented amongst the 'respectable' working class, whilst the former
did better amongst the poorer and unskilled workers. Yet the KPD soon
became a gathering of the unemployed. Communists were inevitably the
most likely to be sacked in the efficiency drives of the 1920s, and by 1932
only 11 per cent of German Communist Party members had jobs.[74]

Adversity only strengthened the KPD's uncompromising attitudes.
Its culture was militaristic and infused with machismo.[75] Its language
was often violent: one newspaper was even named *Rote Peitsche* (*Red
Whip*). Propaganda was an effusion of proletarian fists, leather-coated
marchers and billowing red flags. Its rallies adopted much of the style of
its radical right competitors, and the uniforms and jackboots made it
difficult to distinguish them from the paramilitary Stahlhelm or the
Nazis. Thälmann was even described in the party press as '*unser Führer*'
('our leader'), in imitation of the authoritarianism of the right. At times,
in 1923 and 1930, the Communist party used nationalist language as a
way of attracting support away from the Nazis and others. Even so, the
German Communists were not quasi-Nazis. The party was fundamentally one of class struggle, not national revival, and the Nazis themselves
generally regarded Communists as their main enemies.[76]

The Communist party's militarism was not limited to propaganda. It
had a paramilitary wing, the Red Front Fighters' League (*Rote
Frontkämpferbund*) until it was banned in 1929, and various underground groups after then. Many Communists had guns, brought back
from the war, and sometimes they made their own. In 1921 workers at
the Leuna plant built their own tank, which they deployed against
the police. The German Communists, largely excluded from factories,
became a party of the streets and, especially towards the end of the decade, engaged in brawls and shoot-outs with police.[77] Unsurprisingly,
this martial party was overwhelmingly (70 per cent) male, even though
it had one of the most feminist programmes of all Weimar parties. Even
so, it was too small and isolated to threaten the stability of the German
state in the mid-1920s, at a time when the economy as a whole was
recovering and a liberal politics was still able to incorporate a majority
of interests. As had become clear in the USSR in 1921, militant, sectarian Communist parties were too divisive to appeal to anything more
than a minority. But this only applied in normal times. Everything was
to look very different when the economic downturn came.

V

On 13 May 1928 the *New York Times* published an article entitled 'America's "New" Civilization', which reported on a lecture given by the French academic André Siegfried in Paris. Siegfried had argued that the 'greatest contribution of the United States to the civilized world was "the conquest of the material dignity of life"', through mass production techniques and prosperity, and the journalist praised Siegfried's encomium to the United States. However, the *Times* believed that America's 'contribution to the democratic ideal' and its export of 'a social system free from caste' were of even greater importance than its economic achievements.[78]

Both Siegfried and the *New York Times* expressed a widespread belief that the newly dominant United States, and the laissez-faire democratic model it embodied, had succeeded in overcoming the social divisions of the revolutionary era of 1917–19. Within months, however, this faith proved to be misplaced. In the summer of 1928, the Federal Reserve raised interest rates to restrain a share bubble fuelled by poorly regulated banks; American lending to the rest of the world collapsed. The result was a catastrophic constriction of credit in much of Europe and Latin America; heavily indebted Germany was particularly affected.[79] The economies of the developing world (including that of the USSR) had been suffering for some time from low commodity prices, but the economic crisis worsened when the Wall Street Crash of October 1929 brought the fragile boom to an end in the United States itself.

The result was a sharpening of social and international conflict, as an atmosphere of frantic *sauve qui peut* reigned. Social tensions intensified as workers and middle classes fought over shares of a shrinking national economic cake, whilst international collaboration broke down as states tried to save themselves with protectionist and other autarkic policies. Capitalism's power to integrate the poor and less privileged – whether workers, peasants, or developing countries – into a liberal, free-market order was ebbing. There were now fewer incentives for Communists, Western or Soviet, to cooperate with liberal capitalism, and Communism entered a new radical phase.

The crisis of 1928–9 was, however, only the culmination of tensions between the Communist and capitalist worlds that had been brewing for some years. The 1926 General Strike in Britain led to a deterioration in relations between the Conservative government and Moscow, and in May 1927 the British broke off diplomatic links. Meanwhile, the Guomindang's attack on the Chinese Communists that April was an embarrassing setback for the 'united front' policy, and a major blow to Communist hopes in Asia. German workers were becoming more radical, and in July a failed workers' uprising in Vienna reinforced Moscow's belief that revolution was brewing in the West. From the spring of 1927 the Comintern began to change its line as the Soviet leadership became convinced that its security would be better served by a more militant foreign policy. Moscow began to insist that Social Democrats – especially those like the Germans who had a pro-British foreign policy – be treated as bourgeois enemies, and in 1928 the Comintern declared that a new period of revolutionary politics had begun – the 'Third Period' (following the 'first' post-war revolutionary period and the 'second' stabilization period). Capitalism, it now argued, was tottering; clear lines had to be drawn between revolutionaries and reformists; and the Social Democrats had become 'social fascists'. The new principle of national politics was 'class against class'. Meanwhile the Kremlin became convinced that it could no longer build the economy by relying on trade with the West, but now had to depend largely on the USSR's own resources. The stage was set for a new version of Communism that was both revolutionary and nationalistic. And this model was championed by a Bolshevik leader with a rather different culture and style from Lenin's – Iosif Stalin.

4

Men of Steel

Bolshevik bosses had to wait until March 1928 to see Sergei Eisenstein's completed treatment of 1917 – *October*.[1] Unlike his colleague and rival, the punctual Pudovkin, Eisenstein failed not only to produce his masterpiece on time (possibly because the censor intervened), but he also offered a treatment of the revolution at odds with Pudovkin's Modernist Marxist tale. Whilst Pudovkin dealt with an ordinary 'lad' full of 'spontaneous' feeling who develops a disciplined, rational, socialist consciousness, Eisenstein's film was infused with revolutionary romanticism. He declared that his goal was:

> To restore sensuality to science.
> To restore to the intellectual process its fire and passion.
> To plunge the abstract reflective process into the fervour of
> practical action.[2]

His film is a brilliant rendering of the Radical Marxist temper. His account of 1917 contrasted the inertia and decadence of the Provisional Government with the vibrant energies of the people. And as Eisenstein made clear, the heroism was not individual but collective. The conventional 'leading men' of Hollywood, and indeed of *The End of St Petersburg*, were absent; Lenin's role was fairly minor. The famous storming of the Winter Palace scene, where the masses breached the gates and poured ecstatically into the seat of power, was based not on the revolution itself, but on the carefully choreographed mass festivals of the civil-war period, such as the 1920 'Storming of the Winter Palace', which had deployed its own cast of 10,000. Eisenstein himself had some 5,000 extras at his disposal, live weaponry and the extraordinary tolerance of the authorities. Pudovkin relates how his and Eisenstein's rendering of the iconic storming differed:

> I bombarded the Winter Palace from the [ship] *Aurora*, whilst Eisenstein bombarded it from the Fortress of St Peter and Paul. One night I knocked away part of the balustrade of the roof, and was scared I might get into trouble, but, luckily enough, that same night Sergei Mikhailovich [Eisenstein] broke 200 windows in private bedrooms.[3]

Eisenstein's deputy joked that more people were injured in the cinematic storming (largely the victims of mishandled bayonets) than in the Bolsheviks' actual assault of ten years earlier. The result was a film of extraordinarily propaganda power that did much to create the myth of October 1917.[4] Eisenstein's imagery penetrated global popular culture; indeed only recently it was used in a Western advertising campaign for vodka.

But less appealing today is the real Radical Marxist theme in the film – class struggle. In one of the film's most powerful scenes, a worker flees from the troops after the break-up of the July Days demonstrations. An officer and his girlfriend in a nearby boat spot him and call on a number of well-dressed bystanders to stop the 'Bolshevik'. In the ensuing melee the muscular proletarian is murdered by the violent and angry bourgeois 'mob' – the wealthy women are particularly aggressive, stabbing him viciously with their parasols. As often in Eisenstein's films, the imagery is suffused with machismo, and even misogyny. Eisenstein also insisted on transporting the centrality of conflict to the art of cinema itself: film-making, he argued, must be Marxist and 'dialectical'. His 'montage' technique juxtaposed jarring and paradoxical images to create a new 'synthesis' in the audience, in sharp contrast to Pudovkin's smooth and more conventional 'linkage' method.[5]

However, Eisenstein's film was considerably less well received in the USSR than Pudovkin's. It was deemed to be inaccessible to ordinary people, and his decision to portray Lenin was regarded as an affront to his dignity. Nevertheless, Eisenstein's themes were much more in tune with the developing political order under Stalin than Pudovkin's. The film, a celebration of the energy of revolution, was completed just as Stalin consolidated his power and launched his 'second revolution', and it was screened in the same month as the so-called Shakhty show trial of 'bourgeois specialists' from the Donbass mines was staged. This affair, like *October*, was pure political theatre designed to mobilize the masses against the supposedly continuing influence of the bourgeoisie.

The background of Eisenstein, the Jewish architect's son from Baltic Riga, could not have been more different from Stalin's, the offspring of a shoemaker from Caucasian Georgia. But both were escaping from the more pragmatic Marxism to which Lenin had 'retreated' in 1921 and which seemed to have reached a cul-de-sac by 1927–8. And both were trying to revive the revolution and the class struggles of the civil war, engaging the popular enthusiasm which the regime believed it had once had, and now had lost.

Stalin, predictably, soon abandoned radical class struggle, concluding that it was too divisive, and the message of *October* had soon become outdated. But his use of mobilization and the manipulation of mass emotion continued, despite the twists and turns of party policy. Eisenstein also made efforts to follow the party line, and oddly, given their difficult personal relations, it is by watching the corpus of Eisenstein's films – from the revolutionary Radicalism of *October* (1928), to the more inclusive patriotism of *Aleksandr Nevskii* (1938), to the paranoid search for purity shown in his *Ivan the Terrible* (1944 and 1946) – that one can gain insights into the shifting culture of the Communist Party and the ideas of Stalin himself.

Stalin, of course, did not create Stalinist Communism alone, and we should not exaggerate the role of his personality or background. Stalinism's seeds were embedded in a number of forces, including Bolshevik culture, civil war, and the crises that gripped Russia in the late 1920s, both the fear of a military threat from abroad and disillusionment with Lenin's NEP. But Stalin was able to take advantage of these crises more effectively than any of his rivals. And to understand why requires an understanding of his approach to politics, and a journey back to the region where he spent the first twenty-six years of his life. For in contrast to Lenin, scion of a professional, assimilated cosmopolitan minority within the Russian empire, Stalin had emerged from a veritable cauldron of nationalist and class resentments: Russian Georgia.

11

At the centre of Gori, a provincial town 86 kilometres from Georgia's capital, Tiflis (Tbilisi), is a romantic hill-top fortress. Gorky described it as a place of 'picturesque wildness'. In its courtyard is a spherical stone, from which Amiran – a Georgian Prometheus – is said to have thrown his sword before his cliff-chained incarceration as punishment for challenging the gods (or, in the Georgian legend, Jesus Christ). Each Maundy Thursday Gori's blacksmiths would hammer their anvils to symbolize the renewal of his chains and thus prevent him wreaking revenge on his oppressors.[6]

Ioseb Djugashvili was born in 1878 in the shadow of this castle. He was the son of Beso, a poor artisanal cobbler, and his mother was the daughter of a serf. Georgia was a society awash with stories of Promethean rebellion and vengeance, unsurprisingly given its history. A mountainous borderland, sandwiched between empires, it had a long history of foreign invasion, culminating with the Russians, who had ruled for the previous eighty years. Periodically it had attempted liberation and therefore acquired a well-established warrior tradition, idealized, Walter Scott-style, by romantic nationalist writers.

Ioseb grew up at a time of particularly high tension between colonizers and colonized, as Tsar Alexander III sought to impose Russian over local cultures. When Ioseb entered the religious school in Gori, the teaching medium was still Georgian, but within two years Georgian teachers had been displaced by Russians; Georgian was only permitted to be taught twice a week.[7] His next school, the seminary in Tiflis and the main higher-education institution in Georgia, was run by Russian priests in a reactionary disciplinarian style: any progressive thinking was extinguished by censorship and the Georgian pupils were regarded as inferior. Stalin remembered them 'snooping, spying, prying into one's soul, humiliation'.[8] This priestly regime became an ideal breeding ground for Georgian revolutionaries. As another Bolshevik alumnus commented, 'not one lay school, nor any other type of school produced so many atheists . . . as did the Tiflis seminary'.[9] The seminary was also a highly effective manufacturer of Georgian nationalists, the young Djugashvili amongst them. At the age of sixteen he had several romantic nationalist poems published in the nationalist journal *Iveria*, and when this was closed down by the authorities, he published in a more leftist journal.

Yet Georgia was not only a land of resentful nationalists resisting oppressive Russians. It was also one of the most ethnically diverse regions of the empire, where Armenian and Jewish merchants, Georgian nobles, peasants and artisans, and Georgian, Russian, Azeri and Turkish workers all rubbed shoulders with Russian officials and soldiers. It was, moreover, riven by class and status tensions. The emancipation of serfs had been fiercely resisted by the impoverished Georgian nobility, and nobody was satisfied by the resulting settlement.[10] Ioseb was therefore adrift in a highly stratified society in which he suffered social humiliations. In June 1891, for instance, he was not allowed to matriculate because his family could not pay his fees; it was only the charity of the hated priests that allowed him to continue his education. He was also keenly aware of the social failures of his uneducated father, of whom he spoke with some contempt. Although Beso was clearly ambitious and had, by moving from country to town, raised the status of the family, he also drank, went bankrupt and was forced into lowly factory work in Tiflis. He died in a drunken brawl when Ioseb was eleven.[11]

It is no surprise, then, that Ioseb's early nationalism was intertwined with an entrenched resentment of elites, as was suggested by his choice of Koba, the bandit hero of Georgian legend, as a hero. Like many Georgian nationalists, he revelled in the medieval Georgian epics about heroic knights and the romantic novels based on them. And *Patricide* by the nobleman Aleksandr Qazbegi was a particular influence, its hero Koba, according to a friend, becoming a 'God for him'. Ioseb 'wanted to become another Koba, a fighter and hero as famous as he', and he was later to take the name as his revolutionary *nom de guerre*.[12] Qazbegi had something in common with Bakunin – an aristocrat who romanticized the peasantry – and he even abandoned his privileged life to live with the mountain Georgians. In *Patricide*, Koba joins a group of outlaws-cum-adopted brothers, who avenge the poor but virtuous mountain dwellers by defeating the brutal Russian officials and their Georgian noble collaborators who oppress them. For Ioseb, Koba was a suitable role-model, for several reasons. He had little respect for his weak father and was therefore reliant on the male 'brotherhood' networks that were so important in the South Caucasus.[13] He was also a confident, domineering child, who had to be the boss in any group – the head of a new family of brothers. Banditry, moreover, was not just something to be enjoyed in bygone chivalric romances – it was rife in rural Georgia. Stalin's behaviour as an adult makes it difficult to avoid the conclusion that he was unusually vindictive, suspicious and willing to engage in violence. But he also grew up in an environment where rebelliousness and violence were commonplace.

Despite this violent and picturesque background, it is important to be wary of exaggerating Stalin's image as a reckless, unfettered 'Bandit King'. Stalin had a calculating, devious side, and was by no means the most radical amongst the seminary students. He also admired modernity, and Marxism became for him, as for his fellow Georgian Marxists, a way of transforming an angry resentment of injustice with a strategy for achieving that modernity. And in the Georgian context, modernity meant Russia. For although the radical Georgian intelligentsia loathed Russian imperialism, they regarded its culture as superior to their own, as it embodied the modernity the Georgian radicals craved. The future of Georgia lay in casting off a past of warring nobles and fractious clans, and embracing a unified state within a socialist Russia. For such radicals, an internationalist Marxism was infinitely preferable to a chauvinist nationalism that might, in the Georgian context, spark civil war and invasion from the South.[14] The Georgian Stalin always had a very firm grasp of the lessons of colonial subordination. As a member of a 'backward', stratified society confronting a much more powerful foreign empire, he was to stress the importance of national spirit and unity, even when he had transferred his allegiance from Georgia to Russia.

Despite emerging as a star pupil, excelling in Logic and Slavonic ecclesiastical singing, Ioseb remained a rebel, and could not escape the seminary quickly enough.[15] The Georgian Marxist underground was his natural home. Yet he found his party colleagues, most of whom backed the Mensheviks in downplaying social division, complacent, and he was soon looking for a new political home.[16] Lenin's Bolsheviks provided an ideal new brotherhood. They were more militant and radical than the Mensheviks – especially Bogdanov and the Bolshevik left, with whom Stalin sided in 1905.[17] Moreover, they were more Russian than the largely Georgian and Jewish Mensheviks. Stalin rapidly assimilated himself to the more 'modern' culture, and from 1907 never again published in Georgian. In nineteen years the ambitious boy from provincial

Gori had made the enormous cultural journey to national Tiflis, and onwards to imperial Petersburg. Ioseb had become Iosif.

After the 1905 revolution Stalin stuck closely to Lenin, making himself useful as a man with influence amongst Georgian and Azeri workers, though even then his brittle egocentricity made him unpopular with many of his fellow revolutionaries.[18] He was effective, and became known as the party's expert on the minority nationalities. He was also willing to do Lenin's bidding. Even when he seemed to be closer to the Koba of old rather than the new Marxist man, organizing the 'expropriations', or armed robberies in Georgia, to bolster Bolshevik funds, he was doing so at the behest of Lenin. In 1912 he was rewarded by appointment to the party's Central Committee, and, after a lengthy period in Siberian exile, he returned to the centre of the leadership in 1917. After the seizure of power, he was made Commissar for Nationalities.

The contrast between Lenin and Stalin – 'man of steel' – is a subject on which much ink has been spilt. Whilst some have denied any real divisions, others have detected in Lenin a more liberal figure.[19] The most influential contrast, first drawn by Trotsky, set Lenin the intellectual revolutionary against Stalin the dull but cunning bureaucrat. The views of both, of course, changed over time, but some differences are evident, less in their ideology than in their broader political and cultural outlook. Both Lenin and Stalin were revolutionaries, both saw the party as a conspiratorial, vanguard organization, and both were prepared to use violence to achieve their goals – though Stalin was undoubtedly the more brutal of the two. However, Stalin, whilst accepting the Bolshevik vision of a disciplined, industrial society, tended to stress the power of ideological or emotional commitment, whereas for the more Modernist Lenin 'organization' was more central.[20] Stalin was therefore more comfortable than Lenin with using the campaigning methods of the Radical left, whilst at other times, he was willing to exploit the powerful force of nationalism – a force he understood well as a former Georgian nationalist.[21] By the late 1920s he had also become much more hostile to any sign of ideological disunity than Lenin had ever been.

Stalin's image of the future society also departed from Lenin's. When Lenin tried to describe the party or the socialist future, he often looked to the factory or the machine. Stalin's default model, however, was much more militaristic, and his favoured political metaphors were military, religious or organic.[22] His vision of the party was the product of an odd encounter between *The Communist Manifesto* and chivalric romance. As early as 1905 he called for the party to lead a 'proletarian army', in which every member would cultivate a belief in the party programme. It was to be a 'fortress', 'vigilant' against alien ideas. Its gates were only to be open to the truly faithful, those who had been 'tested'; to accept people who lacked commitment was tantamount to the 'desecration of the holy of holies of the party'.[23] Stalin's party was one of warrior monks, and in 1921 he compared it to the 'sword-brothers' (*Schwertbrüder*), the crusading order founded by the Baltic Bishop of Livonia in 1202 to convert the Slavs.[24]

By the time of the civil war, Stalin's approach to the party had been transferred to the field of geopolitics.[25] If the party was the seat of ideological purity, the holy of holies, the rest of the world was arranged around it in Dantean concentric circles, with virtue diminishing with distance from the centre – geographically, ideologically and socially. Russia was near the divine centre, advanced, cohesive and on the right side of history; the periphery of the USSR – Ukraine, the Caucasus, Central Asia – was in purgatory, more backward, nationalistic and peasant-dominated; and beyond purgatory lay the inferno of hell, the lands of the evil, foreign bourgeoisie. The main goal of the party – that band of knightly brothers – was to purify itself, imbibe the spirit of militant and transformative Marxism, and then disseminate it across the USSR, before venturing abroad at some time in the future. In the meantime, the priority was self-defence against the pernicious foreign and bourgeois influences penetrating its unstable borderlands.

Stalin had a particular interest in geopolitics and Russia's borderlands, but his view of the world had much in common with the culture of the party that emerged from the civil war. His belief in the centrality of ideas and ideological commitment made sense to the Red Army Bolsheviks, who understood the vital importance of morale in war. Any chink in ideological unity could lead to defeat.

It is therefore not surprising that Stalin relished war when it came; even though his role was merely to collect food supplies in Southern Russia, he quickly transformed himself into a military commissar, substituting suit and tie for the martial attire of collarless tunic, breeches and tall boots – an ensemble he favoured thereafter.[26] His behaviour was brutal and cruel, and in some ways his militaristic, mobilizing political style was closest to Trotsky's.[27] This may have been one reason for their mutual loathing, but there were others: he was deeply hostile to Trotsky's (and indeed Lenin's) use of upper-class tsarist officers.

Stalin accepted the NEP retreat. But contemporaries should not have been entirely surprised when he eventually emerged as the destroyer of NEP. As disillusionment with NEP spread throughout the party, Stalin was ideally poised to devise an alternative course with appeal within the party. And that new path amounted to nothing less than a second Bolshevik revolution.

III

In the classic Soviet novel *Cement*, written between 1922 and 1924, the proletarian writer Fedor Gladkov tells the story of Gleb Chumalov, a civil-war hero, who returns home from the fighting to find that his beloved cement factory is idle and decaying. The locals have turned to goat-herding and selling cigarette-lighters (typical petty-bourgeois activities in the Bolshevik imagination). Gleb sets about trying to restore the factory, applying the radical heroism imbibed during the war to economic recon-struction. One of his fellow Communists, an anti-NEP utopian, is prone to reminisce about the war: 'If you only knew how I love the army. Those were the most unforgettable of my life, like the October days in Moscow. Heroism? It's the fire of revolution.' To which Gleb replies:

> That is so ... But here on the industrial front we must also have heroism ... The mountain has fallen, crushing man like a frog. Now, for a real big effort, shoulder to the wheel, and shove the mountain back into its place. Impossible? That's precisely it. Heroism means doing the impossible.[28]

But Gleb has to struggle with resistance in all quarters. Cossack bandits rebel and Whites attack, only to be repulsed. Kleist, the old German engineer, has collaborated with the Whites and is initially sceptical of Gleb's plans. But Gleb, in a scene deliberately reminiscent of Bely's *Petersburg*, plays the role of a revivified Bronze Horseman, placing his hands on Kleist's shoulders and infusing him with the will to help the industrial effort. However, it soon transpires that the most dangerous enemies are not foreign experts, but home-grown bureaucrats. Shramm, the head of the Council of the People's economy, though nominally a

Communist, has the 'soft face of a eunuch', with a 'gold pince-nez perched on an effeminate nose', and is full of bourgeois affectation. He loves luxury and consumes corruptly acquired delicacies with his decadent cronies. He accuses Gleb of being a dreamer who is guilty of 'disorganizing enthusiasms' but is himself a passionless technocrat, signalled by his monotonous mechanical voice.[29] Nevertheless Gleb is not to be deterred, and sets about mobilizing the workers to rebuild the factory. He is at once a human dynamo and descendant of the medieval Russian knight (*bogatyr*), the hero of the old Russian epics. Shramm, meanwhile, is exposed as a saboteur and arrested, and in the final scene the factory is opened in front of a blood-red banner declaring:

We have conquered on the civil war front.
We shall conquer also on the economic front.[30]

Few today would read Gladkov's *Cement* for pleasure; nevertheless unlike some other 'proletarian' literature, it was not merely a *Pravda* editorial in novelistic garb. Despite its unpromising title, it had literary pretensions, was written in a highly emotional, even purple style, and became enormously popular. Party leaders praised it – Stalin himself was its main promoter. And though Gladkov has Gleb formally endorsing NEP, the novel is chiefly notable for capturing the disappointments common amongst many party members. And as the novel's parting slogan illustrates, it both describes the new problems facing the regime, and suggests a way of solving them. The Soviet regime, having defeated internal 'bourgeois enemies', now faced (or thought it faced) external ones; and having achieved some measure of economic stability after the chaos of civil war, now had to think about economic growth and international competition. Gleb's solution was to return to the methods of the civil war, when bands of committed party members had supposedly mobilized the 'masses' in a 'class struggle'. And by the end of the 1920s, many Communists agreed.

Cement also revealed the profound contradictions embodied in NEP. Although Lenin and Nikolai Bukharin, NEP's great supporter, told Communists that they must 'learn from' in order to compete with the bourgeoisie, the regime still defined itself as the 'Dictatorship of the Proletariat', and was based on class favouritism. 'Class aliens' – the aristocracy and bourgeoisie – and 'former people' – priests and supporters of the old regime – were deprived of the vote (7.7 per cent of the urban population by 1927–8), and found it difficult to enter university. And whilst everybody agreed that NEP was temporary, there were deep disagreements over how long it was to last. Radicals, like Gleb (and Gladkov), may have formally acquiesced in NEP, but they were profoundly out of sympathy with its principles. Meanwhile, more technocratic Communists – like Shramm – were convinced of the need for rational management and class reconciliation.

Both views coexisted within the collective party leadership that emerged during Lenin's final months. The majority supported NEP's survival, but of these only the intellectually gifted but politically weak Nikolai Bukharin was deeply committed. Other leaders, one by one, began to defect to the radical left oppositions. The first was Trotsky in 1923 – an unlikely convert to the left given his defence of harsh discipline and tsarist officers during the civil war. Lev Kamenev and Zinoviev formed their own opposition in 1925, and in 1926 all three joined together in a 'United Opposition', which berated the pro-NEP leadership of Stalin and Bukharin for its neglect of 'class struggle', egalitarian 'democracy' and international revolution.

This division between more inclusive technocrats and partisan radicals was hardened by the peculiar structure of the new Soviet system, which became the foundation of all Communist regimes thereafter. Although the small circle of leaders in the party's Political Bureau (Politburo) decided all major issues, below them the power structure was divided into two parallel hierarchies – the party and the state. The state's duty was to administer the country, and it tended to adopt a practical, managerial approach. It was generally run by party members with a Modernist bent – Communists like Shramm – and employed non-party bourgeois specialists. The party, by contrast, was to act as the ideological kernel of the state, to oversee policy and make sure that the regime retained its ideological spirit.[31] In practice, of course, their roles often overlapped, and both sides, each with a different value system and culture, struggled for influence, sometimes viciously.

NEP, therefore, was an unstable order. Whilst some officials happily spent their time trying to make 'state capitalism' work, others were deeply unhappy with the class compromises they had to make. They hated the regime's relative inclusiveness, its toleration of merchants, street markets and conspicuous consumption. As one commentator, an academic, explained:

during War Communism we recognized only one social category within our camp – the 'good'. 'Evil' was consigned strictly to the enemy camp. But then came NEP, injecting evil into the good ... and disrupting all. No longer waging an open war against each other, good and evil coexist today in the same collective.[32]

The 'evil' he referred to was not just political, but moral and cultural, and even psychological. As *Cement* demonstrated, amongst many in the party virtue was intimately linked with class origin. The bourgeoisie was regarded as effeminate, selfish and luxury-loving; the proletariat as masculine, collectivist and self-sacrificing. For many Bolsheviks, Communist society could only be built by the virtuous 'new man', willing to sacrifice himself or herself to the common good. The real danger was that the market, and with it bourgeois influence, would corrupt workers, contaminating them with selfishness, smug philistinism and a shallow hedonism. So despite Marx's, and some Bolsheviks', claims that morality was an entirely bourgeois phenomenon, and would wither away under socialism, most Bolsheviks (like many other Marxists) were highly moralistic. Women's behaviour was especially targeted as an index of virtue. One supposed expert, writing in the newspaper *Komsomolskaia Pravda* (*Komsomol Truth*), opined: 'Contemporary female fashions are conditioned reflexes for the arousal of enflamed emotion. That is why it is essential to battle for the expulsion of "Parisian fashions" from our lives and for the creation of hygienic, simple and comfortable clothing.'[33]

So, whilst the party leadership and economic managers preached collaboration with the bourgeoisie, the party as an organization was obsessed with maintaining its ideological purity at a time of 'retreat', much as it was in Western Europe. As has been seen, Social Democratic parties had long shared some of the features of exclusive religious sects. The notion of 'conversion' to Marxism was a common one, as was the conception of the party member's life as a journey from disorganized revolutionary 'spontaneity' to a disciplined 'consciousness'.[34] And once the party was in power, it was determined to make sure that all of its members had had the same experience. Those entering the party had to give an account of their lives, often in written autobiographies. They were expected to admit to earlier political 'sins' and show that they had truly converted. One student, Shumilov, described how he had read illegal Marxist literature when in a German prisoner-of-war camp. As a result he had 'experienced a spiritual rebirth'; he 'experienced the revelation of the essence of Being', rejecting his old Christianity and embracing Marxism.[35]

Once members of the party, Communists were subjected to a whole range of tools and methods designed to keep them pure and exclude 'alien' ideological influences. The most important of these was the 'purge'. Until the second half of the 1930s, the purge was not automatically connected with arrest and repression; those who fell foul of the purge were either expelled from the party or demoted to a lower status (for instance, from full member to 'sympathizer'). First applied in the party in 1921, and extended to other institutions afterwards, the purge was a regular process, intended to check that party members were committed and morally pure, though of course it could be used to remove leaders' opponents. Party members were questioned about their attitudes, their past and their knowledge of Marxism before a commission of three. Questionnaires were filled out, and members questioned on their past thoughts and behaviour. In 1922 and 1923 the Sverdlov Communist University in Moscow replaced termly exams with purges, in which academic achievement was judged alongside 'party-mindedness' and political or moral 'deviations'.[36] In 1924, purges were extended to all universities, and poor academic standards or political mistakes could lead to expulsion from the party.

Another way of discovering revolutionary commitment can be seen in the academic seminars of Communist universities. Academics were 'worked over', or subjected to aggressive questioning in public meetings; if they were discovered to be in error, they had to confess their sins. This was the root of the 'criticism and self-criticism' campaigns of the Stalinist period, and influenced the 'struggle sessions' used later by the Chinese Communist Party, experienced by the Chinese students of Moscow's Communist University of the Toilers of the East.[37] Such confrontational methods of interrogation also had much in common with the 'agit-trial' – a form of theatrical propaganda developed in the Red Army. These mass spectacles in which, for instance, soldiers participated in 'trials' of actors playing capitalists and Whites, were to become the basis of the Stalinist show trial.[38]

However, alongside detailed inquiries into individuals and their views, purges relied on the cruder criterion of class background, for it was assumed that proletarians were more collectivist and virtuous than the bourgeois. But defining class was not as easy as it sounded. Were workers from large factories to be favoured because they were 'purer' than those from small workshops? Was the class of one's parents to be decisive, or could one overcome a bad class background by working in a factory or joining the Red Army? Members of 'exploiting' classes had to repudiate their parents if they were to gain admission to university by publishing an announcement in a newspaper: 'I, so-and-so, hereby announce that I reject my parents, so-and-so, as alien elements, and declare that I have nothing in common with them.' But this was not guaranteed to work. Inevitably, applicants for the party or university invented proletarian backgrounds for themselves, whilst denunciations for concealing class background proliferated.[39]

Despite the practical difficulties of 'proletarianization', however, party institutions became increasingly obsessed with class and ideological purity. Under Lenin, absolute unity had also been demanded, but by the end of the 1920s, any opposition was seen as a real evil, a danger to the party that needed to be extirpated.[40] Communists increasingly resented the continuing influence of the bourgeois specialists in state administration. Following the so-called 'Lenin Levy' of workers into party ranks of 1924, party cells in factories were often very proletarian in composition, and could be very hostile to bourgeois specialists and the managers who worked with them. But particularly radical was a new 'proletarian' intelligentsia, angry at the continuing influence of the old bourgeois intellectuals, or 'fellow travellers' as Trotsky termed them. The NEP was a period of relative cultural liberalism compared with the 1930s, when great poets like Osip Mandelstam and Anna Akhmatova could be defined as 'fellow travellers' and were able to publish. But this was deeply resented by many of the new 'proletarian' party intellectuals.

The militant, civil-war culture of class struggle had retreated from society at large to the confines of the party after 1921, much as had happened in Western Europe. The difference, of course, was that the Communist party was in power. The gap between official ideology and a reality of trade, merchants and unemployment was therefore stark. The NEP merely reinvigorated radicals' class hatred and socialist radicalism.

The main supporters of this radical line within the party leadership were the members of the leftist United Opposition, and they subjected the leadership's policies to harsh criticism. But in late 1927 Stalin and Bukharin succeeded in having them removed from the party: in October Trotsky and Zinoviev were expelled from the Central Committee, and from December purges of the left took place throughout the party. Trotsky was exiled to Kazakhstan in 1928, and left the USSR in 1929, for Turkey, France, Norway and, finally, Mexico.

However, paradoxically, the defeat of the United Opposition coincided with the victory of much of its programme. Now Stalin had worsted his great enemy Trotsky, he could steal the left's ideas, though he gave them a more nationalistic colouring. The deteriorating international environment after 1926 was central to his calculations. The NEP strategy seemed most convincing in the mid-1920s, at a time of relative peace with the West, because it promised growth through foreign trade. But worsening diplomatic relations only strengthened those who favoured a more self-reliant economic policy. Many Bolshevik leaders were convinced from 1926–7 that the British and the French were planning an invasion with the help of East Europeans. This was, of course, untrue, and the fears seem enormously exaggerated in retrospect. But Stalin, ever suspicious of the foreign 'bourgeoisie', and seeing the world through the eyes of the former colonized Georgian, seems to have been genuinely fearful. If the Soviet Union was to 'avoid the fate of India' and not become a colony of the West, he warned, it had to build heavy industry and increase its military budget.[41]

In these circumstances Stalin adopted much of the left's critique of NEP, and concluded that the Plan was not delivering the industrial development the USSR required. The NEP strategy was a fundamentally slow and gradual one: the peasantry would be allowed to profit from producing food, and as they used their profits to buy industrial goods – such as textiles and tools – their increased prosperity, it was reasoned, would benefit industry. At the same time the government could export now-plentiful grain in exchange for much-needed imported machinery. However, whilst grain production did improve and industrial production increased to pre-war levels, this was not a strategy that was going to deliver rapid industrialization – especially at a time when international grain prices were low.

In 1927 a poor harvest and food shortages forced the leadership to make a decision: to maintain the prices paid to peasants for grain, at the expense of industrialization, or to cling on to ambitious investment targets and use state power (and ultimately force) to extract grain from the peasantry, thus effectively ending the market in grain and destroying NEP. Stalin chose the latter. Echoing his modus operandi as food commissar in the South during the civil war, he went on a highly publicized visit to Siberia to 'find' grain, though in reality he had already decided where it was – in the coffers of 'selfish' kulak hoarders. The party, he declared, had to wage a class struggle against kulaks; poor peasants were to be mobilized against the rich proprietors to seize the hidden food, so contributing to the industrialization and defence of the USSR.

Stalin's revolution was not confined to agriculture. It was a grand ideological campaign, an opportunity to end the retreat of 1921 and 'leap forward' to socialism on all fronts, much as the Radical United Opposition had proposed. The market was to be outlawed, and with it all forms of inequality, between intellectuals and workers, and between workers themselves. At the same time the USSR was to be dragged out of its backward state and brought into an advanced socialist modernity. The era was described as one of radical 'Cultural Revolution'. Religion and peasant 'superstition' were to be eliminated, and 'backward' ethnic cultures brought up to the level of the advanced Russians. The party was to be reinvigorated with messianic zeal so that it could mobilize the masses to achieve miraculous feats of development.

Stalin encountered stiff resistance from Bukharin and his allies, accused of being a 'Right deviation', and at first he faced a majority of opponents in the Politburo. He had embarked on what he was to call the 'Great Break' with the past. Prometheus had again been unbound, as both modernizer and violent revolutionary.

IV

In his memoir *I Chose Freedom* (written in 1947 after his defection to the United States), Viktor Kravchenko reminisced about his time as a 23-year-old technical foreman and Communist Youth (Komsomol) activist in a Ukrainian metallurgical factory during the year 1929:

> I was . . . one of the young enthusiasts, thrilled by the lofty ideas and plans of this period . . . We were caught up in a fervour of work at times touched

with delirium ... Industrialisation at any cost, to lift the nation out of backwardness, seemed to us the noblest conceivable aim. That is why I must resist the temptation to judge the events of those years in the light of my feelings today ... the nagging of the 'outmoded liberals', who only criticised while themselves remaining outside the effort, seemed to me merely annoying.[42]

Kravchenko recognized that he was one of a minority. He was a typical activist in the new Stalinist order. From working-class origins (his father had taken part in the 1905 revolution) and educated under the new regime, he was determined to bring modernity to his country. He was precisely the sort of person Stalin intended to occupy the vanguard of his new revolution. Stalin saw socialism as a something that would be spread from the 'advanced elements' to the 'backward' by a committed, quasi-military force. But post-revolutionary socialism was also intimately linked with industrialization. With his slogan 'There are no fortresses in the world that working people, the Bolsheviks, cannot capture', he deliberately transferred the radical Communism of the revolution to the industrial front.[43] Industrialization was a semi-military campaign, designed to defend the USSR against aggressive imperialists. As Stalin declared with a certain prescience in 1931, 'We are fifty to a hundred years behind the advanced countries. We must close this gap in ten years. Either we achieve this, or they will do us in.'[44]

The First Five-Year Plan was drawn up in 1928, and marked the beginning of the end of the market economy. But the term 'plan', with its scientific connotations, is misleading. Whilst it certainly bristled with figures and targets, they had often been plucked out of thin air by Stalin himself and were impractically ambitious.[45] They are better seen as appeals for heroic effort. Stalin was encouraged in his ambitions by Marxist economists, who applied Engels' curious notions of dialectical materialism to economics: utopian plans, they claimed, were entirely feasible because Marxism had proved that revolutionary 'leaps' forward were a verifiable natural phenomenon and therefore equally applied to the economy.[46] The old 'bourgeois' science, they insisted, had been discredited; a new 'proletarian' science, which took account of the willpower of the masses, would replace it. This, then, was a militarized 'command' economy based on theorized wishful thinking, not a genuinely planned one.

The Stalinists' first objective was to render the party and the state suitable instruments for their socialist offensive. Officials had to be loyal and true believers; any 'rightist' sceptics were to be removed. In practice, this meant purges, usually on the basis of class background. The Shakhty trial of 'saboteur' engineers in 1928 was designed to show how dangerous the bourgeois specialists were, and many were sacked or arrested.

However, the Stalinists hoped that their 'revolution' would be popular, and the next stage was for the suitably purged and re-energized party to mobilize the working class and poor peasantry. The sober bourgeois disciplines that Lenin had been so eager to impart under NEP were scrapped; the populist militarism of the civil-war era returned. Regular work was replaced by 'storming' (*shturmovshchina*) – working intensively to fulfil plans, usually at the last minute. The party organized 'shock work' brigades in which workers took 'revolutionary vows' to achieve production records. Money, partly because there was so little, partly because it violated ideological principles, was not much of an incentive. In many factories production 'communes' were created, where wages were shared equally, echoing the *artel* of old. Self-sacrifice and the achievement of socialism were to be reward enough.[47]

Workers, however, were given some incentives, even if they were not straightforwardly material ones: higher status, upward mobility and the opportunity to vent their fury against unpopular bosses. Stalin explicitly declared that his 'Great Break' would not just be an economic revolution but also a social one. Denunciations of bourgeois specialists were encouraged by the party, and detachments of reliable workers were sent out from factories to root out bourgeois and bureaucratic attitudes in government. The obedient and committed (as long as they were 'workers') had much to gain from these purges, for the regime was committed to replacing the bourgeoisie with a new proletarian 'red' intelligentsia. Indeed, this was an age of social mobility.[48] Many of the Communists who came to rule the Soviet Union in its years of senescence, the so-called 'Brezhnev generation', retained an unflinching loyalty to the regime precisely because they had benefited so much from education and promotion during the 1930s.

The regime, however, was not content to target the bourgeois specialists; it also had its sights on the supposedly 'bureaucratic' Communist managers – the Shramms of the factory – whom it believed had become too close to the specialists. Stalin inaugurated a nationwide campaign of 'self-criticism' and 'democracy', which entailed bosses submitting themselves to popular criticism. In part, this was intended to put pressure on sceptical specialists and managers to fulfil the state's ambitious targets. But there was also another motive: if workers were to 'feel that they were the masters' of the country, as Stalin put it, they would be more committed to a self-consciously revolutionary regime, and therefore to their work.[49] This was not a return to the workers' control of 1917, but even so, some workers, organized by the local party 'cell', were given more influence over the production process, whilst the bosses and specialists were the targets of criticism and could easily fall victim to charges of 'sabotage'. As Kravchenko, who edited a factory newspaper at the time, remembered, 'self-criticism' was certainly manipulated, but was not mere rhetoric:

> Within the limits of the party line, we enjoyed considerable freedom of speech in the factory paper . . . Nothing that might throw a shadow of doubt on industrialisation, on the policy of the Party, could see print. Attacks on the factory administration, trade-union functionaries and Party officials, exposés of specific faults in production or management, were allowed, and this created the illusion that the paper expressed public opinion.[50]

These strategies of mobilization had mixed success. Some do seem to have been enthusiastic shock-workers. They approved of the party's revolutionary rhetoric, hated the old managers and specialists, and could expect privileges and favours from the regime. John Scott, a twenty-year-old American who went to work at the massive Magnitogorsk metallurgical complex in the Urals in 1931, remembered the war-like atmosphere and the spirit of self-sacrifice that it encouraged:

> In 1940, Winston Churchill told the British people that they could expect nothing but blood, sweat, and tears. The country was at war. The British people did not like it, but most of them accepted it.
> Ever since 1931 or thereabouts the Soviet Union has been at war . . . In Magnitogorsk I was precipitated into a battle . . . Tens of thousands of people were enduring the most intense hardships in order to build blast furnaces, and many of them did it willingly, with boundless enthusiasm, which infected me from the day of my arrival.[51]

Many others, however, saw the campaigns as a drive to force people to work harder for less pay.[52] Stalin had hoped to finance industrialization by squeezing the peasantry; in reality it was workers who paid the real price, because the other half of the 'Great Break' – the collectivization of agriculture – was such an utter catastrophe. Workers were labouring harder for much less money: between 1928 and 1933 their real wages fell by more than a half.[53]

If the Bolshevik vanguard had some limited success in mobilizing the factories, its attempts to transform the countryside ran into almost universal opposition. This was hardly surprising, as collectivization amounted to a wholesale assault on the peasantry's values and traditional way of life. It had, of course, long been Marxist doctrine that the smallholder peasant was 'petty-bourgeois', and that farms should ultimately be run like socialist factories. It was commonly believed that bigger was better; and collective farms made for greater efficiency through mechanization. But collectivization also became entwined with the party's need to resolve the grain crisis. Collective farms, controlled by the party, allowed the regime to impose its power on the countryside and force reluctant peasants to produce, and relinquish, their grain for the cities.

Collectivization involved seizing land from 'kulaks', and this category swiftly expanded to include anybody who resisted joining the collective. The fate of the kulaks varied: some were imprisoned in the expanding prison system (Gulag); others were given poor land; others were deported to towns to work in factories or on construction projects; many died on their journey to their place of exile. Unsurprisingly, the process of collectivization soon assumed the form of a new civil war – between the Bolsheviks and the peasantry. Some peasants, the young, poor, or former Red Army soldiers, saw advantages in supporting the campaign, but the vast majority were opposed. And as local party and Komsomol bodies began to falter from the end of 1929, the regime was forced to send out tens of thousands of urban worker-activists to bolster the collectivization campaign, a manoeuvre reminiscent of the Jacobin Revolutionary Armies' expeditions to seize grain. These volunteers were convinced that they were on the right side of history, bringing modernity to the benighted masses. A member of a later detachment, Lev Kopelev, remembered their terrifying certainty:

I was convinced that we were warriors on an invisible front, fighting against kulak sabotage for the grain which was needed by the country, by the five-year plan. Above all, for the grain, but also for the souls of these peasants who were mired in lack of political consciousness, in ignorance, who succumbed to enemy agitation, who did not understand the great truth of Communism . . .[54]

Campaigns against religion were a central part of this 'war' for the 'souls' of the peasantry. After a period of harsh persecution during the civil war, the regime had established an uneasy *modus vivendi* with the Orthodox Church by the mid-1920s. However, with the 'Great Break' came a renewed assault. In 1929 all church activities apart from religious services were banned – from charitable work to church processions – but more violent attacks were also commonplace. Enthusiastic Komsomols and activists from the League of the Militant Godless engaged in acts of iconoclasm and vandalism, whilst church bells were melted down and valuables confiscated.[55]

Such campaigns only reinforced the conviction of most peasants that collectivization was a satanic assault on a moral, Christian way of life. One rumour, circulating in the North Caucasus in 1929, presented an apocalyptic prediction of the future under the collective farm:

> In the collective farm . . . [they] will close all the churches, not allow prayer, dead people will be cremated, the christening of children will be forbidden, invalids and the elderly will be killed, there won't be any husbands or wives, all will sleep under a one-hundred-metre blanket. Beautiful men and women will be taken and brought to one place to produce beautiful people . . . The collective farm – this is beasts in a single shed, people in a single barrack.[56]

Rebellions were widespread and women were often in their vanguard, aware that they would not be subject to the sort of immediate repression their menfolk would suffer. So, in January 1930 in Belogolovoe, a village in the Western region, eight Communist activists arrived at the church to take away the bell and were attacked by a group of local women, who beat them up and stopped them from continuing their work.[57]

The Bolsheviks were bound to win the war of collectivization through brute force, but they lost the peace. Profound resentment of the collective system remained. Peasants, who had been used to organizing work themselves, allocating land through a council of heads of households, were now obliged to obey the command of state officials. Although they were paid for their labour in principle, in practice wages came from whatever was left after all dues were paid to the state. With neither money nor autonomy as incentives to work, they responded to their masters' demands with resentful foot-dragging. Kravchenko, then a member of a grain detachment, was shocked by the 'appalling state of neglect and confusion' on the farm he visited, and ordered the farm's president to assemble the board:

> In half an hour the men and women theoretically in charge of the collective were in the yard. The look on their faces was not encouraging. It seemed to say: 'Here's another meddler . . . what can we do but listen?'
>
> 'Well, how are you getting along, collective farmers?' I began, eager to be friendly.
>
> 'So-so . . . Still alive, as you see,' one of them said in a surly voice.
>
> 'No rich, no poor, nothing but paupers,' another added. I pretended that the irony was over my head.[58]

Stalin's response was much more vindictive. Determined to maintain industrialization, which required grain exports and food for workers, he ordered that extremely high grain targets be set in 1931 and 1932, despite poor weather. Between 1932 and 1933 he launched a savage attack on allegedly 'enemy' groups within the peasantry, who were waging a 'silent war against Soviet power'. Through all this upheaval, Stalin insisted on taking grain from the countryside, even if it was the seed grain for the following year, and families hiding food were punished severely. The result was famine. A letter from a peasant in the Volga region in 1932 to the authorities revealed the despair and devastation in the countryside:

> In the autumn of 1930 the land was all ploughed and the following spring sown, and the harvest OK, a good one. The time came to gather the grain, the collective farm workers reaped the harvest without any hitches . . . but it came time to deliver to the state and all the grain was taken away . . . And at the present time collective farm workers with small children are perishing from hunger. They don't eat sometimes for a week and don't see a piece of bread for several days. People have begun to swell up with hunger . . .

And all the males have departed, despite the fact that in the near future the
spring planting is coming.[59]

Stalin's callous pursuit of industrialization at the cost of immense suffering led to a devastating famine, in which an estimated 4–5 million
died.[60] This was one of the most destructive events in Soviet history,
and one of the first of many disasters caused by the dogmatic agrarian
policies of Communist regimes.

The regime was faced with a serious crisis. Food was running out in
the cities and strikes were breaking out. The harsh exploitation of the
peasantry was partly responsible for the shortages, but so was the
wastefulness of the new command system as a whole.

During the early years of the Stalin era, a group of journalists working
for *Krokodil* (*The Crocodile*) – an officially sanctioned satirical magazine – came up with an inspired hoax. After securing clearance from the
secret police (the OGPU, the Cheka's successor) and Stalin's economic
trouble-shooter, Lazar Kaganovich, they created a fictitious industrial
organization, which they called 'The All-Union Trust for the Exploitation of Meteoric Materials'. They then set about furnishing it with essential items: they tricked the State Rubber Stamp Trust into issuing them
with a stamp, and printed impressive stationery, complete with a fake list
of directors drawn from comic characters in Russian literature. Suitably
stamped letters were sent out to various industrial organizations raising
the exciting prospect of a new source of special, high-quality metals –
meteorites. The All-Union Trust for the Exploitation of Meteoric Materials, the letter claimed, had established, scientifically, that meteorites
would fall in various locations in Central Asia. They knew, they claimed,
precisely when and where they would land and could supply the ensuing
detritus to favoured partners in Soviet industry. Industrial officials
throughout the USSR took the bait. Letters of interest flooded in. The
Furniture Trust offered office refurbishment in exchange for the precious
metals; the State Phonographic Trust proposed phonographs and records
to entertain the expeditionary parties as they travelled through the Central Asian wilderness to recover the meteoric material. Armed with these
and more substantial offers, they were granted a large credit by the State
Bank. But they went a step too far when they approached the Deputy
Commissar for Heavy Industry for help in constructing a factory to
process the metals. The Deputy Commissar, less credulous than most,

smelt a rat and locked them in his office. Eventually the OGPU were summoned, and they, in the spirit of the hoax, made a show of pretending to arrest the meteoric entrepreneurs. Much to the hoaxers' chagrin, however, Kaganovich's sense of humour did not stretch to allowing them to publish the story – it would have been too humiliating for the Soviet Union's industrial elite. Instead the officials' punishment was limited to ridicule within the confines of the corridors of power.[61]

This story, told by a *Krokodil* cartoonist to Zara Witkin, an American engineer working in Moscow at the time, reveals much about the nature of the economic system created in the early Stalinist period. The command economy might best be described as a 'hungry state' – its appetite for resources, whether raw materials, labour, or industrial goods, was limitless.[62] The logic of this system explains why the industrial officials were so easy to dupe. Charged with fulfilling wildly ambitious plans to produce heavy industrial goods, they were blithely unconcerned about costs and practicality, because they simply could not go bust. Profit and loss were immaterial. As long as there was a chance that the meteoric materials were as good as promised, they had little reason to hold back. The ravenous industrial economy swallowed everything that came within reach; it is no surprise that it salivated at the prospect of the meteoric metals.

The First Five-Year Plan built some of the great industrial behemoths of the Soviet economy, such as the metal plants in Magnitogorsk in the Urals and Kuznetsk in Siberia. According to official figures, output doubled in many parts of heavy industry. However, this was achieved at enormous cost. The unrealistic targets, the 'storming' labour methods, and the deployment of semi-trained workers and engineers created shortages, waste and chaos. 'Self-criticism' and 'class struggle' were also damaging practices which soon escaped party control. In Leningrad (the renamed St Petersburg/Petrograd) as many as 61 per cent of shock-worker brigades were electing their managers, and bosses complained that workers were refusing to obey them.[63] The Plan was declared to have been achieved after four years, but in reality 40 per cent of plan targets were unfulfilled.[64]

Chaos and poor economic performance forced Stalin to retreat, and in June 1931 he announced the beginning of the end of his revolution. He declared that the class war against the bourgeois specialists was officially over; the authority of managers was restored and the fervour of party activists and secret police reined in: as Kaganovich declared, from now on the ground had to shake whenever the Soviet manager entered the factory. Stalin was also eventually compelled to abandon his economic utopianism. The Second Five-Year Plan of 1933 was, whilst still ambitious, more modest and pragmatic.

Most significantly, this was also the beginning of the move to greater inequalities that marked mature Stalinism. Stalin severely trimmed his erstwhile enthusiasm for the achievements of 'labour heroism'. Workers had to be paid according to how hard they worked; they were not yet ready, he declared, for equal wages and appeals to self-sacrifice. These, it now appeared, would only be practical under full Communism, not the lower phase of socialism that the USSR currently occupied.[65] During the late 1920s special rations had been given to higher officials, but these privileges were extended to other officials, engineers and some other members of the 'socialist intelligentsia' in the early 1930s. Wages also became more differentiated, though engineers and technicians still only received 1.8 times the average worker's salary.[66]

Greater class peace might have been declared in industry, but it was to be almost another two years before it came to the countryside. Only disastrous famine and urban unrest forced Stalin to retreat in May 1933. Party officials were told to scale down repressions in the countryside, and in 1935 the regime began to compromise with the peasantry. Peasants were permitted to sell some of their produce on the local market, and on the collective farms wage incentives were improved.[67] Though dubbed 'neo-NEP' by critics, this was not a return to the market of the 1920s. The distribution of most goods was now firmly in the hands of state bureaucrats, and remained so until the end of the USSR; peasants continued to resent the regime, and as a consequence agriculture remained a serious drag on the Soviet economy – as it did wherever collectivization was attempted. Peasants only worked with any energy on their private plots, and in 1950 almost a half of all meat was produced on them, though they constituted a tiny proportion of the land.

Yoking together radical revolution and economic development in pursuit of a 'great leap' to Communism had failed. The militant party, far from mobilizing the whole population behind the regime, had caused chaos and division. Discontent also emerged within the party elite, and it may even be that some regional party bosses tried to persuade the

Leningrad party leader, Sergei Kirov, to mount a challenge to his leadership in early 1934. In some ways, Stalin's experience was similar to that of Lenin in 1921: like Lenin, Stalin had to retreat from a divisive policy of class conflict to one that embraced a larger proportion of the population. Unlike Lenin, though, Stalin did not embrace a technocratic socialism. Rather he continued to manipulate mass emotion by other means.

V

In 1938, ten years after *October*, Eisenstein completed *Aleksandr Nevskii*, the story of the medieval Prince Aleksandr Iaroslavovich of Novgorod, who resisted the Swedes and invading Teutonic and Livonian knights in 1242.[68] It has a simple narrative: attacked by brutal Teutonic religious fanatics, the citizens of Novgorod debate what to do. Churchmen, merchants and officials counsel capitulation. But Domash, a noble, urges resistance, and the town entrusts Aleksandr with its leadership. Nevskii insists that the townspeople cannot defend Novgorod alone, but must arm the peasantry, and Ignat, the master armourer, eagerly contributes to the war effort. Ignat's peasant infantry finally defeats the Teutonic knights on a frozen Lake Chud, employing a pincer manoeuvre. In one of the most influential scenes in the history of cinema, the Battle on the Ice, the Russians lure the knights onto the lake where the weight of their armour causes the ice to crack. Courage and cunning (and Russian weather) therefore allow the simple, peasant Slavs to defeat the technologically sophisticated, but hubristic Teutons.

Aleksandr Nevskii, like *October*, was a party-commissioned historical drama, intended to stiffen Soviet resolve against the resurgent German threat. But in all other respects the two films could not have been more different. Stylistically *Aleksandr Nevskii* was much more conventional. With its Hollywood-style narrative and minimal use of montage, its hero was an individual, not the masses; its setting and imagery were archaic, not modern; and patriotic unity, not class struggle, is its theme: its original title had been *Rus* – the old name for the Russian people.

Eisenstein's film was a cinematic reflection of the fundamental ideological changes Stalin and his circle had wrought in the mid-1930s. Like Aleksandr Nevskii, Stalin was intent on resisting the Germans; he was never under any illusions about the Nazis' objectives, and the rise of

Hitler to power in 1933 reinforced his conviction that the divisiveness of the Great Break could not be repeated. And just as Aleksandr insisted that the urban population alone could not defeat the Teutons, Stalin now moderated his old civil-war reliance on a vanguard group of militant party members to spread Communism. From the mid-1930s Communist ideology was gradually refashioned to attract a broader spectrum of support, including the peasantry and the skilled (Eisenstein's armourer). This, of course, entailed replacing a highly divisive class message with a more inclusive one. Stalin pressed for the end to discrimination on the basis of class background, declaring in 1935 'a son does not answer for his father', and he favoured the return of the children of kulaks to the collective farms.[69] In 1936 the new constitution announced that the USSR had achieved 'socialism', meaning that the old bourgeoisie had been defeated, whilst the 'former people' were now enfranchised. Specialists and scientists, previously suspect, were now to be given back some of their old power and status. Though Stalin never formally declared the 'class struggle' over (it was only on Stalin's death that the Soviet leadership was prepared to declare social peace), and the party remained a 'vanguard', he was unmistakeably implying that the internal class enemy had been largely defeated, and that most of the Soviet people could unite against the enemy beyond the USSR's borders.

Nonetheless, Stalin was not prepared to adopt Lenin's recipes for class peace, neither envisaging society as a well-oiled machine nor reasserting the market inequalities of NEP. The Plan remained, and Stalin's Soviet Union would remain a land of revolutionary heroes rather than philistine merchants.[70] The future of the USSR lay with characters of the type that featured in *Aleksandr Nevskii*: proud citizens, defending their nation against foreign threats, with the help of experts, but organized hierarchically by leaders with an almost aristocratic military ethos. The model of socialism was shifting again, from the fraternal band of true believers of the late 1920s, towards a more inclusive conventional army.

The USSR, then, was transformed from a land of angry siblings, completing an interrupted revolution against aristocratic or bourgeois fathers (represented in *October*). It was, rather, supposed to be a society of friendly brothers, big and little, the older guiding the younger. Society was hierarchical, but it was also fluid, and one's place in it depended on political 'virtue' rather than birth. Big brothers were leading their less developed siblings to the shining future of Communism; the more politically 'conscious' – the party 'vanguard' (generally of non-bourgeois class origin) – were 'raising' the less conscious; a new Soviet 'intelligentsia' (a term that now meant anybody with a higher education) was organizing workers and peasants; and amongst ordinary people, a new cadre of worker and peasant heroes was emerging – most notably the 'Stakhanovites', the imitators of the extraordinarily productive hero-miner Alexei Stakhanov.

This was, then, a more 'meritocratic' – or perhaps 'virtuocratic' – version of the old tsarist 'service aristocracy', whereby the state gave status and privileges to those who displayed 'virtue' and served it. The party elite and other favoured people, like some Stakhanovites, were given comfortable apartments and access to consumer goods and special food supplies. A new symbolism of hierarchy was also introduced in the mid-1930s, which had echoes of the tsarist era. Before 1917 civil servants had ranks and uniforms, but they were abolished as signs of the *ancien régime*, as were the old military ranks. But in 1935 ranks were reintroduced in the Red Army, signified by epaulettes and other decorations. Special uniforms were also given to workers in a range of areas, from the waterways to the railways; meanwhile a plethora of medals, orders and prizes was awarded to people at all levels in the hierarchy – from the Stalin Prize, the equivalent to the Nobel, at the top, to 'hero of socialist labour' for Stakhanovites and lesser workers.[71] The socialist value system was merging with an aristocratic one: the 'new socialist person' was now described as the person of 'honour', earned through service and heroic self-sacrifice.[72] However, in contrast to tsarist Russia, this heroic, aristocratic ideal was supposedly open to all. Everybody, in theory, could become an 'honourable' person, both members of the party and 'non-Party Bolsheviks' – even if some were more honourable than others.

The party's attitude towards nationalism shows the same combination of greater inclusiveness and hierarchy. Stalin realized how powerful a force nationalism was, but had to find a set of ideas and symbols that appealed to everybody – a difficult task given that the USSR was in effect an empire rather than a single nation state, and included a large number of ethnic groups from Russians to Ukrainians, Tajiks to Georgians. Stalin's solution was to return, to some extent, to the tsarist past and appeal to a Russian nationalism, whilst rejecting the tsar's Russian chauvinism. He and his ideologists therefore fabricated a 'Soviet patriot-ism'. At its core was the Russian identity, stripped of such ideologically unacceptable elements as Orthodox Christianity and racial superiority. Audiences of *Aleksandr Nevskii* would therefore not have surmised that Aleksandr was a saint of the Russian Orthodox Church; indeed the principal religious figure in the film, the monk Ananias, is depicted as a snivelling traitor.

According to the new Soviet patriotism, Russia was the 'first among equals', within a union bound together by 'peoples' friendship'. In the 1920s, the Bolsheviks had been very wary of emphasizing Russianness, and had tried to attract non-Russian support by encouraging the devel-opment of minority cultures and languages, and even discriminating in favour of non-Russians. But from the early 1930s, Stalin began to alter the balance to benefit the Russians, though in a manner that fell short of Russification.[73] Non-Russian languages continued to be taught, and ele-ments of non-Russian traditions were added to the Russian core. During World War II cinematic epics based on the lives of national heroes were made for the major minorities: *Bogdan Khmelnitskii* for the Ukrainians, *Georgii Saakadze* for the Georgians and *David Bek* for the Armenians.[74] A new 'Soviet' history was being created in which the benign fraternal Russians led their neighbouring 'little brothers' towards modernity and greatness. Unlike Nazi nationalism, which emphasized innate racial and cultural superiority and exclusivity, Soviet nationalism, at least in theory, saw history as an escalator; all nations could reach the summit of his-torical development if they followed the Russian example.

A selective, socialist version of nationalism was carefully manufac-tured by party ideologists – a type of 'National Bolshevism'.[75] History was pillaged for heroes who could be shoehorned into a progressive story of Russian modernization and state-building; however unreliable a historian, Stalin always thought carefully about the best way to mobil-ize the population. Well aware that a pantheon of politically acceptable historical heroes was going to appeal to a broader section of the popula-tion than the old dry and divisive class-based propaganda, he convened a meeting of historians in March 1934 to discuss the teaching of history in schools. He railed at the old textbooks with their dry structuralism:

These textbooks aren't good for anything . . . What . . . the hell is 'the feu-dal epoch', 'the epoch of industrial capitalism', 'the epoch of formations' –

it's all epochs and no facts, no events, no people, no concrete information, not a name, not a title, and not even any content itself . . . History must be history.[76]

The new 'National Bolshevism' seems to have had some success in expanding support for the regime beyond the narrow party sect, and had more with the onset of war. *Aleksandr Nevskii*, Eisenstein's only box-office hit, became especially popular. Withdrawn shortly after its release when the Nazi–Soviet pact was concluded, it was shown again following the German invasion, and audiences welcomed the heavy-handed anti-German message. As a Muscovite engineer who saw the film told the local newspaper: 'May the contemporary "mongrel knights" remember the tragic and shameful role played by their forefathers, the "crusader-scum".'[77] Amongst non-Russians it may have been less effective. But the War provided a powerful external enemy to meld the 'Soviet people' together.

The regime's values had become strikingly less egalitarian than those of the early 1930s, and the new medieval and aristocratic imagery worried some. But the ideology was still, in theory, inclusive and modern. Virtue in the 'new socialist person' included 'culture' and 'Enlightenment', alongside political reliability and a collectivist mentality. The concept of 'culture' was inextricably linked with the notion that humanity was progressing along a steeply ascending path from 'backwardness' – poverty, filth, ignorance and coarseness – to a bright new modernity of comfort, cleanliness, education and politeness (though politeness was not always a virtue in party circles).

This new idea of 'culturedness' – universalizing rather than rejecting a semi-bourgeois lifestyle – is especially obvious in the new socialist 'consumerism' of the period. Marx, of course, was no ascetic, and had promised that plenty and abundance would accompany the coming of Communism. But there were other, more immediate reasons why the leadership began to emphasize consumption. The urban unrest caused by food shortages in 1932–3 forced the leadership to accept that it would have to aim at providing a decent standard of living, and the new emphasis on payment according to work done demanded that workers have something to spend their hard-earned money on. The Stakhanovites were the models of the new 'culturedness'. They were labour heroes, fighting for socialism, and they were rewarded with 'honour', medals and the collected works of Lenin and Stalin. But they also earned higher wages than the average, and were able to live a more comfortable lifestyle. As Stakhanov's party-boss mentor Diukanov explained, 'Now that we have begun to earn decent wages, we want to lead a cultured life. We want bicycles, pianos, phonographs, records, radio sets, and many other articles of culture.'[78]

The new age of consumption was made official with Stalin's constantly repeated slogan of 1935: 'Life has become better, comrades, life has become more cheerful.'[79] The economy, however, remained overwhelmingly oriented towards heavy industry, and many consumer goods were only available to parts of the socialist managerial and Stakhanovite elite. But some efforts were made to give a wider group at least a taste of the good life. That 'good life' was, in part, a copy of capitalist consumer culture – a culture that reconciled mass production and choice. But the party's objective was not a 'consumerist' society, in the sense we use that word today – that is, one in which people measure their status by the consumer goods they own, and compete with each other to buy more and better. Rather, consumer goods were, like education, things that would allow the Soviet people to live the good, 'cultured' life, worthy of heroes; a few people could enjoy them now, but eventually everybody would. Also, most importantly, the goods reflected a status hierarchy founded on politics and ideology, not one based on wealth, as in capitalist societies. Stalin's ideal was a society in which people were motivated, and rewarded, according to their heroic self-sacrifice, not money. As he explained, 'Soviet people have mastered a new way of measuring the value of people, not in roubles, not in dollars . . . [but] to value people according to their heroic feats.' After all, 'What is the dollar? A trifle!'[80]

It was, however, the state that was to judge people's achievements, and their rewards, and underlying Stalin's ideal society was a fundamentally paternalistic outlook: the state was the father, giving rewards to its children depending on how well they behaved. Paternalism was absolutely central to Stalinist propaganda, and its most visible element – Stalin's leadership cult. The Soviet 'welfare state', the schools, hospitals and social protection which were seen by many as amongst the main advantages of the new order, were all commonly presented as gifts from father Stalin to his grateful children, rather than the just entitlements of a hard-working citizenry. As *Komsomol'skaia Pravda* declared,

'The Soviet people know to whom they owe their great attainments, who led them to a happy, rich, full and joyful life . . . Today they send their warm greeting to their beloved, dear friend, teacher, and father.' Meanwhile, school pupils chanted, 'Thank you comrade Stalin, for a happy childhood!' Some responded to these signals, and the tsarist-era habit of sending supplicating petitions to the authorities became a common one.

The first signs of Stalin's leadership cult were evident in 1929 as he sought to marginalize Bukharin and the 'Right', but it really began to flourish in 1933 when Stalin, vulnerable after the failures of the 'Great Break', used the cult of his image to consolidate central control. The cult was largely directed at ordinary workers and peasants, and not so much at the white-collar workers, who were thought to be too sophisticated for it. Though embarrassed by its incongruity in a socialist society, Stalin realized that it had a real resonance; in a widely publicized interview with the 'fellow-travelling' German-Jewish writer Lion Feuchtwanger, Stalin conceded that the cult was 'tacky', and joked about the proliferation of mustachioed portraits. But, he explained, it had to be tolerated because workers and peasants had not attained the maturity necessary for 'taste'. The party tried to discourage some of the more extreme manifestations of paternalism, which they saw as redolent of the old regime. Whilst ordinary citizens' letters often referred to Stalin as *diadia* ('uncle') and *batiushka* ('little father' – a term used of the tsars) these epithets never became part of official language. The official cult depicted Stalin as a hybrid Marxist intellectual and charismatic magus – 'great driver of the locomotive of history' or 'genius of Communism', but these images had far less purchase than the popular notion of Stalin as father of the nation.

There was, though, no necessary contradiction between the paternalistic idea that Father Stalin looked after the nation, and a belief in social mobility. Pasha Angelina, the first woman tractor brigade leader and a famous Stakhanovite, reconciled the two in a verse (*chastushka*) recited at a regional conference in 1936:

> Oh, thank you, dear Lenin,
> Oh, thank you, dear Stalin,
> Oh, thank you and thank you again
> For Soviet power.

Knit for me, dear Mama
A dress of fine red calico.
With a Stakhanovite I will go strolling,
With a backward one I don't want to.[81]

In line with the official message, Pasha thanked Father Stalin for helping young, ambitious people who helped themselves – people like herself. Like an idealized form of the tsarist 'service aristocracy', the state awarded privileges and rewards in return for service. But it was a short step from a world in which one father presided over a fluid hierarchy of virtue, to a fixed, unchangeable pyramid of superior fathers and subordinate children.

This transformation became increasingly apparent in ethnic politics: Russia emerged more and more as the superior nation, ruling over a graded ethnic hierarchy. And whilst the USSR was not the continuation of the tsarist empire by other means, several features of the *ancien régime*, albeit in diluted form, were recreated. After 1932 all citizens had their class and ethnic status inscribed in their passports, and this affected how the state treated them. Peasants, in theory, could not leave the countryside without permission (an echo of the restrictions binding their serf ancestors); class background continued to affect educational and career chances; and party bosses started to become a privileged, 'proletarian' stratum. The *nomenklatura*, as they were known, with special housing, shops and food supplies, was becoming a new privileged status group, with distinct echoes of a tsarist estate.[82]

In Stalinist culture, also, the figurative 'Soviet family' increasingly looked like one of fathers and sons rather than bands of brothers. Soviet heroes did populate official discourse, but they differed from those of the 1920s: unlike Gladkov's Gleb, they never attained full maturity as Soviet leaders; they were impulsive and spontaneous figures who always needed the fatherly guidance of mentors in the party. The most famous hero of this type was Pavel Korchagin, the hero of Nikolai Ostrovskii's semi-autobiographical novel, *How the Steel was Tempered*, of 1934. Set in civil-war Ukraine, the novel tells of Korchagin's extraordinary willpower: he fights against all the odds, narrowly avoiding death on several occasions, and even continues to struggle for the common cause when paralysed. Although his character, like steel, is ultimately 'tempered', he remains immature throughout his life: he is poorly educated and unruly at school; he puts class above love, breaking up with the petty-bourgeois Tonia, but only after a great deal of agonizing; and he remains devoted to the Communist cause, but only following a period of suicidal depression. He is guided by several party mentors in the course of his heroic career, and never himself becomes a party boss, schooled in Marxism-Leninism.[83] Korchagin was only one of the most prominent of the son-heroes who populated 1930s Stalinist culture, both within literature and outside it. Arctic explorer pilots ('Stalin's fledgling-children') and hero-worker 'Stakhanovites' were all shown as valued, but junior, members of the Soviet family. Presiding over the new 'Soviet family' were several grandfather-heroes. Aleksandr Nevskii, Peter the Great and other historical figures were now revalorized, but they too knew their place as modest forerunners of the *ur*-father, the great Stalin.

Stalin, however, was not the only father within the party. The USSR became a *matrioshka*-doll society and 'lesser' fathers appeared in a seemingly endless hierarchy. Many local bosses, their high status earned by their service during the civil war, behaved like 'little Stalins', with their own patronage networks – or so-called 'tails' – which they dragged behind them when moved from one post to another. They encouraged their own cults, copied from the great *vozhd* (leader);[84] like him, they claimed credit for every achievement that had taken place in their region. Sometimes these cults loomed much larger in the popular consciousness than Stalin's own. In 1937 one collective farm-worker, when asked 'Who is the boss now in Russia?', answered 'Ilyin' – the chairman of the local village soviet; it seems that he had never heard of the supreme *vozhd*.[85]

Stalin's attempts to spread the appeal of an aristocratic military heroism effectively authorized an increasingly paternalistic political culture. The noble warriors of *Aleksandr Nevskii* were powerful role models. Nevertheless it would be an exaggeration to suggest that Stalinist Russia had simply reverted to the *ancien régime*. Party members were expected to absorb not only military heroic values, but Lenin's almost Protestant ideal of sober asceticism. Party members were expected to follow a strict moral code. They were also, unlike Peter's nobles, expected to master science – of the conventional 'bourgeois', rather than utopian Marxist variety – and the leadership placed enormous emphasis on the creation of a new cadre of 'red experts', indoctrinated with an ideological message strictly controlled by the party.

The new union of quasi-aristocratic father figures and quasi-bourgeois scientists was abundantly clear in the regional and local elites of the USSR. After the chaos of the early 1930s, Stalin now stressed strict obedience in the economy. Engineers and managers acquired high status, and party officials, once encouraged to adopt a suspicious, 'vigilant' attitude to them, were now expected to help and support them. The party had been partially 'demobilized', whilst its officials and managers now became a more coherent and unified administrative elite. Viktor Kravchenko, who had become an engineer at the new metallurgical plant in Nikopol in the Ukraine in 1934, describes well his entry into the new elite, and his tense relations with the workers:

> Personally I was installed in a commodious five-room house about a mile from the factory. It was one of eight such houses for the use of the uppermost officials . . . here was a car in the garage and a couple of fine horses were at my disposal – factory property, of course, but as exclusively mine while I held the job as if I had owned them. A chauffeur and stableman, as well as a husky peasant woman who did the housework and cooking, came with the house . . .
>
> I wanted sincerely to establish friendly, open relations with the workers . . . But for an engineer in my position to mix with ordinary workers might offend their pride; it smacked of patronage. Besides, officialdom would frown on such fraternization as harmful to discipline. In theory we represented 'the workers' power' but in practice we were a class apart.[86]

Kravchenko's observation that a 'new class' was emerging in the USSR – the *apparatchiki*, with new, bourgeois tastes – was a common one amongst critics of Stalinism, and became central to the Trotskyist analysis (although Trotsky himself never went so far as to allege that the Communists had become a new bourgeoisie). Undoubtedly, during the 1930s a new, powerful social group had emerged. Stalin's own policies were, in part, responsible: he had deliberately reasserted control after the chaos of the early 1930s by strengthening a new hierarchy, with party bosses and Communist experts, often of Russian, proletarian or poor peasant background, at the summit. Unconscious paternalistic attitudes from the tsarist era may also have played a part. But more important was the absence of any authority genuinely independent of an increasingly unified party-state apparatus, whether an autonomous judiciary or a propertied class. In abolishing the market, the regime gave enormous powers to party bosses and state officials, at all levels of the system; they exerted huge influence in economic as well as political life. Moscow attempted to control this burgeoning bureaucratic power with a panoply of 'control commissions' to investigate corruption. Moreover, everybody was supposed to check up on everybody else – party leaders on state officials, the secret police (in 1934 renamed the NKVD) on the party, and the party on itself, through purges, 'self-criticism' campaigns and elections. But in reality officialdom was very difficult to control. Local cliques could protect themselves, persecuting critics.

The 'retreat' from the militant fraternity of the early 1930s had therefore created a highly contradictory system: the rhetoric of equality was still present, but it coincided with a new value system of reward according to achievement, and in practice fixed, almost *ancien-régime* hierarchies were emerging. This system was probably more stable than either the tense standoff of the NEP period, or the violent radical enthusiasms of the late 1920s, for it established a group of white-collar, educated officials committed to the objectives of the regime. But it also created tensions, as, for different reasons, both the supreme leader above and ordinary people below became increasingly hostile to the new bureaucracy.

VI

In the summer of 1935, an ambitious 22-year-old student at the Sverdlovsk Mining Engineers' Institute, Leonid Potemkin, tried to show his effectiveness as a student leader by arranging a group holiday on the Black Sea coast. However, after consultation with the Institute's All-Union Voluntary Society of Proletarian Tourism and Excursions, he discovered it was too expensive for most students. He therefore put a proposal to the Director of the Institute: the Institute should organize a 'socialist competition', and give a holiday subsidy to the students who did best in their annual military training classes. The idea was a good one because it gave the Institute ideological cover to help its students. The Director readily agreed, and, as Potemkin recorded in his (private) diary, he threw himself into the tasks with enthusiasm:

I'm so pleased with the training course. Here I am, a middle-rank commander of the revolutionary, proletarian Army. My heart clenches up with
joy. I am all wrapt in ardour and impatience to work with my platoon . . .
I motivate people with my mood . . . No shouts or cursing. But a strictness
that is inseparable from mutual respect, but at the same time by no means
subordinate to it . . . But if I do have a defect, it is that I'm still not always
sufficiently cheerful and self-confident. I need to develop my role and my
mission and elevate them in the light of consciousness.[87]

Potemkin was Stalin's ideal 'middle-rank' citizen. He had embraced the
new morality of competitive virtue, and had absorbed Stalinist ideas
about leadership – a mixture of strictness and mobilizing enthusiasm.
He also had a 'mission' to contribute to society. He was determined to
become a New Soviet Person, partly because he could see there were
advantages for him – as his skilful manoeuvring over his student holiday showed – but also because he wanted to remake himself and society.
He came from a poor background (though not formally 'proletarian';
his father was a postal employee), and he had to leave school to earn a
living. He remembered how he had been 'weak-willed, sickly, physically
ugly, and dirty . . . I felt that I was the lowest, most insignificant of all
people.'[88] But the new system allowed him to enter higher education
despite his poor qualifications, and he was determined to better himself,
whilst improving society. His diary was an essential tool in this self-
transformation – a place where he could reflect on his mistakes and
successes and vow to do better next time.

We cannot say how many Potemkins there were. He was an unusually successful product of the system, and became an explorer and pros-
pector for metals, ending up as Vice-Minister of Geology between 1965
and 1975. But his attitudes may not have been unusual amongst the
new white-collar 'intelligentsia'. This group was given concrete advantages: from the early 1930s, many of lowly origin benefited from the
massive expansion of white-collar jobs and from the purges of the late
1930s. They were being given a new status: as the new 'command staff'
of the regime, they were entrusted with the transformation of the USSR.
At the same time, however, they were being offered a messianic 'mission', together with a way of transforming themselves into 'conscious',
'advanced' people who were taking part in the making of history. Some

had doubts, as will be seen, and hid them; others had strong incentives to suppress them, surrounded as they were by a very powerful value system. Some even accepted the Bolshevik view that any critical thoughts were signs of class alien and enemy influence, and had to be removed through internal self-criticism, often practised by keeping diaries.[89] Responses to the regime were therefore complex, and are difficult to categorize as simple 'support' or 'opposition'.

A survey of Soviet citizens who had left the USSR during and after the war, interviewed in Harvard in 1950-1, provides some evidence that certainly suggests that Potemkin's attitudes may not have been that unusual for somebody of his social position.[90] Regardless of the many complaints they had about specific policies and low living standards, most people of all classes approved of industrialization, and considerable state involvement in industry and welfare – although they favoured the mixed economy of NEP, not the total state control imposed by Stalin. But the younger and better educated amongst them were more collectivist than workers and peasants. The regime was clearly having some success in integrating this influential group into the system.[91]

The Harvard interviews suggest that the regime was less successful in absorbing workers as a whole into the new order – perhaps unsurprisingly given that wages, whilst higher than in the crisis years of 1932-3, were still by 1937 only 60 per cent of their 1928 level. The picture, however, was again complex. Despite the end of class discrimination in the mid-1930s, the regime's rhetoric still gave workers high status, and they could take part in the idealism of the times. Workers were told that this was 'their' regime, and John Scott found that despite complaints about food and supplies, Magnitogorsk workers still accepted that they were making sacrifices to build a system superior to a capitalism that was in crisis.[92] There were strong reasons to become committed 'Soviet workers', playing by the rules and learning how to use official Bolshevik language to better themselves.[93] A particularly attractive prize was elevation to Stakhanovite status, at least in the early years of the movement when the wages and benefits were good.

Workers also had new educational opportunities. Scott found that twenty-four men and women in his barracks were attending some course or other, from chauffeuring and midwifery to planning. The more ambitious and politically loyal could enrol in the Communist Higher

Education Institute (Komvuz) to prepare for a career as an official, though the quality of that education was dubious. Scott, who attended the Magnitogorsk Komvuz, found that the students were barely literate and learnt a particularly dogmatic version of Marxism-Leninism:

> I remember one altercation about the Marxian law of the impoverishment of the toilers in capitalist countries. According to this law, as interpreted to the students of the Magnitogorsk Komvuz, the working classes of Germany, Britain, and the United States ... had become steadily and inexorably poorer since the beginning of the Industrial Revolution in the eighteenth century. I went up to the teacher after class, and told him that I happened to have been in Britain, for example, and that it seemed to me that conditions among workers there were unquestionably better than they had been during the time of Charles Dickens ... The teacher would have none of me. 'Look at the book, Comrade,' he said. 'It is written in the book.' ... The Party made no mistakes.[94]

There were also, though, many reasons for dissatisfaction, and foot-dragging was commonplace. Some workers also resented the new hierarchies, especially as promotions depended on foremen and managers who often behaved arbitrarily. Stakhanovism sharpened the tensions between workers and managers, and amongst workers themselves: the factory administration decided which workers would be Stakhanovites, and their partiality could lead to discontent and envy. That could be directed against managers or individual Stakhanovites, who were sometimes the victims of intimidation.

Many workers had more general objections to the end of egalitarianism in the early 1930s. Already angry at party privileges, many were even more incensed by the new official acceptance of inequalities, which seemed to have little to do with socialist morality. One Leningrad worker declared in 1934:

> How can we liquidate classes, if new classes have developed here, with the only difference being that they are not called classes. Now there are the same parasites who live at the expense of others. The worker produces and at the same time works for many people who live off him ... There are many administrative workers who travel about in cars and get three to four times more than the worker.[95]

Much working-class criticism of the regime, therefore, came from the 'left', and perhaps most worryingly for the party, the terms used were often strikingly similar to the revolutionary language of 1917. Sharp divisions were perceived between those at the top (the *verkhi*) and those at the bottom (the *nizy*), and objections to them were as much moral and cultural as economic: those at the top were 'aristocrats' who 'insulted' the workers and treated them like 'dogs'. As during the Russian revolution, social divisions were sometimes seen less as Marx's 'class' tensions based on economic differences than as cultural conflicts, between *ancien régime*-style estates.

Even so, this was far from a revolutionary situation. Serious strikes did occur in the early 1930s – especially during the famine of 1932–3 – and workers could express their discontent passively, by 'going slow', but many accepted the system and tried to do their best within it. Surveillance and repression also effectively headed off any real opposition.

The hierarchies of the mid-1930s had a more mixed effect on women. The state, partly because it wanted to encourage births and population growth, abandoned its earlier denunciations of 'bourgeois patriarchy' and embraced the traditional family. Divorce was now frowned on, and families given financial incentives to have children – much as happened in Western Europe in this period. The authority of parents was also strengthened. The cult of Pavlik Morozov – a child who denounced his kulak parents to the authorities – went into abeyance. It seems that this rehabilitation of the family was popular amongst many women, though less well received was the ban on abortion.[96] Also, despite its rhetoric about family values, the Stalinist state was still determined that women should work, and they found themselves assuming a 'double burden', expected to follow a traditional role in the household, whilst working long hours in factories and on farms.

Less integrated into the Soviet order, and much less contented, were the peasants. Although life had improved since the virtual civil war of the early 1930s, and the consolidation of farms into collectives did allow some facilities like schools and hospitals to be built, many peasants were disgruntled and bitter. They might have accepted that collective farms were here to stay, but many felt like second-class citizens. Living standards were much lower than in the towns and peasants did not receive the benefits enjoyed by workers. Arvo Tuominen, a Finnish Communist who was a member of a grain procurement brigade in 1934, found that peasants were extremely hostile to the regime: 'My first impression, which remained lasting, was that everyone was a counter-revolutionary, and that the whole countryside was in full revolt against Moscow and Stalin.'[97]

Andrei Arzhilovskii, formerly a 'middle' peasant (and old enough to remember pre-revolutionary Russia), was one of the disillusioned – understandably, as he had spent seven years in a labour camp for allegedly campaigning against collectivization. When he was released he kept a diary in which he recorded his alienation from the system and the people around him:

> Yesterday the city celebrated the ratification of Stalin's Constitution ... Of course, there's more idiocy and herd behaviour than enthusiasm. The new songs are sung over and over, with great enthusiasm ... 'I Know no Other Such Land Where a Man Can Breathe so Free'.[98] But another question comes up: can it be that people under a different regime don't sing or breathe? I suppose things are even happier in Warsaw or Berlin. But then maybe it's all just spite on my part. In any case, at least the finger pointing [i.e. the anti-kulak campaign] has ended.[99]

A particular complaint amongst peasants was the abuse of power by collective farm officials. A secret police investigation of 1936, for instance, gave a long account of the 'filthy, brazen, criminal, hooligan-like actions' of a collective farm chairman in Southern Russia, Veshchunov, who regularly harassed the women farm-workers. When one of them married a certain Mrykhin, they needed the Chairman's permission for him to join the collective farm – a tricky proposition as he had a criminal record. Veshchunov agreed to admit him if his wife slept with him first. She asked her husband, 'What on earth should I do, go to bed with Veshchunov and buy you off, or you will be sent back to the Urals?' Mrykhin agreed that this was the only thing to do. There had been complaints to the local prosecutors, and Veshchunov had been brought to trial, but he had been acquitted; the decision was then overturned, and the charges upheld, but he was still in post. Officials had influence and were remarkably difficult to remove.[100]

However, amongst those most alienated from the regime were undoubtedly the prisoners of the Gulag, the huge complex of labour camps, supposedly designed to 're-educate' recalcitrants through work. In 1929 the leadership replaced institutions for long-term prisoners with work camps, designed to extract minerals in Siberia and other remote areas of the USSR where it was difficult to attract free labour. The Gulag soon expanded rapidly with the collectivization campaigns, as hundreds of thousands of kulaks, priests and other 'enemies' were imprisoned. By World War II, they had become subjects of an enormous slave state, and a central part of the Soviet economy, with a shocking 4 million people in the whole Gulag system.[101] Prisoners were forced to do heavy labour in the harsh climate, and they only received full rations if they fulfilled their work plan. Those who did not often became ill, and were even less capable of meeting their targets. Many were therefore, in effect, worked to death. One prisoner, writing in the earliest, and worst, period of the Gulag, sent a complaint to the Red Cross (naturally intercepted by the police) about the appallingly cruel treatment:

> Soon they started to force people to work in the forest, with no exception for mothers and sick children. There was no medical care for seriously ill adults either . . . Everybody had to work, including ten- and twelve-year-old children. Our four-day pay was 2.5 pounds of bread . . . After 30 March children were sent to load lumber . . . Loading lumber proved disastrous: bleeding, spitting of blood, prolapse, etc.[102]

Given the different treatment received by various groups within the Soviet population, it was inevitable that attitudes towards the regime varied enormously. But one message emerges from the evidence we have, much of it collected by the party and the secret police: a resentment of high-handed and privileged officials.[103] And Stalin himself was well aware of this, for he regularly received secret police and party digests of popular opinion. He, of course, had no objections to strict, harsh discipline and he was prepared to mete out a great deal of violence himself, but he accused his officials of alienating, rather than mobilizing, the citizenry.[104]

It was not only the pretensions of the 'little Stalins' that angered a vengeful Stalin. He also believed that they were frustrating his efforts to prepare the economy for war. Just as Count Potemkin built fake 'Potemkin villages' along the River Dnepr to convince Catherine the Great of the value of his Crimean conquests, so local party bosses exaggerated their economic achievements and lied about Plan fulfilment in their reports to Stalin and Moscow. Officials protected one another, and whistleblowers or anybody who broke ranks paid a heavy price. The leadership's demand that party officials support managers had led to 'collusion' to hide mistakes.[105] And at the same time, these officials had their protectors within the top leadership in the Kremlin, among Stalin's inner circle.

Stalin, determined to increase his power over the party, now insisted that there were drawbacks to the 'retreat' of the early 1930s and the accompanying 'demobilization of the ranks' of the party, as he put it in 1934.[106] The party, it's leader now aggressively warned, was in danger of becoming impure, much as it had during the NEP, and was losing its transformative power. This time, though, the dangers came from enemies and spies within the party. The party needed to purify itself, regain its messianic role, and rearm itself ideologically to prepare for the coming war.

VII

In May 1936, two months before Stalin sent the 'Secret Letter' detailing the activities of the 'enemies of the people', and thus initiating the bloody purges we call the 'Great Terror', Soviet cinema audiences were treated to another political melodrama: Ivan Pyrev's *Party Card*.[107] It tells the story of one of the virtuous but simple 'children' of the Stalinist era, the fair-haired Anka, who falls victim to an evil enemy, Pasha Kuganov. But unlike the enemies of the late 1920s – the obviously bourgeois specialists and kulaks – Pasha's true nature is hidden. He arrives in Moscow from the provinces with a shabby wooden suitcase, the very image of the humble but ambitious Soviet 'new man'. He is handsome (although, tellingly, rather dark), hard-working, and soon becomes popular in the factory; he then marries Anka, a good proletarian girl, defeating his rival in love, the good (and fair-haired) Communist Iasha. But it soon becomes clear that Pasha is not what he seems. A former lover reveals that his father was a kulak, a detail he has deliberately concealed by elaborately faking Communist virtue. His perfidy is compounded when he steals Anka's party card and gives it to a foreign spy. When the card is recovered, the party puts Anka on trial for negligence, for as the film makes clear, the card is a 'symbol of honour, pride and the struggle of each Bolshevik' and it is the sacred duty of all party members to guard their party cards with their lives. Eventually, though, Pasha's wicked nature is finally revealed to Anka. The foolish girl, who put romantic love over her duties to socialism, has been taught a lesson by the party; armed with a pistol, she hands her husband over to the secret police.

For a viewer today the film seems bizarre, with its obsession with the apparently trivial party card – a document lent almost sacred significance in the film. Equally strange is the notion that the USSR was threatened by a phalanx of foreign spies armed with these stolen documents. Even at the time some found the film incredible. The Mosfilm studios, describing it as 'unsuccessful, false and distorting Soviet reality', refused to distribute it.[108] Only Stalin's intervention secured its release, and he clearly had a better sense of popular taste. *Party Card* had a real resonance with some of its audience, who expressed disgust at the sentimental and unreliable Anka. The press was full of discussions of the film, and the great film-maker Fridrikh Ermler explained to a friend how much it had affected him, even undermining his trust in his wife: 'You see, I saw this film and now, more than anything I'm afraid for my party card. What if someone stole it? You won't believe it, but at night I check under my wife's pillow to see if maybe it's there.'[109] To understand the politics of the time, and in particular one of the most traumatic, and mysterious, events in Communist history – the 'Great Terror' – we could do worse than watch the strange and sinister *Party Card*.

The Terror of 1936–8 still mystifies historians, because it seems so irrational, and profound disagreements amongst scholars over its origins and nature remain.[110] That Stalin should have ordered the arrest and executions of hundreds and thousands of party members and ordinary people, many of them perfectly loyal to Soviet power, and, moreover, precisely the educated experts and experienced officers he needed to help him win the approaching war, seems inexplicable.

Clearly, Stalin's psychological peculiarities played an enormous role. He was deeply suspicious, and seems to have been willing to believe some of the extraordinary conspiracies he charged people with, even as he cynically concocted others. He was the figure who ordered the killings, and his thinking will always remain difficult to fathom. However, many, at all levels of the party and society, participated in the Terror, and these complex events make more sense if we also understand the radical, messianic aspects of Bolshevik culture, and its response to the threat of war. As in the late 1920s, the leadership claimed that the best way to counter the foreign threat was to purify the party, removing 'enemies' and 'waverers' from it, so it could then 'remobilize' a newly militant society against the foreigner. But the fear of internal enemies was much greater than before, and the Terror was a much more controlled, less 'inclusive' campaign than the 'Great Break' of the late 1920s. Leaders did try to whip up the 'masses' against 'enemies', but the Terror was an organized series of arrests and executions, carried out in secret by the police.

The first signs of the search for 'enemies' within the party emerged in the aftermath of the murder of the Leningrad party leader, Sergei Kirov, on 1 December 1934. We still do not know for sure whether Stalin was involved, but whoever was responsible, Stalin sent the rising party official Nikolai Ezhov to investigate the murder, with a view to blaming it on the local secret police or his former opponent, Zinoviev. Lev Kamenev and Zinoviev were imprisoned and the case closed. Even so, Ezhov – partly because he had his own ambitions within the NKVD – continued to warn of the continuing dangers from the former oppositions, and by early 1936 Stalin allowed him to reopen the case of the Kirov murder.[111] In July 1936 Stalin and the Politburo issued a 'Secret Letter' to all party organizations, announcing that a grand conspiracy between Trotsky, Kamenev and Zinoviev had been discovered. It was this letter, and the subsequent show trial in August, that launched the first campaign in the 'Great Terror'.

We still do not know why Stalin let Ezhov off the leash when he did. It is most likely that he cynically smeared people he wanted to purge, but it is possible he believed in the conspiracies. Certainly the Stalinists commonly argued that any ideological doubts 'objectively' aided the enemy, and were therefore tantamount to a real crime. As Stalin declared in November 1937, anyone who 'with his deeds or his thoughts – yes also with his thoughts – attacks the unity of the socialist state will be mercilessly destroyed by us'.[112] But whatever Stalin's intentions, the search for 'enemies' was presented as part of a broader campaign to purify and mobilize the party, and this is how it was understood by party organizations.[113] And the leadership was especially concerned that this new party activism should reinvigorate the economy, for with Hitler in power in Germany, war was becoming more likely.

The first sign of serious efforts to galvanize the economy came in August 1935, when Alexei Stakhanov, a miner in the Donbass, dug 102 tons of coal in one shift, fourteen times the average. This kind of stunt had been staged before, but it was Stalin's response that lent it enormous significance. Stalin hailed Stakhanov's achievement as a sign that the age of mobilization had returned. Workers were again capable of heroic feats; they were only being held back by conservative and bureaucratic technicians. Predictably, the 'Stakhanovite movement' soon acquired a strongly anti-elitist character. Whilst workers were given incentives to become Stakhanovites, the campaign was unpopular amongst managers and technicians, who had to reallocate resources so that the Stakhanovite brigades could achieve their records, whilst maintaining normal production in the rest of the factory. Naturally, they were the scapegoats when things went wrong, especially now that the party and secret police were again in the ascendant. As Kravchenko, one of those engineers tasked with staging a Stakhanovite event, recorded:

> Engineers and administrators as a class were being denounced, day after day, for supposed 'conservatism', for 'holding back' the pace-setters ... Our authority kept falling. Politics, flying the banner of efficiency, had the right of way. Communist and police officials had the final word against the engineer and the manager, even on purely technical problems.[114]

It was therefore no surprise that the search for 'enemies' within the party soon led to the economic managers, accused of 'wrecking' the economy – especially as some of them had been closely associated with Trotsky in the past. The Shramms condemned by Gladkov in the 1920s were being attacked again. But they were not the only targets. The party was urged to search for anybody who showed signs of 'bourgeois' corruption, or who might not be activist and politically enthusiastic enough. It was not sufficient to be a 'narrow-minded' and 'pragmatic' official 'blindly and mechanically' obeying orders from above, as Stalin put it in 1938. Party officials were also, like Anka, blamed for lack of 'vigilance'.

Given the broad definition of the 'enemy', it was very likely that the purge would spread throughout the party. Denunciations proliferated, and virtually any failing could be interpreted as a sign of hostile intent. Expulsion from the party followed, and then, in many cases, arrest by the NKVD, imprisonment and possibly execution.

Responses to the Terror amongst the party faithful varied. Evgenia Ginzburg, an academic, historian and writer, and the wife of a regional party boss in Kazan, Tatarstan, simply could not understand the hysteria. She was damaged by a rather distant association with another historian, Elvov, and was accused of making 'Trotskyist' errors in an article on the

1905 revolution. After expulsion from the party she was summoned to the office of a Captain Vevers of the NKVD, who berated her as an enemy. 'Was he joking?' she remembered. 'He couldn't possibly mean such things. But he did. Working himself up more and more, he shouted across the room, pouring invective on me.'[115] The reaction of the play-wright Aleksandr Afinogenov, however, was very different. As the histo-rian Jochen Hellbeck has shown, when expelled from the party Afinogenov struggled to understand it, and, despite doubts, saw his expulsion as an opportunity to destroy the negative, bourgeois parts of his personality and transform himself into a virtuous party member. 'I killed the self inside me – and then a miracle happened . . . I understood and suddenly saw the beginning of something altogether new, a new "self", far removed from previous troubles and vanity.'[116] Unexpectedly, he escaped the police and arrest, and was restored to the party, convinced of its justice. Afinogenov may not have been typical of party members, but others also believed that the purge was an essential tool to purify the party, even if 'mistakes' were made in particular circumstances.

The Terror also made sense to others, lower on the social scale. There was a populist element to it, and the leadership now tried to whip up antagonisms against the elite. For the first time in years, Stalin announced that party committees were to be subjected to multi-candidate elections, in which the rank and file were allowed to criticize their bosses. He doubtless hoped that criticism 'from below' would reveal what was really happening in the regional cliques, but would also replace any disobedient officials with loyal enthusiasts. He also probably realized that he could improve the standing of the regime amongst ordinary people, hostile as they were to the privileged officials.

Stalin was returning to the strategies of the late 1920s, and he was stirring up the deep resentments many ordinary people felt for local elites, as John Scott remembered:

> . . . chaos reigned in the plant. A foreman would come to work in the morning and say to his men, 'Now today we must do this and that.' The workers would sneer at him and say: 'Go on. You're a wrecker yourself. Tomorrow they'll come and arrest you. All you engineers and technicians are wreckers.'[117]

However, the leadership was determined that this did not become a reprise of the 'Great Break'. They resolutely tried to ensure that any 'self-

'criticism' remained under strict control, even if that proved difficult in practice.

In the spring of 1937 the Terror moved into its second phase, and the arrests of the party bosses and their clients began. Stalin may have planned this all along, but the NKVD also responded to evidence, often the result of denunciations, that the 'little Stalins' were not fulfilling economic targets.[118] In the spring of 1937 Stalin may also have been convinced, possibly by Gestapo disinformation, that Marshal Tukhachevskii and the military high command were conspiring with the Germans. So despite the threat of war, the cream of the officer corps was arrested. And from that summer Stalin sent his close allies from Moscow to the regions to preside over the arrest and replacement of most of the powerful regional party bosses.

The bosses themselves, however, were closely involved in the Terror. Under pressure to find enemies (and desperate to save themselves), they tried to emphasize the threat from 'class aliens' and anybody with a 'spoiled' past, especially the former kulaks. Moreover, Stalin accepted the regional bosses' demands for a mass repression of ordinary people with 'bad' backgrounds. He was also probably afraid of a 'fifth column' of anti-Soviet kulaks who might join the Nazis if they invaded.[119] In the summer of 1937 the Terror entered a new, third phase, that of the 'mass operations'. Stalin and the Politburo, in collaboration with regional bosses, issued secret quotas of arrests and executions, based on class, political and ethnic background. Most of these victims were former kulaks, priests and tsarist officials; they also included vagrants and other 'undesirable' groups. 'Unreliable' ethnic minorities who were thought to be in danger of allying themselves with enemies across the border – such as Germans, Poles and Koreans – were also persecuted. The mass operations were responsible for by far the largest number of those executed and imprisoned during the period; official figures, almost certainly underestimates, record 681,692 executed and 1,575,259 imprisoned in 1937–8, many, though not all, for political crimes.[120]

The result was chaos and economic crisis, as managers and officials fell victim to the arrests. Labour discipline collapsed, as officials refused to impose their authority on workers for fear of being criticized. The first serious attempt to rein in the ideological purge of the party came in January 1938. But the trials continued, including the third Moscow trial of Bukharin and other leaders. Meanwhile mass operations against kulaks and ethnic minorities went on well into 1938, and it was only towards the end of the year that Stalin effectively halted the Terror, though repressions continued on a smaller scale. Nikolai Ezhov was blamed for the 'excesses' and he was arrested and executed, charged, amongst other things, with 'leftist overreaction'. He went to his execution convinced of the rightness of the Terror.

VIII

Eisenstein's response to the Terror was naturally much more ambivalent and sophisticated than the true-believer Ezhov's, and he dealt with this difficult, and dangerous, issue in his last films, the historical dramas *Ivan the Terrible* parts I (1944) and II (1946).[121] The reputation of the sixteenth-century tsar Ivan IV had been rehabilitated in the 1930s as a ruler who had defeated Russia's enemies and unified the country. His deployment of his personal bodyguards, the *oprichniki*, to wage a war of terror against the disloyal boyar nobility was commonly seen as a 'progressive' development in the building of the Russian state. Naturally, parallels between Ivan and Stalin, between the *oprichnina* and the Terror, were obvious to the intelligentsia and party elite.

Eisenstein sought to justify Ivan/Stalin. But at the same time he wanted to give some tragic complexity to the character. In *Part I*, Ivan is shown having doubts about the violence he was unleashing, even against his own family. But these are soon overcome; he easily convinces himself that his personal sentiments must be sacrificed to Russia's greatness. But the sequel's atmosphere is very different. Ivan is now overtly self-lacerating, and the film wallows in an expressionist world of claustrophobic interiors, sinister intrigue and extreme emotion. In the projected *Part III*, Ivan is even shown banging his head on the floor in remorse beneath a fresco of the Day of Judgement, as his confessor and henchmen read out lists of his victims.

Eisenstein's friends were astounded at his extreme foolhardiness. How could he take such risks? And unsurprisingly Stalin, who had welcomed the first part, was outraged at the second and projected third. He excoriated the film for portraying the *oprichniki* as some kind of 'Ku Klux Klan', and presenting Ivan as if he were a vacillating Hamlet. Yet Eisenstein did not totally misjudge the *vozhd*. After a course of self-criticism he was permitted to remake the films, but died before he could restart the project.[122]

Eisenstein had little insight into Stalin's own psyche; the *vozhd* felt no guilt about the violence he had unleashed. But *Ivan the Terrible Part II* does capture some aspects of the world created by the Terror. *October*'s simple emotions of class struggle and vengeance had yielded to a far less confident, interior politics – one in which men's souls had to be interrogated in search of inner doubts and hidden heresy.

Stalin used show trials and purges until his death in 1953, but he was never to repeat the Terror on such a scale. Throughout the 1930s the regime had oscillated between the militant desire to transform society and a willingness to live with society as it was, and that tension continued. Ideological campaigns continued after the War, but the Terror was the last time the USSR experienced such an intrusive effort to force ideological unity on the party and society as a whole. The Terror also marked the end of populist attacks on officialdom, so evident in the late 1920s and more muted in the later 1930s. In 1938 and 1940 labour discipline laws restored the power of managers and technicians, and the regime increasingly emphasized the more inclusive principles of ethnicity and nation, rather than class. The system known as 'high Stalinism' – highly repressive, xenophobic and hierarchical – was emerging from the violence and tumult of the 1930s, to become so powerful on the world stage.

The Terror remained a blot on Soviet Communism's escutcheon until its demise. Khrushchev, in admitting its injustice in his 'Secret Speech' of 1956, seriously damaged the reputation, and the legitimacy, of the Soviet model of socialism, but at the time the Terror did not have as great an effect on views of the Stalinist regime, within the USSR or outside, as one might expect. Those who were already hostile – particularly on the Trotskyist left – denounced the bloodletting. But there were strong reasons amongst the Western centre-left not to make the Terror a significant issue: at a time of appeasement, the USSR was the only real ally against the radical right. The struggle against Nazism was to give Soviet Communism another chance.

5

Popular Fronts

I

In May 1937, as Stalin and Hitler fought a proxy war in Spain, Paris was the setting for an International Exposition designed to promote peace and reconciliation. A 'Monument to Peace' was constructed in the Place du Trocadéro, and an 'Avenue of Peace' linked it to the pavilions of Nazi Germany and the Soviet Union. On one side, Boris Iofan's Soviet pavilion was topped by Vera Mukhina's statue of a worker and a woman collective-farmer, marching together and purposefully brandishing a hammer and a sickle. Opposite loomed Albert Speer's massive neoclassical tower, crowned by an imperial eagle grasping a swastika. Speer (who seems to have had a secret preview of the Soviet plans) deliberately designed his edifice as a riposte to the Communist pavilion.

Some have seen both pavilions as manifestations of 'totalitarian art', and they undoubtedly showed a certain monumental bombast; both embraced a populist, and indeed somewhat conventional, aesthetic, and the German exhibition showed an obsession with work and heroism every bit as intense as the Soviet one.[1] Yet despite the similarities, the differences were striking.[2] The German eagle was a symbol of empire, and within the pavilion society was shown as a static, peaceful hierarchy. The huge and prominent painting *Comradeship*, by Rudolf Hengstenberg, may have suggested parallels with Communist collectivism, but it portrayed building workers clearly subordinate to a dominant architect in an old-fashioned artisanal setting. By contrast, the USSR's pavilion, with its monuments to machines and striving workers, sought to present itself as a more dynamic society, albeit one presided over by the great leader Stalin. There were also subtle differences in the pavilions' depiction of reason and progress. The Soviets crammed their

building with worthy and didactic exhibits lauding economic development and social change. The Nazi pavilion, though filled with the latest
German technology, adopted a consistently mystical and religious *mise
en scène* – the building itself an odd mixture of classical temple, church
and mausoleum. Indeed, the overall aesthetic of each pavilion recreated
stark differences in values. Whilst the Nazi pavilion was self-consciously
conservative, its sculptures and architecture neo-classical, and its interior evoking the heavy nineteenth-century bourgeois style, the Soviet
pavilion mixed neo-classicism with modernist touches; its architecture
suggested an American skyscraper rather than a classical temple, whilst
within, modern photomontage jostled with more conventional socialist
realist painting.[3]

The Soviet pavilion represented several crucial features of Stalinist
ideology to the outside world. Bolshevism was the force of progress,
bringing Enlightenment to the world (though the images of Stalin himself looked distinctly cultic). The ideal society was one devoted to collectivism, work and production, and its creation – the industrial working
class – was now the hero of history. In this vision economics was paramount, and little, if anything, was left of the earlier utopian dream of
liberation. All of these themes were reprised in the *Short Course* of party
history (1938), largely written by Stalin himself and propagated throughout the Communist world. Here one found the approved version of
Marxism outlined in crude, dogmatic form. History followed its determined course: the Soviet Union had achieved 'socialism', Marx's lower
phase of Communism, and the rest of the world would follow. This
was a system where wage inequalities remained, and the state was all-
powerful. Any plans for its withering away were postponed to the very
distant future.

Both the German and Soviet pavilions were much larger and more
grandiose than those of the other countries; visitors complained about
'the bad manners, the excess of pride and the vain pretensions' they
displayed.[4] In striking contrast to both was the pavilion of the Spanish
Republican government, which displayed a rather different approach to
the ideological struggles of the time. Much more modest in scale, it was
built in an unalloyed modernist style. Like the Soviet pavilion, it used
photomontage to teach its visitors about the government's worthy social
programmes.[5] But unlike the USSR's effort, it also embraced the artistic
avant-garde, displaying works by some of Spain's leading artists,

including, most famously, Pablo Picasso's iconic *Guernica*. Picasso, an artist of the left who became a fully paid-up Communist in 1944, had produced the painting as a condemnation of fascist aggression, showing the sufferings of the Basque town as it was bombed to destruction by German aircraft only a month before the exhibition opened.

The pavilion was built by the ruling Spanish Popular Front – an alliance of Communists, socialists and left-liberals – who had tried to bury their differences to resist General Franco's nationalists and their Nazi and Italian Fascist allies. It was just one of a number of Popular Fronts established in the mid-1930s when the Comintern, fearful of fascism, abandoned its harsh anti-Social Democratic line of 1928. The Spanish pavilion reveals a great deal about the ethos of the Popular Fronts. They attracted the support of some of the most prominent intellectuals and artists, and embraced people of diverse political and aesthetic schools: from left-liberal to Communist, from avant-garde to populist, from 'bourgeois' liberal to social democratic.

There was, however, a rather less radical interpretation of the Popular Front embodied at the Exposition by the French exhibitions. At that time, the French government was headed by the socialist Léon Blum with the support of liberals and Communists. The French did not have a pavilion of their own, but various galleries and museums mounted shows, amongst which was a huge exhibition of French art since the Gallo-Roman period.[6] The message was unashamedly patriotic – a patriotism conspicuously endorsed by Communists. Moscow, it now seemed, was happy for Communists not only to adopt a pragmatic, gradualist road to socialism, but also to embrace nationalist rhetoric along the way.

The Popular Front governments, of which there were three before World War II – in Spain, France and Chile – were short-lived. However, during World War II anti-fascist Popular Fronts of the left were revived, and they remained strong until the onset of the Cold War in 1946–7. Their popularity was a consequence of a far more violent phase of European social conflict. The economic crisis of the 1930s radicalized both right and left as a bitter struggle broke out over who was to bear the brunt of the Depression. Radical nationalists argued that organized labour was using democracy to undermine the state, and called for a new authoritarian politics to impose social and racial hierarchy, which they achieved on the Nazis' victory in Germany in 1933. In these conditions, a more Modernist and seemingly more inclusive version of Communism became attractive to many on the left. Only Communist discipline, they believed, was capable of confronting such a powerful right-wing force, and now Moscow was no longer so sectarian, that discipline could be used to defend democracy and the values of Enlightenment.

The period between 1934 and 1947, therefore, was one of considerable Communist success in the West – especially in France and Italy – and in parts of Latin America. This was the era when Communism, and with it the USSR, became fashionable amongst the West European and American intelligentsias. But despite such enthusiasm, the Popular Fronts were always shaky edifices, ready to splinter into many factions, as illustrated by the stark differences between the various Expo pavilions. The Spanish embrace of the avant-garde coexisted uneasily with the Soviet-style realist agitprop, displaying in aesthetic form the continuing tensions between a disciplinarian Stalinist Communism and a more Romantic and radical left. Meanwhile French hopes that the Exposition would embody a rallying of the left and liberal centre were crushed when a wave of strikes disrupted work, and on the opening day several of the pavilions were fenced off or covered in scaffolding – an ominous portent of the social tensions that were starting to destroy the French Popular Front itself.

Despite these difficulties, the Popular Fronts remained appealing to some. As long as the radical right was the main threat, much of the liberal left was prepared to overlook Bolshevik authoritarianism and Stalin's cynical foreign policy. After 1946–7, however, the tensions between the culture of Stalinist Bolshevism and that of the non-Communist left became too sharp. With the defeat of the Nazis, the aggressive behaviour of the Soviets and local Communists in Central and Eastern Europe, and the creation of a new form of capitalism more favourable to labour in the West, Communism seemed neither so necessary nor so attractive. It is no surprise that the Popular Fronts were not to survive the War for long.

II

The Comintern's sectarian 'class against class' policy of 1928 was founded on a profound misinterpretation of Western politics. It assumed that the workers of the West were becoming more revolutionary; that capitalism was on the verge of collapse; and that fascism – the last gasp of a dying bourgeoisie – was a fleeting phenomenon that would soon crumble along with capitalism. Given this erroneous analysis, it made sense for the Comintern to urge Communists to intensify the struggle against the bourgeoisie, including the Social Democrats, and thus hasten the end of liberal regimes. This is why, at a time when the radical right, and especially the Nazis, were going from strength to strength, the Communists' fire was, puzzlingly for many, directed against the moderate left, not the right.

Even at the time, some Communist leaders, especially those in small parties which needed broad alliances, despaired of this policy. Representatives from the American Communist Party, the CPUSA, threatened to ignore Moscow's instructions in 1929, but were met with threats from Stalin.[7] The party was soon purged and the 'rightists' expelled, as were all foreign Communists who opposed the new line. In several countries, the policy was another disaster for Communist parties. Almost half of the members of the pro-Communist Czech 'Red Unions' left to join the Social Democrats;[8] in Britain, party membership collapsed, from 10,800 in 1926 to 2,555 in 1930. The new policy of fomenting revolution and encouraging unofficial strikes simply made it more likely that Communists would be thrown out of work.

Nevertheless, the new policy had some supporters amongst local Communists desperate to believe that the time was ripe for revolution. And in Germany, the confrontational politics of the 'Third Period' was particularly popular in the Communist party, as was the denunciation of the Social Democrats as 'social fascists'. Membership of the party soared, from 130,000 in 1928 to 360,000 by the end of 1932, when it received over 5 million votes, almost 17 per cent of the electorate. The vicious internecine struggles between the Social Democrats and the Communists simply reinforced Communists' view that the Comintern policy was right. On May Day 1929, the Communists ignored a ban on outdoor marches, imposed by the Social Democratic Berlin police chief, Zörgiebel. The result was a battle between Communists and the police, over thirty deaths and 1,228 arrests. To the Communists, it was clear that the Social Democrats were tantamount to fascists.

Street battles between the Communists and the authorities intensified in the late 1920s and early 1930s. It was in this atmosphere of violence that the young Erich Honecker – later the leader of Communist East

Germany – grew up. Born in 1912, in a small town on the Saar, Honecker came from a radical Social Democratic family that became Communist. He himself was a Communist virtually from the cradle. As a child he collected money for strikers, and was told to march at the front of demonstrations – it was thought that the police would not fire on children. In his youth he was a member of a workers' gymnastics club and played in a Communist party brass band. Although he was a roofer by trade, like most German Communists he never found a job; his life was politics. He was sent to the Lenin School in Moscow at the unusually young age of eighteen, where his end-of-year reports were lavish in their praise: 'A very talented and diligent comrade'; 'Understands very well how to relate theory to the class struggle in Germany'. Honecker returned, a fully fledged Marxist-Leninist, to become leader of the Saarland Communist youth league in 1931.[9]

Honecker's – and Stalin's – belief in class struggle and the imminence of revolution was reinforced by the Depression that followed the crisis of 1928–9. In Germany industrial output fell by a catastrophic 46 per cent; in France by 28 per cent. Most governments made the problem worse by following the laissez-faire market orthodoxy of the time and slashing state spending. Welfare was cut, increasing the numbers of the poverty-stricken and reducing economic activity still further. The Keynesian solution (adopted after World War II) of state spending to compensate for private caution was not yet widely accepted, and few defended it with conviction. Meanwhile, international attempts to coordinate a response also failed, as states panicked and pursued narrowly nationalistic agendas. Although the collapse of the gold standard in the early 1930s helped the recovery of European economies, the effects of the Depression reverberated throughout the decade.

It is then not surprising that many came to believe that liberal capitalism had no answers to the problems of the era. The system seemed incapable of providing employment for the mass of America's and Europe's people. The intellectual tide turned and the liberal optimism of the 1920s evaporated. To many on the centre-left it seemed that the Soviet Union, with its (official) growth figures of 22 per cent per annum, had something to teach the West. (The extraordinary levels of waste and low workers' living standards in the USSR were not yet widely known.) Even liberal elites were impressed by Soviet success. In 1931, the British ambassador to Berlin wrote that everybody was talking about 'the menace represented by the progress made by the Soviet Union in carrying out the First Five-Year Plan, and the necessity of some serious effort being made by the European countries to put their house in order before Soviet economic pressure becomes too strong'.[10]

The response of those on the radical right to the crisis of liberal capitalism was inevitably very different. For them, both liberalism and Communism were responsible for fragmenting the nation and thwarting legitimate imperial ambitions: liberalism was responsible for political conflict and economic crisis, whilst Communists preached divisive class struggle. The solution, for the Nazis, the Italian Fascists and their imitators in Eastern Europe and elsewhere, was a militarized, masculinized, mobilized nation. This model, of course, had much in common with the Stalinist one. The difference was that for the right, property rights had to remain largely intact, as did social and professional hierarchies. 'Left' Fascists and Nazis also hoped for a serious attack on liberal capitalism and its market-based ethos, but they were generally ignored and, in the case of the Nazis, purged. The far right did garner some working-class support. But radical-right regimes, broadly speaking, favoured bosses over workers; independent trade unions were banned and wages remained low.

As the economic crisis intensified, support for both Communists and the radical right increased, especially in Germany. Politics was becoming a zero-sum game: the left was insistent that welfare benefits be maintained; the right believed that labour was destroying the nation by resisting the necessary retrenchment. Compromise became difficult. The Social Democratic Party did tacitly support the Catholic Centre Party Chancellor Brüning after September 1930, for fear of triggering elections that might increase Nazi representation. But this alliance antagonized the supporters of both sides. Communist support increased amongst workers – almost overtaking the Social Democrats in the November 1932 elections – whilst Germany's elites began to look for authoritarian solutions to the increased unrest. In July 1932, Von Papen, Brüning's successor, staged a coup against the elected Social Democratic government of Prussia claiming that it could not maintain order, and it looked as if parliamentary democracy was doomed. It was perhaps at this point that a united left could have fought back – as Von Papen indeed thought might happen. But the Social Democrats were too demoralized and committed to legality, the better-armed Communists would not have supported them had they resisted, and even a joint force of the left would have stood little chance against the army.[11] The way was open for the appointment of Adolf Hitler by President Hindenburg in January 1933. Stalin and the Comintern's 'class against class' policy certainly played a role in that disastrous outcome, but it was just one factor amongst many.

The Nazis swiftly moved to destroy parliament and liberal rights, banning both Communists and Social Democrats and imprisoning thousands. The Nazi takeover was only one of several right-wing authoritarian takeovers in the inter-war period. The Italian Fascists had banned the socialist left as early as 1924; Hungary, Albania, Poland, Lithuania, Yugoslavia, Portugal and Spain had all been run by authoritarian governments before the Depression, whilst following the Nazi takeover liberal democracy was abandoned in Austria, Estonia, Latvia, Bulgaria, Greece and (again) Spain. But the attack on the German left was particularly devastating. At one stroke, the largest Communist party outside the USSR and the most influential Social Democratic party in Europe were destroyed.

Events in Berlin inevitably led many Communists to question the Comintern's 'class against class' line. Surely it was now evident that the main enemies were the fascist and Nazi right, not the Social Democrats? At the same time, the Social Democrats became disillusioned with their centrist liberal allies. The decision of the German establishment to embrace the Nazis was merely one example of liberals' 'appeasement' of the radical right. Just as the Communists were rethinking their strategy, the socialists were moving to the left. The time was ripe for a rapprochement between the comrades and the brothers.

III

In 1936 the Soviet film industry produced one of its most successful blockbusters – *Circus*.[12] Scripted by a team of eminent writers, including Isaak Babel, and directed by Grigorii Aleksandrov, one of Eisenstein's collaborators on *October*, it was a fine example of the 'socialist realist' Hollywood-style musical comedy. It told the story of an American singer and dancer, 'Marion Dixon' (a cross between Marlene Dietrich and Ginger Rogers, played by the most popular actress of the era, Liubov

Orlova), who is hounded out of the United States by the racist inhabitants of 'Sunnyville' because she has had a child by an African-American. Dixon is rescued by a German impresario, Von Kneischitz, but his intentions are exploitative, not charitable: he sees her as a money-spinner in his circus tour of the Soviet Union. Dixon propels the circus to the heights of popularity. But she then falls for her co-star, the acrobat Martynov, and decides that she wants to stay in the USSR. The callous Hitler-lookalike Von Kneischitz, worried about losing his main attraction, is desperate to keep her. In the film's climax, during a dance extravaganza featuring rockets, spacemen and dancing girls, he brings her black child into the circus tent, expecting that the Soviet audience, shocked, will drive her out of the USSR. But to his consternation they welcome the infant. Skin colour, the circus-master tells us, whether black, white or green, is of no consequence in the land of the Soviets. Representatives of the various nationalities of the USSR in traditional dress pass the smiling toddler from group to group, each singing a lullaby verse in their own language; most pointedly, given Nazi policies at the time, the Jewish actor Solomon Mikhoels was shown singing a verse in Yiddish. The film ends with Marion Dixon and her fellow circus artists miraculously appearing in the midst of a Red Square rally, holding aloft red flags, Politburo portraits and the black child, as they pass Stalin standing on the Lenin Mausoleum. Whilst they march, they sing 'The Song of the Motherland', a hymn to ethnic equality that was so popular it almost became the unofficial national anthem of the USSR.

A great deal of the film is taken up with Hollywood routines, whether Charlie Chaplinesque slapstick or Busby Berkeley-style dance numbers. But the film skilfully interweaves a political message into the popular entertainment: the Nazis – racist and capitalist – and the Soviets – humanist and socialist – are competing for the soul of the naïve Westerner; after a period of slavery beneath the heel of Von Kneischitz's 'fascism', Marion becomes convinced that life is better under Soviet socialism. Timed to celebrate the Soviet Constitution of 1936, the film showed the USSR to be a unified nation, free of ethnic and class conflict, and bearer of the values of the Enlightenment. This was a happy, free society in which any open-minded Westerner would love to live, from whatever social milieu – even petty-bourgeois circus artistes were welcome. The USSR was ready to ally itself with all 'progressive' forces, of all classes. The only enemies were a small group of racist fascists and reactionary elites, represented by the aristocratically named Von Kneis-chitz (*kniaz* is Russian for 'prince').

Circus was mainly designed for a Soviet audience, and it became the hit of the year. But it was also seen in Eastern and Western Europe – especially after the War – and articulated the new Popular Front policy that had become orthodoxy by 1936. Yet it took some time after the Nazi seizure of power in 1933 to bury the differences between the Second International and the Comintern; the poisonous conflicts of the past were not easily overcome.

At a local level, however, the advantages of an anti-fascist alliance seemed clear. The left in France was most enthusiastic. As the Depression hit, politics became more polarized, and a violent demonstration by the radical right on 6 February 1934 forced the resignation of the centrist Radical Party premier Édouard Daladier. Six days later, the trade unions, socialists and Communists launched a general strike against the right and in defence of democracy, fearing a repetition of events in Germany. The united action impressed the Bulgarian Comintern official Georgi Dimitrov, and he had several meetings with Stalin to persuade him of the need for a new line.[13]

Stalin remained hostile to Social Democracy, and he seems to have accepted Dimitrov's line only very reluctantly.[14] His approach to foreign policy was similar to his domestic policy: the USSR, had to remain a unified 'citadel of the revolution';[15] it had to preserve its ideological purity and be ready to spread socialism when the time was ripe at some time in the future.[16] Indeed, in 1927 Stalin explicitly compared the USSR with Jacobin France: just as 'people danced to the tune of the French revolution of the XVIII century, using its traditions and spreading its system' now people 'dance to the tune of the October revolution'.[17] Class peace and inclusiveness could therefore not go too far. However, given the weakness of the USSR, only 'socialism in one country' was feasible, and the Soviets might have to forge alliances with bourgeois forces in order to preserve it. Ultimately Stalin believed in the inevitability of war between the socialist and capitalist camps, but that war had to be postponed until the Soviet Union was ready for the battle.[18] World revolution would eventually happen, he was convinced, but it was most likely to occur at a time of war, preferably between the 'imperialist' powers.[19] In the meantime, it was unlikely that new revolutions would occur, especially in Western Europe, where the masses had been fooled by 'bourgeois democracy'.[20]

Eventually Dimitrov and others, including the Italian party leader Palmiro Togliatti, won Stalin over, and they were helped by a change in Soviet foreign policy, which now favoured an alliance with France and Britain against Germany. At the end of the year, Stalin acceded to the new policy, which was finally endorsed by the Comintern in the summer of 1935.[21]

According to the Comintern decisions of 1935, Western Communist parties were only allowed to ally themselves with parties committed to a radical, anti-capitalist programme, as a prelude to revolution.[22] But in practice the Popular Front policy allowed Communist parties to join moderate socialist governments and defend liberal democracy against fascism. They desisted from agitation for a proletarian, Communist revolution, at least in the foreseeable future, and they were also allowed to appeal to local nationalisms in their efforts to win support.

Communist parties throughout the West adopted the mantle of national unity and reconciliation, in line with the new emphasis on patriotism within the Soviet party. Even in the United States, Communism became remarkably respectable. Although the party was closely controlled by the Comintern, it claimed to have inherited 'the traditions of Jefferson, Paine, Jackson and Lincoln', and worked with a broad range of organizations from trade unions to churches and civil rights groups.[23] The Popular Fronts' inclusive attitude to ethnicity appealed to many second-generation immigrant workers who had suffered from the Depression and identified themselves as a 'working class'.

The party that followed the Popular Front line most enthusiastically and successfully was the French one, under the leadership of Maurice Thorez. Thorez was born in 1900 and brought up by a family of Jacobin Socialist miners in the department of Nord. A studious child, he did not work in the mines for long, and had a number of short-term jobs.[24] But his real life was the Communist Party, and he worked his way up the hierarchy, carefully observing and obeying the demands of Moscow. His Communist critics saw him as bland, submissive and docile, and he certainly lacked charisma. But his calm manner and beatific smile proved ideal for winning over sceptical socialists and liberals. This was not the rabid class warrior of conservative nightmares. His image did not provoke the bourgeois anxiety aroused by the Jewish and seemingly more threatening Socialist leader, Léon Blum.

Thorez also always made sure he attended public gatherings wearing a *tricolore* sash underneath his suit jacket: the Communists now stressed their French roots. They presented themselves as the successors to the patriotic Jacobins, whilst the fascists were the equivalents of the old aristocratic émigrés, linked to foreign reactionaries. In June 1939 they even celebrated the 150th anniversary of the French Revolution with a grand Robespierrian festival, in which 600 liberty trees were planted by Phrygian-capped children.[25] The Communists also used populist Jacobin language. They spoke of the 'struggle of the little people against the big', and their enemies were the 'two hundred families' – a small quasi-aristocracy rather than the whole bourgeoisie.[26]

The Communists' new image allowed them to play an important role in French politics for some time, as a non-revolutionary leftist party.[27] However, the nature of the party itself did not change. Like other Communist parties, it aspired to be a 'total' institution for its members, in some ways like a religious sect.[28] Like the Soviets, the French learnt party doctrine, wrote autobiographies describing their political and personal histories, and subjected themselves to ideological self-criticism.[29] They were expected to keep the party's secrets and treat the outside world with 'vigilance' and suspicion, a potential source of contamination. Their social and family lives were often entirely bound up with the party. They were to remain a vanguard, ready to bring the revolution when the time came – though levels of participation varied, depending on one's position within the party.

Whilst maintaining their purity, the French Communists were now expected to cooperate with the outside world, and they did so just as workers were being radicalized by the Depression. The result was thousands of new members. A party of 40,000 in 1934 swelled to one of 328,647 in 1937. The French Communist Party had taken over from the German as the leading party outside the USSR. In May 1936, the Popular Front of Socialists, Communists and liberal Radicals gained a majority in the elections, and Léon Blum became Prime Minister, supported by the Communists from outside the cabinet.

However, it was the Popular Front in Spain that, at least temporarily, contributed most to the increasing prestige of international Communism. Here, politics was even more polarized than in France; indeed, some areas of Spain had much in common with the old agrarian states where Communism had been so successful in the years after World War I. In particular, the question of land redistribution was still unresolved.

Landless peasants, especially in the South, were attracted to a decentralizing radical socialism, whilst other radicals, in the Socialist Party, the
anarcho-syndicalist parties and the quasi-Trotskyist Workers' Party of
Marxist Unity (POUM) also had a good deal of support. But so too did
the Right, with its heartland amongst the small-holding peasants of the
North and the centre. When the left, a shaky alliance of left-liberals,
socialists, anarcho-syndicalists and the small Communist party, won
elections in February 1936, a social revolution was sparked in many
rural and urban areas. The left's victory, in turn, provoked a military
coup, led by the authoritarian conservative General Francisco Franco.
The sharp social divisions within Spain had precipitated a civil war; and
within a week a domestic conflict had become an international one,
when Mussolini and Hitler sent military aid to Franco's rebels.

Stalin was faced with a dilemma. The Spanish Republicans were
without foreign friends: Blum in France was too afraid of antagonizing
the Germans, and a Conservative British government would not expend
any effort defending such a leftist government. Only the USSR could
halt Franco in Spain, and therefore prevent the balance of power shifting in favour of the fascists. However, Soviet support for revolutionary
Spaniards might worry the French and British establishments, and scupper any chance for a collective security treaty against Hitler.[30] Stalin
dithered for some time, but eventually decided to send arms and commissars, whilst insisting that the Popular Front should not aim for
socialism. Stalin wrote to the Socialist Prime Minister, Largo Caballero,
advising him that the 'parliamentary road' was more suited to Spanish
conditions than the Bolshevik model; he urged him to take account of
the interests of rural and urban middle classes, and to forge links with
liberals. For the Soviets, winning the war and keeping bourgeois allies
had to take priority over socialist revolution.

This led the Spanish Communist Party to adopt a more pragmatic,
gradualist policy than many in the Popular Front, including, at times,
Caballero himself. But by the end of 1936, it seemed that the Communist strategy had been triumphantly vindicated. The Communists
acquired a large, cross-class membership;[31] and their centralized, militarized approach to politics seemed to be more effective than the more
democratic, divided and chaotic Socialist and radical forces. The
Comintern also organized over 30,000 volunteers from over fifty nationalities, to fight for the Republic – the International Brigades. Many of

these volunteers were Communists and workers. In November 1936, as Franco's Nationalists advanced on Madrid, Caballero despaired of victory and abandoned the capital. But General Miaja remained, and he, together with the International Brigades and the Communist Party, were vital in helping the population to defend the city. Soviet arms (however small in number) and Communist organization and discipline, it seemed, had saved democracy against fascism.

IV

Nineteen thirty-six was perhaps the high point of Communist prestige in the West. The Communists, unlike the French socialists and the British Labour Party, seemed to be the only force willing to act decisively against the forces of extreme reaction. Moreover, since the mid-1930s Western intellectuals had fallen in love with the Plan. Communists now had a disciplined and rational image, the heirs of the Enlightenment. They were no longer the revolutionaries of the post-World War I period, or the militant sectarians of the 1920s. Their Marxism was much more Modernist and rationalistic.

Eric Hobsbawm, the Austrian émigré historian and one of the most incisive Communist memoirists of the period, captured this atmosphere of seriousness. He had taken part in the German Communist Party's militant street marches in Berlin in 1932–3 as a youth, but the Communism of the British party, which he joined in 1936 when he went to study at Cambridge, was very different:

> Communist Parties were not for romantics. On the contrary, they were for organization and routine . . . The secret of the Leninist Party lay neither in dreaming about standing on barricades, or even Marxist theory. It can be summed up in two phrases: 'decisions must be verified' and 'Party discipline'. The appeal of the Party was that it got things done when others did not. Life in the Party was almost viscerally anti-rhetorical, which may have helped to produce that culture of endless and almost aggressively boring . . . sensationally unreadable 'reports' which foreign parties took over from Soviet practice . . . The Leninist 'vanguard party' was a combination of discipline, business efficiency, utter emotional identification and a sense of *total* dedication.[32]

Many non-Communists were also attracted by this ethos of disciplined and clear-headed statism that could counter fascist irrationalism and pull the world out of Depression. Leftist intellectuals flocked to the USSR to see the 'Great Experiment'. In 1932 Kingsley Martin, the editor of the British leftist magazine the *New Statesman*, declared that 'The entire British intelligentsia has been to Moscow this summer.'[33] Soviet eagerness to welcome and impress visitors with well-crafted propaganda trips only fuelled the enthusiasm. Hundreds of travel books appeared; over 200 French intellectuals visited in 1935, and the Communist philosopher Paul Nizan gave a lecture tour of France, describing the marvels he had witnessed.[34]

The 'Soviet Union' the visitors saw was a blend of their own utopian preconceptions and the Potemkin-village socialism presented by their guides. They admired the welfare state, the mass education, and the rational organization of leisure. They envied the high status that intellectuals (at least the obedient ones) enjoyed in the USSR. But most of all they loved the Plan. The Soviet regime was, in their eyes, a Saint-Simonian paradise, where hard science and efficiency informed a moral vision of social transformation.

The British socialists Beatrice and Sidney Webb are the most notorious examples of this type of enthusiast. Technocrats and elitists, they were champions of a rational, modernizing socialism, but enemies of revolutions, which they saw as violent, anarchic and irrational. In the 1920s they had been opponents of the USSR, but Stalin's First Five-Year Plan delighted them, and in 1932, in their seventies, they went on a tour of the Soviet Union. The result of their researches was a massive, detailed work of over a thousand pages, *The Soviet Union – A New Civilization?*, published in 1935.

By the time of the second edition in 1937 the publishers had removed the question-mark. The Webbs' 'new civilization' was a land of committees, conferences and consultations. They could have been writing about the London County Council, to which Sidney had devoted so much of his career. They read reams of official documents, including the Stalinist Constitution of 1936, and assured their readers that full provision was made for elections, democracy and accountability; it would be entirely wrong to call the Soviet Union a 'dictatorship', they declared.[35]

Writers like the Webbs were eager to accept the reassurances of the Soviet authorities for political reasons. Others succumbed to cruder manipulation. The minor French landscape-painter Albert Marquet proved a much more awkward case for the All-Union Society for Cultural Relations with Foreign Countries (VOKS), the body that hosted foreign visitors. He was not interested in politics, and was certainly not a Communist; his guides reported that he was irritable and unimpressed. But things changed when he visited the Museum of Contemporary Western Art in Leningrad. He was gratified, and surprised, to see that his own paintings were prominently displayed as part of the permanent exhibition, alongside works by Matisse and Cézanne. What he was not told was that VOKS had arranged for them to be taken out of storage especially for his visit. Marquet went on to attend various stage-managed meetings with young artists who claimed to value him as a mentor, and he was favoured with wide press-coverage. On returning to France, his attitude had been transformed: 'I did like it in the USSR . . . Just imagine, a large state where money does not determine people's lives', he gushed. In a terse report, VOKS congratulated itself on the success of its elaborate efforts: 'The Soviet artistic community was widely involved with this work [the Marquet visit]. The work went according to plan.'[36]

But for some visiting fellow travellers it was not manipulation or credulity that led them to overlook political repression and violence. They simply saw it as necessary and inevitable. The African-American singer Paul Robeson declared in 1937: 'From what I have seen of the workings of the Soviet Government, I can only say that anybody who lifts his hand against it ought to be shot.' Similarly, the New York Times correspondent Walter Duranty, who notoriously denied the existence of famine in 1932–3, believed that violence was inevitable in a backward country like the USSR, though he was also interested in ingratiating himself with his hosts to further his career.[37] Others deliberately hid the negative sides of the Soviet experience because they did not want to undermine the anti-fascist cause. The French writer André Malraux was a revolutionary romantic, and had little sympathy with the disciplinarian Communist culture of the Comintern. In private he was scathingly critical of the USSR, but he remained a firm supporter in public.[38] The English historian Richard Cobb, who lived in Paris at the time, explained the political choices as they then appeared to the liberal left:

My first sight of France was [a fascist] Action Française strong-arm team in full spate, beating up a Jewish student. And this was a daily occurrence. It is difficult to convey the degree of hate that any decent person would feel for the pimply, cowardly *ligeurs* ... France was living through a moral and mental civil war ... one had to choose between fascism and fellow-travelling.[39]

The Chilean poet Pablo Neruda used a similar language of unavoidable, difficult choices, although he, unlike Cobb, became more committed to the Communist cause. In his memoirs he recalled how his time in Spain convinced him to support the Communists:

> The Communists were the only organised group and had put together an army to confront Italians, Germans, Moors and [Spanish fascist] Falangists. They were also the moral force that kept the resistance and the anti-Fascist struggle going. It boiled down to this: you had to pick the road you would take. That is what I did, and I have never had reason to regret the choice I made between darkness and hope in that tragic time.[40]

Neruda was not alone, and the Spanish Civil War was central to the revival of Communism's popularity in Latin America. There were, of course, close cultural links with Spain, and many went to fight in the civil war; Spanish exiles also played a large part in improving Communism's fortunes there after years of failure.

Communist parties had been founded after 1917 throughout Latin America, and attracted many intellectuals, but as in many countries outside the developed world they did not flourish in the 1920s. Extreme repression by authoritarian states, backed by the influential Catholic Church, explains much of their weakness, but so does the Comintern's narrow obsession with the proletariat – a tiny class in most Latin American states. They therefore found it difficult to compete with broader populist parties, and to harness the radicalism of the peasantry. Some Marxists, like the Peruvian José Carlos Mariátegui, formed a socialist party that sought to unite a broad front of workers, intellectuals and indigenous peasants, but he was strongly condemned by the Comintern for his populism. The Comintern did support two uprisings in El Salvador in 1932 and in Nicaragua in the late 1920s and early 1930s – both of which had strong peasant participation. Neither succeeded, and the Comintern played very little role in the rebellion of the Nicaraguan Communist leader, Augusto Sandino.

Prospects for Communist parties improved after the beginning of the

Comintern's Popular Front policy, especially where there was significant industry and a powerful labour movement. In Mexico, a relatively weak Communist party forged an informal alliance with the reforming social-ist President Cárdenas, and in Chile Communists actually won elections in 1938 as part of a Popular Front government under the left-liberal Pedro Cerda. In Chile, as in Mexico, Communists benefited enormously from their role in the Spanish war.[41]

V

Not everybody on the left, however, saw Spain as a vindication of Comintern strategy, and it exacerbated what was to become a major split in international Communism – that between Stalinists and Trot-skyists. Active in exile in Turkey, then France, Norway and Mexico, Trotsky became one of the main Marxist critics of Stalin. He despaired of the popularity of the USSR amongst the Western intelligentsia: 'Under the pretence of a belated recognition of the October revolution, the "left" intelligentsia of the West has gone down on its knees before the Soviet bureaucracy.'[42] Yet by the time he wrote this, in 1938, the love affair between Soviet Communism and Western leftist intellectuals was already beginning to sour. The Moscow show trials of 1936, 1937 and 1938 and the purges of the Comintern bureaucracy had an ever-greater cumulative effect and deeply disturbed many Communists and fellow travellers. Paul Nizan refused to discuss them, even with his friends Jean-Paul Sartre and Simone de Beauvoir.[43]

However the crisis of the Popular Front policy, and particularly events in Spain, were the main causes of disillusionment. The Popular Front was a shaky compromise. Communists were dropping their old revolutionary goals, temporarily, to appeal to reformist socialists. But at the same time they remained an anti-liberal, disciplinarian party that sought to retain working-class support. This was the essence of Soviet Communism, and for Stalinists the iron discipline of the party was what gave the party its advantage in the fight against fascism. It was a tricky, and ultimately impossible, balance to maintain.

It was Communism's 'realism' and moderation that initially caused problems for the Comintern, as it found itself having to deal with an eruption of popular radicalism. In France, Blum's government came to power amidst massive strikes and factory occupations; Trotskyist groups within the Socialist Party were even arguing that the time was ripe for revolution. The Popular Front granted significant concessions to workers in the Matignon agreements, including the 40-hour week, but the strikes continued. Maurice Thorez supported Blum: now the workers had gained so much, they should 'know how to end a strike'. But afraid of being outflanked from the left, the Communists soon began to go along with worker demands and relations with the liberals and Socialists became tense. Meanwhile, Blum's decision not to intervene on the Spanish Republicans' side for fear of triggering a European war led to further conflict. The Socialists began to fear Communist strength (as also happened in Chile, where socialists began to worry that Communists were exploiting popular radicalism, to their disadvantage).[44] However, it was the centrist Radicals, believing workers had won too much at Matignon, who ultimately destroyed the Popular Front, and in 1938 Blum was forced out of power.

In Spain, the Communists were less willing to make compromises with the more radical left, for here Soviet security was at stake. The victory of the left in the 1936 elections was, in some areas, accompanied by a social revolution: anarcho-syndicalist-inspired workers took over factories and expelled their owners; peasants seized land, and set up collectives and cooperatives. Just as Lenin had rejected factory councils in 1918, the Communists were convinced that egalitarian experiments merely undermined the war effort. Victory demanded centralization and economic efficiency. They argued that the time was only ripe for a market socialist (or 'NEP') type of regime, ruled by a coalition of 'progressive forces', including elements of the bourgeoisie, with private ownership permitted. At the same time, they were virulently hostile to the leftist-Communist POUM, led by Trotsky's old associate Andreu Nin. Therefore they and their ally, the technocratic Republican Prime Minister Juan Négrin, attracted a great deal of support from middle-class groups anxious about the power of workers and anarchists.[45] In May 1937 the Republican government, with Communist support, moved against the anarchists and POUM in Barcelona. Resistance was crushed, and the Soviet secret service, which had a significant contingent in Spain, sent its assassins to murder Nin and arrested other remaining POUM activists.[46]

George Orwell, like many of his generation, was eager to help the Spanish Republic. But unlike most, he ended up with the Trotskyist

POUM, by chance rather than ideological conviction. Orwell was in Barcelona during the May days, and his account of his experiences published in 1938, *Homage to Catalonia*, proved one of the most powerful and influential denunciations of Soviet-style Communism of the era. Initially he had disagreed with his POUM comrades' hostility to the Communists. As he observed, the Communists 'were getting on with the war while we [POUM] and the Anarchists were standing still'. But after experiencing Communist and Republican oppression in Barcelona, he changed his mind. He now declared that the Communists were at fault for stifling popular radicalism: 'Perhaps the POUM and Anarchist slogan: "The war and the revolution are inseparable", was less visionary than it sounds.'[47] He reasoned that the Communists' social conservatism alienated the Western working class, which might otherwise have put pressure on governments to support the Spanish Republic, whilst undermining a potential revolution in the territory occupied by Franco.

The debate over 'who lost Spain?' continues.[48] The Soviet secret police's obsession with purging enemies on the left doubtless undermined support for the Republic. But probably more significant in democracy's defeat were the paucity of help from abroad and the strength of Franco's German and Italian allies. Stalin, it seems, remained committed to Spain to the end, but he had to husband his resources for the defence of the USSR against Germany, and against Japan, which had invaded China in July 1937.[49]

Trotsky was one of the unexpected beneficiaries of the Spanish Popular Front's failure. Soviet behaviour in Spain, together with the show trials, fuelled disillusionment on the left, and Trotsky attracted Communist dissidents to his cause. The murders of Nin and other supporters gave the movement its martyrs, though its greatest martyr was to be Trotsky himself, killed with an ice-pick by one of Stalin's assassins in August 1940. In 1938 Trotsky founded the Fourth International, a new force on the left to rival the second, social democratic, and the third, Communist, internationals.

Trotskyism was a leftist, Radical branch of Bolshevism, and its ideas were typical of the various left oppositions that had existed within the Soviet party since 1917. It championed a revival of 'socialist democracy', and denounced Stalinism for its authoritarianism. But it did not advocate pluralist, liberal democracy. It adhered to the Marxist-Leninist commitment to the single, vanguard party, though politics and the

economy were to be run in a participatory way. Trotsky was also reluctant to be too harsh on the Stalinist system itself. He argued that a
'bureaucratic caste' had emerged under Stalin, but he insisted that this
was not a 'new class'; the USSR had not become a 'state capitalist' system, but was still a 'workers' state', even if a 'degenerated' one. In the
international sphere, Trotskyism was more optimistic and revolutionary
than Stalinism, and it was deeply hostile to the nationalism underlying
Popular Front politics. His theories of 'permanent revolution' and 'combined and uneven development' both justified a revolutionary politics in
the developing world. Unlike Stalinists, who stuck more rigidly to Marxist phases of development, Trotskyists believed that underdeveloped,
agrarian societies could skip phases and make rapid revolutionary leaps
to socialism. They always, however, insisted that only the proletariat
could be in the vanguard, even when leading the bourgeoisie and the
peasants in their 'permanent revolution'.[50]

The membership of the Fourth International was tiny – optimistic
official figures put it at 5,395 – and almost half of its members were
members of the Socialist Workers' Party of the United States (SWP).
Trotsky's Radical Marxism, and his defence of workers-council democracy, was predictably appealing in the more libertarian culture of America, where the discipline-obsessed Second and Third Internationals had
been weakest. And Trotskyism was to be highly influential amongst
American intellectuals, especially the 'New York' group. Saul Bellow,
Irving Howe, Norman Mailer, Mary McCarthy and Edmund Wilson all
at one time had connections or sympathies with Trotskyism.[51]

Yet many American Trotskyists found even Trotsky too indulgent
towards Stalinism, and in 1939–40 the Socialist Workers' Party was
shaken by an acrimonious debate on the nature of the USSR. The party
split, and Max Schachtman created a new 'Workers' Party', more hostile
to Stalinism than the orthodox Trotskyists. He, like several other American Trotskyists, were to become Cold Warriors, and by the 1960s were
to constitute the core of an influential group of militant liberals – the
'neo-conservatives'. Elsewhere, Trotskyism was to come into its own as
a powerful force during the 1960s and 1970s, as the USSR became less
attractive. Even so, the movement retained a deserved reputation for
endless disputes and splits.

The Trotskyists were the first serious champions of the idea that
Nazism and Stalinist Communism had to be compared, and were both

'totalitarian' regimes; and their analysis appeared prescient when, on 23 August 1939, Berlin and Moscow concluded a pact. In fact, the treaty was not the product of a real friendship, but of Stalin's belief that he had no alternative.[52] The British had little real interest in a formal anti-Hitler military alliance, whilst Stalin could not risk war with Germany. But Stalin also had no qualms about the alliance, and, as in the past, hoped that socialism would benefit from a war within the 'imperialist' camp. Speaking to Dimitrov, he exulted that Hitler was 'throwing the capitalist system into chaos'; 'the pact of non-aggression helps Germany to a certain extent. In the next moment we will incite the other side.'[53] At the same time, the Comintern declared the end of the Popular Front. Stalin was not planning imminent revolutions, but he did believe that war might lead to future revolutions, and the Comintern line became strongly anti-bourgeois.[54] Meanwhile, the Red Army was in a position to spread socialism by force into the Baltic, Polish and other lands taken by the Soviets as a result of the pact. The Popular Front line, the Comintern now declared, was heresy; the evils of Anglo-French imperialism were denounced; and anti-fascist propaganda was banned.

Unsurprisingly, the pact caused a crisis in Communist parties. Harry Pollitt refused to accept the new Comintern line, and was replaced by Rajani Palme Dutt as leader of the British Communist Party.[55] In France, a third of the Communist Party's parliamentary delegation resigned. Paul Nizan was one of those who left the party in disgust. Nevertheless, despite deep reservations, the Communist parties bowed down before the demands of Soviet foreign policy.

However, the reconciliation between Moscow and Berlin was bound to be short-lived, despite Stalin's conviction that he could successfully avoid war until the imperialist powers had weakened each other. And with Hitler's surprise attack on the USSR on 22 June 1941, the Comintern performed yet another *volte-face*. Anti-fascism was back, the USSR was now the ally of Britain and then America. And again, despite the debacle of the Nazi–Soviet pact, many on the Western left saw the Soviet Union and its brand of Communism as the only saviour of the world against an aggressive, authoritarian right. World War II was to be the Popular Front's finest hour.

VI

If Tsar Nicholas II was set, and failed the 'exam' set by the Great War, his successors were faced with an even more difficult challenge in 1941 – an 'all-round test' of 'our material and spiritual forces' as Stalin put it. Afterwards Stalin, at least, was in no doubt that he, and the system he had created, had passed with high honours: 'The lessons of war are that the Soviet structure is not only the best form of organization . . . in the years of peaceful development, but also the best form of mobilization of all forces of the people to drive off the enemy in wartime.'[56] Not only that, but the USSR had saved civilization, and the West, from Nazi domination.

Stalin's argument was not wholly implausible. In 1914 Russia was a poor, largely agrarian country, and could not mobilize the men and materiel to defeat its invaders. By 1941, Russia was still far more agrarian and much poorer than its rivals, but despite enduring a far greater burden of fighting and casualties than in World War I, its economy did not collapse. The USSR lost about 27 million people in all, including 10 million military personnel, compared with 350,000 British and 300,000 American military losses. The old Soviet view that the USSR won World War II virtually single-handed is, of course, false. All efforts in the war were interlinked; the Soviets received significant aid, direct and indirect, from their allies; and the Axis powers were very likely to lose against a coalition that could draw upon the combined resources of the United States, the British Empire and Russia. Even so, as Stalin never tired of pointing out, the Germans had to pour many more resources into the Eastern front than other fields of battle.

The contribution of the Communist system itself is more difficult to assess. During the war it displayed all of its weaknesses and its strengths. The narrow centralization of power in the hands of Stalin himself contributed to a catastrophic misjudgement in 1941. Stalin refused to accept the Germans were planning to attack despite a great deal of evidence to the contrary.[57] Hitler's Operation Barbarossa caught the Soviets by surprise and was a huge blow that brought the Germans rapidly to the gates of Moscow.

Compounding the problems caused by Soviet centralization was the persistent Communist mistrust of professional elites. The Red Army's leadership lacked the depth of experience of its German rival: few tsarist officers were employed in the Red Army in the 1930s, and most of its upper echelons had only learnt their skills during the civil war. The purges of 1937–8 had further undermined the army: about 20,000 officers out of 142,000 were arrested. The ineffectual Kliment Voroshilov – one of Stalin's inner circle and a political crony – also contributed to the disastrous defeats at the beginning of the war as Defence Commissar. Finally, the sheer harshness of the Soviet regime itself had a seriously detrimental effect, alienating many, especially in non-Russian rural areas. In 1941–2 the Red Army suffered from mass desertions as between 1 and 1.5 million recruits joined the German forces.[58]

However, certain features of Soviet Communism, no matter how distasteful, proved their worth in wartime. The break-neck industrialization of the 1930s may not have been 'necessary' – there were alternatives – but by the late 1930s the Soviets were out-producing the Germans; by the late 1930s, the USSR was probably the largest defence producer in the world, with massively more of everything than the Germans even then, other than air power.[59] The centralized administrative system also had advantages. Unlike its tsarist predecessor, the Soviet government was able to control and direct food and industrial goods throughout the war, thus avoiding mass civilian starvation whilst maintaining defence production. The regime even succeeded in organizing the transport of huge industrial plants eastwards, far beyond enemy lines. It seems, moreover, that the very ruthlessness of the regime and the efficiency of its police system helped to stem the collapse of order. 'Blocking detachments' shot thousands of deserting soldiers; in the course of the war 990,000 soldiers were punished by military tribunals, 158,000 of whom were sentenced to death.[60]

There was a great deal of popular collaboration with the Nazis, especially amongst non-Russians, but there was also considerable support for the Soviet regime, something the Germans had not expected. German treatment of their Slavic subject populations as racial inferiors to be exploited strengthened the Soviets' ideological claims. Communism seemed to be the only bulwark against the law of the jungle, the equation of might and right. The picture is somewhat obscured, however, by the ideological shifts of the period. The 'Communism' of the war was not the same as the 'Communism' of the 1930s. War against the Germans forced the party to adopt a more inclusive politics, going even further than it had in the mid-1930s. The Communist sectarianism and ideological purism, so pronounced during the Terror of 1936–8, were much less evident. The regime began to make peace with groups it had previously stigmatized – especially peasants and priests – for this was to be a national struggle in which everybody was included, whatever their class background. Even kulaks imprisoned in the Gulag were released to fight in the Red Army, earning their reintegration into Soviet society in the process. Startlingly, Stalin's first speech after the outbreak of war addressed his people not only as 'comrades' and 'citizens', but 'brothers and sisters'. As the writer Ilya Ehrenburg explained in an article in *Krasnaia Zvezda* (*Red Star*), the Red Army newspaper, in 1941, 'all distinctions between Bolsheviks and non-party people, between believers and Marxists, have been obliterated'.[61] Koba's band of brothers (and sisters) was far larger and more inclusive than had been countenanced before.

Stalin realized he needed to mobilize Russian nationalist feeling, even more so than in the past. '*Za Rodinu! Za Stalina!*' ('For the Motherland! For Stalin!') was the new battle-cry. And the 'enemy' was no longer the smug, top-hatted bourgeois but the screeching German parasite/rodent/demon. In 1941 state persecution of Russian Orthodoxy was halted, and in 1943 Stalin restored the patriarchate, in the hope that support might be garnered amongst the Orthodox in Eastern Europe after the war. Senior Orthodox clergy now effectively became part of the *nomenklatura*; the three most senior churchmen were given chauffeured cars.[62] As the Germans encroached on Russian soil, many were prepared to unite behind the Communist banner in the defence of hearth and homeland.

Wartime Marxism-Leninism bore not only the savour of nationalism but also a hint of liberalism. Restrictions on private plots were relaxed, and peasants were allowed to sell produce from this land on the open market. Cultural policy too became more forgiving – big-band jazz was now fully accepted and American tunes were played by front-line groups.[63] The Red Army came increasingly to resemble conventional bourgeois armed services, and officers were given more power. But the most remarkable departure from revolutionary Communism was the dissolution of the Comintern in 1943. This gesture was designed to appease the Allies, proving that the USSR had no desire to spread the revolution to the West. But possibly as influential in the decision was Stalin's waning interest in international Communism.[64] Since 1941 he had seen greater potential in the All-Slavic Committee, which had enjoyed success in Eastern Europe – the centre of Stalin's post-war ambitions.

This more inclusive politics proved capable of attracting the support of those previously alienated by earlier 'class struggles'. As the popular novelist Victor Nekrasov later remembered: 'We forgave Stalin every-thing, collectivization, 1937, his revenge on his comrades . . . With open hearts we joined the party of Lenin and Stalin.'[65] Yet if the war had encouraged prodigal sons to return to the Soviet family, it also produced new black sheep.[66] The party still demanded ideological uniformity, and campaigns of purification and purging continued; however, the 'enemies' were now defined in largely ethnic rather than class terms – especially peoples accused of collaborating with the Nazis. Whole peoples were deported: the Volga Germans, Chechens, Ingush, Crimean Tatars, Kalmyks and Karachais. Others suffered from more limited but still traumatic purges, including the populations of the Baltic States and western Ukraine. Much of this was carried out with great brutality, and the resulting hatreds were deep and long-lasting. Indeed, the rebellions of the Balts and west Ukrainians contributed to the collapse of the USSR in 1991, and the Chechens and Ingush remain a thorn in Russia's side to this day.

It was to be some time, however, before the backlash came, and meanwhile, to the west of the Nazis, Western Popular Fronts generated support by 'Communizing' a politics that was, in its fundamentals, more liberal. The experience of Nazism radicalized populations subject to its rule. The Nazis' 'New Order' was a far-reaching ideological project that sought to create a European empire of racial hierarchies. Hitler, capti-vated by the example of the British Empire, explained that what India was for the British, Ukraine would be for Germany.[67] The Germans were also much assisted by collaborators, many of them from local conservative elites.

These circumstances – an imperial power imposing its rule by force and relying on collaborators from amongst the old social elites – were, of course, ideal for Communists. Communists were militant, well-organized, and used to underground political activity. Moreover, in the chaotic conditions of war, freed from the intrusion of Moscow and the Comintern, local Communists were able to adapt their message to local conditions. Communists were amongst the most committed members of the resistance to Nazism. In some places they were indeed the only political force prepared to resist the occupations. Socialists' response to Nazi occupation depended on particular circumstances, and they were not as consistently anti-fascist as the Communists; in Denmark they collaborated, and in France the majority of Socialists sympathized with Marshal Pétain's anti-Communism. Communists were at the forefront of the resistance in the countries where they subsequently became prominent, especially in Italy, France, Greece, Czechoslovakia, Albania and Yugoslavia.

Yet, despite their strength, Communist parties in Western Europe, with Moscow's full agreement, were determined to remain part of a Popular Front alliance – both to win the war and, more importantly perhaps, to win the peace. They therefore had to discourage the revolutionary expectations of their followers. In 1941 the French Communist Party pursued a policy of assassination which led to bloody German reprisals and antagonized local populations. They soon decided to adopt less militant tactics, and by 1943 had joined De Gaulle's cross-class provisional government.

The keenest supporter of the Popular Front policy was the Italian leader Palmiro Togliatti. Indeed, his character – a mixture of shrewd, cautious politician and well-read intellectual with broad cultural interests – made him the ideal figure to navigate both the dangerous world of the Comintern high-command and the more pluralistic terrain of Italy, where Communism was always likely to be a minority force. Togliatti was the son of a lowly state clerk, born in Genoa. He was a friend of Gramsci's and with him a member of the Radical Ordine Nuovo group after World War I.[68] With Gramsci's arrest he became leader of the Italian Communist Party, though he continued to live in exile in Moscow. He soon emerged as a major figure in the Comintern hierarchy, and was its representative in Spain during the civil war. But he combined loyalty to Stalin with a willingness to think seriously about why the Comintern's Communism had proven to be so fragile in Western Europe. His analysis was based on a partial interpretation of Gramsci's *Prison Notebooks* – a new sacred text for his party which he alone had seen in Moscow after Gramsci's death in 1937.[69] Gramsci, learning from the failures of the early 1920s, argued that Western Communist parties had to abandon the Bolshevik strategy because circumstances were so different. In Russia the state was all, so a Leninist seizure of power, or 'war of movement', was essential; in the West, civil society was much stronger, and revolution would only come through a long-lasting 'war of position'. This 'war' entailed Communists and the working class campaigning to establish not only social but also cultural leadership of society. Togliatti brought Gramsci's ideas to an Italian party that had won wide support during the resistance and was therefore well-placed to become a national party. Its strategy was to establish 'hegemony' (or all-encompassing influence) over society as a whole – the family, the countryside, the workplace and the arts – and not just the state. Togliatti, however, was much less radical a Communist than Gramsci. Gramsci never abandoned revolutionary politics, and he would not have approved of Togliatti's alliances with a whole range of bourgeois groups, including middle classes and peasants, and at the highest level even the Christian Democrats. Like their French comrades, the Italian Communists sought to situate themselves in the traditions of leftist nationalism – the tricolour, Garibaldi and the Risorgimento. Fundamental social transformation was to be put off to the distant future; parliaments and capitalism had to stay.

Togliatti's party was no more democratic than Thorez's, and he was almost as loyal to Stalin. But the Italian Communists' culture was new. Whilst the French party remained the sectarian, worker-oriented organization of the 1930s, Togliatti, in contrast, took advantage of Mussolini's destruction of the old Italian party and was effectively able to refound it. He brought in a group of Communist leaders from an intellectual background who had not grown up in a Bolshevik culture, and who lent Italian Communism an air of urbanity, modernity and cosmopolitanism.[70]

Togliatti's strategy had a great deal of success; it appealed to a generation of left-leaning intellectuals, angered at Fascist collaboration; its record in the resistance was impressive; and there was a vacuum in the centre-left. The Communist party's membership rose from 5,000 in mid-1943 to 1,771,000 in late 1945, most of whom were workers and peasants; in addition it had 5 million affiliated trade unionists. Even so, it could not deliver enough votes to be successful in elections, and remained in opposition (in alliance with the socialists).

The other successful Popular Front Communists were the Czechs. Like the French and the Italian parties, they had already been a significant political force before the War. Leading the resistance, they joined the non-Communist President Beneš's government. Stalin promised Beneš his backing as Prime Minister after the war, as long as he was prepared to outlaw collaborationist political forces.

Between 1944 and 1945 Stalin was a firm supporter of Popular Fronts. Indeed, he was even more willing for Communists to take part in bourgeois governments than in the 1930s, especially in Italy and France, where he wanted them to oppose any attempts by the British or the Americans to interfere. He continued to believe that Communist takeovers in the West would be unlikely for some time, and he insisted that Communists avoid frightening talk of world revolution. For Stalin in 1945, as in 1935, the security of the USSR was paramount, and despite the defeat of the Germans he concluded there was no room for complacency. The Soviet economy had been shattered by the war; estimates suggest it lost about 23 per cent of its physical capital.[71] Stalin was terrified that an aggressive Germany would rise, yet again, from the ashes. But he was also facing a new rival, both wealthier and intent on shaping the post-war order – the United States. In 1945, however, Stalin still believed that peace, and even collaboration, between East and West would be possible for some time to come.

The gilded wartime reputation of the USSR was reinforced by the new, emerging centre-left consensus in much of Europe. The Nazi experience had discredited the radical right, but efforts were also made to learn lessons from further back in history. The extreme radicalization of politics of the 1930s was blamed on the laissez-faire economics of the 1920s. The emerging post-war consensus viewed markets tempered by regulation and planning as a better model; states were also to spend money on social welfare. These intellectual shifts benefited the moderate Popular Front Communists. They even gained substantial numbers of votes where they had previously been very weak – 10.6 per cent of the electorate in Holland and 12.5 per cent in Denmark.

However, Communists were strongest in those West European countries which had seen significant resistance movements. In France and Italy (and, briefly, Finland), Communists took over from the socialists as the main party of the left, where they remained for some decades. By 1946, the French Communists had gained 28.6 per cent of the vote, the Italians 19 per cent, and the Finnish Communist-led alliance 23.5 per cent. All three parties took part in post-war Popular Front governments reflecting, in part, a benign 'Uncle Joe's' lionization in the West.

The cultural and ideological trade went the other way as well. Soviet citizens had little contact with the outside world in the 1930s, but during and after the war millions of soldiers saw the world of capitalism with their own eyes. They were stunned. The gap in living standards was enormous. The Soviet writer Konstantin Simonov described the encounter as an 'emotional and psychological shock'.[72] This could generate anger: the defeated Germans were still living better than the victors. But it also exposed soldiers to the attractions of a less austere way of life. The Western films taken from the Germans as reparations or 'trophies', and widely shown in the USSR, also portrayed Western culture, music and fashion. Soviet youth – contemptuously labelled the 'stylish' (*stiliagi*) by party activists – were particularly smitten.

In 1945–6 it looked as if the 'second' Popular Front would be more successful than its failed predecessor. It is perhaps worth imagining what a Paris Exposition after the War would have looked like, had a shattered France had the resources and confidence to organize one. The pavilions would have been constructed and arranged very differently from 1937. The German tower would have been in ruins; Italy, France and Czechoslovakia would have built edifices along the lines of the left-patriotic French exhibitions of 1937. And close to them would have been a refurbished Soviet pavilion. It might have looked as if the Popular Front had won. But two other pavilions would have told a different story. The old Spanish pavilion, which showed so strikingly the tensions between radical leftism and the authoritarian Soviet Communism, would have survived, but would have been taken over by the new Communist regime in South-Eastern Europe – Tito's Yugoslavia. And a new and immense American building would have replaced the old German pavilion as the main rival to the Soviets. This competitor was to be much more successful than the Nazis in destroying the Popular Front project, and with it Soviet influence in Western Europe.

VII

In 1944 Stalin had such faith in the Popular Front model that he decided to make it the centrepiece of his East European policy. As in the past, security lay at the heart of Stalin's thinking. He wanted a buffer zone to protect the Soviet Union, and the advances of the Red Army in 1944 and 1945 gave him one. The Americans and the British accepted that the Soviets were to have some sort of sphere of influence. Churchill and Stalin concluded the secret October 1944 percentages agreement, which allowed the Soviets to dominate Bulgaria, Romania and Hungary, in exchange for British power in Greece. It was also accepted, implicitly, that the USSR would dominate Poland, whilst the Anglo-Americans had France and Italy. Yet Stalin, anxious to remain on good terms with the Allies, also agreed at the Yalta conference in 1945 to allow free elections in the countries occupied by the Red Army.

How could these very different agreements be reconciled? Stalin thought the answer lay in the creation of pro-Soviet leftist governments – 'people's democracies'. Like the Spanish Republican government of 1936–9, they would be broad coalitions of non-fascist forces, elected through the ballot box; they would not try to establish radical socialism, limiting themselves to redistribution of the large gentry estates, whilst control of internal security and intelligence would make sure that they pursued the foreign-policy interests of the USSR. And to Stalin, a Soviet-led Popular Front in Central and Eastern Europe looked far more feasible than it had in Spain. Ideas of pan-Slavic unity could marry local nationalisms with Soviet interests; the USSR, for instance, supported the creation of homogeneous ethnic states and the expulsions of Germans from Czechoslovakia and Poland. Also the experience of fascism had driven liberals to the left. As Stalin put it in a conversation with the Bulgarian Dimitrov at his dacha in January 1945:

> The crisis of capitalism is evident in the division of the capitalists into two factions – one *fascist*, the other *democratic*. The alliance between ourselves and the democratic faction of the capitalists came about because the latter had an interest in preventing Hitler's domination, for that brutal state would have driven the working class to extremes and to the overthrow of capitalism itself.[73]

Did Stalin think that Popular Fronts were for the long term, or did he plan rapidly to sovietize Eastern Europe? Ultimately he expected Popular Front democracies to become fully socialist states, but in countries under the occupation of the Red Army he thought this process would be a peaceful rather than a revolutionary one. Communist parties would gradually take over, though the timetable was left unclear. As he told Dimitrov, the Bulgarian Communists were only to adopt a 'minimum 'programme', as it would give them a 'broader basis' of support and would be a 'fitting mask for the present period', but later the 'maximum programme' would be appropriate.[74]

In 1945 the prospects for Communists in the Soviet sphere of Europe looked rosy, especially in three countries: Yugoslavia, Czechoslovakia and Bulgaria. It is likely that had the Yugoslav Communists held an election, they would have won it, and it has been estimated that the Bulgarian Communists had the support of between a quarter and a third of the population (though they won the elections through intimidation), whilst in 1946 the Czechoslovak Communists took a massive 37.9 per cent of the vote (and did even better than that in the Czech regions). Even in less hospitable lands, such as Hungary, Communists were strong; the Hungarian party secured almost 17 per cent of the vote. The War had pushed Eastern Europe to the left as it had the Western half of the continent, discrediting Nazi imperialism and Western liberal appeasement. Moreover, the inter-war Central and Eastern European regimes had not made much of a success of development: neither the more liberal policies of the 1920s nor the economic nationalism of the 1930s had helped the region to catch up with the West. The Communists' confidence in state action, planning and welfare thus seemed very appealing.

But there were also serious obstacles to the planting of pro-Communist Popular Fronts on East European soil. Most countries had been deeply suspicious of the USSR before 1945: Romania, Hungary and Bulgaria had taken the German side in the War, and Poland had a long history of poisonous relations with Russia. But everywhere, centre-right parties were reluctant to work with Communists. On their side too, local Communists did not help the process of coalition-building, as they were often deeply unhappy about sharing power. The German Communist Gerhard Eisler, for instance, remarked of democracy: 'Free elections? So that the Germans could again elect Hitler?'[75] Local Communists often saw the Popular Front as a brief transitional phase on the way to imminent socialism, and naturally tried to persuade the Soviets of the advantages of pure Communist rule.

However, the Soviets themselves had a significant share of responsibility for the failure of the Popular Fronts. As in the 1930s, their insistence on giving absolute priority to the interests of the USSR turned many potential sympathizers into enemies. To begin with, Soviet determination to enforce reparations on Germany by dismantling factories in the Eastern sector and exporting them to the USSR was deeply unpopular. In the Soviet-occupied zone of Germany, administrators consistently placed economic exploitation over winning German hearts and minds. On one occasion, Red Army soldiers even interrupted a showing of the uplifting *Circus*, marching its worker audience off to dismantle a German factory for shipping to the USSR.[76] In addition, widespread and unpunished rape, committed by Soviet soldiers, created deep loathing of the occupier, especially in Germany. At the same time (as had happened in Spain) Communist-controlled security services launched purges not only of collaborators but, increasingly, of any opponents of the Communists.

The Russians even began to alienate close friends. Jakub Berman, a Polish Communist leader who had been one of Wolfgang Leonhard's instructors at the Comintern School during the War, found Soviet high-handedness irritating, but tried to explain it to a sceptical interviewer in the early 1980s:

> the Soviets were only doing this, and giving us advice, out of concern for us; they wanted our revolution in Poland to take the form they were familiar with, the best one in their view, because it was victorious. They couldn't, after all, shed their mentality and jump into someone else's. I'm deeply convinced of that and I wish you would enter into their way of thinking. I know it's not easy . . .[77]

Other Communists were less understanding, and saw the Russians as imperialists, pure and simple. For Milovan Djilas, a leader of the Yugoslav Communists, the Russian response to complaints about Red Army behaviour displayed 'arrogance and a rebuff typical of a big state towards a small one, of the strong toward the weak'.[78]

It was, however, by no means clear in 1945 that the Popular Fronts would be so short-lived. Their development depended on local circumstances. In Poland, it was clear before the War ended that Stalin was determined to impose a decisive Communist influence. Mistrusting the London-based Polish government, he sent Moscow-based Polish Communists with the Red Army to set up a government in Lublin, recognized by the USSR. The Soviets then systematically repressed all elements of the non-Communist resistance.[79] Even so, Communist control did not mean the imposition of the full Soviet system – plans, collectivization and the end of all independent organizations. This did not happen in most of Central and Eastern Europe until 1947–9.

In Eastern Germany, similarly, the decisive role of the Red Army ruled out the creation of a serious Popular Front. Communists led by Walter Ulbricht, amongst others, were flown in from the Hotel Lux, and told to forge alliances with the Social Democratic Party (SPD). However, the army itself was the main authority in the Soviet zone, and as the revived German Communist Party failed to establish itself, the Russians forced a 'merger' between the two parties, to create a Communist-dominated Socialist Unity Party (SED). The Russians increasingly ruled through the Communists, who were widely regarded as their stooges.

In Romania, the Soviets had hoped that their moderate social policies, and willingness to work with those parts of the elite untainted with pro-German sympathies, would win over local opinion. Yet liberals, socialists and elites resisted Soviet demands and were reluctant to work with Communists, some of whom were pushing for radical land redistribution. The Popular Front on the ground clearly was not working, and each side tried to secure the support of the great powers: the Communists told the Soviets that the West was intervening on the side of the liberals and undermining the Yalta agreements, whilst the liberals alleged that the Soviets were Communizing Romania. In February 1945 negotiations had ceased, and the Soviet emissary, former show-trial judge Andrei Vyshinskii, angrily instructed King Michael to install a Communist-dominated government. Storming out of the meeting, he slammed the door so hard that he cracked the plaster on the wall.[80]

More solidly based were the Popular Fronts in Hungary and Czechoslovakia. The Hungarian Communists, part of a leftist government, presented themselves as nationalists and did not press for radical social change. Meanwhile in Czechoslovakia, the Communists were the strongest in the region. The betrayal of Czechoslovakia by the Western powers at Munich and the victory of the Red Army over the Nazis gave the Czechs a particular reason to feel sympathetic to a new socialist course. There was also a great deal of sympathy for Stalin's Slavic nationalist project after the Nazis' imperial racism.[81] As Zdeněk Mlynář explained when he described why he had become a Communist in 1946 at the age of sixteen:

> during the German occupation . . . I lived in a state of unconscious fear. As a Czech, I knew that the Nazis considered the Czech people an inferior race, and if Hitler emerged victorious, my fate might be the same as that of

my Jewish classmates . . . The main victor in the war had been Stalin; those
in power in the Soviet Union were Communists . . . At that time I automatically considered this system better, more just, and stronger than the
one under which I had lived up to that point. I had a rather vague notion,
but one I couldn't get rid of, that most likely this was the prototype of the
future.[82]

Yet here also the Popular Fronts lost support as they were beset from
left and right. Workers and poor peasants wanted more radical change,
whilst the majority of the population feared Communist redistribution.
It was no surprise that the conservative smallholders' party won the
Hungarian elections of 1945 with 57 per cent of the vote, compared
with the Communists' almost 17 per cent.[83] The Czech Communists
also lost support. The Soviets and their Communist allies soon realized
that only rigged elections and intimidation would secure the Popular
Front's power.

The main threat to the Popular Front model in Central and Eastern
Europe therefore came from the centre and right – as it did in Western
Europe. Here, the 1939–45 War had different effects from those of
1914–18. Whereas World War I had mobilized workers and peasants in
vast armies, who then demanded compensation once the fighting was
over, the Nazi occupations had shattered working-class organizations,
already weakened by Depression and right-wing regimes; and whilst
World War I had discredited the failed, aristocratic elites, the chaos of
World War II had given local notables a new role in defending their
communities, at the same time creating a new group of officials and
bureaucrats.[84] Perhaps most importantly, the violence, which had
affected civilians as well as soldiers, had shown at its most devastating
the consequences of the social conflict that had lasted since 1918. Most
wanted a quiet, private life; they might have wanted planning and
welfare, but there was little desire for a radical transformation of society.
Figures like Togliatti and Thorez understood this, and were intent on
remaining within a liberal political consensus.

Yet the Popular Front was also challenged from the left, by a more
Radical Communism – largely in Southern and South-Eastern Europe.
Here Communists led the partisan struggle against the Nazis. They had
mobilized peasants who favoured land redistribution, and supported a
more radical social revolution. Conditions were closer to Western

Europe in 1917–19 than elsewhere: old, narrowly based elites had been seriously discredited and the Communists alone seemed untainted. This world favoured not masters of the 'war of position' like Togliatti, but militants of the Béla Kun type. In Greece, the Communists created a powerful resistance organization, EAM-ELAS, which could not reach a compromise with the British-backed monarchist resistance. The conflict led to a vicious civil war. Stalin refused to help the rebels, sticking to the percentages agreement, and the fighting continued until 1949.

The Communists were more successful in Bulgaria. Though not as large a group as in Greece, they had been actively involved in resistance. Stalin tried to persuade them to include their rival Agrarians in a Popular Front, but they only did so reluctantly, and were determined to destroy their opponents and rule alone.[85] The Bulgarian Communists' room for manoeuvre was, however, limited by the occupying Red Army. Tito's Yugoslav Communists, in contrast, had liberated the country themselves, and were in a stronger position to ditch the Popular Front. They also had the confidence to challenge Stalin's unrevolutionary but politically overbearing model of Communism.

Tito's friend-turned-enemy, Milovan Djilas, began his work on Tito's life with the sentence: 'Tito was born a rebel.'[86] Tito came from a family of respectable, though indebted Croatian peasants, and he was proud of their history of rebellion against the Hungarian gentry.[87] He was a charismatic man with a quick intellect and a dandyish style – as a child he wanted to be a tailor. He was, however, apprenticed to a locksmith. As a youth he travelled around Europe looking for work, ending up in the Daimler-Benz factory south of Vienna, where he mutilated his finger in an accident – a badge of his working-class origins. However, as with so many Communists of his generation, it was the Great War and the Bolshevik revolution that radicalized him. Like Béla Kun, he was drafted into the Austro-Hungarian army, taken prisoner by the Russians, and joined the Red Guards in Russia during the revolution. He then returned to Yugoslavia, where he joined the Communist party, was imprisoned in 1928 and tortured, and on his release became an organizer for the Comintern in the Balkans. He spent some time in Moscow ensconced in the Hotel Lux, and gave lectures at the Lenin School on trade unionism. One of his tasks was to organize the (illegal) transport of volunteers to fight in Spain. He based his office in Paris. Fighters could secure visas on the pretext of seeing the 1937 Exposition, and it was then easy to smuggle them into Spain. Later in 1937, he benefited from Stalin's purge of the Comintern, and was appointed head of the Yugoslav Communist Party. From this position he led the resistance to the Germans.

According to Djilas, admittedly not a neutral observer, Tito 'was conspicuously without a[ny] particular talent except one – political'.[88] But Djilas was willing to concede that this sole talent was a powerful one. Tito was not a deep thinker. Despite reading basic Marxist texts in prison and in the Comintern school in Moscow, he was weak on ideological issues and was embarrassed by his poor education. Nor was he a rousing speaker. But his strength lay in his self-belief, energy and charisma. He identified wholly with the Communist cause, partly because he was steeped in the Comintern's culture. As Djilas remembered, with some condescension, his 'speech and delivery overflowed with clichés and concepts inherited from Marxism and folk wisdom'.[89] But Tito also saw Communism as a system for the aspirational and ambitious: it helped lowly people like himself to better themselves.

> In the Communist messianic historical role of the working class, Tito found personal and sacrificial social meaning . . . Whenever he used the phrases 'the working class', 'workers', 'working people', it sounded as if he were talking about himself – about the aspirations of those in the lowest ranks of society to the glamour of government and the ecstasy of power.[90]

Tito's confidence and political nous helped him to establish an independent Communist regime, free of Soviet domination. Unlike rival resistance groups, the Communists stressed multi-ethnic harmony – a powerful message after the vicious conflicts between Serbs and Croats during the war. Tito also succeeded in securing international support, from both Churchill and Stalin, in 1945. However the fact that he came to power through Yugoslav, rather than Soviet, efforts allowed him to follow an independent, more radical line than other East European regimes. The 'Popular Fronts' in Yugoslavia and its satellite Albania were complete shams from the start, despite Stalin's efforts to broaden them. Tito engaged in brutal massacres of opposition forces, and began to pursue ambitious Stalinist planning and radical reforms in the countryside. He also backed the insurgent Communists in Greece.

Tensions between the Soviets and Yugoslavs were in part caused by a clash of cultures, between a young Communism in its Radical puritanical phase, and a mature, more inclusive Communism that had made some compromises with the broader population. A dinner, organized by Marshal Koniev for Yugoslav Communists visiting the Ukrainian front, encapsulated the differences between the two. Djilas recounts how much the Soviet officers enjoyed the extravagant feast of caviar, roast pigs and cakes 'a foot thick', washed down with plenty of vodka. The Yugoslavs, however, 'went as if to a great trial: they had to drink, despite the fact that this did not agree with their "Communist morality"'.[91] Stalin, though, had hoped that Slavic unity would attract the Yugoslavs into the Soviet fold. As he told Djilas, 'By God, there's no doubt about it: we're the same people.'[92]

Stalin himself was less concerned with Tito's radicalism within Yugoslavia than with his threat to Soviet international dominance. Yugoslav help for the Greeks threatened to scupper the agreement with Churchill, giving the Allies an excuse for intervening in turn in Bulgaria and Romania. Stalin was further angered by broader Yugoslav ambitions in the Balkans: Tito's involvement in Albania; his conclusion of an agreement with Bulgaria in 1947 without Moscow's permission; and his claims on lands in Italy and Austria. In early 1948 Stalin engineered a series of threatening encounters with the Yugoslavs. In one letter, delivered by the Soviet ambassador, the Yugoslavs were warned: 'We think Trotsky's political career is sufficiently instructive.'[93] Yet Tito refused to give in to Soviet bullying, and the Yugoslavs were expelled from the Comintern's replacement – the Cominform – on 28 June, the anniversary of the assassination of Archduke Franz Ferdinand in Sarajevo. Neither side wanted the split. For Tito it was a 'bitter psychological and intellectual blow', which, so he believed, brought on the gall-bladder attacks that plagued him for the rest of his life.[94] Yet the split also damaged Stalin's authority in Central and Eastern Europe. A leader in the Soviet sphere had stood up to Moscow and survived.

The Greek and Yugoslav models were not a significant threat to the Popular Fronts. There were pockets of Radical Communism in Southern Europe: the Italian Communists, especially, had an important – though minority – left-wing. But the parties of Western Europe were wedded to moderation. Even so the radicalism of the Left contributed to fears that the moderation of the Popular Fronts in the West was a sham. This fear was a major factor in the transition from uneasy peace to the Cold War and the end of the Popular Fronts.

VIII

Debate still rages on the causes of the Cold War, that epochal struggle between liberalism and Communism, and this is not the place for a detailed discussion. A traditional Western account blamed a millenarian Communism or nationalistic Stalin, driven by the search for global domination; a 1960s 'revisionism' accused a greedy capitalism, desperate for world markets; but neither explains a complex reality.[95] Neither side desired conflict, but given the mistrust between the Soviets and the West, which had prevailed throughout the War, it is no surprise that the alliance broke down. Stalin's behaviour was probably most destabilizing, for whilst he hoped that peace with the West would last for some time, he never abandoned his ideologically inspired view that capitalism and socialism were in conflict, and the latter would ultimately prevail. He also behaved opportunistically, seeking to expand his sphere of influence.[96] For their part, the Americans and the British acted in ways that frightened a suspicious Stalin.

Stalin, as always obsessed with the weaknesses of the Soviet borderlands, was primarily intent on securing a sphere of influence around the USSR. To the west, there would be a stockade of 'friendly' East European states, including, he hoped, a pro-Soviet, united Germany; to the east territories lost earlier to the Japanese and now reclaimed, in Manchuria and the Kuriles; and possibly to the south an enclave in Northern Iran, influence in Turkey and the Bosporus and trusteeship over former Italian colonies in North Africa. This was a maximum programme, and Stalin realized that achieving it would be a struggle, but he was probably confident that a great deal could be secured by agreement with the Allies.[97] The United States would be given the Western hemisphere and Pacific, whilst Britain and the Soviet Union would reach agreement based, as the foreign minister Maxim Litvinov put it in November 1944, on 'amicable separation of security spheres in Europe according to the principle of geographic proximity'.[98]

The power and ambitions of the United States were much greater. The Americans were determined to stop a repeat of the 1930s by preventing any one power dominating the whole of Eurasia; isolation, as the war had shown, only allowed enemies to build up their resources and ultimately threaten the United States. A huge network of bases was constructed worldwide, and America showed its technological and military superiority by exploding the atom bomb. America was just about prepared to accept the Soviet domination of the area the Red Army occupied in Eastern Europe, but no more. If the Soviets controlled Western Europe and Japan, they might use their resources to challenge America, just as the Nazis had done.[99]

Conflicts over many of the Soviet demands strained relations between the United States and the USSR in the course of 1945, but their immediate geopolitical interests were not necessarily incompatible. On the face of it, the informal division of Europe in 1945 could have worked; Stalin won some of his demands and lost others. Truman's judgement of Stalin at Potsdam – 'I like Stalin. He is straightforward. Knows what he wants and will compromise when he can't get it'[100] – was being borne out. Stalin was indeed willing to make concessions, pulling troops out of Manchuria and Czechoslovakia.

In 1946, however, relations began to deteriorate more seriously. In part, Stalin's inconsistency, brinkmanship and opportunism were responsible.[101] In attempting to extend Soviet influence in Iran and Turkey, he fuelled suspicion of his motives and his intentions became difficult to predict; the Soviet realization that the United States would not give it aid without imposing political conditions also contributed to tensions. But an important force underlying the change in relations was the ideological nature of the conflict, and the obsession of both sides with what might be called 'ideological security' – an anxiety that made peace very unlikely.

Stalin, as has been seen, had been obsessed with this issue for many years, and it appeared especially worrying to him after the War, for the relaxation of ideological controls alongside greater contact with the West had generated expectations of further liberalization as reward for wartime sacrifices. This was something that Stalin, now fearing a possible struggle with the United States, would not permit. For him, liberalism would open the USSR to Western influences, and only a wholly ideologically committed population could resist a Western challenge. In a speech of 9 February 1946, he warned of the possibility of this new struggle. It was a defensive speech, addressed to a domestic audience.[102] But American observers interpreted it as a sign of aggressive intent. This in turn triggered anxieties about Soviet subversion and the internal stability of the United States. The deputy head of the American mission

in Moscow, George Kennan, wrote his highly influential 'Long Tele-
gram' less than a fortnight after the speech, arguing that Stalin planned
to 'roll back' American influence through Communist subversion in the
West. Stalin, he suggested, might not be an ideological fanatic, but he
was a security fanatic; he had a 'neurotic view of the world affairs',
fuelled by a 'traditional and instinctive' Russian sense of insecurity,
intensified by Communist ideology and an 'Oriental secretiveness and
conspiracy'. Stalin's USSR was bound to launch a sustained campaign
to destabilize the West, and its main weapon was a network of collaborators within Western Communist parties:

> Efforts will be made ... to disrupt national self-confidence, to hamstring
> measures of national defense, to increase social and political unrest, to
> stimulate all forms of disunity ... poor will be set against rich, black against
> white, young against old, newcomers against established residents etc.[103]

America had to respond by 'containing' Soviet power within its current
borders, whilst preserving ideological unity and confidence within the
United States.

Kennan's analysis of Stalin's thinking in early 1946 exaggerated
Moscow's ambitions in Western Europe. Stalin and the Western Communist parties remained committed to Popular Fronts even as relations
between the two sides deteriorated. The Soviets did not support the
radicals in Greece and were unhappy about Yugoslav pretensions. But
the Americans' anxieties were understandable. From their perspective,
Communism was on the march throughout the world – in Europe and
Asia. They might not be able to do anything about Eastern Europe, but
the USSR had to be contained within its sphere of influence. And as
Western Europe suffered from economic collapse after the War, the
Truman administration became increasingly worried about the West's
ideological security.[104] Conditions in the winter of 1946–7 were bad
(though not catastrophically so), and American officials warned that
unless the United States provided aid and support, Communists would
exploit the disillusionment. According to the newly founded Central
Intelligence Agency (CIA) in September 1947, 'the greatest potential
danger to U.S. security' lay in the 'possibility of the economic collapse
of Western Europe and of the consequent accession to power of elements subservient to the Kremlin'.[105] Communists were particularly
strong in Italy. Once they came to power, it was feared, they would use

the unscrupulous bullying tactics they were employing in Eastern Europe. What the Soviets had failed to achieve by force of arms they might gain by internal subversion.

The new American attitude further strengthened hard-line opinion within the Soviet leadership, including Stalin's.[106] Their suspicions seemed to be borne out when Truman began to challenge Communism in the Western sphere of influence from early 1947, and in the more radical South, this included military force. Congress was asked for aid to Greece and Turkey and the 'Truman Doctrine' promised American support for all 'free peoples', throughout the world, 'who are resisting attempted subjugation by armed minorities or by outside pressures'.[107] In 1948 plans were also made for a military intervention in Italy if the Popular Front won the elections. Secret paramilitary groups were to be supported and Sicily and Sardinia occupied.[108] But, in general, the Americans relied on the carrot rather than the stick. In 1946 Kennan himself had described Communism as a 'malignant parasite which feeds only on diseased tissue', and which could best be challenged by 'courageous and incisive measures' to 'solve internal problems'.[109] This was the principle that lay behind the European Recovery Program, better known as the Marshall Plan, announced in June 1947.

The Marshall planners were learning the lessons of the failures of laissez-faire free markets in the 1920s and nationalistic protectionism in the 1930s. To avoid a new Nazism, Washington elites believed international cooperation and free trade were essential. Also, the prosperity of the United States demanded European, and especially German markets. These economies therefore had to be restored through massive injections of aid, and protectionism resisted. But at the same time, the Marshall planners were trying to reconstruct Western Europe along more leftist lines. Pure free-market capitalism, they were convinced, would only push workers into the arms of the Communists. The working class, which had remained so marginalized and insecure in the 1920s, had to be absorbed into the political system and given higher living standards. The Marshall aiders' goal was a functioning market economy, but they were convinced that only state regulation and collaboration between labour and capital would create it. They therefore involved trade unions, as well as employers, in the planning; if both capital and labour were committed to growth and high living standards for all, they argued, the old class struggles of the past could be overcome.[110]

The Marshall Plan was part of a general move towards a more regulated and egalitarian economic system, and at home Truman was determined to expand the welfare benefits of the New Deal, whilst increasing the military preparedness of the United States. The result was a new, massively expanded 'military-welfare state'.[111] Internationally, too, statist principles were to operate in a new financial system established at the Bretton Woods conference of 1944. Efforts were made to return to the global markets of the pre-1914 era, but without unregulated capitalism and the discredited gold standard, which had put so many restrictions on wages and economic growth in the 1920s. The Americans ran a system of fixed exchange rates, with the dollar at the centre, whilst a new institution – the International Monetary Fund (IMF) – was established to help states in temporary financial difficulties. This was, then, a highly controlled system in which states had the whip hand, not private banks. It was remarkably successful in reviving the economies of the 'West' (including Japan), but it was founded on an implicit bargain: the United States secured powerful allies in the war against Communism, but at the cost of helping to build up their domestic industries and to compete in world markets. In the longer term, America's competitors – and especially its former enemies, Germany and Japan – benefited at the superpower's expense. But immediately after the war, the United States, massively wealthier than the rest of the world, could afford the deal. America was building a set of alliances, the so-called 'Free World', strong and wealthy enough to resist Communism.

Marshall Aid was not as important economically as its cheerleaders claimed; nor was the European economic crisis as dire as the Americans thought. But the Plan had a profound political impact. It forced Western Europeans to choose between capitalism and Communism. And it showed that capitalism had changed: it was finally trying to end European social conflict by making serious concessions to the working class. Liberals were now offering an attractive alternative to the Popular Front – a coalition that included reformist socialists but excluded Communists.

The Marshall Plan put all Communists, including the Soviets, on the defensive. They knew it would be popular, but it came with strings attached, and Moscow rightly saw it as a mechanism that would pull Central and Eastern Europe into an American economic sphere of influence. The Americans offered participation to everybody, including the

Russians and East Europeans, and initially Molotov thought that the Soviets might be able to neutralize Marshall Aid, detaching it from American leadership. But when he discovered that this was impossible, he and Stalin concluded that America was determined to destroy Soviet influence in its buffer states.[112] The Czechoslovak Popular Front's enthusiastic reception of the Marshall Plan only proved to Stalin that it was designed to lure East Europeans out of the Soviet camp. The Czechoslovak Communist Prime Minister, Klement Gottwald, was summoned to Moscow and angrily instructed to denounce the Marshall Plan, as were all Communist parties and all other countries under Soviet control (except partitioned Austria).

The Marshall Plan was decisive for Stalin, and convinced him that the emergence of two blocs was unavoidable.[113] America, he concluded, was trying to revive German industrial power and use it to build an anti-Soviet coalition in Europe. In response he decided that Soviet security required the sovietization of Central and Eastern Europe. He let local Communists off their leashes, and the Popular Fronts were destroyed, one by one – most dramatically in the 'Prague coup' of February 1948, when Gottwald forced Beneš to accept a single-party Communist government. Local Communists had no qualms about abandoning democracy. Jakub Berman justified the Communists' undemocratic behaviour decades later, when the Communists themselves were being challenged by the Polish Solidarity trade union:

> you can also accuse us of having been in the minority, and yes, we were. And so what? . . . That doesn't mean anything! Because what does the development of mankind teach us? It teaches us first of all that it was always the minority, the avant-garde, that rescued the majority, often against the will of that majority . . . Let's admit it honestly: who organized the uprisings in Poland? A handful of people. That's simply the way history is made.[114]

As Berman makes clear, many of the Stalinist leaders were true believers, convinced that the Soviet system was best for their countries. They were eager for the rapid transition to socialism. Most of the new leaders, the 'little Stalins' of the new order, had spent a good deal of time in the Hotel Lux and other Comintern establishments: Poland's Bolesław Bierut, Czechoslovakia's Klement Gottwald, Hungary's Mátyás Rákosi and Bulgaria's Vulko Chervenkov – Dimitrov's brother-in-law – had all spent long periods in exile in Moscow. Only two were 'locals': Romania's Gheorghe Gheorghiu-Dej, a railway engineer who helped to lead the party from a Romanian prison cell, and the now pro-Soviet Albania's Enver Hoxha, a teacher educated at the University of Montpellier, forced to become a tobacconist when sacked by the Italian occupying forces.

This group of Communist leaders was joined in October 1949 by Walter Ulbricht, another Hotel Lux resident, who led the new East German state, the German Democratic Republic (GDR). Germany and Austria had been split into occupation zones after the war, and the Americans, British and French had precipitated the formal division of Germany in June 1948 by announcing plans to create a separate West German state out of their zones, introducing a new currency. Stalin had responded by cutting off Berlin – a jointly administered city within the Soviet zone – in an attempt to force the Allies to back down. Between then and the following May the Allies organized a massive airlift to keep West Berlin from starving. But Stalin was ultimately not prepared to go to war and his bullying tactics failed. Germany, the centre of the struggle between classes in the 1920s, by the 1940s had become the cockpit of the struggle between systems.

Stalin was determined to mobilize his new empire to meet the Western threat. Central and Eastern Europe's economies were to be rebuilt according to the Soviet model of the late 1920s and 1930s. Agriculture was to be collectivized, heavy industry built and consumption squeezed. Popular Front moderation was over. Governments drew up five-year plans in all of the Soviet satellites in 1949–50, and as in the Soviet Union, this policy was combined with 'class struggle' against kulaks and the bourgeoisie.

The end of the Popular Fronts, and the creation of a Communist empire in Central and Eastern Europe, was confirmed at the founding conference of the Cominform in the Polish town of Szklarska Poręba in September 1947. Purportedly an organization for sharing information between Communist parties, it was not designed to be a successor to the Comintern, spreading international revolution. Rather it included only the East European parties and a few strategically important West European parties, and was to subject them to the dictates of Soviet foreign policy.[115] Stalin had become convinced that the relatively loose supervision over European Communist parties had to end. He knew that his demands would be unpopular amongst national parties, and he kept the purpose of the meeting secret. The Polish leader Gomułka made his dissatisfaction clear, but he had little effect. Parties were to be subjected to stricter supervision, and were to mobilize against the American threat. The Popular Fronts were dead, and in their place was a new doctrine of international struggle between 'two camps' – the capitalist and the socialist.[116]

In the East, the Marshall Plan damaged the Communists, but they could rely on force to keep them in power. In the West, Communists just had to do their best in very adverse circumstances. Even though the French and Italian parties were becoming powerful political forces in 1946 and early 1947, Cold War tensions undermined their position. In May 1947 they were expelled from the coalition governments, and the Cominform then commanded them to take a more militant line, not to foment revolution but to mobilize opinion against American influence.[117] In 1947, Stalin called on them to organize strikes, and the following year they were told to take part in 'peace' coalitions against the United States. The Communist parties were inevitably damaged by the new line. The Italian Communist leadership, which stood to do very well in the 1948 elections, hoped that the Soviets would take a softer line on the Plan or to offer their own aid as an answer to Marshall.[118] But the Soviets ignored them. As the Italians understood, the Marshall Plan and the Americans would play a central part in the Christian Democrats' election campaign. General Marshall himself threatened that all aid would be cut off in the event of a Communist victory, and the Catholic Church mobilized Italian-Americans to write over a million letters both to family members and to total strangers, warning of the Communist threat. The Prague coup proved to be the final straw in frightening voters away from Communism, and the Christian Democrats soundly defeated the leftist bloc. The Italian Communist Party remained the largest leftist party, but, like its French sister party, it would be banished from the corridors of power for several decades. The Finnish party was the last to leave government, in 1948.

IX

On May Day 1950 a group of men in quasi-military garb, wearing armbands decorated with red stars, seized control of a small Wisconsin mill-town, Mosinee. They set up roadblocks and arrested the town's mayor, Ralph Kronenwetter, dragging him from his bed at gunpoint, clad in polka-dot pyjamas and dressing-gown. The mayor accepted his defeat, and urged his fellow townspeople to surrender, standing in the newly named 'Red Square' on a platform emblazoned with the slogan 'The State Must Be Supreme Over The Individual'. The leader of the insurgents, the derby-hatted Commissar Kornfeder, then declared Mosinee a part of the 'USSA' (United Socialist States of America), and issued a decree nationalizing industry, abolishing all political parties except for the Communists, and banning all civic and church organizations.[119]

This was Communism American-style – though a Communism staged by the conservative veterans' organization, the fiercely anti-Soviet American Legion, rather than the CPUSA. The citizens of Mosinee had to suffer the torments of Communism for one day only. They were participants in one of the many political pageants of the era staged to demonstrate the dangers of the Communist threat. Out-of-town Legionnaires, dressed as Communists, deliberately 'unfamiliar' to locals, invaded Mosinee. After hearing a speech in which their leader declared 'we count the hours when the poor and downtrodden workers will rise and overthrow the whole rotten regime of the United States!', they embarked on their campaign of repression. Recalcitrants – including three nuns – were put in 'concentration camps'; libraries were purged; the film *Guilty of Treason*, a drama about the show trial of the Hungarian Cardinal Mindszenty running at the local cinema, banned. Other, more commonplace aspects of the American way of life were also disrupted: sports fields were 'confiscated', restaurants served only black bread and potato soup, and the price of suits and coffee more than quintupled. Rationing was enforced, and the *Milwaukee Journal* showed a six-year-old looking dolefully at a shop-sign that read 'Candy for Communist Youth Members Only'.

The Mosinee occupation was organized by Legion officials, but ex-Communists also played a leading role. Joseph Kornfeder was an immigrant tailor of Slovak origin, who had been a Communist between 1919 and 1934 and had been trained at the Lenin School. He was joined in the performance by Ben Gitlow, a former General Secretary of the CPUSA who had been purged during Stalin's anti-rightist campaigns of the late 1920s. Mayor Kronenwetter, a Democrat, was initially unhappy about what he thought was a 'Republican idea', but he finally agreed to go along with the plan.

1. Revolution in Paris. Eugène Delacroix, *July 28: Liberty Leading the People* (1830) – the classic representation of the French revolution of July 1830, and of the French revolutionary tradition as a whole. The term 'socialism' was first used in the aftermath of the revolution.

2. Marxism in Berlin. A cartoon commenting on the emergence of the Social Democratic Party as the second largest party in parliament during the elections of 16 June 1898. The horsemen of the apocalypse drown the traditional parties in a flood of Social Democratic votes.

3. Marxism-Leninism in Moscow. Lenin speaks at the unveiling of a memorial to Marx and Engels in Voskresenkaia Square, Moscow, November 1918.

4. Ten Days that Shook the World. Sergei Eisenstein's mythic 'reconstruction' of the storming of the Winter Palace in 1917, in his film *October*, 1928.

5. Red Cavalry. 'On Your Horse, Proletarian!' Russian civil war poster, 1919.

6. Communist famine. Starvation in 1921, partly caused by Bolshevik grain requisitions.

7. The revolution spreads westwards. Lenin points to the West, above the slogan, 'A Spectre Haunts Europe, the Spectre of Communism'.

8. *Death to World Imperialism*, by Dimitry Moor, 1919. Workers and soldiers struggle for power while the monster of imperialism stifles the world economy.

9. A modern utopia. Model of the monument to the Third International, by Vladimir Tatlin, 1920. Never built, and probably unbuildable, it was designed as a headquarters for the Comintern and became an icon of constructivist architecture.

10. The French example. Ho Chi Minh speaking at the Congress of Tours, 25 December 1920, where the French Communist Party was founded. Ho was one of many Communists of the developing world who joined the French party.

11. 'International Red Aid' poster, condemning 'imperialist terror' in French Indochina and calling for a 'workers' enquiry'.

12. Guerrillas in Asia. A young Mao speaking before his fighters.

14. In 1935, Stalin is much larger than anybody else, and the message is more elitist. The slogan reads: 'Cadres decide everything' – it is now officials and particular heroic workers who are being glorified.

13. The changing image of Stalin. In this poster of 1931 Stalin is the same size as the workers he is marching with. The slogan reads: 'The reality of our programme is living people, it's you and us together'.

15. In 1952, Stalin is alone in the poster, in front of one of his 'wedding-cake' buildings. It reads: 'Glory to the Great Stalin, Architect of Communism'.

16. 'Criticism and self-criticism'. A Soviet cartoon of 1931 encouraging workers to denounce their bosses. It tells the story of a worker whose tools are broken and who finds there are no spare parts. The shortages are blamed on a Soviet bureaucrat, who is advised by a sinister bourgeois specialist with a moustache.

17. The Gulag. Prisoners work on the White Sea–Baltic canal, the first major project built by forced labour, between 1931 and 1933. Tens of thousands died in its construction.

18. The collective farm. A propaganda photograph of happy peasants marching, shoeless, to the collective farm.

19. Moscow's favourite little brother. A Red Army soldier shakes hands with a German worker in this German Communist poster. The slogan reads: 'The Soviet Union, Ten Years' (1928).

20. Civil war. Members of the English 'Tom Mann' International Brigade, fighting in Spain, pose before their red flag. Barcelona, 1936.

21. The war of ideologies. The German and the Soviet pavilions face each other at the Paris exposition of 1937, either side of the Eiffel Tower.

LES HOMMES DES TRUSTS
ONT VENDU LA FRANCE A HITLER
ILS ONT LIVRÉ SON PEUPLE A L'ENNEMI,
ILS ONT RAMASSÉ DES MILLIARDS SUR LES CHARNIERS

IMPOSONS LA CONFISCATION DE LEURS BIENS
LA NATIONALISATION DE LEURS ENTREPRISES
**VIVE LA REPUBLIQUE
VIVE LA FRANCE**
LE PARTI COMMUNISTE FRANCAIS

22. Communist anti-fascism. A
French Communist poster of 1946
presents businessmen as Nazi
collaborators and calls for the
nationalization of their firms. The
text reads: 'The cartel businessmen
sold France to Hitler'.

23. Communism in Italy. Communist
sympathizers in a Turin factory during
the 1948 election campaign, which the
Communists lost.

24. Communist occupation.
A Russian woman
policeman directs traffic
at the Brandenburg Gate,
shortly after the Red Army
entered Berlin in 1945.

The following month, a strikingly similar drama was shown – this time in the cinemas of the USSR. Mosfilm's *Conspiracy of the Doomed* was set in a generic East European country ruled by a multi-party Popular Front.[120] Again, a foreign-led conspiracy to stage a political revolution was at the centre of the story. This time, though, the Americans were the villains. MacHill, the outwardly charming but cynical American ambassador, leads a sinister coalition intent on removing the Communists from government and forcing the country to join the Marshall Plan. His collaborators include the Social Democrats (as MacHill gloats: 'I've overthrown so many governments with the help of the Social Democrats'); the Vatican and Cardinal Birnch (modelled on Mindszenty); the treacherous Cristina, head of the right-wing Christian Unity Party; Tito's untrustworthy ambassador; and an American vamp, the Chicago journalist Kira Reichel. They hatch a number of dastardly plots: to assassinate the heroine of the film, the Communist Deputy Prime Minister Hanna Likhta; to bribe the population with the baubles of American culture (a 'peace train' arrives, complete with jazz band and advertisements for Lucky Strike cigarettes); and to organize a food shortage to ensure complete dependence on the West. But the Communists fight the coup, mobilizing the masses against the insidious dollar, in defence of moral virtue and national independence. They storm the parliament and drive out MacHill together with the reactionary parties, crying, 'The Marshall Plan is our death! We don't want to wear the American dog-collar.'

Both the Mosinee occupation and *Conspiracy of the Doomed* show the themes, and the flavour, of the new Cold War politics – both East and West. The era of the Popular Front is clearly over, and former allies are now deadly enemies: in the United States Communism is equated with fascism, whilst in the USSR social democracy has again become 'social fascism'. In its place, the state enforces unity founded on a mixture of nationalism and universal ideological principles: 'Americanism' and 'Soviet values'. Any threats to this order are highly dangerous. Sympathy with a radical left in the West, or with liberalism in the East, had to be rooted out, as it might be connected with sinister conspiracies hatched by the rival superpower. Political elites used the ideological war for their own purposes, but no one person created it. The new obsession with ideological security explains the bizarre obsession with spies and conspiracies. And the outcome of that obsession was a lengthy interlude in the European 'civil war'. Internal struggles between classes had been recast as conflicts between geopolitical blocs.

Both sides, then, tried to discipline society and mobilize it for the new ideological war.[121] But the effect of that mobilization was much greater in the Soviet bloc than in the West, and the balance between repression and persuasion varied. Repression was by far the most intense in the Soviet bloc, as will be seen in Chapter Seven. In the Western sphere, it involved most violence in Southern Europe. The American-backed monarchists in Greece and the authoritarian Spanish regime used force to suppress Communists, whilst Italy in the late 1940s saw harsh police repression of the left.[122]

In America itself, Communists were discriminated against, not repressed, and some 10,000–12,000 Communists, real or alleged, lost their jobs.[123] Three months before the Mosinee invasion, Wisconsin's own senator, the Catholic Irish-American Joe McCarthy, had delivered his first famous speech claiming he knew of fifty-seven Communists within the State Department. He soon became the symbol of the 'Red Scare' that swept American politics, but he was one of a number of powerful individuals and organizations who launched purges of Communists.[124] Truman himself instituted loyalty tests for his administration in 1947, though he disapproved of McCarthy; employers and trade-union anti-Communists removed activists connected with Communism; J. Edgar Hoover's Federal Bureau of Investigation employed an extra 3,500 people to investigate 2 million federal employees; and Congress's House Un-American Activities Committee launched 135 investigations between 1945 and 1955, including, most famously, into Hollywood.

Moscow did have a network of spies operating in America, some at high levels, and it used the (tiny) CPUSA, whose activities it broadly controlled. However, the extravagant fears of Communism in the period had more to do with fears about ideological security, and their use by various political forces, than the damage caused by spying. McCarthyism had precedents in the Red Scare of 1919–20, but the Cold War placed the issue of Communism near the centre of American politics.[125] So, although the onset of the Cold War brought with it the entrenchment of a New Deal-style economy, it weakened the American left. In 1942 polls showed that 25 per cent of Americans favoured socialism and 35 per cent were open-minded; in 1949 only 15 per cent supported it, whilst 61 per cent were hostile.[126]

In Western Europe, the anti-Communist crusade was more muted. Western Europe did not see the extremes of anti-Communist witch-hunting, and McCarthyism in the United States only dented America's image in Europe. The 1953 tour of European capitals by McCarthy's minions Roy Cohn and David Schine, purging libraries in American embassies and other government institutions of 'dangerous' leftist works like Henry Thoreau's classic *Walden*, went down especially badly.[127] Yet politics was profoundly affected by the Cold War. Communists were marginalized, and Social Democracy returned to the strong anti-Communism of the immediate post-World War I period. Some West European socialist parties still included Marxist talk of class struggle in their programmes, but in reality they were becoming profoundly reform-ist forces.

Cold War liberalism was remarkably successful in achieving its main goals: destroying the Popular Front, presenting Communism as the enemy, and providing an alternative that attracted much of the popula-tion. It proved to be a powerful engine of social integration. In Western Europe and the United States, workers were finally absorbed into the political and economic community. In the United States, excluded ethnic groups, especially African-Americans, Catholics and Jews, found the anti-Communist crusade helped them gain acceptance in a Protestant-dominated polity.[128] Both Catholics and Jews had strongly sympathized with the victims of late-Stalinist Communism: Jews, once the most pro-Communist of all ethnic groups, understandably became the most hostile when their confrères became targets of Stalin's post-war 'anti-cosmopolitanism'.[129] The Vatican, of course, had long been strongly anti-Communist, but Catholics also responded to the sufferings of their brothers and sisters in Eastern Europe.

American Cold War liberalism also managed to retain its ideological attractiveness in Western, and increasingly Eastern, Europe. The United States did establish an informal empire, but American wealth and its liberal ideology allowed it to avoid the exploitative excesses of the nineteenth-century European empires. This was an 'empire by invita-tion', the embossed card issued by both elites and organized labour.[130] In much of Europe and Japan, it could present itself as a genuine pur-veyor of universalist values, selflessly seeking to help those under its protection achieve modernity. East of the 'iron curtain', Stalin's approach was very different. As will be seen, the relative liberalization of the wartime period was soon replaced by a new form of Communism that exaggerated the paternalistic, statist and xenophobic elements of the Stalinism of the 1930s.

The ideological conflict between Communism and the West was therefore being reconfigured, from a social conflict within the blocs, to a geopolitical struggle between them. 'Cold war' between the super-powers was accompanied by a 'cold peace' within. Politics was stabilized, class conflicts tamed. A lake, once choppy, was frozen. The ice was thicker in the North-West of Europe, the USA and the USSR, more fragile in Central and Eastern Europe. It was also thinner in Southern Europe. Greece had shown the weaknesses of British and American power, Yugoslavia the USSR's.

This, though, applied largely to the global 'North'. In the 'South' – and especially Asia – the situation was very different. Internal conflicts there continued to be violent and inequalities stark. Nationalists confronted European empires, whilst highly unequal and divided agrarian societies generated calls for fundamental social change.

Neither the American nor Soviet blocs found it easy to absorb this turbulent part of the world, but as the War ended it seemed as if the United States might be in a better position to compete for influence. It was massively wealthier and had the power to project force anywhere. It could also appeal to nationalists, as it initially rejected the imperialism of its European allies: as the United States National Security Council explained, '19th-century imperialism' was no longer acceptable because it was 'an ideal culture for the breeding of the Communist virus'.[131]

The post-war Soviet Union, meanwhile, was poorly equipped to spread its influence in this newly radicalized world. The Comintern's strategy since the revolution had largely been aimed at Europe: the Popular Front had been fashioned to appeal to European left-liberals, and the Cominform was entirely focused on Europe. Meanwhile Stalin's approach to the developing world was founded on a mixture of *realpolitik* and scepticism about the readiness of agrarian non-European societies to achieve socialism in the near future. He did not want to encourage independent Communists in their revolutionary ambitions, partly because they might challenge Moscow's pre-eminence, partly because they might alienate the Western powers and undermine the wartime agreements on the division of Europe. He therefore refused to help the Greek or Vietnamese Communists, and was also initially reluctant to recognize Mao Zedong, the leader of the Chinese Communists (though in early 1948 he became more enthusiastic about the opportunities for revolution in China).[132] His betrayal of indigenous Communists was most striking – and counterproductive – in Iran, where the Communist-led Popular Front Tudeh party (the largest in the country) was eager to take power. Stalin had no interest in an Iranian revolution, and insisted that it was premature: his objective was a 'bourgeois' Iranian state, friendly to the USSR and prepared to grant it oil concessions. He put pressure on Tehran, using the presence of Soviet troops in the North and support for the Azeri independence movement, and the Tudeh was forced to follow the Soviet line. Stalin's policy, however, was a spectacular failure, destroying the prospects of Communist influence. The Americans put pressure on the Soviets to withdraw their troops, and by 1947 the Tudeh had been banned and the Shah was moving into the American orbit.

In East and South-East Asia, however, Stalin had less direct power, whilst the local Communists were more confident. There Communist parties had melded the Soviet tradition with indigenous ideas, stressing the anti-imperialist elements of Lenin's and Stalin's legacy. And it was this synthesis that was to give Communism a new lease of life. In the West, Communism had found fertile soil largely in tension between social classes. In Russia, Communists benefited from both class conflict and a powerful desire to improve the status of a 'backward' nation. But in Asia – the next centre of global Communism – it had emerged largely in a different context: the conflict between the empires of the West and the colonies of the South. And to understand these powerful, new versions of Communism, we need to return to the aftermath of World War I. For this catastrophic war had brought not only a crisis of Europe's elites, but also of its overseas empires.

6

The East is Red

I

In June 1919 a 29-year-old native of French Indochina, Nguyen Tat Thanh, entered the Palace of Versailles. According to some reminiscences, he wore a morning suit, but if he did it was a hired one. He was a far from eminent figure, working as a retoucher of photographs and fake Chinese antiques. In his hands he held a petition, which he hoped to deliver to President Wilson and his fellow peace-makers. Entitled 'The Demands of the Annamite [i.e. Vietnamese] People', it was a relatively moderate document, demanding political autonomy (rather than independence) for the Vietnamese and equal rights with their French imperial masters.[1] It was signed with a pseudonym, Nguyen Ai Quoc – 'Nguyen the Patriot'. Nguyen had hoped that it would be included on the conference agenda, and he had some reasons for optimism. Towards the end of the war, Wilson had championed the principle of self-determination of oppressed peoples, and although he did not explicitly mention non-Europeans, colonial nationalists were optimistic it would be applied to them. But Nguyen merely received a polite letter from Wilson's senior adviser promising to draw it to his attention. Wilson probably never saw it, but even if he had it would have had little effect. Versailles endorsed self-determination for the European subjects of the old empires, but not for their colonial subjects.[2]

Nguyen's response to this rebuff was to transfer his hopes from Wilson to Lenin. He soon joined the French Socialist Party and in December 1920 became a founder member of the French Communist Party. He then left Paris for Moscow in 1923, where he may have studied at the Communist University of the Toilers of the East (KUTV) or 'Stalin School' – the Comintern school for Asian Communists and the sister institution to the Europeans' Lenin School.[3] Within a few years he had become an important Comintern figure (a regular resident of the Hotel Lux), and had accepted a new revolutionary *nom de guerre* – 'He Who Enlightens', or 'Ho Chi Minh'.

Ho Chi Minh was not the only Asian intellectual disappointed in Wilson. The Chinese Chen Duxiu hailed him in 1919 as 'number one good man in the world', but went on to co-found and lead the Chinese Communist Party.[4] The young Mao Zedong, a political activist in provincial Hunan, found the betrayal at Versailles shattering, and set up a journal, the *Xiang River Review*, in which he published his thoughts on the tragedy. Mao urged his readers to study the 'Russian extremist party' which, he believed, was spreading revolution throughout South Asia and Korea – his first reference to Bolshevism.[5]

Yet in truth, any alliance between Wilson and Ho Chi Minh was doomed to failure. Wilson was undoubtedly eager to keep European imperialism in check, but had little real interest in colonial peoples and their rights. He regarded them as 'underdeveloped peoples', who would very slowly move towards independence, presided over by benign Westerners; he particularly admired British imperialist methods and, more generally, was a cultural Anglophile. He would not have regarded tumultuous nationalist revolutions as the way forward. Moreover, as an American Southerner, he shared many of the racist assumptions of his background. It is therefore no surprise that he acquiesced in the demands of his European and Japanese allies; he accepted that their empires should survive, and, albeit reluctantly, agreed to the transfer of the eastern Chinese enclave of Shandong in China from the defeated Germans to the victorious Japanese.[6]

Moreover, if Wilson was no radical, Ho Chi Minh was certainly no liberal. The son of a disgraced government official, he left Vietnam in 1911 and travelled the world, working as a ship's kitchen hand. Embarked on what was effectively a 'grand tour', he visited the colonial world and then spent extensive periods living in the United States, London and Paris. Already resentful of the French imperial presence in Vietnam, his experiences allowed him to generalize his critique of imperialism, and witnessing the humiliations of African-Americans in the United States and of Africans and Asians in the European empires sharpened his consciousness of white racism. By the time he reached London he was already seen as a radical. The great French chef Auguste Escoffier spotted him in the kitchens of the Carlton Hotel, and offered to teach him how to cook if he abandoned his revolutionary ideas. Ho agreed to learn the art of patisserie, but spurned Escoffier's political advice. He became involved in an organization to improve the conditions of Chinese labourers, and protested in favour of Irish independence.[7] On arriving in Paris in 1917 Ho became active in labour and socialist circles. He was a reserved figure, amongst the French at least. The French socialist Léo Poldès rather patronizingly described his 'Chaplinesque aura', 'simultaneously sad and comic'. 'He was *très sympathique* – reserved but not shy, intense but not fanatical, and extremely clever.'[8] But one of his fellow nationalists described Ho Chi Minh as a 'fiery stallion'.[9] And by 1921 he had concluded, partly (he claimed) as a result of reading Lenin's *Theses on National and Colonial Questions*, that only violence and socialism would free his people.[10]

Ho was in Paris at a time when the old order was under attack in the colonial periphery, as well as in Europe. In parts of the British Empire, the Great War had a similar effect to the one it had in Europe. Almost a million Indian soldiers had fought in British armies, whilst tens of thousands of Chinese went to Europe to work on the home front. Indians and Chinese, like the European working classes, felt that they should have some compensation for their sacrifices. At the same time, it was clear to many Asian nationalists that Europe had been hugely enfeebled by war, and the international balance of power was changing. As Ho wrote presciently in 1914, 'I think that in the next three or four months the destiny of Asia will change dramatically. Too bad for those who are fighting and struggling. We just have to remain calm.'[11]

As Ho realized, war was weakening old hierarchies throughout the world. In Europe, this took the form of social revolutions; outside it, anti-colonial revolts: 1919 saw rebellions against the British in Egypt, Afghanistan and Waziristan (in today's Pakistan), Gandhi's civil disobedience campaign in India, and the declaration of an Irish republic. Further East, the Korean March 1st movement and the May 4th movement in China protested against resurgent Japanese imperialism.

Communism was in some ways a useful vehicle for frustrated anti-colonial movements. European empires generally operated through local collaborating elites, and the Communist claim that domestic inequalities were closely connected with international injustice was a powerful one. Working classes were tiny, of course, but Lenin had justified revolution in backward Russia on the grounds that it was a semi-colony of Europe. Stalin was also a man of the colonial periphery, and was keenly aware of the importance of imperialism in the Bolshevik rise to power. The Comintern therefore soon threw its support behind anti-imperial movements.

However, from the beginning, Asian Communists encountered difficulties competing with nationalist movements that could deploy patriotic messages and fused local political cultures with modern state-building more effectively. Nor were they helped by the Comintern's sectarianism and exclusivity. Moscow was convinced that revolutionary prospects were best in Europe amongst the industrialized working class. The colonial world, they believed, could not achieve socialism for some time to come and had to concentrate on the anti-imperialist struggle, in alliance with bourgeois nationalists if necessary, with the aim of establishing independent 'democratic republics'.

The first congress of the Comintern in March 1919 had little to say about colonial upheavals. Hopes for revolution in Western Europe were still high. By the following year, however, it was becoming clear that Western Europe would not fulfil its revolutionary promise. However, the Bolsheviks hoped that nationalist movements, especially in Soviet-ruled Central Asia, might provide vital allies at a time when their own regime was so weak. The second Comintern congress in the summer of 1920 therefore devoted a great deal of time to the colonial question, and many more non-European delegates were invited. Its conclusions were reinforced by another Comintern congress – this time specifically devoted to the colonial question – held in the Caucasian town of Baku, the First Congress of Peoples of the East. It was attended by a diverse band of Communists, radicals and nationalists representing thirty-seven nationalities, most of them from the former Russian and Ottoman empires.[12]

It was in Baku that sharp divisions emerged between the Eurocentric Soviets and more radical Asians. Lenin, who opposed Popular Fronts so strongly in Europe, thought them the ideal recipe for 'backward' Asia. Communists, he urged, should forge alliances with bourgeois nationalists and radical peasants to fight for freedom; socialism proper had to be put off to the distant future. His analysis, however, was vigorously opposed by the more radical Indian Narendra Nath Bhattacharya (a.k.a. M. N. Roy). Before World War I Roy had been a member of a Bengali anti-British terrorist organization. He had then fled to the United States and Mexico, where, during its revolution in 1917, he became a socialist – converted by the Russian Communist Mikhail Borodin – and founded the first Communist party outside the USSR. In 1919 he decided to go east, as he put it, to 'witness capitalist Europe collapsing, and, like Prometheus unbound, the revolutionary proletariat rising to build a new world out of the ruins'.[13] What he saw, though, was the failure of the Western revolutions. Whilst in Berlin in 1919–20, he realized the future for Communism lay in the colonial world, and not in Europe. As he reminisced:

> Having personally experienced the debacle of the German revolution, I could not share the optimism that the proletariat in a number of countries would capture power as soon as the World Congress meeting in Moscow sounded the tocsin ... the proletariat would not succeed in their heroic endeavour to capture power unless Imperialism was weakened by the revolt of the colonial peoples.[14]

From that time, Roy resolved to open up 'the second front of the World Revolution' in the colonial world.[15]

It followed, in Roy's opinion, that Communists should not just rely on bourgeois nationalists, who, he argued, were too closely allied with the 'feudal' order. Instead they had to mobilize a potentially radical working class, which Roy insisted was developing in Asia. The argument between Lenin and Roy came to a head over their assessment of the Indian nationalist leader Mohandas Gandhi. Lenin saw him as a revolutionary, whilst Roy claimed, not implausibly, that he was a 'religious and cultural revivalist' and was 'bound to be reactionary socially, however revolutionary he might appear politically'.[16]

Lenin began to question his old views of Asia. He decided against endorsing a single strategy and encouraged Roy to write his own theses, which the Comintern then approved together with his own. And over the next eight years the Comintern followed an uneasy hybrid course combining both Lenin's and Roy's lines. Alliances with bourgeois nationalists were the preferred course, but at the same time the Comintern focused on workers rather than peasants. However, although a hybrid course would prove to be inspired, it was not this one. Indeed, it was only once the Comintern influence waned that local anti-colonial leaders, amongst them Mao Zedong and Ho Chi Minh, created a new and successful Asian model of Communism. Like the Communism Stalin had forged by the 1940s, it merged Communism with nationalism. But unlike the Stalinist model, with its hierarchy so redolent of the tsarist service aristocracy, it developed a more egalitarian radicalism and a more inclusive approach to the peasantry. By the 1930s and 1940s, this radical Communist nationalism came to be enormously attractive to generations rebelling against their Confucian heritage. In 1919 China experienced what can perhaps be seen as a cultural revolution, as momentous in its impact as those espoused by Rousseau in the eighteenth century and Chernyshevskii in the nineteenth. And within three decades China was to become a second pole of Communist influence to the East, spreading its revolution to much of the Confucian world and beyond.

II

One of the most famous works of modern Chinese literature is a short story by the writer (and future Communist sympathizer) Lu Xun. In 'The Diary of a Madman', written in April 1918, the narrator tells of his gradual realization that all of his fellow countrymen are in fact cannibals: 'I have only just realized that I have been living all these years in a place where for four thousand years they have been eating human flesh.' 'When I was four or five years old', he recalls, 'my brother told me that if a man's parents were ill, he should cut off a piece of his flesh and boil it for them if he wanted to be considered a good son . . .' Determined to investigate he begins reading histories of China, but he only sees the characters 'virtue and morality' which are rapidly replaced by the characters 'eat people'. The story finishes with the madman desperately hoping that all is not lost: 'Perhaps there are still children who haven't eaten men? Save the children . . .'[17]

'The Diary of a Madman' is a scathing attack on Confucianism, the value system that had been the foundation of Chinese culture and politics for 2,000 years. Confucianism was a philosophy of order, hierarchy and strict moral codes. At its heart was a model of society based on the paternalistic family: subjects had to obey rulers, children parents, and women men. Everybody in the hierarchy had to behave 'morally' – i.e., according to their station – and education, enormously important in Confucian thought, was principally intended to perfect behaviour. At the summit of the social and political hierarchy was the Emperor, governing through gentleman-bureaucrats who had passed lengthy examinations in classical literature and Confucian principles. Their mastery of Confucian texts, it was believed, bestowed on them the moral legitimacy to rule.

Lu Xun's response to the society he lived in was typical of his generation of intellectuals – a rebellious anger, setting the frustrated outsider against a society of all-encompassing cruelty and hypocrisy.[18] Everybody in Lu Xun's universe is perceived as a link in a rigid chain of being, forced to be both oppressors and victims. As Lu Xun's younger contemporary Fu Sinian wrote, 'Alas! The burden of the family! . . . Its weight has stifled countless heroes!' 'It forces you to submit to others and lose your identity.'[19] But Confucianism did not just provide personal misery for China's ambitious youth. Lu Xun and his contemporaries believed that it weakened China, creating a slavish and enfeebled people. As another young rebel, Wu Yu, explained: the Confucian family system rendered 400 million people 'slaves of the myriad dead, and thus unable to rise'.[20] The answer was a complete cultural revolution.

This searing cultural and political critique is strongly reminiscent of those articulated by Chernyshevskii and in some respects Rousseau. For Lu Xun as for them, the cruelty of the family and the old hypocritical and repressive order was intimately linked with the weakness of the nation. Like Rousseau's France and Chernyshevskii's Russia, China was a once-great *imperium*, now humiliated by its rivals. For centuries the Chinese state was relatively untroubled by its neighbours, and it did not need to develop the political structures and taxation system for a powerful military force. As a result, when the much more warlike European states arrived in the nineteenth century, the Chinese were forced to acquiesce in foreign colonization. The British, French and Germans secured footholds on the Chinese mainland – especially in Shanghai – enclaves where foreigners had privileges not granted to Chinese. Meanwhile, Japan, recently and dramatically 'modernized', had also become an imperial power, seizing control of Southern Manchuria and the old Chinese vassal state of Korea. These defeats had brought a revolution against the Qing dynasty and with it the Chinese empire, which collapsed in 1911. But the revolution had hastened, not staunched, China's decline. The new leader, the head of the nationalist party (the Guomindang), Sun Yat-sen, was soon replaced by the conservative Yuan Shikai, and after Yuan's death in 1916, central rule in China collapsed, degenerating into a congeries of warlord-governed regimes – an empire no more. It was in this weakened, divided state that it faced the peace-makers at Versailles. On 4 May 1919, the news that the Japanese had been awarded the ex-German colonies inspired 3,000 students to gather in Tian'anmen Square, before moving on to stage a more destructive protest in Beijing's diplomatic quarter. More importantly, Versailles focused the minds of Chinese students and intellectuals on the need to revive China. These were the people who were to become the founders of Chinese Communism.

The May 4th movement (preceded by the similar 'New Culture' movement of 1915) proposed largely cultural solutions to China's plight: Confucianism had to be replaced once and for all with a 'new culture'. Rather like Chernyshevskii's 'new people', the new Chinese had to escape from the bonds of the traditional family into a world of freedom and Romantic love. At the same time the very ethos and behaviour of Chinese had to be made modern. Just as Chernyshevskii had decried the Russians' *aziatchina* or 'Asiatic values', so the May 4th intellectuals despaired at what they (and Westerners) saw as an ingrained Chinese servility. Chen Duxiu (born in 1879), the dean of humanities at Peking University and an influential leader of the New Culture movement, urged young Chinese to 'be independent, not servile' and 'aggressive, not retiring'.[21]

But where were these models of behaviour to be found? For some, like Chen, the answer was in Western culture. Chen, the son of a minor official and himself educated for the Confucian examinations, now rejected ancient Chinese culture wholesale. The Chinese had to learn from 'Mr Science and Mr Democracy'. But others, like Li Dazhao (born in 1888), the librarian at Peking University and, with Chen, a co-founder of the Chinese Communist Party, were less enamoured of Western liberalism and science. Li was from a rather less exalted background – a rich peasant – and by the time he was at school the old Confucian examination system had been abolished. He therefore had less emotional investment in rejecting the past, and sought rather to adapt Chinese culture, not replace it wholesale. He put more faith in the 'will of the people' than in liberal capitalism or constitutional politics. Indeed, he was one of the first to welcome the Russian revolution as a model for China. So whilst both Chen and Li were to become Communists, they came to represent different wings of the movement. Chen's was closer to Lenin's Modernist socialism, with their interest in modern, centralized organization. Li's was a more radical socialism, with a belief in the power of the people's will to transform society.[22] Backward China might not be economically ready for socialism, but as an oppressed 'proletarian nation' it undoubtedly possessed the energy for revolution. Li's Romantic version of Marxism was to be an enormous influence on a young visitor from Hunan, also from a rich peasant background, to whom he gave a job as assistant librarian on his first visit to Beijing in 1918 – Mao Zedong.

Interest in socialism and the Russian path intensified after the perceived betrayal by the West at Versailles. The Soviets themselves enormously enhanced their reputation in China when, in 1920, they abandoned all Russian claims on Chinese territory. But it was always likely that intellectuals would find Bolshevism more appealing than liberal talk of constitutions and rights. They may have been rebels against Confucianism, but they were products of Confucian culture, and admired socialism's commitment to self-sacrifice and social solidarity.[23] As recent ex-Confucians, they appreciated Marxism's claim to provide a complete understanding of the world and society, and also its lofty disapproval of commerce. And, of course, they also welcomed the important role it gave to an intellectual elite: the socialist vanguard was not too far from the Confucian literati-gentlemen, spreading virtue through education and moral example.

Communism flourished amongst urban intellectuals in other parts of the Confucian world as well. By the end of the 1920s, Communists were at the forefront of the anti-Japanese nationalist movement in Korea, although they were soon repressed by the colonial authorities.[24] The fusion of Confucius and Marx was clearest in Vietnam – another region in the Confucian cultural sphere. As in China, a new generation questioned the Confucian verities of their parents. Trained at French-run rather than traditional Confucian schools, they began to criticize the old thinking and blame their culture for their weakness in the face of French oppression, and in 1925–6 Vietnam's cities saw a rash of radical student demonstrations against French rule. Ho Chi Minh, from his base in Southern China, exploited this dissatisfaction, but he also understood the importance of reconciling Communism with Confucian culture. In 1925, with Comintern help, he set up the Vietnamese Revolutionary Youth League as a broad, cross-class party. He stressed nationalist rather than Communist goals, though he also formed a secret inner group committed to the victory of Marxism-Leninism in the long term. Ho's Marxism had a strongly Confucian flavour, and he even attempted, rather unconvincingly, to reconcile the two great sages, Confucius and Lenin:

> If Confucius lived in our days, and if he persisted in those [monarchist] views, he would be a counter-revolutionary. It is possible that this superman would rather yield to the circumstances and quickly become a worthy follower of Lenin.
>
> As far as we Vietnamese are concerned, let us perfect ourselves intellectually by reading the works of Confucius and revolutionarily by reading the works of Lenin.[25]

His *Road to Revolution* devoted a whole chapter to the ideal moral behaviour of the Communist. Lenin would never have used such an explicitly moralizing language, as morality was always to be subordinate to the needs of the revolution. Ho himself sought to be seen as a Confucian 'superior man', with all of his qualities;[26] and the leadership style of this mandarin's son was in stark contrast to that of the rebellious peasant, Mao.

In other parts of Asia it proved more difficult to embed Marxism in the local culture. Japan, although part of the Confucian cultural universe, had developed a more militaristic political culture than its bureaucratic Chinese counterpart; the ideal of a world ruled by scholar-administrators who had mastered the laws of history was rather less appealing to its martial elites. The Communists also found that in Japan, unlike China, Vietnam and Korea, it was impossible to merge Marxism with nationalism. A powerful and successful Japanese nationalism, fostered by political and military elites, already flourished, and Japan had an empire of its own. The Comintern was implacably hostile to the emperor cult – a central feature of Japanese nationalism. Japanese Communists pleaded for the Comintern to relax its rigid line, but in vain, and such wranglings meant that the Communists in Japan were easily presented as foreign stooges and were subjected to harsh repression.[27]

The Indian Communists found it equally difficult to adapt to the local culture. Some, like Roy, exulted in rejecting Hindu mores such as caste, and Communists were often depicted as an alien, foreign force as a result. They were also unlucky in their rivals – a relatively liberal British imperial administration, expert in dividing its opponents, and Mohandas Gandhi's nationalist Congress party. Gandhi created a highly successful nationalism, blending a curious mix of mildly progressive though anti-modern socialism with Hindu traditions. He succeeded in forging a powerful coalition of the dominant peasantry and urban middle classes whilst retaining the moral high ground by using a pro-poor rhetoric and rejecting violence. Intellectuals with some sympathy for the USSR and the Modernist Marxism of the Plan – like India's first Prime Minister, Jawaharlal Nehru – were persuaded to stay within Congress, and remained faithful to a fundamentally liberal view of politics.

In the early 1920s, Japan, as the most industrialized country in Asia, had been seen by the Comintern as the most hopeful place to see a proletarian revolution. But by the mid-1920s, the Comintern's attention had moved to China. How, though, could a small group of students and academics, eager to transform Chinese culture, have any effect on such a diffuse society? Their initial strategy was remarkably similar to that of the Russian agrarian socialists of the 1870s. They tried to put their ideals into practice, by setting up 'work-study societies', which often involved communal living. They also tried to urge workers and peasants to boycott Japanese goods, or reform the Confucian family system.[28]

However, they found that most ordinary people were not interested, and the work-study societies were also short-lived. For many, the May 4th movement seemed to have failed. Culture and education would change nothing. China remained weak and divided; its population ignorant and deferential, its rulers corrupt and selfish. Lu Xun's powerful story of 1921, 'The True Story of Ah Q', expressed the despair of his generation. It is the story of a petty thief living in a village during the last years of the Qing Empire. He is a pathetic figure, frequently beaten and bullied by his neighbours, and he retains his self-esteem by bullying those who are weaker than him. After alienating the local gentry family he moves to the city, where he joins a gang of thieves and hears about the 1911 republican revolution. On returning to the village to sell stolen goods, he tries to frighten the gentry by pretending that he is himself a revolutionary. However, real nationalist revolutionaries descend on the village and join forces with the gentry to arrest him for a theft he has not actually committed. The story ends with the execution of Ah Q. Ah Q is China, at the mercy of its more powerful neighbours. But he is also the unenlightened poor Chinaman, pathetically ignorant of his humiliating position within an entrenched social hierarchy.[29]

It was this awareness of the enormous difficulty of transforming China that led many of the May 4th generation from a Romantic socialism or anarchism to Bolshevism. There was at first a great deal of ignorance about the ideology. When Li Dazhao wrote one of the first articles about it in November 1918, the subject was so alien that the printer transliterated the word 'Bolshevism' into the Chinese characters for 'Hohenzollern'.[30] However, what little was known of Marxism appeared extremely appealing at this time of crisis: it was committed to uniting a disorganized and fissiparous nation; it was not afraid to use violence; and, unlike a nationalism based on the nineteenth-century European model, it identified selfish elites as the main obstacle to national rebirth. On 1 July 1921 Chen Duxiu echoed Lu Xun's pessimism about the Chinese, and his Promethean frustration with their supposed passivity. They were 'a partly scattered, partly stupid people possessed of a narrow-minded individualism with no public spirit who are often thieves and traitors and for a long time have been unable to be patriotic'. Democracy was impractical. Instead 'it would be best to undergo Russian Communist class dictatorship. Because in order to save the nation, make knowledge widespread, develop industry and not be stained with a capitalist taint, Russian methods are the only road.'[31]

Given their admiration for the Soviet example, it is no surprise that Chinese Communists looked to Moscow and the Comintern for help. Indeed the Chinese Communist Party (CCP) was essentially a joint Chinese–Soviet venture from the beginning, largely set up by Chen Duxiu and the Russian Comintern representative, Grigorii Voitinskii. Formally established in Shanghai in July 1921, it sought to absorb many of the study groups in the cities of China, and to subject them to Bolshevik-style discipline. But from the very beginning there were tensions between the Chinese and Moscow. Of course, 'Bolshevization' was a fraught process everywhere, and initially it was easier than in the West because the Chinese Communists welcomed the discipline they thought they lacked. Yet the cultural differences between the Russians and the Chinese were probably greater, and the power of locality, lineage and personal networks even stronger in China, than elsewhere. Moreover, Moscow was imposing a much more gradualist strategy on Asia than Europe, so the gap between the goals of the Comintern and of the locals was bound to be that much greater. The conflict between Lenin's alliance strategy and Roy's proletarian radicalism, far from being resolved, continued to dominate Chinese Communist politics throughout the 1920s.

III

In 1923 a young Russian emissary to China, Sergei Dalin, wrote about his experiences in the Komsomol newspaper *Komsomolskaia Pravda*. 'Matters are discussed without a chairperson or secretary and everyone speaks whenever they like or feel it necessary,' he complained. Discussion was endless, and the Chinese were reluctant to come to decisions. When, during one debate, Dalin suggested that each side sum up for five minutes before holding a vote:

> They fell silent, opening their eyes wide at me, so that I looked in the little mirror hanging on the wall to see if there was dirt on my face. Suddenly, they all began to laugh . . . Evidently, no one had ever made such a proposal in thousands of years of Chinese history. Later I learnt that Chinese refrain from a final decision until everyone is in agreement.[32]

Dalin's complaints were typical, and despite the Comintern's efforts to create a Bolshevik-style party, it ran up against opposition from Chen and others, who were determined that the party remain a relatively broad church. The Comintern did not always use the best techniques to achieve its aims – some officials, like Voitinskii, were sensitive and popular amongst the Chinese; others, like the Dutchman Hendricus Sneevliet, who had had considerable experience in Dutch-ruled Indonesia, were more overbearing. One Chinese Communist who worked with him remembered: 'He left the impression with some people that he had acquired the habits and attitudes of the Dutchmen that lived as colonial masters in the East Indies.'[33]

One way of inculcating Bolshevik methods and attitudes was by sending Chinese Communists to Moscow for training. At its height, the Communist University of the Toilers of the East had 1,500–2,000 students at any one time. Its curriculum was very similar to that at the Lenin School for Western Communists, although language problems complicated things, and students had to slave endlessly over their Russian. Learning new forms of behaviour was also fraught with difficulty. Students here, as in other party institutions, were expected to undergo 'self-criticism', or 'study-criticism'. Students had to criticize their fellows, and then submit to criticism themselves. This 'emotionless struggle' would help them to eliminate bad thoughts. By the 1930s, these 'struggle' sessions were exported to China itself, and became a central part of Communist Party practice. But in the early years they were deeply unpopular, breaking with the traditional Chinese emphasis on 'face' and group consensus.[34]

However, the Soviet–Chinese relationship was not only damaged by these questions of centralization, but by a more fundamental political question – the relationship between Communism and nationalism. Chinese intellectuals were attracted to Communism because it could be yoked to the nationalist cause. It seemed like a way of reviving a weak China. But how could class struggle be reconciled with national unity?

The Comintern answered the question by following its highly gradualist line. A cross-class 'national bourgeois' revolution would have to unite China first. In 1923, the Comintern therefore decided to support not only the Communists but also Sun Yat-sen's nationalist Guomindang, which was looking for foreign friends. The Guomindang received a dedicated Soviet adviser, Mikhail Borodin, and Red Army officers taught Guomindang and Communist soldiers at the Huangpu Military Academy on an island south of Canton. Nationalists also joined Chinese Communists at the Sun Yat-sen University of the Toilers in China in Moscow, founded in 1925.[35] The Comintern persuaded the Guomindang and the Communists to join together in a 'United Front'; the Communists would become a 'bloc within' the Guomindang that would, at some time in the future, take over the whole party.

The Guomindang welcomed both Soviet military aid and advice. It even reorganized the party along centralized Bolshevik lines, underlining the appeal of the Soviet organizational blueprint in Asia. But it was divided between a left, committed to the Communist alliance, and a right, closer to the Chinese elites. On Sun's death in 1925, it looked as if the centre had won, when Chiang Kaishek, the head of the military section at the Huangpu Academy, took control. Chiang was at first a great admirer of the USSR, which he visited in 1923, and his son was a member of the Komsomol. But he never supported social revolution, and he soon found himself in conflict with the Soviet advisers and the Guomindang left, whom he believed were conspiring against him.[36]

Chen Duxiu and the Communists were initially reluctant to follow the Comintern's advice and join the United Front with the Guomindang. In 1923 Chen went along with the policy, but as the Guomindang moved to the right, and local elites began to resist social reforms, he began to press for the end of the alliance. All 'selfish' elites, including the gentry and the bourgeoisie, were now the enemy. China would only be strong and united when these elites were overthrown by the proletariat.

The decisive move to the left came on 30 May 1925. A strike at a Japanese-owned factory was put down forcibly by the foreign-controlled, principally British or Indian Shanghai police. Twelve workers were killed, and the 'May 30th movement' – demonstrations and boycotts of foreign goods – spread throughout China's cities. The events seemed to be straight out of a Marxist-Leninist textbook; the links between imperialist and class oppression seemed crystal-clear. Communism became more fashionable amongst writers and intellectuals, and membership of the party swelled to 60,000; it was on the verge of becoming a mass party for the first time. The Communists also enjoyed some success in organizing trade unions in the cities, and began to achieve real breakthroughs in the countryside. As Guomindang armies took over ever vaster swathes of China, peasant associations took the opportunity to challenge their landlords' control, which worried the gentry who were the Guomindang's natural supporters. The Communists, naturally, were eager to help.

The nationalists soon had their revenge. In 1926 Chiang Kaishek launched his 'Northern Expedition' – a military campaign to unite China and defeat the warlords. His National Revolutionary Army, trained and financed by the Soviets, marched up the Chinese eastern seaboard, sometimes defeating, but more often absorbing warlords. An important consequence was that the Guomindang became even more reliant on the gentry and the military, and more hostile to social reform. As Chiang approached Shanghai, the Communists led a pre-emptive uprising of some 200,000 striking workers, seizing power from the local warlord ruler. But in the spring of 1927 Chiang's forces captured Shanghai and finally destroyed the United Front. With the help of businessmen, city fathers, the authorities in the international settlement, and the notorious Green Gang mafia, Chiang arrested and killed large numbers of Communists and their sympathizers.

The Shanghai massacre marked a catastrophic end to the Comintern's attempts to manipulate Chinese politics, and it led to vicious recriminations in both China and Moscow. Chen Duxiu was made the scapegoat and removed, but the destruction of the Chinese Communist Party really demonstrated the bankruptcy of both Lenin's and Roy's ideas. Stubbornly committed to Lenin's United Front, the Comintern had provided finance and training for the very army that was to massacre the party. But the Chinese Communists were also guilty of Roy's proletarian utopianism. They set about organizing urban worker revolution, even though the Chinese proletariat was tiny and workers often felt greater loyalty to secret societies and lineages than to their 'class'. More-over, the Chinese Communists lacked their own military force but believed they could hold their own against rivals armed at Comintern expense. Failed insurrections in Indonesia in 1926–7 also convinced the Comintern that urban revolutions were premature in Asia.

The Shanghai massacre was followed by a 'white terror'. Communists were purged from the Guomindang, and the remaining Communists fled to the mountains, where they established Communist 'base areas'. There were over a dozen of these, but they were far from the centres of power. Comintern blunders seemed to have destroyed the Communist prospects that only two years earlier seemed so rosy.

But the defeat and the enforced sojourn in the countryside, far away from the Comintern's influence, were ultimately to be the making of the Chinese Communists. Expelled from the towns and persecuted by the Guomindang, they were forced to refashion themselves.

IV

In the winter of 1918 a 25-year-old man from the provinces sat in a crowded lecture hall in Peking University, at that time the centre of the extraordinary intellectual and cultural unrest of the period. He was listening to one of the most Westernizing leaders of the New Culture movement, Hu Shi. At the end of the lecture, excited by these new ideas, he went up to Hu to ask a question. On hearing his strong southern dialect, Hu enquired whether he was really a student, and learning that he was, in fact, only a lowly library assistant at the University, gave him the brush-off.[37] The young librarian was Mao Zedong, who had left his native Hunan and was in Beijing for a few months, before his mother's illness forced him to return home to his ancestral village. Mao was just one of many young, idealistic Chinese, desperate to take part in the revival of their country and learn about new, foreign ideas. And despite his humiliating treatment by Hu, it was in fact his provincial, rural origins that fitted him to adapt those ideas to Chinese soil far better than more educated and sophisticated students.

The parallels between Mao and Stalin are striking. Both were from lowly backgrounds, and neither had spent much, or any, time in the West, and had to establish themselves amongst more cosmopolitan and better-educated Communists; both were suspicious of the educated intelligentsia (though Mao's hostility was more extreme); both spent their youths on the periphery of great but declining empires, amidst a politics of angry nationalism, and then made their way, by a tortuous route, to the imperial centre; both were interested in military issues from an early age, and established themselves as leaders during civil wars; both were ruthless political Machiavellians; both were clever but educated only to a relatively low level in a traditional system that stressed the importance of morality and ideology, whether Orthodox or Confucian. And both had a belief in the power of ideas in politics, and were initially on the Radical side of the Marxist movement.

They were both also stubborn and rebellious, and had developed a deep contempt for their fathers. Mao saw his father as a narrow-minded, greedy tyrant, who exploited the poor; he refused to live with the wife chosen for him, and later he claimed that he had learnt the importance of rebellion from his relations with his father. Mao's interest in rebels is evident in his love of the *Water Margin* (also known as *All Men are Brothers*), the classical Chinese tale of the 108 bandit-'brothers' who fought for the poor against unjust officials – a heroic romance reminiscent of the Koba tales Stalin was so attached to. He told the journalist Edgar Snow that he had much preferred them to the Confucian texts, and often read them in class, hidden by a classic when the teacher walked past.[38] Mao himself, like Stalin, would have known of peasant bandits near to home. As the Qing Empire decayed, Hunan, like Georgia, had its own bandits: secret brotherhoods that fought the landlords.

But we should not press the parallels too far. Georgia of the 1870s and 1890s Hunan were very different places. Mao, unlike Stalin, was an eager participant in a movement of cultural revolution against a hierarchical Confucianism – the May 4th movement – and his attitudes to a whole range of issues – family, society, culture – were much more egalitarian and radical than his elder comrade's.

Whilst Mao shared Stalin's sardonic sense of humour and his use of coarse language, he was reserved amongst his peers. People who met him saw an intense, private figure. As the American writer and *Manchester*

Guardian correspondent Agnes Smedley wrote of her first meeting with him in the 1930s:

> His dark, inscrutable face was long, the forehead broad and high, the mouth feminine. Whatever else he might be, he was an aesthete . . . As [the military leader] Zhu [De] was loved, Mao Zedong was respected. The few who came to know him best had affection for him, but his spirit dwelt within itself, isolating him. In him was none of the humility of Zhu. Despite that feminine quality in him he was as stubborn as a mule, and a steel rod of pride and determination ran through his nature. I had the impression that he would wait and watch for years, but eventually have his way.[39]

When he was only eighteen, Mao had an opportunity to emulate his warrior heroes by enlisting in the Republican army in Hunan's capital, Changsha, to defend the 1911 revolution. He was not involved in the fighting, but he still faced considerable hardships and risks. After six months he was demobilized, and had to decide what to do with his life. He thought about enrolling in a police school, registered as a trainee soap-maker, and enrolled at a business school, which he left when he learnt that the courses were all in English. He passed the exams for a prestigious Middle School, specializing in Chinese history and literature, but found the regime too restrictive and disciplinarian; he finally ended up at a teacher training college, which he enjoyed, graduating in 1918.

He used his years at the college to extend his reading. At a time when China was in intellectual and political ferment, he was typical of nationalist students of his time in seeking ways to revive China. Like members of the New Culture movement, he believed that the Chinese had to shed their servile mentality. Assertiveness and willpower were the answers. But Mao's solutions also had a distinctly military colouring, and he continued to see the world through the eyes of the young soldier and reader of heroic romances. In his first article, written in 1917, he wrote:

> Our nation is wanting in strength: the military spirit has not been encouraged. The physical condition of the people deteriorates daily . . . If our bodies are not strong, we will tremble at the sight of [enemy] soldiers. How then can we attain our goals, or exercise far-reaching influence?[40]

The discipline of physical exercise – which Mao himself practised every day – would strengthen the will, and in turn willpower, combined with a proper moral outlook, would give the Chinese the strength to rise up against their imperial oppressors. Unlike the Confucian 'superior man', whose deportment was 'cultivated and agreeable', exercise had to be 'savage and rude'.[41] Mao was perhaps justifying his own, rather earthy peasant character. But he was also combining a Confucian interest in ethics with a fashionable Social Darwinism imported from the West. Mao's remedy for national decline was much the same as his French and Russian predecessors' had been: to destroy the old elitist culture and forge the people into a quasi-military fraternity.

Like many of his contemporaries, Mao began as a vague anarchist, but it is no surprise that he should have been one of the first to conclude that the Russian 'extremist party', as he called it, had the real answers. His observation of what he saw as the corrupt and selfish Hunanese gentry convinced him that any reform that relied on them was hopeless.[42] In 1921 he went though the options available to China, and argued that all models – from social reformism to moderate Communism – would fail to change China. Only 'extreme Communism' with its 'methods of class dictatorship' 'can be expected to deliver results'.[43]

Mao soon became a successful Communist party organizer in Hunan. He embraced the United Front strategy, and worked for the Guomindang in the office of its central Propaganda Department. But after the crisis of 1927, when the Communists were forced out of the towns into the countryside, Mao was well prepared to take advantage of the new conditions. His attention returned to the military, and soon he urged the Communists to build a military force to counter the Guomindang. As he famously declared, 'We must be aware that political power grows out of the barrel of a gun.'[44]

Mao also had a deep interest in the countryside and its social tensions. He was not sentimental about rural life, but, as his doctor reminisced, 'Mao was a peasant and he had simple tastes.'[45] Like other southern Chinese peasants, he never brushed his teeth, and merely rinsed his mouth with tea (in later life they became completely rotten and black). Foreign visitors were sometimes disconcerted when he took his clothes off in mid-conversation to search for lice.[46] From 1925 onwards, Mao became increasingly convinced that the peasantry had to play a decisive revolutionary role. He never abandoned the Marxist doctrine that the working class and the party were the vanguard, and that socialist society would be modern and industrial.[47] But he argued that Communist strategy should be focused on the countryside, because the 'feudal-landlord class' was the main bulwark of the warlords and the foreign imperialists.[48]

Initially, Moscow took a dogmatic Marxist-Leninist line, opposing this emphasis on the peasants. But by the end of 1927, and with the disaster of its United Front policy clear, it had accepted the new strategy. Mao himself established a base in the Jinggang Mountains, before being forced to move it to the Jiangxi–Fujian border in south-western China, near the town of Ruijin. On 7 November 1931, the anniversary of the Bolshevik revolution, the first Communist state in China was inaugurated: the 'Jiangxi Soviet Republic'. The ceremony took place in a clan temple outside the capital Ruijin, the regime's headquarters. A parade was organized, which included a figure symbolizing a 'British imperialist' with two prisoners in chains – India and Ireland. Mao, standing with others on a Soviet-style podium and surrounded with red flags and hammers and sickles, was declared President of the new Republic.[49]

It was in this period that the party developed the notion of the guerrilla 'people's war', which was to be so important in adapting Communism to the conflicts of the Third World. The Central Committee of the CCP issued a 'General Outline for Military Work' in May 1928, which explained the strategy in detail: the Communist 'Red Army' was to mobilize local peasants into Red Defence Detachments to fight against local landlord militias and the Guomindang, whilst confiscating land and distributing it to the poor. Meanwhile, the party was to be dominant and would perform 'agitation and propaganda' amongst the soldiers; relations between officers and soldiers were to be egalitarian; and efforts were made to exclude the petty-bourgeoisie from the army. The Jiangxi bases were to be the germ of a Communist state, whilst supplying the Red Army and resisting Guomindang incursions.[50]

This, then, was a very different model of military organization to the conventional European one – and indeed the one taught by the Soviets at the Huangpu academy. It was paradoxically Chiang Kaishek and the Guomindang who were more impressed by Soviet ideas than the Communists were, and they tried to create a hierarchical, all-encompassing national structure to mobilize the population for military and labour service. According to their *baojia* system, all households were to be registered through a complex bureaucratic organization supervised by a mixture of central envoys and local elites.

The Guomindang's effort had some successes, and was by no means

doomed to failure.[51] But given the political chaos of the time, the proliferation of armed gangs, and the weakness of central government, its
top-down approach was over-ambitious and could easily be frustrated
by disobedient local officials. The Communist strategy, in contrast, was
a local rather than a national one, and was only likely to succeed at a
time of extreme political disruption. But it was effective at knitting
together a society pulverized by war, whilst forging disparate military
groups into coherent forces.[52]

Mao was just one Communist military commander of many, but he
became a particularly successful and committed practitioner of the guerrilla 'people's war'. He had joined Zhu De, a former mercenary and
opium addict who had gone to Germany and then returned, a secret
Communist, to train officers in the Guomindang. Mao learnt about military science from him, and together they formed the 'Fourth Red Army',
which became an effective guerrilla force. Rather than confronting a
stronger enemy in conventional battle formation, their strategy was to
retreat, luring their enemy into their heartland and attacking them when
they were far from their supply lines.

Meanwhile, Mao applied himself to a thorough sociological analysis
of the peasantry. He saw the peasantry as a 'sea' of sympathy and sustenance, essential if the Communist fish were to swim freely. But he realized that the crude Marxist class divisions of 'rich', 'middle' and 'poor'
peasants would not help him, and might even alienate the rural population. In 1930, therefore, he carried out a massive and exhaustive survey
of the peasantry of several areas, including Xunwu;[53] he itemized the
numbers of shops and the 131 consumer goods available in them, as well
as the professions and political attitudes of the inhabitants. He soon
concluded that the rich peasants were a tiny, isolated minority; the party
could therefore draw 'on the fat to make up the lean' – that is, redistrib-
uting the land of the rich to the poor – without upsetting the majority.[54]
Even so, Mao had no qualms about using violence, and organized 'Red
Execution Teams' to kill landlords and other 'counter-revolutionaries'.

Communist rule could therefore be violent and chaotic. The Communist armies that arrived in Jiangxi and other base areas were rag-tag
groups of intellectuals, Guomindang defectors, bandits, criminals,
workers and peasants. They were then confronted with the task of
imposing their control over a fractured political landscape whilst simultaneously trying to resist frequent Guomindang attacks. Meanwhile,

secret societies, lineage brotherhoods, rival villages and a plethora of Guomindang and Communist militias all competed for power.

The leadership itself was also highly divided – as was the norm in the Communist party. Despite Mao's military success, Moscow and the Shanghai-based Communist party thought him much too revolutionary and undisciplined. In 1929 the Comintern had tried to impose control over the Chinese Communists, by sending Wang Ming and the so-called 'Returned Students', trained at the Sun Yat-sen University in Moscow, to run the party, and they in turn were intent on imposing control over this stubborn maverick. They disliked Mao's preference for informal, guerrilla war, preferring more conventional military action. And they tended to favour attacks on cities to Mao's rural methods. Mao's appointment as President of the Jiangxi soviet was actually a clever way of promoting him out of harm's way.[55]

By 1934 Mao had effectively been sidelined by the Muscovite group. Paradoxically, however, it was Chiang Kaishek who came to his rescue. Chiang's fifth campaign against the Jiangxi republic was successful, and the Communists were forced to flee. The tortuous search for a new base area, which took them from the south-western region of Jiangxi to the northern region of Shaanxi and the city of Yan'an, became known as the Long March. Mao yet again showed his prowess as a military leader and the success of his guerrilla methods, swiftly re-establishing himself as a contender for sole leadership.

In future years Mao skilfully transformed the Long March into the transcendent moment in Communist mythology. Mao became a Moses, leading his chosen people to the Promised Land, enduring enormous suffering on the way.[56] In fact, Mao and the central leadership had a rather more comfortable journey than most, because they were borne in litters (though they did work on intelligence and strategy at night; Mao, like Stalin, was a nocturnal worker). Even so, the Long March was an extraordinary feat. Six thousand miles were covered in a year – about seventeen miles a day, over what was often very difficult terrain. They were pursued by the Guomindang, and were especially vulnerable at river crossings. Of the 86,000 that set off, only a few thousand reached the safety of Yan'an.

As the Communists fled from Chiang's armies, more dangerous enemies were gathering their forces. The Japanese, their economy ravaged by the Great Depression, now sought captive markets in China. Meanwhile, of course, Nazism had forced the Comintern to change its line. Moscow now pressed Mao and the Yan'an government to create a Popular Front with the Guomindang in order to resist the Japanese. Mao, unsurprisingly, was hostile to the idea. In 1936 he gave in to Comintern pressure, however, taking part in campaigns against the Japanese, but he resisted Moscow's continuing attempts to force him into a close alliance with the nationalists. He insisted on maintaining the independence of the Communist Party, expanding the Communist base areas, and following his tried-and-tested guerrilla tactics.

The Long March had enhanced Mao's prestige, but he was still part of a collective leadership, and the Comintern was still trying to assert its authority. Again, Stalin sent Wang Ming to re-establish Moscow's chain of command and to force Mao to accept the Popular Front policy. For a time Mao was under serious threat; it may be that Stalin was planning to implicate him in a planned trial of Comintern 'rightists' in 1938.[57] But Mao was rescued by renewed tensions between Chiang and the Communist party, and by the capture of Wang's capital, Wuhan, by the Japanese – Mao's strategy of fleeing to distant Yan'an was vindicated. By the end of 1938, Mao had secured Moscow's support as party leader, though it was only in 1943 that Mao's dominance was wholly secure. And it was in this period, holed up in Yan'an, that Mao established himself as pre-eminent leader, and began to forge a new radical Communist amalgam.

The Yan'an region had been the cradle of Chinese civilization, but it had become one of the most isolated and poorest parts of China. The landscape was rugged, the earth yellow. Edgar Snow, the American journalist, tried to convey the effect to his distant readership, using the common references of European modernist culture:

> There are few genuine mountains, only endless broken hills, hills as interminable as a sentence by James Joyce, and even more tiresome. Yet the effect is often strikingly like Picasso, the sharp-angled shadowing and coloring changing miraculously with the sun's wheel, and toward dusk it becomes a magnificent sea of purpled hilltops with dark velvety folds running down, like the pleats of a mandarin skirt, to ravines that seem bottomless.[58]

The town of Yan'an, meanwhile, was an ancient stronghold, far from the sophistication of the cities of the eastern seaboard, with massive crenellated walls, dominated by a white pagoda on a hill. But it was precisely its distance from cosmopolitan civilization that made it ideal for Mao's new Communist community. Mao had always been mistrustful of big cities, and felt much more at home in this provincial backwater.

Yan'an was also an ideal place for Mao to establish himself as the prophet of a new, 'Sinified' Marxism.[59] Mao, who had had so much trouble from Moscow-educated Communists, realized that he needed to establish a theoretical justification for his independent line; it was not enough to be a military leader and expert on mobilizing the peasantry. In the next few years he sought to establish an agreed party history that vindicated his alleged 'deviations', and he wrote several works of Marxist philosophy, which were to become the foundations of 'Mao Zedong Thought'.

Mao's untrained Marxism was idiosyncratic, and did not stick to the rigid, dogmatic language that was taught in Moscow. Agnes Smedley commented on his style:

> Mao was known as the theoretician. But his theories were rooted in Chinese history and in experience on the battlefield. Most Chinese Communists think in terms of Marx, Engels, Lenin and Stalin, and some take pride in their ability to quote chapter and verse of these or lecture on them for three or four hours. Mao could do this too, but seldom attempted it. His lectures ... were like his conversations, based on Chinese life and history. Hundreds of students who poured into Yan'an had been accustomed to drawing their mental nourishment only from the Soviet Union or from a few writers of Germany or other countries. Mao, however, spoke to them of their own country and people ... He quoted from such novels as *Dream of the Red Chamber* or *All Men are Brothers* ... His poetry had the quality of the old masters, but through it ran a clear stream of social and personal speculation.[60]

It was intrinsically difficult to translate Marxist concepts into Chinese; words like 'bourgeois' or 'feudal' could not just be imported unchanged as they could into European languages. The word 'proletariat' itself was rendered by the Chinese characters for 'without property class' (*wuchan jieji*), blurring the distinction between the urban and rural poor, and making it easier to treat the peasantry on a par with industrial workers. But Mao went further, and deliberately used traditional Chinese terms to describe Marxist ideas. For instance, he used the old term for 'autocracy' (*ducai*) as an equivalent for '[proletarian] dictatorship';[61] he also used the Confucian concept of 'Great Harmony' (*datong*) as synonymous with

'Communism', combining a Marxist theory of history with a traditional Chinese notion of a future golden age.[62] The works of Marxist philosophy he wrote in this period were also full of Chinese concepts. His discussions of dialectics and the conflict of opposites – though central to a view of Marxism so concerned with struggle – were also reminiscent of Daoist theories on the presence of opposites, *yin* and *yang*, in all things.[63] Mao read Soviet textbooks on dialectics carefully, but his annotations often showed he wanted to relate general abstractions to concrete, Chinese circumstances.[64]

Yet the 'Sinified Marxism' of this period was less specifically Chinese than is sometimes thought.[65] It was, in fact, a version of egalitarian Radical, mobilizing Communism suited to a guerrilla force that needed to gain the support of peasants. It tended to see the power of human will and ideological inspiration as important, and not just economic forces;[66] it argued that peasants could be as revolutionary a force as workers (although it never denied that the industrial working class would ultimately inherit the earth); and it embraced the principle of the 'mass line', the notion that the party had to practise socialist 'democracy' and 'learn from' the masses (although, of course, this was far from liberal democracy; the more libertarian elements of the Marxist tradition were absent from Mao's thought, and Chinese Marxist thought more generally).[67]

In practice, the Communism that prevailed in Yan'an combined idealism and pragmatism. It was a strongly egalitarian system: everybody, even leaders, was expected to perform some form of manual labour, and lived in the draughty caves outside the town. New arrivals at Yan'an were housed eight to a cave, and life consisted of productive work, military training, theatrical performances and, perhaps most importantly, long, intense political discussions in study sessions. There were inequalities: Mao's cave was larger than most and had excellent views, and salary differences did exist.[68] These hypocrisies attracted criticism from some of the more idealistic urban intellectuals who had flocked to Yan'an, hoping to find the radical equality they had demanded during the May 4th movement. Some complained of the absence of political principle and passion amongst Yan'an's officials; others – especially the writer Ding Ling – protested at officials' attitude towards women: despite claims to the contrary, women were not treated as equals in Yan'an.[69] Although Ding Ling did not say so openly, the promiscuous Mao, who had a callous attitude towards his many wives and girlfriends, was a major culprit. However, compared with its Soviet Communist counterpart of the later 1930s, Yan'an's culture was puritanical and egalitarian, as was fully on show in the Yan'anites' dress: men and women wore either military uniforms or the Sun Yat-sen suit, a military-style outfit based on the Japanese student uniform, and popular amongst both Communists and Guomindang officials (it later came to be known as the 'cadre suit', or the 'Mao suit' in the West).

Nevertheless, the Communists, whilst puritanical, could not be doctrinaire, because they needed the support of the peasantry as a whole. They therefore made every effort to avoid alienating local elites. The 'three-thirds' system of government allowed traditional bosses to retain some influence, giving Communists only a third of seats on village councils, with the second third reserved for non-Communist 'progressives', and the final third open to anybody, as long as they were not Japanese collaborators. Most of the richer peasants were also allowed to keep their land. The poorer, meanwhile, benefited from lower rents and taxes, and seem to have welcomed the guerrillas who were sent to live and work amongst them to improve the local economy. Yan'an's combination of ideological flexibility and activism seems to have attracted support among both peasants and elites.[70]

Initially the atmosphere amongst the Communists in Yan'an itself was also relatively tolerant. But with the outbreak of the Japanese war in 1937 and the influx of new recruits from widely diverse backgrounds, Mao insisted on greater ideological unity, and he became especially suspicious of the bourgeois 'individualism' of intellectuals from Guomindang areas. From 1939 onwards he followed Stalin's example in using ideological texts as tools to make party officials conform, ordering the translation of Stalin's 1938 *Short Course* of Communist party history and writing his own supplements on the Chinese experience. Senior officials were then expected to read and learn the texts. However, by 1942 Mao had decided that the whole party had to be trained, to 'rectify' their thoughts. Only if Communists truly internalized the ideology would they have the commitment to win the war and establish Communism.

'Rectification' was a Chinese variation on the Soviet party 'purge', though it was much more elaborate, probably reflecting a Confucian belief in the importance of moral education and correct thinking.[71] Party members were instructed to study twenty-two texts of ideology and party history, most of them written by Mao himself, which members were told to relate to their personal experience. They filled out question-naires, which asked them to give accounts of any instances of 'dogma-tism', 'formalism' and 'sectarianism', and to describe their plans for thought reform. They were also expected to denounce others in so-called 'short broadcasts'. These documents were then checked by leaders, and the group then held a session in which individuals were publicly criti-cized and confessions made. Eventually most errant party members were received back into the fold, their thoughts supposedly reformed.

As in the Soviet Union, some accepted that purges were necessary, and that their thoughts had needed reform. Dou Shangchu, a regimental commander of the People's Liberation Army, admitted that the rectifica-tion had forced him to change his old-fashioned attitudes to marriage; his future wife would have to be politically reliable and somebody he loved, not just an obedient homemaker.[72] Others found it deeply unpleas-ant. As one Yan'an veteran reminisced: 'You had to write down what X or Y had said, as well as what you yourself had said that was supposed to be not so good. You had to dig into your memory endlessly and write endlessly. It was most loathsome.'[73]

The rectification soon escalated into a more violent campaign of repres-sion.[74] This was partly because the Communists were under increasing military pressure from the Guomindang, following the effective end of the alliance in 1941, and paranoia reigned. But Mao and his own Ezhov – Kang Sheng – were also responsible. The sinister Kang – Mao's 'pistol' as he was sometimes called – came from an elite background and was a cultivated man: a poet, calligrapher, connoisseur of erotic literature and Song dynasty pots. He had lived in the Hotel Lux throughout much of the 1930s, and had worked with the Soviet secret police to spy on the Chinese in Moscow. He was one of the Returned Students flown to Yan'an with Wang Ming, and had an unusually cosmopolitan appearance, wear-ing a moustache, a Soviet-style black leather jacket, and with a preference for high black leather boots and riding crop. He also had a fondness for black Pekinese dogs and employed the chef who had prepared delicacies for the last emperor.[75] Yet despite his Soviet connections and pantomime-villain habits, Kang enjoyed a close relationship with Mao, whom he helped with his poetry and calligraphy. He soon became the head of the security service in Yan'an, the euphemistically named 'Social Affairs Department'. Kang claimed that the rectification campaign had exposed the presence of spies in the party's ranks, and with Mao's support he launched a 'rescuing the fallen' campaign, which used torture, round-the-clock interrogations and terrifying mass 'struggle' meetings to force confessions. This was no repetition of Stalin's Terror – there were relatively few executions – but the campaign, which Mao had promised would be educational, not repressive, caused deep anxieties amongst some leaders. Ultimately Mao was embarrassed by the episode and apologized for 'excesses'.

The 'rescue' campaign may have done more to damage Mao within the party than help him, but by 1943 his power was secure. After years of expert manipulation of party politics, he had emerged triumphant, and he had established a new charismatic form of leadership – the first leader to rival the status of Lenin and Stalin.[76] 'Mao Zedong Thought' was declared to be the ideology of the party, and the famous anthem 'The East is Red' was adapted from an old love song:

> The East is Red, the sun rises.
> In China a Mao Zedong is born.
> He seeks the people's happiness.
> He is the people's Great Saviour.[77]

It is important to remember, though, that despite his pretensions Mao was not the only guerrilla leader during the period, and Yan'an was not the only Communist base. Chinese Communism was a polycentric movement, and the Long Marchers left behind a number of smaller armies scattered throughout Southern and Central China which succeeded in tying down many of Chiang Kaishek's forces. Their experience was very different to that of the Yan'anites, and they were forced to adopt different tactics, eschewing peasant mobilization and relying on traditional 'feudal' and clan networks.[78]

It was the Yan'an experience, however, that was ultimately to prove most influential on the party. In future years Mao was to try to resuscitate its spirit, most notably during the Cultural Revolution, but in the shorter term it gave the party the cohesion to exploit the chaos of the war. But the Japanese invasion of China in 1937 was perhaps most crucial in delivering ultimate victory to the Communists. The Communists could present themselves to the peasants as defenders of their localities against the Japanese.[79] They therefore enlisted the support of some

Chinese in guerrilla actions, whilst avoiding head-on military confrontations. Meanwhile, the conventional military machine of their Guomindang rivals was worn down by the superior Japanese forces.[80]

The Communists had used the war against the Japanese to expand the areas under their control, but when the Japanese were defeated in 1945 they were still in a relatively weak position, largely confined to the north-western periphery of China. The Guomindang controlled most of China, including the urban centres, had the support of the United States and was recognized by the USSR, which tried to force the Communists to forge another United Front with the nationalists. When the Soviets withdrew from Manchuria in the spring of 1946, fighting for control soon broke out between the Communists and the Guomindang, and the Chinese civil war began. The Communists played a weak hand well. They benefited from renewed Soviet help, but they also had some success in mobilizing peasants against landlords with promises of rent reductions, though it did take some time to persuade them to break with tradition and challenge their landlords.[81]

From 1946, Mao pressed for radical land redistribution in Communist-occupied areas, and this undoubtedly helped the People's Liberation Army (PLA) to secure support and recruits in some areas, especially the North. Communist 'work teams' arrived in villages and set up Poor Peasant Associations, with whose help they would try to determine the class of the villagers. They would then encourage poor and middle peasants to participate in 'struggle meetings', in which they would 'speak bitterness' against, and often physically attack, their landlords. In one village in the northern Shanxi province the main target was Sheng Jinghe, the wealthiest man in the community, who had grown rich from money-lending and skimming from gifts to local temples:

> When the final struggle began Jinghe was faced not only with those hundred accusations but with many many more. Old women who had never spoken in public before stood up to accuse him. Even Li Mao's wife – a woman so pitiable she hardly dared look anyone in the face – shook her fist before his nose and cried out: 'Once I went to glean wheat on your land. But you cursed me and drove me away ...' Jinghe had no answer to any of them. He stood there with his head bowed.
>
> That evening all the people went to Jinghe's courtyard to help take over his property ... People all said he must have a lot of silver dollars ... So

then we began to beat him. Finally he said 'I have 40 silver dollars under the *kang* [brick bed].' We went in and dug it up. The money stirred up everyone ... We beat him again and several militia-men began to heat an iron bar in one of the fires. Then Jinghe admitted that he had hidden 110 silver dollars ... Altogether we got $500 from Jinghe that night.

All said: 'In the past we never lived through a happy New Year because he always asked for his rent and interest then and cleaned our houses bare. This time we'll eat what we like', and everyone ate his fill and didn't even notice the cold.[82]

As this episode shows, long-festering resentments could explode into violent anger, and peasants sometimes behaved in a more radical way than the Communists intended.[83] In areas occupied by the Communists, richer peasants were often influential supporters, and the Communists could not afford to lose them. And in Southern China, where the Communists were weaker, there was much less conflict between rich and poor. Other leaders – and especially Mao's number two, Liu Shaoqi – pressed, successfully, for a less divisive approach.[84] Liu was born near Mao's native village in Hunan, and knew him as a youth. But he was better educated and more cosmopolitan than Mao, and went to study in Moscow at the Stalin School in the early 1920s. Like Mao, he had had his arguments with Moscow in the 1930s, but he remained on the Modernist side of the Marxist divide. He saw the rational, bureaucratic state he had witnessed Lenin trying to build as the model for the new China, not Mao's sect-cum-guerrilla band. By late 1947 Mao himself agreed that class struggle had to be moderated in the name of national consensus: rent reductions could be more effective in dividing the peasantry from the Guomindang.[85]

The peasantry, then, was difficult to mobilize, and the party's propaganda, featuring serried ranks of peasants marching to power, red banners aloft, was far from the truth. Most peasants were observers of, not participants in, revolution, and many obeyed the Communists because they were punished if they did not.[86] Much more important in Mao's victory were the Communist fighters themselves. It was youth, rather than poverty, that predicted peasants' willingness to join the Communists, though the party itself discriminated against the wealthier, and by the end of the civil war the ranks of the party largely comprised poor peasants.[87]

The most systematic contemporary study of Chinese Maoist guerrillas was carried out by the American anthropologist Lucien Pye, who interviewed sixty Chinese former Communist insurgents, most of them party members and low-level officials, in British Malaya in the early 1950s.[88] The Communists he encountered were 'an exceedingly alert group of people with very active minds'.[89] Most were from a lowly background, though they were not from amongst the poorest. They were better educated than the norm (though only to school level), and were eager to better themselves. Yet their prospects were limited. Most were skilled workers, many on foreign-owned rubber plantations, and had little chance of betterment.[90] They were dissatisfied with their status and the way their superiors treated them. They were also trying to realize their ambitions in a rapidly changing world. This led them, like the May 4th generation of urban intellectuals, to question their parents' Confucian values. They were convinced that their parents' world of filial piety and ritual would condemn them to low status and poverty; they wanted to be modern. They therefore relied more on peers than elders. Friends and male comradeship were important to them, and they often had charisma, becoming the informal leaders of their peer-groups.

They also lived in a chaotic world where politics mattered. With the Japanese invasion, the lives of ordinary people were clearly and directly affected by the world of high politics. Many of them had lost family members during the occupation. They felt they needed to become involved in politics, both to protect and to advance themselves. One option was to join one of the many community associations – secret societies, clans and trade organizations. But the Communist party offered something different. It was perceived as more reliable than traditional associations in helping its members; it seemed to make sense of the politics of the time and had a clear strategy. It was modern, yet not Western and 'imperialist', it was committed to the ordinary person – people like them[91] – it was well-organized and powerful, and it promised to help the Chinese assert themselves. As one said, 'I thought their propaganda said that if I joined them, I would be like those who were running China. I knew the Communists were very powerful in China and no one dared oppose them.' Communism and the October Revolution had shown how a poor, weak nation could suddenly become one of the great powers: as another explained, 'Until the Chinese learned about the Russian Revolution, we were no good at politics and we made fools of ourselves. However, now the Chinese Communists have learned from the Russians how to have a revolution, and no one laughs any more about the Chinese revolution.'[92]

Once they joined the party, Communists felt they had influence in the world: 'It was as if I climbed on the back of a tiger,' one declared. 'It was very exciting and I had the power of the tiger; I moved as he moved.' They did not at first object to party customs such as rectification. As eager self-improvers they were happy for the party to correct them, though they soon became anxious that group criticism might lead to a loss of status within the party. Indeed, for Communists brought up in a Confucian culture, a primary attraction of the party was the moral education it offered: 'The political commissar told me he would help me learn about Marxism-Leninism, so that I would be able to get rid of my bad habits,' one remembered.[93]

Maoist Marxism-Leninism served a number of other functions for the guerrillas. It could be a source of emotional sustenance in battle. The political commissar would frequently give long political lectures before fighting started, and each soldier would step forward with a clenched-fist salute, promising to sacrifice his life to the Marxist-Leninist cause. According to one soldier, 'When we had all finished making our speeches, and I had told them that I wasn't afraid to die a true revolutionary, it didn't seem as though it would be very serious if we were all killed. That's how fierce Marxism-Leninism is.' The ideology was also seen in another way: as a special, esoteric knowledge, which showed how history worked and how to win the political struggle. The Malayan guerrillas were particularly impressed that the Communists had shared this valuable knowledge with them, unlike the selfish Westerners who kept the secrets of their success to themselves:

> Marxism-Leninism teaches one how to carry out a revolution and what history will be like. The Communists have books that tell how to be successful politically, and they let everyone read them so that if you want to help them you will know what to do. The democracies keep everything secret and tell no one what their plans are. Who knows what the strategy and tactics of Wall Street are? If I had wanted to work for the democracies against the Communists, how would I have known what to do?[94]

Within China itself, the Communists were one of a number of forces – regional, liberal, student and secret society – opposing a Guomindang that was divided, compromised by discredited elites and corrupt.[95] Massive amounts of collaboration between Chinese elites and the Japanese during the war split the Guomindang's supporters, and the party was shattered by the war against the Japanese. Nationalist administrators after the war were widely seen as greedy – imposing unpopular taxes – and unable to meet the expectations for social justice that were then so common, in Asia as in Europe. The nationalists found themselves suppressing student demonstrations and rural unrest, whilst Chiang Kaishek's attempts to strengthen central state control also alienated regional elites.

The Communists did attract much peasant and even some urban support, but their cohesiveness was perhaps their main advantage. Ultimately their victory was a military one, and it was by no means a foregone conclusion. Both sides made strategic errors, but Chiang Kaishek's were more serious.[96] He was forced to retreat to Taiwan, where the Guomindang ruled for many decades. In the spring of 1949 Mao found himself travelling from the village of Xibaipo in Hebei province – the Communist headquarters since 1947 – to the old imperial capital of Beijing. Mao was clearly nervous. He joked that it was rather like making the journey to sit the imperial mandarin exams,[97] for whilst the trip was a relatively short one geographically, in cultural terms it was equivalent to the Long March. Mao had to transform himself from guerrilla leader to master of one of the largest states on the globe.

V

On 1 October 1949 Mao Zedong ascended Tian'anmen, the Gate of Heavenly Peace to the old Forbidden City in the centre of Beijing, and addressed a crowd of about 30,000, famously declaring: 'The Chinese people have now stood up!' His audience stood in the square in front of the gate, waving the new Chinese flag – red with four small yellow stars surrounding a larger star in the upper left-hand corner. Speaking in his high-pitched voice, he announced the foundation of the People's Republic of China. It was followed by a military parade, made up of thousands of civilians, some holding portraits of leaders, others playing waist-drums and dancing the traditional Northern Chinese *yangge*.

The ceremony had been carefully planned, and every element was there for a reason.[98] It owed much to the Soviet demonstrations for the anniversary of the October Revolution in Red Square, but, unlike them, it also had a strong peasant, folk element. Meanwhile, the parade's symbolism carefully combined Soviet Communism and Chinese nationalism. October was the anniversary of both the 1911 revolution against the Qing and the Russian revolution, whilst the red of the flag referred both to Communist revolution and China's red earth. The stars also showed that the Communists were committed to national unity: they represented the four classes of 'the people' – the national bourgeoisie, the petty bourgeoisie, the workers and the peasants, surrounding the great Communist Party, all of whom were to be part of the Chinese 'New Democracy'. Mao was showing that the new regime was Communist, unashamedly nationalist, and pro-peasant.

October 1949 marked the culmination of the post-war reddening of the East. As in Europe, the end of Axis-power rule helped the anti-imperialist Communists, as did the serious damage done to old elites by collaboration. China joined two other states – North Korea and Vietnam – as part of the new Asian Communist brotherhood. All three regimes had close similarities, and differed from their East European confrères. They were created by peasant parties, operating in Confucian societies that had fought guerrilla wars against imperialist powers. Yet each state was born in rather different circumstances. If China was Asia's Yugoslavia – a Communist state born out of an anti-imperialist guerrilla war – North Korea was closer to East Germany – a regime largely created by superpower *realpolitik* and partition. The Vietnamese revolution, meanwhile, had a strong urban element, and had similarities with its Russian predecessor.

The North Korean regime was created under the auspices of Soviet troops. The Americans had proposed that Korea be divided on the eve of the Japanese surrender in August 1945, allocating the portion north of the 38th parallel (bordering the USSR) to the Soviets and the South to themselves. The North then followed an East European path: a Popular Front followed by Communization. In February 1946 a Communist-dominated central government was established, led by Kim Il Sung ('One-star Kim'). However, we should not press the East German parallel too far, for the regime soon secured a good deal of autonomy.

Kim Sŏng-ju (he adopted his *nom de guerre* in 1935) was born in a village near Pyongyang in 1912 into a Christian family. His father was a member of a Christian Korean nationalist organization, and may have been imprisoned by the Japanese. On his release in about 1920, the family emigrated to Manchuria, joining a large Korean émigré community. Kim's cultural background was therefore eclectic: he was Korean, born in a state ruled by the Japanese, was educated in Chinese schools in Mandarin, but also returned to Korea for two years at the age of eleven to attend a Christian school – indeed he was for a time a Sunday school teacher, a fact not recorded in his official biography.[99] He followed his father into nationalist politics, joining a Marxist group at school in 1929 and, after a brief time in prison, joined a Chinese Communist Party-led guerrilla force in 1931 to fight the occupying Japanese. He rose through the ranks, and became a regional commander of the guerrilla army.

He spent most of his youth outside Korea, then, but it would be a mistake to see him as a 'foreigner'. He, like many of his fellow guerrillas, saw himself as a Korean nationalist – though one fighting for international Communism under the leadership of the USSR. There were close links between Eastern Manchuria and the lawless borderlands of North Korea, and Koreans were involved in the guerrilla struggle against the Japanese throughout the region. It was in this tough guerrilla milieu – fighting against an extremely resourceful and harsh Japanese enemy – that Kim's politics were forged.

By 1940, however, the Japanese were winning, and Kim, like many other fighters, was forced to seek refuge over the border in the Soviet Union. Kim flourished during his five-year sojourn there and embraced Soviet life with enthusiasm – he seemed to prefer the culture of the Red Army to his former guerrilla life. He received training at the Khabarovsk infantry officer school, and became a captain in the Red Army. He fathered two sons and a daughter during this time, to whom he gave Russian names. His elder son was called Iurii. The man who came to be known as Kim Jong Il was known as Iurri Irsenovich (Il-sung-ovich) Kim for the first few years of his life.

Kim seems to have wanted to continue his career in the Red Army, but on the fall of the Japanese the Soviets had different ideas for him. They had begun to mistrust the North Korean nationalists whom they were trying to work with, and decided to impose a more reliable, Communist leadership; the 33-year-old returnee was an ideal candidate, even though initially he was not keen.[100] He was introduced to the public in October 1945 at a ceremony to honour the Red Army. He had been billed as a venerable, heroic guerrilla leader, and many confused him with a semi-mythological, Robin Hood-style fighter. When they saw him, naturally, they were deeply disappointed:

> [He was] a young man of about 30 with a manuscript approaching the microphone . . . His complexion was slightly dark and he had a haircut like a Chinese waiter. His hair at the forehead was about an inch long, remind-ing one of a lightweight boxing champion. 'He is a fake!' All of the people gathered on the athletic field felt an electrifying sense of distrust, disappoint-ment, discontent and anger.
>
> Oblivious to the sudden change in mass psychology, Kim Il-sung con-tinued in his monotonous, plain and duck-like voice to praise the heroic struggle of the Red Army . . . He particularly praised and offered the most extravagant words of gratitude and glory to the Soviet Union and Marshal Stalin, that close friend of the oppressed peoples of the world.[101]

Kim, then, was a Soviet puppet, but the Soviets were not interested in micro-management, and left much of the day-to-day administration to the Koreans.[102] Despite his inauspicious start, Kim proved able to man-age the factions within the party – his own 'Manchurians', the 'Koreans' who had stayed under the Japanese, the 'Soviet' Koreans who had lived in the USSR, and the 'Yan'an' Communists who had been attached to the Chinese Communists in China.[103] As will be seen, he also laid the foundations for a regime that attracted a great deal of support by forging together Communism and Korean nationalism.

Just as Korea was being divided in August 1945, another Communist regime was rising from the ashes of Japanese rule, in Vietnam. But unlike the Koreans, the Vietnamese Communists came to power as part of a genuine, indigenous revolution – a mixture of the Chinese guerrilla revo-lution of 1949 and the Bolshevik urban revolution of 1917.[104] Ho Chi Minh had always been a radical in the Comintern, on Roy's side of the debate with Lenin (though Roy did not like him), but he had become increasingly dissatisfied with the Soviet obsession with the urban work-ing class. With Mao's success from the mid-1930s, Ho learnt from the Chinese experience, distancing himself from the old Moscow template. He visited Yan'an in 1938 (though he did not meet Mao himself), and then sent two young party members, Vo Nguyen Giap and Pham Van Dong, there to a CCP school.[105]

The Vietnamese soon began to follow the Chinese recipe. They formed a 'base area' in the border regions to the North, created a guerrilla army, and in 1941 transformed the Communist movement into a nationalistic, cross-class Popular Front force (including landlords and officials), now called the League for the Independence of Vietnam – the 'Vietminh' – with an extensive rural organization. They then began to plan a peasant uprising against the French imperial administration, which was cooperating with the Japanese. Communists were told to merge with the peasants, dress like the locals, and translate Vietminh manifestos into vernacular verse. They took advantage of peasant resentment at the disruption of traditional agriculture, first by French colonial exploitation, and then by brutal Japanese exactions. Most help to the Communists, however, was the famine of 1944–5, which was made worse by Japanese wartime exactions and not helped by the French, who attracted most of the blame.[106] In March 1945 central control of the country was weakened further when the Japanese launched a coup against the French administration and set up a puppet government under Emperor Bao Dai. When the Japanese finally surrendered to the Americans in August, the Vietminh were in an ideal position in the North, with strong support in both Hanoi and the countryside, and merchants and officials stood by as they took over. In the South, the Vietminh also took control, although there they had more serious nationalist rivals.

On 2 September 1945 Ho stood in Ba Dinh Square in Hanoi, dressed in a humble khaki suit and blue canvas shoes, and declared the independence of Vietnam, under Communist control. His speech quoted both the American declaration of independence of 1776 as well as the French declaration of the rights of man of 1791.[107] Ho still hoped that he might secure American support by signalling that he was still committed to a broad, non-ideological government in the medium term; Stalin had not yet given the Vietnamese Communists any recognition or aid. However, when the French returned to the South with British help soon after the declaration of independence, nationalist groups began to withdraw their support for the Vietminh. The Communists, with strong support in the North, were soon on the defensive in the South, and by 1947 the Vietminh were fighting another anti-colonial war against a French-backed regime.

The subsequent restoration of European colonial rule after the defeat of the Japanese enraged and emboldened Communists throughout Asia. In many places they were able to exploit the economic disruption in the countryside caused by the war and harsh Japanese exploitation. But outside China, Vietnam and Korea, they were generally unable to fuse Communism with an attractive nationalism. The Indonesian Communist Party took part in fighting against the Dutch, but it had little success. The indigenous socialist leader Sukarno, who sought to combine a non-Marxist socialism with Islam, was much more able to forge such a diverse archipelago together than the Communists. The Communist Party was finally crushed after a failed rebellion in eastern Java in 1948. It was only when it adopted a less revolutionary approach in the 1950s that its fortunes revived.

More serious were Communist insurgencies in American and British colonies, though, confined as they were to particular groups of the population, they also ultimately failed. The Americans granted independence to the Philippines in 1946, handing over power to a wealthy collaborator landed elite. Its attempts to disband the Communist-led People's Anti-Japanese Army ('Huk' for short) precipitated a peasant rebellion in central Luzon. The Huks, though, were relatively few. The Americans also decided that Communism was best fought by addressing social problems, and persuaded the Manila government that land reform could blunt the Communists' appeal. The revolution was soon tamed by a judicious mix of repression and reform.[108]

The Malayan Communist uprising failed for similar reasons. The appeal of Maoism and guerrilla warfare took hold amongst the Chinese in Malaya – like the Malays, about 40 per cent of the population – after the beginning of the Japanese invasion of China in 1937; it was then, at the age of fifteen, that their future leader Chin Peng first became interested in Communism.[109] During World War II, the Malayan Communist Party, like the Vietnamese Communists, formed a guerrilla force to fight the Japanese and even received British support. But the British were soon to alienate the Chinese community, first promising them full political rights and then, when the War was over, reneging on that promise under pressure from the Malays. The Communists took up the Chinese ethnic cause, and fought a guerrilla insurgency against the British from 1948.[110] They were, however, at a disadvantage compared with the Vietminh. Their support was largely limited to the Chinese, especially the poor, excluded rural population without secure land rights, and the British, like the Americans in the Philippines, generally took a more conciliatory line than the French and the Dutch. They sought to win 'hearts and minds' of potentially Communist villagers.[111] And as well as declaring their intention of giving Malaya independence, they embarked on the costly resettlement of half a million Chinese squatter peasants into highly defended 'new villages', which gave them higher living standards and starved the guerrillas of support.

Despite these setbacks, Communists had established a powerful position in East and South-East Asia by 1950. On the face of it, they had benefited from the very forces that had helped Communists in Europe in the 1940s: they were at the forefront of a struggle against imperialist occupiers and their collaborators amongst local elites. They had also used similar guerrilla or partisan strategies, retreating from the cities into the countryside and harrying their more powerful enemies. But the outcomes were very different, much depending on the role of the Red Army. In the West, Communist parties were defeated electorally and returned to political isolation; the Central, Soviet zone embarked on projects to build Soviet-style socialism; and in South-Eastern Europe and Asia, more independent, radical Communisms emerged.

The Communist 'bloc' was therefore highly diverse – much more so than many in the West appreciated at the time. Even so, for a few years from 1949, Communist regimes, most of them closely allied with Moscow, ruled a third of the earth's population. Few would have predicted such an extraordinary outcome only eight years before, when the Nazis were at the gates of Moscow and Communism was on the verge of collapse.

7

Empire

Like Shelley's Ozymandias, all great imperial rulers have built monuments to celebrate their power, from the Roman emperors' aqueducts and triumphal arches to the grand memorials and gothic railway stations of the British Empire. The Soviet empire was no exception. Despite the removal of most of the Marx and Lenin statues that adorned (or blighted) the former Communist world, remarkably prominent monuments are still scattered throughout the former Soviet sphere of influence. The most recognizable of all are the Stalinist 'tall buildings'. These colossi of Stalinist gothic were planned between 1948 and 1953, and had Stalin lived longer there would have been many more. Eight were planned for Moscow, though only seven were actually built (a nostalgic pastiche of the eighth, the luxurious 'Triumph Palace' apartment building, was built in Vladimir Putin's Moscow in 2003). The most monumental is the massive 5,000-roomed Moscow State University building on the Lenin Hills.

Similar enormous buildings, 'gifts from Comrade Stalin', were planned for the satellite states. Only one, the Stalin Palace of Culture and Science in Warsaw, was completed (built to accommodate 12,000 people, it now houses, amongst other things, a bowling alley). But the ex-Communist world contains a number of smaller versions, from the Hotel International in Prague to the Soviet Friendship buildings in Beijing and Shanghai. Scores of other grand buildings were also built in a similar style; amongst the most striking were the Casa Scînteii in Bucharest and the Stalinallee (today Karl-Marx-Allee) in East Berlin.[1] These symbols of Communist power were the *pointes d'appui* of the Soviet sphere of influence at its most extensive, when it encompassed much of the Eurasian landmass, from the Baltic to the South China Sea in the period between Mao's victory in 1949 and the Sino-Soviet split in the late 1950s.

Moscow's tall buildings also tell us much about post-war Stalinism. Gargantuan hybrids of Manhattan-skyscraper gothic and neo-classical bombast, studded with ornamentation from the medieval Muscovite past, they combined modernity, empire and nationalism.[2] But they also indicated a politics that was increasingly emphasizing local, mostly Slavic cultures over internationalism and universalism.[3] Stalinist buildings in every state tried to incorporate, in a minor way, 'national forms' – whether Byzantine features in Romania or Renaissance motifs in Poland and Czechoslovakia. They were also designed to boost the prestige and power of élites; these offices and apartment blocks were clearly not designed to provide housing for the cramped masses after the destruction of war.

All of these massive structures were stone embodiments of a post-war 'High Stalinism', an exaggerated version of the order first seen in the mid-1930s, both paternalistic and technocratic. The remnants of Radical, anti-bureaucratic Marxism, still evident even during the Terror, had now largely disappeared. This hierarchical model was also applied to the whole of the Soviet bloc. Indeed there was something distinctly imperial about it. Of course, the USSR never called itself an empire, and it was deeply hostile to 'imperialism', which, following Lenin, was still seen as 'the highest stage of capitalism'. Unlike many empires, it did not justify hierarchy on the grounds of ethnicity but as a reflection of different levels of socialist attainment. Russians were at the top of the tree because they were the most progressive people, not because they were racially or culturally superior. In practice, however, the USSR's relationship with its satellites in Eastern Europe was typically imperial, and its politics and culture were increasingly those of an imperial state. A hierarchy of power, centred in Moscow, extended to all Soviet-bloc states; Russians had higher status than other nationalities; and socialist societies were becoming highly stratified, with the most loyal (or at least politically reliable) party members at the top. In some parts of the bloc, such a system required high levels of coercion and intimidation to keep it in place.

Anxiety about maintaining control over a USSR and Eastern Europe devastated by war and lessons learnt from the Terror all fed the Soviet leadership's appetite for a fixed and ordered culture. At the same time, fears of foreign invasion and the desperate desire to raise international status reinforced inequalities at home. Khrushchev remembered, with some contempt, Stalin's anxieties that Westerners would look down on the Soviet Union: 'What will happen if they [foreign visitors] walk around Moscow and find no skyscrapers? They will make unfavourable comparisons with capitalist cities.'[4]

According to the Stalinist post-war vision, then, top officials were to live and work high above the ordinary people – a service aristocracy of technical experts and ideological visionaries, guiding the state machine towards a glorious future. At the same time, however, the Soviet leadership hoped to combine discipline with dynamism. Alongside the tall buildings, the Communist-bloc regimes built vast squares to accommodate huge parades of supposedly enthusiastic people. Assembling the people, or as many of the people as possible, in elaborate state festivals and marches was, of course, reminiscent of Jacobin France. But the ceremonies of the late Stalin era acquired a particularly Soviet colouring. The original model was the Lenin Mausoleum – repository of the great man's mummified corpse – which served as a tribune on which leaders stood to welcome the masses processing though Red Square. Bulgaria followed the Soviet example most closely, with the construction of Dimitrov's Mausoleum in 1949 and the ceremonial September 9th Square in front of it. Tribunes and squares were also built in Budapest, Bucharest and East Berlin. Only Prague, relatively undamaged by war, escaped Comrade Stalin's generosity.[5] Meanwhile the Chinese built their own Stalinist spaces on their own initiative, with Soviet assistance. During the 1950s the vast space in front of the Tian'anmen gate podium – what is now Tian'anmen Square – was built, destroying countless ancient buildings and walls.

How, though, could mass enthusiasm be generated within such a rigid political hierarchy? The contradiction was most visible in Warsaw, where the base of the enormous Palace of Culture served as the tribune for the mass parades. This highly unpopular building, symbolizing, as it did, not only Russian domination but also party and bureaucratic privilege, was hardly going to generate feelings of commitment amongst the ordinary workers marching past every May Day. Stalin had, of course, wrestled throughout the 1930s with the problem of how to mobilize the masses whilst subjecting them to discipline, and he had sought to do so through appeals to inclusive patriotism rather than class. The Stalinist regimes therefore sought to merge local nationalisms with Soviet Communism, but inevitably the task was a difficult one.

The Stalinists were therefore left with a problem: the economic system demanded high levels of heroism and self-sacrifice from workers and peasants, but it depended on repression and harsh discipline, wielded by white-collar workers and officials. Even more than in the USSR of the 1930s, the post-war Soviet system seemed to operate in the interests of the 'socialist intelligentsia' rather than the workers and peasants. This had its advantages, as it attracted young, ambitious people eager to advance themselves and develop their countries. At the same time, however, many ordinary people were deeply alienated, as were the non-Communist middle classes. The socialism Stalin exported throughout his empire therefore, like his buildings, looked monumental, but had serious cracks behind the façade.

The balance between repression and mobilization, and levels of support, differed in the various parts of the Communist bloc, however. It was at its most rigidly disciplinarian in the USSR itself. In Eastern Europe, in contrast, Communist parties were more dynamic, for they were transforming their societies and 'building socialism' from scratch. But the violence inevitably alienated many, and the be-medalled patriarchs found it increasingly difficult to inspire ordinary people. And as the hoped-for dynamism turned to *stasis*, Soviet socialism looked less like universal progress and more like Russian imperialism. The late-Stalinist model was most appealing in China – part of the USSR's 'informal' empire – for it was seen as more effective in building a modern state than the more egalitarian 'guerrilla' socialism of the civil-war period. But here also the drawbacks soon became abundantly clear, and the way was soon prepared for a sharp rejection of the Stalinist vision.

II

In 1951 a certain Mishchenko, of the Molotov military academy in the city of Kalinin (formerly, and now, Tver), reported on the visible poverty in its centre:

> If the secretaries of the . . . party committees take a walk along the streets of the regional centre [Kalinin], they would notice that some kind of beggar is sitting on almost every street corner. It gives the impression that the centre of the town of Kalinin is beggarly. Citizens of the countries of

the [Communist] people's democracies study at the Molotov Academy. There is one indigent near the post office, who without fail seeks them out and begs. They will go home and say that the town of Kalinin is full of beggars.[6]

Mishchenko's priorities were typical of the late-Stalinist elite. Poverty and inequality within the USSR were less important than international status, and after World War II Stalin sacrificed the living standards of Soviet citizens to the needs of the crippling Cold War arms race. The Soviet Union was, of course, a victorious power, but its triumph had been a Pyrrhic one. At the end of the conflict it was at a huge disadvantage in its competition with the enormously wealthier United States: with a massive 23 per cent of its assets destroyed and 27 million lives lost, it was faced with the task of rebuilding with a devastated population.[7] Labour shortages were especially bad in the countryside, and contributed – together with drought and harsh state grain requisitions – to the famine of 1946–7 in which between 1 and 1.5 million died. The Soviet state was barely able to cope with the chaos, disorder, poverty and criminality in the aftermath of war. And at the same time it was faced with the task not only of rebuilding but also of creating a virtually new, technologically advanced military complex. By the end of the 1930s, the USSR had more or less eliminated the technological gap with Germany, but the challenge was far greater in the mid-1940s now that American weaponry had become atomic.

The USSR faced all of these tasks at a time when the 'ideological preparedness' of the population, as the official jargon put it, was seriously dilapidated. The wartime experiences of many Soviet soldiers presented a major challenge to the values of the regime. Some had fought in partisan units, where they had become used to a degree of equality and autonomy. More importantly, millions of soldiers had visited the West, and were in a position to question official propaganda. One political officer, charged with repatriating Soviet citizens who had sought sanctuary in neutral Sweden, reported that, 'After they have seen the untroubled life [in Sweden], certain individuals among our repatriated [citizens] draw the incorrect conclusion that Sweden is a rich country and that people live well.'[8] But some even claimed that they were better fed and treated as German prisoners of war than they had been in the Red Army. Unsurprisingly Stalin suspected all ex-prisoners of war of anti-Soviet thinking, and on their homecoming many were despatched to the Gulag.

Faced with deteriorating relations with the West and disunity at home, the Stalinists imposed a regime that reinforced the nakedly coercive elements of the pre-war order and depended on patriotic, rather than class mobilization. The speech which George Kennan saw as an attack on the West signalled the end of wartime liberalization in the spring of 1946. The entire country was now to be mobilized to reconstruct the economy. Problems of labour shortage were addressed by increasing the levels of unfree labour beyond those already seen before the War. About 4 million students aged between fourteen and seventeen, mainly from the countryside, were conscripted into factory jobs, where they worked for nothing but their board and lodging.[9] One of the greatest contributions was made by the Gulag – the vast archipelago of labour camps, most of them in remote Siberia. Prison labour had also played a major part in the economy in the 1930s, but the system now became much more extensive under their post-Terror boss, the secret police chief Lavrentii Beria. The whole prison system, which is estimated to have included some 5 million in 1947, provided some 20 per cent of the industrial labour force and over 10 per cent of the USSR's industrial output.[10] But Stalin's firm belief in the economic importance of the camps was wrong: they were extremely wasteful and unproductive – inevitably given that conditions were so poor and the prisoners treated so callously. Certainly, in comparison with the mid-1930s, the Gulag was more technocratically organized, but this was hardly a rational way to run an economy. In her brilliant pen-portrait of one Gulag director, Kaldymov, Evgenia Ginzburg, a worker on his Siberian state farm during the War, vividly illustrated how technocracy and a belief in the Stalinist hierarchy combined to produce extraordinary cruelty. Kaldymov, a child of peasants, had benefited from the inter-war social mobility and had become a teacher of Dialectical Materialism before an embarrassing family scandal led him to move to Siberia. Nevertheless, in the eyes of his bosses he was a good director:

> judging from fulfilment of the plan – he made quite a respectable job of running a state farm in the taiga with its convict labour force . . . [He] used to run his enterprise on a work-intensive basis, relying on slave labour and a rapid turnover of 'worked out contingents'.

He was totally oblivious to his own cruelty . . . Take, for example, his dialogue with Orlov, our zootechnician, which one of our female workers who was forking manure near the dairy farm happened to overhear:

'What about this building? Why has it been left empty?' inquired Kaldymov.

'It had bulls in it,' Orlov replied, 'but we have had to put them elsewhere. The roof leaks, the eaves are iced up, so it isn't safe to put cattle in it. We will be doing a proper repair job on it in due course.'

'It's not worth wasting money on such a pile of old lumber. The best thing would be to use it as a hut for women.'

'What are you saying, Comrade Director? Why, even the bulls couldn't stand it and began to fall ill here!'

'Yes, but they were bulls! No question, of course, of risking the bulls!'

This was not a joke, nor a witticism, nor even a sadistic jibe. It was simply the profound conviction of a good husbandman that bulls were the foundation of the state farm's life and that only extreme thoughtlessness on the part of Orlov had prompted him to put them on an equal footing with female prisoners.

In his sanguine swinishness, his fixed belief in the solidity and infallibility of the dogmas and quotations he had learned by heart, Kaldymov would, I think, have been fearfully surprised if anyone had called him to his face a slave owner or slave driver. The Jacob's ladder that supported on its lowest rungs the prisoners and near the top the Wise and Great One, with the official cadre members like the state farm director somewhere in between, seemed to him utterly irreversible and sempiternal. His firm conviction of the unchangeability of this world, with its hierarchy and its accepted rituals, could be sensed in every word and gesture of the director.[11]

Given these attitudes to prisoners, it is no surprise that millions died of starvation and over-work. Figures remain uncertain and one based on official archives – of 2.75 million for the whole Stalin era – is certainly too low.[12]

Conditions, though not quite so harsh in ordinary factories, were certainly grim, with workers much poorer than before the war; prices were raised and rations cut in September 1946. In many ways, the regime was returning to the strategies of the late 1920s and early 1930s, forcing workers to finance industrialization through low living standards, but the methods were different: the leadership eschewed populist appeals for fear of undermining managers. And whilst Stakhanovism survived, the leadership largely relied on coercion. Managers were given more powers over workers than in the 1930s and labour discipline was harsh. Workers were no longer free to change jobs, and anyone who tried to was liable to be punished for 'labour desertion'. However, the system was less draconian in practice than the legislation suggested. Managers did not always enforce their powers because they needed the cooperation of the workforce. Moreover, there was remarkably little sign of labour unrest. Workers undoubtedly resented the postwar hierarchical order, but protests were muted, and demoralized workers and peasants tried to evade controls by going slow or running away from their jobs.[13] A letter of complaint sent to Moscow gives a sense of the dire conditions and the inequalities in the city of Vodsk:

> In the city from early morning all the people are on the search for water, the pumps don't work, we take water from the open man-holes wherever they are ... For a population of 50 thousand we have only one functioning bathhouse ... there are huge queues to get into the bath and they are only made up of the damned directors of the city ...[14]

As this complaint suggests, the early 1950s were a much better time for bosses. Efforts by the police to control them were discouraged, and corruption flourished.

From 1946 Stalin did launch ideological campaigns of purification against 'deviations' amongst the 'socialist intelligentsia', but rather than anti-elite, they were nationalistic and xenophobic in content. The first victims of the post-war ideological campaigns were two literary journals – *Leningrad* and *Zvedza* (*Star*) – and two writers: the poet Anna Akhmatova and the humorous short-story writer Mikhail Zoshchenko. In a major decree on patriotism in literature in August 1946, the ideological chief Andrei Zhdanov described Akhmatova as a 'mixture of nun and harlot ... a crazy gentlewoman dashing backwards and forwards between her boudoir and her chapel'; Zoshchenko was denounced as a 'vulgar and trivial petty-bourgeois', who 'oozed anti-Soviet poison'. But the centre of the charges was that they, and other literary figures, had 'slipped into a tone of servility and cringing before philistine foreign literature'.[15] However, it was the beginning of the Cold War proper in early 1947 that led to full-scale patriotic campaigns. Purge commissions, now given the distinctly retro name of 'honour courts' (named after tsarist military courts), were set up in offices and bureaus to 'eliminate servility to the West'.[16]

This new cultural xenophobia blighted several areas of intellectual life, and most famously affected genetics, in the person of the notorious bogus 'biologist' Trofim Lysenko. Lysenko came from a peasant family and had no scientific training, but he claimed that his practical knowledge as a peasant more than made up for the absence of formal education. During the late 1920s and 1930s he had been a beneficiary of the Radical Marxist idea that ideologically inspired scientists 'from the people' were superior to academically trained specialists. His main invention was 'vernalization' – soaking and chilling winter wheat so that it would grow in the spring. The results were unimpressive, but Lysenko skilfully exploited the political atmosphere of the time. He also developed an ideological justification for his new approach. Changes in the environment, not just genes, could improve plants – a doctrine that accorded with Marxist ideas on the importance of the environment over heredity (genetics was damned by association with eugenics and Nazism). Lysenko fought a long-running battle with geneticists in the Academy of Sciences throughout the later 1930s, but failed to secure political support; Stalin was not then prepared to endanger economic development by subordinating scientific research to Marxist speculation. However, by the summer of 1948, at the height of the Berlin crisis, he was more willing to sacrifice science to patriotism. At that point Stalin was determined to establish a clear difference between a 'progressive' Soviet science and a 'reactionary' bourgeois science.[17] Soon after this Lysenkoism became the new orthodoxy, blighting Soviet biology for two decades.

Stalin was, however, more circumspect about subjecting physics to such ideological tampering because he was unwilling to risk the atomic project. Even so, science became increasingly bound up with national pride. The *Great Soviet Encyclopaedia* informed its readers that Aleksandr Mozhaiskii, not the Wright brothers, built the first aeroplane; Grigorii Ignatiev invented the telephone; A. S. Popov the radio; V. A. Manassein and A. G. Polotebnov penicillin; P. N. Iablochkov and A. N. Lodygin the light-bulb.

Stalin and his propagandists were of course tending the seed of a nationalism they had planted some time before, in the mid-1930s. This was not Russian nationalism pure and simple, but a Soviet–Russian amalgam, intended to integrate all official Soviet nationalities into a single harmonious whole. But the Russian element in the mixture became far greater after the War, and in one respect particularly it came strikingly close to the state nationalism of Tsar Nicholas II – its anti-Semitism.

Jews, as an ethnic group, had not been victimized by the Soviet regime before World War II, and were not specifically targeted by the 1936–8 Terror. Indeed, as has been seen, Jews were one of the most pro-Communist peoples in the USSR, and throughout the world. As a highly educated and urban group, they were also overrepresented in the upper echelons of professional and cultural life. Nevertheless Stalin frequently manifested crude prejudices about many ethnic groups, including Jews. Khrushchev, hardly a model of political correctness himself, described him as having a 'hostile attitude towards the Jewish people', recalling Stalin's mimicking of a Jewish accent 'in the same way that thick-headed backward people who despise Jews talk when they mock the negative Jewish traits'.[18] But this was no ideological racism, Nazi-style. Jews were numbered amongst Stalin's closest associates (and he would tolerate no anti-Jewish prejudice when the Jewish Kaganovich was within earshot). Anti-Semitism was, he said in 1931, 'an extreme form of racial chauvinism', 'the most dangerous rudiment of cannibalism'.[19] And during the War, the Soviet leadership set up the Jewish Anti-Fascist Committee – a typical Popular Front-style organization designed to attract worldwide Jewish support for the Soviet war effort, chaired by Solomon Mikhoels. Even so, the War strained relations between Jews and Slavic nationalities: the sufferings of the Jews at the hands of the Nazis – and their collaborators – intensified the sense of their ethnicity, whilst the revived Russian nationalist messages of the period encouraged a popular anti-Semitism.[20]

Initially the Soviet leadership was happy merely to indulge this traditional anti-Semitism. But Stalin took more extreme measures when international politics intervened. The USSR had supported the foundation of Israel in 1948. The Zionists, after all, were socialists, and many had been born in the Russian empire; Stalin hoped that Israel would become a bridgehead for Soviet influence in the Middle East. But he also worried that Israel might act as a magnet for the loyalties of Soviet Jews. The arrival of Golda Meyerson (later Meir) in Moscow – born in Kiev but brought up a three-hour drive from Mosinee in Wisconsin – as the first Israeli ambassador to the USSR caused particular anxiety when it provoked spontaneous Jewish demonstrations of support. And when it became clear in 1949 that Israel was firmly in the American sphere of influence, Soviet Jews were transformed, overnight, into potential fifth columnists, and became victims of discrimination and even repression. Like the Germans, Poles and Koreans in the 1930s, they were seen as conduits for foreign influence, in this case Israeli, and therefore American. According to Stalin, 'Jewish nationalists believe that their nation has been saved by the United States (there they can become rich, bourgeois and so on)'.[21]

Many were caught up in the witch-hunt. The Anti-Fascist Committee was closed down, and Mikhoels murdered by the secret police. The film *Circus* was re-edited and Mikhoels' performance of the Yiddish lullaby verse excised. Jews who embraced Yiddish culture were now 'bourgeois nationalists', those who were more assimilated were 'rootless cosmopolitans'. Various 'conspiracies' were discovered; some leading figures were arrested, including Molotov's Jewish wife; many more lost jobs or were unable to continue their studies. Most worrying for Soviet Jews was the 'discovery' of a supposed plot by a 'spy group of doctor-murderers'. These 'monsters in human form' – all of them Jews – had allegedly assassinated Soviet leaders, including Zhdanov (who had died of a heart attack in 1948). The so-called 'Doctors' Plot' was made public at the beginning of 1953, months before Stalin's death; fortunately for Soviet Jews, the anti-Semitic campaigns did not survive him.

Some have seen these events as a fresh outbreak of the purges of the 1930s. They did have some similarities with the ethnic cleansings of the earlier period, but they were very different from many of the repressions, which had at their core the revival of 'class struggle'. They were much more targeted and there were many fewer victims. Also the new message now being broadcast was of patriotic unity, not class division. These purges then were not a threat to the vast majority of party bosses, technical experts and other previously suspect elites. Stalin had learnt the lessons of the 1930s Terror. Never again would he allow mass 'criticism from below', nor would he try to mobilize the population with campaigns for ideological purity. The carrot of unequal wages and the managers' stick was replacing appeals to worker heroism.

The new balance of power between elites and masses was reflected in the continuing embourgeoisement of culture. Paintings dwelt lovingly on elaborate lampshades and curtains, and soft pink replaced red as the dominant colour. Novelistic heroes were no longer puritanical scourges of bureaucracy, but bluff and easy-going pragmatists. Whilst the appearance of a piano in a 1920s novel was always a sure sign that its owner was a bourgeois enemy, in the 1940s and 1950s pianos were approved of as markers of culture and education. Even Pasha Angelina, the famous Stakhanovite woman tractor-driver of the 1930s, had transferred her enthusiasms from the cultivation of wheat to cultivating her daughters' pianistic virtuosity. In 1948 she wrote a magazine article in which she related that her youngest daughter, the delightfully named Stalinka, wanted to follow in her sister's footsteps:

> 'Mama, mama, when I grow up like Svetlana, will I play the piano too?'
> 'Of course you will.' I listened to Stalinka with excitement and happiness. My childhood was different: I couldn't even think of music.[22]

It would be misleading to see late Stalinism as a restoration of the tsarist *ancien régime*, populated with a new elite; this was a much more modern society – integrated, socially fluid and welfarist – than tsarist Russia. But after the War, Stalin went further than many other Communist leaders in jettisoning the remnants of radical socialism and embracing hierarchy, bolstered by *ancien régime* trappings and symbols. It was this model that was, at least in principle, exported to the USSR's empire and its spheres of influence. However, the circumstances in Eastern Europe were rather different. East European Communists were introducing a wholly new social and political system, and inevitably pursued a more revolutionary politics, eliciting much opposition, but also some enthusiasm for the new order, at least for a time.

III

The Joke, the Czech writer Milan Kundera's 1967 novel, is the story of Ludvik, a bright and popular student during the Stalinist period of Czechoslovak history, whose life is ruined by a minor mistake. He is a keen party member, and a true believer, though his motives are mixed:

> The intoxication we experienced is commonly known as the intoxication of power, but (with a bit of good will) I could choose less severe words: we

were bewitched by history; we were drunk with the thought of jumping on its back and feeling it beneath us; admittedly, in most cases the result was an ugly lust for power, but (as all human affairs are ambiguous) there was still (and especially, perhaps, in us, the young), an altogether idealistic illusion that we were inaugurating a human era in which man (all men) would be neither *outside* history, nor *under the heel of history*, but would create and direct it.[23]

Yet far from being history's master, he becomes its victim. For a 'tiny crack' opened up 'between the person I had been and the person I should (according to the spirit of the times) and tried to be'.[24] Whilst he can be earnest and committed at party meetings, he adopts a teasing, cynical persona when flirting with his fellow student Marketa. Marketa is a very different type of true believer, a straightforward, unsophisticated and humourless enthusiast. Much to Ludvik's chagrin, she sends him a postcard praising the 'healthy atmosphere' of callisthenics, discussions and songs. Upset that she prefers party propagandizing to him, he sends a jokey riposte: 'Optimism is the opium of the people! A healthy atmosphere stinks of stupidity! Long live Trotsky! Ludvik.' But for the party this is no joke, and he is denounced as a Trotskyist and a cynic, whose nihilistic attitudes are sabotaging socialism. Stripped of party membership and with it his university place, he is forced to work in a labour brigade in the mines. Initially he attempts to rehabilitate himself – but he ultimately lapses into angry contempt for the shallow, folksy nationalism now being propagated by the party. The bitterness stays with him, and lays the ground for another series of disastrous jokes.

Kundera's novel was loosely based on his own experience. The son of a famous pianist, he joined the party in 1948, a true believer, and has even been accused of informing on a Western spy; he was then expelled in 1950 for making a politically incorrect comment. He was therefore ideally placed to capture the atmosphere amongst educated youth during the revolutionary years of the early 1950s. For whilst the old Popular Front generation of Communist leaders was either assiduously conforming to the Moscow line or enduring purges and show trials, a younger group of enthusiastic Communists was coming to the fore. In part this was typical of the swing to the left in many countries amongst an anti-Nazi post-war youth, East and West. But their place on the periphery of a more successful Western Europe also explains their choices. The Stalinist model could appeal to young and educated people in developing countries, for whatever its failings it seemed to provide a recipe for catching up. The conservative counts and generals and liberal professionals who had ruled most of Eastern Europe between the wars had been strikingly unsuccessful in improving their economies. After the disasters of the inter-war period, when the poor, weak and divided countries of the region had been at the mercy of an aggressive Nazi Germany, loss of liberty seemed to some to be a price worth paying for development and Soviet protection.

Moreover, Communism promised free education and an expanded state with large numbers of professional jobs – precisely what the ambitious, self-improving middle classes were seeking after the deprivations of Depression and war. Some groups with a middle-class background did suffer under late Stalinism. Class quotas were applied to education – the playwright and future dissident (and President of the Czech Republic) Václav Havel was one of the victims. Others suffered more directly in deportations and other persecutions. In 1951, for instance, many thousands of bourgeois were deported from Budapest to make way for workers in the new industrial plants.[25] But High Stalinism never permitted class struggle to threaten economic productivity. The educated generally retained high status as long as they were loyal. And except in Poland (where over 70 per cent of the professional and business class had been killed during the War) and East Germany (where many fled to the West), the old middle classes were remarkably successful in clinging on to their dominant positions. In Czechoslovakia there was relatively little anti-bourgeois discrimination. In Hungary there was some, but in 1956 60–70 per cent of professionals still came from the old middle and upper classes. The regime, desperate to fill technical jobs, was often happy to turn a blind eye to the air-brushing of biographies. One girl, expelled from grammar school because she was labelled a member of the dangerous element of the bourgeoisie – the 'x-class' as it was informally called – was told that if she worked as a labourer for a time she could shed her bad background and return to school.[26]

The Captive Mind – an analysis of the thinking of the Polish intelligentsia by the dissident Czesław Miłosz – explored these mixed motives: a sense that history was on Communism's side, a moral commitment to national development, and self-advancement. He described the attitude of 'Alpha', a well-known writer:

Alpha did not blame the Russians. What was the use? They were the force of History. Communism was fighting Fascism; and the Poles, with their ethical code based on nothing but loyalty, had managed to thrust themselves between these two forces . . . A moralist of today, Alpha reasoned, should turn his attention to social goals and social results . . . The country was ravaged. The new government went energetically to work reconstructing, putting mines and factories into operation, and dividing estates among the peasants. New responsibilities faced the writer. His books were eagerly awaited by a human ant-hill, shaken out of its torpor and stirred up by the big stick of war and of social reforms. We should not wonder, then, that Alpha, like the majority of his colleagues, declared at once his desire to serve the new Poland that had risen out of the ashes of the old.[27]

For people like Alpha and Marketa, therefore, the regime seemed to be the harbinger not only of modernity, but also of morality. The Stalinist social model elevated self-sacrificing labour over all else. Production, not selfish consumption, was to lie at the centre of life. As if to prove the point, the numbers of shops fell and advertising entirely disappeared. And what shops there were became bill-boards for the regime of labour. The façades of the shops in Warsaw's 1952 Marszałowska Residential District bore a huge narrative sculpture, depicting the heroic workers who had built the complex; there was no representation of the products sold inside.[28] Production also lay at the centre of the massive new socialist cities of the period, like Nowa Huta outside Krakow in Poland, and Sztálinváros in Hungary, both built around huge steelworks.[29] In the latter, the whole city plan was arranged around the twin poles of political and productive power: at one end of the main street lay the party headquarters and city hall and at the other the steel plant. The ideal of the large, collectivist factory was also brought to the countryside, through collectivization. As in the USSR, these campaigns were accompanied by repression of 'kulaks', and were also highly unpopular amongst the small-holding peasantry, now corralled into collectives and forced to give more food to the state for lower prices.

Indeed, despite valorization as the 'owners' of the state, workers and peasants tended to be the groups most disillusioned with Communism, for it was they who bore the brunt of Eastern Europe's 'revolution from above' after 1949 – a revolution even more rapid and radical than the USSR's in the 1930s. This economic revolution probably damaged living standards even more than in the 1930s USSR (although the income per capita was higher). Except in the more developed Czechoslovakia, investment in the industrial Plan was set at between 20 and 27 per cent of national income, compared with 9–10 per cent before.[30] Consumer goods were no longer a priority, and collectivization contributed to dire food shortages.

For Communist leaders such suffering was the inevitable price of development; without foreign help there was no alternative to reducing consumption to fund investment. The Polish secret police chief, Jakub Berman, explained:

> We had to see this realistically, and the whole thing boiled down to solving the puzzle of whether to build at the expense of consumption, which could bring the risk of upheavals along with it, and indeed this happened in 1956, or not to build and resign ourselves to a situation with no prospects.[31]

Others, though, were sceptical of Berman's reasoning. For critics, the Five-Year Plans were imperialist projects pure and simple, designed to extract resources for the Soviet military effort. The huge sums taken by the USSR in reparations reinforced these views: between $14 billion and $20 billion (thus more, possibly, than the $16 billion given by the United States to Western Europe under the Marshall Plan).[32] Most of these reparations came from East Germany, but all the satellites' economies were affected. The euphemistically named Council of Mutual Economic Assistance (Comecon), founded in January 1949, was also designed in such a way that economic cooperation furthered Soviet interests.

The perception that the USSR was an imperial power, squeezing the economic lifeblood from its East European colonies, was deeply damaging to the Communist regimes in those countries. Communism had always been most successful when it could enmesh itself within local nationalisms, and the Stalinist regimes did try to present themselves as indigenous. However, their attempts to drape themselves in national colours were often unconvincing, and soon, as Kundera demonstrated, even loyal Communists developed a bitter contempt for the Russians. As Czesław Miłosz wrote, many Polish intellectuals privately harboured 'an unbounded contempt for Russia as a barbaric country'. Their position was 'Socialism – yes, Russia – no'.[33] Rather like Béla Kun in 1919, they came to believe that East Europeans were actually far better able to realize socialism than Russians because they were more civilized, intelligent and organized. But unable to say so openly, they hypocritically praised Russian literature, songs and actors at every turn.

The harsh political controls could be especially unpleasant and humiliating for East European Communist elites. Show trials and purges were initially used against non-Communist rivals. The most notorious case was the trial of the Bulgarian Agrarian Party leader, Nikola Petkov, in 1947, whose 'confession' had to be published posthumously because he refused to cooperate at his trial. It was the defection of Yugoslavia's Tito from the Soviet bloc in 1948, though, that brought about the wave of repressions and trials. Tito's lèse-majesté was a serious challenge to Soviet control, and there was a real possibility that other Communists would follow him. Wolfgang Leonhard, for instance, escaped from Berlin to Belgrade, after a severe attack of 'political tummy-ache' as he called it. He now decided that Stalinist Communism, with its special party canteens and housing, was unbearably hypocritical.[34]

Moscow responded by launching violent campaigns to root out potential 'Titoite' influences in East European Communist parties. Communists who had not spent some time in exile in Moscow were at particular risk. NKVD experts in staging show trials were sent to the satellite states to share their expertise in repression. The show trials and purges of alleged Titoites were particularly intense in those countries near Yugoslavia – Hungary, Bulgaria, Romania and Albania. In Poland, Władisław Gomułka was also accused of Titoism in 1951, because he had objected to the harsh centralization of the Cominform and called for a national road to socialism. He, though, escaped execution.

Together with anti-Titoism, Stalin and his secret police brought with them anti-Semitism. And many East European regimes were often happy to seek popular support by scapegoating Jewish Communists: anti-Semitic campaigns were especially pronounced in Poland, East Germany, Romania and Czechoslovakia. In the latter, the number two in the party, Rudolf Slánský, was accused of both Titoism and Zionism. His show trial in November 1952 was meticulously scripted and prepared, and indeed a dress rehearsal was recorded in case one of the defendants should retract his confession.[35]

Repression was, however, difficult to direct and control. As in 1936–8, Moscow was interested in political biographies and ordered the East European parties to investigate the pasts of Communists who might be susceptible to Titoism or who had prior links with the West. But the outcome of those investigations could be shaped by locals who wanted to settle personal scores or do favours to friends, as they had been in the Terror of the 1930s. The East European terrors therefore had a logic to them, yet they also appeared unpredictable and arbitrary, creating confusion and fear. In East Germany, for instance, several Communists found themselves under suspicion because they had lived in exile in the West during the Nazi period; perhaps, their accusers argued, they had been 'turned' by Western spies. The inmates of concentration camps were also investigated; some were accused of cowardice, others of recklessness. And it was in these kinds of cases that local politics could come into play. Erich Honecker, the future East German leader, received a party reprimand for escaping from a Nazi prison without party permission, but this had no further consequences; Franz Dahlem, however, a serious rival to Walter Ulbricht, found himself stripped of all his offices and threatened with a trial as a result of allegations that he had tried to stop an uprising in the Mauthausen concentration camp.[36] And in Albania and Romania, Enver Hoxha and Gheorghe Georghiu-Dej were able to turn Stalin's repressions into opportunities to strengthen their own networks of clients at the expense of loyal 'Moscow' Communists.

East European Communists had, therefore, been granted their wish. Stalin had destroyed the Popular Fronts, put them in power and allowed them to embark on full sovietization. But they had paid a high price. They did have considerable powers over their countries, but their influence ultimately derived from Moscow – it was, as Gomułka commented, 'a reflected brilliance, a borrowed light'.[37] Leaders even found that they were expected to synchronize their lives to coincide with Stalin's eccentric daily routine. Jakub Berman remembered how he would go to work at 8 a.m., return home for lunch with his wife and daughter between 3 and 4 p.m., and then go back to the Central Committee for 6 where he would work until midnight or 1 a.m. Stalin remained at his desk until late in the night and his subordinate leaders had to be there in case he phoned. Every high official had to follow the same schedule.[38]

In Moscow, the heads of East European parties were treated as subordinates in an imperial court, rather than heads of state in their own right. One of the most unsettling of experiences was the invitation to dine at Stalin's Kuntsevo *dacha* on the outskirts of Moscow. These dinners went on all night, and the senior guests often found that they were the entertainment. According to one, Stalin tried to get them drunk so they would spill secrets. He also subjected them to practical jokes, for instance arranging for tomatoes to be left on chairs so 'when the victim sat on it there would be loud roars of laughter'.[39] On one occasion, Beria wrote the word 'prick' on a piece of paper and attached it to Khrushchev's overcoat.[40] There was much hilarity when, about to leave, he put it on; the brittle Khrushchev was less amused. Film-viewing and dancing were also regular features of the tense evenings. Berman – who kept his job in charge of the Polish security services despite being a Jew – was more indulgent of the bizarre soirées. He found they could be useful:

BERMAN: 'Once, I think it was in 1948, I danced with Molotov –' [*laughter*]

INTERVIEWER: 'Surely you mean with Mrs Molotov?'

BERMAN: 'No, she wasn't there; she was in a labour camp. I danced with Molotov – it must have been a waltz, or at any rate something very simple, because I don't know the faintest thing about dancing, so I just moved my feet to the rhythm.'

INTERVIEWER: 'As the woman?'

BERMAN: 'Yes, Molotov led; I wouldn't have known how. Actually, he wasn't a bad dancer. I tried to keep in step with him, but what I did resembled clowning more than dancing.'

INTERVIEWER: 'What about Stalin, whom did he dance with?'

BERMAN: 'Oh, no, Stalin didn't dance. Stalin wound the gramophone, considering it his duty as a citizen. He never left it. He would just put on records and watch.'

. . .

INTERVIEWER: 'So you enjoyed yourselves.'

BERMAN: 'Yes, it was pleasant, but with an inner tension.'

INTERVIEWER: 'You didn't have fun, really?'

BERMAN: 'Stalin really had fun. For us these dancing sessions were a good opportunity to whisper to each other things that couldn't be said out loud. That was when Molotov warned me about being infiltrated by various hostile organizations.'[41]

Not all Communists were as tolerant as Berman. The widow of the Czech minister Rudolf Margolius remembered: 'Our lives, permeated by insecurity, became hopeless drudgery.' Even the President, Klement Gottwald, had taken to drink, drowning his pangs of conscience, so the gossip went.[42] As the realities of the High Stalinist order became clear, many early enthusiasts became disillusioned.

IV

The Cold War and behaviour of the Soviets in Eastern Europe also dam-aged the Western Communist parties. Communists remained a signifi-cant force in only three countries – France, Italy and, to a lesser extent, Finland. They attracted a triple alliance of industrial workers, intel-lectuals and a traditional peasantry determined not to be absorbed into the free market.[43] Elsewhere these conditions were absent, and Com-munism soon withered – especially in Northern Europe, where the Social Democrats had a strong presence.

The French and Italian parties – Western Europe's biggest – also suf-fered declining membership numbers after 1948. In France, member-ship estimates show a fall from some 800,000 party members in 1948 to 300,000–400,000 between 1952 and 1972. Yet the French Commun-ist Party benefited from its 'outsider' status, challenging the entrenched Parisian establishment; it took 26.6 per cent of the vote in the 1951 elections, and in 1956 55 per cent of Parisian workers voted Communist.[44] The turn towards High Stalinism in the USSR did not discomfort the French party too much, for its social conservatism and anti-intellectualism, its strict discipline and its Manichaean outlook all remained close to the Stalinist worldview. It proceeded to create a counter-culture, free of the influence of America and consumerism. Morality was strict and puritanical, and every aspect of life was politi-cized. For members, the party continued to be the centre of intense emotional involvement. The writer Domenique Desanti found Commu-nist life completely absorbing; she and her fellow Communists felt themselves almost wholly cut off from the outside world.[45] The party had its own parallel society – its organizations for youth and sport, its children's holiday camps – to keep people in the fold.

Despite its closed and dogmatic culture the party attracted support beyond its committed membership. Some of the most famous intellectuals in France became fellow-travelling sympathizers – even, paradoxically, existentialists like Jean-Paul Sartre whose philosophy celebrated individ-ual responsibility. There were a number of reasons for this apparent contradiction. The Communists' resistance record was undoubtedly important, as was their influence amongst the virtuous proletariat, and, oddly, their anti-intellectualism.[46] Simple anti-Americanism and snobbery about Coca-Cola and other accoutrements of the new consumer culture also had a place. But imperialism was also a major issue. The French, supported by the United States, were fighting an anti-nationalist war in Vietnam and the Communists were the only major domestic force to oppose the fighting. It was this issue that helped push a semi-detached Sartre towards the Communist party between 1952 and 1956; he had undergone a 'conversion' and had developed a 'hatred' of the bourgeoisie.[47] High Stalinism was, ironically, benefiting from anger at Western imperialism; moral outrage was being transferred from inequalities at home, to inequalities abroad. As Sartre was later to write in his preface to Franz Fanon's great anti-imperialist polemic, *The Wretched of the Earth*, Europe was a 'pale fat continent', and the Third World was the future.[48]

The consequence, of course, was that the progressive left was often willing to ignore repression in the Eastern bloc in the fight against what it perceived as the more brutal repression in the South. The most notorious case was the controversy over Viktor Kravchenko's memoirs, *I Chose Freedom*, with their lengthy account of the Terror and discussion of the Gulag. When they were published in French, the party's journal *Les Lettres françaises* accused Kravchenko of being part of a CIA conspiracy to discredit the USSR. Kravchenko sued in 1948, and a galaxy of non-Communist intellectuals spoke in defence of the French party and the USSR. Even though Kravchenko won, the damages were small and the moral victory belonged to the French Communists, who continued to follow a slavishly pro-Moscow line.[49] Lysenko, socialist realism and Russian xenophobia were all defended by the French comrades. Similar to the French party was the Finnish. After its electoral defeat in 1948, it retreated into its own world, nurturing a workerist political culture. It continued to be highly successful in elections – in 1958 it took 23.3 per cent of the vote and became the largest parliamentary group.[50]

If the French and Finnish leaderships followed Moscow's change of line happily, their Italian comrades were much less content about it. Palmiro Togliatti's old strategy of cross-class alliances was now heresy, and he was forced to bow to the Kremlin, fearful of being ousted by his more orthodox rival Pietro Secchia. He remained leader, but the Stalinists were in the ascendant in the party organization, and Stalin's portraits could be seen much more commonly in party offices than Gramsci's.[51] Yet in many ways the Cominform's Manichaean approach to politics suited the times. The Catholic Church – with the Christian Democratic Party and the organization of Catholic laypeople, Catholic Action – became the centre of a militant opposition to Communism, and in July 1949 Pope Pius XII excommunicated all Communists. The Church continued to present elections as a choice between 'Christ or Antichrist', rather than conventional political parties, and Communists in turn feared the emergence of a pro-Catholic fascist regime, rather like Franco's in Spain.[52] The Communists and the Catholic Church therefore faced each other as rivals, each with its own self-enclosed social and political world.[53] In this atmosphere of confrontation, the popularity of Stalin was perhaps not surprising

The two largest Communist parties of the West therefore survived the crisis of 1947–8 as major political forces. They lost support, but politics was polarized enough to sustain them in their bunkers. Stalin's 'two camps' view of the world still made sense to many, even though his behaviour made it more difficult to admire the USSR. On the other side of the Soviet sphere of influence, in China, meanwhile, the Communists also found Soviet high-handedness and *realpolitik* difficult to stomach. But there the Soviet model was much more attractive, promising an alternative to 'backwardness', division and foreign occupation.

V

In December 1949, Mao boarded a train and prepared to take his first journey abroad. His destination was Moscow. The ten-day trip was kept secret until his arrival, and the strictest security was observed. The train was escorted by two others occupied entirely by soldiers, in front and behind; guards were also posted along the entire route. Mao was accompanied by only a small delegation, but he had also brought an eclectic selection of presents for Stalin, ranging from white cabbage and radishes from Shandong, to embroidery and cushions from Hunan. Whether Stalin ate and appreciated the cabbage we do not know.[54]

The new master of Red China, now fifty-six, was to meet the great *vozhd* of world Communism for the first time on the occasion of Stalin's seventieth birthday. Mao hoped to secure aid and recognition and a new Sino-Soviet treaty, to replace the one signed by Chiang Kaishek and approved by the Americans and British at Yalta in 1945. Despite its significance, though, the trip was far from the slick PR opportunity of the modern state visit. Indeed, it was one of the most bizarre encounters of the post-war era, as the two protagonists danced a tense *pas de deux* over the course of two months. Trouble started at the railway station, when Stalin failed to welcome Mao in person, against the usual protocol. The leaders did speak later that day, but Stalin made it clear he was reluctant to conclude a new treaty. He was happy to give aid, but did not want to risk upsetting the Yalta arrangements, and thus give the Americans an excuse to unpick them. Stalin also mistrusted Mao. So soon after the Yugoslav split, Stalin was worried that this guerrilla leader who had caused Moscow so much trouble over the years might well turn out to be a disloyal Asian Tito. Mao was sent to a state *dacha*, bristling with bugging devices so that Stalin could observe him and make up his mind. On one occasion he sent Molotov to find out 'what kind of guy he is'. A patronizing Molotov reported back that he was a shrewd peasant leader rather like the eighteenth-century Russian rebel Pugachev. He was 'naturally' not a proper Marxist, and had not even read *Capital*. Even so, Molotov's impression was broadly positive.

Mao, left 'stewing in his own juices', as his Russian minder put it, became more and more frustrated. Used to the privations of a guerrilla army, he hated the trappings of Western comfort, moaned about the European pedestal toilet, and ordered that his soft mattress be replaced with hard planks. He repeatedly tried to arrange another meeting with Stalin, but in vain. 'Am I here just to eat, shit and sleep?' he complained. He even told colleagues that he was under house arrest and might never be allowed back to China.

Stalin did, however, make a fuss of Mao at his birthday celebrations in the Bolshoi Theatre. Mao was placed at Stalin's right hand, and was the first foreign leader to speak. Stalin clearly realized that he had a great deal to gain from association with a man who had brought Communism to a quarter of the world's population. Eventually, fearing (unnecessarily) that Mao might do a deal with the Americans, Stalin agreed to the treaty. Mao was forced to make concessions, accepting an independent Mongolian People's Republic, but he had got his way. Soviet aid and advisers went to China; the Chinese recognized the Soviets as their 'elder brothers'.

However, the tension continued. Mao decided to recognize Ho Chi

Minh's government in Vietnam, and Stalin felt he had to do the same, even though he did not want to antagonize the French. Stalin also continued to suspect Mao of colluding with the Americans. After one frosty meeting Stalin invited Mao, with a number of Soviet Politburo members, to his *dacha* for one of his bizarre soirées. He tried to break the ice in his customary way, by starting up the gramophone and presiding over an all-male dancing session. But Mao was not in the mood to party. As his translator remembered, 'Although three or four men took turns trying to pull Chairman Mao onto the floor to dance, they never succeeded ... The whole thing ended in bad odour.'[55] A couple of weeks later the Soviets compounded the embarrassment by inviting the Chinese to Reinhold Glière's 1920s ballet about revolutionary China, *The Red Poppy*. It told the story of a Soviet marine who met a Shanghai prostitute, and then converted her to Marxism-Leninism. Mao, hearing of the patronizing plot and the dubious title (to Chinese ears it seemed to be associating Communism with the evil of opium), did not attend. It is just as well he did not. His secretary, who went in his stead, was deeply offended by the yellow face-paint worn by the Russian dancers playing Chinese characters. To him it seemed that the Chinese were being portrayed as monsters.

In this fraught visit we can see the acute tension between Stalin's ageing Communism and the younger, Radical Communism to the East. There were, of course, strong reasons for the USSR to seek close relations with China, despite the long-standing difficulties between Stalin and Mao. Communism in Asia gave Stalin real opportunities. He already had a close ally in North Korea; in North Vietnam, Ho had drifted away from Moscow towards Beijing, but Stalin could influence events in Vietnam through China. And whilst Mao was difficult to manage, he still recognized Stalin's suzerainty over the world Communist movement. Mao, moreover, however frustrating he found the Soviets' patronizing attitude, still saw them as the source of the magical blueprint for transforming China. Stalin's *Short Course* of party history continued to be an enormously important text for Mao: in Yan'an its stress on ideological unity and conformity had been uppermost; now it was just as valuable as a route-map for development. By 1945 the *Short Course* was one of the five 'must read' books for Chinese Communist officials for the transition to socialism.[56] The USSR, it was commonly believed, was fundamentally the same as China, only about thirty years ahead; as the slogan of the mid-1950s went: 'The Soviet Union's Today is Our Tomor-row'. The *Short Course*'s narrative of Soviet history could plausibly be mapped onto China's: there had been a revolution and civil war, and now was the time for an NEP-type period; then would come 'socialist industrialization' (1926–9 according to the *Short Course*'s idiosyncratic chronology), 'Collectivization' (1930–4) and finally the 'struggle to complete the building of the socialist society' (1935–7). China, it was widely believed, would follow the same stages, though the timetable was rather more controversial.

In 1949 the Chinese – and Soviet – leadership were agreed that the time was not ripe for socialist ambition. China, Mao and his colleagues believed, was still vulnerable to foreign invasion. And the Communists, who had not yet conquered Tibet and Taiwan, were therefore not yet ready for internal conflict. The Guomindang officials of the old regime were kept in place whilst liberal intellectuals, with their valuable expertise, were treated well. Private ownership was retained, and whilst land was taken from landowners the objective was not equality but improvements in productivity through consolidating farm size. This was defined as the era of 'New Democracy': the state was a 'people's democratic dictatorship' under the guidance of the proletar-iat but including the bourgeoisie; purges were confined to only the avowedly anti-Communist.

As in the USSR in the 1920s, there were different views about how rapid China's journey to socialism would be (though this time Stalin was a supporter of gradual reform). Those with the closest connections with Moscow – Liu Shaoqi, his ally and fellow Hunanese Moscow-educated Communist Ren Bishi, and Zhou Enlai (a leader with strong Soviet links since the 1920s) – all hoped that 'New Democracy' would last between ten and fifteen years, during which time they could build a state and economy on the Stalinist model.[57] Liu was an especially import-ant influence. He visited Moscow in June 1949, before Mao's trip, and toured scores of ministries and institutions to learn how they worked. He then returned to China with some 220 Soviet advisers primed to set up Chinese organizations in the Soviet image. However, rather more important than the relatively modest number of advisers were transla-tions of a wide range of Soviet 'how to' books.[58] It was from these handy socialist manuals that the Chinese learnt how to run factories and offices. Textbooks were much more effective than tanks in exporting the Soviet model of modernity.

Liu's visit to Moscow turned out to be much more harmonious than Mao's, as he shared a much closer affinity with Stalin. Mao, in contrast, with his nostalgia for the guerrilla socialism of Yan'an, continued to prefer radical solutions. He was impatient to push history forward towards industrialization and socialism.

As in the USSR of the late 1920s, the threat of war helped the radicalization of Chinese politics. In April 1950, Stalin, uncharacteristically, agreed to support Kim Il Sung's invasion of South Korea, and when, after initial North Korean successes, the Americans (leading a United Nations force) landed and drove them back, the Chinese reluctantly agreed to intervene.[59] The war continued for over two years. The struggle was a huge burden on China. It was a conventional war of mass armies, planned and partly financed by Moscow, but fought largely by Chinese soldiers. Three million Chinese fought there, and over 400,000 died – Mao's eldest son, Anying, was amongst them. China itself spent between 20 and 25 per cent of its budget on the campaign and the war caused enormous hardships on the front and at home.

The Korean War had the effect of accelerating calls for rapid industrialization, and Mao began to discuss the need for a Five-Year Plan as early as February 1951. But war legitimized radicalism more generally, and strengthened the supporters of violent 'class struggle'. For example, the land reform of 1949 and 1950 had begun to stall as party bosses found it difficult to enforce redistribution against the opposition of landlords, clans and temples, and the war became an opportunity for the party to accuse foreign enemies of colluding with the bourgeoisie within. Land reform quickly escalated into violent 'class struggle'. 'Speak bitterness meetings', public humiliations and straightforward violence – not always endorsed by the authorities – became common. Meanwhile, 43 per cent of the land was redistributed to 60 per cent of the population. Although this undoubtedly strengthened support for the new regime, it did so at an enormous human cost. It has been estimated that between 1 and 2 million died in these land reform campaigns.

The Chinese Communists were not yet imposing collective farms on the population, but in some ways they were even more radical than their Soviet predecessors in the early 1930s. Determined to root out old identities of class, clan and region, they put enormous efforts into categorizing the rural population by class, and class labels – whether landlord, rich peasant or poor peasant – became crucial in determining people's lives. Between 1951 and 1953 the CCP extended 'class struggle' to the towns with the 'Campaign to Suppress Counter-revolutionaries', the 'Three Antis' campaign against corrupt officials, the 'Five Antis' against the big 'national bourgeoisie' and a thought-reform campaign against intellectuals. These campaigns often involved extreme violence.[60] The suppression of counter-revolutionaries campaign alone led to between 800,000 and 2 million deaths, and countless more were dragged before mass public trials. As in the countryside, the party was often successful in mobilizing the majority against the minority; between 40 and 45 per cent of all Shanghai workers sent denunciations against 'counter-revolutionaries' to the authorities. According to one report, 30,000 attended one accusation meeting in Beijing directed against the 'five major tyrants' – a group of local bosses. As they had done in the land campaigns, the Communists mobilized the respected elderly to denounce their 'enemies':

> As the criminals entered, suddenly mass feeling erupted with the sounds of curses and slogans that shattered the earth and sky. Some spit on the criminals. Others burst into violent tears . . . One eighty-year-old woman came forward on her walking stick, confronting the accused: 'You never thought you'd see today! Hah! I never did either. The previous court system belonged to you, but now Chairman Mao will repay us our blood debts!'[61]

In September 1952 Mao announced to his colleagues that the era of NEP-style reconstruction was drawing to a close and the time was ripe for China to embark on building socialism. The First Five-Year Plan, when the socialist sector of the economy would begin to squeeze out the capitalists, began in 1953. Shortly thereafter, in 1955, collectivization was launched.

Now that he had decided on a full-blown Five-Year Plan, Mao was happier to accept the need for a move towards the High Stalinist model. In February 1953 he declared 'there must be a great nationwide upsurge of learning from the Soviet Union to rebuild our country'.[62] The graded hierarchies of the Soviet service aristocracy were now introduced wholesale; engineers were the new kings of the workplace, whilst the party organization was marginalized. Enormous industrial plants were started with Soviet help. But most striking were the changes to the People's Liberation Army, as Soviet-style ranks and insignia replaced the old civil-war guerrilla-style of army.

The Stalinist model was not, however, followed to the letter. The Chinese, so reliant on peasant support, were unwilling to exploit the peasantry too harshly in the interests of heavy industry. Overall, though, the USSR became the accepted model, and the enthusiasm for all things Soviet soon penetrated beyond the party elites. In urban areas, especially amongst the educated, the pro-intelligentsia High Stalinism of Moscow inevitably proved to be far more attractive than the peasant socialism of Yan'an. Russian novels were widely read in translation and Russian films were shown throughout the country. Ostrovskii's *How the Steel was Tempered* had the highest sales of all, and its hero, Pavel Korchagin, became an example for all to emulate. From 1952 several schools established 'Pavel classes' as part of a 'Reading good books, learning from Pavel' campaign, whilst a 1956 Soviet film, dubbed into Chinese, was shown throughout China the following year to celebrate the anniversary of the October revolution. There is some evidence that Ostrovskii's book was genuinely inspirational amongst young people, in part because Korchagin was such a flawed hero; his poor behaviour at school and his impulsiveness made him easier to like than the remote and improbably virtuous Chinese 'new socialist men'. Korchagin represented revolutionary romanticism, tempered with some realism.[63]

Cinema became a major conduit of Soviet ideas into China; by 1957, 468 Soviet films had been translated and shown in China, seen by almost 1.4 billion Chinese. These films propagated a number of messages. The heroism of the little man – people like Korchagin – was one, but the films also popularized 'modern' ideas, such as gender equality.[64] *How the Steel was Tempered*, like many other Soviet films, showed women fighting and working alongside men. China's first female tractor driver, Liang Jun, claimed that the film inspired her to seek work. The Soviet Union, as seen through film, seemed like the acme of modernity. As the historian Wu Hung remembers:

> Thinking about the early 1950s, it seems that everything new and exciting came from the Soviet Union and anything from the Soviet Union was new and exciting. Repeated over and over in schools, parks and on streets was the slogan: 'The Soviet Union's Today is Our Tomorrow'. It was both exhil-

arating and uncanny to see your own future written on someone else's face, especially when this 'someone else' had yellow hair and pink skin ... My mother, along with all her colleagues at the Central Academy of Drama, immediately permed her hair into numerous curls to resemble those of the robust Russian heroines ... Fused with my memory of my mother's hair-style during that period was a kind of dress that people called a *bulaji* (a phonetic rendering of the Russian word [*plat'e*, or 'dress']). It had short puffed sleeves, a buttoned-up collar and a wide, floating skirt, and was always made of colourful fabric with cheerful patterns, again associated with the 'revolutionary spirit' of the Soviet Union.[65]

However, as Wu Hung illustrates, the Soviet 'modernity' transmitted to China was of a particular type. In fashion, as in many other areas, the official embrace of the 'Soviet model' after 1953 marked a transition rather similar to the one that the USSR underwent in the mid-1930s: from the more egalitarian, guerrilla socialism to a more 'joyous' and aspirational society. In the late 1940s, the 'Lenin suit' – a female version of the Sun Yat-sen suit, based on the Soviet Red Army uniform – had become popular amongst female revolutionaries, and was common attire amongst urban women in the early 1950s. But in 1955, inspired by the Soviet model and fed up with Yan'an-style austerity, several leading cultural figures, including the poet Ai Qing, launched a dress reform campaign. For Ai Qing the Sun Yat-sen and Lenin suits did not 'harmonize at all with ... the joyful tenor of life'. 'In the Soviet Union,' he explained, 'if there are six or seven girls walking along together, they will all be wearing different styles of dress', whereas Chinese children 'dress up like little old people'.[66]

Despite a great deal of press coverage in 1956, the dress reform campaign was not entirely successful, and many women clung to their Lenin suits. In part, the reason was economic: full skirts demanded more material than Lenin suits. But expense was not the only reason; popular values were not yet in tune with this departure from Yan'an guerrilla socialism. One of the supporters of dress reform explained the enduring popularity of the Lenin suit amongst women:

> they have linked together cadre suits and progressive thinking, cadre suits and simplicity of lifestyle, cadre suits and frugality ... Although this is all erroneous, there is no denying that in it we find encompassed the desire of women for progress and for equality with men in life and work, as well as a

view of simplicity and frugality as the core elements of Chinese aesthetics.[67]

The conflicts over revolutionary fashion mirrored the continuing tensions within Chinese politics. Mao was willing for a time to embrace the Soviet model, but he never jettisoned his guerrilla values, and it was not long before he would turn against the tide from Moscow.

A different blending of the Chinese-style peasant guerrilla tradition with Soviet-style hierarchy is evident in Communist North Korea. Kim Il Sung himself had been immersed in both Chinese and Soviet Communist cultures, but Korean political culture was crucial in forging this very specific model of Communism.[68]

Like the Chinese party, the 'Korean Workers' Party', as the Communist party was called, was predominantly a peasant-based party, and had secured considerable support from the poorer peasantry with its land reform of 1946 (which was very similar to the Chinese Communist land reforms in Manchuria during the civil war). Its kinship with the Chinese party was also evident in the enormous emphasis it placed on 'self-criticism' and 'thought unity'. Korea's Confucian culture contributed to the stress on ideas and thought, but the Japanese colonial administration's efforts at ideological 'conversion' – something many Communists experienced in prison – may also have been influential.[69]

At the same time, however, Kim found the High Stalinist model attractive. The Japanese had left the North with the foundations of a heavy industrial economy, and the regime launched a typically Stalinist programme of industrialization, helped by Soviet experts and technical training. By the end of the 1940s, Korea had become part of a broader Soviet economic empire, exporting raw materials in exchange for manufactured goods.[70]

Kim's personality cult also had echoes of Stalin's and Mao's, though its extravagance and intensity were of a different order, and here non-Communist sources were crucial.[71] Stalinist and Maoist imagery and language were certainly present – Kim was compared, like Mao, with the sun (though this may also have owed something to the Japanese emperor cult) – but so was Confucian familial imagery. Kim's 'revolutionary lineage' was praised, and he was presented as the father of the Korean people. Korean Shamanistic folk religion also played a part: Kim was presented as the 'mother' of the nation, and had a magical control over the weather and harvests. He was also, moreover, hailed as a transformative philosopher-king who gave 'on-the-spot guidance', advising workers how to use lathes and peasants how to improve their crop-yield. North Korea is still littered with thousands of signs commemorating his inspirational visits (including perilous raised sections on highways, which mark the many places where Kim gave 'on-the-spot guidance' on road construction). Finally, Christian elements penetrated the cult: his biographer wrote that a shining star marked his rise to the leadership, and he shed 'precious blood' to save the nation.

A curious mixture of High Stalinism and Korean tradition was also evident in the social order. The post-war Stalinist model of the factory was replicated, complete with Stakhanovism and sharp wage differentials, but the inequalities and social distinctions were to become much more rigid than in the USSR or China. Korean political culture may have been influential here. Although influenced by Confucianism, the Korean Chosŏn dynasty (which ruled until the Japanese took power in 1910) had preserved a hereditary aristocratic elite, unlike in China, where Confucian ideas of educational merit were much stronger.[72] The rigid Communist hierarchy of 'core class', 'wavering class' and 'hostile class' was therefore reminiscent of the Chosŏn dynasty's tripartite division of society into the *yangban* (literary and martial classes), commoners and outcastes or slaves, and heredity remained crucial in determining people's life-chances.[73] As will be seen, these hereditary hierarchies had also emerged in China, but Mao was determined to undermine them. Kim, in contrast, buttressed them, a hierarchical outlook which was reflected in the extraordinary use of two different words for 'comrade': '*tongmu*' for equals and '*tongji*' for superiors (the Chinese Communist Party only used one word – '*tongzhi*').

Kim and his fellow Communist leaders were to create a form of Communism with strong local roots that were to prove remarkably resilient. It was to become one of the most *ancien régime*-like of all Communist powers, and its social structure proved unusually rigid. But all Communist societies in the late Stalinist period had strong elements of hierarchy, and they inevitably undermined the hopes of many potential supporters for a new era of modern social relationships and justice.

VI

At the age of seventeen, Edmund Chmieliński left his home village in Central Poland to join a youth labour brigade and work in the new 'socialist city' of Nowa Huta, outside Krakow. Chmieliński had been traumatized by war: his father had been killed and at the age of eleven he had been interned in a Nazi slave labour camp. On his return to his home village he was confronted by poor prospects: he was at the bottom of the village hierarchy, treated badly by his teachers and the local priest. His uncle, a Communist youth organizer, offered him an escape route, even though his mother tried to keep him in the village:

> My decision was unalterable. I wanted to live and work like a human being, be treated the same as others and not like an animal . . . There was no force or might that could keep me in the village that I hated so much, which had looked down on me throughout my childhood.[74]

When he arrived, Chmieliński was issued with a new khaki uniform, complete with cap and red tie. 'Sometimes I furtively looked at myself in the mirror and I couldn't get over how different I now appeared.' He was now an equal, part of a new army of labour. Equal rations were given to everybody at dinner, and 'all of us were equal'. For the first time, he fell asleep 'completely happy'. Although the work was hard, and Chmieliński was surprised that his brigade was expected to build a huge plant with only very basic tools, he became an enthusiastic Stakhanovite labourer, engaging in heroic 'socialist competition' to reconstruct the country after the War:

> I firmly believed that with a common effort we would build in a few years a splendid city in which I would live and work . . . I didn't count the hours of work. I built as though I was building my own house. I believed that I was working for myself and my children.[75]

However, his story ended in tragedy. He won a scholarship to study at a vocational school, but even so he could not afford all the fees. He had a nervous breakdown, blaming trade union and party bosses for the injustice, and ended up a homeless alcoholic. He rejoiced when the old regime was removed after the rebellion against the Stalinist order in October 1956.

Chmieliński's memoir, written in 1958, after the High Stalinist period but still under Communism, was undoubtedly influenced by the ideological nostrums of the time, but its account of youthful enthusiasm is corroborated by others, and indeed makes sense. Chmieliński believed Communist promises of a new system, of a semi-militarized 'guerrilla' society of equals, all striving for the common good, which would bring personal education and advancement, and it is no surprise he was taken with the vision. However, like many others he found the new order much more stratified, unjust and harsh towards the poor than was promised. The dreams of many young Communists like Chmieliński foundered when confronted with the reality of the hungry state and the 'new class'.

Young and ambitious people like Chmieliński, desperate to escape from rural backwaters, were precisely the sort of people willing to be forged into new socialist people – much as they had been in the USSR of the 1930s. And there were real benefits to conformity. Large numbers of managerial and technical positions were waiting to be filled in postwar Eastern Europe, especially in Poland and the GDR, and levels of social mobility in this period were much higher even than in the West (which was witnessing its own golden age of mobility). Chmieliński may have found that mobility had its limits, but many others were able to afford an education and join the ranks of middle-management.

Established, older workers, however, had fewer incentives to become part of the regime's new labour army. They remained loyal to older working-class cultures that the Communists were trying to break.[76] The late-Stalinist order in industry was an even more authoritarian and non-egalitarian version of the one developed in the USSR in the mid-1930s. It was founded on a rigid hierarchy: plans and work-targets (norms) were laid down by the ministry at the centre, and then communicated down the line of command to be implemented by managers and foremen. Each worker was given what was effectively a mini-plan to fulfil, and was paid according to how much he or she produced. Bosses were therefore given even greater powers than they had wielded under the capitalist system. In practice, shortages of labour, and the bosses' need to secure workers' cooperation, prevented managers from throwing their weight around too much. But workers still resented their powers, especially over the allocation of jobs, where they could show favouritism. For example, a worker's pay very much depended on whether the norm was easy to fulfil or not, and shortages of materials could make it impossible for the worker, however heroic, to make a reasonable wage.

Unequal pay was also a source of resentment. It was common to pay workers on a piece-rate system; and this gave power to foremen and bosses who could decide who was to be given the easy and who the difficult jobs. And at the same time that technicians and bosses were given higher pay and privileges (such as special shops), older, more equal wage scales were scrapped. This was particularly controversial in the GDR where many of the technical specialists were former Nazis who had been fired in 1945 and then rehired. According to one party report, party members were deeply hostile to these policies: 'The intelligentsia must be brought to account once and for all. The preferential treatment of the intelligentsia is bullshit. The stores where the intelligentsia have the right to go shopping must be smashed.'[77]

Especially unpopular were the Stakhanovites who cooperated with managers to over-fulfil their norms, and, just as in the USSR in the 1930s, this put pressure on all workers to do the same. One worker at the United Lighting and Electrics Factory in Northern Budapest, János Sztankovits, had been deported to the USSR after 1945 and worked in a Soviet factory, where he became a Stakhanovite worker. On his return to Hungary he resisted becoming a Stakhanovite there as well, telling party agitators that 'Stalin could stick his shift up his arse, I worked for him for three years for free, I wasn't even given proper clothes, I was freed, and why should I work for him again?' He was now in serious trouble, and had no option but to cooperate and become a Stakhanovite, and he received the higher wages that came with it. His fellow workers were naturally angry that he was prepared to over-fulfil the norm, telling him to 'go back to the Soviet Union, if you like it so much there'.[78]

The Communists could, of course, justify this inequality according to Marx's ideological scheme: in the lower phase of socialism, the principle 'to each according to his work' would operate. But, understandably, many saw the new order as a betrayal of the socialist values the party proclaimed so loudly, and Marxism gave them a ready-made language of protest. One anonymous letter of January 1949 from a worker to Hilary Minc, the Polish Minister of Industry, signed 'A follower of the Teachings of Marx and Engels', declared:

You announce that the factories in which we work are our exclusive property, only ours – and how does it turn out that we are only miserable
servants with a lower wage rate than in private factories. And after all, if
this is our property, then the income which the factory gives should be
divided among the workers, and we would pay a tax like the private
factories pay. You don't like it, do you? For then there wouldn't be money
to build you palaces in which there are dozens of square metres of space for
each bureaucrat. . .[79]

There was one area of life, though, where the regime was too egalitarian
for many workers' tastes: the place of women. The Communists pressed
for women to be employed in all jobs – even those that were traditionally done by men. Some women did become party activists and hero-
workers, but the obstacles were enormous. Male workers often
successfully resisted the employment of women, and women tended to
be confined to traditionally female roles, whilst earning less than men.
Meanwhile, the life of the hero-labourer, working all shifts to over-fulfil
the plan, was difficult to reconcile with family life.[80]

This was not the only concession the regime had to make to East
European workers. In many places, pre-existing socialist cultures gave
workers the confidence to resist the Communists; in the GDR, for
instance, old Social Democratic workers were at the forefront of complaints.[81] In some cases, the ideal of creating a 'new socialist man', full
of enthusiasm for Communist ideology, was more or less abandoned.
The Polish sociologist Hanna Świda-Ziemba noted that as long as workers worked, ideological incorrectness was permissible:

In my contacts with workers at the time I was struck by their freedom of
expression, their aggressive attitudes toward their superiors and the system
of the time – shown sometimes very sharply at public meetings . . . This was
not a matter of personal courage in that community, but the result of the
ruling ideology, and also the social practice of the Stalinist system.

In contrast with the intelligentsia, who were expected to follow the
party line, 'The duty of the workers instead was essentially work, the
realisation of the six-year plan. Views and opinions could be expressed
without punishment, and instead the slightest sign of real refusal to work
could be dealt with under many different types of regulations. . .'[82]

If East European Communist regimes, dealing with a pre-existing industrial workforce, had to make compromises with workers, the Chinese Communists were in a much stronger position. In 1949, manufacturing had largely taken place in small-scale workshops. It was the Communists themselves who created large-scale industry – much as the Soviets had done in the 1930s – and their large factories and plants were modelled on those found in Soviet textbooks. This made it much easier for the regime to mould its workforce. Moreover, as the gulf between rural and urban economies was even greater than it had been in Eastern Europe and the USSR, the Chinese economy enjoyed a huge labour surplus. Nevertheless, the regime could not provide industrial jobs for all-comers, but those who did find work with relatively high wages and benefits soon rose to the top of the labour hierarchy. Below them was a group of less privileged and unprotected workers in smaller plants, whilst at the very bottom came the mass of the peasants, who after 1955 were effectively tied to the land. Realizing their privilege, the urban working class proved far more receptive to the party's intensive propaganda effort.

Despite this, many aspects of High Stalinism became deeply unpopular in Chinese factories. The Soviet piece-rate and wage system, introduced between 1952 and 1956, was not only difficult to organize in circumstances where skilled managers au fait with its complexities were scarce, but also caused intense hostility amongst workers used to more egalitarian wage regimes. A rigid, Soviet-style eight-grade scheme that was applied throughout China's various regions was endlessly criticized for its arbitrariness. Efforts to categorize the labour force according to the eight grades reached absurd lengths: the managers of one Shanghai department store tried to determine salespeople's 'skill levels' by giving them a 'blind taste test' designed to assess their judgement of a range of tobaccos – non-smokers were naturally disgruntled.[83] Meanwhile the powers given to managers fed smouldering resentments, especially in the case of formerly private-sector firms where the old 'capitalist' owner was officially dubbed a new 'socialist' manager. These various grievances constituted a powder-keg of anger, which would explode the moment Mao began to question the hierarchies of the so-called 'Soviet model' of management in the late 1950s.

This kind of crisis came much earlier in Eastern Europe, as the governing regimes ratcheted up pressure on workers whilst real wages fell. In Hungary, for example, wages declined by an estimated 16.6 per cent between 1949 and 1953. Workers tended to express their dissatisfaction indirectly, for example by going AWOL, frequently changing jobs, and foot-dragging. But occasionally full-blown strikes would break out, necessitating forcible repression; 31.6 per cent of those imprisoned in Czechoslovak jails for 'political crimes' were workers.[84] By the early 1950s, it had become clear that the Communists' attempts to mobilize workers into their new army of labour had stalled badly. If they were so singularly unsuccessful in their appeals to the supposed labour vanguard, it was hardly likely that the 'backward' peasantry would prove more willing recruits to the new Communist project.

VII

In April 1952 a Chinese traveller, far more humble than either Mao or Liu, visited the Soviet Union. Geng Changsuo, a peasant from the village of Wugong (about 120 miles south of Beijing) first reached Moscow, where he enthusiastically celebrated May Day in Red Square, and then travelled to Ukraine, where he and his delegation inspected various collective farms, including the model October Victory Collective. Geng and his fellow Chinese were flabbergasted by the riches on show: the water, electricity, plentiful food and clean solid houses equipped with telephones. Geng was even more impressed by what was presented as the source of this wealth – the miraculous tractor – which achieved what 150 Wugong peasants with 150 animals and 150 ploughshares would struggle to complete.[85]

Geng was an earnest party member, committed not only to helping his own family and clan, but the village as a whole. He neither smoked nor drank or gambled, and with his low, confident voice and down-to-earth manner, he was the ideal Communist village leader. During the War he had organized a voluntary cooperative of poor peasant families who pooled their resources and were able to diversify into rope production, which they then sold on local markets. The cooperative prospered in the early 1950s as more and more families joined, and Geng soon attracted the attentions of the party leadership. From 1951 Mao had been trying to coax Chinese peasants into embracing fully socialized agriculture, and Geng, after his state-sponsored study-tour in the USSR, returned a convert and true believer, not only in Soviet collectivism, but more generally to the Soviet version of modernity. Advertising his passion for all things 'modern', he shaved off his beard and moustache, sported Western-style tailoring, and began to learn to read and write. He soon embarked on a mission of proselytization, explaining how collectivization and mechanization – and especially the '*traktor*', transliterated as '*tuolaji*', a word the Wugong peasants had never heard before – had brought the USSR prosperity. These same villagers were exhorted to join an expanded, village-size cooperative.[86]

When Mao pressed for full Soviet-style collectivization (the consolidation of small farms into large state-owned units) in the summer of 1955, Geng became one of the first collective farm chairmen. However, the policy was a step too far for Geng and his fellow peasants, and the collective farm proved to be a very different proposition from the much less ambitious peasant cooperative. Peasants' income, which had hitherto come from selling their produce, now came entirely in the form of wages from the labour they gave to the collective farm. Under this system only a few large families with many wage-earners could earn the income they had enjoyed before. Moreover, the Chinese drew directly from the Soviet model, using the collectives to extract more and more resources from the countryside for industrial investment. Peasant living standards suffered accordingly. Even so, Geng and the other Wugong leaders, desperate to retain their status as model villagers, banned all private plots, and pressed on with full-scale collectivization.

More revolutionary, perhaps, than even its economic consequences was the political impact of collectivization. The power of Geng and people like him over peasants' lives (already considerable) now became vast. Village leaders exercised exclusive control over all of the land; they allocated jobs to peasants; and they gained privileged access to all state resources. One popular verse tersely captured the new relationship between rank and resources:

> First rank folk
> Have things sent to the gate.
> Second rank folk
> Rely on others.
> Third rank folk
> Only fret.[87]

Geng was one of the more honest and altruistic officials, and put much effort not only into persuading peasants of the advantages of the collective farm but into making the system work. Education was expanded, and unlike many villages, Wugong acquired, for the first time, a rudimentary welfare system. However, even the virtuous Geng was soon wrapped in all the trappings of local bossdom, for alongside schools and welfare, Wugong could also now boast its own village security apparatus. The new police force was led by the feared 'Fierce Zhang', a former poor peasant, who recruited a rough and ready cadre of local toughs to keep order. When, for example, a group of villagers uprooted 1,500 cotton plants in protest at the low price for cotton being offered, this security force used torture to flush out the culprits. In other Chinese villages abuses by officials could be even worse. Now village leaders' powers fused with traditional patriarchal attitudes into a new quasi-feudal code, which could include an informal *droit de seigneur* over mainly poor women. Rapes were widespread: two of Mao's former bodyguards, for instance, rewarded with high office in Tianjin, used their power to terrorize local women. They were ultimately executed for their crimes, but many others escaped justice.[88].

The story of Geng Changsuo and Wugong village encapsulates many of the hopes and disappointments of what was called the 'Soviet model' in China. Some aspects of collectivization could appeal to some peasants: the tractors and the large-scale agriculture all promised the riches small-scale agriculture could not deliver, whilst education and welfare promised integration and opportunities in the broader national community. But collectivization soon created a new hierarchy: a powerful privileged stratum which often behaved arbitrarily and exploitatively. The peasantry, as a whole, remained at the bottom of the social hierarchy, isolated from the rest of China and tied to the land, over which they exercised much less control than they had before. Meanwhile, rural resources were sucked out of agriculture and pumped into heavy industry, whilst the incentive system damaged productivity, laying the ground for food crises in the longer term.

Soviet Eastern Europe had experienced collectivization in a similar, though even more traumatic way. China escaped violent 'dekulakization'; the Chinese Communist Party succeeded in persuading (or pressuring) peasants into joining collectives without a full-blown class-struggle campaign. (In all probability this was because peasant resistance had been broken earlier during the violent land reform campaigns.) Eastern Europe, however, following the Soviet 1930s blueprint more closely, launched collectivization and dekulakization simultaneously.

Pressure to join the collective was often intense, and in some areas, coercion was explicit. In others, it was less direct: peasants would find that they could only buy non-agricultural goods in state shops if they were collective-farm members. As one Bulgarian peasant put it, 'Of course, you did not *have* to join the cooperative, unless you wanted shoes on your feet and a shirt on your back.'[89] Even so, as in the USSR of the 1930s, there was a good deal of resistance. Peasants mistrusted the detachments of officials sent from the towns to impose the collectives, and refused to give inspectors information about who owned what. It was not, moreover, easy to persuade peasants to denounce their influential wealthy neighbours: in the Romanian village of Hîrseni in the Olt Land region of south-eastern Transylvania, for instance, party officials tried to persuade the poor peasant Nicolae R. to denounce his allegedly kulak (*chiabur*) neighbour Iosif Oltean, who had promised him 20 kilograms of wool and 10 of cheese in return for work, but had only delivered a nugatory quantity of poor-quality wool. Nevertheless, Nicolae defended his neighbour: 'Oltean was a good man who helps us poor people, even if he was greedy.'[90]

Peasants were profoundly alienated by the loss of their land. The new Marxist-Leninist ideology, which regarded labour as the prime virtue, was diametrically opposed to the moral economy of many peasants, which saw landowning and economic independence as a mark of status. But the high food-delivery quotas demanded by the state to feed workers and finance industrialization were, if anything, even more unpopular than dekulakization or collectivization. One woman peasant from the Hungarian village of Sárosd, south of Budapest, remembered her misplaced hopes that she could deliver enough tax to the state by growing 1.7 hectares of sunflower seeds: 'One came home without a penny. Everything went to taxes, not enough was left even to buy an apron.'[91] On the collective farm itself, pay was low and conditions were poor. One peasant from the Bulgarian village of Zamfirovo remembered:

It was terrible. I remember nearly collapsing in the fields one day during the wheat harvest. We worked all day in unbearable heat, doing everything by hand just like before ... The work was hard and the pay very low – only 80 *stotinki* a day and any pay in kind was deducted from that. People were worse off. Even the poorest people who joined the cooperative with little land felt worse off. I remember one summer somebody came to the fields to sell beer and sodas and even though we were dying of thirst no one could afford to buy them.[92]

As in China, the weakly constrained power of the new village political elite inflamed peasant anger further. Quotas depended on the whims of collective farm officials. Meanwhile peasants found that people higher up in the political hierarchy were given more credit for their collective-farm work than others. Life became intensely political, as villagers' future became dependent on relationships with the new bosses.

Some resisted the harsh policies, and rebellions and demonstrations broke out in several areas. One of the most violent and disruptive was in the Bosnian Bihać region in May 1950, though elsewhere they rarely posed any real threat to the authorities. A more common way of resisting collectivization was simply to leave agriculture altogether – something that some East European governments, desperate for industrial labour, encouraged.

Resistance and resentment slowed the pace of collectivization, and by the time of Stalin's death it had made surprisingly little headway in Eastern Europe. In Czechoslovakia, for instance, only 43 per cent of the agricultural population were employed on collective farms of some sort, whilst in Poland the figure was a mere 17 per cent. Indeed, it was only in the early 1960s that collectivization was completed, and then only after serious concessions had been made to the peasantry – allowing private plots and giving peasant households the right to organize the use of labour, for example. In Poland and Yugoslavia, collectivization was simply scrapped, and the countryside reverted to small private farms.

In 1949, the Communist Party organization in the East German town of Plauen drew up one of its regular reports on popular opinion. It concluded that whilst the highly qualified workers and technical intelligentsia were reasonably content, the 'broad masses' of the population – workers and peasants – were not.[93] And by 1953 there is a great deal of evidence that this distribution of happiness held for much of Soviet Eastern Europe. Efforts to break peasant cultures were inevitably unpopular. Meanwhile the High Stalinist system, in which a 'new class' of bureaucrats was set above the labouring classes as official resource-extractors for the ever-ravenous state, could not be sustained for long, especially in societies with indigenous socialist traditions of a pre-Soviet provenance.

In the closing years of the High Stalinist era, the Soviet satellite regimes became increasingly reliant on naked coercion to force through unpopular economic policies. In 1950 in Poland, and 1952–3 in Romania, Bulgaria and Czechoslovakia, currency reforms effectively confiscated people's savings, and in Czechoslovakia they led to a wave of protests.[94] By 1953, it has been estimated that between 6 and 8 per cent of all adult males in Soviet Eastern Europe were in prison. It was no surprise that the High Stalinist system did not long survive its architect's demise.

8

Parricide

I

On a bright summer's day in June 1962, beneath the shadow of the monumental Moscow University building, a good-humoured and avuncular Nikita Khrushchev released a goldfish into a newly constructed pond. Shortly afterwards, a young child was given a giant key on behalf of all Pioneers – the 'Key to the Land of the Romantics', as the press put it. Both were part of the opening ceremonies for the new Pioneer Palace – a centre for the party's children's organization on the Lenin Hills. The massive 56-hectare park and large, airy building were to be a children's wonderland – a 'children's republic', where the 'children are masters' and adult discipline was to be as light as possible. The project's creators claimed that children would teach each other, using peer pressure to maintain discipline.[1]

This was all a long way from late Stalinism. Stalin loved to be shown patting children's heads but handling goldfish in public would have been beneath his dignity. The building itself was also a sharp contrast to its forbidding Stalinist neighbour. In the modernist 'International style' created in the 1920s, it was decorated with modern sculptures and reliefs, some in a primitivist, child-like style, not with the old neo-classical figures of muscle-bound workers. It was low-rise and deliberately 'democratic', with large glass windows and doors on all sides – open to the joyful children running in from the surrounding park.

The Pioneer Palace was ideology in concrete. It showed the form of Communism Khrushchev wanted to take the place of High Stalinism: modern and internationalist; free of the archaic nationalism of the early 1950s;[2] and yet also Romantic, full of the possibilities of human creativity. According to the journalists of *Komsomolskaia Pravda*, it was built 'by people who are Romantics, and this Romantic Pioneer style of life must splash over the walls of the palace'.[3] It was centred round the welfare of its people, rather than the power of the state. Most importantly, though, it was to be a building for children free of parental restraint. It embodied the values of equality and fraternity and was to be inhabited by children who disciplined themselves. Khrushchev loathed the old 'aristocratic', status-obsessed Stalinist style. He thought the Moscow University building was church-like, 'an ugly, formless mass'.[4]

Khrushchev was only one of the Communist leaders to seek an alternative to the harshness and hierarchy of Stalinism. Once the old patriarch of Communism was dead, the heirs realized that the old system must change. Coercion was no longer working and growing privileges and inequality were causing anger. At the same time, the legacy of mass violence and the Stalinist party's continuing commitment to 'struggle' against 'enemies' were narrowing the regime's base of support. The system had to become more inclusive. More generally, many reacted powerfully against the Stalinist economic determinism – the view that everything, including values, morality and human lives, had to be sacrificed to building a modern, industrial society. The old cruel dogmatism, they argued, had to be replaced by a more 'humane' socialism.

What, though, was this to mean in practice? Some called for a more Pragmatic Communism of limited markets and individual rights. This was especially appealing in Soviet Eastern Europe but most party leaders were not ready for this compromise. For it would undermine the ruling party and threaten its 'leading role' in politics, whilst challenging the old command economies. Others sought a more technocratic, Modernist model. Another answer, more appealing to Communist leaders, was to seek to broaden the regime, whilst restoring its revolutionary dynamism. The band of brothers had to be reassembled and the spirit of collective will revived. The great ideological innovators of the 1950s – Tito, Khrushchev and Mao – all embarked on a 'great leap backwards' to the Radical Lenin of 1917 or even the Romantic Marx of the 1840s.

Yet the photographs of the Pioneer Palace's opening ceremony present a rather different picture to the image of relaxed self-discipline depicted in *Komsomolskaia Pravda*. To the modern eye the atmosphere looks distinctly militaristic: uniformed children stand in ordered ranks, bearing flags and drums. And here lay the difficulty facing Stalin's 'sons'. Whilst their ideal might have been a people working creatively and cooperating in an easy spirit of peace and harmony, they hoped to achieve this whilst constructing powerful states and efficient economies. In the absence of market incentives, a resort to semi-military mobilization therefore remained attractive. This was Mao's solution, and a military, guerrilla Communism, complete with accompanying 'class struggle', became the foundation of his strategy. Khrushchev was determined to avoid violence, but even he found it impossible to pursue a Radical Communism whilst escaping the bullying, military party culture of his youth; only Tito really broke from it, but at the cost of drifting towards the market and into the Western sphere of influence.

It is therefore no surprise that the death of Stalin brought not peace, but a 'thaw' that exposed some of the 'frozen' tensions within the Communist world, whilst fragmenting his vast empire. Indeed the fifteen years after Stalin's death were some of the most turbulent in the Communist history and the most dangerous of the Cold War, when the world came closest to nuclear conflagration. The first challenge to Stalin's orthodoxy, though, had come whilst he still lived – with the break with Tito in 1948.

II

In his memoirs, Milovan Djilas recalls:

> One day – it must have been in the spring of 1950 – it occurred to me that we Yugoslav Communists were now in a position to start creating Marx's free association of producers. The factories would be left in their hands, with the sole proviso that they should pay a tax for military and other States' needs 'that remained essential'.

He then revealed his new idea to the ideologist Edvard Kardelj and the economic chief Boris Kidrič 'while we sat in a car parked in front of the villa where I lived'. Kidrič was sceptical, but eventually they took it to the boss:

> Tito paced up and down, as though completely wrapped up in his own thoughts. Suddenly he stopped and exclaimed 'Factories belonging to workers – something that has never yet been achieved!' With these words, the theories worked out by Kardelj and myself seemed to shed their

complications and seemed, too, to find better prospects of being workable. A few months later, Tito explained the workers' self-management bill to the [Yugoslav] National Assembly.[5]

Djilas was describing the first of many 'returns to Marx' of the 1950s, as Communists tried to find an alternative to Stalinism. Djilas's account of eureka moments, fevered discussions about Marxism in the backs of cars and sudden decisions in party villas tells us a great deal about the closed nature of Tito's leadership. Yet his story of the origins of the new Yugoslav model of Communism is not entirely convincing. Tito and the leadership had been looking for new models for some time before the break with the USSR. More importantly, the rhetoric of 'self-management' was highly misleading. Djilas and his friends were doubtless sincere in trying to find a democratic Marxism, and their ideas caused enormous excitement amongst Western socialists. But in practice, Yugoslav self-management had little to do with the Romantic Marx's ideas of democratic participation in management, or even the workers' control of Lenin's *State and Revolution*. The reforms were the beginning of Tito's move towards the market, and the Yugoslav model showed how difficult it was to re-radicalize Marxism in Europe after Stalin.

As in China, the roots of the Yugoslav Communism are to be found as much in the experience of partisan warfare as in Moscow and the Comintern. But in Yugoslavia, with its ethnic and economic diversity, two models of governance emerged as the War ended. The first, in the relatively peaceful and prosperous Slovenia (where most fighting had finished with Italy's collapse in 1943), was moderate and pragmatic. Local assemblies were relatively democratic, land redistribution was limited, and the state used money to give people incentives. The second, in the poorer, war-torn Bosnia-Herzegovina and Macedonia, was more radical and egalitarian. Here shortages and inflation had destroyed the value of money. Communists resorted to rationing, ideological enthusiasm, and the mobilization of labour teams to keep the economy going.[6]

Tito's objective in the first few years of Communist rule was to combine the Pragmatic Slovenian and Radical Bosnian models and apply them to the rest of Yugoslavia. Many policies of the early years echoed Lenin's NEP. Tito, apprehensive about alienating his peasant supporters, eschewed collectivization, whilst Kidrič's Five-Year Plan of 1947 (an enormous set of documents weighing one and a half tons) was not modelled on Stalin's. It was an amalgam of hundreds of local plans; the centre used financial incentives, not political commands, and budgets were expected to balance. At the same time, however, Tito wanted rapid development for his poor and vulnerable country – something moderate NEP-style policies would not achieve. So the Communists decided to rely on voluntary, unpaid 'shock work' to push the economy forward. The Communist Youth League was particularly active, and led 62,000 young people in building the Brčko–Banovići Youth Railway. Several idealistic Communists from around the world also joined the labour platoons, much as their predecessors had flocked to Spain in the 1930s – one of them was the future Cambodian Communist leader Pol Pot, who was studying in France at the time. For Yugoslavs, however, participation was not always voluntary, and conditions were poor. Nevertheless some enthusiasm persisted; as one worker declared, 'although we are tired, together, and with song, it is easier'.[7] This type of mobilization, though, had its disadvantages for Tito. In its enthusiasm for social transformation, the Youth League often encouraged the unauthorized persecution of 'class aliens', something the leadership did not want.

This schizophrenic combination of two very different approaches continued until 1947, at which stage Tito understood his real vulnerability. A wily operator, Tito had secured foreign aid from both the Americans and the Soviets after 1945. With the beginning of the Cold War, though, Western aid stopped, and following the break with Moscow in 1948 Yugoslavia was left friendless and threatened by a possible Stalinist coup. Paradoxically, Tito resisted Stalin by emulating him with a much more centralized, militaristic strategy. These years saw some of the harshest repressions of the period, including purges of 'Cominternists' and the foundation of the 'Naked Island' (Goli Otok) prison camp for political opponents. The old idealism came under severe strain. Djilas commented angrily to the security chief Aleksandar Ranković: 'Now we are treating Stalin's followers as we treated his enemies', to which Ranković replied despairingly, 'Don't say that! Don't talk about it!'[8] Repression, though, was combined with pro-worker campaigns rather similar to Stalin's in the early 1930s. The party encouraged workers to criticize managers and experts, at the cost of losing control of the workforce.

These years were grim ones for Tito and his circle, constantly terrified of assassination, Soviet invasion and economic collapse. But in 1950 salvation arrived in the form of American aid. It was the United States, keen to have an ally in the Communist world, that decided to 'keep Tito afloat', and the Americans, the International Monetary Fund and World Bank all provided loans. Loans, of course, had to be repaid, and that meant that budgets had to be balanced, which in turn made more radical socialist experiment impossible. Military-style mobilization had to give way to strict accounting and efficiency. Meanwhile the regime decentralized power, and officially transferred all property from the state to so-called 'worker councils'. The Yugoslav Communist Party was renamed, in a bow to democratic sensibilities, the 'League of Communists of Yugoslavia'. But this was still a one-party state, and 'worker self-management' was not management by workers at all. In practice managers and officials were in control, and they had to keep within budgets set by the centre. This much-trumpeted democratization of the workplace was actually a reversion to the Slovenian wartime model, and far from being a return to Marx, this was rule by managers and financial controls.

After 1950, Yugoslavia was neither a command nor a market economy but something in between; the state managed the economy by regulating prices and issuing credits rather than by political diktat. In some ways, it continued to behave like a typical Communist state: the regime poured money into heavy industry, and used redistribution to soften inequalities, especially between the richer Croatia and Slovenia and the poorer Macedonia and Montenegro. But it had scrapped collectivization, and was, to all intents and purposes, part of the Western economic world. For a time, this mixture of markets, socialism and American aid was remarkably successful, and in the 1950s Yugoslavia posted the highest growth rate in Eastern Europe. The country was also the most open and liberal of all Communist states. Western tourists visited and Yugoslavs worked abroad, bringing back Western influences with them. At the same time, tensions between the republics were held in check by memories of wartime blood-letting, and by Tito himself. Tito, Serbian Orthodox and Croat, embodied 'Yugoslavism', and his almost monarchical style appealed to many, even as it alienated others. Djilas, a puritan and intellectual, excoriated Tito's vanity and love of luxury – his thirty-two palaces, his lavish banquets and receptions, his perma-tan, dyed hair and dazzling false teeth.[9] But he conceded it had a rationale:

By taking up residence in palaces, by ruling from them, he attached himself to the monarchic tradition and to traditional concepts of power ... Pomp was indispensable to him. It satisfied his strong *nouveau riche* instincts; it also compensated for his ideological deficiency, his inadequate education.[10]

Djilas was expelled from the Central Committee for his democratic scruples in 1954. But he acknowledged that Tito's monarchical style appealed to a rural population accustomed to traditional forms of authority. Tito's regime, caught as it was between the East and West, the urban and the rural, presented a remarkably diverse set of faces to the world. To the urban intelligentsia, party idealists and the Western left it was the home of an authentic democratic Marxism; to the United States and Western business, it had reconciled socialism with the market; and to the peasants, it was a government of ancient heroes. Folk poets celebrated the break with the Soviet bloc (and the Hungarian Communist leader Rákosi) in pseudo-epic verse:

> O Rákosi, where were you
> When Tito spilled his blood?
> You rested in the coolness of Moscow,
> Whilst Tito fought the war.
> Pretend now to be a democrat!
> If a battle develops again,
> The old story will repeat:
> Our Tito will be the leader,
> And you will hide again.[11]

As will be seen, beneath the prosperity and Tito's bravura confidence, all was not as happy as it seemed. Nevertheless, by 1956 Tito could afford to be satisfied. Since the perilous and gloomy days of 1948–9, he had steered Yugoslavia towards independence and wealth. He had even gained international prestige with his own special form of Marxism. He became a major figure in the 'Non-Aligned' movement of states outside the Soviet and Western alliances, and by 1955 he had made peace with the USSR. The transition from the Stalinist model was to be rather more traumatic in other East European states.

III

On the morning of 1 March 1953, after a boisterous evening of food, drink and cinema that lasted until 4 a.m., Stalin was discovered on the floor of his bedroom. He had suffered a severe stroke. Members of the party's inner circle – Georgii Malenkov, Beria, Khrushchev and Red Army boss Nikolai Bulganin – were called to his bedside, but it was some time before they summoned the doctors. This may have been deliberate. They had become increasingly worried about Stalin's unpredictability and vindictiveness in his final years. But it is more likely that they were too frightened to act.[12] In the poisonous atmosphere of the Soviet leadership, overt ambition and pushiness could attract severe punishment. The extreme centralization of power Stalin had spent so much of his life perfecting may well have killed him.

Stalin's death came as an emotional shock to friends and enemies alike. For Stalin was not just a political boss; he was the embodiment of a whole system – ideological, cultural, political and economic. Fedor Burlatskii, later one of Khrushchev's main advisers and, privately, no admirer of Stalin's, tried to sum up his mixed feelings:

> His death shook everyone in the Soviet Union to the core, even if the emotions it aroused were varied. Something that had seemed unshakeable, eternal and immortal was gone. The simple thought that a man had died and his body had to be consigned to the earth hardly entered anyone's head. The institution of power, which lay at the very foundation of our society, had crumbled and collapsed. What would life be like now, what would happen to us and to the country?[13]

Burlatskii's thoughts were probably shared by many of the middle-aged lieutenants of world Communism who attended the funeral, including Togliatti, Thorez and Zhou Enlai, as well as the Soviet inner circle. All were aware that the USSR was in a poor state. Living standards were low, there was little new housing, and consumer goods were scarce. Agriculture was a disaster – harvests were poorer than before World War I – and much of the nation's food was produced outside the collectives on the tiny proportion of land given over to individual plots. The prison system was massive, and Beria, charged with making the Gulag pay, despaired at the cost of managing the 300,000 guards and the low productivity of the prison labour.[14] Riots and protests in the camps were common: in early 1954 inmates in the Kengir prison in Kazakhstan took over the camp for forty days before being eventually subdued by tanks and aerial bombing. Relations with the West were also tense, forcing the regime to expend scarce resources on guns, not butter. The Korean War dragged on, only repression kept Eastern Europe stable, and the USSR lagged behind the United States in airpower and nuclear capability. Stalin's successors all agreed that his security-obsessed worldview had merely caused fear and resentment abroad, and had ultimately undermined Soviet security.

There was, however, no agreement on what was to replace Stalin's old order. Of the influential leaders that succeeded Stalin – Beria, Malenkov and, very much in the rear, the poorly educated party secretary, Nikita Khrushchev – Beria and Malenkov had most in common. They were on the Modernist side of the party, and believed that repression and persecutions, especially of intellectuals and experts, were counterproductive – economically and politically. On Stalin's death they probably worked together to install Malenkov as head of the state apparatus and senior leader.

It was Lavrentii Beria who took the initiative in the days after the funeral, and he immediately launched a radical programme of change. At first sight, he was an unlikely reformer. As Ezhov's successor as head of the secret police, he was directly involved in torture. But he was a talented administrator and was largely responsible for the success of the Soviet atomic project. He also had a deep contempt for the party apparatus – it was full of useless 'prattlers' and 'parasites'.[15] Power, not agitprop, would make the USSR great.

Beria had no moral qualms about repression, but he realized how economically irrational it was. On Stalin's death he began to review Stalin's fabricated cases. He told his fellow party leaders that over 2.5 million people were languishing in the Gulag who were no threat to the state, and proposed the release of over a million non-political inmates. Forced labour, he argued, was less efficient than free; the Gulag had to be drastically reduced.[16] At the same time, he challenged the Russian chauvinist and imperialist elements of late Stalinism, condemning discrimination in favour of Russian personnel and language – something he felt keenly as a Georgian.[17]

Most dramatic and controversial, though, were Beria's foreign policy proposals. He and Malenkov were convinced that the health of the economy depended on serious concessions to the West, and they had some success in winning over their colleagues. Soon after Stalin's death, the USSR helped to bring the Korean War to an end and restored relations with Tito's Yugoslavia. More controversial, however, were Beria's proposals for the future of the GDR, where unrest was rife and thousands were continuing to leave for the West in response to Walter Ulbricht's harsh policies. Beria, it seems, proposed that the Soviets cut their losses and abandon socialism there completely: 'Why should socialism be built in the GDR? Let it just be a peaceful country. That is sufficient for our purposes.'[18]

Malenkov probably had sympathy with Beria's ideas, but the old Stalinist Molotov was strongly opposed, as was Khrushchev. Beria became vulnerable on the issue, partly for ideological reasons, but largely because his colleagues did not trust him. They were right not to. He was clearly manoeuvring for the top job and might well have killed them had he succeeded. Once Khrushchev and Malenkov had come to this conclusion, they began to conspire against him, securing the support of the army, together with the old guard Molotov and Kaganovich. Charged in a typically Stalinist manner with being a British spy, Beria was executed as an enemy of the people.

The triumvirate had become a duumvirate, and Khrushchev and Malenkov were now left to fight it out. Malenkov came from an old officer family, and was academically successful. He had a technical education, and, according to his son, saw himself as an enlightened autocrat, the leader of a Soviet 'technocracy'.[19] Sophisticated and intelligent, the patrician British ambassador Sir William Hayter recorded that whilst there was 'something creepy about his appearance, like a eunuch', he was 'quick, clever and subtle', an 'extremely agreeable neighbour at the table'.[20]

Malenkov's outlook was a broadly technocratic, Modernist one. The Plan would remain, but the regime would motivate people to work by offering higher living standards and financial incentives, not by repression, and so investment had to be reallocated from heavy industry and defence to consumer goods. Industry also needed to be more efficient, and that required less party interference in the economy and a slightly more liberal attitude towards the intelligentsia. Malenkov encouraged scientists to vent their grievances, which pre-

dictably provoked a flood of attacks on Lysenko and Stalin's ideolo-
gized science.

Malenkov also continued to defend a less confrontational foreign
policy, and was committed to serious détente with the West – though he
did not pursue Beria's controversial proposals on East Germany. He
used the testing of the new Soviet hydrogen bomb in August 1953 to
argue both that the USSR was now strong enough to seek peace, and
that the old East–West confrontation had to be superseded. Any war
between the United States and the USSR, he declared in March 1954,
would mean nuclear conflagration and 'the destruction of world civilization'. In making this statement, Malenkov was implicitly challenging
Marxist-Leninist orthodoxy: in these new conditions, he was calling for
a new world of pragmatism, in which the United States and the USSR
engaged in 'long-term coexistence and peaceful competition' between
the two systems, rather than Stalin's international 'class struggle'
between two hostile camps.[21]

The brief influence of Malenkov after the death of Stalin therefore
presented the West with a real opportunity to reduce Cold War tensions,
and it was an opportunity it missed – as Charles Bohlen, the American
ambassador in Moscow at the time, admitted.[22] The respected World
War II general Dwight Eisenhower had been elected American President
in 1952 in an atmosphere of recriminations over Truman's alleged 'loss'
of China and the Soviet acquisition of the atomic bomb in 1949, and he
promised to wage a more vigorous, but cost-effective, struggle against
Communism. A committed Christian, he saw the Cold War in highly
ideological terms, as a war in which 'the forces of good and evil are
massed and armed and opposed as rarely before in history', as he
declared in his inaugural address.[23] His Secretary of State, John Foster
Dulles, had a similar view, though he was, if anything, even more confrontational as he feared the power of Communism in the Third World.
Containment, he argued in 1952, had had its day. The United States had
to 'roll back' Communism.

At first, therefore, Washington was determined to use Stalin's death
and the tensions within the Kremlin to weaken the USSR. Eventually
Eisenhower did make some proposals to reduce the threat of nuclear
war, but few serious efforts were made to achieve détente. It may be that
any lessening of tensions was impossible because too many leaders, on
both sides, saw the conflict in absolute ideological terms, and were

suspicious of the motives of the rival superpower.[24] Even Malenkov retained deep suspicions of the capitalist West. But had Eisenhower followed Churchill's advice in May 1953 and held talks with Malenkov without conditions in that year, the Kremlin's more hard-line Cold Warriors might have lost influence.

As it was, Malenkov found himself under increasing pressure from the ambitious Khrushchev, and in January 1955 he was sacked as Prime Minister, accused of 'rightism' and condemned for neglecting the struggle against the international bourgeoisie. The West now had to deal with a much less easy-going leader – Nikita Khrushchev – whose vision of 'peaceful competition' was a more ideologically committed and confrontational one.

Sir William Hayter's first impression of Khrushchev at a dinner for the then British Prime Minister Clement Attlee was predictably less flattering than his view of Malenkov. He found him 'rumbustuous, impetuous, loquacious, free-wheeling'. In a deft if patronizing pen-portrait sent to his London bosses, he described Khrushchev as a combination of a peasant from a nineteenth-century Russian novel – shrewd and contemptuous of the master (*barin*) – and a 'British trades union leader of the old-fashioned kind', with a 'chip' on his shoulder; the result was a leader 'suspicious of the *barin*, now transformed into the capitalist powers of the West'.[25] Hayter's remarks were undoubtedly snobbish, but this product of the British class system understood the importance of hierarchy and status, in both the USSR and the international arena, better than many others.

Of all Communist leaders, Khrushchev's background was one of the poorest. He was born into an illiterate peasant family in Kursk province in April 1894 and for much of his youth lived in deep poverty. His father was a seasonal labourer in the mines, and at the age of fourteen, after a parish school education, Nikita followed him to work in the industrial town of Iuzovka, named after its founder, the Welsh businessman John Hughes. This was a huge cultural transition, and Khrushchev was eager to become a modern person. He began as an apprentice fitter, and like many first-generation workers developed an enthusiasm for all things mechanical that lasted for the rest of his life.[26] He even built his own motorcycle out of spare parts he managed to find around the town.[27] His first proper job was in a factory linked to the mines where labour radicalism was strong, and he soon became involved in illegal trade-union activities. He was the type of person likely to become a Communist leader and reminds one of Stalin and Tito – popular, gregarious, a natural leader, ambitious and eager to better himself.

Khrushchev was a politician of a strongly populist hue. He joined the Bolshevik party in 1918 (rather later than one would expect), became a political commissar in the Red Army, and after the civil war returned to the Iuzovka mines as deputy manager. He had the classic 'democratic' style prized at the time – spurning the office and report-writing to roll up his sleeves and help the workers out. It is no surprise that he briefly joined the Trotskyist opposition in 1923, a lapse which he managed to survive. Even though he had clearly found his niche as a party activist, he always wanted to make up for his lack of education and at one time had ambitions to become an engineer. He made two attempts to return to college: in the early 1920s he went to a party 'workers' faculty' (*rabfak*) to prepare him for a course at mining technical college, and in 1929 he went to the Industrial Academy in Moscow. Each time he found the academic demands a struggle, and returned to full-time party work. The Radical Marxist politics of the late 1920s were especially appealing to him and the populist Khrushchev could support Stalin's 'Great Break' with genuine enthusiasm. He was rapidly promoted and by 1932 was effectively running the Moscow party organization as Kaganovich's deputy. One of his most high-profile jobs was overseeing the construction of the first two lines of the Moscow Metro, with its people's-palace-style stations bedecked with chandeliers and statuary. He was the ideal early Stalinist party boss: enthusiastic, mobilizing, down in the tunnels day and night, driving his workers on to achieve extraordinary feats despite immense hardship and numerous accidents. He was also prepared to implement Stalin's repressions, and benefited from them when he replaced the purged boss of the Ukrainian party in 1938. Like many other party members, however, he became disillusioned and angry as he saw people he knew to be innocent accused and killed. He reportedly told an old friend at the time, 'When I can, I'll settle with that Mudakshvili in full' – combining the word for 'prick' (*mudak*) with Djugashvili (Stalin).[28]

Khrushchev's attitude towards Stalin's legacy was therefore more complex and ambiguous than that of his colleagues. Beria and Malenkov saw Stalin's repressions as irrational, and had no trouble cutting themselves loose from the Boss. Khrushchev, in contrast, had a more emotional reaction: Burlatskii remembered that he was always moved by the fate of individuals, and frequently launched into long, guilt-ridden monologues on the victims of the Terror.[29] He was as determined as his colleagues to replace Stalinist dogmatism and xenophobia with a new world of science and modernity, but he had been forged by the party of the 1920s and 1930. He was a true believer in the ideals of military-style Radical Communism – the collective, socialism, achieving great things by force of will. So whilst determined to abandon violence, he tried to revive the mass mobilizing spirit that had so often been its progenitor.

The differences between Malenkov's and Khrushchev's reform programmes soon became obvious. Whilst Malenkov was willing to sacrifice guns for butter Khrushchev insisted that it was perfectly possible to have both. To square the circle he looked to the mass mobilization methods of 1930s Moscow, proposing a massive expansion of the area devoted to grain and maize, especially in Western Siberia and Kazakhstan – the so-called 'Virgin Lands Programme' of 1954. This was a typical Khrushchev solution. It was massively ambitious, claiming to solve the food problem at a stroke; and it relied on the self-sacrifice of some 300,000 young Komsomol 'volunteers' who were sent to these remote regions in specially chartered trains. And for a time it appeared to be a huge success – the 1958 harvest was almost 70 per cent above the 1949–53 average.

Khrushchev's solutions may have seemed naïvely optimistic to some, but they were, in fact, in greater accord with the party's culture than Malenkov's, which appealed principally to the urban managerial and educated classes. This popularity was easy to explain: Khrushchev was not asking the USSR to retreat before a more powerful West, risking a 'roll-back' of Communism. Nor was he challenging entrenched military and heavy industrial interests. And he was also giving the leading role to the Communist Party and the Central Committee. After 1945, Stalin's lack of interest in grand ideological campaigns had led to a decline in the party's influence in relation to state administrative bodies, but Khrushchev promised to put it back at the very centre of Soviet politics. It is no surprise that he had no trouble winning over the party's Central Committee in engineering the fall of Malenkov.

Khrushchev now had the power to impose his new vision, and he did so in a momentous act of parricide: his denunciation of Stalin at the twentieth party congress in February 1956. As Mao justly commented,

Khrushchev did not just criticize Stalin, he 'killed' him. There were various reasons for this brave, if reckless, step. In part, Khrushchev was motivated by raw politics: although Khrushchev had taken part in the Terror, his rivals, Molotov and Kaganovich, were far more closely implicated, and any attack on Stalin was effectively an attack on them. Nevertheless, there was clearly an idealistic motive to the speech. Khrushchev was convinced that the party's moral stature was central to its success, and the only way to restore that stature was to admit the horrors of the past and start anew.

On 25 February, after an exhausting ten days of Congress speeches, the Soviet delegates were asked to stay for an extra meeting. The speech Khrushchev gave at this 'secret' session was probably the most extraordinary in the history of the Soviet Communist Party. His excoriating denunciation of the *vozhd* lasted for four hours. In it he detailed Stalin's responsibility for the torture and murder of 'honest and innocent Communists'; his cruel deportation of whole peoples; his vainglorious recklessness during the war; and his treachery towards Leninist principles. Khrushchev delivered the speech at a highly emotional pitch, at one point even berating Stalin's old associates: 'Hey you, Klim,' he sneered at Kliment Voroshilov, 'cut out the lying. You should have done it long ago. You're old and decrepit by now. Can't you find the courage and conscience to tell the truth about what you saw with your own eyes?'[30] Yet despite this language, Khrushchev's was a controlled and calculated attack. Stalin alone, with his 'cult of personality', was responsible for the Terror; he had gone to the bad from the mid-1930s, after which he had built the foundations of the Stalinist system. The party had been his victim, and now he had gone, it would be resurrected, pure in spirit.[31] It was evident that neither the party, nor the Plan, nor the collective farm would be threatened by Khrushchev's denunciation.

The audience was stunned. Accustomed to achingly dull speeches larded with ideological clichés, they could not believe their ears. Ageing party bosses, realizing its incendiary impact, reached for their heart medication. But the speech was also, of course, fundamentally implausible, for it would be extremely difficult to condemn the post-1934 Stalin without also discrediting the whole system which he, and Lenin before him, had built. Moreover, as Khrushchev well knew, the 'secret' speech could not be confined to Communist Party circles and was bound to become widely known. Soon there was a rash of 'demagogic' speeches and Stalin statues were vandalized. Meanwhile demonstrations broke out in Georgia, in defence of its disgraced son.[32] But the greatest impact, predictably, was on the region where the hold of Soviet Communism was at its weakest – in Eastern Europe.

IV

In 1953 a Russian theatre company staged a production of *Hamlet* in Budapest. Even though few would understand the Russian-language performance, this was an important ceremonial occasion, when the imperial power would demonstrate its generosity and cultural prestige to the cream of Hungarian society – on this occasion, the Communist ideology chief, József Révai, was in attendance. This time, though, there was one major difference from the past. Although the old Communist leaders were still in power, Stalin was dead. A journalist, sent to cover the performance, remembers:

> Everybody knew that nobody would understand anything, but it was packed, and I was there from the radio. We were behind Révai's box and there was a scene where the ghost is talking to Hamlet and the actor was just repeating '*Gamlet, Gamlet*' [the Russian pronunciation of 'Hamlet'], and there was an incredible murmur of '*Gamlet, Gamlet, idi siuda, davai chasy!*' [Russian for: 'Hamlet, Hamlet. Come here. Give me your watch!']
> ... everybody in the audience thought they alone were murmuring that stupid thing, and then the actor also said, '*Gamlet, Gamlet, idi siuda, davai chasy!*' That was the Russians in forty-five: *idi siuda, davai chasy!* I'll never forget Révai's face; it lengthened and paled. Then the entire audience was whispering, '*Gamlet, Gamlet, idi siuda, davai chasy!*'[33]

This may have been a minor revolution, but it was a revolution all the same. The Hungarian intelligentsia were telling the Soviets what they thought of them: they were not the high-minded missionaries of a superior civilization they claimed to be; they were crass imperialists, no different from the Red Army occupiers of 1945 who had seized Hungarians' valuables – including their watches – as war booty.

In Hungary, especially, such anti-imperialist mutterings amongst the middle classes following Stalin's death were predictable. Hungary, along with Poland, presented the most united opposition to Moscow. All social classes could identify with their powerful nationalisms, in which anti-Russian feeling featured strongly. Elsewhere societies were more divided. In East Germany – where much of the old elite had been killed or had fled to the West, and Czechoslovakia – where indigenous Communism still had a hold – middle-class groups were less angry. Here it was workers who rebelled. And paradoxically it was generally not hard-line Stalinists who provoked these revolts but Malenkov-appointed reformists. For Moscow's liberalizing reforms often helped the middle classes and peasants rather than the workers. Workers may have been disadvantaged under High Stalinism, but they did not do well from market reforms either.

Stalin's death put all of the 'little Stalins' under pressure. Beria and Malenkov had an extensive intelligence network and realized how fragile Soviet rule was in Eastern Europe. Reform was deemed essential to shore up the crumbling empire. East European leaders were bullied into adopting a 'New Course' – a mixture of technocratic and decentralizing reforms. East Germany, the biggest worry for Moscow, was the first in line. The rigid Ulbricht – whom even the conservative Molotov thought 'somewhat blunt and lacked flexibility' – was summoned and told of the Kremlin's 'grave concern about the situation in the GDR'.[34] In June 1953 he reluctantly introduced reforms, which helped small and medium-scale enterprises, lessened discrimination against the bourgeoisie, and relaxed controls in the countryside. They did not, however, improve workers' wages or reduce Plan targets. On 16 June the labourers building the monumental Stalinallee boulevard protested, sparking two days of working-class strikes and risings throughout East Germany. Only Soviet troops rescued the regime. Ulbricht beat a rapid retreat and made concessions to the workers, but the incident was profoundly embarrassing for this alleged workers' state.

Czechoslovakia witnessed similar unrest in the same month and for much the same reasons. Shortly after attending Stalin's funeral, Klement Gottwald died (probably from an alcohol-related illness), and a new collective leadership took power. The veteran trade unionist Antonín Zápotocký, a Malenkov protégé, became President, and Antonín Novotný, a member of Khrushchev's client network, party boss. Zápotocký pleased peasants with the end of forced collectivization, but his simultaneous currency reform hit workers' living standards. The result was serious unrest in the Lenin (now, and formerly, Škoda) car plant in

Plzeň – strikes, the burning of Soviet flags and demands for free elections. Repression was swift and brutal, but again the workers ultimately got their way and received higher wages.

All leaders in the Eastern bloc were forced to bend to the winds of change coming from Moscow. Collective agriculture was relaxed, whilst in some places collective leaderships replaced the little Stalins, at least in theory. Even so, old Stalinist regimes remained in control, and in Romania, Bulgaria, Albania and Poland reforms were limited.

It seemed, by late 1954, that the East European regimes had largely weathered the storm of Stalin's demise with a mixture of concessions and repression. There was one notable exception – Hungary – and here the problem was Moscow's indecision. Like Ulbricht, the Hungarian leader Rákosi was summoned to Moscow and forced to accept the Malenkov ally, Imre Nagy, as Prime Minister. Nagy, his avuncular bourgeois appearance only marred by a luxuriant Stalin-style moustache, was a veteran Comintern official who, like Béla Kun, converted to Bolshevism whilst imprisoned by the Russians during World War I and was a resident of Moscow in the 1930s. Unlike Kun, however, he was a more Pragmatic Marxist and a follower of Bukharin's pro-peasant ideas.[35] A struggle between Nagy and Rákosi ensued, Nagy seeking to push through the New Course and Rákosi, supported by much of officialdom, seeking to sabotage it. The conflict ended in 1955 with Malenkov's, and with him Nagy's, fall, and the return of Rákosi. But the obvious instability at the top quickly spread to all classes and bred popular dissent. The Hungarian intelligentsia, who had been relatively passive, high up in Stalin's imperial edifices, now seemed willing to join the workers. The young poet Sándor Csoóri expressed their feelings of guilt in 1953, remembering how he had lived 'on the topmost heights' ignoring the 'harsher reality' of his people staggering 'among over-fulfillings' and 'miraculous' Plan targets.[36]

The apparent stabilization of the old order in Eastern Europe after Stalin's death was therefore rather fragile. Even so, Khrushchev still tried to replace the old paternalistic relationship between the USSR and its satellites with a more fraternal one – for both moral and economic reasons. In April 1956 he abolished Stalin's instrument of control, the Cominform, and he also sought to repair relations with Yugoslavia. From 1955 he wooed Tito assiduously, trusting that their common hatred of Stalin would persuade Tito to rejoin the Soviet bloc. He sincerely hoped that the Secret Speech would draw a line under the past, reunify the bloc, and legitimize a new cohort of East European leaders committed to the New Course.

However, it proved difficult to heal the wounds inflicted by Stalinist imperialism. Tito welcomed the diplomatic rapprochement, but he refused to give up his ideological independence, and continued to promote the Yugoslav model as an alternative to the Soviet one. Meanwhile, in Eastern Europe itself, Moscow's more liberal policy threatened to destabilize Communism, and Soviet control.

The first crisis developed in Poland. The Secret Speech had killed not only Stalin's reputation, but also Poland's party leader Bierut, who was ill in hospital; on reading the text after the session he was so shocked by Khrushchev's *lèse-majesté* that he succumbed to a fatal heart attack and died. The new leader, Edvard Ochab, bent to the Malenkovian line and implemented moderate New Course reforms, but they failed to prevent popular rebellion.

As in East Berlin and Plzeň, it was workers who started the protests, this time in Poznań. Low living standards lay at the root of the discontent, and as so often in Communist systems, workers condemned Communists from the 'left' for exploiting them as the capitalists had done. As one older worker complained:

> I have slaved all my life. I've been told that before the war it was the capitalists who profited from my work. Who profits now? ... It is a treat when I give the children butter on their bread on Sundays. It was never so bad as that before the war.[37]

Many believed that the Russians, not the Polish Communists, were really profiting from the exploitative system. Butter, it was alleged, was being shipped eastwards; 'Glory to our Polish railway workers!' Poles joked. 'If it weren't for them, we'd have to carry our coal to the east on our backs.'[38]

The Poznań riots of June 1956 were put down, but war then broke out within the party between the Stalinists and reformers led by Gomułka, now released from gaol. Pressed by an increasingly angry public opinion, the Polish Communist Party planned to install Gomułka as First Secretary and remove the Soviet-imposed Minister of Defence, Marshal Rokossovskii. The Soviets were seriously concerned. They regarded Gomułka as anti-Soviet and Khrushchev even feared that

'Poland might break away from us at any moment.' On the morning of the crucial Central Committee meeting on 19 October, a delegation including Khrushchev, Mikoian, Molotov, Kaganovich and Marshal Koniev (the commander of the new Warsaw military pact of Communist states) flew to Warsaw in a dramatic move to forestall the reformist coup. At the same time Soviet troops were moved to the border. Talks between the Russians and the Gomułkists continued into the night. The explosive Khrushchev was furious at what he saw as the Poles' rude resistance; indeed he was so incensed that on his arrival in Warsaw he had shouted and shaken his fist at Ochab in full view of the airport staff.[39] However, despite his apparent weakness, Gomułka prevailed. He may not have had superior military power, but he had the party, the secret services and much of the nation behind him. He insisted, moreover, that he had no intention of ending party control or taking Poland out of the Soviet bloc. Reform would be limited to decollectivization, liberalizing economic reforms, freedoms for the influential Catholic Church, and limited 'socialist democracy'. The uninvited guests returned to Moscow, apparently reassured, but the following day Khrushchev's anger returned and he ordered that troops be sent in. Mikoian, realizing that he might regret it, managed to delay the final decision, and Khrushchev again changed his mind.[40] An invasion had been averted – just.

Hungary was less fortunate because the party was more divided. Hard-liners had more influence, convinced by the failures of 1919 that only harsh, Stalinist methods could break the reactionary classes. The reformist Communists, unlike their Polish comrades, therefore did not have the power to defuse popular discontent. Khrushchev forced Rákosi to resign in July 1956, but imposed another leader with hard-line connections, Ernö Gerö. Unrest continued, and on 23 October demonstrating workers raided the civil defence weapons stores in their factories. Gerö panicked, and Soviet troops were called in, which only stoked the unrest. The Communist power structure, highly divided, disintegrated within a few days; revolutionary committees and worker councils filled the vacuum. Gerö tried to recover the situation by appointing Nagy as Prime Minister but it was too late. Nagy could no more control the popular anger than Gerö; if he was to stay on the crest of the revolutionary wave he had to become ever more radical.

Delacroix would have recognized the Budapest of October 1956. As Miklós Molnár, a Communist and participant in the Hungarian Uprising, has written, this was 'perhaps the last of the revolutions of the nineteenth century. Europe will probably never see again this familiar and romantic picture of the rebel, gun in hand, cries of freedom on his lips, fighting for something.'[41] Hungary's was a genuinely spontaneous, cross-class revolution; it included many different political strands, from radical left to radical right. There was no time to develop a coherent programme. Initially, the rebels had no plans to destroy one-party rule but only to modify it; to transform an austere, unforgiving and imperial socialism into a more humane and national one. The rebels' first manifesto of 23 October even adopted the rhetoric of Leninism to condemn the current regime. Béla Kovács, a former chair of the old peasant Smallholder Party, urged that the changes of 1945–8 be preserved: 'no one should dream of the old order. The world of counts, bankers and capitalists is gone for good; anyone who sees things now as if it were 1939 or 1945 is no authentic Smallholder.'[42] Doubtless, had the insurgents actually formed a government, tensions between democratic socialists and nationalists would have surfaced rapidly.

The Hungarian events could not have been more painful for Khrushchev. 'Budapest was like a nail in my head,' he remembered.[43] Intent on transforming Stalin's empire into a fraternity of nations, he now had to make a stark choice between brutal imperialism and humiliating retreat. The choice was made all the more embarrassing because simultaneously the old colonial powers, Britain and France, were secretly helping Israel against Nasser in Egypt, in their ill-fated attempt to restore neo-imperial influence in the Middle East. On 30 October the Presidium took an extraordinary decision: to accept that Hungary could go its own way; they would rule out force, withdraw troops and negotiate.[44] But this idealistic line lasted for precisely one day. As the Presidium met, violence on both sides in Hungary was escalating. Nagy could no longer channel popular resentment into reformist Communism and had bowed to popular pressure, calling for the withdrawal of Hungary from the Warsaw Pact and the creation of a multi-party Popular Front government. From Moscow's point of view there was now a real risk of revolutionary contagion. Disturbances broke out throughout the region, and Romania closed its border with Hungary as students from its Hungarian minority demonstrated in Transylvania. Khrushchev was terrified that the West would intervene; his whole reforming project would collapse and the Stalinist hard-liners would have been proved right.

According to one witness, Khrushchev told Tito that people would say 'when Stalin was in command everybody obeyed and there were no big shocks, but that now, ever since *they* had come to power . . . Russia had suffered defeat and the loss of Hungary.'[45]

On 31 October, Khrushchev reversed his earlier decision. János Kádár, a reformist who had been imprisoned by the Stalinists, was taken to Moscow and persuaded to return to Hungary with Soviet tanks, on condition that there would be no return to the old order once the rebellion had been put down. On 4 November Warsaw Pact forces entered Hungary and Nagy fled to the Yugoslav embassy. Resistance was heavy. By the 7th – the thirty-ninth anniversary of the October Revolution – Kádár had established his new regime after some 2,700 had died in the fighting. Repression was harsh. Twenty-two thousand were sentenced, 13,000 imprisoned, about 350 executed, most of them young workers. Some 200,000 managed to escape to the West.[46] Nagy was not so lucky. He was tricked into leaving the Yugoslav embassy and arrested, imprisoned and finally executed in 1958.

Nineteen fifty-six devastated the reputation of Soviet Communism in Eastern Europe; harsh repression of workers' councils and revolutionary committees looked like counter-revolution, not progress. For many East Europeans, Russia and its satellites seemed the very reincarnation of the reactionary post-Napoleonic Holy Alliance.

V

Nineteen fifty-six was also damaging for Communism in Western Europe. Khrushchev looked like an ageing imperialist, not that different from the Socialist French Prime Minister Guy Mollet and his Conservative British counterpart Anthony Eden, who had invaded Egypt at the same time. The Hungarian invasion triggered mass defections in all parties. The Italian Communist Party lost 10 per cent of its membership and Eric Hobsbawm, who remained a Communist after 1956, remembered how difficult it was to deal with the reality of Soviet violence, both past and present. He and his fellow party members 'lived on the edge of the political equivalent of a collective nervous breakdown':

It is difficult to reconstruct not only the mood but also the memory of that traumatic year . . . Even after half a century my throat contracts as I recall the almost intolerable tensions under which we lived month after month, the unending moments of decision about what to say and do on which our future lives seemed to depend, the friends now clinging together or facing one another bitterly as adversaries . . .[47]

The party that had the greatest difficulty, though, was the one most closely identified with High Stalinism – the French. Maurice Thorez did his best to limit the effect of the Secret Speech. He had, in fact, been shown it before it was delivered but kept its contents secret; when it was published five months later he even denied its authenticity. The French party was eventually forced to accept that Stalin had made errors, but insisted that he had also achieved much. The term 'the party of Maurice Thorez' was abandoned, redolent as it was of Stalin's cult of personality, but Communist leaders supported the invasion of Hungary, precipitating the defection of Sartre and other intellectuals. The French party remained workerist, loyal to the USSR and relatively closed, though it did make some concessions, finally accepting that a 'peaceful transition to socialism' was possible. Thorez even moved towards a form of alliance with the Socialists, and on his death in 1964, Waldeck Rochet established a much more consensual leadership style. By 1968, the party's membership was creeping up again, to 350,000.

Italy's Togliatti, predictably, had a very different response to de-Stalinization. He welcomed Khrushchev's speech, and indeed went further in his critique (though he still supported the Hungarian invasion). The Soviet model, he declared, was no longer to be obligatory; the Communist world should become 'polycentric' – allowing a number of diverse approaches to Communism. The denunciation of Stalin in 1956 weakened the hard-liners, but Togliatti now had to hold the ring between reformists surrounding Giorgio Amendola, who called for the party to forge alliances with the socialists, and a left-wing associated with Pietro Ingrao that favoured a more populist and radical politics. Both sides were demanding a more inclusive party, but this tension, between a more pragmatic, parliamentary road, and a more radical, participatory Marxism, was to divide the party for some time to come.

The party retained a large membership, and its culture remained vibrant and relatively inclusive at a local level. At its heart lay the 'festival' (*festa*). Initiated to finance and distribute the party newspaper, *L'Unità*, the *feste de l'Unità* were modelled on the church *feste* and competed with them, as a boastful Communist pamphlet from the Bologna region makes clear:

> What incenses the clerics!
> – 276 sectional *feste*
> – 1500 cell *feste*
> – an unprecedented Provincial *festa*
> – 28 million [lire] in contributions[48]

The Communist festivals were a mixture of community bonding, entertainment and politics, in that order. They would begin with a procession, the people bearing red flags and banners rather than statues of the Virgin. They would then enter the site of the *festa*, filled with propaganda stalls and posters on the struggle for justice, in Italy and internationally. But at its centre would be long tables laden with local food and drink, cooked by the comrades (both women and men). To add to the egalitarian atmosphere, party bosses would serve ordinary members at table.[49]

The *feste* reinforced the bonds of community, and Italian Communism was expert at making itself the centre of working-class and peasant neighbourhoods. In some areas, such as Emilia-Romagna in central Italy, a very high proportion of the adult population joined the party. This was far from the Leninist party – a vanguard committed to ideology and revolution. One joined the party to indicate broadly defined socialist values, and because your friends and neighbours were also members. The party might also be able to help out with housing and welfare. The Italian party had similarities with the nineteenth-century German Social Democrats: excluded from power at the top (though not in local councils), it abandoned revolutionary goals, and created its own cultural world.

Even so, from the 1950s economic change began to erode the party's support, which had hitherto relied on traditional impoverished groups such as Central Italian sharecroppers.[50] Its culture also came under assault from a new consumerism, and it did not always respond well to the challenge. Togliatti had concentrated on securing high cultural prestige and winning over intellectuals, and the Communists were less willing to make concessions to popular culture than their rival Catholics.

So, whilst they did organize a series of beauty contests for the coveted title of 'Miss New Life' (*Miss Vie Nuove*), their contest was less popular than the Church's. Communist intellectuals were unable to hide their suspicion of consumerism and popular music, raging, for instance, against the music of Elvis Presley and the 'hysteria and paroxism' it allegedly caused.[51]

Despite the events of 1956, both the French and Italian Communist parties remained powerful political forces. In France, the mass of the membership seemed unperturbed by Hungary, and in Italy membership remained above 2 million for much of the Cold War era, with a youth wing of some 400,000. In the Eastern bloc, too, the violence of that year if anything stabilized politics, and led to a more viable *modus vivendi* between Communist regimes and society over the next decade. Most East European governments established a more liberal, less austere form of Communism from the late 1950s, and after a period of repression Hungary itself was to become one of the most relaxed countries in the bloc. For their part, potential rebels in Eastern Europe realized they had to make the best of the situation. American covert actions before 1956 had encouraged some to believe that they might intervene, but their refusal to do so in that year showed there was no real plan to 'roll back' Communism. The lake had refrozen and the cracks could no longer be seen, but the ice would never again be so thick.

Eastern Europe was the first region to be 'stabilized' after the revolutionary period that followed Stalin's death. Yet it was some time before the turbulence in the USSR itself was to come to an end. The forces Khrushchev unleashed in Eastern Europe were so powerful he had to use violence to suppress them. But he had barely started his project to transform the Soviet Union.

VI

On 13 May 1957, Khrushchev attended a day-long discussion of Soviet writing at the Writers' Union – a sign of the extraordinary seriousness with which the party treated literature. A number of novels, including Vladimir Dudintsev's *Not by Bread Alone* of 1956, had elicited vicious attacks from influential Stalinists. The writers listened in trepidation, not knowing which side the leader would take. They were to be disappointed.

Khrushchev gave a typically rambling two-hour-long speech, which descended into farce when an elderly Armenian writer interrupted to complain about the shortage of meat in her homeland. Yet the message of the speech was clear: Dudintsev and other writers had been taking their criticism of Stalin too far. It was evident that Khrushchev had not read the book, but had been briefed on it by conservative advisers. Mikoian tried to convince him that Dudintsev was actually on Khrushchev's side, but failed. He stuck to the view that the novel was slandering the Soviet system. But within two years he had changed his mind; though still critical of the novel, he now declared that it was, nevertheless, ideologically acceptable.[52]

It was no surprise that Khrushchev should have spent so much time worrying about *Not by Bread Alone*. It was an extraordinarily popular novel: 'Everywhere, in the subway, in the streetcars, in the trolley-buses – young people, adults, and seniors' were reading it. Mounted police, fearful of unrest, patrolled meetings organized by readers to discuss it. Journals were flooded with letters calling for a purge of the targets of the book – the bureaucrats. Some used language strongly reminiscent of the 1937 Terror. A bricklayer from Tashkent wrote that the novel showed the need for struggle against 'hidden enemies, the survivals of capitalism in the people's and our own mind'.[53]

It is unsurprising that Khrushchev and his advisers found the novel so difficult to categorize, for it was a *roman à thèse* (and rather a crude one at that) which understood and sympathized with Khrushchev's almost Romantic ideas, but also explained why it would always fail. The novel is the story of Lopatkin, an idealistic young physics teacher of the late 1940s. He designs a machine for the centrifugal casting of drainpipes, but although the machine is excellent, he is thwarted at every turn by Stalinist bureaucrats. Chief villain is the ambitious careerist Drozdov. Drozdov is a typical Stalinist of the post-Stalin imagination. He is socially aspirant and a lover of luxury who refuses to associate with ordinary people. He is also a philistine technocrat, whose bed-time reading includes Stalin's very un-idealistic chapter on dialectical materialism in his *Short Course* of party history. Drozdov describes his philosophy thus: 'I belong to the producers of material values. The main spiritual value of our time is the ability to work well, to create the greatest possible quantity of necessary things . . . The more I strengthen the [economic] base [of society], the firmer our state will be.'[54] For Lopatkin, this is an extreme form of 'vulgar Marxism'. Men need ideals; they cannot live 'by bread alone'. Lopatkin, though, is in a small minority: cynical bureaucrats hound him and steal his ideas, and eventually succeed in having him banished to a prison camp. Whilst he is there, his friend Professor Galitskii constructs his machine and shows that it works, and when he is released, he is rehabilitated and given a prestigious job. But the corrupt circle of bureaucrats – a 'hidden empire', as Dudintsev calls it – remains in power, as materialistic and cynical as ever. They accuse Lopatkin of being a selfish individualist. Now he is a success, why doesn't he re-enter the 'Soviet collective' of good ol' boys, and buy himself a car and a *dacha*?[55] The novel ends with Lopatkin leaving industry to enter politics, vowing to fight the bureaucrats.

Not by Bread Alone was typical of the novels of its time. It condemned the callous technocracy it saw as typical of late Stalinism, and called for a new Romantic Marxism of creativity, feeling and democracy. This was also the message of Ilya Ehrenburg's *The Thaw* of 1954, whose title came to define the whole period. The theme chimed with Khrushchev's view that in everybody lay an innate creativity. If only officials encouraged it to flourish, economic miracles would ensue. In many ways, of course, this Romantic message was close to Stalin's campaigns against bureaucracy in the late 1920s. But Dudintsev, like Khrushchev, refused to return to the old class-struggle rhetoric of the 1930s. As in the past, the villains were the bureaucrats, but the hero was now an educated person, not a horny-handed worker. Even so, the novel's overall message was deeply disturbing for Khrushchev. Dudintsev was implying that the elite could not be reformed. The system would be saved by *individual* creativity; the Soviet 'collective' had been corrupted by greed and selfishness.

It turned out that Dudintsev's pessimism was more realistic than Khrushchev's utopianism. Khrushchev hoped to revive the idealistic campaigns of the 1920s and 1930s, stripping them of class conflict and workerist exclusivity whilst purging them of the old Stalinist austerity. But he and his allies found themselves confronting a bureaucracy intent on preserving its power; a population more interested in bread than Marxist enthusiasm; and a disaffected intelligentsia, often idealistic but slowly losing its faith in the virtues of the collective spirit.

Khrushchev outlined his new vision of Communism in a long speech at the twenty-second party congress in 1961. Like Tito, he was appealing to a radical Marxism with some elements of Romantic utopianism, and it is notable that editions of the early Romantic Marx were now appearing in Russian for the first time. For Khrushchev, Lenin and Stalin had, in effect, postponed Communism to the distant future. 'Socialism', with its inequalities of income, its use of money to incentivize people to work, and its all-powerful state, would continue for some time. But Khrushchev was impatient, and believed the Soviet people had waited long enough. In 1959 he set up a commission to look into how the USSR might speed up the journey to Communism. It came up with a new party programme, which predicted that the party would build Communism 'in the main' by 1980. Khrushchev had hoped that the programme could promise all of Marx's desiderata, the withering away of the state included. But wiser heads prevailed, and all talk of withering was removed. 'Communism' in the 1961 USSR denoted a combination of collectivism, a society in which work would become 'genuine creativity', and consumption (a rather loose translation of Marx's material 'abundance'). Even so, this was a far cry from the Romantic thinking of the 1840s. Society would be disciplined, but 'that discipline will depend not on any coercive means, but on fostering a feeling of duty to fulfil one's obligations'.[56] This would transpire within the next twenty years, but Khrushchev insisted that the time was ripe for the end of repression immediately. Indeed, the 'class struggle' was formally ended. The 'Dictatorship of the Proletariat', founded by Lenin, was abolished. The USSR now included all classes, and was described as an 'All-People's State'; one class, the proletariat, and its vanguard, the party, no longer lorded it over the others.

How, though, could Khrushchev reconcile the dream of creative work and the promise of outpacing Western living standards? Marx's Communism did indeed promise material abundance: 'From each according to his ability, to each according to his need.' But the principles of Western consumerism had more to do with desires than need. Also, Western consumer culture – with its focus on the home, the nuclear family and the individual – was deeply corrosive of Communist collectivism. The Czech Zdeněk Mlynář understood how dangerous Khrushchev's new consumerist goal was for the Communist system:

Stalin never permitted comparisons of socialism or Communism with capitalist reality because he argued that an entirely new world was being built
here that could not be compared with any preceding system. Khrushchev,
with his slogan 'Catch up with and surpass America', changed the situation
fundamentally for the average Soviet citizen . . . After that . . . a comparison
was indeed made . . . He wanted to strengthen people's faith in the Soviet
system, but in fact the practical comparison with the West had the opposite
effect and constantly weakened that faith.[57]

The scale of the task confronting Khrushchev became evident in the
dramatic 'kitchen debate' between Khrushchev and US Vice-President
Richard Nixon in 1959. As part of Khrushchev's new 'peaceful competition' between ideologies, the Americans were allowed to stage an exhibition in Moscow's Sokolniki Park, which included a model six-room
ranch house, its kitchen packed with the latest appliances. The two leaders, equally brittle and belligerent, found themselves confronting one
another. Khrushchev was rattled when told that a typical American
steelworker could buy this $14,000 house. In a reply that convinced no
one he blustered: 'You think the Russians are dumbfounded by this
exhibition. But the fact is that nearly all newly-built Russian houses
have this equipment. You need dollars in the United States to get this
house, but here all you need is to be born a citizen.'[58]

Khrushchev did what he could to make the boast come true. The most
visible signs of change were the thousands of new low-rise apartment
buildings in the towns. They were small and cheaply built – they soon
acquired the nickname 'khrushchoby', merging 'Khrushchev' with the
word trushchoby ('slums'). But this was an enormous advance on Stalinist housing policy, which had poured resources into a few high-prestige
skyscrapers, leaving ordinary people to live in cramped communal apartments, sharing kitchens and bathrooms. Khrushchev's goal was to give
every family (admittedly often multi-generational) its own apartment. Yet
he was insistent that greater consumption should not engender petty-
bourgeois individualism. The authorities encouraged public dining rooms,
neighbourhood committees, apartment-block wall newspapers and 'open-
door days', when families would invite anybody from the building to
drop in and engage in wholesome sociability. Sewing and knitting were
discouraged as dangerously individualistic activities.[59]

The modernist buildings themselves were an implicit attack on old

High Stalinism. The USSR now endorsed a version of the modernism of the 1920s and 1930s – the high point of international Communism. It was engaged in an ideological competition with the West, and needed to present a more modern and cosmopolitan image.[60] The fussy, elaborate style of late Stalinism was regarded as 'petty-bourgeois', philistine kitsch – the type of art liked by the crass Drozdov and his philistine chums. Officials even launched campaigns to persuade ordinary Soviet people to throw out their sets of miniature carved white elephants – an ornament as popular amongst Soviet households as the china flying ducks that populated Western living rooms in the 1960s.[61]

The greatest symbol of the modernity of the Communist project, however, lay not in the boxy apartments that clustered around the metropolises of Eastern Europe, but in the sputnik satellite floating in the vastness of outer space. The Soviet space project had its origins in early scientific utopianism, and especially in the work of the pioneering theorist of space travel Konstantin Tsiolkovskii and his Society for Studies of Interplanetary Travel founded in 1924. In the 1930s Marshal Tukhachevskii championed the cause of rocket science. But with his disgrace in 1937, many of his scientist protégés were imprisoned and some even executed. In the early 1940s the baton of the space project passed to Malenkov, and the scientists – including several previously arrested as 'enemies of the people' – were now recruited for the atomic missile project. By the 1950s the entire programme, which had benefited enormously from hardware and expertise developed by the Nazis, had come under the protection of Khrushchev, who hoped to transform the Soviet armed forces and end its reliance on soldiers and tanks. The world became aware of the first spectacular success of the Soviet rocket programme when, on 4 October 1957, radios broadcast the beeps from the first sputnik artificial satellite. More triumphs were to follow: the first journey into space by an animal (a dog – 'Laika') and then, most impressively, the first human space journey by the pilot Iurii Gagarin in April 1961.

Khrushchev marked Gagarin's mission with the most lavish public celebrations since 1945 and could not hold back his tears at the ceremony. For him, the success of Gagarin's 'Vostok-1' ('East-1') rocket was proof that the USSR had become a modern country. The Americans were rattled. The Democratic Senator Henry 'Scoop' Jackson, a militant Cold Warrior, declared that the sputnik launch was a 'devastating blow'

to American power and called on President Eisenhower to announce a
'week of shame and danger'. Convinced that there was a huge 'manpower gap' between Soviet and American scientists, Jackson and his
allies persuaded a tight-fisted president to sign the National Defense
Education Act into law. Federal spending on education doubled and
included massive funds for science and the study of the Communist and
developing world – laying the foundations for American pre-eminence
in higher education and advanced research.

The space programme might have planted in the minds of its enemies
the idea of the USSR as a land of enlightened, rational citizens, but the
transformation of image into reality proved a far greater challenge. After
a period of relative tolerance during wartime and the late Stalinist period,
Khrushchev returned to the atheism of the 1920s and 1930s, closing
churches and introducing new courses on 'scientific atheism' into universities. Party propagandists, in their efforts to spread atheism, declared
the Gagarin journey proof-positive of God's non-existence.

The Soviet Union, then, had spectacularly reclaimed its earlier status
as the acme of modernity after the 'dark ages' of post-war obscurantism. But how was modernization – of both defence and living standards
– to be paid for? Khrushchev's solution lay in his new, more inclusive
and non-violent form of mobilization. He was convinced that would
achieve much more than either Stalin's bullying or capitalism's incentives. He relaxed the old disciplinarian regime in factories, and workers
were given more freedoms in the hope they would work harder. He was
also determined to shake up complacent officialdom. But this emphasis
on inclusivity and participation did not amount to the end of the privileged position of the Communist Party. Indeed, he expected the party to
take a leading role in mobilizing the masses. One of his first initiatives
was to scrap the industrial ministries – the home of the arrogant Drozdovs as he saw it – and give power to local party bosses through new
regional economic councils. Khrushchev expected that party people, as
ideological enthusiasts, would be much better able to enthuse the masses
than the staid state bureaucrats. The old 1930s campaign style was
back. Party officials, desperate for promotion, made impractical promises to achieve economic miracles. Even the disgraced Lysenko returned,
as Khrushchev believed his promises to improve wheat output.

Predictably, Khrushchev's faith in the rapid 'leaps' was sadly misplaced. His first campaign – the Virgin Lands grain programme – had

run aground by 1963, as the land planted was prone to drought, and was less fertile than average. Promises of enormous feats of production were shown to be fraudulent. The party leader of the Riazan region promised to triple meat production, and was made a Hero of Socialist Labour on the strength of his utopian plans. But it was then shown that he was actually buying meat from neighbouring regions and passing it off as his own. When exposed, he committed suicide in shame.

Nor did Khrushchev's attempts to recast the relationship between officials and workers meet with success. He replaced Stalinist repression and individual 'piece rates' with new collective incentives (linking wages to the factory's overall success), but with little success: workers did not feel inspired to work harder when they, individually, had little control over the performance of the factory as a whole.[62] Meanwhile, Khrushchev found that party bosses were no more capable of inspiring heroism in ordinary people than state bureaucrats. A disillusioned Khrushchev – like Stalin in the 1930s and Gorbachev in the 1980s – increasingly moved from seeing party bosses as allies against a recalcitrant state bureaucracy, to blaming them for the failures of his grand projects. These party men were as conservative as the Drozdovs in the old economic apparatus, he complained, arguing that the answer was an infusion of new blood. He ordered that a fixed proportion of officials be compulsorily replaced at each party election, and divided the party apparatus into two – one in charge of agriculture and one industry. Both of these reforms were deeply unpopular amongst party officials, who understandably saw them as a threat to their jobs and status.

Khrushchev's early popularity also declined as he failed to meet his economic promises. Food price-rises in 1962, designed to improve incentives and living standards for the peasants, hit workers, triggering strikes and unrest in many Soviet cities. Most serious was a strike at the Budennyi Electric Locomotive Plant in the Caucasus town of Novocherkassk. Workers complained that they could no longer afford meat and sausage. One official told them, in an inversion of Marie Antoinette's advice, they should be satisfied with cheap liver pasties, and the workers replied with a new slogan: 'Make sausage out of Khrushchev'.[63] Echoing Bloody Sunday in 1905, the strikers marched to the town centre, loyally bearing portraits of Marx, Engels and Lenin, and were confronted by soldiers. Shooting started when they refused to leave, and twenty-three were killed. Khrushchev was worried that the unrest would spread if it was left unchecked.[64]

Novocherkassk had brutally illustrated how conditional workers' support was. The urban educated classes – Khrushchev's most fervent early supporters – also soon fell out of love with their hero. Ludmilla Alekseeva, a teacher who was later to become a dissident, remembered the circle of friends of her youth, her *kompaniia*. They saw themselves as descendants of the intelligentsia of Chernyshevskii's era, but unlike them 'weren't burdened by guilt before the common people, since we were just as poor and deprived of rights as our compatriots who hadn't reached our level of education'. Alekseeva pointed to an increasing split between the educated, urban middle classes and the party. She recalled how her friends were divided into two groups: the 'physicists' were the descendants of the Modernist Marxists, but were now deeply sceptical of all ideology: 'all this blather about social justice, democracy, equality, "the people", proletarians-of-the-world unite. Look where it got us: there's nothing to eat. We are up to our throats in shit, and you are still chitchatting.'[65] The 'lyricists', in contrast, were scornful of this obsession with atoms and neutrons. These Romantics wanted to know about the meaning of life and 'how to live'. Amongst this group a few remaining enthusiasts for Marxism could be found, though theirs was an eclectic unofficial Marxism – a mish-mash of Karl Kautsky, Rosa Luxemburg and the Frankfurt School's Herbert Marcuse.

Both Alekseeva's physicists and lyricists had initially found much in Khrushchev's 'de-Stalinization' to admire, but they were soon disillusioned. Khrushchev, like Beria and Malenkov, accepted that the rigid dogmatism of the Stalinist era had been destructive, and that the regime had to have a more inclusive attitude towards the technical intelligentsia. He allowed work to be published which would never have seen the light of day before, like Solzhenitsyn's powerfully bleak account of a Gulag prisoner's life, *One Day in the Life of Ivan Denisovich*. But the rehabilitation of Lysenko and the criticism of Dudintsev disappointed his erstwhile supporters. In his memoirs, Khrushchev regretted that he had not courted the intelligentsia more, but the problem was in part a cultural and generational one: the poorly educated party official of the 1920s and 1930s had little in common with the urban sophisticates of the 1960s. The clash of cultures is well illustrated by his tirade at an exhibition of modern art in Moscow:

'You're a nice-looking lad, but how could you paint something like this? We should take down your trousers and set you in a clump of nettles until you understand your mistakes. You should be ashamed. Are you a queer or a normal man? . . . We have a right to send you to cut trees until you've paid back the money the state has spent on you. The people and the government have taken a lot of trouble with you, and you pay them back with this shit.'[66]

More dangerous for Khrushchev than the relatively quiescent intelligentsia, though, were his fellow leaders. They found his ambitious goals, ideological enthusiasm and impulsive behaviour deeply threatening. His behaviour on the foreign stage was especially unsettling and embarrassing. Khrushchev had promised to convert the old East–West military confrontation into peaceful ideological competition, but he presided over the most tense and dangerous period of the Cold War. His leadership was marked by a series of crises: Hungary in 1956; his attempts to drive the West out of Berlin in 1958, culminating in the construction of one of the greatest symbols of the Cold War confrontation – the Berlin Wall of 1961; and, most serious of all, the Cuban Missile Crisis of 1962.

It would be unfair to place all of the blame for the warming of the Cold War at Khrushchev's door. The world of the early 1960s had become much more ideologically charged than that of a decade earlier. The true believer Mao was snapping at Khrushchev's heels, whilst Fidel Castro's Cuban revolution of 1959 announced the arrival of a new generation of Third-World Communists. Meanwhile, though the policies of President John F. Kennedy, elected in 1960, were marked by a great deal of flexibility, he was determined to negotiate from strength. He also injected a new energy into the struggle against Communism in the Third World, and was willing to use covert military action. Khrushchev, determined to retain the ideological leadership of world Communism, responded to these challenges impulsively, with none of Stalin's fearful caution.

Khrushchev was also trying to mount an ambitious foreign policy on the cheap, reluctant as he was to cut living standards, and he hoped to reduce spending on the conventional military whilst building up nuclear weapons. Yet his plans did not go smoothly. Red Army officers were naturally unhappy at the proposed cuts in manpower, whilst the construction of long-range Intercontinental Ballistic Missiles (ICBMs) proved much more expensive and difficult than he had expected. In 1962 – a year of disappointing economic performance, price rises and social unrest – Khrushchev had to find a cheap and quick way of improving the strategic balance, at a time when the United States was installing missiles in Italy and Turkey. His solution was to put 'one of our hedgehogs down the Americans' trousers', as he vividly put it: placing intermediate and medium-range missiles in newly Communist Cuba.[67] It was American technological superiority, though, that unravelled Khrushchev's plan. Spy planes revealed the build-up, and American and Soviet ships confronted each other in the Caribbean. The superpowers were 'eyeball to eyeball', as Dean Rusk said, and the world was the closest it has ever been to nuclear catastrophe. Khrushchev blinked first, and the ships retreated. He extracted some concessions from the Americans: they withdrew the missiles from Turkey and promised, informally, not to attempt another Cuban invasion. But Kennedy insisted that the Turkish missile deal not be made public, and so Khrushchev was unable to rebuff criticisms that he had humiliated the USSR. He had lost face within the Soviet leadership, before the Americans and the Chinese, and faced the anger of the Cubans.

The Cuban Missile Crisis proved to be a turning point in the Cold War. Warnings of the dangers of nuclear weapons, made by Malenkov and others in the mid-1950s, could no longer be ignored. Meanwhile Khrushchev, and the USSR's leadership of world Communism, was deeply damaged, and within two years he was facing a plot against him. Yet his foreign-policy failures were not the only reason for his weakness. His conflicts with party bosses were also important. Khrushchev believed that his policies were not working because they were being undermined by self-interested officials. His colleagues suspected, probably rightly, that he was planning a purge of party bosses by organizing elections to which they would have to submit.

On 13 October 1964 Khrushchev returned from the Caucasus to a meeting of the Presidium, where his colleagues condemned him for his unreliability and voluntarism, and called for his removal. Khrushchev did not fight, and even tearfully accepted some of the criticisms. He peacefully went into retirement on 'health' grounds. His successors, led by party boss Leonid Brezhnev, Prime Minister Aleksei Kosygin and Nikolai Podgornyi changed course. Promises of imminent Communism were abandoned. Populism gave way to the power of officials, and

Khrushchev's term for the USSR – the 'All-People's State' – was abandoned. Brezhnev returned life-time job security to insecure officials. Khrushchev's non-violent version of the radicalism of the 1930s had failed; Dudintsev's 'invisible empire' had struck back.

As the Lenin Hills Pioneer Palace was opening its doors in 1962, it was already clear that the peaceful version of Radical Marxism it expressed was failing. The Communist Party was clearly not going to enthuse the people and drive them to work harder. It was no longer the messianic organization of the late 1920s, and the declaration of class peace at home and abroad ensured it was even more difficult to engage popular enthusiasm. Confronted with an enemy – whether within or without – people are often willing to make sacrifices, but Khrushchev did not want violent class struggle, and the West was not an immediate threat. Khrushchev was increasingly forced to behave like a Soviet Father Christmas, promising treats and abundant consumption, rather than as a Marxist Moses, leading his people to a land of justice and equality. The early 1960s was still a time of optimism and faith in socialism. But by throwing down the gauntlet (or rubber glove) to Nixon at the kitchen debates and explicitly setting out to compete with the West over living standards, Khrushchev had only succeeded in planting the seeds of future ideological decay.

Khrushchev always saw himself as a radical, and his disgruntled Central Committee colleagues agreed. But to Communists forging a new wave of revolutions in the developing world, Khrushchev seemed to have lost his revolutionary élan. He had backed down over Cuba, and by rejecting class struggle he had deprived Communism of its moral and emotional energy. The most vocal critic of Khrushchev's 'revisionism' was Mao, for the Chinese party still believed that it was building socialism, and harsh measures were still required. Also China had not suffered anything as traumatic as the Soviet 'Great Break' or Terror of the 1930s, and class struggle still seemed virtuous and necessary. China, though, was soon to make up for its lack of experience. In the following decade it was to suffer disasters unprecedented in the Communist world.

VII

Between 1958 and 1959, as part of China's utopian 'Great Leap Forward' into modernity, a grand architectural project was completed – Beijing's 'Ten Great Buildings'. Five of them were museums and exhibition halls; the other five included Beijing's railway station and government hotels and guest-houses. Even though this was five years after Stalin's death and the Soviet bloc had embraced modernism, the style adopted in Beijing was unashamedly Stalinist – though leavened with Chinese features such as pagoda roofs. These, though, were not the elaborate wedding-cake buildings of 1950s Stalinism, but were closer to the more austere Soviet architecture of the mid-1930s – more like the 1937 Paris pavilion.[68] As in architecture, so in politics: whilst the Chinese rejected the rigid hierarchies of the late-Stalinist style, they were closer to the Radical Marxism of the early Stalin.

Mao was ambivalent about Khrushchev's act of parricide. On the one hand, he disliked the paternalistic culture of High Stalinism as much as Khrushchev did. Relations between the Soviet Union and China, Mao complained, had been akin to those of 'father and son, cat and mouse';[69] Stalin had behaved like an old-style Confucian 'mandarin' and Khrushchev's Secret Speech was like a 'liberation movement'. Mao also at first liked the forthright Khrushchev, recognizing in him a fellow rough-and-ready Marxist from the provinces. It was good, Mao asserted, when comrades from the localities replaced comrades from the centre, because 'at the local level the class struggle is more acute, closer to natural struggle, closer to the masses'.[70] However, as this observation revealed, he had fundamentally misunderstood Khrushchev. Khrushchev may have been a radical, but he had abjured class struggle, whilst Mao most certainly had not. Mao's view of Stalin, though critical, was never as harsh as that of the Soviet leadership. In February 1957 Mao formulated a more favourable – and remarkably precise – assessment of Stalin: he was 70 per cent a Marxist, 30 per cent not a Marxist. Moreover, Mao was not pleased that Khrushchev had embarked on his act of parricide alone, without consulting the fraternal parties. Khrushchev himself, he concluded, was adopting the arrogant, imperial mantle of the old patriarch.

In the mid-1950s all was set fair for the Chinese Communists. The party had its enemies, but it also attracted wide support as a force for justice and economic development. The political situation was stable; the USSR was helping its younger brother. Soviet aid, which had been relatively modest under Stalin, had swelled, and in 1959 it amounted to an extraordinary 7 per cent of Soviet national income.[71] Mao showed his continuing vigour – despite his sixty-two years – by taking three well-publicized long-distance swims in the Yangtze River.

Something, though, had to be done to flatten the old hierarchies inherent within High Stalinism. Mao looked anxiously at the rebellions sweeping Eastern Europe between 1953 and 1956, and was determined that they should not erupt in China. He and other Chinese Communist radicals had been unhappy about emerging inequalities for some time. The transformation from a guerrilla to a professional army was particularly galling. Army officers were behaving like petty feudal lords, using their soldiers as servants and even exercising *droit de seigneur* over local women. Mao's solution was to bring soldiers closer to local peasant communities by, for example, donating their excrement to the villages for fertilizer, or helping them in pest-eradication efforts. Naturally, professional, technically proficient officers found this political interference and slanting of military priorities deeply irritating.

Mao's general approach, though, was closer to Khrushchev's, or even Malenkov's – at least initially. The party, he concluded, needed to be 'rectified' but this was not to be an old-style class struggle, for that might undermine the pace of economic development. Rather, this was to be a 'liberal' purge. Bourgeois intellectuals, rather than the 'red' classes – workers, peasants and party activists – would be invited to offer their criticisms. And it would not be done through abrasive and confrontational 'struggle sessions', but 'as gently as a breeze or mild rain'. Officials would be cut down to size, but every attempt would be made to avoid a revival of Communist puritanism and dogmatism, as had happened in Yan'an in 1943. A 'hundred flowers' were to bloom in culture and 'a hundred schools of thought contend' in science.[72]

At first, intellectuals sensibly kept quiet. They feared retribution from party bosses if they spoke openly. Mao, though, eventually persuaded them he was serious. For a five-week period from May Day 1957, they obeyed Mao's calls for frank and open criticism. Mao, predictably, did not like what he heard. The criticisms were vitriolic. Corruption, rigged elections and party arrogance were all targets, as expected, but so was collectivization, the party's monopoly of power and slavish emulation of the Soviet Union. In Peking University a 'Democracy Wall' was plastered with posters attacking the party. Mao soon realized that his liberalizing revolution had got out of control and was undermining the legitimacy of the party itself. He soon performed an abrupt *volte-face* and launched a brutal attack on 'rightists'. Over 300,000 intellectuals fell victim to censure, their careers ended.

Mao was never again to follow Khrushchev's strategy of controlled liberalization; indeed, it was only to be repeated after his death. From thence forward, as far as Mao was concerned, intellectuals were irredeemably anti-Communist. Nevertheless, he continued to look for an alternative to what he saw as the Stalinist order now embedding itself in China. He found it by going back to the guerrilla socialism of Yan'an and in radical class struggle.

The drawbacks of the old Stalinist model were particularly glaring in the economy. How was China to overcome the disparities with the West – and indeed with the USSR? On his second trip to the USSR in 1957 Mao had been deeply impressed by the Moscow University building, but Stalinist methods seemed unlikely to help China reach those heights of wealth and culture.[73] Stalin's strategy had involved squeezing the rural sector (and workers) and pouring these resources into heavy industry. But there was a problem applying this to China. Chinese agriculture was much poorer and less productive than the USSR's had been in 1928, when Stalin began his economic transformation. In truth, there was not much of a surplus to extract. How was the state to pay for industrialization?

Mao's solution was the 'Great Leap Forward' of 1958. This campaign was even more utopian than Stalin's 'Great Break', though it did have a certain logic to it. China was abundant in one resource only – peasant labour – and Mao was determined to exploit it to the absolute limit. The theory of the Great Leap was that the peasantry would achieve huge productivity improvements in agriculture by, for example, building irrigation systems, whilst simultaneously constructing industry. Unlike most models of development, industrialization was to happen not in towns, but in the countryside. Peasants were to achieve these ambitious feats as part of revolutionary armies led by party activists. The hope was that the self-sacrificing spirit of the revolutionary war could be reignited and transferred to the economy. At the same time the use of guerrilla-style work brigades would dissolve the political inequalities of 'feudalism' and Stalinism. As Mao explained:

> Our revolutions follow each other, one after another . . . After a victory, we must at once put forward a new task. In this way, cadres and the masses will forever be filled with revolutionary fervour, instead of conceit. Indeed, they have no time for conceit, even if they like to feel conceited.[74]

This rhetoric was, of course, eerily familiar; indeed it echoed Stalin's in the late 1920s: willpower could achieve anything when properly mobilized; there was no fortress the Bolsheviks could not storm. But Mao's ambitions were far in excess of anything even Stalin could have imagined. The British economy, it was announced, would be surpassed in fifteen years, and as enthusiasm intensified this timetable was compressed. In September 1958, Mao claimed that China would catch up with Britain the very next year.[75] Moreover, Mao asserted, China was on the threshold of full Communism.

In the cities, the Great Leap took the form of a more utopian and participatory version of Stalin's First Five-Year Plan. It was a time of 'democracy': criticisms of managers and specialists by party activists were energetically encouraged. Expertise was no longer privileged; everybody, from the poorest peasant to the highest academician, could be a specialist – or in the regime's famous slogan, both 'red' and 'expert'. But the real focus of the Great Leap was the countryside. 'People's Communes', created out of groups of villages, were charged with organizing the peasants for the great tasks Mao had set them. More than 100 million men and women were mobilized in semi-military units to work on irrigation, reforestation and anti-flood projects, often far from home. Peasants were also encouraged to build industry in the countryside, constructing small steel-furnaces. Bu Yulong, a rural official from Henan province, who volunteered to build steel furnaces some distance to the south of his village, remembered the martial atmosphere:

> We were divided into companies of 180 people, like a military company. Indeed, everything was a copy of the military system. We were soon given green military uniforms and the running of daily life was also militarized. Every morning, a bugle blew to rouse everyone.[76]

All able-bodied people were expected to participate, and this raised the question of who was to look after children, cook and perform domestic tasks. Here again the Communes stepped in. Nurseries and schools were built on the assumption that the promised rise in productivity would pay for them. Food was free, and everybody ate in public dining halls. Wage-rates were flat, no longer linked to productivity; self-sacrifice, not money-grubbing, would motivate the heroic Chinese people. The Great Leap was not just to be economic, but cultural as well. Theatres for the performance of regional opera sprang up, and millions of men and women were encouraged to write poetry and so break the stranglehold of the old elite on culture; state scribes travelled the country to collect this new people's literature.

To begin with, the Great Leap Forward had some support in the countryside. One villager from Zengbu village in Guangdong, Southern China, recalled the altruism of the time:

> The people's consciousness was so high at the beginning of the Great Leap Forward that we wanted to do everything in a collective manner. There was no need even for shop-assistants in the shops because people could be trusted to leave the correct amount for the goods they had taken.[77]

Bu Yulong also found the collectivism of the era exhilarating:

> I'll never forget the excitement when I saw my first furnace . . . Our output was hardly high, yet a big celebration took place in Zhugou. Firecrackers were let off and drums beaten. Some read out their poems:
>
> Our spirits rise higher than the rockets;
> Our will is stronger than the iron and steel;
> We are counting the limited days until we overtake Britain and America.[78]

But rapidly disillusionment set in. So many were working on irrigation projects and steel production, there were not enough hands to bring the harvest in. Meanwhile, free dining in communal halls contributed to food shortages. Also the backyard steel-furnaces produced sub-standard steel, and targets were only fulfilled by confiscating pots and shovels and melting them down. This was only one symptom of the effect Mao's wild optimism was having. Party bosses had come under intense pressure to promise the earth, lie about their achievements and cover up failures. Mao seems to have fallen for all this fraudulent activity. His doctor, Li Zhisui, recalls how they both took a train trip into the Hebei countryside and marvelled at the transformation they saw. Peasant women, dressed in colourful clothes, were at work tending luxuriant crops, whilst everywhere they looked steel furnaces lit up the skies. But Dr Li soon realized that this was a giant Potemkin village – the furnaces, it transpired, had been specially constructed along the route, whilst rice had been brought from distant fields and temporarily replanted to give an impression of abundance. Paddy-fields were so over-planted that electric fans had to be brought in to keep the air moving through the rice and stop it from rotting. As Li commented bitterly, 'all China was a stage, all the people performers in an extravaganza for Mao'.[79]

Most of Mao's colleagues went along with the Great Leap, convinced by the vastly inflated successes reported by local officials. But by early 1959 doubts were setting in, and even Mao was worried. When he visited Shaoshan, the village of his birth, he was saddened to discover that the local Buddhist shrine – much visited by his mother – had been destroyed: the bricks had been taken to build a backyard furnace and the wood used as fuel.[80] Mao made some adjustments in May; the communal dining halls, for instance, were no longer compulsory. Nevertheless, the Leap continued, and when the head of the army, Marshal Peng Dehuai, called for a retreat in July 1959, Mao, stung by the criticism, insisted on re-radicalizing it. Peng was condemned for 'rightism', and officials were again pressured to open communal dining halls. The waste therefore continued, and at the same time the peasants were forced to pay taxes levied on falsely inflated production figures.[81] Huge resources were now being extracted from agriculture: industrial investment soared from 38 per cent in 1956 to a massive 56 per cent in 1958, much of it at the expense of the peasantry. The result was a catastrophic famine: according to some estimates, between 20 and 30 million people died between 1958 and 1961 – one of the most devastating famines in modern history.[82]

By 1960, the party leadership, including Mao, had accepted that the Great Leap had been a disastrous failure. And a further blow was delivered to Mao's prestige by the break with the USSR (and with it Khrushchev's withdrawal of financial and technical help). Mao's guerrilla radicalism made Khrushchev look like an arch-reactionary, especially in foreign policy. Mao berated Khrushchev for his doctrine of 'peaceful competition' with the West, and for his willingness to ally himself with non-Communist Third World leaders, like Nehru in India. Chinese forces shelled the island of Quemoy, occupied by Chiang Kaishek's Nationalists, and Mao even declared that full-scale nuclear war would not be such a disaster; socialism would rise from the rubble; the Americans' bomb was a 'paper tiger'. Alarmed by Mao's recklessness, Khrushchev refused to assist him in a nuclear weapons programme. By 1961 the Communist bloc was irrevocably split.

Mao's position after the end of the 'Great Leap' in 1960–1 resembled Stalin's after the 'Great Break' in 1931–3. He realized that his vaulting ambitions and populism had caused chaos. He also accepted that 'retreat' from Radicalism towards a more technocratic form of Communism was necessary. The Great Leap was abandoned. Most of the backyard steel furnaces were dismantled and 6 per cent of the land was given back to peasants for cultivation as private plots. Liu Shaoqi, Deng Xiaoping and Zhou Enlai – more Modernist Marxists – took control, whilst Mao lost both face and influence. The new collective leadership's main objective was to restore order after the chaos of the Leap. Democracy campaigns were abandoned; piece rates returned; expertise was valued again; and old elites were re-established in the countryside. The inequalities that Mao had inveighed against crept back.

Local bosses reasserted their authority much as their Soviet predecessors had done in the mid-1930s: with police and paper. Passports, identity cards and files recorded details of every individual, including those essential pieces of information – class and political background. Since the revolution, people had been categorized as members of the 'five red types' (workers, poor and lower-middle-class peasants, revolutionary cadres, revolutionary soldiers and dependents of revolutionary martyrs), or of the 'five black elements' (landlords, rich peasants, counter-revolutionaries, bad elements and rightists – plus, implicitly, intellectuals). When, from the mid-1960s, local parties began to take more control of the economy, these categories began to matter a great deal. A university education, a good industrial job, or the risk of being 'sent down' from the town to the countryside to work as a peasant all depended on which of these categories one occupied. The Chinese leadership was inadvertently creating a new Communist *ancien régime* where everybody was allocated an unchangeable status – with the 'proletariat' at the top and the 'black elements' at the bottom – at least in the towns.

Class discrimination happened to some extent everywhere in the Communist world in the early phases of the regimes, but it was more systematic in China than in the Soviet bloc. This was because both Communists and society differed in each region. Lineage, clan and patronage were more dominant in China than in the USSR, and Communist leaders, many of them former members of the anti-patriarchal May 4th movement, believed these traditions were at the root of China's backwardness. They therefore used rigorously imposed class labels as a way of breaking the old order. But once they became the rulers, 'red' clans emerged, and used the class-label system to entrench their power.

But as the *ancien régimes* often discovered, fixed, inherited status hierarchies fuelled resentment. All those who were excluded from the 'red' establishment – whether people with a bad class background or the migrant workers who lacked the secure jobs and welfare benefits of tenured workers – had reason to feel angry with a rigid system they could not change. The Chinese Communist Party was paradoxically creating a new alliance of revolutionary groups that had every reason to stage a revolution against the new Communist 'class'; and the leader of that revolution was to be none other than Mao himself.

By the mid-1960s, Mao had become deeply unhappy about the policies of Liu Shaoqi, Deng Xiaoping and Zhou Enlai. These leaders were, he believed, presiding over new inequalities based on class inheritance, differential wages and educational merit. Mao, in contrast, never abandoned his guerrilla socialism and his belief that China could only be revived by altruism and self-sacrifice. Mao identified his legacy with equality in China, and became more radical with age. What, he fretted, would happen after his death? Would the Communism he had created be hijacked by right-wing 'revisionists' within the party, as had happened in Germany in the 1890s or the USSR after Stalin? As he said to Ho Chi Minh in 1966, 'We are both more than seventy, and will be called by Marx [i.e. die] someday. Who our successors will be – Bernstein, Kautsky, or Khrushchev – we can't know. But there's still time to prepare.'[83]

Challenges from abroad, as the Vietnam War threatened to spread to China, also convinced Mao of the need to return to guerrilla Communism. He decided that he had to root out the forces of the 'right', partly by purging officials at the top, but largely by changing the attitudes of the whole of society. Patriarchal hierarchy, clan domination, technocracy and money-grubbing were to give way to the reign of virtue, when people worked altruistically, for the good of all. Such were the goals of Mao's most disastrous campaign: his 'Great Proletarian Cultural

Revolution'. As the 'sixteen points' that launched the campaign in 1966 declared:

> Although the bourgeoisie has been overthrown, it is still trying to use the old ideas, culture, customs and habits of the exploiting classes to corrupt the masses, capture their minds and endeavour to stage a comeback. The proletariat must . . . change the mental outlook of the whole of society.[84]

In some ways, then, Mao was (unconsciously) following Stalin's path in the 1930s. Having led disastrous economic 'leaps', both had been forced to restore order, which in turn entrenched officials and other leaders. Both then tried to increase their power over the party, by undermining any potential rivals in the leadership. At the same time they launched ideological campaigns, purging non-believers or 'rightists' from the bureaucracy – Stalin in the Terror and Mao in the Cultural Revolution. Both campaigns also rapidly escalated out of control. But Mao was much more radical in his methods and goals. Stalin preserved hierarchy, and relied on the secret police; Mao returned to the guerrilla socialism of Yan'an and mobilized the masses in the hope of creating the new socialist man. Mao, then, was not merely imposing his will on the party; he was launching, as he saw it, a Communist revolution within a Communist state – a revolution that in effect became, uniquely, a civil war *within* the Communist Party, and amongst the population as a whole.

Typically for Chinese politics, this devastating revolution from above began in a rather subtle, oblique way, on 10 November 1965. A play, the *Dismissal of Hai Tui from Office*, about the removal of a virtuous Ming dynasty official by a tyrannical emperor, became the subject of a campaign of press criticism, orchestrated by Mao and his wife, Jiang Qing. They claimed it was an Aesopian attack on the Chairman, alleging that parallels were now being drawn between Hai Tui and Marshal Peng Dehuai. They then used the case to condemn a group within the leadership whom they accused of right-wing 'revisionism', including Peng Zhen, the party boss and mayor of Beijing and a close ally of Liu Shaoqi, and Lu Dingyi, the head of party propaganda. Speaking in March 1966, Mao used the vivid language of ancient myth:

> The central Party Propaganda Department is the palace of the Prince of Hell. It is necessary to overthrow the palace of the Prince of Hell and liberate the Little Devil . . . The local areas must produce several more [monkey

kings] to vigorously create a disturbance at the palace of the King of Heaven.[85]

Soon Mao was using more radical language and levelling more fundamental criticisms at the 'revisionists' within the party. On 16 May, the first Cultural Revolution circular described them as 'representatives of the bourgeoisie' and 'people of the Khrushchev brand still nestling in our midst', and called for a mass campaign against them.

Naturally local party bosses became anxious, and they, with Liu Shaoqi's support, tried to blunt the campaign, leading Mao and the radicals to raise the stakes. Mao now called for the creation of so-called 'red guard' groups – many made up of students – as a new vanguard to attack revisionism in the party and, more generally, the 'four olds' within society as a whole – 'old ideas, old culture, old customs, and old habits of the exploiting classes'. In August Mao himself donned a red-guard armband, and 13 million red guards from across the country visited Beijing in eight mass rallies, all brandishing their 'Little Red Books' of Mao quotations.

Throughout China, young red guards – often schoolchildren – rampaged through the streets. They enforced puritanical morality, forcing women to cut their hair and remove jewellery; they changed shop-signs and street names (the British Embassy now stood on 'Anti-Imperialism Road', the Soviet Embassy on 'Anti-Revisionism Road'); and they broke into 'bourgeois' houses and smashed or looted their belongings. Gao Yuan, the schoolboy son of a provincial official, remembered:

> With a red flag reading 'Red Guard' fluttering at the head of our column, we set out for the centre of town. Most of us carried the little red book, as we had seen the Beijing Red Guards doing in pictures in the newspapers . . . As we marched, we bellowed the new 'Song of the Red Guards':
>
>> We are Chairman Mao's Red Guards,
>> Tempering ourselves in great waves and winds;
>> Armed with Mao Zedong thought,
>> We'll wipe out all pests and vermin.
>
> . . . we reached three elaborately carved marble arches that straddled the street. The [Qing-era] triple archway had stood there for two hundred years . . . Although I had happy memories of playing under the shadow of the arches, I did not feel too bad about destroying them. Of all 24 Chinese

feudal dynasties, I disliked the Qing most . . . it was under the Qing that the Western powers had begun to subjugate China with opium and gunboats . . . To the clamour of 'Smash the four olds' the resplendent structure came down and smashed into a pile of broken stone.[86]

Mao's Cultural Revolution, then, bore striking similarities to the Soviet 'Cultural Revolution' of the late 1920s, in that it combined a populist attack on 'capitalist' backsliders in the party with a sudden 'leap' to modernity. Culturally, the impact was devastating, just as the closure and demolition of churches in late 1920s Russia had been. However, cultural figures – most vocally Mao's wife, Jiang Qing – also made serious efforts to create a new Chinese culture. Traditional opera was an early target of these cultural modernization campaigns. Jiang complained that opera, a very popular art form, was full of 'cow ghosts and snake spirits', and false values such as 'capitulation' to 'feudal' power-holders. She encouraged Communist writers to write new works, in which 'emperors, ministers, scholars and maidens' were replaced with heroic workers, peasants and soldiers.[87] These revolutionary operas, though heavily influenced by Soviet revolutionary romanticism, were also saturated with older stylized models, especially in the accompanying music. In 1966 Kang Sheng declared that five 'modernized' operas, together with two ballet dramas and a symphony, now constituted China's 'eight model performances'. The magnificent eight were shown endlessly to Chinese audiences, both on stage and on film. Initially, the operas were popular; however, because relatively few were produced, audiences were soon seeing the same operas again and again, and unsurprisingly boredom set in. As the joke went, the culture of the Cultural Revolution amounted to 'eight-hundred million people watching eight shows'.[88]

Though very self-consciously modern, the 'new' culture of the Cultural Revolution also harked back to the guerrilla socialism of Yan'an. Seven of the eight model performances concerned the Chinese revolutionary experience, and their heroes and heroines were often soldiers dressed in revolutionary-era fatigues. Indeed, military uniforms soon became the height of fashion, especially amongst the young. As one who lived through the period remembered, 'real army uniforms were few . . . I was ten at that time, and pestered my mother for a uniform. All she could do was buy some wrapping cloth (a coarse cloth used for wrapping items for the post, which didn't need cotton coupons), and dye some for me and my brothers.'[89]

The Cultural Revolution's guerrilla socialism was, then, a sharp departure from Stalinism. Society was to be completely reordered, with the virtuous at the top, not the well-educated or the well-connected. Prestige based on educational achievement was an early target. Now not only 'feudal' hierarchies but also 'meritocracy' had to yield to a type of 'virtuocracy'.[90] The ideal was now one of extreme altruism, and even the formerly lionized fictional hero Pavel Korchagin was now censured by Chinese critics for his self-indulgent romanticism and complaints about his illnesses.

The new order particularly affected schools and universities. Following Mao's belief that merit as tested by exams merely reinforced class divisions within society, political activism was to count for more than educational achievement. Students confronted an entirely novel set of incentives, where political virtue, not intellectual distinction, would gain the rewards of prestigious urban jobs.

Students were amongst the most enthusiastic supporters of the Cultural Revolution. But towards the end of the year official attention shifted to workers, who were now encouraged to embark on vocal campaigns against their bosses. Liu Guokai, a member of a group of rebels in a Guangzhou factory, described how 'had-it-bad' factions (often contract workers with their poor pay and benefits) responded eagerly to Mao's signals by rebelling against 'had-it-good' groups (the workers with secure jobs and their allies, the managers). On 25 December 1966 protestors closed down the Ministry of Labour in Beijing, and the next day Jiang Qing supported them, berating the Vice-Minister for treating them as the Cinderellas of the working class:

> She said: 'The Ministry of Labour is simply the Ministry of the Lords. Even though the country has been liberated for so many years, the workers are still suffering so much; it is unbelievable. Does your Ministry of Labour know about this or not? Do you mean to say that contract workers are the offspring of a stepmother? You, too, should work as a contract worker.' Saying this, Jiang even burst into tears.[91]

On hearing that the Cultural Revolution group now supported their cause, contract workers throughout the land rose up to demand the end of their subordinate status. They also, more generally, demanded less high-handed, more 'comradely' and dignified treatment by officials.[92]

The Cultural Revolution reached the countryside last of all, though the inhabitants of some villages had experienced the 'remoralization' of politics as early as mid-1965. When Chen village, in Guangdong province, was visited by party 'work teams' from the towns sent to spread Mao's radical message, individual piece-rate wages gave way to a work-points system designed to encourage collective labour and reward. At the same time local political structures, based on kinship networks and family favouritism, were shaken up. One such network was that of Chen Qingfa, nicknamed 'Hot Sauce' after his temper and his willingness to resort to physical violence during an argument. However, rural power structures did not really change until the most radical phase of the Cultural Revolution in 1967. In Chen village, Qingfa's rival, Chen Longyong, with the help of radical urban students sent to the countryside, seized control and imposed a terrifying reign of virtue. Longyong, who rejoiced in the nickname 'Old Pockmark', came from a more modest background than Qingfa, and had the support of poorer peasants excluded from village politics. He was also more puritan in his lifestyle and morals. He decried clannishness; he zealously organized collective labour and was more respected than the luxury-loving Qingfa. But the Cultural Revolution allowed him to wage a moralistic terror against 'bad' people, including Qingfa and even some of the radical students, and he soon alienated many of the villagers. They may have found Qingfa's rule corrupt, similar to the gentry of old, but they also found it more 'human' than Longyong's harsh and vengeful behaviour.[93]

Mao and his allies, however, did not always find it so easy to replace the Qingfas with the Longyongs. Local bosses successfully protected themselves by deflecting the Cultural Revolution campaigns away from themselves and on to 'class alien' outsiders – much as their Soviet predecessors had done in 1937. Mao's attacks on the 'bourgeoisie' were deliberately misinterpreted as a campaign against the 'black' bourgeois classes – who had long suffered discrimination – rather than one against their own class of newly bourgeois 'red' groups. So, for instance, worried local bosses set up their own red guards, made up of 'red' students (i.e. those of 'good' class backgrounds, like Gao Yuan), to persecute the old 'black' bourgeoisie and their offspring. The campaigns of class discrimination were pursued with fanatical consistency. Visitors to restaurants were forced to complete questionnaires on their class origins, whilst bourgeois surgeons were afraid to operate on proletarians in case the procedure went badly and they were accused of 'class revenge'.[94]

Party officials justified these highly self-interested distortions of Mao's campaigns by reinterpreting Mao's warnings of revolutionary decay using the dogma of 'blood pedigree theory'. Blood pedigree was the notion that virtue was not only a class-specific but also an exclusively inherited characteristic. The 'red' classes and their children were genetically good, whilst the 'black' classes were forever tainted across the generations. Class was reinterpreted as something akin to caste or race. The theory was summed up in a verse couplet:

If the old man's a hero, the son's a good chap,
If the old man's a reactionary, the son's a bad egg.[95]

This, of course, was the exact opposite of what Mao had in mind. He and his radical supporters condemned blood pedigree theory as 'feudal', and stated that class was about attitude, not blood. It was, Mao insisted, possible for the 'black' classes to be more virtuous and 'proletarian' than the 'red' ruling groups; indeed, he argued, it was the 'reds' who were fast becoming a new privileged class, similar to the old bourgeoisie. However, Mao – like Trotsky – never categorically declared that the party elite had become a new bourgeois class, for to do so would have been tantamount to calling for a full-blown revolution against the Communist Party, endangering the entire regime.[96] Mao was, therefore, always studiedly ambiguous; though he encouraged the 'black' classes, he never wholly disowned the 'reds'.

Such equivocation contributed to chaotic civil war, with both sides insisting that only they were following the true will of the Chairman. The former bourgeoisie, allied with underprivileged workers and other stigmatized 'blacks', advanced their claims to revolutionary virtue by forming their own red guards. An Wenjiang, the son of a lowly seaman who was studying at Fudan University, Shanghai, decided to join one of the rebel red-guard groupings to counter the violence of the establishment red guards – known as 'Scarlet Guards':

Before the movement, I had been quiet, obedient, and almost shy in class, but only because my free and reckless nature had been suppressed. Given the opportunity, I grew radical, daring, and enthusiastic ... I can't deny there was a selfish element, a desire to show off, in my becoming a rebel leader, but it was mostly a conviction that the son of a working-class man should be allowed to participate in revolution.[97]

On 24 August 1966, An's red guards were thrilled when a large poster with Mao's declaration 'Bombard the Headquarters' (of the Communist Party) appeared on the campus. As he remembered, 'we regarded it as a victory for our rebel groups' for it was a call to attack the elite, and 'near midnight, 1,400 of us marched off in high spirits to invade Shanghai's drama academy at the invitation of its rebel minority'. Two days later, however, the establishment Scarlet Guards staged a massive 40,000-strong rally, claiming Mao supported them. An decided to go to Beijing by train 'to see Chairman Mao and understand the real situation'. He was assured by the red guards of Peking University that the Chairman was indeed on the rebels' side, and he returned to Shanghai, full of radical zeal.[98]

This civil war dynamic soon spread throughout China as rival red guard units fought for dominance. Most institutions and workplaces – schools, universities and factories – had their competing red guards. As Mao later recalled, 'Everywhere people were fighting, dividing into two factions; there were two factions in every factory, in every school, in every province, in every county ... there was massive upheaval in the country.'[99] The young were most active in the red guards, but much of the urban population was sucked into the revolutionary turmoil. By the end of 1966 the 'blacks' were in the ascendant, but the 'reds' continued to defend themselves.

Mao understood perfectly well that the Cultural Revolution was generating extreme violence, and saw that Beijing and the central party were losing control. Nevertheless he would not retreat, determined as he was to foment a real revolution from below against the party bureaucracy, not merely a purge from above. For once perfectly unambiguous, Mao, entertaining guests at his birthday party on 26 December 1966, proposed a toast: 'To the unfolding of nationwide all-round civil war!'[100] This heartless insouciance was also evident in Mao's justification of the chaos and violence that engulfed China: 'it's a mistake when good people beat up on good people, though it may clear up some misunderstandings, as they might otherwise not have got to know each other in the first place.'[101] For Mao, disorder was less dangerous than allowing the old elite to remain in power.

The most decisive signal that the tide had turned against the 'reds' and in favour of the radicals and the 'blacks', was the 'January Storm' of 1967 in Shanghai. Here, unusually for China, the rebels were not students like An Wenjiang, but largely unprivileged workers. The local party had amassed battalions of red guards to oppose them, but the 800,000 members they claimed to have could not defeat the rebels. On 30 December 1966 some 100,000 rebels attacked 20,000 establishment red guards and after four hours' fighting were victorious. On 5 February Mao approved the end of the local party's power, and its transfer to a new organization – the Shanghai People's Commune, modelled on the Paris Commune of 1871.

The January Storm buffeted the whole country. The young Gao Yuan, a child of the party establishment, now became a victim of the violence he had previously meted out to others. When he awoke one morning and went out to buy food, he was shocked to see notices posted around the town centre, declaring that 'the time is ripe to seize power from the counter-revolutionary Party Committee and government' – an elite that included his father. The rival 'black' red guard group, the so-called 'Mao Zedong Thought Red Guards', broke into his house and held his father in the painful 'jet-plane' position for two hours – kneeling down, his arms outstretched and a red guard foot on his back. They then ceremonially 'crowned' him with the cap of an old-style feudal official, as worn by actors in traditional operas, to symbolize his ejection from office.[102] Across the land, political factions subjected their enemies to similar public humiliations, torture and even death. Meanwhile in Beijing a secret police-style organization established by Mao, the Central Case Examination Group, investigated and purged the so-called enemies of the Cultural Revolution Group. Liu Shaoqi and Deng Xiaoping were now denounced as 'China's Khrushchevs'.

The high point of Mao's radicalism came in the summer of 1967, when, realizing that the conservatives were winning, he ordered local military authorities to 'arm the left'. The results were predictable: the casualties in local battles between conservatives and radicals rose to the thousands. By the end of August Mao had begun to accept that the 'great chaos' had become too dangerous, and he launched a new campaign to 'support the military and cherish the people' – using the army, which had previously allowed the radicals free rein, to restore central control. Mao toured China establishing new revolutionary committees, thus restoring the shattered party organization, but it was a lengthy process. Competing factions had to be united and radical red guard movements suppressed. The army itself now embarked on a campaign of purging and killing – rather more systematically than the red guards had. This was the period when the Cultural Revolution was at its most bloody and brutal. It was only in September 1968 that the last of the stabilizing revolutionary committees was put in place.

Alongside political centralization went a restoration of cultural order – especially when it came to the thorny question of Mao's own cult. As was often the case in Communist regimes, Mao's cult had emerged during periods of threat, when the leadership needed to consolidate its power – in Yan'an in the early 1940s, and during the leadership crisis surrounding the Great Leap Forward. However, with the Cultural Revolution the leadership began to lose control of a cult that was becoming ever more extravagant – far outstripping that of Stalin.[103] As political power crumbled, rival red guards outdid each other to show loyalty to the Chairman, and competitive sycophancy pushed the cult to extreme levels. In some places life became dominated by expressions of loyalty to the Chairman: 'Quotation gymnastics' were held, in which participants competed to show their knowledge of *Quotations from Chairman Mao*, and many meetings began with a 'loyalty dance'. Some rural expressions of devotion had even more explicitly ritual or religious overtones, with the building of 'Quotation Pagodas' housing 'instruction tablets'. Mao's words were being treated as if they were Buddhist sutras. The Cultural Revolution leadership in Beijing disapproved of the uncontrolled use of the cult, recognizing that it was really being used to further the ambition of local bosses, and so ultimately weakening Mao. As Kang Sheng explained:

> At present the loyalty dance is being danced everywhere. They say it is loyal [to] Chairman Mao, but in reality it is opposing Chairman Mao . . . There further exists 'loyalize' this, 'loyalize' that, wasting the nation's wealth. This is loyal [to] oneself, giving oneself political capital.[104]

Soon, the army made serious efforts to control the cult, imposing rigid codes and practices on its use and thus depriving it of spontaneity. The new 'three loyalties and four boundless loves' movement encouraged revolutionary committees to establish strict liturgies, setting out precisely how citizens should show their devotion to Mao. Most extraordinary were the authorities in the Hebei city of Shijiazhuang, who prescribed a detailed set of rituals for all shop sales staff. Before shops opened in the morning, they were to 'seek instruction' from the Chairman's works and in the evening they were to 'report back' on the day's events before a portrait of the Chairman. They were also given a catechism of Mao's quotations, suitable for opening conversations between salesperson and customer. A sales-clerk welcoming a worker customer, for instance, might say, 'Vigorously grasp revolution', whilst the customer would respond, 'Energetically promote production', completing the quotation; an elderly person, on the other hand, would be greeted with the phrase 'Let us wish Chairman Mao a long life!', and would be expected to reply, 'Long live Chairman Mao! Long live, long live!' Naturally these rituals caused deep anxiety, for punishments could be harsh for those who made mistakes. One teacher from Fucheng County in Hebei Province was sentenced to nine years' imprisonment because he had initially written in his diary that a Mao quotation had given him 'boundless energy', and then changed the phrase to 'very much energy'.

In the cities, the 'three loyalties and four boundless loves' movement ended in June 1969, and by then the worst of the violence was over. Nevertheless many remained in prison or exiled to the countryside until the official end of the Cultural Revolution, with Mao's death in 1976. Estimates suggest that at least a million people died and many more suffered through torture or humiliation in the Cultural Revolution. The lives and the prospects of millions of others were blighted, as a generation of youths was deprived of education. Feng Jicai, the son of a former banker, stressed the long-lasting psychological damage wrought by the persecutions:

> The greatest tragedy of the Cultural Revolution was its torture of people's souls ... My father suffered badly ... In the seventies, after countless struggle sessions, he developed a strange problem. At night, he would wake from his nightmares and begin to scream. It was a small place. When he screamed, no one could sleep. But he dragged on until 1989.[105]

However, the Cultural Revolution had resolved absolutely nothing. Mao, like Stalin, had hoped to remobilize the country to build a new society, but only violent chaos had ensued. Political leadership in Beijing remained weak and the economy had been wrecked. The Cultural Revolution officially may have continued until 1976, but it was already clear as early as 1968 that the old Radical class struggle waged against the Communist bureaucracy had brought disaster to China and its people.

With sputnik's launch in October 1957, the international reputation and self-confidence of Communist regimes reached their zenith. As in Frazer's *Golden Bough*, it seemed as if the sacrifice of Stalin, the mythical king, had permitted a reinvigoration of the system. The use of rocket technology to conquer space for the whole of mankind suggested that Communists really had devoted their energy to the service of peace and humanity rather than war and division. By the late 1960s, however, it was clear that efforts in Yugoslavia, the USSR and China to expand the appeal of the regime beyond the rigid Stalinist party, whilst finding new forms of radical mobilization to achieve economic successes, had failed. Tito had, to all intents and purposes, abandoned mobilization and was beginning his journey to the market and the West; Khrushchev found it difficult to escape the crude militarized methods of the 1930s; whilst Mao's extremism had demonstrated how fearsome and destructive a highly radical, egalitarian Communism could be. But at the same time as these three Communist regimes were finding it difficult to transform their own societies, they found new opportunities abroad, in Latin America and an Africa in the throes of decolonization. And they were joined by a new Communist competitor in the struggle for the hearts and minds of the Third World: Cuba.

9

Guerrillas

Early in 1954, a young Argentinian was to be found in the centre of Guatemala City peddling bulb-illuminated pictures of Guatemala's 'black Christ'. As the icon particularly appealed to the numerous poor Indians of the city, the trade was surprisingly lucrative. The idea of manufacturing the icons had originally come from Antonio 'Ñico' López, a Cuban exile and sometime participant in Fidel Castro's failed coup of 1953. But it was the Argentinian Ernesto Guevara (nicknamed 'Che' after his frequent use of the indigenous Guaraní term meaning 'hey, you') who sold them. Though a qualified doctor, Che had been unable to get a job, and he was forced to make ends meet however he could. In a letter home, Guevara described his sales patter: 'I am selling a precious image of the Lord of Esquipulas, a black Christ who makes amazing miracles . . . I have a rich list of anecdotes of the Christ's miracles and I am constantly making up new ones to see if they will sell.'[1]

Guevara and López were just two of an eclectic group of Latin American leftists – from Venezuelan Social Democrats to Nicaraguan Communists, from opponents of the Argentinian strong-man Juan Perón to rebels against the Cuban dictator Fulgencio Batista – who had come to see the new radical Republic of Guatemala. Rather like the Europeans who had flocked to Republican Spain eighteen years before, many Latin Americans on the progressive left saw Guatemala, ruled by the socialist Jacobo Arbenz, as the hope of the continent. Guevara himself, still only twenty-six, was a charismatic figure, brave or reckless depending on one's perspective. But he could also be a tough disciplinarian; he endorsed the Stalinist position on the legitimacy of violence, and his brusque and moralistic manner alienated some. This austere demeanour, however, was leavened by a self-satirizing sense of humour: one of his favourite literary characters was Cervantes' Don Quixote, the ridiculous would-be knight errant, fighting for hopelessly lost causes.[2]

Born to an aristocratic but now impoverished family, Che was a sickly child, whose severe asthma had turned him bookish – he often retreated to read in the family bathroom to escape his chaotic environment. Though physically fragile, he was determined to overcome his physical weakness through willpower and brain-power, and as a youth he set off on his now-famous motorcycle tours of the Latin American continent, when he saw the enormous inequalities between indigenous Indians and affluent whites.

However, for Che such inequalities were not merely about race, or even class. Like many Latin American intellectuals, he saw them as the consequence of imperialism and colonialism, and of the power of the United States over the continent: its companies' capitalist exploitation of natural resources, and its cadre of local dictators who maintained semi-imperial control. Pablo Neruda, the Chilean Communist-sympathizer and Che's favourite poet, captured this anger in his 1950 poem 'The United Fruit Co.', in which he painted a picture of swarms of tyrant-flies feasting on the rotten fruit of imperialism and corruption.[3]

It was Arbenz's attempts to nationalize the vast lands of *el polpo* ('the octopus') that had attracted many radicals to Guatemala, including Guevara:

> I had the opportunity to pass through the domains of United Fruit, convincing me once again of just how terrible these capitalist octopuses are. I have sworn before a picture of the old and mourned comrade Stalin that I won't rest until I see these capitalist octopuses annihilated. In Guatemala I will perfect myself and achieve what I need to be an authentic revolutionary.[4]

El polpo, however, proved resilient, and it was not United Fruit that capitulated but the Arbenz regime. Local conservatives fought back, assisted by the American CIA, which directed a year-long campaign of political and military subversion against Arbenz. Guevara was determined to stay and defend the 'Guatemalan revolution', braving the aerial bombing of Guatemala City just as the Communists had defended Madrid. But Arbenz refused to fight and fled the country. Guevara himself, sheltering in the Argentinian embassy, only narrowly avoided arrest at the behest of the American Secretary of State, John Foster Dulles, who was determined to stop revolutionaries regrouping elsewhere. In September 1954 he fled to Mexico.

The fall of Arbenz galvanized the Latin American left, just as the fall of Republican Spain had radicalized it in the 1930s, and Communists took advantage. As in the 1930s, Moscow allowed Communists to ally themselves with other 'bourgeois' forces and Communists argued that their combination of modernity and hard-headed discipline could best rid their countries of foreign imperialism. For Che Guevara, certainly, Soviet-style Communism provided the answers, and he criticized Arbenz for failing to embrace Stalinist ruthlessness and organization. His uncompromising approach might have been expected given his upbringing. His father had led campaigns to support the Spanish Republic and, as a child, Che had named their family pet dog Negrina after the pro-Moscow Spanish President Juan Négrin.[5]

Even so, there were naturally enormous differences between 1950s Latin America – with its history of foreign interventions – and 1930s Europe, as there were between the Communisms of the period. Communism had become a much more diverse movement, and the success of Asian Communism offered an alternative, rural guerrilla model of revolution to the Third World. From the mid-1950s Moscow began to lose control of international Communism to rival capitals, and Havana, following Castro's and Che's Cuban revolution of 1959, was to be one of them. Che, who had once signed a youthful letter to his aunt 'Stalin II', gradually became disillusioned with the Soviet tradition, and his *nom de guerre* certainly suggested he had a different revolutionary style. 'Hey, You' was no 'Man of Steel', but a much more Radical, even Romantic Marxist.

Che became an iconic figure, and for a time Cuba became one of the most attractive models for radical nationalists. But the Cubans were not alone: the 'parricidal', post-Stalin regimes of Tito and Mao were competing fiercely to attract the new, nationalist Third World leaders. And under Khrushchev, the Soviets themselves were presenting a more idealistic face. They had also abandoned their old Stalinist sectarianism and adopted a more inclusive strategy, forging alliances with non-Marxist-Leninist groups. This was a fluid era in which Soviets, Chinese and Cubans supported an eclectic range of left-wing groups – Radical Marxist guerrillas, Soviet-style modernizers, moderate Communists willing to collaborate with nationalists, and non-Marxist nationalists. After a long period of Stalinist neglect, Communism was now speaking to a wider audience in the Third World at a time when the West was also presenting a more attractive face under the leadership of John F. Kennedy. However, Cuba's guerrilla Communism was no more successful in sustaining itself than the other Romantic Communisms of the 1960s, whilst the new Communist activism in the Third World caused instability and frightened its opponents, leading to a backlash and a string of Communist defeats. The era of optimism, on both sides of the ideological divide, was not to last.

II

Almost a year after the fall of Arbenz, on 18 April 1955, twenty-nine delegates from Asian and African countries assembled in the West Javan city of Bandung to hear Indonesian President Sukarno's thunderous welcoming speech:

> Yes, there has indeed been a *'Sturm über Asien'* [Storm over Asia] – and over Africa too . . . Nations, states have awoken from the sleep of centuries. The passive peoples have gone, the outward tranquillity has made place for struggle and activity . . . Hurricanes of national awakening and reawakening have swept over the land, shaking it, changing it, changing it for the better.[6]

Sukarno's 'Storm over Asia' was a reference to Pudovkin's 1928 film of that name, a drama about a Mongolian descendant of Genghis Khan who, in 1918, switches allegiance from the imperialist British to the Bolsheviks.[7] There were, then, echoes of the old Comintern in Bandung, and, like the Baku conference of 'Peoples of the East' of 1920, it was seeking to unite the global 'South' in the struggle against imperialism. However, this was categorically not a Communist congress. The Mongolians had not been invited, nor had any other nationalities deemed too close to the Soviets – whether the Soviet Asian republics or the North Koreans. Of the Communist regimes, only the Chinese and North Vietnamese were there. And whilst some of the leading delegates – India's Jawaharlal Nehru and Indonesia's Ahmed Sukarno – were socialists (and Nehru had a great deal of sympathy for Soviet-style planning), they were indigenous nationalist socialists, determined to meld socialism with local political traditions, rather than Marxist-Leninists. Being nationalists, they also refused to identify themselves too closely with any bloc, whether Eastern or Western. Indeed, some delegates were strongly anti-Communist – six of the twenty-nine had recently aligned themselves with the United States and Britain. Carlos Romulo, representative of the Filipino regime that had recently suppressed the Communist Huk rebellion, famously quipped: 'The empires of yesterday on which it used to be said the sun never set are departing one by one from Asia. What we fear now is the new empire of Communism on which we know the sun never rises.'[8]

The Chinese refused to accept that their Soviet allies had an empire in Eastern Europe, and the meeting was a fraught one, as delegates argued about the conference's attitude towards the superpowers. However, Zhou Enlai made a masterful attempt to charm the Bandung leaders, presenting China as a moderate, tolerant friend of the global underdog. He recognized that Marxism-Leninism was a rarity in the new decolonized world, and that compromises were required if China was to have any influence. Romulo complained that he behaved as if he had 'taken a leaf from Dale Carnegie's tome on *How to Win Friends and Influence People*'.[9] But Zhou had more respectable theoretical backing for his charm offensive than Dale Carnegie: the Chinese Communists were in their ideologically moderate 'New Democracy' phase, and were happy to sanction Communist alliances with bourgeois nationalists.

Bandung saw the birth of the 'Third World' as a new entity, independent of both the 'First' West and the 'Second' East. The conference agreed on the need to escape economic dependence on the First World – described by Sukarno as colonialism in modern dress – through economic cooperation. It also resolved to fight against the dangers of nuclear war. In his rousing speech to the conference, Sukarno urged the African and Asian South to deploy the 'moral violence of nations in favour of peace', standing up to the militarism of the two Cold War blocs.[10]

The Bandung Conference marked the entry of an identifiable 'South' into world politics, and the power of anti-imperialism. Though the old empires were clearly waning, many were clearly determined to hang on, or at least retain influence after decolonization by shaping the politics of the successor states. By the early 1960s, only a few states remained under white control – the Portuguese colonies, mostly in Africa, South Africa and Rhodesia. Nevertheless, many Third World leaders still saw imperialism as a powerful force, and notions of 'neo-colonialism' and informal empire were much discussed, especially in connection with the United States and its prominent role as the new supporter of old, pro-Western collaborators.

However, debates at Bandung also underlined how far Stalin's Communism was tarred with the imperialist brush, opening the way for the Chinese and the Yugoslavs to challenge the USSR as the true and legitimate leader of global Communism. Even more worrying for the Soviets was a meeting the following year on the Yugoslav island of Brijuni between Tito, Nehru and Nasser. There plans were made to turn the Third World into a foreign policy bloc with a 'plague on both your houses' stance towards the superpowers. The founding of the 'Non-Aligned Movement' in 1961 in Belgrade was the result.[11]

Khrushchev was swift to respond to the challenge. He and his ideologists were convinced that decolonization provided enormous opportunities for Soviet socialism. The USSR, he believed, could provide an attractive model to Third World nationalists – one that combined a long record of anti-imperialism, a commitment to social justice, and technological progress symbolized by the Virgin Lands project and sputnik. With Soviet encouragement, he argued, bourgeois 'progressive' nationalists would gradually move into the socialist camp; meanwhile, as their economies developed and working classes became stronger, anti-imperialism would become anti-capitalism. This transition, Khrushchev insisted, could be peaceful; it need not necessarily be a violent, revolutionary one, involving vanguard parties and class struggle. The progressive Third World was to be a 'zone of peace'.[12]

Shortly after Bandung, therefore, Khrushchev hurriedly organized a series of state visits to Yugoslavia, India and Burma, aimed at restoring the Soviets' image amongst the anti-imperialist left; he also sent an emissary to the Middle East to forge links with Nasser. This marked a dramatic departure from the late-Stalinist view of all non-aligned leaders as potential enemies,[13] and it necessitated a major change in Soviet doctrine, for with the end of the Popular Front in 1947 the USSR had seen the world as divided into 'two camps'. Khrushchev announced the end of the old Stalinist worldview at the twentieth party congress in 1956. The USSR, he proclaimed in 1960, was happy to see 'national democratic states', in which Communists forged alliances with left-wing 'bourgeois' nationalists.[14]

This was, in effect, a version of the old 'united front' policy, with 'bourgeois' nationalist governments taking the place of nationalist parties. The new policy took the form of increased aid to Nehru's India, Nkrumah's Ghana, Sukarno's Indonesia and Ben Bella's Algeria. But from a propaganda perspective, Khrushchev's most effective intervention was in formerly Belgian Congo (Congo-Léopoldville, later Zaire). On giving the Congo independence in 1960, the Belgians, with the support of the Americans, had backed an insurgency against the elected left-wing nationalist Patrice Lumumba. Lumumba's capture and assassination in 1961 was a setback to Soviet policy, but he became a martyr to the cause of Soviet-backed anti-imperialism, and his death resonated throughout Africa.

Following the Sino-Soviet split of the late 1950s, meanwhile, the Chinese provided stiff competition to Moscow in its quest for Third World influence. In the early 1960s, Zhou Enlai and Liu Shaoqi crisscrossed Africa and Asia, and visited large numbers of non-aligned leaders from Burma to Egypt, from Algeria to Ethiopia. The Chinese now presented themselves as a radical alternative to the Soviets and strong opponents of the policy of 'peaceful coexistence' with the West. In 1965, Lin Biao, the radical military leader, argued that Chinese guerrilla experience was much more suited to freedom struggles in agrarian societies than the Soviet model. Their old strategy of 'encircling the cities by first liberating the countryside' could be applied to the whole world: the West constituted the 'world's cities', whilst Latin America, Africa and Asia were the 'world's countryside'.[15] People's wars had to be fought against feudalism and imperialism.

The Chinese message was an appealing one for many Third World Communists. As the head of the powerful Indonesian Communist Party, Dipa Aidit, told a foreign Communist delegation, Communist regimes like the Soviet one would inevitably become '"rich fat cats" at the expense of backward countries and will lose their revolutionary spirit'. He was particularly exercised by the fact that he had paid much more for a shirt in Moscow than in New York, and even then the quality had been distinctly inferior – proof-positive that the Russians were even more money-grubbing than the Americans.[16] The Indonesian party was one of the main allies of the Chinese, but Beijing also funded the Vietnamese and a number of African and Middle Eastern non-Communist regimes and independence movements.

The 1960s Third World 'united front' of indigenous socialists and Communists, like its 1920s predecessor, was highly unstable, for the renewed prestige of international Marxism increased Communist support in many post-colonial societies, which inevitably threatened nationalist leaders. Nasser responded by brutally suppressing the Egyptian Communists in 1959, and Abdel Karim Qassim of Iraq, a left-wing nationalist leader who came to power in 1958 in collaboration with the Communists, soon began to regret the alliance. For whilst there were only about 25,000 Iraqi Communist Party members, affiliated mass organizations boasted some million members, about a fifth of the population.[17] One of the most striking examples of tensions between left nationalists and Communists occurred in India, where the Communist Party of India (CPI) won elections in the highly caste-divided southwestern state of Kerala in 1957, partly with the support of low-caste groups. The CPI, with Moscow's support, pursued a non-revolutionary set of policies. Indeed its plans for land reform were strikingly similar to Nehru's own ideas. Nevertheless, it soon encountered serious opposition from conservative groups, and especially from the powerful Catholic Church, which opposed its education policies. The Catholics formed a 'Liberationist' militia, and local Communists responded. In 1959 the threat of a Catholic *coup d'état* forced the Communist Chief Minister Elamkulam Namboodiripad to call on the centre for help, and Nehru took advantage of the crisis to dismiss the government in July.[18]

Khrushchev's efforts to improve the image of the USSR amongst Third World leaders benefited enormously from the Americans' deep mistrust of Third World nationalism. In the years after the War, the United States agonized over how to deal with the radical South. Its leaders understood that European imperialists and conservative local elites were fuelling popular radicalism, and yet they were afraid that nationalists – many of whom were demanding land redistribution and other social changes – might ally with Moscow. In the early years, the Americans generally maintained their anti-imperial position. In 1949, for example, Secretary of State Dean Acheson warned the Netherlands that it would be deprived of Marshall Plan aid and military help if it used force to re-impose its rule on Indonesia. Indonesian independence rapidly followed.

However the 'loss' of China to Communism in 1949 had a major impact on American policy – it was a devastating trauma, and loomed over American foreign policy for years. Washington's belief that it could 'contain' Communism throughout the world was shaken, and policy-makers increasingly moved from idealism to *realpolitik*; from the optimistic belief that Third World states could be converted to American-style liberal democracy, to a pessimistic fear that anybody who did not fully support private property, the free market and the American alliance was likely to defect to Moscow. The result was a tendency to exaggerate the Communist threat and regard all socially radical nationalisms as potentially dangerous. This attitude led in turn to a strategy of supporting European empires or narrowly based conservative elites, which naturally fuelled Third World fears of 'neo-colonialism', a condition in which the vintage European empires seemed merely to have been replaced by a new American model. Unsurprisingly, this apparently seamless connection between European empire and American hegemony helped Moscow and Beijing increase their influence amongst Third World nationalists.

Perhaps the most long-lasting result of this change in Washington was the jettisoning of serious efforts to lessen economic inequalities between the First and the Third Worlds. Whilst there was never any serious chance of a Marshall Plan for the South, the British liberal economist John Maynard Keynes had persuaded the Bretton Woods conference of 1944 to extend the benefits of the new financial system in that direction, by establishing an International Trade Organization with the power to stabilize the commodity prices on which poor countries depended so greatly. However, the ratification of Keynes's plan by the United States Congress was delayed, and after 1949 suspicion of international organizations in the United States was such that it was never passed. Its replacement, the General Agreement on Tariffs and Trade (GATT), offered no support for commodity prices. The result was growing economic inequality between the industrial North and agrarian South, as improving technology depressed agricultural prices whilst industrial prices rose. The economies of the South did grow during the 1950s and 1960s, but much more slowly than those of the industrialized North.[19] Many poor countries found themselves trapped, unable to rise up the ladder of development.

Of more immediate importance, though, was the change in American foreign policy. In 1953, as the USSR began to move away from Stalin's Manichaean power politics, the new administration of President

Eisenhower embraced *realpolitik* – at least insofar as the Third World was concerned. The administration accepted that anti-Western feelings were growing, and were the result of 'racial feelings, anti-colonialism, rising nationalism, popular demand for rapid social and economic progress' and other deep-seated causes.[20] And it was sometimes acknowledged that the United States needed to win hearts and minds, to wean nationalists away from Communism. But 'soft power' was less central to American policy under the Eisenhower administration than the use of force, often in the form of military aid to strong men and dictators. Secretary of State Dulles was convinced that Communism was an 'internationalist conspiracy, not an indigenous movement' (even in Latin America where there was, as yet, little Soviet involvement), and he favoured firm action.[21]

One of the main features of Eisenhower's Cold War strategy in the Third World, therefore, was the use of the CIA to stage *coups d'état* against nationalists deemed to be too close to Communism. The first attack on a popularly elected government targeted that of the nationalist President of Iran, Mohammed Mossadeq. Fearing that he would deliver oil supplies to the Soviets, the CIA organized a successful coup in 1953.

Mossadeq, however, was not alone. The United States found itself facing a whole series of popular nationalist leaders in the Middle East, committed to destroying European influence, and willing to make tactical alliances with the USSR. Sometimes the Americans intervened successfully, for instance saving the regime of the Lebanese President Camille Chamoun against radical challengers. Other cases were more difficult: Nasser nationalized the Suez Canal in 1956, provoking the bungled British, French and Israeli invasion.

By the 1950s, the United States even found itself moving closer to a state that was regarded by Third World nationalists as the most egregious example of imperialism and racism: South Africa. Despite CIA warnings about increasing African opposition to apartheid, American relations with South Africa actually strengthened during the 1950s as Washington sought strategic and economic advantages.

But it was Vietnam that offered the most stark example of the United States' assumption of the mantle of the old European empires. President Roosevelt had been hostile to the continuation of French rule after World War II, but in 1950 Truman performed an about-turn: fearful

379

that Communist victory in Vietnam would lead to the serial collapse of pro-Western regimes throughout South-East Asia, the Americans reluctantly compromised their anti-imperialist principles and recognized the French-backed South Vietnamese Bao Dai regime. In 1953 Eisenhower went further and approved the financing of most of the French campaign. But even that could not stop the French defeat at Dien Bien Phu in 1954 and their withdrawal from Vietnam. Neither the Russians nor the Chinese wanted war to continue against the Americans, and they therefore pressed a reluctant Ho Chi Minh to agree to a temporary partition of Vietnam into North and South, pending elections (which were never held). He would control the North, whilst the South would be run by the American-backed Ngo Dinh Diem – a nationalist politician who had parted from Bao Dai in the early 1930s.

For some time it looked as if the American strategy had worked. Diem, who had good anti-French credentials and local support from the Catholic Church, had some initial success in entrenching his government.[22] And for some time neither Moscow nor Beijing was eager to revive the war, whilst the North Vietnamese were distracted by a Chinese-style land reform whose violent excesses had become deeply unpopular within the party.[23] However, Hanoi became increasingly worried that the division of the country would become permanent, and at the same time the underground Communists in the South, the National Front for the Liberation of South Vietnam (NLF, sometimes called the 'Viet Cong'), exploited resentment at the heavy-handed policies of Diem. In 1959, under pressure from the Viet Cong, the North decided to escalate the war.

The United States may have succeeded in distancing itself from European imperialism by backing Diem's temporarily stable regime in South Vietnam in 1954, but in the same year it seemed as if Washington were following a Marxist-Leninist manual on how to be an imperialistic capitalist: it really did look as if it was promoting imperialism, and that imperialism really was the highest stage of capitalism. Jacobo Arbenz's threat to the interests of United Fruit led to lobbying in Washington – the company's tentacles reached the New York law firm of John Foster Dulles and his brother, Allen, the head of the CIA. More worrying to the White House, however, was Arbenz's willingness to work with the Guatemalan Communist Party, and despite minimal Soviet involvement, the administration was convinced that Guatemala threatened to become a launching-pad for Communism across the continent. The covert CIA campaign of subversion, 'Operation Success', finally toppled Arbenz in 1954.[24] The operation may have lived up to its name in the short term, but it would eventually have a profoundly damaging effect on America's image. In Latin America, it helped to push some of the post-Bandung generation towards radicalism, and the first sign of this process was evident only 90 miles from the shores of the United States, in Cuba.

III

As the Americans had feared, after his fall, Arbenz's radical supporters merely fled the country and continued their struggle elsewhere. Flushed out of Guatemala, Che Guevara, his Cuban friend Ñico López and other radicals made their way to the Mexican capital. Mexico City hosted a number of revolutionaries, including Fidel Castro and his brother Raúl, who were in exile but planning to return to Cuba. Che, unlike Fidel, was now a convinced Marxist, but he was still willing to join Fidel's liberation movement. As Castro remembered:

> Our little group there in Mexico liked him immediately . . . He knew that in our movement there were even some petit-bourgeois members and a bit of everything. But he saw that we were going to fight a revolution of national liberation, an anti-imperialist revolution; he didn't yet see a socialist revolution, but that was no obstacle – he joined right up, he immediately signed on.[25]

The son of a Spanish immigrant who had leased land from United Fruit and planted sugar, Fidel Castro was from a wealthy, but far from aristocratic or well-connected background. He was a rebellious child, and his politics were profoundly different from those of his Franco-sympathizing father. Nevertheless, he valued the 'military spirit' of his Jesuit boarding school, and he enjoyed the 'kind of healthy, austere life I lived in those schools'.[26] Whilst studying law in Havana, he became involved in radical politics – though he had little in common with the Cuban Communist party (PSP), which had forged alliances with Batista in the 1940s. Rather, he joined the Ortodoxo party with its roots in the radical nationalism of the nineteenth-century poet-cum-revolutionary José Martí.

Cuban intellectuals felt the power of American neo-imperialism and capitalism particularly keenly. Following the end of Spanish rule in 1898, Cuba was occupied for four years by the United States, and even after formal independence it remained tightly tied to its northern neighbour. Indeed, its economy was almost wholly integrated into that of the United States. It was highly dependent on income from sugar exports to the United States (and sugar quotas depended on the goodwill of the American Congress), and foreigners owned a large number of the plantations. Havana itself was a cosmopolitan city, full of American expatriates, who were blamed by nationalist moralizers for transforming the city into a centre for organized crime, gambling and sex tourism. It seemed to many educated Cubans that their country was trapped by sugar and the United States in a position of permanent subordination. Only radical change could restore its self-respect.

The immediate target of the nationalists, however, was the corrupt American-backed dictator Batista. The Ortodoxo party – with its demands for social and land reform – soon became Batista's main opponent. Castro proved a tireless revolutionary: after his exile following the failed 1953 coup, he rallied his small force, now dubbed the '26th July Movement', and returned from Mexico to Cuba in 1956, on the *Granma* (*Grandmother*) – a rusty motorized yacht. The landing was a disaster, and only twenty-two revolutionaries of the original eighty-two managed to regroup, eventually establishing a base in the inaccessible Sierra Maestra – a poor region in the east of the island with a long-established tradition of peasant rebellion. From here Fidel and his band waged a guerrilla war, whilst at the same time urban rebels – the *llano* – carried out a campaign of strikes and violence in the towns.[27] However, the failure of the urban general strike in the spring of 1958 weakened the *llano* and increased the power of Castro and the rural guerrillas. Batista responded to the guerrilla violence with more violence and support for him ebbed away, not only within Cuba but also in Washington. On New Year's Eve, Batista, correctly sensing which way the tide of history was flowing, fled, and Castro and Guevara entered Havana two days later.

Compared with the Vietnamese and Chinese revolutions, the Cuban revolution was remarkably swift and easy. The roots of Batista's support were shallow, whilst the opposition included a large, vocal urban middle class, and links between towns and the rural proletariat were stronger than elsewhere in Latin America. Castro was buoyed by enormous popular support for an end to the Batista regime, and he insisted that his was a nationalist revolution, not a Communist one. Indeed, in a speech on 1 January, he placed his revolution firmly in the tradition of past nationalist risings:

> This time Cuba is fortunate: the revolution will truly come to power. It will not be as in 1895 when the Americans intervened at the last minute and appropriated our country ... No thieves, no traitors, no interventionists! This time the revolution is for real.[28]

Castro announced a cabinet of liberals headed by Judge Manuel Urrutia, and declared that his regime would be 'humanist', not capitalist or communist. Unlike Raúl and Che, he was no Communist; indeed Che wrote in 1957: 'I always thought of Fidel as an authentic leader of the leftist bourgeoisie.'[29] As late as May 1959, Castro could declare that 'capitalism can kill man with hunger, while Communism kills man by destroying his freedom'.[30] And the 26th July Movement's economic programme was not initially that radical.[31] It proposed a relatively moderate land reform and the development of domestic 'import substitution' industries to diversify away from sugar. Castro was clear that national capitalists – excluding the big landowners and foreign companies – were part of the revolution, and many capitalists saw great opportunities in the new regime's industrialization policies.

Nevertheless, Castro's 1959 revolution was far more radical than his 1953 coup had been. Che Guevara – radical by temperament and immersed in Marxism – was clearly an important influence, and many of his views were shared by Raúl. But the tough guerrilla life of Sierra Maestra, where Castro's *compañeros* ('comrades') lived in close proximity with poor peasants for the first time, also had an impact; it forged an egalitarian revolutionary culture.[32] It was in Sierra Maestra that the guerrillas adopted their trademark unkempt beards, a 'badge of identity' which became such an essential part of the revolutionary image in the 1960s and 1970s.[33]

In contrast to 1953, therefore, the rebels of 1959 were committed not just to nationalism and industrialization, but also to ruling in the interests of the 'popular classes' (*'clases populares'*) as opposed to the propertied *'clases económicas'*.[34] Unsurprisingly, the poor now harboured high hopes, and the guerrilla forms of mobilization that had emerged in the Sierra Maestra encouraged them. They therefore demanded more radical reforms, and Castro's Rebel Army, which had a great deal of power on the ground, was sympathetic to them.[35] There also seems to have been popular support for the summary trials and executions of Batista's supporters, presided over by Che Guevara himself. Some of Che's old Argentinian friends were dismayed by his transformation from curer of the sick into violent dispenser of revolutionary justice, but he was unapologetic; as he told one of them, 'Look, in this thing either you kill first, or else you get killed.'[36]

Inevitably this radicalism alienated many, including liberals, the propertied and the United States. Washington was naturally suspicious of Castro's revolution, fearing his Communist connections, but, initially reassured by his anti-Communist statements, it had recognized his regime. However Castro's emerging commitment to economic nationalism and land redistribution inevitably fuelled conflict with Cuban-based American-owned firms. The trials and executions of Batista supporters, and the cancellation of elections, also convinced Washington that Castro had been lost to Communism and could not be won back. Relations with the United States deteriorated, and by March 1960 Eisenhower had asked the CIA to plan a coup with the help of anti-Castro émigrés.[37] They were determined that Castro should suffer the fate of Arbenz five years before.

In 1959 the Cubans and the Soviets knew little of each other, but in March 1960 Castro, convinced that the Americans were about to invade, asked for a meeting with the now well-travelled and cosmopolitan Anastas Mikoian, who happened to be in the region. Mikoian arrived in Havana, and they hit it off: the Cubans saw the USSR as a source of economic and military aid, and Khrushchev's Politburo regarded the Cuban revolution as a chance to extend their influence, and to infuse some youthful spirit into the ageing body of Soviet Communism.[38] Mikoian excitedly described Castro as 'a genuine revolutionary, completely like us. I felt as though I had returned to my childhood.'[39] The Soviets agreed to send arms and oil in exchange for sugar, and despatched a group of Spanish Communist officers who had lived in exile in Moscow since the end of the Spanish Civil War to reorganize the Cuban army.[40]

Castro was right to fear American intentions. Eisenhower and Dulles were indeed planning to support a full-scale émigré military invasion with American air cover, but the Cubans had a piece of luck in the form of a change of regime in Washington. With the election of John F. Kennedy, American foreign policy was again more synchronized with that of the USSR. Kennedy came to power – much as Khrushchev had – promising a new way of pursuing the struggle with the rival super-power that would be both more idealistic and more intelligent. Shocked by the 'loss' of Cuba, the greatest defeat since the 'loss' of China a decade before, he was determined to jettison the crude military methods of the Eisenhower era and to distance himself from European imperialism and its epigones in apartheid South Africa. As he explained, America had to be 'on the side of the right of man to govern himself . . . because the final victory of nationalism is inevitable'.[41]

Under Kennedy, Washington began to acknowledge more fully that Communism could be the product of economic and political inequalities. Modernization theory, as developed by academics like the Kennedy adviser Walt Rostow, was the answer. Rostow and his followers maintained that all societies were on a similar 'modernizing' path to liberal democracy, but in the transitional stage, before they reached full maturity, they could catch the disease of Communism. The best solution was to accelerate the process of modernization, and the interests of the world were best served by trying to promote rapid development through financial assistance and the promotion of democracy.[42] In 1961 Kennedy even mobilized thousands of youths to spread American modernization throughout the world through the 'Peace Corps' and its 'community development' programmes. Hard power – the military option – remained, but it had to be conducted through intelligent counter-insurgency campaigns, tempered with appeals to hearts and minds, or soft power.

When it came to Cuba, Kennedy had real doubts about Eisenhower's planned invasion, and feared that if it went wrong it would damage America's reputation. Even so, he was as eager as his predecessor to eradicate Communist influence from the United States' backyard and decided to go ahead, though with a more covert, guerrilla-style operation and without air cover. The hope was that strategic landings by armed exiles would provoke spontaneous sympathetic uprisings amongst ordinary Cubans. The result, the 'Bay of Pigs' landing of April 1961, was a complete fiasco. The expected pro-exile uprisings failed to materialize, and Castro's civil defence forces proved highly effective. Most of the invaders were captured, and the image of the United States in the Third World further besmirched. The Bay of Pigs invasion was also counterproductive, and merely pushed Cuba even further into the Soviet sphere. Castro was convinced that another invasion was imminent (and indeed new plans were being drawn up in Washington). Meanwhile, the CIA embarked on a long series of outlandish attempts to assassinate Castro – from exploding cigars to fungus-infected diving suits – and even to damage the supposed source of his charisma, his beard; Castro has claimed that over the years 600 attempts have been made on his life by the CIA and Cuban émigrés.[43]

Greater reliance on the Soviet alliance was accompanied by a turn towards a more disciplined style of government at home, as the Cubans became convinced that the informal, participatory rule through the Rebel Army was not suited to national defence and state-building. Diverse revolutionary organizations were integrated into a single body, the Integrated Revolutionary Organization (ORI), and Castro increasingly relied on the well-organized old Cuban PSP Communists to provide an administrative infrastructure.

The culmination of the Soviet alliance was Khrushchev's offer to station nuclear weapons on Cuban soil. Castro seized the opportunity, believing that the Soviet nuclear umbrella would finally guarantee his revolution against an American attack. But the subsequent Soviet capitulation to American threats during the missile crisis of October 1962 (without consulting Cuba) was deeply disappointing for Castro; and whilst Kennedy gave a verbal assurance that invasion would not be attempted again, he did not trust the American. Meanwhile, ample proof had been provided that the USSR could not be relied upon. Castro proceeded to turn against the Soviets. Earlier that year, Castro had asserted his control by purging the PSP Communists and along with Che Guevara he had made it clear that the harsh, technocratic Marxism which underlay the Stalinist model was no longer welcome in Cuba. 'Humanist Marxism', as Che called it, would be the alternative. This was a version of Romantic Marxism, though one that was not afraid to use an explicit language of morality. Che defined his Marxism with explicit reference to the young Marx, in whose works he was steeped:

> Economic socialism without communist morality does not interest me. We are fighting against poverty, yes, but also against alienation. One of the fundamental aims of Marxism is to bring about the disappearance of material interest, the 'what's in it for me' factor, and profit from men's

psychological motivation ... If communism fails to pay attention to the facts of consciousness, it may be a method of distribution, but it is no longer a revolutionary morality.[44]

In practice, the Cuban regime sought to blend the struggle against poverty and state weakness with mass participation just as Radical Communists had in the past – through guerrilla Communism (in Cuba termed *guerrillerismo*). Citizens, or unselfish 'new men', were to be soldiers in an egalitarian, brotherly army of labour, giving their all so that Cuba might achieve extraordinary levels of development. This, then, was an ascetic Communism. Cubans were mobilized to work for their homeland for little individual reward. But collective reward was a different matter, and huge efforts were made to improve education and health for the whole population, and especially for the countryside, which was the main beneficiary of the new regime. The literacy campaign of 1961 became one of the iconic movements of the era. Some 250,000 school and university students were trained, mobilized in 'literacy brigades' and sent to the countryside for six months to live with peasants, where they would teach – and 'revolutionize' – the illiterate. As so often in Communist history, campaigns like these, appealing to youthful idealism, seem to have been enormously popular, whilst also transforming the lives of the illiterate.[45] One American visitor remembered the atmosphere of celebration when the students returned to Havana for a week of games, cultural activities and parades:

> Dressed in the remnants of their uniforms, often wearing peasant hats and beads, and carrying their knapsacks and lanterns, the *brigadistas* swarmed into the capital, singing and laughing and exchanging stories of their experiences. The similarities between the joyous return of the literacy army and the triumphal entry of the guerrilla troops only three years earlier was not lost on the population.[46]

Public expressions of joy, of course, were central to all Communist regimes, as Milan Kundera showed so well. But it is no surprise that Cuba was especially appealing to the global left at the time. Cuban Communism was as puritanical and militaristic as any other form of guerrilla Communism, and non-conformity and dissent were punished, most notoriously in labour camps established between 1965 and 1969. But in the early years the Cubans were more successful than many other

Communist regimes in emphasizing the enthusiasm and heroic spirit brought by militarism, at the expense of its more unpleasant features – violence and repression. This was partly a matter of leadership and the culture of the party: Che and Castro tried to present their Marxism as one that genuinely relied on persuasion and 'consciousness', and unlike Mao and the Chinese leaders, they had not been brought up within a Soviet-influenced party culture of institutionalized self-criticism and purges. But it was also the result of the relative ease with which the revolutionaries took power, owing to the weakness of internal opposition. The peasants of the southern region of Escambray did rebel during a six-year-long insurgency, which was put down by force. But many opponents simply left the island. After the revolution and between 1965 and 1971, many of the middle class migrated to the United States, with the agreement of both governments. The Cubans therefore avoided the systematic 'class struggle' or mass persecution of the bourgeoisie seen in so many other Communist regimes.[47] Meanwhile, the sense of being a David besieged by a bullying American Goliath inevitably bolstered the legitimacy of Castro in the eyes of those left behind, at least for a time.

Yet Cuban Communism was far from free of the other great disadvantage of Radical Marxism: the economic trauma and dislocation it tended to bring in its wake. The direction of economic policy became clear very early on, when Che emerged not only as the main strategist of agrarian reform, but also Minister for Industry and head of the Cuban Central Bank. Che relished the incongruity of this last appointment, and humorously claimed that he had got the job by accident: at the cabinet meeting to decide on the post, Castro had asked for a good '*economista*' to volunteer, and was surprised when Che put his hand up. 'But Che, I didn't know you were an economist!' he exclaimed, to which Che replied, 'Oh, I thought you needed a good *comunista*.'[48] Che actually went on a crash course in economics, but the Communist won over the economist. Like all voluntarists before them, Che and Castro insisted that harnessing popular willpower would permit Cuba to leap from agrarian poverty to Communist plenty, and the regime pursued a highly ambitious policy of rapid industrialization. Predictably it ran into a combination of chaotic central planning, American sanctions and the loss of middle-class expertise to exile. Che himself later admitted that 'We dealt with nature in a subjective manner, as if by talking to it we could persuade it.'[49]

The result, by 1963, was economic crisis, and Che found himself fighting a losing battle against Soviet-supported technocrats who favoured a less ambitious, more Modernist approach. Che, wholly unsuited to the practicalities of economic management, became disillusioned – according to one of his friends his spirit was 'smothered under the mountains of statistics and production methods'.[50] It was during these debates over the direction of the economy that he began a fundamental reconsideration of the Soviet Union. Che recalled to another friend how he had been converted to Marxism in Guatemala and Mexico by reading Stalin's works: they had convinced him that 'in the Soviet Union lay the solution to life, believing that what had been applied there was what he had read about'. But when he actually worked with the Soviets 'he realized they had been tricking him'; the result was a 'violent reaction' against Stalinism in 1963–4.[51]

Castro, however, took a more pragmatic view, and had more sympathy with the Soviets. From 1964 he realized that Che's recipes were too ambitious: labour enthusiasm alone could not make tiny Cuba into a self-sufficient, industrial power; Soviet-style material incentives and the Soviet market for Cuban sugar would be needed for some time. Che, defeated, gave up on his efforts to apply guerrilla Communism to the economy, and decided to employ it in a more appropriate area: spreading the Cuban model of revolution to the rest of Latin America and Africa. He resigned all of his offices, even renouncing his Cuban citizenship, and spent the rest of his short life as a revolutionary nomad. But the reconciliation between Cuba and the USSR was to be short-lived. Following the Sino-Soviet split and the fall of Khrushchev in 1964, the USSR seemed to be an increasingly unreliable protector, and from 1965 Castro yet again began to pursue a radical politics of mass mobilization to develop the Cuban economy. After zigzagging between Radical and Modernist Marxism, the Cubans were to retain their guerrilla model of economic development until the end of the decade, but they were now to do so under the auspices of a disciplined, vanguard party: the Cuban Communist Party, founded in 1965. The early experiments in participatory democracy of 1959–60 were finally at an end. Even so, the Cubans avoided following the more technocratic Soviet model for some time. They believed their revolution was uniquely democratic and suited to the developing world, and were committed to exporting it.

IV

Shortly after the revolutionaries had taken power, Che Guevara dictated his thoughts on his experiences, and they were published in May 1960 under the title *Guerrilla Warfare*. This was partly a 'how-to' manual. Guerrillas were instructed in the use of Molotov cocktails, as well as the best ways of bringing social reform to their peasant hosts. Advice was also given on what to wear and carry – a hammock, a piece of soap and notebook and pencil (for writing messages for fellow guerrillas) were all recommended. But Che was also defending a rural guerrilla strategy as an exemplar for all Southern revolutionaries, regardless of the peculiarities of the Cuban revolution, and carefully ignoring the importance of the Cuban urban insurgency. Placing himself in the guerrilla Communist tradition, from Mao's Yan'an to Ho Chi Minh's struggle against the French and the Americans, and explicitly distancing himself from the Soviet tradition (and even from the anti-German partisans of World War II), Che was arguing that the *foco* – the small, vanguard guerrilla band – could ignite revolutionary fires throughout the Third World.[52]

The book was primarily written for revolutionaries in Latin America. In part, Castro and Che regarded it as their duty to help the oppressed throughout the continent. But there were also strong practical reasons to foment revolution abroad. As Castro explained, the United States 'will not be able to hurt us if all of Latin America is in flames'.[53] Castro did signal that he would abandon his support for foreign revolution in return for peaceful coexistence with the United States, though it is unclear whether he would have kept to this promise. But whether seriously meant or not, his overtures came to nothing. Kennedy continued to support anti-Castro forces, and his successor from 1963, Lyndon Johnson, was even more unwilling to compromise.

Efforts to spread the revolution were directed by 'Comandante' ('Commander') Che Guevara. The Cubans trained more than 1,500 revolutionaries from the continent, but more important than practical help was the galvanizing example of Cuba itself. As a leader of the Venezuelan Communist Party remembered, the Cuban revolution was like a 'detonator'.[54] The ease with which the Cubans had taken power gave rise to extraordinary optimism. It seemed that the *foco* could swiftly seize power everywhere. One Venezuelan guerrilla recalled that he took to the mountains believing 'our war was going to be a Cuban-style war'; 'We thought that the solution to our problems was no more than two or three years away.'[55]

The Cuban example inspired numerous Communist guerrilla movements to take up arms across the continent, whether Castroist, Maoist, pro-Soviet Communist or Trotskyist. However, most were small and lacked popular support. They only had any real impact in Venezuela, Guatemala and Colombia, where brief periods of left-wing success had been followed by the victory of the right.[56] In Guatemala, a series of dictatorships had followed Jacobo Arbenz's rule, and following the suppression of a left-wing military revolt in 1960, two officers set up a guerrilla group in alliance with pro-Soviet Communists and then Trotskyists. In Colombia, the Communist party had controlled peasant enclaves for some years, and when the military succeeded in putting them down in 1964–5, the Communist Revolutionary Armed Forces of Colombia (*Fuerzas Armadas Revolucionarias Colombianas*, or FARC) emerged to fight back. Meanwhile, the Venezuelan guerrillas, supported by the Communist party despite Moscow's displeasure, benefited from their participation in ousting the Pérez Jiménez dictatorship in 1958, and then from some popular resentment at the economic austerity imposed by the democratically elected centre-right.

Nowhere, however, did the guerrillas pose a serious threat to the regimes. In Venezuela, a mixture of liberal democracy and repression damaged them. Elsewhere, guerrilla forces were no match for governments' military forces. Kennedy and his successors were determined to thwart Cuban plans for revolution and poured money into local militaries, even if that meant setting aside his more ambitious plans for modernization and democracy. Between 1962 and 1966, nine military coups took place in Latin America, and in at least eight they were designed to replace governments that were felt to be too left-wing or soft on Communism.[57]

Divisions within the Communist world also played a part in the failure of the *foco*. At first, the Soviets tolerated the Cubans in Latin America, but they soon decided that they were becoming too expensive, their plans were unrealistic, and they were spoiling relations with the United States at a time when Moscow sought détente. Local Communist parties in other Latin American countries also resented what they saw as

Havana's unrealistic ambitions. Most followed Moscow's gradualist line: Communists and workers had to unite with peasants and the bourgeoisie, rejecting a sudden Cuban-style leap from 'feudalism' to 'socialism'. Nor did the Chinese help the insurgencies, despite their guerrilla origins. Their relations with Cuba were poor, and whilst Maoist groups did spring up – usually made up of extreme hard-liners – they secured little practical support from Beijing.[58]

By the mid-1960s, it was clear that rural guerrilla revolution on the continent was failing, and the Cubans realized they had to retreat. They had, however, already found another outlet for their revolutionary energies – Africa. The Cubans felt a strong link with Africa: about a third of its own population could trace connections through ancestors brought to the island as slaves. The revolutionaries had formally abolished all racial discrimination in Cuba, and believed they had a mission to do the same abroad. But to the Cubans, Africa was also a continent where the United States seemed vulnerable, a power on the wrong side of history as the continent threw off European imperialism.

V

In December 1964, Che Guevara embarked on a three-month tour of the radical nationalist states of Africa, and in January 1965 he reached Brazzaville, the capital of the formerly French Congo. In 1963 the first self-proclaimed Marxist regime in Africa had taken power in an insurrection there, and the new government of Alphonse Massemba-Debat was happy to host the Popular Movement for the Liberation of Angola (*Movimento Popular de Libertação de Angola*, known as the MPLA), which was struggling against Portuguese rule in its south-west African colony. The meeting was a tense one. The MPLA wanted Cuban help, but Che was determined to pour all of his resources into the war in the neighbouring Congo-Léopoldville, where the Simbas ('Lions') – leftist followers of the assassinated Patrice Lumumba – were staging a remarkably successful rebellion against the American- and Belgian-backed regime. Che proposed that the MPLA send their fighters to Congo-Léopoldville and learn from Cuban trainers on the ground, in the course of the fighting. Naturally the MPLA, and its leader, the doctor and poet Agostinho Neto, were unenthusiastic about fighting somebody else's war, but despite their differences, the prevailing atmosphere was a good one as the MPLA were a Marxist group, and they had much in common with Che.[59] As one of the MPLA leaders at the meeting remembered:

> We wanted Cuban instructors because of the prestige of the Cuban revolution and because their theory of guerrilla warfare was very close to our own. We were also impressed with the guerrilla tactics of the Chinese, but Beijing was too far away, and we wanted instructors who could adapt to our way of living.[60]

Che was not only impressed by the Angolans' Marxism, but also by their apparent strength. He sent one of his associates to their training camp, where he saw an impressive guerrilla force, little realizing that what was being paraded before him was a continuous loop of the same men. He should have spotted the ruse, for the Cubans had done exactly the same thing when parading before journalists from the *New York Times* in the Sierra Maestra.[61] But the Cubans were fooled, and Che relented, agreeing to send instructors to the MPLA in Congo-Brazzaville.

The following month, Che had a much less successful encounter with African guerrilla fighters in Dar-es-Salaam, the capital of Tanzania, which under the African socialist Julius Nyerere had become the main centre for exiled fighters in the anti-imperialist struggle. The Cuban embassy gathered a meeting of about fifty people from a number of liberation movements, all seeking Che's support. Che's proposal that they all send their guerrillas to Congo-Léopoldville was received in an atmosphere that was 'worse than cool', as he remembered. His audience objected that their duty was to defend their own people, not help other liberation movements. But although Che insisted that they had a common enemy – imperialism – and a blow against it in Congo-Léopoldville would help everybody, he was forced to concede that 'no one saw it like that'. Eduardo Mondlane, former United Nations diplomat and leader of FRELIMO (*Frente de Libertação de Moçambique*) – the guerrilla movement fighting the Portuguese in Mozambique – was especially angry. At the end of the meeting, 'the farewells were cool and polite', and Che concluded: 'we were left with the clear sense that Africa has a long way to go before it reaches real revolutionary maturity. But we also had the joy of meeting people prepared to carry the struggle through to the end.'[62]

Che's efforts to persuade his audience to contribute to the Congo-Léopoldville war were a failure, as was the expedition of black Cubans he led to help the Simbas. The insurgency was defeated in 1965, and the Cubans were driven out. But his encounters in Brazzaville and Dar-es-Salaam had given him a good idea of the state of the left in Africa, from the 'Marxist' government of Brazzaville to the African socialist state of Tanzania, from the Marxist insurgents in Angola to the non-Marxist guerrillas of Mozambique. His judgement – that nationalism in Africa was radically anti-imperialist but not 'mature' (by which he meant fully 'Marxist') – was broadly accurate.

Nyerere was the most common type of nationalist leader in the independent parts of Africa of the early 1960s: a non-Marxist, indigenous socialist of the Bandung generation. African socialists had much in common with the Russian agrarian socialists of the nineteenth century. Just as the latter had seen Russian peasant society as a communitarian idyll, so Nyerere and his fellow socialists believed that African society was naturally collectivist. Nyerere claimed that 'the idea of "class" and "caste" was non-existent in African society', and Africa's unique concept of 'familyhood' (*ujamaa*) would help the continent develop a special form of socialism.[63] Such philosophies were inevitably attractive to leaders who had inherited states riven by ethnic divisions from the European empires. For them, Marxism, with its love of class struggle, was much too aggressive a creed for their fragile new states, whilst the small vanguard party seemed to be unsuited to countries that were so divided along ethnic lines. The all-inclusive 'mass party' was, for a time, much more attractive.

Some African leaders did move towards a more Marxist politics, believing that only a more ambitious state would promote economic development and prevent continuing neo-colonial subjection. European and American interventions also pushed African socialists to the left, and the Lumumba assassination played an equivalent role in Africa to the toppling of Arbenz in Latin America. Guinea's Sékou Touré, Ghana's Kwame Nkrumah, Algeria's Ahmed Ben Bella, and Mali's Modibo Kéïta all, therefore, moved towards a more radical, quasi-Marxist politics. Africa's weaknesses, they were convinced, would have to be resolved by a more determined, centralized state. As Nkrumah explained, 'socialism is not spontaneous. It does not arise by itself.'[64] By 1961, he had established an 'ideological institute' to indoctrinate ruling party officials, and in 1964 he had launched a Seven-Year Plan for industrialization.

However, Ghana retained a mixed economy and foreign capital was welcomed. And whilst questioning their old optimistic African socialism, and welcoming Soviet, Chinese and Cuban aid, these leaders were not ready to embrace a full-blown internationalist Marxism. Marxist influence was still weak in Africa, and it flourished only in particular conditions. The Marxist Congo-Brazzaville had an unusually large urban and literate population of civil servants and students, and they were receptive to Western ideas and responsive to the highly charged events in neighbouring Congo-Léopoldville. Political forces also reflected a French prototype, and as in France the Communists had a great deal of power over the trade unions. To these urban dwellers, a French-style Marxism promised modernity and independence. President Massemba-Debat was relatively moderate, but more radical Marxists, connected with the party's youth group, soon became influential as the regime tried to consolidate its power. By the middle of 1964 Congo had a single Marxist-Leninist-style party and an ideologically trained 'Popular Army'. Moreover, on the failure of Che's mission to Congo-Léopoldville in 1965, some of the Cubans crossed the border to Congo-Brazzaville, and had a further radicalizing effect on the regime.[65]

The influence of Marxism is perhaps least surprising in the guerrilla groups that confronted the Portuguese empire in Angola, Mozambique and Portuguese Guinea (renamed Guinea-Bissau on independence). The Portuguese, under the authoritarian dictator António de Oliveira Salazar, were determined to hold on to their empire and the long struggle inevitably radicalized politics. But there were other reasons why Marxism should have appealed in the specific conditions of Portuguese Africa.

VI

To the guerrillas of Mayombe.
  who dared challenge the gods
  by opening a path through the dark forest,
  I am going to relate the tale of Ogun,
  the African Prometheus.[66]

Thus began the novel *Mayombe*, written in the early 1970s by a white Angolan fighter in the Marxist MPLA forces, Artur Carlos Maurício Pestana dos Santos, better known by his *nom de guerres,* 'Pepetela'. As the dedication makes clear, the novel is about Promethean modernity and war, for Ogun is an African warrior god. It is the story of a group of guerrillas fighting the Portuguese in the dense forest of Mayombe, and much of it is taken up with everyday life. But it also includes interior monologues by the characters that reveal the continuing tensions within the guerrilla band. One of the novel's main themes is the effort to forge a modern Angolan people and end the divisions of tribe and the racist colonial past. The novel shows how, eventually, the guerrillas succeed in overcoming these differences, but the continuing tribalism and racial prejudice of the fighters are made very clear to the reader. As Theory – the half-Portuguese, half-African former teacher with a highly ideological *nom de guerre* – explains at the beginning of the novel:

> In a universe of yes or no, white or black, I represent the maybe . . . Is it my fault if men insist on purity and reject compounds? . . . In the face of this essential problem, people are divided in my view into two categories: Manichaeans and the rest. It is worth explaining that the rest are rare; the world generally is Manichaean.[67]

But despite Theory's complaints about Marxism as practised by MPLA guerrillas, Marxism in theory became enormously attractive to the *mestiços* (mixed race) and *assimilados* – the small group of Africans and Indians educated in Portugal to help administer the colonial state – because it gave class pre-eminence over race.[68] For people who had been placed in a rigid racial hierarchy between Portuguese *civilizados* and African *indígenas*, Marxism provided an opportunity to forge bonds with black African workers and peasants. It also promised to create a modern integrated state, capable of standing tall in the world. Moreover, after the war the *mestiços* and *assimilados* had particular reason to be angry, for they faced competition for jobs from new immigrants from Portugal.

At first, these nationalists' main interests were largely cultural: 'de-Portugalizing' and 're-Africanizing' Angolan culture. But they were always self-conscious modernizers, seeking to create large, European-style states out of numerous tribal groups. It is therefore no surprise that they moved towards Modernist, Soviet-influenced Marxism, especially as one of the few forces to oppose the Salazar regime was the underground Portuguese Communist Party, which established an Angolan party in 1954. And even though – like the French Communists – the party did not wholly condemn the empire or defend national liberation until 1960, many modernizing nationalists came into its orbit.[69]

Marxism had a particular influence on the Portuguese Africans who studied in Lisbon, and especially on a group of friends who met regularly to discuss African affairs and included Agostinho Neto, the future leader of the MPLA, and the Cape Verdean agronomy student Amílcar Cabral, the future leader of the African Party for the Independence of Guinea and Cape Verde (*Partido Africano para a Independência da Guiné e Cabo Verde* – PAIGC). However, their commitments to Marxism varied. Neto became a member of the Portuguese Communist Party and remained an orthodox, pro-Soviet Marxist throughout his life, whilst Cabral's Marxism was much more flexible.[70]

On their return to Africa, it became increasingly clear that the Portuguese were not going to give up their colonies without a fight. In 1961 political activists and local youths in Angola's capital tried to release political prisoners from Luanda's Bastille – the São Paolo gaol; they failed and the police stood by whilst the Portuguese settlers exacted an extremely bloody revenge. Nationalists now became convinced that they had little choice but to retreat to the countryside and resort to the gun.

Apart from modernizing socialists, a host of other nationalist movements emerged, some seeking to create a supposedly 'traditional' Africa of chiefs and 'tribes', and others promoting a particular ethnic group. In Guinea-Bissau, the pragmatic Cabral succeeded in absorbing all of these resistance fighters into his inclusive and highly successful PAIGC. Similarly, in Mozambique, the modernizing nationalist Eduardo Mondlane created a broad coalition in FRELIMO. A former United Nations diplomat, Mondlane was much less influenced by Marxism and was closest to Nyerere's socialism. FRELIMO was a coalition of three nationalist organizations, whilst Mondlane used his considerable diplomatic skills to smooth over ideological and ethnic conflicts. The MPLA, the most Marxist and pro-Soviet of all, was least successful in establishing itself as the single Angolan nationalist party, and it faced serious anti-Communist rivals: the ethnic nationalist FNLA (*Frente Nacional de Libertação de Angola* – representing mainly the Bakongo ethnicity) and then Jonas Savimbi's breakaway UNITA (*União Nacional para a Independência Total de Angola*).[71]

In the course of the 1960s, all three modernizing parties – the Angolan MPLA, the Guinean PAIGC and the Mozambican FRELIMO – became more radical, marginalizing the traditionalist groups, whilst launching their own versions of Maoist guerrilla war. The MPLA moved to the left in 1963, and in 1964 Cabral defeated the traditionalists in the PAIGC. Even so, Cabral's Marxism was still relatively undogmatic, whilst FRELIMO did not fully move into the Marxist camp until the early 1970s.

In South Africa, too, Communists developed a flexible Marxism so they could collaborate with African nationalists in the struggle against apartheid. The Communist Party of South Africa (CPSA) was a long-established one, and in the 1920s it had considerable success in attracting black African members.[72] However, by the 1940s it found its revolutionary proletarian ideology had little resonance amongst African workers, many of whom were rural migrants.[73] The increasing militancy of the African National Congress (ANC), and the apartheid government's banning of the Communist party in 1950, led them to rethink their doctrine. The new, underground party, the South African Communist Party (SACP), formed in 1953, declared that South Africa suffered from a 'colonialism of a special type': because there was no black bourgeoisie, it was possible for a 'proletarian' Communist party to ally itself with non-Communist nationalists.[74] The SACP had given itself theoretical cover to enable it to forge an alliance with the ANC, and both parties had overlapping memberships. The SACP had considerable influence on the struggle against apartheid, despite its small numbers, and members of both parties – including the ANC's Nelson Mandela – formed the guerrilla organization *Umkhonto we Sizwe* ('Spear of the Nation'), which began its campaign of political violence in 1961.

VII

By the mid-1960s the guerrilla Communism promoted by Mao, Ho Chi Minh and Che had therefore acquired a foothold in Africa – mainly in the Portuguese-controlled South – but elsewhere it struggled to survive, and it no longer seemed like the force of the future as it had in the late

1950s. Much stronger in this era were the non-revolutionary, 'united front' parties, which were prepared to collaborate with left nationalists. Such parties boasted the largest memberships in the non-Communist Third World in the early 1960s: the Sudanese party was the second largest, benefiting from its good record in the struggle for independence and commanding support amongst students, some peasants, and workers (especially on the railways).[75] The Iraqis came third. But largest of all was Dipa Aidit's Indonesian Communist Party, which had recovered after the 1948 Javanese debacle by adopting a more moderate, inclusive set of policies. It forged an alliance with Sukarno, and by 1965 it had an extraordinary 3.5 million members, whilst another 17 million or so joined its trade unions and other mass organizations (out of a population of 110 million).[76]

On the face of it, therefore, it seemed that the great powers could be satisfied: the Soviet 'national democratic state' and Chinese 'new democracy' were paying dividends in delivering mass Communist support, whilst the United States did not have to worry about a powerful revolutionary strain of Communism. In reality, though, all three powers were deeply dissatisfied with the Third World 'united fronts', because their global influence was largely dependent on nationalist leaders over whom they had no direct control, and who could defect to the other side at any moment.

The United States was the most discontented – understandably given many Third World nationalist leaders' overt sympathy for the Communist bloc. And Washington became particularly determined to change the status quo from late 1963, under Lyndon Johnson. Several in the administration had concluded that Kennedy's encouragement of 'modernization' and liberal democracy had been counterproductive and had only helped the left, especially in Latin America.[77] It seemed as if Communism was advancing in the Third World, and Washington could not risk a liberal policy. But Johnson's personality probably led him to favour military solutions even more than Kennedy. Though undoubtedly committed to improving relations with the Soviets, he suffered deep anxiety about the humiliation of the United States, and his own personal humiliation. One of his greatest fears was that he would lose face after the 'loss' of another China or Cuba to Communism,[78] and so he responded very harshly to any sign of left-wing nationalist advance.

Whatever the reasons for the change in policy, Johnson presided over a sustained American offensive against radical nationalist governments throughout the global South. The United States encouraged coups in Brazil (1964) and Ghana (1966), and in 1965 invaded the Dominican Republic, helped its client Mobutu Sese Seko to defeat the Lumumbist insurgency in Congo-Léopoldville, and welcomed the toppling of Algeria's Ben Bella. In the same year, most fatefully, Johnson responded to Ngo Dinh Diem's deteriorating position in South Vietnam by sending in ground forces and escalating the bombing campaign.

The clearest – and most violent – attack on the Communist 'united fronts', however, occurred in Indonesia. In 1963 Sukarno moved sharply to the left in response to popular unrest at famine and economic collapse, and angered that the Americans had accepted the foundation of Malaysia as an independent state. He strengthened his alliance with the Chinese without, and Dipa Aidit's pro-Beijing Communists within. The Communists took advantage of their new power by launching a campaign of rent reduction for peasants, which in turn sparked off a violent reaction by landlords and anti-Communist Muslim organizations.[79] The Communists, who had no military force of their own, were forced to moderate the campaign, and they became increasingly anxious about the possibility of a military coup against Sukarno. Therefore, when a group of junior army officers mounted their own coup against the generals, the Communists probably supported them, though the facts are unclear.[80] The rebel officers failed; the commander of the army's strategic reserve, General Suharto, took control, and proceeded to launch a violent campaign against the Communists. Commandos were sent to kill suspected party members and sympathizers, and Suharto also exploited social tensions generated by the Communists' rent reduction campaign. Whole villages were destroyed in the resulting massacres, and scholarly estimates of the numbers killed range from 200,000 to 1 million.[81]

The United States was pleased to see the end of Sukarno, and it supported General Suharto in his violent campaigns against the Communists. Meanwhile for the Communist bloc – and especially the Chinese – the destruction of the powerful Indonesian party was a disaster. The events had distinct echoes of the Guomindang's massacre of the Chinese Communists in Shanghai in 1927. And just as that catastrophe had led Stalin to reconsider the 'united front' strategy of forging alliances with 'bourgeois' nationalists, so the Indonesian events cast doubt on the collaborations which Zhou Enlai and Khrushchev had championed from the mid-1950s. The Soviets had been disappointed with the strategy for some time. Khrushchev's optimistic view that support for left-wing nationalist leaders would help the transition to Soviet-style socialism was clearly false; the Soviets had spent time and precious resources nursing leaders like Nasser, only for them to turn against their benefactors. Even the relationship with Castro had turned sour, and the series of defeats in Indonesia, Ghana and Algeria only reinforced the conviction that the Soviet approach had to change. The Chinese, who had particularly close relations with the Algerians and Indonesian Communists, were similarly dismayed.

The response of the two Communist powers was to withdraw from the Third World – for a while – but for rather different reasons. The Chinese became increasingly absorbed in the domestic politics of their own Cultural Revolution, and as a result of that upheaval their foreign policy became strident, uncompromising and ineffective. In the USSR, meanwhile, the fall of Khrushchev had discredited Third World adventures, and Leonid Brezhnev had little interest in them. And when, in the late 1960s, the Soviets renewed their assault on the global 'bourgeoisie', they were to abandon Khrushchev's faith in united front-style alliances in favour of orthodox Marxist-Leninists.

VIII

After his failure in Congo, Che Guevara abandoned Africa, seeking new revolutionary opportunities in Latin America. He returned to Bolivia, where he had travelled as a youth, and tried to apply his *foco* theory of guerrilla warfare there. It was, predictably, a failure, and in October 1967 he was tracked down, caught and executed by the Bolivian army with the help of the CIA. His emaciated corpse was preserved and displayed to journalists in an ultimately misguided PR exercise to prove that he, and the guerrilla Communism the Americans so feared, was truly dead. Walt Rostow wrote a triumphant letter to Johnson, asserting that the death of Che 'marks the passing of another of the aggressive, romantic revolutionaries like Sukarno, Nkrumah, Ben Bella . . . It shows the soundness of our "preventive medicine" assistance to countries facing incipient insurgency.'[82]

But the dead Che proved to be just as, if not more, potent than the live one. With his matted hair and beard, wan features and drawn face, many pointed to the resemblance between Freddy Alborta's photograph and Mantegna's *Lamentation over the Dead Christ*. And in a strange reprise of his youthful trade in Catholic trinkets, he too became a source of relics, as local women cut off locks of his hair and kept them as charms. The Cuban regime exploited the cult of the new revolutionary martyr, and Che's image – especially Alberto Korda's famous 1960 photograph of a determined Che looking into the distance – became a powerful symbol during the student revolts of the late 1960s and 1970s. The 1965 song to mark Che's departure from Cuba, '*Hasta siempre, Comandante*' ('Farewell, Comandante'), also became a popular anthem on the radical left, sung by, amongst others, the American folk-singer Joan Baez.

The idealism of the late 1950s and early 1960s, represented by Che, was therefore to remain a powerful force during the rebellions of the late 1960s, as will be seen in Chapter Eleven. But in some ways Rostow was right: the death of Che was a sign that the romantic era was coming to an end, at least in the capitals of the superpowers. Different as their politics were, Khrushchev, Mao, Tito, Che and even Kennedy believed that they were fighting an ideological struggle for hearts and minds. From the mid-1960s, however, statesmen in Moscow and Washington were concluding that the times were much more dangerous; the new era demanded not a Peace Corps or guerrilla bands, but traditional armies and vanguard parties. And in Moscow, this conservative thinking was only reinforced by a revolutionary challenge within the Communist bloc itself – the 'Prague Spring' of 1968.

10

Stasis

I

On 21 August 1968, as Soviet and other Warsaw Pact tanks rolled into Czechoslovakia, the Romanian leader Nicolae Ceauşescu addressed a crowd of 100,000 from the balcony of the Central Committee building in Bucharest. The USSR, he declared, was guilty of aggression and Romania would not be sending troops to join her Communist allies, even though she was a member of the Warsaw Pact. His announcement was met with roars of approval, and his stand seemed like a truly courageous one, for Romania might have been at risk from a Soviet invasion. Ceauşescu, together with Alexander Dubček, now led the most popular Communist regimes in Eastern Europe. Nevertheless, his alliance with the Czechoslovak reformers was a strange one in ideological terms. Whilst the Communists of the 'Prague Spring' were moving towards a more liberal form of Communism, only one year earlier Ceauşescu had abandoned a much less liberal reform package, and within a few years would preside over one of the most authoritarian of Eastern Europe's regimes. The plaudits and praise he enjoyed were not rewards for any great liberalization but were bestowed in recognition of his patriotic valour in standing up for little Romania against an overbearing Soviet neighbour.

The drama of August 1968 revealed the crisis the Communist bloc found itself in following the failures of Tito, Khrushchev and Mao to revive Communism by looking to various Marxist forms of 'democracy', with doses of militant radicalism and party-led mobilization. What was the way forward? The bloc fragmented. One group, including Romania, clung to a version of High Stalinism, complete with mobilization and harsh austerity, though they draped it in their own national colours. At the other extreme, Communists like Dubček looked to a more pragmatic, even liberal Marxism which even allowed markets and pluralism. In the mid-1960s Moscow also tried to liberalize its economy to a limited degree. But the experiment was short-lived, and the Prague Spring discredited such experiments. By the end of the 1960s the nature of the Soviet bloc was best seen in the image of the tanks rumbling into Prague. It had lost any dynamism the system once had, and now devoted its energies to stability at any cost.

II

In 1974 Edgar Papu, a Romanian literary critic, wrote an article in the Bucharest journal *Twentieth Century* that elaborated a rather far-fetched theory. He called his idea 'Romanian Protochronism'. Papu argued that, throughout history, literary movements and styles commonly believed to be West European in origin – the baroque, Romanticism, the ideas and styles of Flaubert and Ibsen – could actually be found in Romanian literature first. Protochronism became an enormously popular idea in Romanian culture in the 1970s and 1980s, and was endorsed by Ceauşescu himself.[1]

Protochronism, of course, had been seen before, in the Soviet claims of the late 1940s that Russians had invented the telephone and the lightbulb. This was no accident. Romania was essentially importing a version of High Stalinism: a politics of hierarchy and discipline was wedded to an economics of industrialization and an ideology of nationalism. It was joined in this strategy by Albania, on the other side of the Balkans. Both Romania and Albania were non-Slavic agrarian societies; both were far away from the flashpoints of Central Europe and the impracticality of Soviet invasion gave them room for manoeuvre; and both parties saw Khrushchev's Soviet Union as the new imperialist power – a threat to their national autonomy.

Why did they have such a strange, counter-intuitive view? Surely Stalin, not Khrushchev, was the imperialist? Khrushchev had indeed made real efforts to extend a new spirit of fraternity to Stalin's empire. The old diktats gave way to greater freedom for local Communists. Stalin had treated East European party bosses as if they were vassals in a patrimonial court, and their visits to Moscow were almost private affairs, rarely publicized. Now the relationship was much more equal. Visiting party leaders were treated as heads of state on official visits, and were spared the humiliations and post-prandial dancing sessions of the late-Stalinist court. Khrushchev also abolished Stalin's old nocturnal timetable. Certainly, the Soviets continued to exert direct influence in their satellites' security services and military, and they made it clear that there were boundaries to the freedom: capitalism and a multi-party system were out of the question. But Khrushchev's reconciliation with Tito in 1956 marked a major change. The Soviets now accepted that Stalinist ambitions for a monolithic bloc were over; as they now declared, the 'paths of socialist development vary according to the country and the conditions that prevail there'.[2]

The economic logic of the bloc had also altered under Khrushchev to a less imperialistic direction. The old exploitation gave way to subsidies.[3] By the late 1950s it was the USSR that was transferring wealth to its satellites, not vice versa – most notably when Khrushchev gave János Kádár 860 million roubles' worth of aid to prevent the Hungarian regime from collapsing during the anti-Communist strike wave of 1956–7. The subsidies increased with time and by the 1970s and 1980s had become a serious drain on the Soviet economy.

At the same time, however, Khrushchev began to take the economics of the Soviet bloc more seriously. He was not satisfied with Stalin's loosely articulated congeries of militarized buffer states. Inspired by the example of the European Economic Community founded by the Treaty of Rome in 1957, Khrushchev sought to create something more ambitious. In the early 1960s he tried to introduce a 'socialist division of labour' into Comecon – encouraging the national economies to concentrate on areas where they enjoyed a comparative advantage. But to the poorer nations this policy really did look like imperialism. Stalin may have seemed like a pillaging imperialist to the developed states of north-eastern and central Europe. But to the agrarian states of south-eastern Europe, he had offered a route to wealth and independence: the command economy. Khrushchev, in contrast, threatened to condemn them for ever to impoverished agrarian dependence, supplying food to the richer North. From the perspective of non-industrialized countries, Khrushchev's demand that they confine themselves to producing food and primary products for the needs of the Soviet economy would imprison them in permanent inferiority.

The Romanian Communists were always likely to find nationalism alluring because they had unusually shallow political roots.[4] Most Communist leaders in the inter-war period were from Romania's ethnic minorities (many were Jews) and when they came to power they were under intense pressure to establish some appeal to the majority population. The ethnic Romanian 'local' Communist Georghiu-Dej – a former railwayman (and accomplished Machiavellian) – eventually seized the leadership, successfully outmanoeuvring the Jewish 'Moscow' Communist Ana Pauker. While Stalin lived Georghiu-Dej followed a slavishly pro-Soviet line. But weakened by the denunciation of Stalin in 1956, he increasingly looked to nationalism to bolster his regime. Lacking a committed group of Communists in its middle ranks, the Romanian party found itself increasingly reliant on officials with strongly nationalistic views. This was a nation with a traumatic recent history: it had been heavily bombed, many of its Jewish citizens had been massacred, it had lost hundreds of thousands of men fighting alongside the Germans, and it had permanently lost substantial territories – including Bessarabia to the USSR – resulting in substantial population transfers. It is no surprise that questions of national integrity and status should have been central, even to Communist politics.

Georghiu-Dej gradually began to distance Romania from the Soviet Union, negotiating the withdrawal of Red Army troops in 1958 and refusing to take sides on the Sino-Soviet split. The final break came in 1962 when Khrushchev tried to launch his new division of labour within Comecon. The Romanians responded by issuing a 'declaration of autonomy' in 1964 and began to pursue an independent foreign policy (though within the Warsaw Pact), forging links with Yugoslavia, France and even the United States. On the death of Gheorghiu-Dej the following year, his successor Ceauşescu continued the new nationalist line, which he justified with an intensely chauvinistic ideology.

Ceauşescu, born in 1918, the son of poor, ethnically Romanian peasants and apprenticed to a cobbler at the age of eleven, had little education. By the age of fifteen, however, he had been elected to the Communist-led Anti-Fascist Committee. From then on he was in and out of prison, where he received an education in Marxism and became part of the Dej faction. On becoming premier in 1965 it seemed that Ceauşescu would probably combine a new nationalist ethos with some form of cultural and economic liberalization, and he tried to gain the support of intellectuals through a limited cultural relaxation. But this was always likely to be temporary. Ceauşescu had been committed to heavy industrial development, quoting the nineteenth-century historian A. D. Xenopol – 'to remain only agricultural is . . . to make ourselves for all time the slaves of foreigners' – and many agreed with him.[5] Meanwhile, the Prague Spring convinced Ceauşescu of the dangers of liberal political reforms, and the popularity of his opposition to the Soviet invasion demonstrated the power of Romanian nationalism.

The tenth party congress of 1969, at which Ceauşescu delivered a marathon speech lasting five and a half hours (punctuated every half an hour by a waiter in a white jacket bringing a glass of water), marked the beginning of his complete control of the party, and the launch of an exceptionally extravagant leadership cult.[6] By 1974 he was being compared to Julius Caesar, Alexander the Great, Pericles, Cromwell, Peter the Great and Napoleon.[7] In many ways this was just a more extreme version of Tito's multifaceted cult, in which the leader posed both as ascetic revolutionary for the party members, and as new king for the peasantry. The principal difference was the elevation of various relatives to high positions, and of his wife, Elena, to cultic status. This was, of course, typically monarchical; as the joke went, if Stalin had created Socialism in One Country, Ceauşescu had established Socialism in One Family. Yet Elena's virtues were not merely uxorious, but, importantly, scientific. She pursued a career as a research chemist, and from the 1970s was described as 'eminent personage of Romanian and international science', 'Academician Doctor Engineer [*Ingener*] Elena Ceauşescu' (hence commonly called 'Adie' by the impertinent).[8] She was also credited with the invention of a major new polymer, though when asked to discuss her researches in public she became mysteriously tongue-tied.

Like other Communist leaders in Balkan societies, then, Ceauşescu projected an eclectic mixture of political messages: monarchical, scientific and Communist. He even briefly flirted with Maoism, visiting China in 1971, though he did this largely to establish his independence from Moscow. But trumping all these conflicting attributes of Romanian Communist ideology was ethnic nationalism. In the 1970s, Ceauşescu set about creating an ethnically homogeneous state. Jews were allowed to emigrate, as were Germans (for a price, paid by the West German government), whilst efforts were made to assimilate the resentful Hungarians. Ceauşescu's chauvinism was clearly difficult to marry with

Marxism, though the Romanians did their best, dredging up some obscure jottings by Marx which seemed to condone Romanian claims to Bessarabia.[9] But it seems to have been very popular, and the Romanian regime was remarkably successful in attracting intellectuals to its cause.

On the other side of the Balkans, the Albanian Communists did not espouse such a crudely ethnic nationalism. They had little interest, for instance, in the rights of the Kosovar Albanian minority in Yugoslavia. But like the Romanians, they welcomed the Stalinist model as a way of building national strength.

Born ten years before Ceauşescu in 1908, Enver Hoxha was a small landowner's son from southern Albania, and he always claimed that his uncle, an old Albanian patriot, had imbued him with an ardent belief in 'Albanianism'. Hoxha won a government scholarship to study sciences at Montpellier University, and from there he went to the Sorbonne to study philosophy. He was one of the many Communist leaders of the developing world – including Ho Chi Minh, Zhou Enlai and Pol Pot – who were inducted into Communist culture by the French Communist Party, and it was there that he began to see Stalinism as a solution to Albania's backwardness. When he returned to Albania, he briefly taught French. But when he refused to join the Fascist Party during the Italian occupation he was sacked. He then set up a tobacconist's shop which became a centre of undercover Communist activism.

He was a confident, articulate figure, who, like Tito, liked to dress well. Indeed, sartorial issues lay behind his conflict with the equally vain Tito: when he visited Tito in June 1946, Hoxha was appalled at his arrogance and jealous of his extravagance – his palatial surroundings, white and gold uniform and 'haughty' manner. He and his fellow Albanians felt humiliated and patronized. So whilst Tito complained about Soviet imperialistic arrogance, Hoxha saw Tito as the real imperialist. Yugoslav attempts to dominate the region soured the relationship further, and Albania was delighted when Tito broke from the USSR in 1948. Inevitably, therefore, the Soviet–Yugoslav rapprochement of 1955 spoiled Soviet relations with Albania, and Hoxha was further angered at Khrushchev's attempt, as he saw it, to consign Albania to the status of a permanent agricultural ghetto within Comecon. From 1960 relations between Albania and the USSR deteriorated. The formal break came in 1961, with Hoxha denouncing Khrushchev in typically vituperative language as 'the greatest counter-revolutionary charlatan and clown the world has ever known'.[10] In that year the Third Five-Year Plan launched an intensive programme of Albanian industrialization, and industrial output rose from 18.2 per cent of national income in 1960 to a massive 43.3 per cent in 1985.

To his orthodox Stalinism Hoxha added a number of other elements. The first was the ethnic and clan politics of Albania. The party systematically favoured the southern Tosks, of whom Hoxha was one – a group that had resented the suzerainty of the northern Ghegs for some time. And within the Tosks, Hoxha depended on a close-knit group of clans. Of sixty-one members of the Central Committee in 1961, there were five married couples (including Hoxha and his wife), and twenty were related as sons-in-law or cousins.[11] In glaring contrast to this traditional 'tribal' politics was an adherence to Maoism, a tendency that emerged in the 1960s as Albania forged links with China in one of the more curious alliances of the era. Hoxha's 'Maoism', however, was rather closer in spirit to late Stalinism than Chinese Communism. The works of Mao were used to justify his purges, and he also shared Mao's love of and talent for vitriolic invective. His campaigns, however, were highly controlled, and bore few signs of Mao's populism.

The most controlled of the High Stalinist states, however, was undoubtedly North Korea. After the end of the Korean War, and Stalin's death, direct Soviet influence declined, but Kim continued to use High Stalinist policies, combined with Japanese and indigenous traditions for nationalist objectives. The Korean War had left a deep, unhealed wound in the form of the border dividing North and South; Kim Il Sung faced a threat from the American-backed South, and he himself continued to dream of reunification under his control. After the end of the war a technocratic 'right' emerged within the leadership, which argued for a more balanced, consumer-oriented economy, but they were soon defeated and purged. Kim insisted on an industrial and military build-up under the slogan, 'Arms in the one hand and a hammer and sickle in the other!'[12] It was unclear how one hand could manipulate both a hammer and a sickle but in 1958 – the year of China's Great Leap Forward – Kim believed 'Great Break'-style storming could overcome any obstacles. He called this the 'Chollima' campaign, after the magical winged horse from Korean mythology that could cover extraordinary distances at great speed.

Kim was worried about threats from his Communist neighbours to the North – the USSR and China – as much as from the capitalist South; he was therefore determined to build up his defences during the turbulent years of the late 1950s and early 1960s, when Khrushchev's criticisms of Stalin left him dangerously exposed. Setting out to free himself from the vagaries of Communist-bloc politics, in 1955 Kim began to marginalize Marxism-Leninism, and his philosophy of *Juche* (usually translated as 'self-reliance'), became the new ideology of the regime. *Juche*, in effect, meant national spirit. The main evil in the *Juche* universe was 'flunkeyism' (literally 'serving the great-ism' (*sadae juŭi*)) – sycophancy towards foreigners and their culture. This echoed the High Stalinist crime of 'servility to the West', but this time the targets were the Russians themselves. Kim decried 'poets who worshipped Pushkin and musicians who adored Tchaikovsky'; 'flunkeyism was so rampant that some artists drew foreign landscapes instead of our beautiful mountains and rivers' – he was particularly outraged to find a painting of a Siberian bear in a local hospital.[13] His old connections with the Soviets and the Red Army were downplayed, and Kim Jong Il's official biography was doctored – now he had been born in Korea itself, not the USSR. Iurii Irsenovich Kim had never existed.

Kim initially deployed *Juche* during the tensions with the USSR in the early 1960s. But later, during the Cultural Revolution, it was China that became more of a threat. In 1967 radical red guards, seeing in North Korea the 'feudal' Communism they were so eager to extirpate, and criticizing Kim for failing to be anti-Soviet enough, began to condemn the regime as 'revisionist' and corrupt, and a dispute simmered over the Sino-Korean border.

Kim responded by emulating aspects of Mao's leadership cult. North Koreans were now expected to demonstrate the passionately intense emotional attachment to the 'Great Leader' that the red guards showed to Mao. However, Kim never copied the chaotic populist mobilizations of Maoist China. Indeed the country has retained his hierarchical order: according to a grim Korean quip, the population was divided into 'tomatoes' – those who are red to the core; 'apples' – red on the surface but susceptible to ideological improvement; and 'grapes', who have no chance of redemption. Heredity and class background (*songbun*) still play a role in Korean society: the top 'core class' are largely the descendants of the workers, peasants and Communists of the 1940s and 1950s, and occupy good jobs; the 'wavering class' have opportunities to secure promotion, possibly through the military; whilst the 'hostile class' are seen as outcastes, and have lowly jobs. However, observers disagree over the strength of *songbun* and people's ability to circumvent it – as over so many other aspects of this mysterious and isolated society.[14]

Social hierarchy has been reinforced by ideological controls, and the population continues to be treated as a labour army. Life was, and is, hard. North Koreans generally have to leave for work at 7 a.m., attend political study sessions and meetings between 8 a.m. and 9 a.m., work for eight hours with a rest period of three hours at lunchtime, and then attend more study sessions and self-criticism meetings until 10 p.m. (except for mothers with young children who are excused), returning home between 10.30 and 11 p.m. The military model extends to all aspects of everyday life. Everybody is allocated a set of clothes, suited for their work and position, once a year on Kim Il Sung's birthday, and whilst there are subtle differences in quality according to rank, the styles are all very similar, creating an extraordinary uniformity. They are also of mediocre quality, many of them made of 'vynalon', a locally invented synthetic textile derived partly from limestone. Food has been rationed, and droughts, combined with agricultural mismanagement and exports of grain to earn foreign currency, have caused serious shortages and even famines.[15]

Despite these crises, however, the regime has survived. After the Cultural Revolution, relations with China improved, and North Korea became more secure internationally. Domestically, too, the regime has been remarkably stable. Defectors report dissatisfaction, especially amongst those social groups that are not favoured by the *songbun* system, but there is a significant privileged group that benefits from the regime. The regime's nationalist credentials, its determination to preserve its isolation from the rest of the world, the state's intrusiveness, and the power of the leadership cult – now under the auspices of Kim Jong Il – have all contributed to its survival, despite a severe deterioration in living standards.

All three regimes on the periphery of the Eurasian landmass found they could use their own versions of High Stalinism in pursuit of nationalist ambitions. But the Central and East European core was travelling in precisely the opposite direction. As relations between East and West gradually improved from the 1960s, the failures of Khrushchev's

Romantic Communism left them open to the influence of the market and the capitalist world.

III

The second part of Kundera's *The Joke* is set in the 1960s. Ludvik has long been released from his mining labour battalion and has become a successful academic in a research institute. A journalist comes to interview him about his work, and it transpires that she is Helena, the wife of Zemanek – the party boss who presided over his youthful expulsion from the Communist Eden. Still bitter, Ludvik decides to take his revenge by seducing Helena and breaking up her marriage. But though he succeeds in winning Helena, he fails to wound Zemanek, who is involved in an affair himself and is delighted at Helena's departure. He also discovers that Zemanek has become a popular reform Communist. His cruel joke aimed at his old enemy has backfired on him. A last encounter with his old friend, the folklore enthusiast Jaroslav at an ersatz folk festival – the 'Ride of the King' – reveals that the Slavic folk tradition, now commandeered by the Communist regime, has been emptied of all meaning; it has become a hopelessly vulgar, kitschy entertainment gawped at by uncomprehending teenagers. Though temporarily transported by their love of music, Ludvik's and Jaroslav's brief idyll ends when Jaroslav has a heart attack.

Ludvik is again a victim of his incomprehension of the world around him and, more generally, mankind's inability to control events. His first joke backfired because he did not understand the puritanism of the late 1940s, whilst his second 'joke' fails because he does not realize how far those ideals have decayed by the 1960s. The marriage of Helena and Zemanek, which began as an idealistic Communist union, is a sham. The folk tradition has been deeply corrupted by the state. Ludvik discovers that a world without values is as abhorrent as one of intolerant mass joy.

Kundera, writing in 1965, captured the changes in Eastern Europe since the end of High Stalinism. In most states, the terrifyingly idealistic enthusiasms of the late 1940s had yielded to a less repressive but more cynical era. The rebellions of the mid-1950s had forced many of the socialist regimes to retreat from High Stalinism, and they had achieved some stability. However, now they had jettisoned their old ambitions, there was a danger they would merely become repressive and infinitely less successful versions of their Western counterparts.

Immediately after the shock of 1956, it looked as if the Eastern bloc might be subject to new campaigns of revolutionary purity. Khrushchev was sensitive to Chinese criticisms, and the Moscow conference of Communist parties in 1957 launched a new push for collectivization after the brief post-Stalin pause. Except in Poland, where Gomułka managed to ditch collective farms completely, most East European countries completed collectivization by the early 1960s. Yet this was to be the last gasp of ideological optimism in the region. Never again would there be such a concerted advance along the road to Communism.

The loosening of the imperial reins brought much greater diversity to Eastern Europe in the late 1950s and 1960s. Whilst Yugoslavia, Romania and Albania had escaped Soviet control, even within the Soviet sphere variations were large – from a liberal Hungary at one end of the spectrum to an immobile Bulgaria at the other. But beneath the surface they all resembled each other in one respect: Communist parties throughout the region were retreating, and in doing so they were forced to become a different type of animal. The more egalitarian militias or guerrillas of the Soviet First Five-Year Plan and of the Chinese 1950s and 1960s had never been much of a model in Eastern Europe, but even the more orderly armies of High Stalinism no longer seemed to be suitable. One Hungarian low-level party official, interviewed in 1988, put the problem starkly:

> We inherited the structure of the period when it was really a war-like goal to get this country in shape. To start something. That required a large concentration of will-power and force on the part of the party. It was possible only if the party worked with a soldier-like punctuality and discipline. Now the biggest problem of the party is peace. There are no tasks. We are a combat-troop, and there is no war ... So, for the present problems, the party is like a bull in a china shop. It attacks everything, wants to fight, to battle, and so on, when the problems have been different for a long time.[16]

The remaining Radical elements of High Stalinism were dropped in favour of technocracy and creeping markets. Communists were now much more likely to be professionals and managers than workers. In 1946, only 10.3 per cent of Yugoslavia's Communists were white-collar workers; by 1968 the proportion had more than quadrupled to 43.8 per cent.[17] Secret policemen remained but they were less visible.

The Communist authorities also made fewer efforts to remould their populations and create the new socialist man. They sought, rather, to establish a workable *modus vivendi* with the rest of society. The first renegotiation was with the industrial working class, the most rebellious and threatening force. Stalinist efforts to bully workers into increasing productivity were abandoned, and the influential grouping of male skilled workers in heavy industry was bought off with incomes approaching those of educated white-collar employees. Rapidly, therefore, the regimes' pro-worker rhetoric, so evidently hypocritical in the Stalinist period, began to mean something. But as will be seen, these concessions had their drawbacks. Factories became even less productive, and opposition to market-style reforms became more entrenched. The concessions also fuelled resentment amongst professionals, who felt that their educational achievements were not being recognized.

Communist parties also retreated before entrenched peasant cultures. In Yugoslavia and Poland collectivization was permanently abandoned, but even where collectivization was the norm, efforts were made to accommodate the traditional peasant household. Private plots expanded, and soon made a major contribution to food supplies.

Religion also flourished after the new retreat. No longer were the churches and (in Bosnia) mosques treated as inherently anti-Communist. The Polish Catholic Church did particularly well out of the 1956 crisis and became a major force, seizing a great deal of autonomy. In Hungary Kádár reached agreement with the Vatican in 1964, whilst in 1958 the East German leadership tried to come to some understanding with the influential Protestant churches. Yet the Communists never fully made their peace with God. Relations with the churches were always tense, and churches were riddled with spies and informers. Only in Orthodox Romania did Gheorgiu-Dej follow Stalin's wartime strategy and co-opt the Church. By 1971, his successor Ceauşescu had put medieval images of St Stephen on Romanian postage stamps.[18]

But perhaps the greatest beneficiaries of the retreats – at least for a time – were the urban middle classes; the early 1960s was one of the freest periods of the Communist era. Khrushchev's second and even more forthright denunciation of Stalin at the twenty-second party congress in 1961 reverberated throughout the Soviet sphere of influence. Solzhenitsyn and Kafka could even be read in conformist Sofia – for a time. Only Poland bucked the trend. After a liberal period in 1956–7, when Gomułka even allowed competition between candidates in parliamentary elections, the party cracked down, seeking refuge in anti-intellectualism and anti-Semitism.

But if the comrades were retreating, and no longer serious about creating full Communism, what on earth were they for? How could they justify their monopoly of power to the population, or to themselves? Nationalism, of course, had long been part of the Communist repertoire, and the Polish regime embraced it more fully after 1956. But nationalism itself could be hazardous. Polish nationalism, for example, was strongly entwined with an anti-Communist Catholicism and anti-Russian sentiment; Hungarian nationalism was difficult to disentangle from old revanchist demands for pre-World War I territories – demands that were naturally unacceptable to its now socialist neighbours; and nationalism in the GDR was now irredeemably besmirched by Nazism. In multi-ethnic states like Yugoslavia and Czechoslovakia (and the USSR), nationalism, far from fostering cohesion, could be dangerously corrosive. Slovenes and Croats increasingly saw Yugoslavia as a Serb project and became vocal liberalizers in the 1960s, whilst Slovak discontent at Czech domination helped to bring about the Prague Spring in 1968.

The real alternative to Radical and Romantic mobilization in most of the Soviet bloc, however, was the promise to improve consumption. Abandoning the promise of a Communist utopia to justify self-sacrifice and austerity, Communist leaders now claimed that they were the best people to deliver higher living standards, whilst distributing them equitably. The 'Communism' which Khrushchev promised would be attained by 1980 was widely interpreted as a society of material plenty rather than an idyll of Marxist creativity.

Efforts to please the consumer began in the 1950s; it was then that some East Europeans finally enjoyed the self-service supermarket – developed before the War in the United States and exported to Western Europe during the Marshall Plan era. In Warsaw the grand neo-classical Stalinist shops were joined by a low-rise modernist, American-style self-service store, the 'Supersam', in 1959. As the supermarket's inventors in Depression-era America intended, it brought liberation and autonomy. Shoppers could wander round the store, choosing what they wanted without the need to engage with sullen assistants or join long queues at every counter. However, as any resident of or visitor to the old Eastern bloc will remember, an American consumer culture never flourished, and self-service supermarkets remained the exception.

The socialist car was the real symbol of the aspiration to satisfy consumers. The GDR, under most pressure to compete with the West, was the first country to make serious attempts to build cars for the private market with its plastic-bodied, environmentally unfriendly Trabant (meaning 'satellite', and named after the Russian sputnik), first introduced in 1958. By the late 1980s about 40 per cent of households had cars – higher than any other country in the bloc, but not nearly as many as in West Germany. The USSR followed in the late 1960s, with its massive $900 million deal with Fiat to build a factory in the Volga town of Togliatti in 1966 and produce the 'Zhiguli' or Lada, a version of the Fiat 124.[19] Until then, a tiny 65,000 a year had been made available to the public; that increased tenfold, and by the 1980s, 10 per cent of households owned cars.

However, whilst Communist leaders had hoped that cars would become a sign of the socialist world's ability to provide similar living standards to the West, in fact they became a symbol of their failure: in June 1989 the GDR's secret police, the Stasi, even reported that 'Many citizens view the solution of the "automobile problem" as a measure of the success of the GDR's economic policies.'[20] Cars were expensive, and waiting lists were long: in 1989 customers were receiving Trabants they had ordered in 1976.[21] This was taking delayed gratification too far. The regimes had raised expectations without being able to meet them.

Why did socialist economies find it so difficult to satisfy consumers, even though their leaders were so eager to do so? A story told by Michael Burawoy, an American industrial sociologist who got a job in 1985 as a steel-worker in the October Revolution Brigade of the enormous Lenin Steel Works in Miskolc, Hungary, helps to explain why. In February, it was announced that the Prime Minister was visiting, and production stopped for days as he and his fellow workers cleaned and painted the factory. 'Hordes of young lads from neighbouring cooperatives were swarming around' and soldiers were shovelling the snow. 'It seemed as if the entire land had been mobilized for the visit of the Prime Minister.' Burawoy was supposed to be helping to paint one of the machines – the slag drawer – yellow and green, but there were not enough clean brushes to go round, and he spent his time pointlessly painting shovels with the only tool available: a brush loaded with black paint. The workers were deeply cynical about the whole exercise, seeing it as a typical example of the wastefulness of the system: 'On seeing workers melting ice with a gas flame, Gyuri [a fellow worker] shakes his head in dismay: "Money doesn't count, the Prime Minister is coming."'[22]

Gyuri was right: in socialist economies – even those with strong market elements, like Hungary's in the 1980s – politics mattered more than money and profit. Successful managers were those who expanded their empires (whilst, of course, fulfilling plans), and that meant pleasing the political bosses who controlled the purse-strings. It was essential that a good show be put on for the Prime Minister, however much was spent.

In this struggle for resources, it was the politically influential who were best able to compete – especially the heavy industrial and defence industries. Therefore even after Stalin's death, when the economy was no longer whipped into fulfilling heroic plans, the state continued to neglect the consumer. And without the fear of bankruptcy to rein in their voraciousness, the old industrial interests remained uncontrollably 'hungry', sucking up all the resources and creating shortages throughout the economy – from Burawoy's paint-brushes to Trabant cars.[23]

Thus the main drawback of Communist economies was not always equality and the concurrent poor incentives for workers, as is often thought (in some economies, like the USSR's and the GDR's, from the 1970s incentives were indeed weak, but in others, like Hungary, they were stronger). One of the main problems of the system lay in how capital was allocated – whether it went into productive or unproductive areas. The absence of democracy, combined with the centralization of economic power amongst the planners, allowed well-entrenched interest groups to hijack the honey-pot. This was, at root, the insight of the Austrian right-liberal economist and influential critic of Communism, Friedrich von Hayek.

Inevitably, this rigidity crippled Communists' ability to innovate. Entrenched interests made sure that they took the lion's share of resources, starving new ventures which were to be vital for the economy. By the 1980s, therefore, a massive 20–30 per cent of the Soviet national budget was spent on defence. Meanwhile the Soviet bloc seriously lagged behind in the computing industry of the future. By the 1970s the USSR had a quarter of the world's scientists, half the world's engineers and a third of the world's physicists, but manpower did not make a high-tech economy. The Soviet bloc did develop a serious computer system, copied from an IBM model – the Riad – but, typically, much more energy was spent on producing the computers than helping their consumers in industry to use them.[24] In the 1980s, the number of computers in the USSR amounted to less than 1 per cent of the quantity in the United States: 200,000 to 25 million.[25]

The other main obstacle to the consumer economy – at least in less reformed states – was the Plan, which typically set quantity targets. Factories therefore took the easiest route, producing large quantities of consumer goods of poor quality, which nobody wanted to buy. The result was shoddy, expensive goods that lay mouldering on shop shelves whilst the public competed for the higher-quality, expensive goods on the black market. As the Russian economist Nikolai Shmelev explained in 1987:

> We produce more shoes than any country in the world, but they aren't any good and nobody wants them. We produce twice as much steel as the United States ... layers of bureaucracy and administrative tyranny are responsible for this mess. They prevent producers from caring about the quality of what they produce and from marketing it properly.[26]

Even when efforts were made to improve consumer industries in the 1970s and 1980s, factories were still responding to planners, rather than consumers. Party officials did try to decide what would sell, but sober, puritanical bureaucrats were hardly the ideal people to predict future consumer trends. One member of the Dresden regional administration in the GDR was aware of his limitations, but still, absurdly, found himself having to second-guess fashion-conscious citizens:

> willy-nilly one always hits up against the question: what is actually fashionable? During the last meeting between shops and manufacturers in Dresden, some of the retail outlets were of the opinion that the selection was too stylish and there was a lack of standard wares. Is this opinion right or is it subjective? Of course we cannot answer this question definitively ... [But] the relation between stylish and standard wares should be about 50/50.[27]

By the mid-1960s, it was becoming clear not only that Soviet-type economies were struggling to satisfy the consumer, but that their high growth rates more generally declining. Between 1950 and 1958, Soviet growth per unit of resource was 3.7 per cent, whilst between 1959 and 1966 it had fallen to 2 per cent. What was to be done? Economists increasingly thought about combining the plan with the market, and Khrushchev's fall helped them. Khrushchev had dallied with market reforms, and had introduced them in a very limited way in 1964. But he was, at root, a true believer in collectivist economics and was suspicious of encouraging individual, market incentives. Brezhnev, in contrast, whilst he was no liberal, was much less concerned with ideology. It looked as if Khrushchev's awkward combination of technocracy and Radicalism would give way to a new era of Pragmatism.

IV

The 1970s and early 1980s were some of the most dispiriting years in the history of the Soviet bloc, but, precisely for that reason, they were the golden age of the Communist joke. Two of the best-known capture popular views of Leonid Brezhnev in the early 1980s:

> Brezhnev begins his official speech at the 1980 Moscow Olympics: 'O!' (thunderous applause), 'O!' (thunderous applause), 'O!' (thunderous applause) ... His aide interrupts him and whispers: 'The speech starts below, Leonid Il'ich. That's the Olympic symbol.'

> – Leonid Il'ich is in surgery.
> – Is it his heart again?
> – No, he's having a chest expansion operation. He's awarded himself another Order of Lenin.

No Moscow dinner party in the late 1970s and 1980s was complete without jokes about his idiocy and vanity, and everybody had their own impersonation, complete with his doddery Ukrainian-accented speech. Kundera's Ludvik would have had no problems in the USSR of the 1970s. Even Brezhnev did not care. When told about the chest-expansion joke, he said, 'If they're telling jokes about me, it means they love me.'[28] Yet many of his former colleagues have argued that it was only from the early 1970s that he became the notoriously lazy mediocrity who would brook no criticism, partly as a result of the ill-health that dogged him from 1968. Before then he and Aleksei Kosygin, the Prime Minister, seemed like energetic, pragmatic reformers, willing to break from Khrushchev's old ideological mind-set. As the Czech reformer Zdeněk Mlynář remembered, few of his reformist friends in the Soviet party missed Khrushchev, and they welcomed Brezhnev as an interim leader who might preside over a 'rational line based on expertise'.[29]

Leonid Brezhnev was born into a Russian workers' family in Kamenskoe (now Dneprodzerzhinsk, renamed in honour of Felix Dzerzhinskii, the founder of the Cheka) in eastern Ukraine in 1906. His parents were ambitious for him, and he attended a good classical grammar school. The revolution and civil war disrupted his education, but they also opened up new opportunities; had it not been for the Bolsheviks, he would have undoubtedly followed his father into the steel mill. He joined the Komsomol, worked in factories, and acquired a technical education, eventually graduating as a metallurgical engineer. In 1936 he was elected to the Dneprodzerzhinsk town council, and then had a job organizing metal production for Ukraine's defence industries. It was at this point that he joined the 'tail' of an important party boss – Nikita Khrushchev, the new head of the Ukrainian party. During the war, he continued to put his technical and administrative skills at the service of the party, helping with the dismantling of factories in the western USSR for transport to the East. He also became a political commissar, charged with inspiring and disciplining his troops.

Ultimately Khrushchev took him to the Kremlin on his coat-tails. But Brezhnev's style could not have been more different to his patron's. He was a technical person before he became a party activist, and when he did become a commissar it was during the most nationalistic and least ideologically Marxist period of the party's history. He was therefore more consensual than Khrushchev. He was, indeed, a fairly typical official of his generation who owed his extraordinary social mobility to the party. Like Dudintsev's Drozdov, he was uninterested in ideas, did not enjoy films and disliked reading – acolytes even had to read official papers to him. Some of his pleasures were simple ones: playing dominoes with his security guard and watching football on the TV. But the Brezhnev jokes had some truth to them: he was hilariously vain, loved ceremony and was no puritan. He had accumulated more state awards than all of his predecessors combined; indeed he had more military medals than Marshal Zhukov, who had captured Berlin.[30] Other weaknesses included

25. Learning from big brother. A Soviet engineer instructs his Chinese colleague (1953). The slogan reads: 'Learn the advanced production experience of the Soviet Union, struggle for the industrialization of our country'.

26. Enemies. A Soviet worker catches a saboteur, bribed by American money. The poster (1953) reads: 'Vigilance is our weapon', and was produced at the height of Stalin's xenophobic campaigns.

27. Communist puritans. Virtuous workers, rebuilding Poland after the war, reproach a woman personifying Western consumerism, in Wojciech Fangor's painting *Postaci* (*Figures*), of 1950. Her dress is covered with Western words such as 'Coca Cola' and 'Wall Street'.

28. The power of consumerism. Richard Nixon shows an unhappy-looking Nikita Khrushchev the benefits of the American way of life during their 'kitchen debate' at the American exhibit in Moscow's Sokolniki Park, 24 July 1959.

29. Great Leap Forward. Chinese Peasants operate newly built blast furnaces in the countryside, June 1958.

30. The Great Proletarian Cultural Revolution. Chinese soldiers in a political study group, 1966. The slogan behind reads: 'Open fire on the black anti-party and anti-socialist line!'

31. Execution of an 'enemy' during the Cultural Revolution.

32. Icon of revolution. Pop art version of Alberto Korda's famous photograph of Che Guevara, 1967. The slogan 'Forever, until victory' were the last words Che wrote to Fidel Castro.

33. 'Christ Guerrilla'. Alfredo Rostgaard's poster of 1969 blends Christianity and Marxism into a 'Liberation Theology'.

34. Children of the revolution. A very young soldier of the Popular Movement for the Liberation of Angola (MPLA) sits beneath a portrait of its leader, Agostinho Neto. Huambo, Angola, February 1976.

35. Rebellion.
Protestors burn
portraits of Stalin in
Budapest, 1956.

ncarceration. Strengthening the Berlin Wall
the Brandenburg Gate, 1961.

37. 1968: two faces of Communism.
(*above*) Parisian student protesters carry
portraits of Mao (May); (*below*) Soviet
tanks crush the Prague Spring (August).

38. Brother No. 1. Pol Pot leads a group of guerrillas after his fall from power, 1979.

39. Killing fields. A boy stands beside the remains of some of the Khmer Rouge's victims, collected together in a disused school south of Phnom Penh, 1996.

40. Afrostalinism. A poster of the Ethiopian dictator Mengistu dominates this Soviet-style Addis Ababa square.

ТОВАРИЩИ конец!

Magyar Demokrata Fórum

41. 'Comrades, it's over'. Poster of the Hungarian Democratic Forum, 1989, hailing the defeat of Communism in Eastern Europe.

42. The Fall. The Berlin Wall is breached, November 1989.

43. Communist survivals. A portrait of Mao in Tian'anmen Square Beijing, during the ceremony celebratir the arrival of the Olympic torch, 31 March 2008.

44. Enduring icon. A Cuban boy holds a picture of Che Guevara during a rally marking the 75th anniversary of his birth, 14 June 2003.

45. 'The Fierce One'. Prachandr the leader of Nepal's Maoists, addresses a rally September 2006.

fast cars and the post-Stalin Communist sport of bear-hunting (Stalin had not permitted his lieutenants to shoot). And whilst Brezhnev hardly lived in the luxury enjoyed by today's Russian elites (or indeed Western elites at the time), his lifestyle was very different from the mass of the Soviet people, and inevitably generated resentment – and jokes. In one, Brezhnev's mother visits her son in his luxurious *dacha*. 'This is my house,' he boasts; 'these are my cars; this is my swimming-pool.' His mother gasps with wonder and pride, tinged with anxiety: 'You do live well, Lionechka. But I'm worried for you. What happens if the Bolsheviks return?' As will be seen, the joke turned out to be prescient. Revolutionary Bolsheviks – of a sort – were indeed to return, and Brezhnev's corrupt legacy was to be one of their first targets.

Brezhnev's lack of attachment to ideological shibboleths made him an ideal international negotiator, as did his easy-going character: he once confessed 'charm can take you a long way in politics', and he was resolutely opposed to those he dubbed the 'Soviet Chinese' – the Mao-style anti-Western ideologues within the party. After the erratic and touchy Khrushchev, Brezhnev was welcomed by Western statesmen, and peace-making with the United States was his great achievement, in the raft of nuclear arms control and other treaties of the early 1970s.

Brezhnev's ideological flexibility, together with his own interest in the good life, also gave him a greater willingness to tolerate economic reform in the Soviet bloc, and whilst the reforms in the USSR itself did not go very far, the 1960s saw some of the boldest economic experiments in the region; three parties – the East German, the Hungarian and the Czechoslovak – embarked on serious programmes of economic liberalization, as did the Yugoslavs outside the bloc. The first reformer was the unlikely Walter Ulbricht. Few expected that the old rigid Stalinist, forged in the sectarian German Communist Party of the 1920s, would change in his sixties, but the GDR was on the front line in the economic competition with the capitalist world: before the building of the Berlin Wall in 1961, those dissatisfied could just move to the West – as about a sixth of the population did (an estimated 2.5–3 million). As Ulbricht told Khrushchev in 1960, 'we cannot choose against whom we would like to compete. We are simply forced to square off against West Germany.'[31] In 1970 Ulbricht sincerely believed that the GDR could overtake its Western brother in specific high-tech areas like electronics and machine-building, even though it might not catch up with the economy as a whole – hence the party's surreal slogan 'To Overtake without Catching Up'.

Ulbricht's 'New Economic System' of 1963 was a typical reform of the time and was partially inspired by the economist Evsei Liberman – a technocratic project to introduce market mechanisms into the plan without giving in to the free market. Efforts were made to subject enterprises to market signals to improve their productivity and to make them more responsive to consumers. This would be done by judging them – and financing them – according to their profitability, rather than by how much they produced, and by giving them more powers over pay and bonuses. At the same time Ulbricht challenged traditional party bosses by seeking to promote technically able, educated 'experts' rather than the less well-educated 'reds'. His reform, however, soon ran into the difficulties that bedevilled all attempts at market-style reforms in the Soviet bloc: the objective difficulty of moving from the old system to the new; political resistance; and fears of worker unrest. Economic bureaucrats complained that they were still expected to fulfil plans, but had fewer powers to do so; enterprises spent money on wages to appease workers, and productivity declined; the regime did not have the courage to set higher commercial prices (vital if producers were to respond to the market); and even though Ulbricht did talk about the need to close down unprofitable plants, it was politically impossible to do so, as they had powerful supporters in the party. Ulbricht also discovered that decentralization deprived him of the powers he wanted to force through his ambitious high-tech projects, and he began to reverse the reforms. Soon a powerful opposition had emerged within the party, led by Erich Honecker, whilst Ulbricht's obsession with high-tech industries began to cause shortages and bottlenecks in other areas of production. A combination of economic crisis, mass discontent and Brezhnev's displeasure at Ulbricht's unauthorized détente with West Germany brought Ulbricht's fall, his replacement by Honecker and the end of market reforms.[32]

Serious reform had ended much earlier in the USSR. In 1965, Kosygin introduced a limited version of Liberman's proposals, but they were soon watered down. Brezhnev was a staunch defender of established bureaucratic interests, and the 'hungry' parts of the economy – especially the military and heavy industry – resisted any reduction in their resources.

The Hungarian party introduced the most long-lasting liberal reform, which few predicted after the brutal repressions of 1956–7. Once Kádár had re-imposed Communist rule, he tried to follow a middle course between hard-liners and liberals, and began to seek support for his unpopular regime. The 'New Economic Mechanism' of 1966 and 1968 reduced plan targets to a minimum and freed prices, gradually lifting economic controls until by the 1980s the Hungarian economy was one of the freest in the bloc. A dual economy emerged, rather like the Soviet economy in the 1920s, with cooperatives and a (relatively small) legal private sector allowed to compete with the state-owned economy. The reform gave consumers – at least those with money – real power. The old socialist dilemma of too few goods and too much money was reversed, and the problems of capitalism returned: too little money, too much to buy. Wage differences also increased and inevitably caused some discontent. The Hungarians, then, had created their own 'goulash Communism'; by Communist standards, this was a consumer paradise, and industrial performance also seems to have improved. Even so, this was not capitalism. Market disciplines were weak, and failing firms were not closed down. The state, moreover, still had most of the power.

As long as these reforms promised to improve the popular mood without challenging the party's rule, the Kremlin tolerated them. And yet there were real dangers. After the crises of the mid-1950s, Communist regimes had bought off rebellious workers at the cost of economic efficiency. Liberalization may have had the support of white-collar workers and peasants, but it was bound to hurt workers and poorer regions. After the Russian invasion, Hungary had a united, disciplined party that could cope with these tensions. Yet most Communist states were not so resilient and proved unable to deal with the tensions liberalization brought in its train. Yugoslavia and Czechoslovakia – both with more powerful Communist traditions than Hungary, but plagued by ethnic division – showed how dangerous the market could be to Communist rule.

By the mid-1960s the dangers of the market were most obvious in Yugoslavia. The old efforts to unite the Romantic Marx of worker councils with the market had long been abandoned. Instead a Faustian pact had been forged – borrowing cash from the capitalist West to fund socialism in Yugoslavia. The bargain proved hopelessly unequal, and Yugoslavia became increasingly sucked into the capitalist world. Forced to export more and more to pay off debts, efficiency and cost-cutting – and with them higher unemployment – were inevitable. By 1968 almost

10 per cent of the population were jobless – a unique situation in a Communist state. Conflicts broke out between conservatives, committed to greater planning and centralization, and liberals, and, more dangerously, they became linked with tensions between Yugoslavia's republics. Wealthier Croatia and Slovenia resented subsidizing the poorer Montenegro, Macedonia and Bosnia-Herzegovina, especially at a time of retrenchment, and demanded further liberalization and decentralization. Belgrade was beginning to lose control. In 1963 the republics were given more powers; in 1965 the central state's control over the economy was reduced further; and in 1966 the main defender of the old centralized system, the secret policeman Alexandar Ranković, fell from grace. But state control was not replaced with market disciplines. Local party pressure made it difficult to close inefficient enterprises, whilst managers were free to raise wages and borrow money. The consequence was spiralling debt and inflation. By the 1970s, Yugoslavia was in crisis – inefficient, indebted and in danger of disintegration.

Yugoslavia's travails should, perhaps, have warned Brezhnev of the dangers of markets and of integrating East European economies with the West. But Soviet bloc economies were not in debt – yet – and Tito's troubles elicited only *schadenfreude* in Moscow. Brezhnev, however, could not ignore the crisis in Czechoslovakia. The Czechoslovak party was governed by Antonín Novotný – an old Czech party official of a fundamentally Stalinist bent. As Mlynář described him, he combined a 'true belief in the correctness of Communist doctrine and its advantages for workers, with political hucksterism and a talent for bureaucratic intrigue'. He had been closely involved in the Stalinist show trials of the early 1950s, and was so lacking in sentiment that he was happy to sleep between the sheets belonging to Vlada Clementis – one of the Communists he had sent to the gallows (the belongings of the condemned were often sold off cheaply to officials).[33] Nevertheless Novotný forged links with Khrushchev and was prepared to introduce limited reforms in response to economic failure – growth slowed from an impressive 11.7 per cent in 1960, to 6.2 per cent in 1962, to zero in 1963. He allowed more cultural freedoms and rehabilitated the economist Ota Šik, who proposed a number of liberal reforms. Yet the conservative Novotný dragged his feet when it came to implementing them, and workers – who inevitably suffered from reform – were unhappy.[34] As the economy continued to do badly, the intelligentsia also became restive, and a slew of novels appeared, condemning evil apparatchiks in the harshest terms. The party now began to split along ideological and ethnic lines. The poorer Slovaks, who felt very much the inferior partners in Czechoslovakia, and whose economy was doing particularly badly, demanded liberalization (although in practice it would have undoubtedly hurt them). But it was the Prague students who began the crisis, when in December 1967 they protested against poor conditions in their dormitories. The police put the protests down savagely, and Moscow began to get worried.

Brezhnev flew in to Prague for forty-eight hours. Initially, he did not plan to change the leadership, but merely to put pressure on the Czech party. He soon realized, however, that Novotný was not open to persuasion. He seemed to have no idea of the seriousness of the situation, was rigid and did not know 'how to handle people'. Brezhnev told the Czechs that they had to sort the situation out themselves: 'this is your affair'.[35] But his refusal to give Novotný unequivocal backing was fatal to the old regime. The Slovak leader Alexander Dubček replaced him in January 1968, and charged a group of reformist Marxists with formulating an 'Action Programme'.

Unlike the Hungarian reformers of 1956, the reformers had no intention of dismantling the party-state, or leaving the Soviet bloc. Dubček had spent much of his childhood in the Soviet Union, and was deeply attached to his Russian elder brothers. Similarly, one of his main advisers, Zdeněk Mlynář, wrote in 1980: 'I was a reform Communist, not a non-Communist democrat. I didn't try to hide it then, and there is no reason why I should try to do so now.'[36] Multi-party democracy, he believed, would only cause a conservative backlash and endanger the reforms. Yet the reformers were left with the old dilemma: how to reconcile genuine democracy with the guarantee that the party would retain its leading role.

Khrushchev's Romantic Marxist solution had been a programme of moral renewal, to reinvigorate officialdom by means of purges and controlled party elections; officials would then be in a fit condition to mobilize ordinary people. But the Czechoslovak reformers rejected this top-down vision. Whilst they agreed with Khrushchev that the Communist elites were capable of change, they believed it should be through direct democratic pressure from below. The party had to re-earn its 'leading role' by taking account of popular opinion.

They justified their democratic socialism by going back to a non-Stalinist Marxism – both Romantic and revisionist. The post-Stalin thaw had given intellectuals a very different view of Marxism from the orthodoxy that had prevailed since the mid-1930s. Mlynář, one of the first cohort to move into the grand new Moscow University building on the Lenin Hills, remembered how narrow and distorted the Marxism he studied there was: 'it was only in the late 1950s that I finally studied what every Marxist-oriented university should teach its political science students as a matter of course'. Now that he had been able to read the young Marx and Gramsci, as well as Kautsky and Bernstein, 'my former system of Marxist ideology was destroyed'.[37]

Most influential, perhaps, was the young Marx. This Marx, the new generation plausibly argued, was interested in human creativity. But from the end of the nineteenth century, Marxism had taken a wrong turn with Engels, his technocratic view of the world and belief in the inexorable laws of history. Feelings and creativity had been sacrificed to modernity and rationality. Stalin, they argued, had merely continued on this path: for him, any amount of human suffering was tolerable, as long as modernity was built. The time had come for a 'socialism with a human face' to flourish, which allowed people to engage in 'praxis', or creative activity.[38]

This, of course, all sounds like classic Romantic Marxism. But it is significant that Mlynář's memoirs do not see any contradiction between the Romantic young Marx and the Pragmatic Kautsky and Bernstein. As in early 1950s Yugoslavia, the contradictions within different kinds of 'reform' Communism were rarely seen with much clarity. Some of the Czech proposals – like worker self-management – were Romantic in inspiration, and were, of course, rather difficult to reconcile with market reforms intended to empower managers. Others were inspired by a Pragmatic Marxism, with an almost liberal commitment to market reforms and pluralist politics. The reformers called for multi-candidate elections as the only way of revealing popular opinion, and denied they wanted to vote the Communists out. Multi-candidate elections also had wide public support. But would the elections not undermine the Communist system? Opinion polls showed that they would not, and an overwhelming majority of the population rejected any fundamental change; only 6 per cent believed that political parties opposed to the system should be permitted to stand. Even so, this was not a ringing endorsement of the

Czechoslovak Communist Party. When asked whom they would vote for in the event of free elections, the Communist Party came top with 39 per cent, a new, unspecified political party received 11 per cent, and 30 per cent of people refused to answer or did not know. When only non-party members were counted, however, only 24 per cent supported the Communist Party.[39]

Even so, the reformers believed that they had finally found the philosopher's stone: a way of uniting the whole people behind the Communist party. Dubček remembered his deep emotions as he watched the May Day parade from his democratically low tribune:

> I will never forget the May Day celebration in Prague in 1968 . . . After years of staged productions, this was a voluntary "happening". No one herded people into columns marching under centrally designed and fabricated catchwords. This time people came on their own, carrying their own banners with their own slogans, some cheerful, some critical, some just humorous. The mood was relaxed and joyful . . . I was overwhelmed by the spontaneous expressions of sympathy and support from the crowd as they passed the low platform where the other leaders and I were standing.[40]

Most of the Soviet bloc's leaders, though, were profoundly unhappy. Everything looked fine in May, but what would happen after September, when the Action Plan envisaged free elections? This looked like a recipe for the collapse of Communist rule. Gomułka asked: 'Why not draw conclusions from what happened in Hungary? That all began in a similar way.'[41] Brezhnev, ever the consensualist, was desperate to avoid Soviet action, and he reluctantly endorsed the Action Programme. But as time went on, it seemed to Moscow that Gomułka and the hardliners were right. Dubček's pluralism seemed to be unleashing a wave of criticism. Especially worrying for the Kremlin was the 'Two Thousand Word' manifesto signed by leading intellectuals, which implied that the party, full of immoral 'power hungry individuals', could never be transformed into a humane force.

Fears that the party would suddenly collapse as in Hungary in 1956 were exaggerated, but pressures for some kind of Soviet intervention became overwhelming when party bosses started to warn of cross-infection; Petro Shelest, the Ukrainian leader, told Brezhnev that the Prague Spring was destabilizing his own republic, and Brezhnev feared that he was facing a series of falling dominoes.[42] He agonized, and the crisis marked the beginning of his long battle with illness, insomnia and addiction to tranquillizers and sleeping pills. He finally took the fateful decision. In August the 'fraternal' forces of the USSR, Poland, Hungary, Bulgaria and East Germany 'rescued' their helpless sibling from the evils of counter-revolution. They were met with some demonstrations but no serious resistance. As in Hungary, brutal repression followed. The new Czech Communist leader, Gustáv Husák, who like Kádár had been imprisoned by Stalin, agreed to do the Soviets' bidding. Thousands left for the West, were imprisoned or were given punitively menial jobs. Dubček himself became a forestry inspector in Slovakia. Unlike in Hungary, though, short-term repression was not followed by long-term relaxation. The Czechoslovak party kept a tight grip on society until the state's demise in 1989.

In hindsight, we can see Prague 1968 as the writing on the wall for the whole Soviet bloc, and perhaps for old-style socialism throughout Europe. Hungary in 1956, like the Polish 'Solidarity' movement in 1980–1, threatened the Soviet system, but these were cases of anti-imperial rebellion. In both countries, society was largely united in a mixture of nationalist and ideological resentment. But workers could be bought off and opponents imprisoned or intimidated, as happened in Hungary. The Prague Spring, in contrast, exposed the real weaknesses of the Soviet bloc, for it was a movement that had grown up amongst elites *within* the party and its culture – unlike the more nationalistic Hungarian and Polish rebellions which had largely developed outside it. It was fuelled by Communist true believers who principally sought to use reform to restore the party's moral right to rule. And whilst still Marxist, it was moving rapidly towards liberalism – unlike the more radical Western protests of 1968 with which it has so often been compared. As Kundera, one of the participants, has written, 'Paris May '68 was an explosion of revolutionary lyricism. The Prague Spring was the explosion of post-revolutionary scepticism.'[43] These Communists, unlike nationalists and dissidents, knew how to gain power and use it. And it was Communists like these, not nationalist rebels, who ultimately destroyed Soviet Communism.

There was also a more personal and direct relationship connecting the Czech crisis with the ultimate demise of the Communist system. One of Zdeněk Mlynář's closest friends at Moscow University in the early 1950s was a fellow law student – Mikhail Gorbachev. Both were part of a student generation committed to a non-Stalinist Marxism, and in 1967 Mlynář had stayed with Gorbachev, now a party official in Stavropol. Mlynář found his old friend broadly sympathetic to the Czechoslovaks' right to reform, even though his ideas were by no means as radical as his. Gorbachev also visited Prague in 1969, and saw with his own eyes the Czech hatred of their Soviet occupiers. The Soviet authorities were highly sensitive to the potential dangers of Gorbachev's Czech contacts. In 1968 the KGB questioned Gorbachev's friends and fellow students about the friendship, but could not find any concrete evidence of heresy. Two years later he became party secretary of Stavropol region, unimpeded by the organs of state security.[44] It is tempting to imagine what might have happened had they acted on their suspicions. Rather like the tsarist censors who failed to stop the publication of *Capital*, they let slip the person most responsible for destroying the system they were charged to defend.

In the shorter term too, the Czech invasion had momentous consequences for the Communist world – more so even than 1956. It marked the end of the thaw of the 1950s and 1960s as Moscow reversed its old tolerance of different national roads to socialism. In November 1968 Brezhnev first formally enunciated the principle that the USSR had the right to intervene militarily if national Communist parties deviated from the 'principles of Marxism-Leninism and socialism' – the so-called 'Brezhnev doctrine'.

Similarly, the Prague Spring signalled the end of economic reform and cultural liberalization throughout the Soviet bloc. Brezhnev presided over an increasingly conservative order. The ice was not as thick as before 1953, but the choppy water had been stilled. Nineteen fifty-six was, of course, damaging to the reputation of the Soviet bloc, but many Communists still believed that the system retained its dynamism and could be reformed. Between 1945 and 1968, three forms of Communism had been tried in the Soviet bloc: High Stalinism, Khrushchev's mixture of Radical and Romantic mobilization, and the technocratic and market reforms of the 1960s. All had failed or been outlawed, except in Hungary, where goulash Communism remained. What, now, was left?

The system that emerged was described by Brezhnev as 'developed socialism', by Honecker as 'real existing socialism'. Behind these bland phrases lurked a deeply conservative message: socialism was 'developed', not 'develop*ing*'; it was 'real' and 'existing' and so did not need to be improved upon. Khrushchev's talk of an egalitarian Communism arriving as early as 1980 had been quietly forgotten. Perhaps the best way to describe the system in this period is 'paternalistic socialism'. This was a variation on High Stalinism, as it entrenched political hierarchies, even as it lessened economic inequalities. But the party was much less sectarian and violent than its Stalinist forebear. It had jettisoned its militancy and had given up on mobilizing the population for production. The Soviet Union still had major military ambitions, but the Communists were now more committed to satisfying demands for higher living standards.

V

In 1979 Leonid Brezhnev was awarded yet another medal: the most prestigious Soviet prize for literature – the Lenin Prize. Never had the world seen such a combination of statesman, war-leader and litterateur. The prize was given for the ghost-written three-volume memoir of his war exploits at the battle of Malaia Zemlia ('Little Land'), near his home town of Novorossiisk. The incident was a minor one, and Brezhnev had been a rather unimportant political commissar. But his role and the battle's were systematically exaggerated in histories, and they had now became a major part of the official story of the War. Children sang songs about the heroic encounter, and tours of party members trudged around a newly constructed Malaia Zemlia memorial complex.

Of course, the cult of Malaia Zemlia was greeted with general hilarity and occasioned a whole sub-genre of jokes. But it also tells us a great deal about the nature of late Soviet rule. The obsession with medals was typical of the hierarchical culture of the Brezhnev era, and, for the first time, the War became a central part of the regime's propaganda. There was a flurry of memorial building, including the enormous Motherland sculpture in Kiev. War memorials spread throughout the Soviet bloc, and many are still there, despite the efforts of anti-Russian nationalists to remove them.

Brezhnev himself admired Stalin as a war leader, and though he did not rehabilitate him, criticisms stopped. The Terror was simply not mentioned. Brezhnev, though, did adopt aspects of Stalin's style. He took

Stalin's title, 'Secretary General' of the party, and by the end of the 1970s was being described as *Vozhd*. His claims to great literary achievement also echoed Stalin's pretensions to be a leading Marxist philosopher, linguistic theorist and 'coryphaeus [chorus-master] of science'.

Brezhnev was perhaps closest to the late Stalin in his love of hierarchy. After Khrushchev's chaotic attempts to 'flatten' society, Brezhnev was determined to restore the lines of command. Stalin's ethnic hierarchy was also restored. Just as it had during and after World War II, the party now relied on a version of Russian nationalism to replace a Marxism-Leninism very much in abeyance. A vocal Russian nationalist intelligentsia was treated with indulgence, the Central Committee became more Russian, and anti-Semitism crept back into official practice.

Some of the main beneficiaries of the Brezhnev system were the 'cadres' – the socialist service aristocracy. In 1965 János Kádár told Brezhnev that it was unacceptable to operate according to the old Soviet principle of 'today a hero, tomorrow a bum', but he was preaching to the converted.[45] Brezhnev himself enunciated the principle 'stability of cadres', protecting them from Khrushchev's threatening democracy campaigns, whilst in the GDR the technocratic challenge to their position was removed. The result was an entrenched, and increasingly senescent political elite; in the USSR the average age of full members of the Politburo rose from fifty-eight in 1966 to seventy in 1981.

In contrast with the early 1950s, however, political hierarchy was combined with greater economic equality, and a very un-Stalinist willingness to buy off worker discontent. The harsh father of the Stalinist era was replaced by a paternalistic state looking after the economic welfare of its citizens. Workers' wages rose throughout the Soviet bloc, and the gap between blue-collar and white-collar wages declined – in the USSR, for instance, the differential between an engineer and a worker fell from 2.15 in 1940 to 1.11 in 1984. Worker protests in Poland in 1970 at rises in food prices – toppling Gomułka and forcing the new government under Edvard Gierek to give in – concentrated the minds of all leaders. In the GDR, subsidies on basic goods such as food and children's clothes rose from 8 billion marks per year in 1970 to an enormous 56 billion in 1988.[46] In the 1970s living standards rose in most countries in the bloc, which explains the continuing nostalgia for the era.

But how were these improvements to be financed when the productivity of the economies was declining? The answer lay in two rather unexpected places: beneath the ground, and in the banks of New York and London. The oil-price hike in 1973 gave the USSR, a major oil-producer, a massive windfall. It could therefore afford higher living standards and an ambitious foreign policy, even though, according to some estimates, in the second half of the 1970s its growth had slowed to a meagre 1 per cent. For oil-importing Eastern Europe, in contrast, the price increase was a disaster. The USSR found it was forgoing huge export earnings by sending subsidized raw materials, and especially oil, to Eastern Europe; it has been calculated that in 1980 the terms of trade within Comecon transferred a massive $42.8 billion (in 2007 prices) subsidy from the USSR to its East European satellites.[47] But oil also provided salvation, for it flooded the world with Arab petrodollars, funnelled through Western commercial banks and looking for a home. With the petrodollar, the free global financial markets that dominate the world to this day were born, and the regulation of the 1930s was gradually dismantled.

Hayek and his followers argued that private bankers, free of state regulation, were the ideal people to decide on the rational allocation of capital, and were certainly much less inefficient than bureaucratic planners. Driven by profit, bankers would inevitably invest in the most productive projects around the world, rewarding the innovative and hard-working and shunning the stupid and lazy. However, the early behaviour of these new captains of global capital should have warned the world that Wall Street could be as careless with its capital as Gosplan: bankers' time-scales can be short, and far from picking long-term winners, they invested in the ramshackle, over-planned economies of Soviet Eastern Europe.

The banks were encouraged by Western governments, eager to help their recession-stricken industries export goods to Eastern Europe. Communist leaders, for their part, abandoned any remaining ideological qualms and took the cash. It helped them to finance better living standards for their disgruntled populations whilst feeding the hungry states' voracious appetite for industrial investment. Having exhausted domestic resources, they now found a new source of capital abroad. Poland was one of the most ravenous states, and Gierek used loans to build steel mills and plants producing cars under Western licence – like the Fiat Polski – which he hoped to export throughout the Soviet bloc. By 1975 investment had reached a massive 29 per cent of GDP, largely because the party failed to control industry's demand for the new foreign capital.[48] Ceauşescu also hatched grandiose projects, conceived by crony economists and his own children. He borrowed in the hopes he could create a modern, though still planned, economy, exporting petro-chemicals to the Western market. As one commentator has remarked, the ends were those of Adam Smith, the means those of Iosif Stalin. Like the Yugoslavs, the Romanians, even though operating an inefficient economic system, had ambitions to compete on the world market. By the end of the decade much of the Communist world – Eastern Europe, North Korea, Cuba and Communist Africa – was in hock to Western banks, joining much of the non-Communist developing world. East European debts were especially large, and between 1974 and 1979 the Polish debt tripled, whilst the Hungarian doubled. In the 1980s these debts were to cause a major crisis, but until then they helped to finance the paternalistic socialism of the mature Communist regimes.

By the end of the 1960s it was clear that Communism was no longer a radically transformative force, at least in Europe. Many Communists and even ordinary citizens in some countries were still convinced that their system was superior to capitalism, but they no longer expected it to forge radically egalitarian social relations, or to create a dynamic new economy to compete with capitalism: both radical equality and economic dynamism were simply too difficult to reconcile with party dictatorship and the command economy. Ambitions therefore became more realistic: Communism's objective was to be a stable system of economic welfare and justice. Similar trends can be seen in China. Although China remained much more egalitarian than the Soviet bloc until Mao's death in 1976, as early as 1968 it was becoming clear to Mao that the Radicalism of the Cultural Revolution was unsustainable. And as the leadership turned away from its earlier Radicalism, China itself moved towards its own version of socialist paternalism. In many parts of the Communist world, the system found some sort of equilibrium, as Communist regimes learnt how to live in peace with at least most of their people.

VI

In the autumn of 1988, a pair of Hungarian sociologists, Ágnes Horváth and Árpád Szakolczai, both deeply unsympathetic towards the ruling

Communists, were finally given permission to embark on a project most thought impossible: an independent academic analysis of party officials in the district organizations of Budapest – the way they worked, their values, and their psychological profile.[49] But traditional Communist secrecy almost aborted the research even before it began. How, the anxious Communists asked, could non-party people be trusted to study the comrades? Eventually, however, a tiny window of opportunity opened: liberalization had reached the point where the party was willing to be scrutinized from outside – though it was in fact only a matter of months before the party's monopoly ended. Even so, a wary Horváth and Szakolczai sent their results for safekeeping to a number of well-known Hungarian academics as soon as they had a first draft, terrified lest their work be confiscated and suppressed.

The results of their research surprised them. When a group of party 'instructors' – middle- to low-ranking full-time officials – was asked what made them especially well-suited to politics, the replies were remarkably similar. One answered: 'I can make personal connections easily in all areas. I love to deal with people's problems'; another: 'I planned this job as a temporary *service*. I felt I could easily make contacts with people; I have empathy' (italics added). Though, of course, these answers should not be taken at face value, they are remarkably consistent with the results of questionnaires they completed on their personalities and values. The researchers had expected the officials to be typical political leaders: decisive, independent and self-consciously rational problem-solvers. Instead, they saw themselves as particularly flexible, emotional and sympathetic. Moreover, when asked about their values, they were much more likely than other educated people to value individual responsibility, hard work, tolerance and imagination. On the other hand, they were less likely than others to see rules and constraints, whether internal (such as self-control and honesty) or external (such as obedience and politeness) as virtues.

These Hungarian instructors sound like a group of social workers or psychotherapists, rather than the leather-jacketed militants of old. However, these results are less remarkable given how radically Communist regimes in the Soviet bloc had changed since the early 1950s (and in China from the mid-1970s). The party – unlike the more technocratic state organizations – had always prized emotional skills, and the ability to connect with 'the masses'. These were, after all, essential

434

qualities if one was to persuade and mobilize others. But now the heroic era was past, the party increasingly saw itself as an organization committed to looking after the welfare of its citizens, although, of course, it propounded a very particular vision of welfare – moralistic, paternalistic, economically egalitarian and socially conservative. The values endorsed by these Hungarian officials were useful in this type of organization. They wanted to help people, prized personal relationships, eschewed abstract, impersonal rules, and were happy to discriminate, seeing some as more deserving than others. Unlike previous party officials, those of the 1980s were generally highly educated, and Communist parties increasingly presented themselves as scientifically trained professionals. They were not, however, Max Weber's rational bureaucrats; indeed, they strongly disapproved of formal or routinized methods. As one said, 'I consider the most important thing to do . . . is to talk. [Information] from paper – that information smells of paper.'[50]

Therefore, outside the Stalinist periphery, Communist parties no longer treated their populations as guerrilla armies; citizens were not expected to be 'labour heroes'; nor were egalitarian social and gender relations enforced. They were also no longer so concerned with transforming their citizens' internal beliefs, though some regimes, such as the Chinese and the East German, were more concerned with ideological belief than others, such as the Hungarian and Soviet. Rather, the paternalistic party-state looked after the population and used coercion to make sure they stayed in line – they were 'welfare dictatorships', as one scholar has put it.[51] They also gave privileges according to people's 'service' to the state and society – a non-military version of the tsarist and Stalinist 'service aristocracy', which had now been extended from the elite to society as a whole. In some states they were also reminiscent of the 'well-ordered police state' imported into Russia from Central Europe in the seventeenth and eighteenth centuries, in which the 'police' (now the party) were not just responsible for law and order, but also for making sure that the citizenry were both moral and productive.[52]

But this paternalistic structure had its weaknesses. It was very difficult, if not impossible, to ensure that rewards were given in a way that was seen as just. The officials in charge of distributing goods often acted corruptly, helping friends and family. And even if they had been more altruistic (and some parties, such as the East German one, were less corrupt than others), a system founded explicitly on official decisions about who is and who is not virtuous is bound to be vulnerable to criticism. Capitalism, paradoxically, is less vulnerable, because its inequalities can be justified as, in some way, a 'natural' impersonal phenomenon – the product of the iron laws of the market.

The style and degree of paternalism varied from place to place, depending on local political cultures and social conditions. Some of the most intrusive examples were to be found in China. The enormous reservoir of rural Chinese labour gave the regime much more power over the workforce than in the Soviet bloc, where managers found it difficult to stop workers leaving for other jobs. Old Guomindang practices and a Confucian paternalistic culture also had an influence. Neighbourhood committees played a much greater role in all aspects of people's lives than municipal bodies did in the Soviet bloc, and more closely resembled the Japanese neighbourhood police (with its acute personal knowledge of local inhabitants) than Soviet local councils. The lowest rung on the political hierarchy was the residents' small group unit, which looked after between fifteen and forty families, and communicated orders from on high whilst organizing welfare and policing citizens. In the workplace, the *danwei* ('work unit'), like the Soviet *kollektiv*, provided housing, clinics, childcare and canteens for workers, but it had even greater sway, and even relatively low-level factory officials had powers to allocate apartments, bicycle coupons and other rations.[53] To receive these 'favours', workers had to behave in an approved way. Even their private lives were carefully scrutinized. As one worker, interviewed by the political scientist Andrew Walder, explained:

> Workers are usually punished for stealing, bad work attitudes and showing up late, absenteeism without leave, and having sex [outside marriage]. There are no set punishments for different things. Having sex is usually treated very seriously, at least a formal warning . . .[54]

Interestingly, poor performance in the job attracted less strict punishment, although much depended on the attitude and class origin of the worker. As one explained, 'if the person admits guilt and makes a self-criticism, usually the group will recommend leniency, and give the person "help" or education. Usually this is enough, because this is embarrassing for a person.'[55]

In the Soviet bloc, by contrast, such an intrusive approach to private life only extended to party members. Local councils were too remote to have very close contact with their inhabitants, and factories had less control over their workforces. Even so, the post-1964 Soviet system was strongly paternalistic, though socialist paternalism was not the same as the eighteenth-century paternalism of the well-ordered police state. In principle, citizens were not merely expected to be loyal to the party boss, factory manager or collective farm chairman, but had also to behave in a socialist way, that is, to work hard, be virtuous, and participate in collective activities or 'social work' as it was called. For workers, this would involve doing an unpaid shift for some worthy cause or serving on a trade union committee. For academics and professionals, it might include giving evening lectures to workers: the 'social work' given to Alexander Zinoviev, an academic philosopher and dissident commentator on Soviet society in the 1970s, involved drawing cartoons for public 'wall-newspapers' and travelling with an agitprop brigade around the countryside giving lectures.[56]

This kind of 'social work', though, was not done by everybody. Like party culture more generally, it penetrated the upper echelons of society to a much greater extent than society as a whole: in the USSR in the 1960s and 1970s, it was compulsory for party members, whatever job they did, whilst 60–80 per cent of educated people participated, compared with 40–50 per cent of industrial workers and 30–40 per cent of farm workers.[57] Motives were mixed. Many believed social work – especially committee meetings – were pointless and only participated because they were pressured to do so, or because they hoped for benefits. As Zinoviev explained: 'If someone avoids social work, then that fact is noted and measures are taken. And there are several measures, ranging from pay rises and promotion to the solution of accommodation problems, the possibility of trips abroad or the chance of having one's work published.'[58]

Even so, Zinoviev denied that 'social work' was always an empty formality that people were forced or bribed to perform. He insisted that it was often taken seriously: many people did it because it was good in itself, and it raised the reputation of the whole collective. It could also be a displacement activity. Surveys of academics found that older academics who had lost interest in their own research tended to be keener on social work than their younger colleagues.[59]

Like the 'service aristocrats' of old, therefore, some people laboured both for reward and for an ideal of service. For some, this was the essence of mature socialism. One young Komsomol organizer in the early 1980s, interviewed by the ethnologist Alexei Yurchak, though critical of the boring and pointless meetings, insisted:

> Basically, as far as I was concerned, the government's policy was correct. It consisted simply of caring for people, free hospitals, good education. My father was an example of this policy. He was our region's chief doctor and worked hard to improve the medical services for the people. And my mother worked hard as a doctor. We had a fine apartment from the state.[60]

But not everybody was as convinced of the fairness of the system. Frau Hildegard B. from Magdeburg in the GDR was one. In 1975 after a very long wait, she finally received an allotment she had applied for, but at a far higher price than she was expecting. Furious, she protested to the authorities that she deserved better because she had loyally served the state as Chair of the Factory Trade Union Executive Committee. The Chair of the District section of the Association of Small Gardeners, Settlers and Small Animal Breeders wrote back to deny that she had been unfairly treated: all of those ahead of her had been virtuous 'activists' and deserved their privileges. Even so, ultimately he came to a compromise, and gave her a cheaper allotment elsewhere.[61]

The lengthy official response demonstrates the regime's concern to be seen to be acting justly. Any suspicion that privilege was not closely attached to good citizenship was bound to erode general placidity and willingness to play by the rules. However, the more the state abandoned its ambitions to transform society, the more difficult it was to ensure a direct link between reward and service. This was increasingly the paternalism of the acquisitive boss and his clients, not of the loving father and his children. Meanwhile, subordinates realized that they were rewarded more for unswerving loyalty and sycophancy to their superiors rather than more abstract socialist virtue. For even though they no longer aspired to mobilize their workers to build the socialist utopia, bosses still exercised power over the details of everyday life.

When in 1983 the sociologist Michael Burawoy went to work in Hungary's Bánki heavy-vehicle plant, he was struck by the contrasts between it and the Allied plant in Chicago where he had worked a decade earlier. Relations between managers and workers were very different. In the United States, jobs were not secure, but pay was; in Hungary, the reverse was true. It was very difficult to sack people, but workers were paid strictly according to piece rates: if they only produced 50 per cent of their 'norm', they were paid 50 per cent of their wage; in the United States, independent trade unions ensured that workers were guaranteed a minimum of 100 per cent of their wage, whatever they produced. The Hungarian system gave managers and foremen a great deal of power, for they could set the work norms, and therefore pay, and they could allocate the best machines and the easiest work to their friends. So Burawoy, who, as a foreign interloper was given an old machine and a difficult job, only ever achieved 82 per cent of his norm, and earned 3,600 forints, unlike his favoured fellow worker who earned 8,480 forints.[62] The Hungarian poet and leftist dissident-turned-Margaret-Thatcher-admirer Miklós Haraszti, who spent some time in the Red Star Tractor Factory in the early 1970s, described the role of the foreman:

> The foreman doesn't just organize our work: first and foremost he organizes *us*. The foremen fix our pay, our jobs, our overtime, our bonuses, and the deductions for excessive rejects [i.e. low-quality goods]. They decide when we go on holiday; write character reports on us for any arm of the state which requests them . . .[63]

The power of managers varied across the Soviet bloc. In China, factories had a great deal of control over food supplies and housing, and so workers were forced to stay on good terms with bosses. During the 1970s the factionalism of the Cultural Revolution period continued, but it now turned not on ideology but on personal connections. In Hungary in the 1970s, managers had less power over perks such as accommodation, but more over wages. In the GDR, in contrast, piece-rate systems were weaker, but even here managers used incentive structures that divided the workforce between different shifts and brigades. So whilst worker protests did occur, they were isolated and rarely led to factory-wide strikes.

However, it would be wrong to conclude that bosses were all-powerful. As in most paternalistic societies, 'fathers' and 'children' were bound together in a web of informal rules, customs and reciprocities, which meant that managers could not behave entirely as they wished. One worker presented a rather extraordinary picture, in which managers were wholly at the mercy of personal connections:

One's actual power depended on these kinds of ties. A vice-director transferred into our factory had a difficult time getting his orders carried out
because he had no connections. It took a long time for him to build up
these connections before people would listen to his orders. Friendship facil-
itated the carrying out of orders, kind of a way of helping out your friends
by carrying out their requests.[64]

There were also other, more fundamental reasons for the weakness of
managers in late socialist societies. They may have had total control
over wages and perks, but in the Soviet bloc there were simply not
enough workers, and the discontented did not find it too difficult to quit
and find another job. Also managers relied on workers' cooperation and
goodwill to be flexible in an economy marked by chaotic supplies and
shortages. If workers did not cooperate, the factory would not fulfil the
plan and managers would suffer. Collective farm chairmen were in a
similar position. One chief of a collective farm in Romanian Olt Land
explained how difficult it was to get peasants to work for him when
there were other opportunities in local industry and they could work on
their private plots. It was especially difficult to find people to act in positions of responsibility:

> The hardest part of my job is to get other people to work. There are never
> enough team chiefs, so I have to go jawing from house to house, making
> promises to get people to be chiefs. This one needs bottled gas, that one
> wants meat. I can't satisfy them all, but we need chiefs.[65]

This picture – of officials with limited powers, forced to compromise
with their subordinates – is reinforced by the Russian philosopher Alexander Zinoviev's devastating satire on the Soviet system, *The Yawning
Heights* of 1976. For Zinoviev, the dominant force in Soviet society was
not the Kremlin but the *kollektiv* – whether the workshop in a factory,
the collective farm, the academic institute or the apartment block. While
officially appointed from above, managers and officials tended to identify with the collective, not with their bosses. Though managers might
constantly try to exceed their authority and abuse their power, they
were constrained by the fact that their career prospects depended on
how well their subordinates worked, and by the surveillance of the local
party cell and 'the rank and file of citizens who write complaints and
anonymous letters to all sorts of organs'. The power of managers there-

fore tended to be limited to feathering their own nests and those of their 'henchmen' and 'toadies'. It was virtually impossible to change the organization of the enterprise: 'even a small initiative costs managers immense efforts, and quite often the result is a heart attack.'[66]

Zinoviev's account must be treated carefully, for the lives of the academic elite were a world away from those of the ordinary worker or peasant. Even so, he helps to explain the paradox of the mature socialist system: its legitimacy was constantly undermined by endless popular complaints about injustice and hypocrisy, and yet it was remarkably stable (except in a few cases like Poland).

One reason was that people developed a sense of security in the collective, for it was very difficult to sack workers. Moreover Zinoviev could reasonably talk of the 'simplicity of life' compared with the West, for, paradoxically, in these supposedly bureaucratic societies people were in general much less burdened by red-tape than under modern capitalism. Everything was looked after by their workplace, obviating the need to deal with a whole range of separate private institutions (such as banks and insurance and energy companies). Whilst acquiring desirable goods took a lot of time and energy, in most places and at most times a basic standard of living could be counted on. Furthermore, people generally did not have to work very hard (though where a significant black economy emerged, people often worked very hard indeed). And yet the collective was not a stagnant, static place, nor was competitiveness absent. Hard work and overt ambition might not pay off, but there were many opportunities for self-advancement by politicking and forging good relations with bosses.[67]

The relatively undemanding nature of work permitted people to devote time to personal relationships. As Horváth and Szakolczai commented in 1992, whilst the party 'successfully discouraged a large number of people from being able to lead their own lives, express their opinions, and discuss public issues and their interests in a civilised form', its failure to imbue people with a work ethic did leave people with time and space for themselves and their personal relations:

'People don't work here', said Western experts. But it was precisely this distance [from an internal work ethic] that made it possible for a long time, up to the 1970s, for people to preserve in their everyday life, in what remained relatively free from the official world, their personal connections,

the trust toward each other, the immediacy, the inner harmony and autonomy, the ability to live and feel. The 'fight of all against all' mentality which
today characterises all strata of society was earlier restricted to only those
groups that were close to the internal power struggles.[68]

Alongside the official collective, therefore, was the unofficial collective:
friends and family. Indeed, the intrusiveness of Communist regimes, and
their ambition to change friendship into a politically acceptable 'comradeship', only increased the importance of friends as a refuge. Friends
were people you could trust, people who would not report something
you had said or done to the party activists. This was most important
during periods of radicalism, like the Cultural Revolution. As Chinese
remembered about their schooldays in the Mao period, you could trust
friends to mention only 'small things' and 'minor mistakes' in self-
criticism sessions.[69] Even in more normal times, friendship was probably
more important in socialist than other societies. When asked in 1985
which institution had the most authority in their lives, 23 per cent of the
3,500 Belorussian and Estonian young people questioned cited the
collective, 33 per cent said friends, and 41 per cent family. Friendship in
the USSR seems to have been taken much more seriously than in the
West, and indeed there was much more time for it: 16 per cent of people
met friends every day, 32 per cent once or several times a week, and 31
per cent several times a month. American single men, in contrast, met
friends on average four times a month.[70]

Yet however much one might create one's own informal 'collective'
outside the system, the official collective mattered, and there was a clear
tension between the justice and egalitarianism that were supposed to
reign there, and the managerial and party hierarchy that frequently
operated according to personal favours. Workers, especially, tended to
see the power and perks of managers as unjust. Miklós Haraszti found
workers making a very clear distinction between themselves and the
privileged managerial stratum – just as the workers of Stalin's USSR
had in the 1930s:

They, them, theirs: I don't believe that anyone who has worked in a factory,
or even had a relatively superficial discussion with workers, can be in any
doubt about what these words mean . . . the management, those who give
orders and take the decisions, employ labour and pay wages, the men and

their agents who are in charge – and remain inaccessible even when they cross our field of vision.[71]

As Haraszti admitted, whilst all workers felt very separate from managers, they were not necessarily hostile to them. Some accepted that, as technical specialists, they were valuable and necessary, but in all workplaces it was common to find the Radical Marxist view that managers, especially those without obvious expertise, were merely parasites, feeding off the surplus produced by workers. One young worker echoed Lenin's claim in *State and Revolution* that administrative work could be done by a barely literate worker – and could be done better because the worker would be fair:

> 'That lot, what they do, I mean what they *really* do, could be done just as well by an unskilled labourer, all on his own . . . if someone taught him to count. Every morning he could distribute the jobs fairly, working from the list of runs, and take them to the machines . . .'[72]

Industrial and farm-workers were not alone in believing that others were benefiting from unjust privilege. White-collar workers increasingly felt hard done by, especially from the 1970s onwards as the income gap between workers and the educated narrowed. As one East German teacher, Friedrich Jung, recalled, 'he who had neither money nor connections was in poor shape'; and for him industrial workers at large wealthy plants were in a particularly good position because they earned more than teachers and their food and accommodation were subsidized.[73]

So even as incomes became more equal, resentment at unjust economic privilege was endemic, as was revealed by the few independent opinion polls conducted during the 1970s and 1980s. A poll taken in Poland in 1981 showed that 86 per cent of the population saw income differences as 'flagrant', and in Hungary most of the population believed that the party acted 'to a large extent' in the interests of the top party leadership and apparatchiks.[74] Indeed, it seems that as incomes became more equal, people perceived unjust privileges to be greater. Research on Soviet opinion in the Brezhnev era showed that younger generations were more likely than the older to see their era as the most unjust.[75]

Michael Burawoy certainly found anger at inequalities much stronger amongst workers in the Communist world than in capitalist countries.

The workers of the Lenin Steel Works in Miskolc, Hungary, and those of the Allied plant in Chicago all complained about the closure of the old steel furnaces. But whilst the American workers were faced with losing their jobs, 'they still find little fault with capitalism'. Meanwhile 'paradoxically, the furnacemen of the October Revolution Brigade, although more or less insulated from the ravages of the world market and unable to comprehend what it means to be without a job, nevertheless know only too well how to criticize their system', and spent a great deal of time condemning the hypocrisies of socialism.[76] The solution to this paradox lies in yet another paradox: despite the political secrecy and distorting propaganda that suffused Communist regimes, the system was actually much more transparent than capitalism. Zola, rightly, described Capital as a mysterious god, hidden in a tabernacle, rarely questioned or even noticed by ordinary people. In Communist regimes, by contrast, workers were constantly made aware of the principles of socialism through propaganda, socialist competition, 'voluntary' social work and production campaigns, and could always contrast the ideal with the reality. Also the economic mechanisms of socialism were well understood: the state invested in a factory and workers produced a 'surplus', which was then taken by the state, which claimed to distribute it justly for the good of society. So when workers saw bosses awarding themselves privileges, apparently unearned, they felt angry and exploited. Under capitalism, it is very difficult to see where the profit is going or how justly it is being distributed. It is no surprise that workers normally criticized socialist systems for not being socialist enough.

But, as in the past, not only did Communism's paternalistic practices clash with its commitment to equality, but they also contradicted the 'modern' values which the regimes claimed to champion. If 'traditional' societies typically involve non-egalitarian, hierarchical social relations of dependence, deference and immobility whilst in 'modern' societies individuals are supposedly independent and are judged according to their achievements, then we can certainly see elements of a 'traditional' order under Communism. Paternalistic relationships governed collectives; people were often dependent on bosses, and in some socialist societies, people were trapped in their collectives (as in post-Great Leap China and the USSR, where internal passports sometimes made it difficult to move). Meanwhile, women continued to be discriminated against, despite official rhetoric. The militant messianic party could believe in its role when it was building socialism and fighting the class enemy, but when that task had been achieved its function was less clear. It increasingly looked like a traditional status group, less able to run the country than real experts.

Even so, Communist regimes had built societies that were 'modern' in some other ways: they had promoted urbanization, mass education systems and welfare states. Socialist regimes also encouraged a 'modern' attitude towards life, where individuals and families strove to better themselves as part of a broader, national community. As the anthropologist David Kideckel has argued, the peasants of the Romanian Olt Land developed much broader and more diverse networks, covering a wider geographical area, than they had before the War, and peasants were well aware of the importance of bettering oneself. The concept of 'preparedness' (*pregătire*) – the need to do well at school and know about one's work – became much more important under socialism than before. As one worker explained, 'In the past leaders had *pregătire* and workers and peasants didn't. Now it's the opposite.'[77] The older, almost aristocratic aspiration to be a *domn* ('lord') – the generous, stylish and charismatic person who did not work – was still present, but it coexisted with newer models of behaviour. Peasants also adopted a much more pragmatic, utilitarian attitude towards work. The anthropologist Martha Lampland found that between the wars the Hungarian peasants of Sárosd, south of Budapest, were relatively uninterested in markets; status came with independence from others, and the peasants' ideal was to acquire enough land to secure it – a goal that most were too poor to achieve. Socialism, therefore, was unpopular amongst many peasants because it made them dependent on officials. But it also helped to transform their attitudes. Now work was measured and paid for, they developed a much more commercial view of their labour. By the 1980s, the Hungarian village was a place of 'rampant economism and utilitarianism'.[78]

Communist regimes, of course, were perfectly happy with these attitudes, as long as peasants placed the collective above the individual. They had sought to create a new type of modern individual – rational, free from the social ties of the past, and collectivist. And they enjoyed some success. In some cases, Soviet-bloc citizens seem to have been more collectivist than their Western contemporaries, and as will be seen in Chapter Twelve, many citizens of Soviet bloc societies had more egalitarian views than Westerners.[79] However, there were strong forces undermining that collectivism. Opinion surveys in Poland showed that the principle of self-sacrifice for the collective became less important for ordinary people between 1966 and 1977 (although that of equality became more so).[80] Commitment to the collective was also threatened by a new enemy: consumerism. Communist societies were still far from the consumerism of the West, but some were beginning to measure their status by the goods they acquired, rather than by their service to the state.

VII

In 1983, a new, genuinely amusing romantic comedy was released in the USSR, though one with a strong ideological message. *The Blonde Round the Corner* told the story of the romance between Nikolai, an astrophysicist who decides to become a warehouseman in a large Moscow shop, and the real heroine of the film, the shop-worker Nadia, a larger-than-life wheeler-dealer who can fix anything through Moscow's black economy.[81] Her life and relationships turn on her ability to secure 'deficit' goods: she introduces her friends to Nikolai not by name, but by what they can get for her – one is 'theatre tickets', another 'holidays on the Black Sea', and so on. In this parallel consumerist universe, the materialistic Nadia, not the party secretary, is boss. She has so much faith in her influence that she tries to find out whether she might be able to procure the Nobel Prize for Nikolai by bribing the committee members with caviar and other luxuries. Light comedy ends in heavy moralizing: Nikolai, at first captivated by this new world, abandons the monstrous Nadia on the eve of their marriage and, by implication, the selfish and shallow pleasures of consumerism.

The Blonde Round the Corner displayed all of the Communists' anxieties about consumerism: it was a rival universe, with its own hierarchy and values antithetical to those of Communism. Soviet bloc countries all had flourishing black economies by the 1970s; some, such as those of the USSR, Poland and Hungary, were largely tolerated; others, such as the East German, were treated less liberally, but flourished all the same. These parallel economies covered a significant proportion of economic activity – surveys showed that in the USSR of the 1980s, 60 per cent of all car repairs, 50 per cent of shoe repairs and 40 per cent of apartment renovations were done on the black market, many by people moonlighting from their official jobs.[82] But socialist states also legitimized this corrosive consumer culture by establishing special shops where luxury goods could be bought. For instance the GDR's Exquisit and Delikat shops sold such goods for much higher prices than in normal shops, and the Intershops sold goods for Western currency, acquired from relatives in the West.

Consumerism established a different world. People spent a great deal of their time tracking down 'deficit' goods for their apartments, or finding fashionable clothes – especially Western ones. It is no surprise that those jobs which gave access to consumer goods became much more popular in the 1970s. Sociologists found that shop sales jobs like Nadia's, looked down on in the early 1960s, were now much more attractive, whilst conversely higher education was becoming less popular. White-collar workers still generally earned more than their blue-collar counterparts, and some groups, such as the army and top party bosses, were relatively well paid in money and perks. But a new status hierarchy, founded on access to consumer goods, began to rival the old paternalistic one based on service. A survey of Soviet teenagers in 1987 showed that they regarded black-marketeering as the most lucrative job in Soviet society, followed by work for the military, car servicing and bottle-recycling; at the bottom came pilots, actors and university teachers.[83] Similarly, in the GDR, where access to foreign currency sent by relatives was so crucial, the joke went that German socialism had reached a new phase in the Marxist scheme: 'from each according to his ability, to each according to the residence of his aunt'.[84]

As The Blonde Round the Corner showed, this challenge to the old order was resented by those without access to consumer goods. In Poland, where party apparatchiks were themselves involved in the black market, it damaged their prestige. Elsewhere, it was more difficult for middle-ranking party officials to nurture foreign contacts, and consumerism antagonized those who did not have the opportunity or desire to participate in the parallel economy; whilst they had status in the old hierarchy, they were very lowly in the new one.

It was perhaps inevitable that consumer goods would become so central to people's lives when they became more widely available. Most people, in most societies, try to acquire status. But that status was only likely to become associated with consumerism when official socialist hierarchies became less important, and, crucially, when consumer goods were within the reach of ordinary people. People compete with their peers; when the very top elite, remote from most people, had these goods, it was less important to have them, but from the 1950s Communist regimes created the ideal conditions for an obsession with consumer goods. They made greater efforts to spread these goods around, but failed to produce nearly enough to meet demand.

Fascination with consumer goods clearly showed that many Soviet bloc citizens were moving into the Western cultural orbit. Youth culture revolved around Western clothes and music; even though socialist states produced their own clothes (sometimes with Western brand logos on them, such as 'Marlboro' or 'Levi-Strauss'), only foreign-produced clothes were fashionable. However, we should not exaggerate the power of consumerism; Communism was not brought low by the Marlboro cowboy. A survey of attitudes to social prestige in Hungary – the socialist economy with one of the most developed market economies – showed that jobs associated with knowledge (like doctors) had the most prestige attached to them. Commerce and high incomes were much less prestigious.[85]

Also, an interest in consumer goods did not necessarily lead to anti-socialist attitudes. A minority of people were actively involved in the black market – an estimated 15 per cent in the USSR – and they were generally regarded as being an unusual group, more materialistic than normal people.[86] So even though official propaganda relentlessly attacked youths obsessed with Western clothes as materialistic and work-shy, the youths themselves did not see the world in such Manichaean, black-and-white terms. Enthusiastic Komsomol activists were as likely to buy jeans from black-marketeers as dissidents.

The same can be said of that other hugely influential Western import: rock music, though in this case Communists did sometimes have more cause for concern. Rock music was, of course, strongly associated with the youth rebellions of the 1960s, and its lyrics were often imbued with a hedonistic Romanticism – as hostile to the principles of state socialism as technocratic capitalism. In some countries rock music became explicitly oppositional. The punk group Perfect provided the soundtrack to Poland's Solidarity movement in the early 1980s, and the post-invasion Czechoslovak group The Plastic People of the Universe was explicitly dissenting. One of its 1973 songs included the verse:

> Bring your kilogram of paranoia into balance!
> Throw off the horrible dictatorship!
> Quickly! Live, drink, puke!
> The bottle, the Beat!
> ⸱ Shit in your hand.[87]

Some of the group were arrested and tried, accused of 'extreme vulgarity with an anti-socialist and an anti-social impact, most of them extolling nihilism, decadence and clericalism'. During the trial, the defence did not deny their vulgarity, but ingeniously argued that they were just following Lenin's Bolshevik forthrightness, quoting his supposed maxim of 1922, 'bureaucracy is shit'.[88] They failed to convince the judge, however. The musicians were imprisoned, and their case became a cause célèbre, attracting international attention; it also led to the creation of Charter 77, a dissident group committed to forcing the regime to observe law and the constitution, whose most famous member was the playwright Václav Havel.

Most pop and rock music, however, was not so explicitly anti-Communist, and most Soviet bloc regimes in the 1970s were willing to tolerate it – as they rather had to, given the huge numbers who listened to Western radio stations. The East German party sponsored 'socialist realist rock', whilst the Soviets had their own anodyne, politically correct bands, like the Happy Guys – named after the 1930s socialist realist comedy film. The Komsomol produced long lists of banned groups: the heavy metal group Black Sabbath was accused of promoting 'violence' and 'religious obscurantism', whilst the crooner Julio Iglesias, bizarrely, was categorized as a promoter of 'neo-fascism'.[89] However, the implication was that other bands were fine, and Komsomol organizations themselves organized rock concerts. Alexei Yurchak tells of Aleksandr, formerly Komsomol secretary of a school in Yakutsk and then a student at the University of Novosibirsk, who was both unusually committed to the Communist ideal, and enthusiastic about prog rock and the British group Uriah Heep. He wrote, somewhat self-importantly, to a friend whose philosophy teacher had condemned rock music:

Tell your professor of aesthetics that one cannot look at the surrounding world from a prehistoric position ... 'The Beatles' is an unprecedented phenomenon of our life that in its impact on the human mind is, perhaps, comparable with space flights and nuclear physics.[90]

There was, then, no necessary contradiction between Communism and modern popular culture, but Communist parties still reacted to it in a 'prehistoric' way. Khrushchev and his generation had dragged Communism into the space and nuclear age. But modernity had moved on, and the ageing Communist leaders looked increasingly 'prehistoric', just as their politics seemed conservative.

VIII

'I like rightists.' Thus did the *ne plus ultra* of Communist radicalism, Mao Zedong, address the notorious anti-Communist, American President Richard Nixon, during their summit in Beijing on 21 February 1972. Equally implausibly, Nixon, not known for his interest in theory, claimed a desire to discuss 'philosophic problems [*sic*]' with Mao.[91] A mere two years earlier, few would have predicted this extraordinary rapprochement between the most radical force in the Communist world and the 'jittery chieftain of US imperialism', as the Chinese press had dubbed Nixon.

Just over three months later, on 29 May, Nixon met the other Communist bloc leader, Leonid Brezhnev, in the distinctly unrevolutionary surroundings of the Kremlin's St Catherine Hall, an architectural orgy of gilt and crystal. They had come together to sign a range of treaties, including the Strategic Arms Limitation Treaty (SALT) and a document outlining new foundations for US–Soviet relations.

Brezhnev's willingness to make peace was no surprise, given his character and the changes in Soviet thinking since the Cuban Missile Crisis. Also, the détente of 1972 achieved much of what Stalin had hoped for in 1945. The world was formally carved up into spheres of superpower influence. Now that East and West were more equal – at least in military and geopolitical terms – Brezhnev had succeeded in securing the recognition of the Communist empire in Eastern Europe which the Americans had denied for so long.

Mao's reincarnation as a peacemaker is, of course, more unexpected. But both Communist leaders were facing similar difficulties, weakened as they were by the revolutionary explosions of the late 1960s and strategically vulnerable. As Brezhnev was trying to stabilize his bloc after the Prague Spring of 1968, Mao was still restoring order after his own

Cultural Revolution, whilst anxious about military threats from the USSR and India. He therefore had good reasons to turn to the 'right'.

It was Nixon, however, who had most reason to compromise. For after its apparent success in suppressing revolutions in the Third World in the mid-1960s, American power was shaken by resistance in Vietnam. As in 1945 – and indeed 1919 – statesmen negotiating in grand residences and palatial halls could not impose their will on the turbulent South. And even more worryingly for Washington, it found that its opponents in the Third World had attracted sympathizers closer to home – on its own university campuses and in its inner cities. In 1968, from Washington to Istanbul, from Paris to Mexico City, politicians anxiously looked on as a new generation of revolutionaries took to the streets.

11

High Tide

I

In March 1968 a charity fashion show was held in Addis Ababa University's Ras Makonnen Hall in an atmosphere of high tension.[1] It was organized by Linda Thistle, an American Peace Corps volunteer who ran extracurricular activities at the girls' hostel, and followed a show the previous year when a Californian firm had donated modish creations from 'Salon Exquisite' and 'La Merveilleuse' – including the fashionable miniskirt. The 1967 show had generated critical articles in the Ethiopian student press; miniskirts were especially controversial. Whilst some of the arguments were nationalistic or Africanist – fashion shows were 'un-Ethiopian', an 'opium that has contaminated Europe' – denunciations also carried a distinctively Marxist tone. Indeed, such rhetoric had become pervasive in student circles at the time. 'The fashion show is nothing but [an] . . . agency for neo-colonialism . . . an instrument for the creation of [a] favourable market for [Western] luxury goods,' one article thundered.[2] Thistle responded to the criticism by excluding miniskirts and transforming the event into the first African fashion show on the continent, featuring only 'African fabrics'. But the radical students were not to be so easily appeased. Some argued that no fashion show, however nationalistic, could be justified in such a poor country. But questions of gender, and power relations between the male and female students, were also at issue. The men saw the event as evidence that Ethiopian women, seduced by Western mores and decadent lifestyles, were neglecting the more serious business of political discussion and activism. As one, Wellelign Makonnen, explained, 'Our sisters' heads have been washed with western soap . . . American philosophy of life leads nowhere.'[3]

The dispute eventually erupted into a small but violent demonstration. About fifty angry male students gathered outside the hall, abused and slapped the women, jostled foreign visitors, threw rotten eggs at some of the guests, and dragged others from their cars. Soon the police were summoned, violence escalated and the police arrested a number of radical students, including the editor of the student journal, *Struggle*. Meanwhile the University authorities – with the American University Vice-President at the forefront – decided to close the institute. Marxism and anti-Americanism had been a palpable sentiment amongst Ethiopian students for some time. Americans were associated with the increasingly unpopular regime of Emperor Haile Selassie, and a couple of months before the fashion show, the US Vice-President Hubert Humphrey had been prevented from speaking to students by a rowdy anti-Vietnam War demonstration.[4] But the events at the Ras Makonnen Hall signalled the final breach between the student movement and the Selassie regime; many of the students involved would go on to play a central role in the Ethiopian revolution of 1974.

A couple of weeks before, in New York, a young Berkeley graduate, Dona Fowler, read out a petition with sixty-six signatures, which championed the miniskirt and threatened to picket department stores with banners demanding 'Down with the Maxi!' But whilst Thistle's and Fowler's generation was just as angry about Vietnam and 'American imperialism' as its Ethiopian peers (and were indeed just as fond of Marxist sloganeering), their immediate concerns and overall vision of politics could not have been more different. For Fowler and her sisterly protestors, miniskirts symbolized personal and gender liberation, a rejection of the disciplined and masculine culture they believed had prevailed in the United States since World War II. But for Wellelign Makonnen, these garments flaunted a decadent attitude that was holding Ethiopia back; rigorous discipline, not frivolous liberation, was precisely what was needed. Both groups of youth voiced Marxist slogans, but those of the Ethiopians, which harked back to the militant Radical Marxism of late 1920s Russia, contrasted rather sharply with the more democratic, Romantic Marxism of the Americans.

The year 1968 saw the explosion of a whole range of long-established resentments heralding a high tide of revolutions throughout the world. Never before nor again would Marxist language be so fashionable and commonplace, as activists in the global South joined those in the West to struggle against 'imperialism', 'racism' and 'paternalism'. The number of Marxist regimes proliferated and the map of world Communism was at its reddest. And yet beneath the apparent unity, Communism had never been so diverse and disunited. The decade or so after 1968 saw it emerge in all its varieties. It was as if the whole history of the movement had been condensed into one febrile decade: from a late 1920s-style Stalinism in Africa, to a Cultural Revolution Maoism in Cambodia; from the Popular Front Communism of Allende's Chile, to the Marxist Romanticism of the *soixante-huitards*; from an almost Social Democratic Eurocommunism, to Nicaragua's Guevara-inspired guerrilla struggle.

But the sense of Romantic liberation and democracy beckoned by 1968 proved fleeting. Though the defeat of American power in Vietnam had emboldened a vast range of radical political and social forces, the United States and its allies soon rallied. And as Communist movements and regimes became entangled in great power rivalry and Cold War competition, the politics of protest meetings, discussion groups and love-ins gave way to those of guns, bombs and grenades. Khrushchev's Third World 'zone of peace' had become a bloody battlefield.

I I

In the summer of 1964 about a thousand American students from Northern universities – most of them white – travelled to the Southern state of Mississippi as part of a campaign by the Student Non-Violent Coordinating Committee (SNCC) to fight against the racial segregation that prevailed there. During the 'Mississippi Summer', the students lived in communes – or 'Freedom Houses' – or with local black families, registered voters and taught in 'Freedom Schools'.[5] Much of this earnest activity recalled the 'Going to the People' movement of idealistic young Russians in 1874. But unlike the Russian agrarian socialists, these American students were joining an already well-established grass-roots movement and their relations with the local African-Americans were good. Nevertheless, like their Russian forebears, they had to contend with repression. Ten days after they arrived, three students were beaten to death by segregationists (assisted by the local police) and many more were victimized.[6]

The Mississippi Summer was a radicalizing experience for all involved; and it was with anger, therefore, that a group of returning Berkeley students discovered they had been banned by the university authorities from land which they had previously used to set up stalls and distribute political leaflets. When the police turned up to enforce the ban, one student, Mario Savio, led a 'sit-in' around the police car – a technique used in Southern civil rights demonstrations. Attempts by Berkeley to punish Savio provoked the newly formed 'Free Speech Movement' (FSM) to organize massive sit-ins and demonstrations involving an estimated 10,500 of the university's 27,000 students. These remarkable events became a model for student protests that was swiftly exported, making Berkeley, in a sense, the epicentre of the series of rebellions (or even 'revolutions') which swept across America, Europe and beyond and which we call '1968'.

The Berkeley student movement, like its Russian and Chinese predecessors, was an attack on both legally sanctioned inequality – in this case ethnic – and on paternalistic power structures, and in particular the university authorities. Savio explicitly linked civil rights and university politics in a speech of 1965:

In Mississippi an autocratic and powerful minority rules, through organized violence, to suppress the vast, virtually powerless majority. In California, the privileged minority manipulates the University bureaucracy to suppress the students' political expression. That 'respectable' bureaucracy is the efficient enemy in a 'Brave New World'.[7]

Savio's language is strikingly radical, but before the 1964 demonstration he was not known as an especially politicized person. As an Italian-American – one of the ethnic groups that had been so successfully mobilized in the anti-Communist crusade – Savio was a beneficiary of the welfare state of Truman and Eisenhower. He was also attending a university (or 'multiversity' as it proclaimed itself) committed both to technological research – some of it for the military effort – and to social mobility, at least for white Americans. Berkeley was therefore typical of many universities, especially in the Western world, which had rapidly expanded and now counted amongst their students many people from rather modest families with no previous history of higher education. And like the first-generation students in 1860s Russia, they did not always appreciate the rather hierarchical and sometimes alienating educational culture they encountered. As one student recalled, 'We really did speak of Berkeley as a factory. Classes were immense, and you didn't feel that you could get near professors because they were this presence way up in front of the lectern.'[8]

In recent years it has become common to see the student rebellions of the 1960s as naïve and self-indulgent, but whatever our opinion of their objectives, we should not underestimate their historical significance. For like their Romantic student predecessors, they registered a fundamental shift in worldview. Western students of the 1960s and 1970s were taking a stand against all 'fathers', whether at home, in the university or in the state. Within the essentially fraternal communities fostered by student life, young people were questioning traditional hierarchies and authority, challenging prevailing attitudes to women and gay people, and even experimenting with new forms of domestic life in hippie communes.[9] At the same time the feminist and homosexual rights movements challenged traditional patriarchal attitudes. At the centre of their vision, therefore, lay a participatory form of democracy. Much of this iconoclasm was the consequence of a long-term change in the position of young people since the 1950s. With higher incomes and the autonomy of higher education, the young seemed more independent and assertive than in the past.

Moreover, as the elision of the university and the 'factory' illustrated, a critique of gender and ethnic discrimination, along with paternalism, could soon evolve into a more generalized attack on what was perceived by some as the 'military-welfare state' of the post-war era. To their critics it seemed that Western states, though not as regimented as their Soviet-style counterparts, demanded an intolerable degree of social discipline. Factories were governed by the 'Fordist' production line, and corporations had become huge, hierarchical and alienating. In the immediate aftermath of World War II, when many feared Stalinist subversion and accepted the imperative need to rebuild swiftly shattered economies and societies, such discipline had seemed defensible. But as in the Soviet bloc, once the threat of real war retreated, the young were less willing to submit to these constraints for which the compensations of welfare and consumer goods seemed insufficient. As Barbara Garson, the editor of the FSM newsletter, wrote: 'Many people were beginning to say: "I want to do something with my life. I don't want to be a sharply chiseled tool to be used for corporate profit."'[10]

In crucial respects, therefore, the Western student movements differed from their Russian and Chinese forebears: they were suspicious of the very technology, machinery and organizational modernity that their predecessors had so admired. Indeed they were challenging a fundamental element of the Promethean project, as was perhaps not surprising, given the fact that they did not perceive their societies as 'backward' and were uninterested in international competition. In some ways the protests of the mid-1960s, with their attacks on 'imperialistic' and 'militaristic' fathers by rebellious sons and daughters, were closer to the convention-ridiculing Dadaists of World War I than to Chernyshevskii and Lu Xun. The European Situationists of the 1950s and 1960s acknowledged that debt. Convinced that deep down Western men and women were 'alienated' by philistine consumer society, they believed that provocation and 'spectacle' would shock them out of their numbed complacency.[11] The main theorist of the 'Situationist International', Guy Debord, insisted that 'proletarian revolutions' had to be 'festivals' based on 'play' and the indulging of 'untrammelled desire'.[12] Debord's book, *The Society of the Spectacle*, published at the end of 1967, became one of the gospels of Western student revolutionaries.

But as had happened during World War I an essentially aesthetic frustration at bourgeois philistinism evolved into a more political Romanticism, bearing powerful Marxist influences. Indeed, it brought the return of the Lukács–Frankfurt School brand of Marxism to prominence. Herbert Marcuse, a pre-war Frankfurt School luminary who had left Germany for the United States in 1934, was to emerge as philosopher-in-chief of the 1968 student revolt. His *One-Dimensional Man*, published in 1964, was an extreme restatement of the Romantic Marxist worldview, albeit one now exotically blended with Freud. Marcuse argued that modern capitalism was imbued with a technocratic rationality that had fused the 'Welfare state and the Warfare state' to produce a 'society of total mobilization'. Consumerism and hierarchical institutions like corporations, the military and political parties had established a 'mechanics of conformity', people were alienated and autonomy was suppressed whilst the genuinely pleasurable, creative and erotic aspects of life had been outlawed.[13] In Marcuse's rejection of the Modernist Marxism of planning and rationality, one sees a revival of Fourier's phalansteries and the Romantic 'Young Marx'. And given his rejection of the Marxist synthesis of modernity and revolution, it is hardly surprising that Marcuse condemned Soviet Communism as vociferously as he did capitalism. For him both industrial capitalism and Communism were heirs of Nazism – 'totalitarian' orders, ruled by soulless technocratic elites.

Marcuse's deep mistrust of technology and science, and his view of Nazism, industrial capitalism and Soviet Communism as all symptomatic of a 'totalitarian' syndrome, permeated the Romantic left politics and culture of the 1960s. Domineering fathers, Nazis and atom bombs were vividly yoked in the soon cultic poetry of the American Sylvia Plath. And 1960s technophobia haunted the powerful films of Stanley Kubrick. The figure of Dr Strangelove in his 1964 satirical film of that name encapsulated many of Marcuse's themes – a bomb-obsessed German-born scientist and adviser to the American president, whose mechanical arm kept rising in an involuntary Nazi salute.[14] In *2001: A Space Odyssey*, first shown in 1968, technological progress is shown as a sinister force that leads to violence, most famously in the form of the murderous Cyclopean computer HAL.[15] Mario Savio's most famous speech at the Berkeley rallies was full of this Romantic rhetoric:

> There is a time when the operation of the machine becomes so odious, makes you so sick at heart, that you can't take part, you can't even tacitly take part. And you've got to put the bodies upon the gears and upon the wheels, upon the levers, upon all the apparatus and you've got to make it stop.[16]

Marcuse was, however, merely the most prominent of the 'New Left' thinkers – an eclectic group, amongst whom we can count the American sociologist C. Wright Mills, the British historian E. P. Thompson and the Greek-born Trotskyist intellectual Cornelius Castoriadis. In adopting the label 'New Left', they consciously defined themselves against an 'old' left, both Social Democratic and Soviet Communist. Their objections to the old left were numerous; they disliked its obsession with party organization and hierarchy, championing instead free discussion and participatory democracy. But at its root the conflict between old and new left turned on conceptions of equality and power: for 1960s thinkers economic equality alone (a core value of the old left) was simply not enough. More important was a change in authority relations, a cultural revolution and an end to all forms of hierarchy. As Gregory Calvert, a president of the New Left Students for a Democratic Society (SDS) explained, 'revolutionary mass movements are not built out of a

desire for the acquisition of material goods ... Revolutionary movements are freedom struggles born out of the perception of the contradictions between human potentiality and oppressive actuality.'[17]

This opposition to 'economistic' Marxism was closely connected
with disillusionment with the industrial working class, which (at least in
northern Europe and the United States) the radicals believed had been
bought off by the 'warfare–welfare state'. The new revolutionaries
would be an alliance of groups who suffered from legal, political or
racial discrimination in a world dominated by an imperialistic United
States – an alliance of students, African-Americans, Third World revolutionaries, women and homosexuals. As Wright Mills wrote in his
'Letter to the New Left' of 1960:

> Forget Victorian [i.e. Kautskian, technocratic] Marxism, except when you
> need it; and read Lenin, again (be careful) – Rosa Luxemburg too ...
>
> Whatever else it may be, it's not [utopian]. Tell it to the students of
> Japan. Tell it to the Negro sit-ins. Tell it to the Cuban Revolutionaries. Tell
> it to the people of the Hungry-nation bloc.[18]

By the early 1960s the parallels between African-American civil rights
at home and American anti-Communism abroad seemed obvious to
some intellectuals and activists. But it was only with the escalation of
the Vietnam War in 1965 that the comparison became a commonplace.
With the doubling of military conscription, students were inevitably
radicalized. Although deferments were possible, avoiding the draft was
often difficult. Protests began in the universities in 1965, and radical
academics began to cancel normal lectures and organize 'teach-ins',
based on the Mississippi Freedom Schools – day-long seminars on the
war. One Students for a Democratic Society (SDS) member remembered
how powerful the New Left conception of an alliance between students,
blacks and Vietnamese had become:

> 1965 – that was the year for me of the connection between all this rhetoric
> of American values and what we were really doing. The connection between
> civil rights and the Vietnam war. Keeping down a large underbelly minority
> population at home and bombing back to the stone-age a peasant popula-
> tion of another race and culture abroad.[19]

A radical anti-imperialist language became increasingly dominant within
the SDS. As another SDS activist and future terrorist, Cathy Wilkerson,

recalled, it was at this time that Vietnam and a perception of persistent economic inequality led her from liberal democracy to the revolutionary belief that 'we could sweep out the old government ourselves', and 'any "sweeping out" would not be accomplished without a fight, given the violent nature of our government'.[20] By 1967, the SDS leadership – though not always the rank-and-file – was turning to revolutionary Marxism, because, as Carl Oglesby explained, 'there was – and is – no other coherent, integrative, and explicit philosophy of revolution'.[21]

A similar radicalization was occurring in the civil-rights movement. The Vietnam conflict was the cause of a double resentment, as resources were funnelled away from social programmes and into the war, whilst a far higher proportion of blacks than whites found themselves conscripted. Martin Luther King's non-violent strategy which had worked so well in the South did not resonate with the radical youths of the Northern cities where violent riots erupted in the summer of 1967.[22] A new generation of Black Power politicians drew freely from the rhetoric of guerrilla Communists, and in particular the violent Third Worldism of the Martinique-born revolutionary, Franz Fanon. Speaking in London in 1967, one of Black Power's most charismatic spokesmen, Stokely Carmichael, quoted Fanon and Che Guevara in a paean of praise to political violence, adding:

> We are working to increase the revolutionary consciousness of black people in America to join with the Third World. Whether or not violence is used is not decided by us, but by the white West ... We are not any longer going to bow our heads to any white man. If he touches one black man in the United States, he is going to war with every black man in the United States.[23]

The rebellion also spread to America's 'empire by invitation' in Western Europe. Anger at events in Vietnam was central to all student protests there, particularly once TV screens began to fill with images of airborne, mechanized violence. Opposition to the war grew rapidly in those states where the government supported the conflict, as in Britain. One British student remembered: 'There was the bombing and the relentlessness of the bombing ... I think people now probably don't understand that, but it was just terrible. Everything that was progress was being used to destroy ... My feelings were so strong that I feared the sense of my own violence.'[24] Europe's elites began to question their support for the United

States. France's De Gaulle refused to contribute to NATO operations, and the British declared that financial difficulties would force them to reduce their troop commitment in Europe.

The United States, of course, never experienced a Marxist revolution, but 1968 brought a taste of it. At home and abroad waves of rebellion, partly inspired by ethnic nationalism, partly by various very different forms of Marxism, were threatening the American *imperium*. President Johnson, faced with 'guerrillas' in both urban America and Vietnam, was determined to continue welfare at home and warfare abroad. But as in so many empires in the past, a combination of domestic unrest, defeat abroad and financial profligacy provoked a crisis.

The (partial) defeat came in Vietnam, and was of huge symbolic importance. Johnson, convinced that its fall would undermine American credibility and embolden Moscow and Beijing throughout the world, had decided to send American troops into Vietnam in 1965. And he had a point: Vietnam was central to the Cold War conflicts, and America's successful halting of the North Vietnamese advance in 1954 had indeed blunted Moscow's and Beijing's resolve in the Third World for some time. However, as critics argued, by 'Americanizing' the conflict, Johnson had dangerously raised the stakes. Undersecretary of State George Ball's prediction that a military failure would have far worse consequences for American credibility than a peaceful compromise, proved prescient.[25] Though initially pessimistic about the Vietnamese Communists' prospects, Moscow and Beijing were determined to counter American military support with their own, and poured money and weapons into the conflict. The result was stalemate. Meanwhile, American bombing and destruction of forests with chemical defoliants only pushed more South Vietnamese into the arms of the Viet Cong.

In January 1968, in what became known as the 'Tet Offensive' after the Vietnamese term for New Year, 67,000 Viet Cong troops attacked the major cities in the South. It was, in effect, a mass suicide mission, and though it was eventually beaten back, the accompanying media images of Communist fighters attacking and occupying the United States embassy in Saigon were deeply humiliating for Washington, and encouraged radicals everywhere. As one West Berlin student remembered:

It was a world-shaking event that allowed me to imagine what the Russian revolution must have meant for people with socialist ideals. There, next to the American embassy in Saigon, the battle was raging from house to house, the NLF's [i.e. Viet Cong's] flag was flying over Hue. It was said that the students were mainly holding the city. There was no doubt now – the world revolution was dawning.[26]

The Johnson administration was stunned. The Secretary of Defense, Clark Clifford, remembered that 'there was, for a brief time, something approaching paralysis, and a sense of events spiraling out of control of the nation's leaders'.[27] The elite split, with the military demanding more troops whilst Clifford and others called for disengagement. More importantly, the markets began to lose faith in Washington's ability to finance the war, and in March the dollar came under serious strain as investors fled. The old Bretton Woods system that fixed the dollar to gold was under threat.

Johnson was forced into a partial retreat. The war continued, but on 31 March he announced that the escalation was over: bombing was to be limited, military demands for a massive build-up of troops were rejected, and peace talks offered. Meanwhile, he was compelled to accept that the Bretton Woods system, and with it the economic hegemony the United States had enjoyed since 1945, was unsustainable. As the dollar cracked, so did the legitimacy of American global power, both at home and abroad. The spring and summer of 1968 saw the high point of protests throughout the world as the enemies of American power scented weakness. In the United States, the assassination of Martin Luther King in March sparked off riots in 126 cities, whilst in August student protests at the Chicago Democratic Party Convention brought police repression.

Outside the United States, in its Western sphere of influence, the Vietnam War and 'American imperialism' (along with more mundane university governance grievances) became the major targets of student demonstrations. Students fought with police from Rome to Tokyo, from Paris to West Berlin. But the rebellions also took on specific national colourings. In countries with a fascist past – Germany and Italy – students demanded that the guilt of the older generation, which they believed had been suppressed, be exposed. In southern Europe workers played a central role in the revolts.[28] Elsewhere, the rhetoric of civil rights merged with Radical Marxism to fuel nationalistic protests. In Belgium, students protested against the dominance of the French language in Flemish universities. In Northern Ireland, a broad alliance of liberal Republicans, Catholics and Marxists challenged the Protestant ascendancy, drawing on the example of American civil rights. It became more radical as violence increased, and in 1969 Republican Marxists took over the Ulster civil rights movement, casting it as a struggle against imperialism.

Everywhere, though, whatever the local specificities, a Romantic, participatory Marxism was the inspiration – one that set itself firmly against Soviet Marxism (especially coming so soon on the heels of the Soviet invasion of Czechoslovakia). Che Guevara was now joined by Ho Chi Minh in a new pantheon of leftist heroes – Ho's distinction being principally his defiance of the USA; people knew little of his politics. Stalin, however, had definitely been excluded.

The immediate consequence of the 1968 rebellions and the North Vietnamese offensive was the humbling of various Western governments and politicians. Lyndon Johnson announced that he would not seek another presidential term; the Belgian government fell in February; and in France a general strike seriously undermined President De Gaulle, and forced Prime Minister Pompidou to agree to a massive 35 per cent increase in the minimum wage. But the longer-term repercussions of this series of rebellions were more profound. They signalled the unwillingness of the West's youth to fight for control of the global South, whilst also triggering a wage explosion that undermined the economic order established at Bretton Woods. The *soixante-huitards* had then, in effect, signalled the beginning of the end of the post-World War II order.[29]

Nowhere, however, did the movements of 1968 achieve lasting power. In large part this was the result of the diversity of their objectives. Students, concerned with democratizing everyday life, and workers, often more concerned with economic demands, found it especially difficult to forge long-lasting alliances. The New Left's inherent suspicion of conventional 'bureaucratic' politics made it difficult to achieve lasting goals. Shunning party organization, they failed to develop coherent programmes or sustain political victories.

In the short term, the convulsions of 1968 contributed to the electoral victories of the right. Elections in France brought a landslide victory for De Gaulle, and the conservative Republican Richard Nixon won the United States presidency, promising to counter the 'revolutionary struggle to seize the universities of this country'.[30] The West had experienced a revolutionary crisis akin to the failed revolutions of

1789–1815, 1848 and 1918–19; and like them it too was followed by a pronounced swing to the right. Yet it was some time before order was to be restored.

On the radical left, the defeats of the summer of 1968 led to a reassessment of the revolutionary project. Some of the rebels now decided that the New Left was too democratic in these violent times, and more Radical, far-left Marxist parties emerged, mainly Maoist and Trotskyist.[31] Their precise character varied from place to place. Some, like the Maoist *Gauche Prolétarienne* (Proletarian Left) – whose sympathizers included much of the cream of the French intelligentsia, including Jean-Paul Sartre, the philosopher Michel Foucault and the film-maker Jean-Luc Godard – were relatively decentralized.[32] Daniel Singer, a participant in the Parisian *évènements* of 1968, described the appeal of the Maoists:

> There is something of the Russian *narodniki* [1870s agrarian socialists] in the young Maoists. The former preached among peasants; the latter are going to the workers in order *To Serve the People*, to quote the title of their journal. Quotations from the little red book and the cult of Mao were not the ideal means of attracting critical students, but they were attracted by China's Cultural Revolution, with its anti-bureaucratic message and its appeal to youth. Their ideological enthusiasm and personal abnegation enabled the young Maoists to make substantial gains among university and high school students.[33]

More commonly, however, Maoists valued organization and discipline, even more so than Trotskyists. This Radical Marxist obsession with ideological coherence and unity led to endless splits and disputes – so well lampooned in the biblical satire *Monty Python's Life of Brian* (1979), in the absurd rivalry between the Judean People's Front, the People's Front of Judea, the Judean Popular People's Front and the one-man Popular Front of Judea.[34] Yet whilst tiny groupuscules proliferated, the far left was surprisingly popular in some countries. Almost 100,000 activists were involved in Italy, and in Germany polls showed that 30 per cent of secondary and university students sympathized with Communist ideologies – largely of the New Left or far-left variety.[35]

The same conviction that New Leftist participatory democracy had failed inspired the transition to a more radicalized politics of conspiracy and terrorism. If the Vietnamese had won victories through a disciplined Marxist-Leninist party and military force, surely that was the right strategy in the West as well? Such was the thinking of the terrorist Weathermen, the group named after a line in a Bob Dylan song ('You don't need a weatherman to know which way the wind blows') that broke from the SDS in 1969. SDS member Cathy Wilkerson remembered the reasoning behind this decision to build a Marxist-Leninist party, for 'popular democracy must be a luxury that we would have to forgo until the world became a more peaceful place'.[36] Members now trained themselves in martial arts and subjected themselves to Maoist self-criticism sessions. The 'Americong', as they called themselves, sought to 'bring the war home' with violent protests and bombings.

Even so, these extremists were very small in number, especially in America. Marxist terrorists, though, had more impact elsewhere. In Northern Ireland, the Provisional Irish Republican Army (IRA) split from the Marxist Republicans and launched an armed struggle for a united Ireland; in France the *Gauche Prolétarienne* also formed an armed wing. But the most fertile ground for terrorism lay in West Germany and Italy, where they used the argument that the authorities were profoundly compromised by the Nazi or Fascist pasts.[37] In both countries the terrorists were drawn largely from the educated middle class and included a high proportion of women. The most prominent German group was the Red Army Faction (RAF), commonly called the 'Baader–Meinhof Gang' after the charismatic, aggressive and violence-loving Andreas Baader and the well-known left-wing journalist Ulrike Meinhof. Meinhof, who came from an anti-Nazi family, had originally joined the illegal East-German-aligned German Communist Party (KPD) in 1958, believing that it best embodied the anti-fascist tradition, before eventually embracing the New Left.[38]

The real or supposed persistence of fascism in contemporary Germany was not, however, the most inflammatory issue; it was the question of German official attitudes to American-supported regimes in the Third World – though when a student demonstrator was killed during a visit by the Shah of Iran in 1967 the themes converged. From 1970 the group began their campaign of urban terrorism, which continued until the gang's arrest in 1972. Yet even from within prison the RAF's leaders managed to recruit and orchestrate a new group of terrorists. Though their numbers were tiny, the terrorists elicited a notable degree of public support, with a quarter of West Germans under the age of thirty expressing broad sympathy in 1971, and 14 per cent actively willing to help.[39]

Italy's terrorist groups were more numerous and larger and had deeper roots in society. Like the German terrorists, they believed that they were continuing the wartime struggle against a quasi-fascist state, and in the case of Italy they could appeal to the tradition of the wartime Resistance. It was widely believed that authoritarian groups within the Italian state favoured the use of violent tactics against radical students and workers, and that bombings in Milan in 1969 had been organized by neo-fascist groups in collaboration with the police and the CIA to justify a crackdown. For one terrorist, the bombings 'marked a decisive turning point for me as it closed the circle (which until then had still seemed open) between the institutions, the state and the right'.[40]

However, industrial unrest also gave the Italian extreme left their opportunity. Worker unrest formed a much greater part of '1968' in southern Europe than in the North or the United States. Italy saw some of the most radical worker unrest with a strike wave that lasted for two years. Wage demands were important, but so too were more radical, egalitarian demands for self-management. Young workers followed students in demanding participatory democracy, and serious concessions were extracted from employers, including the election of factory councils. The 'Red Brigades' – the most prominent of all terrorist groups – emerged from radicals involved in the rash of strikes that hit urban North Italy in the late 1960s and early 1970s.[41] And though from the mid-1970s repression forced the Red Brigades to become more clandestine, they also became more violent – and more effective in disrupting the state.

Italy was undergoing an economic downturn, but it was not alone in suffering serious industrial unrest. The 1968 disturbances in France were so effective because workers joined with students in a general strike that lasted over a fortnight. The diminished authority of governments after 1968 emboldened workers throughout Europe and the United States, but there were other reasons for their assertiveness. Full employment in some countries and post-1968 inflation gave them power, and also a new radical generation of workers was growing to maturity. Business had invested in new European plants in the 1940s and 1950s, taking advantage of cheap migrant labour, whether from southern Europe in the case of the north-west, or from the countryside within the nation in the case of southern Europe itself. As is so often the case, however, second-generation migrants proved less willing to put up with the hardships their parents had endured. Countries – like Italy – that relied on their own citizens rather than foreign immigrants were especially affected by worker radicalism, because internal migrants linked industrial disputes with broader demands for equality and recognition.[42]

The Vietnam crisis, then, released and radicalized a cascade of pre-existing grievances amongst students, ethnic minorities and workers. But whilst Marxist-Leninist rhetoric became fashionable, the rebels were, in reality, rejecting the orthodox, pro-Soviet Marxism of modernity and political pragmatism. Nineteen sixty-eight – both the student and worker rebellions in the West, and the Prague Spring in the East – was a major challenge to all orthodox Communist parties fearful of being outflanked by a new radical left. For a time the French party condemned the Soviet invasion of Czechoslovakia, but under Soviet pressure it soon accepted the Husák 'normalization'. It also refused to accept that France was experiencing a genuine revolutionary situation, and Waldeck Rochet accused the students of being 'typical petty-bourgeois radicals'.[43] The domestic rebellions, and the Prague Spring after them, led to serious splits within the party, though it retained its 21.5 per cent of the vote in the 1969 elections. The Italian party, in contrast, remained critical of the Soviets (even though it refused to split with them), and succeeded in appealing to some of the more radical student and working-class left. But ultimately the radical left was not tamed, and the Communists were forced to confront them later in the decade.

Latin America experienced a similar series of student and urban rebellions in the late 1960s, under the banner of a similarly eclectic Romantic Marxism. The failures of the guerrilla revolutions in the mid-1960s had undermined the radical left's faith in the Cuban model of the rural *foco*, and guerrilla war was now brought to the towns. Che Guevara's *Guerrilla War* gave way to the *Mini-manual of an Urban Guerrilla* (1969). For its Brazilian author, Carlos Marighella, a former Communist leader and founder, in 1967, of a terrorist organization:

> the accusation of 'violence' or 'terrorism' no longer has the negative meaning it used to have . . . Today, to be 'violent' or a 'terrorist' is a quality that ennobles any honourable person, because it is an act worthy of a revolutionary engaged in armed struggle against the shameful [Brazilian] military dictatorship and its atrocities.[44]

Urban terrorism was strongest in Uruguay and Argentina, where the left faced repressive, conservative military regimes. Some terrorists were Marxist (like the Trotskyist Argentinian People's Revolutionary Army (ERP)), but others preferred a mixture of populist nationalist and left-wing ideas (such as the Argentinian Montoneros and Uruguayan Tupamaros). The Montoneros and the ERP both benefited from the labour militancy that swept Argentina, as it did in so many other parts of Latin America during the period.[45]

Left-wing politics now arrived in a curious convoy of vehicles, sometimes rather surprising ones. In Peru it was the military, which took power in 1968 deploying Marxist theory and pro-Third-World rhetoric, and eagerly supported by the Peruvian Communist Party. Other unlikely Marxists included a group of Catholic priests, amongst whom was the Colombian Camillo Torres – 'Che in a cassock' as he was called. For Torres, the principles of Christianity, notably 'love thy neighbour', 'coincide in action and in practice with some Marxist-Leninist methods and objectives'.[46] Torres, who decided to join a Colombian guerrilla group in the mountains and was killed in 1966, was hardly a typical cleric. Nevertheless, the Catholic Church was so worried about the appeal of Marxism that a meeting of bishops in the Colombian city of Medellín in August 1968 resolved to endorse a socially aware Christianity and fight against the 'unjust consequences of the excessive inequalities between poor and rich, weak and powerful'.[47] The Church authorities were certainly not becoming Marxist, but many 'liberation theology' priests believed that the combined teachings of Karl Marx and Jesus Christ made for a complete education.

Against these competitors, the orthodox pro-Soviet Communist parties of Latin America seemed distinctly unattractive, especially as they generally failed to adapt to new realities. Concentrating on the working class, they neglected the rapidly growing 'under-class' of urban shanty-dwellers. But they did have some successes, most notably their participation in the 1970 Chilean coalition government of the Socialist Salvador Allende, who had been a supporter of Pedro Cerda's Spanish-inspired Popular Front in the 1930s.

The Cubans were also losing their appeal on the continent, especially as economic failures and anxieties about Nixon's election forced them back into Moscow's embrace. Castro refused to condemn the invasion of Czechoslovakia in 1968, and soon he too caved in to Soviet pressure and abandoned the ambitious mobilizing economic policies the Soviets so disapproved of. The 'voluntary labour' and mass mobilizations pursued since the mid-1960s had produced exhaustion and cynicism, and in 1970 Castro was forced to accept a more Modernist, Soviet-style economic regime of labour discipline and wage incentives.[48] In 1972, the notion of a separate Cuban model of socialism was dealt a severe blow when Cuba became a member of Comecon. This did not, however, mark the end of Cuba's activist, independent foreign policy. As the Cubans lost their revolutionary lustre in Latin America, they – together with their new Soviet allies – found new disciples in Africa.

III

In January 1966, the leader of the Guinean guerrilla movement, Amílcar Cabral, gave an optimistic assessment of the state of the world revolution, whilst also condemning Khrushchev's old notion that the Third World was a 'zone of peace':

> the present situation of national liberation struggles in the world (especially in Vietnam, the Congo and Zimbabwe) as well as the situation of permanent violence . . . in certain countries which have gained their independence in the so-called peaceful way, show us . . . that compromises with imperialism do not work . . . that the normal way of national liberation . . . is *armed struggle*.[49]

The charismatic Cabral was speaking in Havana, at Castro's 'First Solidarity Conference of the Peoples of Africa, Asia and Latin America' – the so-called 'Tricontinental Conference'. It was designed to be a Marxist replacement for Bandung, a declaration that the old socialist Third World was dead and had been reborn in more militant form. After the many setbacks of the mid-1960s, and as Communists were being massacred in Indonesia at that exact same time, not all were convinced that the time was ripe for such assertiveness. But Castro agreed with Cabral: the Americans were losing ground in Vietnam, and the time was right for an intensified armed struggle throughout the world.[50]

However, it was not just the new international balance of power that radicalized Third World leaders in the late 1960s and early 1970s.

Marxist ideas from the West played a role, whether communicated through links with the Portuguese, French or Italian Communist parties, or through students studying abroad, as was the case in Ethiopia.[51] Generational change was also important. Many believed that the Bandung generation had not delivered on its promise that a moderate form of socialism would deliver economic development and international prestige. By refusing to challenge local chiefs and 'tribes', critics argued, the indigenous socialists had left in place a powerful class of neo-colonial collaborators who merely served the interests of the old imperial powers. As Cabral explained in his long and densely theoretical speech to fellow revolutionaries, 'the submission of the local "ruling" class to the ruling class of the dominating country limits or prevents the development of the productive forces'.[52]

Cabral was never a dogmatic Marxist-Leninist, but his fluency in its syntax shows how pervasive the Marxist style of thinking had become amongst much of the African left by the late 1960s.[53] And the variety of 'Marxism-Leninism' that was to become so powerful there was in many ways reminiscent of 1930s Radical Stalinism, combining, as it did, anti-imperialist nationalism, a model of development that stressed 'modernity' and the city over 'tradition' and the countryside, and a hard-line willingness to use violence.[54] Of course, African Marxist-Leninists accepted that their 'proletariats' were tiny, but they still clung to the belief that, given the right policies, they could swiftly build a 'Dictatorship of the Proletariat'. A coalition of various progressive classes would take power and build heavy industry, and with it a revolutionary proletariat. These Marxist-Leninists claimed to have the solutions to underdevelopment that the indigenous socialists so conspicuously lacked. Only a vanguard party, they argued, would have the will and focus to remove the local elites who were so selfishly holding their countries back; their commitment to 'class struggle' allowed them to use the violence so necessary to resist imperialists and dislodge their internal bourgeois allies; and their Marxist internationalism would attract funding from the USSR at a time when the Soviets themselves were moving in a more 'Stalinist' direction.

In the last respect at least, the Afro-Communists were right. From the late 1960s, the ideologists in the party Central Committee's International Department (including Karen Brutents and the future Gorbachev advisers Georgii Shakhnazarov and Vadim Zagladin) began to develop an analysis of the reasons for Communism's defeats in the middle part of the decade. They concluded that Khrushchev's 'united front'-style policy and belief in peaceful transitions from indigenous socialism to Communism had been far too optimistic. The frequent American interventions had convinced them that only vanguard parties of orthodox Marxist-Leninists could protect the left in the Third World. But far from being pessimistic, they argued that the prospects for Communism were bright. American difficulties in Vietnam would weaken the West's prestige, whilst continued Western intervention would also strengthen socialism. 'Bourgeois' nationalists, they argued, denied true independence by the neo-colonial West, would have to forge alliances with the still small, but growing working-class and peasant movements. Guided by a party vanguard, pro-Communist nationalists would fight 'reactionary' nationalists, and then engineer transitions to socialism, even in these 'backward' peasant societies.[55] In some ways, then, the Soviet response to the setbacks of 1964–6 in the Third World was a milder version of Stalin's reaction to the failures of the united front in 1927–8: Communists would have to be more sectarian and cohesive; outside the global North, the era was one of 'struggle' between the capitalist and Communist worlds, not peaceful coexistence; and domestically the time could be ripe for a rapid advance to socialist states and economies – in the agrarian Third World, as in the peasant Soviet Union forty years earlier.

One of the first regions to experience the full force of Marxist-Leninist rebellion against the Bandung generation was the Middle East. Israel's defeat of Syria and Egypt in the six-day war of 1967 was a humiliation for Arab socialism throughout the region, whether Syria's 'Ba'athism' or Nasser's socialism. After the war, the Arab states lost influence over the Palestinian nationalist movement, which they had tried to control by supporting the creation of the Palestine Liberation Organization (PLO) in 1964. Yasser Arafat's more radically nationalist Fatah ('Victory') group began to displace its rivals, championing a guerrilla struggle inspired by Franz Fanon and the Vietnamese example.[56] In 1967 Fatah was joined as a member of the PLO by the Popular Front for the Liberation of Palestine, which declared itself a fully Marxist-Leninist party in 1969 and received Soviet backing from 1970.[57] For these Palestinians, the conflict with American-backed Israel was more than just an Arab affair: it was part of the global struggle against imperialism.

Nasser's defeat also contributed to the foundation of the first

Marxist-Leninist regime in the region, in South Yemen. One of the main guerrilla nationalist organizations fighting the British, the Nasser-backed National Liberation Front (NLF), had already become disillusioned with its patron from 1965 when Egypt began to withdraw its support. The NLF regarded itself as a radical party, fighting for the rights of small peasants against landowners, and when the British handed over power to the NLF in November 1967, the People's Democratic Republic of Yemen declared itself a Marxist-Leninist state.[58]

The Vietnamese example inevitably encouraged other peasant-based guerrilla movements in many other regions throughout the world. In West Bengal, rural rebellion against landlords in Naxalbari village were joined by Marxist students from Calcutta, encouraged by Beijing's Cultural Revolution radicalism. The formally pro-Beijing Communist Party of India (Marxist), which had just achieved power in West Bengal, repressed the rebellions, and in 1969 the radical former student Charu Mazumdar formed the militantly Maoist Communist Party of India (Marxist-Leninist) – commonly called the 'Naxalites'.[59]

In Portuguese Africa, too, the guerrilla movements moved further towards Marxism, and from 1970, under the leadership of Samora Machel, the Mozambican anti-colonial front – FRELIMO – finally declared itself a socialist movement. Machel, a former nurse from a family with a long anti-colonial tradition, was not a doctrinaire Marxist-Leninist of the Agostinho Neto type, but he used Marxist language to express a fundamentally moral critique of the Portuguese.[60] And, like the other anti-colonial movements in Portuguese Africa, FRELIMO was conducting a self-consciously Maoist-style 'people's war'.[61] The 'people's war' strategy involved efforts to win over peasants by establishing rural schools and hospitals, whilst also involving peasants in 'mass line'-style 'democracy'. More radical still were the attempts made in guerrilla-liberated areas to dismantle old hierarchies of gender and generation by challenging the power of chiefs and promoting women and younger men in their political organizations and guerrilla bands.[62]

How far these movements really did mobilize peasants is a matter of debate. Communists could find it very difficult to secure peasant support because the political culture they were imposing seemed very alien. As had been the case in 'liberated areas' in 1930s and 1940s China, some peasants benefited from and supported the new order, whilst many more merely put up with Communist rule because they had to.[63] The guerrillas used some violence to control their areas, and the terror seems to have become particularly extensive in parts of Eastern Angola, where the MPLA tried and executed alleged traitors (and even persecuted witches, despite its supposed Marxist hostility to superstition).[64] The Angolan movement was the least successful militarily, and in Mozambique, too, the Portuguese were not seriously threatened by an all-out FRELIMO military victory.[65] Only in the much smaller and less divided Guinea-Bissau did the PAIGC become a government-in-waiting, securing some three quarters of Guinea-Bissau's territory by 1972. Even so, all of the rebels could draw from a deep well of dissatisfaction with Portuguese rule. Economic growth caused divisions between those who had bene-fited from Portuguese rule and those who had not, whilst Portuguese repression alienated many.[66] Naturally Portugal – a small, relatively poor country – found it increasingly difficult to sustain these debilitating wars, which by 1968 consumed 40 per cent of the state budget.

The anti-apartheid guerrilla movement in South Africa was in far worse shape than its Mozambique counterparts at the end of the 1960s. It also had special reasons to welcome the Soviets' renewed interest in the continent, as Moscow had already been giving substantially more assistance to Oliver Tambo's African National Congress (ANC) than it had to the South African Communist Party proper, which it regarded as too independent (and too white).

A weakened United States did not find it easy to respond to this left-ward surge in southern Africa, or to the Soviets' and Cubans' willing-ness to take advantage of it. Nixon and his influential adviser, Henry Kissinger, strongly objected to Kennedy-style efforts to spread democ-racy, convinced they would not work. Both the US President and Kissinger dismissed the global South as a backward, benighted and incorrigibly authoritarian place which had been by-passed by history. Kissinger informed a dumb-struck Chilean foreign minister that 'Noth-ing important can come from the South . . . The axis of history starts in Moscow, goes to Bonn, crosses over to Washington, and then goes on to Tokyo.'[67] The Americans' main concern, therefore, was simply to block Soviet and Cuban influence as effectively as possible, whilst not repeat-ing Johnson's mistakes by intervening directly. Their solution was to franchise out the struggle against Communism in the Third World to a series of loyal 'gendarmes' of various political colourings – from the authoritarian Shah of Iran, Somoza of Nicaragua, Suharto of Indonesia and Médici of Brazil, to apartheid South Africa, and democratic Israel and Turkey – all of whom would be generously rewarded by Washington for their trouble. Efforts were also made to 'Vietnamize' the South-East Asian conflict, withdrawing US troops and creating a pro-American regime that could survive by itself. Finally Nixon hoped that the détente process itself would relieve pressure on American power by dissuading Moscow from intervening in the global South.

Though undoubtedly energetic, Nixon and Kissinger were playing a weak hand; their machinations not only failed to stop the Soviets but left many intellectuals in the Third World enraged and more willing than ever to contemplate Marxist solutions. Moscow, for its part, did not see why détente with the United States should stop it from promoting Communism outside Europe, especially when the United States was continuing to intervene to strangle it (as in Chile in 1973). Moreover, challenged by North Vietnam, Cuba, the European parties and (a much weakened) China, the Soviet authorities became even more determined to retain their international socialist pre-eminence. Party intellectuals in the Central Committee saw opportunities to re-ignite the flame of socialist internationalism at a time when the regime at home was so lacking in ideological sparkle. And the more *realpolitik*-obsessed military regarded the new scramble for Africa as a way of keeping its hand in with the United States in the superpower game.[68]

America's gendarme strategy had serious weaknesses. The alliance it fostered with apartheid South Africa was especially damaging, as it seriously undermined Washington's efforts to maintain the moral high ground in Africa and made it very difficult for African nationalists to feel sympathy with the United States. In Vietnam, meanwhile, Washington's efforts to establish a powerful American-backed figure in Nguyen Van Thieu failed because his base of support was too narrow. His regime collapsed in 1975, two years after American troops had left, and Vietnam united under Communist rule.

Meanwhile, gendarmes could not always be relied on to hold the line in those regions where the United States believed Communism was spreading. In Allende's Chile, Kissinger saw a dangerously attractive Communism, and he was determined to change the regime. But he could not rely on local allies; rather he used economic sanctions and covert support for the opposition. Allende gave his opponents an excuse to intervene when his radical economic policies of land redistribution and nationalization alienated the middle classes and provoked strikes, and in 1973 General Pinochet led a right-wing military coup against the President, claiming that he was rescuing Chile from an economic crisis.[69] He proceeded to ban leftist parties and some 3,200 were killed and 30,000 tortured. The United States' precise role is unclear, but whatever the level of its involvement, the experience of a democratically elected Popular Front-style government being ousted by military force, with the support of foreign backers, had distinct echoes of 1930s Spain. Washington had suffered yet another blow to its standing in the Third World.[70]

There was, however, one area where the gendarme policy at first sight seems to have worked: the Middle East. When, in October 1973, Arab armies attacked Israel, they were repulsed with American help and the Soviets backed down from their threats to send aid to Egypt. The United States, with its Israeli ally, had shown itself to be the master of the region. But this was to be a temporary victory that was soon to lead to a second defeat for the West, arguably as important as Vietnam, if not more so. The Arab oil producers retaliated by raising prices by 70 per cent, and then by imposing an embargo on Israel's supporters, including the United States. The oil price shock demonstrated the drawbacks of supporting regionally unpopular gendarmes. A significant redistribution of the world's resources took place, from oil consumers to producers; indeed it was this that helped finance the Soviets' African adventures.[71] Meanwhile, the West's economies were hit, and the inflation of the late 1960s worsened, increasing labour militancy as workers fought to preserve their wage gains. It seemed as if capitalism itself was in crisis. In the oil-importing parts of the Third World, the shock was even greater, and bolstered the Marxist view that the time was ripe for radical economic change.

One of the first victims of the oil shock was Marcelo Caetano's authoritarian regime in Portugal, and with it the Portuguese Empire in Africa. Caetano had been trying to liberalize the old regime, in the face of resistance from conservatives, but in 1974, weakened by the economic crisis, he was toppled by a politically eclectic group of junior army officers, bitter at the conduct of the African wars. The coup was bloodless, and was dubbed the 'Carnation Revolution' after the red carnations handed out by the rebels to show their peaceful intent. Far from signalling the start of the revolution with banners or bugles, the leaders of the rebellion told their supporters to wait for the broadcast of the Portuguese entry for the Eurovision Song Contest.

A new broad coalition took power, representing conservative officers and more radical junior officers in the Armed Forces Movement (MFA), as well as liberals and Communists.[72] Yet Eurovision ballads were to give way to more martial tunes. Shanty-town dwellers took to the streets, occupying buildings and demanding full state housing provision, whilst landless peasants called for the break-up of large estates.[73] The MFA, the far left and the Communists – who were much more radical than their Spanish and Italian comrades – began a more fundamental redistribution of property, and legalized massive land seizures. In the north the result was violence, as right-wing paramilitaries, with the support of small-holders, attacked the left. Portugal in 1975 had distinct echoes of Spain in 1936, and Kissinger estimated that there was a 50 per cent chance that Portugal would join the Soviet bloc.[74]

However, the radicals were weakened by their poor performance in the elections of April, and by the victory of the moderate socialists. It was clear that most of the poor had achieved what they wanted – basic property rights which they believed were rightly theirs – and did not desire a revolutionary transformation of society. The Communists attempted to mobilize the poor against the socialists, but moderates in the army regrouped and the threat of revolution was headed off. The last Communist-inspired revolution in Europe had failed.

As the revolutionary Communist era finally came to an end in Europe, it was only just beginning in Africa. In 1975 the new government of Portugal granted the colonies their independence; the PAIGC became the ruling party of Guinea-Bissau, and FRELIMO of Mozambique. The road to Angolan independence proved to be a rockier three-way struggle, as the MPLA, backed by the Soviets, fought two regionally based freedom movements – the FNLA and UNITA (both backed at various times by either China or the United States). As the MPLA began to win, South Africa, with the encouragement of Washington, invaded its neighbour. And, though the Soviets were initially unenthusiastic, Fidel Castro sent Cuban troops half way across the world to assist the MPLA, at which point the South Africans retreated, leaving the MPLA holding the field – for the moment at least. Prolonged civil wars soon broke out in both Angola and Mozambique, wars that have been seen as proxy confrontations between the superpowers, but that did not stop their rulers trying to build socialism.

IV

In the short story 'The Secret Love of Deolinda', published in 1988, the Mozambican writer Mia Couto tells of a young Maputo woman, the eponymous Deolinda, who has a dreary job shelling cashew-nuts. Her life, however, is not without its excitements and one day she returns home sporting a badge bearing the 'face of an ever photogenic Karl Marx, as if unburdened by the years'. Her father is not pleased; indeed, not recognizing Marx as the renowned nineteenth-century theorist of world history he assumes he is someone Deolinda has recently met, 'one of those foreigners, who start off as internationalists, and then became aid workers'. 'Never again do I want to see this fellow's snout sniffing your bra,' he tells her. Deolinda meekly obeys and removes the offending object from her bosom to a box under her bed. But every night, before she falls asleep, the badge is retrieved and 'she would kiss the thinker's fleecy beard'.[75]

Couto, a writer deeply critical of Mozambican Marxism (or 'Marxianism' as he called it, 'out of respect for Marx'), saw its manifestation in Mozambique as a variety of cargo cult – an opaque symbol of Western modernity, both worshipped and misunderstood. And certainly the brand of Marxism imported by the Portuguese African Marxists was at the Modernist, Westernizing end of the spectrum. This is somewhat surprising; given FRELIMO's history one might have expected its leaders to pursue a more Radical Maoist approach, applying the experience of the guerrilla war of independence to running their new country. But they firmly adopted a Soviet-style Marxism.[76] This was partly the consequence of the Soviet alliance, but as has been seen, it was also a response to the perceived failures of indigenous forms of socialism. As Mao himself had temporarily concluded in the early 1950s, a nationalist version of Stalinism was a recipe for entry into the modern world of cities and industry. It had supposedly worked elsewhere, so why not in Africa?

If anything, the Africans found it even more difficult to launch this project than the Chinese; their states were even weaker, and more fragmented by lineage, ethnicity and a divisive colonial heritage. As

Couto's short story made clear, whilst the Marxist-Leninist project had great emotional appeal to some, it was even more of a dream in Africa than in its Eurasian homeland.

The conditions for transplanting Marxism-Leninism into Angola and Mozambique were, it must be acknowledged, especially inauspicious. Unlike the French and British colonial empires, which had, at least, left their colonies with functioning legal and administrative systems, the sudden departure of thousands of Portuguese settlers left the new regimes with tiny educated elites and state apparatuses. The new regimes were also forced to nationalize a great deal of industry and land simply to fill the vacuum left by their departing Portuguese owners. But Neto, the Angolan leader and a long-time Stalinist, was more cautious in his efforts to transform the economy than the less orthodox Machel in Mozambique. For Machel, independence was the chance for Mozambique to become truly modern and escape the backwardness he blamed on Portuguese exploitation. As he proclaimed in 1981: 'The victory of Socialism is a victory of science, it is prepared and organized scientifically. The Plan is the instrument of scientific organization of this victory ... Everything must be organized, everything must be planned, everything must be programmed.'[77] Mozambicans had to become modern as well. Science was to replace spirit mediums and rain-making ceremonies.

FRELIMO brought the Plan to a country that may have been even less prepared for it than the Soviet Union of the 1930s, for Mozambique, like many African states, lacked an effective state machine. Soviet and East German expert planners helped the Mozambicans, but expertise in the central office in Maputo could not compensate for a desperate shortage of experienced administrators at all other levels of the economic system. Even the largest state companies struggled: Petromoc, the state oil company, failed to produce accounts for seven years.[78] Meanwhile, large amounts of money were wasted on grand projects, such as the failed attempts to establish an iron and steel industry. FRELIMO's agricultural plans were, if anything, even more ambitious. The regime created huge state farms, which, whilst they increased production, absorbed huge resources. The regime also sought to relocate peasants into new, well-ordered communal villages, with good health services, education and clean houses in neat rows. FRELIMO's officials were convinced that they would improve the lives of peasants, giving them better government services whilst breaking the authority of chiefs, and creating new, modern socialist people. These projects were reminiscent of European Communist programmes – whether Khrushchev's planned 'agro-towns' or Ceauşescu's 'systematization' of villages – but they were also influenced by a general fashion for grandiose transformations amongst regimes of various ideological hues, including socialist Tanzania's 'villagization' programme. Whilst such schemes undoubtedly contributed to Mozambique's successes in education and health, in economic terms they performed poorly and were extremely unpopular amongst the peasants compelled, often by brute force, to live and work there.[79] By the end of the 1970s, the economic environment was bad for all developing countries, but the rigid utopianism of orthodox Modernist Marxism explains a great deal of Mozambique's poor performance.

Nor did the Marxist-Leninist political system help to speed Mozambican development. As the African socialists had predicted, the narrow, sectarian vanguard party proved particularly unsuited to African conditions. FRELIMO cadres may have been well-trained to push through radical programmes, but they were far less successful at securing the general population's enthusiasm for these projects. The resulting conflict increasingly took on an ethnic colouring. Angola was already plagued by regionally based ethnic rivalries inherited from the colonial regime, but the narrow, authoritarian MPLA (its leadership still dominated by whites and *mestiços*) only exacerbated them. Shortly after it came to power, it was challenged by a left-wing coup led by the Enver Hoxha-admiring Nito Alves, a prominent black commander of the guerrilla period who had successfully mobilized Luanda slum-dwellers to agitate for more power. Neto's regime was only saved by the Cubans, but thereafter he chose to impose MPLA-style Marxism-Leninism with Stalinist ruthlessness, savage violence and a brutal secret police.[80]

By the end of the 1970s, the Angolan and Mozambican civil wars were ending, but they were soon to reignite as South Africa and the United States renewed their offensive. In Mozambique RENAMO (*Resistência Nacional Moçambicana* – National Resistance of Mozambique), established by a white settler-ruled Rhodesia with the help of pro-Portuguese exiles, at first had little effect. But after the beginning of African rule in Rhodesia (renamed Zimbabwe) in 1979, South Africa began to pursue a much more aggressive policy against the African National Congress, which was launching attacks from Mozambique.

The regime poured resources into RENAMO, which waged a highly successful campaign of destabilization and sabotage. In Angola, too, a brief lull in fighting led to renewed war with the American-backed UNITA. The war continued throughout the 1980s, fuelled by Angolan oil, superpower competition, and the highly charged ideological conflict between Marxism and South African apartheid.

Angola and Mozambique joined a host of self-declared Marxist-Leninist regimes in Africa. In 1980, seven of Africa's fifty African- or Arab-ruled countries described themselves as Marxist-Leninist (Angola, Benin, Congo-Brazzaville, Ethiopia, Madagascar, Mozambique and Somalia), whilst another nine professed some form of socialism (Algeria, the Cape Verde Islands, Guinea, Guinea-Bissau, Libya, São Tomé and Principe, the Seychelles Islands, Tanzania and Zambia). Altogether about a quarter of the continent's population lived under these regimes. The regimes in Angola, Mozambique and Guinea-Bissau, however, were unusual in coming to power as the result of anti-colonial guerrilla wars, and they had serious ambitions to transform society. All of the other Marxist-Leninist rulers were military, and (bar the Ethiopian case) had far more modest ambitions. Even so, they were very much in the Modernist Marxist tradition – leaching resources from the countryside to fund urban development, favouring city populations over rural ones, and financing a form of welfarism which, with its intense preoccupation with higher rather than mass education, tended to benefit the better-off.

But if socialism in most of these new military Marxist states looked largely rhetorical, one example did not. Ethiopia was to experience one of the last 'classical' revolutions, echoing its French and Russian predecessors of 1789 and 1917. For the last time, an *ancien régime* was to collapse and give way to a radical Marxist politics, highly reminiscent of Bolshevism.

V

In his satirical story, *The Case of the Illiterate Saboteur* (1993), the Ethiopian writer Hama Tuma described the court in which a series of absurd political trials takes place:

Above the judge's chair hung the photo of the Great Chairman of our country. Rumour has it that some overzealous cadres who had the gall to suggest that portraits of Marx, Engels and Lenin had to be hung along with that of the Chairman were executed for the crime of misguided internationalism and stunted revolutionary nationalism. However, it is said that the Wise Chairman, in order to placate the Russians (who as you know have extra-sharp ears), built monuments for Lenin and Marx (poor Engels is still waiting for his!).[81]

Ethiopia was not unusual amongst Afro-Communist regimes in using Marxism-Leninism for its own nationalist ends, and nor was it exceptional in trying to please the Russians. But there was a special affinity between Ethiopia and Russia, which Marxists of the time noted. For Ethiopian revolutionaries lived in a very different country from other African Marxists, who had come to Marxism through the anti-colonial liberation struggle. Like Russians in the early twentieth century, they inhabited a crumbling, stratified *ancien régime* Christian Orthodox empire and felt that they were failing to keep up with their neighbours. The history of Russia was therefore a compelling one, and to some it seemed as if they were merely living through the Bolshevik experience, albeit in speeded-up time.

In 1957, an editorial in a student newspaper declared, 'both Ethiopians and foreigners are looking to us as the generation that will shoulder the great responsibility of putting Ethiopia on equal footing with the rest of the civilized world'.[82] At the time, some believed they might work alongside the Emperor Haile Selassie. Selassie, who had ruled since 1930, apart from a period of exile after the Italian invasion, had been a modernizing autocrat. When he came to power, Ethiopia was an agrarian country largely controlled by aristocrats who enjoyed tax exemptions and labour services from some of the peasantry. It was also a Christian Orthodox empire, which the northern Amharas and, to a lesser extent, the Tigreans dominated, having conquered the non-Orthodox peoples of the south. Selassie tried to reform the regime by developing the economy of this poor agrarian nation by encouraging industry, though it remained small. He also sought to centralize the state and weaken the aristocracy by building up a class of educated officials and a modern army, and the student population rose from 71 in 1950 to about 10,000 by 1973, in addition to those who studied abroad (including some 700 in the United

States in 1970).[83] Of course, this was a risky strategy, as it assumed that the newly educated be both modern in outlook and prepared to serve an autocrat who claimed to be the descendant of King Solomon and the Queen of Sheba. As Selassie's regime became more conservative and repressive, building up his own aristocracy of service whilst preserving many of the powers of the old hereditary nobility, modernizers in the army began to condemn him for allowing Ethiopia to fall behind the decolonized states of Africa. In 1960 they staged a coup, which failed, but which also showed the depths of elite disenchantment. Like its Russian predecessors, the autocracy was increasingly beset by criticism from educated modernizers, peasant rebellions and ethnic insurrection – most seriously in Eritrea.

In Ethiopia, then, an orthodox Marxist analysis of 'feudalism' seemed to make perfect sense, and many students came from relatively humble backgrounds, feeling sympathy for the poor peasantry, and guilt at their privileges, much as their Russian predecessors had. But it was Western, not Soviet, influence that contributed to Marxism's popularity. Selassie's regime was closely aligned with the United States, and Western-educated students were especially influential in bringing back the newly fashionable Marxism from American campuses, as were some of the Peace Corps volunteers.

In 1965 the students in Addis Ababa began a campaign for more rights for tenants and an end to labour dues, with the slogans 'Land to the Tiller' and 'Away with Serfdom', and by 1968, as has been seen, the student movement had linked its own complaints with the struggle against American policy in Vietnam and apartheid in South Africa.[84] By 1971, all ten candidates for a Union of University Students election accepted that Marxism-Leninism was the only possible ideology for Ethiopia;[85] as one unsympathetic observer remembered: 'Marxism was presumed to be an unchallengeable truth . . . every element of youth discontent was defined in Marxist terms. Many did not read about it, but that was beside the point. They were obsessed by it.'[86]

It was an economic crisis that triggered the fall of Selassie: the famine of 1973–4, which the regime responded to incompetently, and the oil price hike. The revolution began in February 1974 with a mutiny of junior army officers, resentful at poor conditions and the high-handed way in which they were treated by their senior officers. Their protests were followed by strikes, and, despite an attempt by the new liberal

Endalkachew government to prepare constitutional reforms, unrest continued until a group of junior army officers, the so-called 'Derg' (Committee), took power in the summer, deposing the Emperor in September.

At first, the majority of the Derg favoured a form of Nyerere-style African socialism – 'Ethiopian socialism' – but from early on an influential group, including the first Vice-Chairman of the Derg, Major Mengistu Haile Mariam, was listening to the vocal and prestigious student Marxist left. Mengistu's background is obscure, but his father seems to have been a pauper of southern origin who worked as a servant to a northern lord.[87] Darker-skinned than most Amharas, he was certainly regarded by many Ethiopians as a 'slave' by origin.

Mengistu felt his lowly background keenly, but he had advantages in politics. He was an expert at judging political situations and hiding his real intentions.[88] And for the French journalist René Lefort his humble origins were a real advantage in the revolutionary politics of the 1970s:

> In the head of any peasant in the south or 'have-not' in the capital . . . he incarnates the revenge that justifies usurpation, Robin Hood ascended to the throne. Like those emperors of the past emerging like robbers to conquer the crown and at last bringing the reign of justice to the people.[89]

But Mengistu, whilst he claimed to champion the poor, was no Romantic populist. He may have had low status and a limited education, but he made serious efforts to assimilate into the elite Amharas, and he had the oratorical skills to express a passionate Amhara-led Ethiopian nationalism. In some ways, his background was not unlike Stalin's: looked down on as a member of a conquered southern nationality in a multi-ethnic empire, eager to assimilate into the 'superior', more modern culture, and thus to make his way to the centre of power.[90]

Mengistu's politics were closely connected with his background. Like Stalin, he understood the power of popular mobilization, but he was also determined to establish an 'advanced' modernity by means of a highly centralized authority and even brutal force – even though he insisted that the Ethiopian revolution could avoid violence (unlike the English Glorious Revolution of 1688, which, he claimed, had resulted in the deaths of hundreds of thousands of people).[91] Although he at first had little knowledge of Marxism, he, and other radical members of the Derg, were eager to secure the support of the Marxist students.

The first significant evidence of the Derg's radicalism was its decision in March 1975 to nationalize the land, handing it over to those who tilled it. The plan, developed by a group of radical officials in Haile Selassie's civil service (many of them educated in the United States), followed the long-running desire of the Ethiopian Marxist left to abolish 'feudalism', and ignored liberal warnings that it would lead to violence.

Just as Stalin had done in the late 1920s, the Derg mobilized urban students to bring the revolution to the countryside, and both regime and students saw the project in very similar ways: as military-style campaigns to bring enlightenment to a backward and superstitious countryside, thus uniting the nation. The word 'campaign' (*zemecha*) used in the title of the 'Development through Cooperation, Enlightenment and Work Campaign' was the one that had described the crusade-style northern Christian conquests of the south in the nineteenth century, and despite their atheism, the students brought with them the arrogance of the past. 'For centuries,' the Derg declared, 'the people in general and the rulers in particular have lived with outmoded beliefs'; 'These dividing ideas worked against progress and enlightenment.'[92]

The Ethiopian students seem to have been as enthusiastic as their Russian predecessors, but unlike them they had a great deal of support from the southern peasants themselves. The peasants were desperate to rid themselves of the domination of the ethnically alien northern military lords (or *neftenya* – 'gunmen'), who had established a highly exploitative regime. The arrival of the *zemecha* students could therefore spark off revolutionary demands and ethnic separatism, which the students often sympathized with. This was precisely what the Derg, committed to the integrity of Ethiopia, did not want, and the result was often the use of force and student disillusionment. However, whilst the students could join with the peasants against the northern landlords, they could also clash with them as they tried to impose 'enlightenment', much as their Soviet predecessors had done. If anything, the ethnic differences between the student 'enlighteners' and the peasants made the violence more extreme. In one episode, the students tried to undermine the power of a local chief, who had religious as well as political significance. According to an American report:

In an act of calculated effrontery the semi-divine and normally secluded *geramanja* was unceremoniously paraded in the streets of a provincial town ... the students deliberately desecrated the *geramanja*'s sacred eating utensils and, after dinner, seated a low-caste *manjo* on his special horse. The outraged followers of the *geramanja* waited until the students had assembled in a school building in the neighbourhood. The building was surrounded and put to the torch.[93]

The Derg, officially, was still pursuing 'Ethiopian socialism', but this looked much more like Marxism-Leninism, and the land reform was welcomed by the student Marxists. From September 1975 the Derg began to formulate a Marxist-Leninist doctrine, and sought to create a more formal alliance with the Marxist parties. But Ethiopian Marxism was divided between the more Stalinist, modernizing Marxism of the All-Ethiopian Socialist Movement (MEISON), largely consisting of ethnic southerners, and the more decentralized Marxism of the 'Maoist' Ethiopian People's Revolutionary Party (EPRP), with a largely northern membership. It is no surprise that Mengistu ultimately allied with the MEISON. Partly as a result, serious conflicts broke out, within both the Derg and the Marxist movement. The regime sought to suppress the EPRP, and it went underground and began a guerrilla campaign, leading to a vicious 'red terror' which lasted for about a year from early 1977. The violence was extreme, and at times spilled into the streets – most notably the massacres that followed the EPRP's attempts to disrupt the 1977 May Day rallies in Addis Ababa.

Mengistu's extremism intensified separatist movements – the Marxist Eritreans, the Maoist-inspired Tigreans and rebels in other regions – and he also came under serious threat from within the Derg. He was further weakened when the United States, which under Kissinger's *realpolitik* had continued to fund the regime despite the Derg's violence, began to reduce aid under the new Carter administration and support Ethiopia's enemy, the formally Marxist regime of Somalia. Meanwhile, the Soviets, who had been supporting Somalia, began to move closer to Ethiopia. The Somalis, sensing weakness now American support was being withdrawn, invaded the Ethiopian Ogaden. However, the war, far from undermining the Derg, only served to consolidate the regime, much as World War II had reinvigorated Stalin's rule. Mengistu was able to present himself as a defender of the nation, and, in an even more striking echo of the Stalinist past, he began to associate himself with the Ethiopian Orthodox church to bring the nation together against the foreigner. In other respects too he adopted the ideology of High Stalinism. He was committed to using force to preserve the multi-ethnic hierarchical Ethiopian state, in which Amharas controlled other ethnicities, and to further signal the debt, he increasingly adopted a monarchical style and was to be seen sitting on a gilded armchair-cum-throne covered with red velvet to watch his military parades.[94]

By 1978, Mengistu, with Soviet and Cuban military aid and the support of the southern peasants who manned his army, had won the Ogaden war. His internal enemies had been crushed, and the separatist insurgents were being contained. He responded to victory by resuming his transformation of the economy, setting high targets for agriculture and building up industry, following a Stalinist strategy. The result was peasant passive resistance and soil erosion, contributing, together with the Tigrean war and drought, to a devastating famine in 1984.[95] Having neglected the disaster, the regime was goaded into action by international outrage (helped by the televised 'Live Aid' charity rock concert), but its solutions caused even more traumas. It decided to relocate the peasants, in a coercive programme of villagization that further increased support for the guerrilla insurgencies now threatening the regime.

Mengistu was one of Stalin's most faithful disciples, and the world was yet again reminded of the devastating effects of this violent form of politics. Again, the hatreds created by a crumbling *ancien régime* had given rise to an angry and destructive modernizing Prometheus. But even Mengistu's cruelty was put in the shade when, a few weeks after the Derg launched its campaign of rural transformation, another Communist regime of extraordinary violence came to power. In April 1975, the Communist Party of Kampuchea (known as the 'Khmer Rouge') occupied Phnom Penh. The Khmer Rouge championed a variety of Communism very different to the pro-urban Afro-Stalinism of Ethiopia. This was a Maoist Marxism – one that used peasants rather than an urban vanguard to pursue goals of modernity and national greatness. The Khmer Rouge was to take Cambodia (or Kampuchea as they called it) into a world more nightmarish even than that of the Cultural Revolution, one pursued with a single-minded violence that ended up destroying the modernity it was trying to create.

VI

In 1971, a French student of Cambodian Buddhism, François Bizot, then touring the Cambodian countryside, was captured by Khmer Rouge guerrillas who were fighting a guerrilla war against the American-backed regime of Lon Nol. Suspected of being an American spy, Bizot was imprisoned in a camp, and his fascinating and subtle memoir of his captivity includes a gripping account of conversations with his captor, 'Comrade Duch', the former mathematics teacher who was later to become the head of the notorious torture chamber, the Tuol Sleng (S-21) prison.[96] Despite the circumstances, Bizot and Duch established a strange rapport, and engaged in an extraordinary debate about Kampuchean Communism. Bizot, an enthusiast for traditional Cambodian culture, challenged Duch with a powerful critique of what he saw as the Khmer Rouge's modernizing Promethean impulse – namely its subservience to Western ideas, its contempt for 'backward' peasants, and its willingness to sacrifice ordinary people on the altar of national greatness: 'If you destroy these structures of peasant society, if you impose a new rational model, don't you risk humiliating them even more than your enemies do?' he asked. Duch, however, refused to accept that the peasantry would resist modernity, and insisted that they would welcome the Khmer Rouge's programme:

> 'Quite the reverse,' he erupted. 'It's because . . . we know that the peasants are the source of true knowledge, that we want to free them from oppression and abuse. They're not like the lazy [Buddhist] monks who don't know how to grow rice. They know how to take control of their destiny . . . This society will retain the best of itself and will get rid of all of the contaminated remains of the current period of decline . . . it's better to have a sparsely populated Cambodia than a country full of incompetents!'[97]

At the same time, however, he declared himself committed to helping those peasants who were willing to shoulder their responsibilities: 'My duty is to lead each of them back to a life of simple pleasures; what more can anyone want from life than a bicycle, a watch and a transistor radio?'[98]

Duch went on to condemn Bizot for hypocrisy, for forgetting that France had created a nation through bloody revolution, just as the massive ancient Cambodian temples of Angkor Wat had involved massive sacrifice:

> For a Frenchman, I find you very timid. Did you yourselves not have a revolution and execute hundreds and hundreds of people? Would you care to tell me when the memory of these victims prevented you from glorifying in your history books the men who founded a new nation that day? It's the same with the monuments at Angkor, whose architecture and majesty everyone admires . . . who now thinks about the price, about the countless individuals who died from the endless labour over the centuries? The extent of sacrifice matters little; what counts is the greatness of the goal you choose for yourself.[99]

Bizot was shocked by Duch's callousness, but his feelings were complex:

> Up until then, I had been convinced by the reassuring image of a brutal executioner. Now the man of faith, staring ahead of himself with an expression combining gloom and bitterness, suddenly emerged in its immense solitude. Just as he revealed such cruelty, I surprised myself by feeling affectionate towards him . . . As I looked at him, tears came into my eyes, as if I were dealing with a dangerous predator I could not bring myself to hate . . . His intelligence had been honed as the tooth of the wolf or the shark, but his human psychology had been carefully preserved. Thus prepared, his masters employed him as a cog in a vast timepiece beyond his comprehension.[100]

Bizot may or may not have been right in his view of Duch's motivations, and in his conviction that Duch was the victim of inhumane bosses. But his record of Duch's views helps us to understand why leaders of the Khmer Rouge such as Duch were prepared to organize such violence. Duch's language – and especially his praise for the achievements of the ancient Angkor civilization – was more explicitly nationalistic than most Communists', and clearly war and Cambodian nationalism are central to any explanation of these events. But his words echo those we have seen in Stalin's and Mao's Radical voluntaristic thinking – that national greatness and economic success could only be achieved if the people became self-sacrificing heroes, whilst the unheroic or the unreliable had to be eliminated. But the Khmer Rouge were Maoist rather than Stalinist in believing in the virtues of the peasantry, at least in the abstract; they did not have the contempt for their culture or the admiration for the urban that Stalinists did. Even so, 'Communist State No. 1', as they called their regime, went even further than Mao in valorizing the Radical over the modernizing side of the Promethean synthesis and in their efforts to mobilize the nation as a peasant guerrilla army at a time of war. The Khmer Rouge also used the enormous resentments of the countryside towards the cities. The consequence was murder and destruction on a massive scale.

The Khmer Rouge's leader Saloth Sâr (better known by his pseudonym 'Pol Pot') arrived at his extremist version of Marxism in the course of a life that was in some respects similar to that of other Asian Communist leaders. He came from a prosperous peasant background (like several other Communist bosses in the developing world); he went abroad as a student, where he encountered Communism, and then returned to a land beset by anti-colonial and post-colonial guerrilla wars. But his outlook was also forged by the peculiar ethnic and social hierarchies of his homeland. Cambodia was a particularly agrarian part of the French Indochinese empire, and the native Buddhist Khmers were largely peasants. The French saw the Khmers as less developed than the Confucian Vietnamese, who filled many of the administrative posts in the country, and Cambodian nationalists became increasingly resentful of their lowly status amongst the dominant Vietnamese and Chinese. As a child in the 1930s, Pol Pot himself had close connections with the more traditional aspects of Cambodian culture: he spent some months as a novice in a Buddhist monastery, where he was given a highly disciplinarian and traditional education. His family also had links with the royal household: Pol's cousin Meak was a member of the royal ballet and became the King's consort, and Pol himself spent some time in the palace. We do not know what he thought of the court at the time, but his later denunciations of the monarchy and its decadence became very harsh.[101] And if he was not aware of it before, he would have understood Cambodians' place in the ethnic pecking order when he went to a French school in Phnom Penh, a city dominated by French, Vietnamese and Chinese. All this may be one reason why he came to believe that Cambodia's status could only be raised by eliminating its traditional culture.

Pol Pot reached adulthood at a time of nationalist ferment, when the French had reimposed control after World War II but tolerated a constitutional monarchy under Prince Norodom Sihanouk. Even though he was a mediocre student, Pol managed to secure a scholarship in 1949 to study in France at the Radio-Electricity Institute in Paris, but he had little interest in the subject. Much more compelling to him were French history and nationalist politics, and Rousseau was one of his favourite authors. However, at a time when the Communist party had so much influence in France, it was no surprise that he should move into the Communist orbit.

Pol attended Marxist discussion groups, and became a member of the French Communist Party. A contemporary recalls that he had a particular admiration for Stalin's idea of the secretive, vanguard party, and for Stalin himself; indeed he hung a portrait on his wall.[102] When he returned to Cambodia at the beginning of 1953, the Vietnamese Communists had extended the anti-French guerrilla struggle across the border, and controlled about a sixth of Cambodian territory. Pol joined the Indochinese Communist Party, founded by the Vietnamese, and joined a guerrilla band for a time, although he probably did not actually fight. Shortly after the French granted independence to Cambodia later that year, he returned to Phnom Penh and became a secret Communist activist whilst working as a teacher. He was popular, and one of his students remembers his mild and personable style:

> I still remember Pol Pot's style of delivery in French: gentle and musical. He was clearly drawn to French literature in general and poetry in particular ... In Paris many years later I watched him speaking Cambodian on the TV ... He spoke in bursts, without notes, searching a little but never caught short, his eyes half-closed, carried away by his own lyricism.[103]

Pol's monastic teaching style was also effective in recruiting the monks, teachers and students of Phnom Penh for the Communist party at a time when Sihanouk, an authoritarian modernizer, was expanding education. In 1962, with the mysterious death of the Communist Party's leader, Pol became acting secretary of the party. But student riots in 1963 forced him to flee to guerrilla camps in the east and north-east of the country. Pol was following the route followed by Mao and the Chinese Communists after 1927, from the town to the countryside.

By the early 1960s Sihanouk, desperate to keep Cambodia out of the Vietnam War, had broken with the United States and forged an alliance with China and North Vietnam, allowing the Vietnamese guerrillas to use his territory. The Vietnamese were therefore not eager for the

Cambodian Communists to attack the Sihanouk regime, a message that was clearly communicated when Pol Pot visited Hanoi in 1965. The radical Pol was looking for support for his insurgency, and resented the patronizing Vietnamese, but he found a much warmer welcome in Beijing when he visited at the end of the year. The Chinese did not want to help him against Sihanouk either, but they were politer, and Pol was excited by the radical atmosphere he saw there. The Socialist Education Movement was in full swing, and the Cultural Revolution was only months away. The 1965 Chinese visit, and a subsequent one in 1970, were to have an enormous impact on Pol's thinking, and would provide him with a new vision. On his return he changed the name of the Communist party from the Vietnamese-style 'Revolutionary Workers' Party' to the Chinese-style 'Communist Party of Kampuchea', and departed from Vietnamese-influenced areas to a more remote Yan'an-type part of the north-east, inhabited by 'tribal' minorities. The Khmer Rouge also began to prepare for an armed struggle against Sihanouk, which they launched the following year.[104]

The prospects for the radicalized Pol's Communists began to look much brighter in 1969–70, partly as a result of Washington's Vietnamese strategy. In 1969 Washington began to bomb Vietnamese bases in Cambodia, thus demonstrating the abject failure of Sihanouk's efforts to avoid war. It also helped to precipitate his fall in a pro-American coup. The Vietnamese, the Khmer Rouge and Sihanouk were now all united against the Washington-backed regime of Lon Nol, and by 1972 the Khmer Rouge controlled about half of Cambodia's territory, mainly in the countryside. Led by teachers and urban people, most of its recruits were young poor peasants, and the classic Maoist methods of self-criticism, study sessions and manual labour were used to forge a united force. It was from this time that the Khmer Rouge began its campaigns against 'feudalism' in its 'liberated' areas, eradicating Buddhism and imposing an extreme egalitarianism and collectivism, symbolized by the demand that peasants wear sets of identical black pyjamas.

In 1973 the constellation of forces changed yet again, as the Vietnamese agreed with the Americans to withdraw from Cambodia, and the Khmer Rouge were left alone, bitter at Hanoi, but continuing the struggle. American bombing intensified, but it probably only increased support for the guerrillas. On 17 April 1975 the residents of Phnom Penh looked on anxiously as the victorious young peasants of the Khmer

Rouge entered the capital – much as the residents of Beijing had in 1949. It soon transpired that they had a lot to be anxious about.

The party that took control of Cambodia looked so unusual that some have doubted whether we should really call it Marxist at all. Several have pointed to the influence of Theravada Buddhism, its collectivism and fatalism, and this was François Bizot's own explanation for this extraordinary movement.[105] As he asked an angry Duch:

> are you not defending a new religion? I've followed your educational sessions. They're not unlike courses in Buddhist doctrine: renouncing material possessions; giving up family ties, which weaken us and prevent us from devoting us entirely to the Angkar [Organization]; leaving our parents and children to serve the revolution. Submitting to discipline and confessing our faults.[106]

The Khmer Rouge's peasant recruits were certainly taught its teachings without reference to Marx or Lenin, and until 1977 it even hid the fact that it was a Communist party, demanding allegiance to the 'Revolutionary Organization' (*Angkar Padevat*) instead. This was partly for nationalistic reasons: the Khmer Rouge was highly xenophobic, and did not want to acknowledge any foreign descent, especially from the hated Vietnamese. As Pol Pot declared in his victory speech: 'We have won total, definitive, and clean victory, meaning that we have won it without any foreign connection or involvement.'[107] But the Khmer Rouge was also extraordinarily secretive. Convinced that they had very little time to carry out a total revolution to prepare for a counter-attack, they continued to behave as if they were fighting a revolutionary war. The government was formed in secret, and the leaders all had code names: 'Brother No. 1' (Pol Pot), 'Brother No. 2', and so on. The first time the public heard the name 'Pol Pot' was during the 'elections' of April 1976, when this mysterious figure was identified, bizarrely, as a 'rubber plantation worker'.[108] Khmer Rouge officials told foreigners that Saloth Sâr was dead.

War and an extreme, resentful nationalism undoubtedly contributed to this secrecy and xenophobia, but so did the example of the Khmer Rouge's erstwhile Vietnamese patron. The Viet Minh also presented itself as a broad nationalist front, and never officially referred to Marxism-Leninism.[109] In other respects, the Khmer Rouge followed Maoist traditions in elevating the peasantry to the status of revolutionary class.

However, the Cambodians went much further. As has been seen, Mao idealized the virtues of the peasantry, but he always remained committed to the ultimate supremacy of the proletariat. The Khmer Rouge, in contrast, saw the poor peasantry as a 'working class', and discriminated against all city-dwellers. One of their first decisions was to order that Phnom Penh and all other cities be evacuated and their residents – over 2 million people – be sent to the countryside to work, under coercion, in collective farms.

It is unclear what the precise motivation was.[110] In large part, it exploited the resentments of the peasantry at the richer, cosmopolitan cities. This was a politics of revenge. As the party explained to its members when beginning the evacuation of the cities, 'The city people have had an easy life, whereas the rural people have had a very hard time . . . The morality of the cities under Lon Nol was not pure and clean like in the liberated areas.'[111] But it was also reminiscent of persecutions in other Communist states in mixing ideology and security. The urban residents were seen as potential opponents, but they were also seen as ideologically corrosive because they had grown up in the 'filth of imperialist and colonialist culture'.[112]

In other respects, however, Khmer Rouge policy was an extreme version of the egalitarian Maoism of the Great Leap Forward. Money was abolished, and everybody, including the deportees, became labourers on collective farms. Urban life was destroyed, the cities emptied, schools closed. The country became one large agricultural labour camp, and the lives of all were devoted to labour and political education. The regime sought to destroy old hierarchies of all sorts. Children were expected to call their parents 'comrade father' and 'comrade mother' and the use of the term 'sir' was banned.[113] Only marriages approved by the party were allowed. Pol Pot even declared that 'Mothers should not get too entangled with their offspring', and communal dining halls were introduced to stop family bonding.[114] At the same time, however, society was divided in new ways, according to class and ideology: the deportees from the towns (the 'new people') were treated as second-class citizens, whilst the 'base people' were divided into two groups: the loyal poor peasants ('full-rights members'), and the semi-reliable (the 'candidates'). Rations and privileges depended on one's status in the new hierarchy, although in theory one could rise through hard work and commitment.[115]

Pol also followed Mao, and the Radical Marxist-Leninist tradition, in his desire to engineer a 'great leap forward' towards agricultural plenty and, ultimately, industrialization. As the Khmer Rouge launched border raids into Vietnam and the conflict with its neighbour escalated, Pol Pot announced his 'Four-Year Plan to Build Socialism in All Fields' in 1976, as part of his strategy to defend the nation. The 'Plan' was one of the most unscientific ever produced in the Communist world. Lacking detail, sloppily constructed and hugely overambitious, it revealed the Khmer Rouge leadership's fundamental lack of interest in the discipline of economics, and depended largely on willpower. 'When a people is awakened by political consciousness,' one official declared, 'it can do anything'; 'our engineers cannot do what the people do'.[116] The hubristic Pol Pot was convinced that 'Democratic Kampuchea' would not just catch up with its neighbours, but become a beacon for all other Communist states. It would truly be 'Communist State No. 1'.

Little came of the industrialization projects, but plans to increase the rice harvest sent about a million workers – many of them the urban 'new people' – to create new agricultural land out of wilderness. Tens of thousands died of hunger and disease, and the Khmer Rouge treated these class enemies callously, declaring in the notorious phrase, 'To keep you is no benefit and to destroy you is no loss.'[117] They were seen as second-class citizens, and could be killed for minor infringements. But all peasants, whether 'base' or 'new', were subjected to high rice delivery targets, and suffered as a result.

However, there were also more Stalinist aspects to Khmer Rouge thinking, as one might expect given the influence of the French Communist party on its leaders. Close contacts were also maintained with North Korea.[118] There was no Cultural Revolution-style mobilization, and the attitude towards 'enemies' also echoed the Stalinist one of the late 1930s: they were to be executed, not re-educated. Like Stalin, Pol Pot argued that success in war required campaigns against hidden internal 'enemies', and he blamed economic failures on the lack of commitment of the 'new people', on enemy 'microbes' that were 'seeping into every corner of the party' and had the potential to do 'real damage'. In a striking echo of Stalin's language, he declared: 'Are there still treacherous, secret elements buried inside the party, or are they gone? According to our observations over the last ten years it's clear that they're not gone at all ... Some are truly committed, others waver in their loyalties. Enemies can easily seep in.'[119] A vast spectrum of people was targeted, some of them previous party loyalists. About 14,000 passed through Comrade Duch's S-21 prison, most of them forced by torture to confess to bizarre conspiracies, and then executed. Meanwhile, the regime launched a series of persecutions of various groups, both 'class enemies' and ethnic minorities.

The violence varied over time, and deaths were higher in some areas than others. But in all, the death toll from murders and famine was horrific: estimates range from 1.5 to 2 million, or 26 per cent of the population.[120] Of course, the regime relied on supporters to carry out the killings, and individual motivations differed. Most were young peasants who had initially been enthusiastic about land reform, and the Khmer Rouge created an atmosphere in which there were strong pressures to mete out violence against 'enemies'. 'Cutting off one's feelings' towards all 'enemies' of the revolution, even they were relatives, was considered a virtue, and killing them was seen as a way of achieving 'honour' in the new society. One 'new person' remembered how his boss believed that 'if he purged enough enemies, he satisfied his conscience. He had done his duty to Angkar [the Organization]';[121] others were pressured into conforming, afraid that if they did not kill they would be suspected of being an enemy themselves.

The nightmare of 'Democratic Kampuchea' came to an end at the beginning of 1979 with a Soviet-backed Vietnamese invasion. Unsurprisingly, the poorly prepared Kampuchean military was no match for its well-armed and battle-hardened neighbours. But the Khmer Rouge, backed by the Chinese, continued the guerrilla struggle throughout the 1980s, until the Soviets withdrew support and the Vietnamese left in 1989.

VII

The experience of Kampuchea and Ethiopia was seriously to damage the reputation of Third World Communism, even amongst Communists themselves. Both the Soviets and the Chinese saw how much these regimes resembled their own militant pasts – histories they were now eager to forget.

The Chinese continued to support the Khmer Rouge militarily, even though on Mao's death they moved away from the radicalism they had once espoused, for they wanted the Cambodians' support against the Vietnamese. Similarly, Soviet policy-makers became increasingly disillusioned with some of their clients. Initial enthusiasts within the party for the African adventures, such as Brutents, Shakhnazarov and Zagladin, found that protégés such as Mengistu refused to take their advice and moderate their ambitions. As they witnessed the purges and the bloodshed, they wondered whether some of these supposedly Marxist-Leninist vanguard parties might actually be self-interested elites, who were not promoting real socialism in the interests of society as a whole, and who had excessively ambitious goals given the level of economic development.

Events in the USSR's southern neighbour, Afghanistan, seemed to confirm this gloomy prognosis. The authoritarian modernizer Mohammed Daoud was alienating both an urban-based left and a tribal and Islamic right. As a consequence, in April 1978, without Soviet involvement, the leftist 'Khalq' ('Masses') faction of the Communist party took power in a coup under Nur Taraki and Hajfizullah Amin. Calling themselves 'the children of history', these urban missionaries of modernity, many of them schoolteachers, tried to bring literacy and progress to the countryside, but their style was insensitive, and they increasingly resorted to force.[122] The Soviets, for whom Afghanistan was of high strategic importance, supported the new regime, but tried and failed to moderate its behaviour. When a rebellion broke out in Herat, spear-headed by Islamist guerrillas, Moscow decided it had to act, and tried to remove Amin. The plot backfired, and Amin killed Taraki, thus leaving the Soviets with a hostile government to deal with. In December 1979, Leonid Brezhnev made the fateful decision to send in the tanks.[123]

The Soviet invasion, then, was a sign of weakness, not strength, as many in the West believed at the time. The optimism of the mid-1970s, when the Kremlin embraced ideological ambition in the Third World, was over. Amongst the Western Communists, meanwhile, the military confrontation between the blocs had been causing deep anxieties for some time, and especially within the Italian party, headed from 1972 by the reserved Sardinian aristocrat Enrico Berlinguer. Italy, like much of Western Europe, was suffering from an economic crisis and social tensions, but its labour unrest was especially serious and the country had the most active terrorists in Europe, mainly of the far left, but also of the far right: between 1969 and 1980, 7,622 violent attacks caused 362 deaths and 172 casualties. Berlinguer was worried about both extremes. The toppling of Chile's President Allende in 1973 convinced him that as the Communists became electorally stronger they would face the threat of a coup. The Spanish Communist party, led by Santiago Carillo, took a similar view following the revolutionary chaos they had seen in Portugal.

Berlinguer was convinced that Communism would only succeed if the conflict between the blocs, and within states, was moderated. His solution was the formation of a third way between Social Democracy and Soviet Communism – a movement that came to be known as 'Eurocommunism'. It would embrace détente fully, including the Helsinki agreements on human rights which the Soviets had signed in 1975 but not adhered to; it would set its face against the militarized Cold War, including Soviet interventions; and it would formally accept multi-party systems and 'socialist pluralism'. The Italians had most support from the Spanish, but they also succeeded in securing French approval. And in June 1976 at the pan-European Communist conference in East Berlin, all three parties claimed political independence from Moscow, and criticized the Soviets' use of military force to spread Communism. In the compromise document, signed by all participants, all mention of the 'dictatorship of the proletariat' had gone, and the term 'Marxism-Leninism' was replaced with 'the great ideas of Marx, Engels and Lenin'. Criticism of NATO was also absent, in deference to the Italians, who now supported membership of the Western military alliance. And in April 1978 the Spanish party became the first Communist party formally to drop the description 'Marxist-Leninist' in favour of 'Marxist, democratic and revolutionary'.

Both the Italian and French parties also forged alliances with rivals at home. Berlinguer launched his 'historic compromise' (*compromesso storico*), designed to unite with the Christian Democrats against the threat of fascism and pull Italy out of crisis. In France, too, the Communists collaborated with François Mitterand's Socialists in 1972, agreeing on a left-wing, but far from orthodox Communist programme. For the first time since the 1940s they were a potential party of government.

However, Berlinguer failed to create a new, successful form of Communism. The Soviets became extremely hostile to it, fearing that the Italians would create a rival Communist centre that might threaten their interests in Eastern as well as Western Europe. 'It is unthinkable to fight Leninism in the name of Marxism', *Pravda* declared. 'Nothing could be more absurd.' The Americans were also suspicious, and continued to see the Eurocommunists as a threat to the West. Meanwhile the Italians were always much more committed to Eurocommunism than the French, whose attitudes and political culture remained more sectarian and pro-Soviet.

The parties' 'Popular Front'-type strategy at home also ran into difficulties. In France, the Socialists were the principal beneficiaries of the deal, as the Communists' old workerist politics looked increasingly stale. In 1978 the Communists, now lagging seriously behind their socialist allies, began to move away from their earlier endorsement of Eurocommunist principles. They took a small role in the Socialist government of 1981, but the decline became inexorable.

The Italian Communists were initially more successful. With 34.4 per cent of the vote in the 1976 election they were not the largest parliamentary bloc, but had succeeded in depriving the Christian Democrats' coalition of a majority for the first time since the War. And though the Communists did not take ministerial positions in the Christian Democrat-dominated government until 1978, they supported it from outside and had considerable influence. But these were difficult times economically. The party behaved much like Social Democratic governments in other countries of Western Europe at the time: it sought to improve productivity through class compromise. Unions were asked to restrain wages, whilst the state in return promised to introduce fair taxes and reorient the economy into more productive areas. At first the unions cooperated and inflation fell. But overall the economic reforms were ineffective, partly because trust between social groups was poor, and partly because the Christian Democrats were not really committed to the alliance.

The Italian Communists' short period of responsibility without power disappointed their supporters. Radical youth were especially hostile to the Communists' support for harsh anti-terrorism legislation: the Communists, much to their disappointment, had become the staunchest defenders of the Italian state. Student demonstrations and terrorism flourished, and, dispirited and divided, the Italian Communist Party ended the 'historic compromise' in early 1979. The Communists' vote fell, and whilst support was to remain relatively high, it was to remain enfeebled until the iron curtain was parted.

However, Eurocommunism was perhaps most damaged by the deterioration in East–West relations towards the end of the 1970s. Revolutions in the Third World and Soviet interventions convinced American political elites that the USSR was taking advantage of détente to spread Communism. Even President Jimmy Carter, committed to improving relations with the USSR and with a Third World policy oriented towards human rights rather than pure security, was anxious about Soviet behaviour. His hard-line National Security Adviser, Zbigniew Brzezinski, was particularly suspicious of Moscow's intentions, and the invasion of Afghanistan strengthened his position against the 'doves'. In Moscow, meanwhile, there was little understanding of how much damage Soviet policies in the Third World were doing to détente. Rigid and unyielding, they continued to pursue a policy of zero-sum competition.

As superpower tensions increased, 'third ways' such as Euro-communism became very difficult to sustain. Relations between Berlinguer and the Soviets deteriorated, and the final blow came with the invasion of Afghanistan;[124] the French party returned to the Soviet fold, whilst the Italians condemned the invasion. Following the imposition of martial law in Poland in 1981, Berlinguer made a final, devastating critique of Soviet Communism: the phase of socialism initiated by the October revolution, he declared, had 'exhausted its progressive force'.

The worsening international atmosphere was ultimately to destroy another 'third way' Communist regime – the Sandinista regime brought to power by the Nicaraguan revolution of 1979. The Sandinistas (the FSLN – *Frente Sandinista de Liberación Nacional*) were a coalition named after the anti-American guerrilla leader of the 1920s, Augusto Sandino. Benefiting from the wide unpopularity of the dictator Anastasio Somoza Debayle, they came to power calling for independence from the United States and a government in favour of the poor. They were made up of three groups, one peasant-based, one urban-based, and the 'Terceristas' – or the 'third alternative', amongst whom were the Ortega brothers, Daniel and Humberto. The Ortega brothers were Marxists, though not of a particularly doctrinaire variety, but most Sandinistas were more populist. In some respects the Sandinistas were following the Cuban path, calling for nationalization, land reform and improved welfare and education; unlike the Cubans, however, they favoured political pluralism and a mixed economy.

Predictably, the regime was popular amongst the poor, but nationalization antagonized the middle classes, whilst relations with the United States were also tense. The Sandinistas were mainly interested in developing their country, but they did welcome welfare aid from Cuba, and the Ortega brothers were keen on supporting the guerrilla groups in El Salvador and elsewhere. Even so, initially there were no hostilities between Washington and Managua; it was only with the intensification of the Cold War after the victory of Ronald Reagan in the US presidential elections in 1980 that Washington unleashed a guerrilla war against the Sandinistas, and Daniel Ortega began to receive aid from Moscow.

By 1979, therefore, the Soviets were becoming increasingly disappointed with their efforts to spread Communism in the Third World, whilst their military interventions – together with the violent Stalinism of some of their clients – were reinforcing the conviction of many of its remaining allies that Marxism-Leninism was too brutal, and Marxism had to be united with pluralism. But despite the increasing lack of confidence in the Communist world, many in the West, frightened by Soviet behaviour, were convinced that the expansion would continue. At the end of 1978, the British right-liberal journal *The Economist* gave an alarming prognosis for the next 'singularly dangerous seven years'. After describing the high level of 'political-military will' of the Russians, Cubans, East Germans and Vietnamese to spread Communism throughout the world, the editorial declared: 'It is not possible to stop the Soviet Union from expanding its military power . . . [But] it is essential to prevent that Soviet expansion from proceeding to the point where it controls the commanding heights, whether nuclear or non-nuclear.' *The Economist* declared this was feasible, but asked, pessimistically, 'can the Americans find in their allies – or in themselves – even a fraction of the will essential to prevent that Soviet expansion from proceeding to the point where it controls the commanding heights, whether nuclear or non-nuclear'.[125]

12

Twin Revolutions

I

On 11 October 1986, the General Secretary of the Soviet Communist party, Mikhail Gorbachev, met President Reagan, for the second time, in a government conference house in Reykjavik. Reagan's style was rather low-key, compared with Gorbachev's garrulous intensity, yet they had much in common. Both leaders were performers: Reagan had appeared in Hollywood B-films, whilst Gorbachev once had thespian ambitions and several of his colleagues commented on his dramatic skills.[1] They were also idealists, true believers in their own systems – Reagan a Christian and militant liberal capitalist, Gorbachev an atheist and convinced Communist. And so paradoxically, and despite their sharp ideological differences, there was an affinity between these two actors on the international stage. Reagan even persuaded himself Gorbachev might be a believer – he told his aide Michael Deaver: 'I don't know, Mike, but I honestly think he believes in a higher power.'[2]

At first the intensity of their particular ideological commitments made agreement difficult. For example, on the morning of the summit's second day a bitter row broke out, as Reagan accused Communists of seeking world domination and Gorbachev angrily defended the Soviet record on human rights.[3] In the afternoon, though, the atmosphere mellowed. Gorbachev proposed sharp reductions in nuclear weapons, and after some wrangling over precisely what was meant, Reagan made an extraordinary declaration: 'It would be fine with me if we eliminate all nuclear weapons.' Gorbachev's response was, 'We can do that. We can eliminate them.'[4] They then agreed to leave their negotiators to draft a treaty. Much to the disappointment of both, the agreement slipped through their fingers, the Russians objecting to the Americans' development of their space-age missile defence system, 'Star Wars'. But the agreement, which shocked many of Reagan's advisers, showed how far things had changed since the 1970s. The tone of these debates was very different to the measured Nixon–Brezhnev talks. Both leaders took ideas seriously and were keen fighters in the ideological struggle. But they also agreed on one fundamental thing: they had to abandon the old *realpolitik* that had brought a massive build-up of nuclear weapons and had threatened the very future of humanity.

Two and a half years later, on 15 May 1989, when Gorbachev went to meet the Chinese leader Deng Xiaoping in Beijing, the atmosphere was very different. This was the first Soviet visit since the Sino-Soviet rift. However, whilst Gorbachev and Deng did sign a treaty, unlike Gorbachev and Reagan in Reykjavik, there was not much meeting of minds. The atmosphere was tense. Students were demonstrating in Tian'anmen Square in support of democracy, and were looking to Gorbachev for support. The technocratic Deng, moreover, was a very different Communist to Gorbachev. The meeting was friendly enough, but there was little real engagement. Gorbachev wrote blandly in his memoirs, 'I think the key to his [Deng's] great influence . . . lies in his enormous experience and healthy pragmatism.'[5]

The two sharply contrasting meetings illustrate how much the three blocs – Soviet, Chinese and American – had changed since the last flurry of summits of 1971–2. Then, as in 1989, the Americans and Soviets had most in common: Nixon and Brezhnev were arch-pragmatists; Mao, the ageing utopian, had been reluctantly forced into pragmatic retreat by the disasters of the Cultural Revolution. By the mid-1980s the new leaders of all three blocs had disowned their predecessors. Reactions against cynical *realpolitik* in the United States and the USSR had brought two idealists to power – Reagan and Gorbachev; in China, by contrast, the hard-nosed Deng represented the absolute opposite of Mao's destructive utopianism. Just as China was losing its revolutionary élan, the United States and the Soviet Union were regaining theirs.

Reagan and Gorbachev embodied the two revolutions that were to change the world in the late 1980s: the liberal capitalist and the reform Communist. Though the second was largely responsible for the final collapse of Communism in its Soviet heartland, it was the first which ultimately won the struggle for global pre-eminence. Both, however, learnt from each other. Cold War hawks adopted some of the strategies (and even the language) of the Marxist-Leninists, whilst Gorbachev was increasingly swayed by liberal ideas.

The Reagan presidency marked the beginning of a renewed Western liberal ideological ascendancy. In the 1980s it looked as if it would achieve world domination, overwhelming China as well. Yet the liberal force that had stormed the citadels of the Kremlin ultimately failed to breach Beijing's Zhongnanhai – the home of China's elite. China's pragmatic leaders had little enthusiasm for any revolutionary talk, whether Maoist or liberal. China also had another model of development to fall back on – the authoritarian capitalism of the so-called 'Asian tigers'. Since Stalin's death the world's tectonic plates had been gradually shifting. The gulf between the West and the Soviet bloc had been narrowing, whilst both had been moving away from China. Gorbachev and Deng may have signed a Sino-Soviet agreement, but in truth 1989 marked a parting, not a meeting, of the two worlds.

II

In the late 1970s, a new genre emerged in China: 'reportage'. A literary form of journalism, it was often highly critical of the Communist Party and the Cultural Revolution. One of the most controversial pieces, 'People or Monsters?', written in 1979, was a fiercely sardonic account of a notorious corruption case in Bin County, Heilongjiang Province. The anti-heroine was the brazenly cynical Wang Shouxin. A sort of Communist Becky Sharp, she had started off as the humble cashier of the local coal company. When the Cultural Revolution arrived it unexpectedly 'brought out in her political urges that had lain dormant for many years'. Deciding to use the momentous changes to her own advantage, she teamed up with a 'former bandit', Zhang Feng, and created a new red guard unit, the 'Smash-the-Black-Nest Combat Force'. She then launched her own personal Cultural Revolution against the main obstacle to her advancement, the company's planner and accountant Liu Changchun – a member of the ruling 'Red Rebel Corps'. Fortunately Wang had ingratiated herself with a top official, who approved a 'debate' between the two. She accused Liu of favouring the 'power-holders' and stressing production rather than revolution. The authorities took her side and Liu was publicly humiliated and then arrested. The way was now open for Wang to become manager and party secretary of the firm. She then began her reign of corruption, using her control of local coal supplies to bribe and bully her way to wealth and power. Shrewd as always, she managed to survive Mao's death, but she eventually fell victim to the party's decision to allow criticisms of the Cultural Revolution in the late 1970s.[6]

The Cultural Revolution, of course, caused many forms of suffering, both physical and emotional. But one of the most long-lasting effects was disillusionment. The regime had used ideals of virtue and self-sacrifice to enthuse the population, and many had taken them at face value. When people decided that their idealism had been exploited by cynics like Wang Shouxin they became bitter. By the early 1970s, Radical Marxism-Leninism had been seriously discredited. Never again would the Chinese Communists return to Maoist class struggle. In fact, the end of the Cultural Revolution was to mark the beginning of a long, serpentine journey from Communism to capitalism.

Stalin's Terror of 1936-8 had brought a similar disillusionment. But the war against the Nazis had restored the Communist regime's *raison d'être*. Stalin was able to call forth popular sacrifice again in the interests of national survival, and thereafter Soviet Communism was inextricably linked with victory. This redemption was not possible in early 1970s China. One option, of course, was to go back to the orderly, Modernist Marxism of the 1950s. But much had changed since then: the Soviet model was looking worn, and whilst China had been engrossed in internecine struggles, its neighbouring rivals had been stealing a march on it. Taiwan and South Korea, the Asian tigers, with their unique blend of authoritarianism, capitalism and export-led growth, had actually achieved 'great leaps forward' and were now far ahead of their stagnating neighbour. Communists – especially those who had suffered in the Cultural Revolution – began to question the Soviet model fundamentally.

The first signs of change could be seen even during the last years of Mao. Officially the Cultural Revolution continued until his death, and its principles were stoutly defended by its four main supporters – including Mrs Mao, Jiang Qing. But the army, under its leader Lin Biao, had brought an end to its ultra-revolutionary phase by 1969, and after Lin's own fall in 1971, politics entered a period of uneasy calm. The agreement with the United States in 1971 showed that Mao was rethinking his strategy, and the change was confirmed by the rehabilitation of the pragmatic Deng Xiaoping and his appointment as Vice-Premier.

Nothing much would happen as long as Mao lived, and indeed towards the end of 1975 the radicals launched a successful attack on Deng, as a 'revisionist' and 'capitalist roader'. The ailing Mao lined up the colourless Hua Guofeng as his successor – the leader of the so-called 'whatever' faction, whose main guiding principle was that 'whatever' Mao said was correct. Hua still clung to the economic policies of the 1950s and 1960s, but the backlash against the Cultural Revolution became too intense.[7] He arrested Jiang Qing and the other members of the vilified 'Gang of Four' and in 1977 allowed Deng to return to his post as Vice-Premier. Deng was then helped by popular pressure to rehabilitate the victims of the purges, and defeated Hua and the 'whateverists' at the end of 1978.

Deng in 1978 was in the same position as Khrushchev in 1956. He needed to criticize the past to justify political change, but knew that if it went too far it could destroy the entire regime. During the power struggle at the top, students put several so-called 'big-character posters' on a wall west of Tian'anmen Square, attacking the 'whateverists' and the Gang of Four. Deng was very happy to have this popular support from 'Democracy Wall' – many of the posters were sycophantic in their praise for him – though he warned the students off targeting Mao himself. But as the criticisms became more radical, he ordered a crackdown in 1979. Deng was establishing clear limits to change and made it clear that he was no political liberal.

Deng's marriage of market reform with strict political control has, in essence, lasted to this day. The 'Four Modernizations' (as the project was called) was an extension of Lenin's Pragmatic Marxist NEP of the 1920s. It contrasted starkly with the Romantic reform Communist tradition that was born with Khrushchev and reached its culmination with Gorbachev. The Chinese leadership had one eye on the success of the capitalist Asian tigers, and another on the lessons of the Cultural Revolution. Mao, he concluded, by assailing the bureaucracy and stirring up mass democracy from below, had hastened civil war and collapse. Deng was determined not to repeat the mistake. He insisted on keeping the heavy-industrial and party bureaucrats on side, winning them over by persuasion, not violent confrontation.

The centrepiece of Deng's programme was to develop a two-track economy. Heavy industry would remain under state control; the party did not try to dissolve the old planning hierarchy with the acid of democracy or markets. Rather, it planted the seeds of the market alongside the inflexible and inefficient state sector. Collectives were abolished and private, family-based agriculture restored. At the same time, entrepreneurs were free to set up businesses – shops, small workshops and factories – with low tax rates and the freedom to hire and fire. Private business activity exploded, and by the end of the 1980s less than 40 per cent of national income came from the state sector – similar to levels in France and Italy. Soon the bureaucrats managing state industries became worried about competition from private business. But they did not try to sabotage the private-sector reforms, as one might have expected, because Deng made a crucial concession: state managers were allowed to set up private firms alongside state firms, using some of their profits. The bureaucrats, who might have been expected to resist market reforms, had thus been given a personal stake in their success.[8] At the same time a number of 'special economic zones' were allowed to offer foreign investors privileged tax and customs treatment. The market, originally seen as the state's junior partner, had begun to take over.

By the end of the 1980s, China had been transformed. The major cities were bright, bustling places; advertising hoardings had replaced the old party banners and political slogans. In place of the old Maoist workerism and austerity was a new enthusiasm for money and business. A journalist-cum-anthropologist, collecting material for a portrait of Chinese life, found how far values had changed when interviewing a garrulous Tianjin peasant woman and her anxious, cautious husband:

WIFE: . . . we've really made it. Townies are useless. We poor and lower-middle peasants are ahead: we've left the working class behind. They were stinking rich for thirty years, but now they're crawling along by oxcart.

HUSBAND: Never mind what she says. Once she starts she doesn't give a damn. The workers are the leading class.

WIFE: Leaders? Sure. But would you become a worker if anyone asked you? . . .

What are you laughing at? We really are rich . . . What's the Communist Party for, if not to rescue the poor from their sufferings?

HUSBAND (with a smile): That'll do. If you go on talking any longer you'll start singing [Cultural Revolution new model] opera.[9]

The reforms certainly had a dramatic effect on the countryside, and were very successful in improving productivity. Even Song Liying, a retired party official from Dazhai in Anhui Province – a model village in the Cultural Revolution period – accepted that life had improved for peasants since the reforms of the early 1980s:

> Before the reform . . . we weren't allowed to grow anything on our back-yard; we weren't allowed to produce anything for sale . . . As a village cadre, I would intervene myself if I knew anyone dared violate the rules. Now, you can do anything you like, raise pigs to eat or sell, make cloth tigers . . . In 1984, with the extra money we had, we bought a small black-and-white TV set. I still remember it was a panda brand. We all thought the electric box was magic with its sounds and images . . .
>
> Nowadays people know how to make good use of time. Before, if you came to our village, you would see people standing around, chatting, playing cards or mahjong. Now, you simply won't see anybody hanging around. They're all working![10]

Underlying the reforms of 1976–89 was an intellectual opening up, especially to the West. This was to be known as the era of 'Culture Fever', when Chinese intellectuals were allowed to debate the merits of a whole range of previously suppressed ideas – from neo-Confucianism to liberalism. It was, however, a preference for technocracy that won out. This seems surprising as the violence of the Cultural Revolution period might have been expected to produce a yearning for 'socialism with a human face' – a humane socialism that did not sacrifice the individual to the greater good. And amongst some it did: a group of Marxist humanists surrounding Wang Ruoshi read a mixture of the young Marx and translations of East European critiques of High Stalinism. However, Mao's extreme Romanticism had discredited even these modestly idealistic attitudes, and a technocratic Marxism was soon in the ascendant. Moreover, following Mao's malign neglect of education and expertise, 'Respect knowledge, respect talent' became the slogan of the day. Far more influential than the young Marx was the American futurologist Alvin Toffler, whose *Third Wave*, published in China in 1983, was a hit; in 2006, *People's Daily* counted Toffler amongst the '50 foreigners shaping modern China's development'.[11] Toffler's appeal lay in his claim that the 'second wave' of industrial society was over, and the world was entering a new era – the 'knowledge society' – in which a radically decentralized economy of diversity and consumer power would be held together by information technology. For Chinese readers, this seemed to promise a new future, free of the old Soviet industrial model. China could leap from the 'first wave' of agrarian society directly to the third wave, by mastering these new technologies.

There were, of course, tensions. The market produced losers as well as winners, and Beijing found it difficult to keep control of the local bosses-turned-businessmen, whilst corruption flourished. Conservatives were naturally unhappy, and the 'zigs' of liberalization were interrupted by occasional 'zags' – old-style campaigns against 'spiritual pollution' and 'bourgeois liberalism'. Workers, in particular, faced lower living standards with the 'smashing of the iron rice-bowl', or the end of the old welfare state. But the party leadership, fearful of disorder, moved very cautiously, and it was only by the end of the 1980s that welfare benefits actually began to be withdrawn. Worker unrest played a major part in the rebellions of 1989, and it almost helped to derail reform. But by then, a reform coalition had been built that included party bosses. Ten years after the end of the Cultural Revolution, China had decisively changed course. A visitor in 1968 would have found the China of 1988 virtually unrecognizable.

Western commentators were surprised by the changes, but in hindsight they should not have been. Despite significant opposition to market reforms, the experience of the Cultural Revolution had been so traumatic that the technocratic and liberalizing 'right' was in a good position to win political battles. In the Soviet bloc, in contrast, the regimes were following a very different course, because they had learnt different lessons from the late 1960s. They had already tried market reform, and it had ended in the Prague Spring. Therefore unlike the Chinese, who gave party bosses incentives to support market reform, they encouraged them to become paternalists, buying off workers and peasants with welfare and consumer goods. This strategy was to prove destabilizing, for it alienated educated, white-collar groups. And it was these groups who had the confidence and the power to challenge the system. The regimes therefore laid the foundations for a revolution within the party against Communism itself.

III

In the early 1980s, a Komsomol organization in a Soviet library convened a meeting to decide whether one of its librarians, who had been moonlighting as a Latin teacher at a religious seminary, should be expelled. Though religious observance was not illegal, and ordinary citizens could attend church, it was a big problem for party or Komsomol members – supposedly still the ideological vanguard. It was, indeed, grounds for expulsion. But these were pragmatic times, and the Komsomol committee was ambivalent. As one of the participants told Alexei Yurchak:

> At first our committee was against expelling that guy . . . Considering his degree, it was obvious that teaching Latin was much more appropriate and interesting for him than doing tedious library work. However, the problem was that . . . he was arrogant and disrespectful and just tried to show that he couldn't care less what we had to say. And unexpectedly, several people in our committee began attacking him for being a 'traitor of the motherland'. One committee member even said, 'And what would you do if you were offered a job by the CIA?' That was a ridiculous thing to say, of course, but at that point all of us started attacking the poor guy. We were not too kind to him.[12]

The episode is highly revealing. Here was a group of educated people, with a liberal, even sceptical attitude towards the ideology; they placed a high value on individual fulfilment in work, and were less driven by puritanical social duty than earlier generations. Even so, the system's collectivism broadly fitted in with their own morality, and they saw it as 'theirs'. Angered by a colleague who seemed so arrogantly to flout the rules of their own little *kollektiv*, they found themselves, much to their own surprise, invoking the harsh dogmas of earlier generations of Communists.

Despite the ebbing of ideological dynamism, many Soviet citizens still saw socialism, fundamentally, as just. Though party and Komsomol members might find party culture boring and pointless, it did not follow that they were cynical about Communism itself. Indeed, amongst many a residual idealism lingered. One Komsomol organizer from the town of Sovetsk, born in 1960, described the tedious routine of the meetings:

I understood perfectly well, and I think everybody did, that the decisions had been made in advance. The meeting had to be sat through . . . You could not talk much, so reading was optimal. Everyone read books. Everyone. And what's interesting, as soon as the meeting began, all heads bowed down and everyone started to read. Some fell asleep. But when a vote had to be taken, everyone roused – a certain sensor clicked in the head; 'Who's in favour?' – and you raised your hand automatically.[13]

But at the same time, though, he believed in Communism and the Komsomol: 'I wanted to be in the Komsomol because I wanted to be among the young avant-garde who would work to improve life . . . I felt that if you lived according to the right scheme – school, institute, work – everything in your life would be fine.'[14]

Many citizens of the USSR in the early 1980s continued to regard the Soviet system as superior in many ways to the one existing in the West. From their limited knowledge of the West, heavily influenced by official propaganda, many concluded that although the USSR might have lower living standards, it was superior in social justice, welfare, stability, morality and education.

Soviet citizens, of course, had the advantage of living in the imperial power. Communism was 'their' system and gave them international standing (with the exception of some disaffected nationalities, like the Baltic peoples). But throughout the bloc (bar Poland), support for broadly market socialist values, if not revolutionary ones, remained strong until the late 1980s. In Hungary in 1983, schoolchildren aged between ten and fourteen were given a list of words, and asked whether they 'liked' or 'did not like' them. Amongst the most popular were 'national flag' (liked by 98 per cent), 'red flag' (81 per cent), and 'money' (70 per cent); amongst the least popular were 'party secretary' (40 per cent), 'revolution' (38 per cent), and 'capitalism' (11 per cent).[15]

Children may, of course, be particularly susceptible to school propaganda, but some of the polls showed that adults were also broadly sympathetic: Hungarians were overwhelmingly in favour of socialist equality; the delivery of welfare by the state; collective farms; and the principle that 'everyone should subordinate his interests to those of the society'. On the other hand, there were also majorities in favour of greater political liberties ('people should be free to say what is on their minds') and greater market reforms.[16] Surveys of émigrés in the 1970s showed that support for this mixture of welfarist socialism and market reforms also applied to the USSR.[17]

Hungary had its own idiosyncrasies. János Kádár was widely popular (87.7 per cent were fully or partly satisfied) as a figure who had defended the interests of Hungarians against the USSR, and this may have distorted poll responses. The position of the parties in the other Communist states varied. Husák's Czechoslovak regime did promote higher living standards and consumerism, but unpublished official polls taken in 1986 show serious dissatisfaction with the regime's ideology and policies. Opinion in the GDR was also much less supportive of the socialist system than in Hungary and the USSR. But Polish opinion seems to have been in a class of its own. Independent polls taken between 1981 and 1986 showed that support for the leadership was a mere 25 per cent, and 50 per cent were unhappy with the system but were unwilling to challenge it. But even in anti-Communist Poland, opinion polls showed strong overall support for broadly socialist values. In a 1980 survey, taken during the Solidarity period, 'equality' was regarded as the second most important value, after 'family', and there was a great deal of support for ensuring more or less equal incomes for every citizen. Democracy was seen as valuable, but it was less important than equality.[18] The Communist regimes may not have created 'new socialist people', but they did create men and women with many socialist ideals which could be used to criticize Communism.

There were, of course, many dissidents throughout the bloc who criticized the regimes from a number of perspectives – populist-nationalist, liberal-democratic and radical socialist. The Soviet bloc countries' signing of the Helsinki accords (which included protection of human rights) in 1975 particularly strengthened liberal groups, whilst the growing environmental movement became the focus of other dissident groups.

Official response to dissidence varied. Repression was greatest in Albania and Romania; Poland and especially Hungary were much more liberal, as was Yugoslavia. Secret policemen were extremely active in East Germany and Czechoslovakia, and Brezhnev's KGB expended much energy persecuting a tiny, but increasingly vocal dissident movement. The show trial of the writers Siniavskii and Daniel in 1966 marked the end of the Khrushchev thaw, and several intellectuals were arrested or exiled. But few sought a return to the days of Stalin. In part this was a pragmatic choice: terror could get out of hand, threaten officials themselves and possibly upset relations with the West. The KGB, therefore, tried to stay within 'socialist legality' and go through some form of due process. That, though, could be embarrassing and unpredictable, so normally the KGB first tried 'advice' – or 'explanatory work' as the jargon described it. If the 'advice' was ignored, the dissident could be expelled from the USSR, as was the case with the conservative nationalist writer Aleksandr Solzhenitsyn, or, as happened to the liberal physicist Andrei Sakharov, sent into internal exile. Alternatively a pliant psychiatrist might be persuaded to furnish a diagnosis of 'sluggish schizophrenia' – a syndrome known only in the Soviet bloc, the symptoms of which included 'reformist delusions'. The dissident would then be sent to a 'special psychiatric hospital' and subjected to painful punitive 'treatments'.[19]

East Germany had one of the best-organized and largest secret police services in the entire bloc – the feared *Staatssicherheitsdienst* (State Security Service), or 'Stasi'. This was a much more extensive organization than the KGB. The Stasi had 91,000 staff to monitor a population of 16.4 million (compared with the 7,000 Gestapo in the pan-German population of 66 million). Moreover, the Stasi was assiduous in building a network of informants, especially within dissident groups; in the eighteen years of the Honecker era, some 500,000 people informed on their neighbours, colleagues and relatives at some point in their lives.[20] Motives for informing varied. Some were coerced (though, according to Stasi figures, only a small minority (7.7 per cent)); others were given rewards; many merely wanted to please the authorities, or hoped that working for the Stasi might advance their careers. But Stasi officers were instructed to use ideologically principled arguments to elicit cooperation from informants as much as was possible, and on many occasions this clearly worked.[21] One informant, 'Rolf' – an idealist who supported the GDR but was unhappy with official policies towards the environment – was told by the Stasi that if he helped them he would be contributing to world peace by preventing espionage. They also promised him that they would look into any environmental complaints he might have. As he remembers:

I used to read the *Weltbühne* [*World Stage*] newspaper at that time and once there was an article in it and yes, it sounds mad, but it said that it was important at that time to do more than just get on with your daily life, that you should do more than just get up and go to work if you wanted to ensure peace. . .

In a word they made use of my, yeah what should I say, my love of peace, maybe that sounds a bit mushy, my concerns for the world, and they said: 'You can help us fight this together.' Yes, and then I said: 'I've got nothing against that.'[22]

Once 'Rolf' realized that the Stasi was manipulating him, he broke off all contact – though that was unusual. It was more common for the Stasi to abandon the informant because they were not providing useful information.

The impact of such information was often devastating. The lives and careers of many were ruined; more rarely persecution resulted in death. The greatest victim, though, was trust. As one who had been part of dissident circles explained: 'These informers determined my life, changed my life over those ten years. In one way or another – because they poisoned us with mistrust. They caused damage simply because I suspected that there could have been informers in my vicinity.'[23] When the files were opened in the 1990s, many discovered that friends or even spouses had been spying on them for years.

With the exception of Poland, the enormous expense and effort devoted to secret intelligence in the GDR and also in the Soviet Union seems bizarre as the number of dissidents was small, as was their influence on broader society.[24] Yet whilst Soviet bloc populations, in most countries, were unwilling to challenge the system, and even supported aspects of it, sharp differences were emerging within society – not between White and Red partisanship, but between white and blue collar. A comparison between Soviet émigrés' views from the Stalin era and those of the 1970s and 1980s shows that whilst a majority in both eras favoured industrialization, a mixed, NEP-style economy, extensive state welfare, and fewer political controls and repression, there were also striking differences. In the Stalin era, the young and the educated were more likely to favour state control and welfare than workers and peasants; in the 1970s and 1980s, it was the exact opposite. Moreover, the divisions between those with and those without higher education hardened into coherent, ideological divisions between the more liberal and less liberal. In the Stalin era workers and peasants were *more* economically liberal than the educated, but people of all social groups were split more or less evenly over whether controls on the press should be kept and freedom of speech restricted. In the Brezhnev and Gorbachev eras, in contrast, the young and the educated were not only more economically liberal than the less educated, but more politically liberal as well. So, in the Stalin era, 55.1 per cent of those with a higher education supported the existing strict controls on the press, compared with 47 per cent of those with a secondary education; in the Gorbachev era, in contrast, 55.7 per cent of university-educated people thought it right to ban certain books, compared with an overwhelming 86.8 per cent of those with less than a secondary education.[25]

Hungarian polls in 1983–4 show a similar ideological division based on education. Sociologists found that 49 per cent of degree-holders favoured a liberalizing 'democratic socialism', compared with only 4 per cent of those with less than a secondary education. The vast majority of the least well-educated supported a number of other ideological positions which were fundamentally anti-reform.[26]

This growing difference between the university-educated and ordinary citizens, and the defection of the intelligentsia, was hardly surprising given the style of socialist paternalism that had prevailed since the 1960s. Since Stalin's death, the party had been quick to respond to worker and peasant discontent by improving their living standards, and that had tended to undermine the privileged position enjoyed by the educated under Stalin.

At the same time, paternalism had undermined the prestige of the party amongst the educated. Throughout the Soviet bloc party bosses of all ranks were still largely people with political rather than technical skills – people like the officials Horváth and Szakolczai interviewed.[27] They were also generally less well-educated than economic managers. And as the economies started to experience difficulties, the educated blamed officials' amateurism and resented having to be subservient to people less well-educated than themselves. Even so, links between the intelligentsia and the Communist parties remained, especially at the very top, and it was through these channels that liberal reformist ideas penetrated the power structure. The educated may have been disillusioned with Communism, but its end was not brought by a broad-based middle-class revolution; it was a much more elitist affair. To look for the roots of the end of Communism, we need to look within the Communist party itself.

IV

When, in 1986, the philosopher and covert 'White' Aleksandr Tsipko first visited the Central Committee building in Moscow's Old Square as a newly appointed ideological consultant, he was stunned to discover a deeply anti-Communist atmosphere at the very heart of the Communist Party:

> French journalists who wrote at the start of *perestroika* that the breeding ground of counter-revolution in the USSR was the headquarters of Communism, the CPSU Central Committee, were right. Working at the time as a consultant to the International Department of the CPSU Central Committee, I discovered to my surprise that the mood among the highest hierarchy of that organisation did not differ at all from the mood in the Academy of Sciences or in the humanities institutes ... It was clear that only a complete hypocrite could believe in the supremacy of socialism over capitalism. It was also clear that the socialist experiment had suffered defeat.[28]

Tsipko, who had completely abandoned Marxism, noted how much things had changed since the pre-Prague Spring years when he worked in the Komsomol's Central Committee. Then there had been a great deal of optimism about the future, and most of his colleagues had been convinced Communist nationalists, or 'Red Slavophiles' as he called them.[29] During the 1970s, however, the atmosphere amongst the intelligentsia had become distinctly more liberal and pro-Western, and many had moved towards Social Democracy. These ideas had also affected the intellectuals who worked in party headquarters – indeed throughout the bloc (and in China as well) 'party intelligentsias' were often in the vanguard of reformist thought. Party intellectuals were very much part of the broader non-party intelligentsia, and shared their more liberal values, but they also had much closer links with foreigners than most people, especially in the USSR. Cosmopolitan in outlook, they were therefore more acutely sensitive than most to the USSR's status abroad. And one group that was to become especially vocal and influential was those party members working in the Central Committee's departments dealing with foreign affairs – in effect the successors of the Comintern. People like Georgii Shakhnazarov and Vadim Zagladin – both future advisers of Gorbachev – realized that the USSR was losing its moral force in the world.[30] They sought high international status for the USSR, but they believed it could only be achieved if it changed and became the leader of a progressive, more liberal Communist movement. By concentrating exclusively on military power, the USSR was forfeiting its prestige, even amongst Western Communist parties. These reformers, initially keen supporters of Soviet involvement in Africa, were especially disillusioned by the militarization of Soviet support for revolutionary regimes in the Third World. They saw the ageing Brezhnev much as the previous generation had viewed the ageing Stalin: a reactionary figure who had detached the USSR from the cause of 'progress'.

A good example of this type of party intellectual was Mikhail Gorbachev's future ideology chief, Aleksandr Iakovlev. Born in 1923 to a peasant family, he had risen through the party, studied in party academic institutions, and become acting head of the Propaganda Department of the Central Committee from 1965. However, in 1972 he wrote an article criticizing all kinds of nationalism – including Russian 'great-power chauvinism' and anti-Semitism. Brezhnev, predictably, was displeased, and Iakovlev was exiled to Ottawa as ambassador to Canada.

His apparent misfortune, though, was in fact his big break. In 1983, a new member of the Politburo, Mikhail Gorbachev, visited Canada, and Iakovlev was in charge of organizing the trip. They got on well, Gorbachev complaining about *stasis* at home, and Iakovlev explaining 'how primitive and shaming the policy of the USSR looks from here, from the other side of the planet'.[31] When Gorbachev took power two years later, Iakovlev was to become one of his main mentors. Their Canadian meeting marked the beginning of an alliance between liberal party intellectuals and Marxist party reformers that was eventually to destroy Soviet Communism.

Ultimately, then, it was this small 'vanguard' alliance of Communist Party politicians and intellectuals that led the revolution against Communism – just as small bands of revolutionary intellectuals had brought Communism to power. But neither group was operating in a vacuum. By the early 1980s the future of Communism in the Soviet bloc looked increasingly grim. The majority of East European countries may have been stable – and, as we have seen, there was still much support for the regimes' socialist paternalism – but the bloc had serious weaknesses, especially in Poland and in the developing world. And when, from the end of the 1970s, international economic conditions deteriorated and the West began its counter-attack, the bloc became extremely vulnerable. In these conditions, a fundamentally conservative leadership was willing to give the reformers a hearing.

V

In 1980, when the Polish Communist Party effectively collapsed before the onslaught of the Solidarity independent trade union, the film director Andrzej Wajda produced his cinematic account of the uprising and its history – *Man of Iron*. The film used documentary footage of the uprising but it was also a conventional film drama. At its core was the relationship between the old worker Birkut and his educated son, Maciek. Birkut is the conscience of the Polish working class, disillusioned with the party, but sharing little sympathy with the student rebellions of 1968 and Maciek's involvement in them. The mistrust between workers and students is reciprocated when the students refuse to support the 1970 Baltic shipyard strikes. When his father is shot by police, Maciek realizes that he has to forge a worker–intelligentsia alliance and becomes an activist in Gdańsk. After many struggles, his goal is achieved with the Solidarity strikes of 1980. And helping to forge this unity is the Catholic Church: Maciek plants a cross where his father fell, and he marries in a church, his (film-maker) wife given away by the leader of Solidarity, the mustachioed electrician Lech Wałesa (played by himself).

Wajda's film reflected the crucial importance of the relations between white- and blue-collar workers. Divisions between the two were one of the main sources of stability in Communist regimes: society was too divided to mount a real challenge to the status quo. Also, many Polish workers, like their Soviet-bloc confrères, broadly endorsed socialist values and benefited from improving standards of living – a theme explored by the prequel to *Man of Iron*, *Man of Marble*. In Poland alone, however, the Communists' paternalistic strategy failed to achieve the stability it needed, largely because nationalism, together with the extraordinary power of the Catholic Church, helped to reconcile white with blue.

Poland, of course, had been the Achilles heel of the bloc for decades, and after the 1956 crisis the Polish party's retreat – on the issues of collectivization, religion and the private sector – was more extensive than elsewhere. Even so, after a period of relative peace, conflict between the party and sections of society resumed after 1968. In that year Gomułka's repression of student dissent alienated the intelligentsia, and in 1970 he antagonized workers with price rises. Strikes were put down by force, but Gomułka, who had survived so many vicissitudes, was forced to stand down. He was replaced by Edvard Gierek, a worker by background, who responded to worker discontent by pursuing one of the most lavish and expensive programmes of socialist paternalism in the bloc, all financed by Western loans. The strategy worked, for a time. Living standards rose by 40 per cent, and the party leaders basked in the public's esteem: in 1975, when asked whether they had confidence in their national leaders, 84.8 per cent replied 'yes' or 'rather so'.[32] Yet in the absence of economic reforms, the massive new industrial investments did not provide the expected returns, and the leadership was forced to make sudden, savage cuts in investment and food subsidies. The resulting 60 per cent rise in food prices in 1976 showed how shallow and conditional popular support for the regime was. Workers' strikes and violent demonstrations again flared up, and were again harshly suppressed. This time, though, the use of repression was more damaging to the regime. Notwithstanding *Man of Iron*, it was 1976 rather than 1970 that precipitated the worker–intelligentsia alliance, and in that year a group of thirteen intellectuals founded the Committee for the Defence of Workers (KOR) to provide legal and other support for strikers, providing a model for many other oppositional groups throughout Poland. By 1980 Poland had a large network of democratic oppositional groups.

Central to this alliance was the Catholic Church – and this is one of the main reasons why Poland was different. As in the rest of the bloc, blue-collar and white-collar groups had very different views on politics: workers favoured equality much more than the intelligentsia, and many of the intellectual dissidents, with their Marxist background, were suspicious of the Church.[33] Nevertheless, the Church successfully placed itself at the head of a nationalist, anti-Communist revival. Its massive nine-year campaign to celebrate the 'Great Novena of the millennium', the anniversary of the coming of Christianity to Poland, saw huge crowds marching behind the Black Madonna of Częstochowa and the Polish crowned eagle. By the mid-1970s, therefore, the dissident intelligentsia was beginning to move towards the Church (with the reforms of the Second Vatican Council). When in 1978 the election to the papacy of Karol Wojtiła, Archbishop of Krakow and a worker in his youth, gave the Catholic Church even greater nationalist credentials, the Polish Communist party confronted a broad social movement united behind a coherent alternative ideology and an effective organization with international reach.[34] The dissident Adam Michnik and the journalist Jacek Żakowski remember the power of this religious nationalism amongst workers:

> On 16 October 1978, I was riding in a taxi when the radio program was interrupted. The announcer, whose voice was dry and nervous, read the official press communiqué stating that Cracow's cardinal Karol Wojtiła had just been elected pope. The taxi driver drove off the road. He couldn't take me further because his hands were shaking from emotion ... In Cracow's market square, Piotr Skrzynecki [a well-known theatre and film director] shouted 'Finally a Polish worker has amounted to something!'[35]

As was clear from Skrzynecki's comment, the intelligentsia and workers were now united behind the Catholic Church, and the Polish regime had to face unusually strong challenges to its authority. Even so, the Polish party's travails were merely extreme forms of the forces buffeting every Communist state in the late 1970s and 1980s. All regimes, except the USSR's, had taken advantage of the opening to the West in the mid-1970s and had borrowed money from Western banks. And all of them found their inefficient smokestack industries unable to pay off those debts with increased exports.

Yet they were suffering, in extreme form, from conditions that affected the whole of the industrialized world. A global glut of heavy industrial goods, new computer technologies, and the oil-price hike all demanded radical changes to an economic project developed in the 1940s and 1950s. At the same time organized labour had been empowered by high levels of employment and the after-shocks of the 1968 rebellions. Wage levels rose as productivity and profitability fell, and business lost faith and refused to invest. Share prices, an indication of economies' levels of optimism, fell by two thirds between the early 1960s and the mid-1970s.[36] Clearly the industrialized world needed a new economic model – one that redirected investment into more profitable, high-tech areas.

Communist regimes found these challenges particularly difficult because, despite their image of power and monolithic unity, they were politically weak. They had been captured by powerful heavy-industrial and defence interests, and also could not risk renewed social conflict with workers. But west of the iron curtain, too, governments, especially of the left, found it difficult to promote reforms that might alienate workers. Meanwhile, business and the conservative right mobilized against the power of labour at home, moves which coincided with a massive American rearmament programme against the USSR. But this was an ideological counter-revolution as much as a military one. Much as Kennedy had tried to compete with the USSR by stressing a new capitalist model of Third World development, so Reagan's United States adopted some of the revolutionary, optimistic style of 1970s Third World Communism in the interests of a right-wing liberalism. After an era of superpower *realpolitik*, ideas again took centre-stage.

VI

In the early 1940s, at the height of debates over the Nazi–Soviet pact, a young Brooklyn-born college lecturer, Irving Kristol, was regularly to be seen in Alcove Number 1 of the New York City College cafeteria, devouring the latest issues of the Trotskyist-leaning magazines the *Partisan Review* and the *New Internationalist*, edited by the Trinidadian Marxist C. L. R James. The Stalinists, meanwhile, occupied Alcove Number 2. Like many New York intellectuals, they were all absorbed in European intellectual struggles, and they remained so.[37] But by the end of the 1970s Kristol had switched sides in the conflict. He was now at the centre of a 'neo-conservative' group of intellectuals, many originally from the Marxist left, who were developing the intellectual firepower for a counter-revolution against the socialist and Third-Worldist vision of equality.

Were the neo-conservatives Trotsky's revenge on the USSR? It may seem far-fetched to seek Marxist roots in neo-conservatism, but a striking number of the writers for *The Public Interest*, Kristol's neo-conservative journal, had been close to Trotskyism. They were now hearty cheer-leaders for capitalism, having become, in effect, a variety of American nationalist (although as promoters of 'universal' American values rather than narrow xenophobes). But they shared a number of Trotskyist attitudes: internationalism, a belief in struggle, the utopian notion of a moral society at the 'end of history', a hatred of Stalinist *realpolitik*, and most importantly, a Romantic belief in the power of ideas and morality to change the world. The Trotskyist journals that Kristol had read so avidly in the 1940s condemned Stalinism from a Romantic perspective – for ignoring the role of mass enthusiasm in socialism – and similarly, neo-conservatives believed in the power of ideological commitment. Yet where Trotskyists hoped to mobilize the proletariat with ideas of collectivism, the neo-conservatives tried to rouse public opinion with a mixture of bourgeois morality and high patriotism. Although, like the old Marxist left, the neo-conservatives maintained links with organized labour, they had been incensed by the student assault on university authorities in 1968, and were outraged by the New Left's support for Communist guerrillas in the Vietnam War.

Kristol and his group, therefore, were the capitalist equivalent of the Romantic Marxists, calling for moral renewal and a mobilization against the Communist threat. But just as Communism was most effective when it combined the Romanticism of the young Marx with the technocratic later Marx, so the capitalist counter-revolution needed rationalistic as well as moral foundations. It found them in 'neo-liberalism', promoted most effectively by another, slightly older Brooklyner – the economist Milton Friedman. Friedman, a former New Dealer, was a militant opponent of the mixed economy created in the aftermath of World War II. He popularized an elegant and coherent vision of the laissez-faire economics propounded by people such as his fellow Chicago professor Friedrich Hayek: states, Friedman insisted, were predatory, corrupt and inefficient, stifling growth and creativity. Their power had to be destroyed and the natural forces of the market allowed to flourish. This ideology was highly technocratic: Friedman even argued that monetary policy – and thus, in effect, economic policy – could be run by a computer, which, free from political pressure, could defeat inflation. But it was also revolutionary. As one of Friedman's students remembered: 'What was particularly exciting were the same qualities that made Marxism so appealing to many other young people at the time – simplicity together with apparent logical completeness; idealism combined with radicalism.'[38]

The two Brooklyners were not themselves close, and indeed there were major intellectual differences between them. Though both were visionaries, and were willing to support forceful attacks on Communism, Kristol's neo-conservatives were more militaristic, moralistic and apocalyptic in their outlook, and were more positive about the role of the state and labour, than the neo-liberals. In the aftermath of 1968, however, they came together in the struggle against Communism, convinced, like the old Leninists, that a vanguard of intellectuals had to attack the old, corrupt state and replace it with something new. Neo-liberals and neo-conservatives united behind a programme of 'revolutionary liberalism' that used the Marxist-Leninists' militant and mobilizational methods against them. And they found their champion in another former New Dealer, now radical anti-Communist – Ronald Reagan.

The continuing erosion of American power and evidence of revolutionary success in the Third World strengthened the credibility of the neo-conservatives. They were convinced that President Carter, in forcing America's gendarmes to respect human rights, was weakening both them and American power. The neo-conservative intellectual Jean Kirkpatrick (later Reagan's ambassador to the United Nations) developed one of the most influential arguments for anti-Communist militancy, by drawing a sharp distinction between 'totalitarianism' and 'authoritarianism'. Unlike 'authoritarian' regimes, she argued, which would evolve into liberal democracy as they modernized, 'totalitarian' regimes would never do so. Therefore if the United States wanted to promote democracy, it had to support authoritarians against totalitarian Communists, however unsavoury the former were.[39]

The climacteric year of 1979 proved to be the turning point. The United States' policy was buffeted by a series of disasters: the Sandinistas' revolution, the Islamist defeat of the Shah of Iran and the Soviet invasion of Afghanistan. All seemed to bear out the neo-conservative analysis of Soviet strength and aggression, and the following year Americans responded by voting to fight back, electing Ronald Reagan president by a landslide the following November.

The crisis of America's economic order, though, was more acute and the response more immediate. Washington's efforts to maintain both defence and welfare spending by printing money succeeded for some time, but the blows to American prestige in Iran and Afghanistan were the final straw, and Washington faced a flight from the dollar and the end of its status as the major world currency. On 14 October 1979 the head of the Federal Reserve, Paul Volcker, implemented the anti-inflationary measures proposed by Friedman and decided to give financiers what they wanted: a massive hike in interest rates, an assault on inflation, and a highly valued dollar. This, together with the so-called 'supply-side' economic revolution, increased the profitability of capital – cutting taxes on corporations and reducing welfare, whilst raising unemployment and weakening the power of labour.[40] More generally, it marked the final end of the economic order established at Bretton Woods in 1944. The Vietnam defeat had shown Washington that it could not maintain its global hegemony by taxing and conscripting its citizens, but only in 1979 did it, almost accidentally, find a viable alternative. International finance would become the fuel of American power. It was this alliance between the United States and global finance that gave it the power to fight a new phase in what is often called the 'second Cold War'. And it was this powerful system that was to bestride the world for almost three decades, until it spectacularly imploded in September 2008.

The United States' final struggle against Communism was therefore largely financed by foreign loans – many of them Japanese.[41] Washington could now fight to regain its global supremacy without demanding sacrifices from its population. However, its objective – rearmament – had less impact on American power than its unintended consequences. In order to fund its massive borrowing, the United States used high interest rates to attract much of the world's capital. That in turn caused a financial famine within the Second and Third Worlds: a $46.8 billion outflow from the G7 industrialized countries in the 1970s became a $347.4 billion inflow in the 1980s.[42] The resulting shortage of capital inevitably hit the indebted, and especially Communist regimes.

Not all Communist states were affected: China, together with other East Asian states, had little debt and benefited from a new liberal trade regime. It was allowed to export cheap industrial goods to the United States, and by the 2000s China was to take the place of Japan as the main source of capital for an indebted Washington. But the USSR's satellites in Eastern Europe and its allies in the South were less fortunate. Their industrial goods were not in demand, and as a group they were the most indebted of all countries. In 1979 Poland's debt service ratio was a massive 92 per cent, and the GDR's 54 per cent, compared with Mexico's 55 per cent and Brazil's 31 per cent, and much higher than a prudent 25 per cent.[43] They now faced crippling interest rates and the withdrawal of loans. As Stalin had anticipated when he rejected Marshall

Aid, succumbing to the lure of Western credit was dangerous. East European Communists were to rue the day they took the Western shilling.

Poland and Romania effectively became bankrupt and suffered the humiliation of having to beg Western capitalists to reschedule their debt; Hungary and the GDR were in less serious trouble, and survived with temporary financing. All had to cut living standards, particularly for the industrial working class – something they found painful. Communist states were weak, and their regimes had little legitimacy. The debt crisis was to corrode it even further.

Predictably, unreformed Stalinism was best able to impose austerity. When Romania defaulted on its debt in 1981 and was forced to request rescheduling, bread rationing was introduced; energy was only available intermittently, and the use of refrigerators and vacuum-cleaners banned. Work was intensified and extended to Sundays and holidays. When petrol became scarce the government, supposedly a harbinger of modernity, was humiliatingly forced to encourage a return to horse-drawn transport. The Securitate developed a Stasi-style network of informants to enforce discipline, and the state intruded ever further into private life, including the notorious compulsory examinations of women to stop abortions and reverse the falling birth-rate.

In the more liberal and decentralized Yugoslavia, in contrast, the federal state's austerity programme only accelerated political disintegration. Deeply indebted, it was forced to go cap in hand for loans to the IMF, which imposed tight conditions in 1982. A previous supporter of decentralization, the IMF now declared, understandably, that if austerity measures were to work, the republics had to be stripped of their autonomous powers to borrow and create money. The wealthier republics – especially Slovenia and Croatia – objected, and struggles between them and their poorer neighbours continued throughout the 1980s, setting the scene for the apocalyptic breakdown of the 1990s.[44] Communist leaders increasingly acted as republican, rather than all-Yugoslav politicians, and local nationalisms replaced Marxist Yugoslavism. Tito's death in 1980 had dissolved some of the country's unifying glue, but the consequences of international debt and IMF intervention did the rest. The bonds holding Yugoslavia together were disintegrating.

In Poland, the debt crisis brought the almost complete collapse of Communist power. When in 1980 the government was forced to impose austerity measures and reduce the distribution of meat, it was met by strikes. The stoppage at the Lenin Shipyard in the Baltic port of Gdańsk was one of the best organized and the workers soon moved from economic to political demands. They erected a wooden cross outside the factory in memory of four workers killed in 1970 and launched a broader movement, 'Solidarity', to fight for social justice and independent trade unions. The strikes, joined by people across the social spectrum, spread and the economy was soon paralysed. The Communists, now led by Stanislaw Kania, had no option but to permit trade union activity entirely free of party control. In August 1980, Solidarity and the party signed agreements which, for the first time since the end of the Popular Fronts of the 1940s, gave non-Communists real power. For the next sixteen months, the Communists and Solidarity faced each other in a tense stand-off.

This could not last for ever. Solidarity was becoming more assertive, and a planned strike in December 1981 raised Soviet fears of rebellion. The Kremlin put pressure on Kania, and the leader of the army, General Wojciech Jaruzelski, to rescue the decaying party by imposing military rule. The Polish leadership was naturally reluctant to take responsibility for an unpopular crackdown, and Kania even seems to have become sympathetic to Solidarity.[45] Moscow decided he had to go, and he was replaced as first secretary by Jaruzelski, who, threatened by a Red Army invasion, agreed to Moscow's wishes.

The military now took power following Jaruzelski's declaration of martial law, killing about a hundred people. Solidarity activists were arrested, and stability was restored. As Jaruzelski had predicted, the measure removed any remaining legitimacy the party still possessed. This was barely a Communist state any more. The military man Jaruzelski, with his signature dark glasses, looked more like an austere version of a Latin American dictator than a Communist party leader; the state and the army now ruled, not the party.[46] Most importantly, the events of 1981 made clear that the limits of Soviet support for Eastern Europe were being reached. The Soviets made it clear to Communist elites (though not to the rest of the world) that the Brezhnev doctrine and the promise of military support for Soviet-bloc regimes were now dead.[47] And although the USSR was forced to give huge credits to Poland in 1981–2, Soviet patience with its unstable East European clients was running out, partly because it was itself feeling poorer; whilst the oil price was still high, it had been falling since 1981. In response to threats that the East Germans would have to borrow more money from the West unless it received greater infusions from the USSR, Nikolai Baibakov, the head of the Soviet planning organization, told them that they had to cut investment:

> I have to think about the People's Republic of Poland! When I cut back on oil there (I am going there next week) that would be unbearable for social-ism . . . And Vietnam is starving. We have to help. Should we just give away South-East Asia? Angola, Mozambique, Ethiopia, Yemen. We carry them all. And our own standard of living is extraordinarily low. We really must improve it.[48]

Communists in Eastern Europe were not the only ones to suffer in the new international economic order. Many Third World states, of all ideologies, were hit by the rises in interest rates and the world recession, as raw material prices fell and debt became expensive. Some Commu-nist regimes in the Third World, though, were especially vulnerable because they were more likely to pursue ambitious policies of economic development and welfare. The debt problem, therefore, especially affected them.

Exacerbating the economic and debt crises was the fact that Com-munist regimes were forced to deal with a newly assertive IMF and World Bank. In contrast to the 1970s, when these international institu-tions counselled state-led development, the United States now used them to impose its neo-liberal vision on the world. In February 1980, Robert McNamara, head of the World Bank, introduced the long-term 'Struc-tural Adjustment Loan' programme for countries in economic trouble. This programme, together with those of the IMF, became one of the most effective weapons of neo-liberalism in the Second and Third Worlds. Under the slogan 'stabilize, privatize and liberalize', money was given only if the state was cut back, the economy was privatized and markets were unleashed.

There were now strong incentives for Communists in the Third World to abandon their economic model. But forces from within the Communist world also influenced them, notably the Chinese embrace of the market in 1978. The defection of the regime which had previously espoused hard-line Communist purism in the Third World, influenced by the success of the East Asian tigers, was a major blow to Marxist-Leninists. The failures of socialist planning also played their part. By the mid-1980s, several pro-

Soviet states were introducing market reforms. In 1984 Guinea-Bissau began cooperating with the IMF, as did Mozambique in 1987, the year after the death of Samora Machel in a plane crash. Even Angola, still involved in civil war with American allies and therefore excluded from IMF aid, introduced market reforms in 1985.

By the mid-1980s, debt and financial crisis had weakened Communism, and had a devastating effect on regimes in the South. But they did not destroy it in its Soviet and East European heartland. Indeed, conservative Communists in the USSR, hostile to economic reform, pointed to debt as evidence of the dangers of capitalism and collaboration with the West. The results of Ronald Reagan's neo-conservative revolution in American foreign policy were similar: they had a major impact in the South, but a much more ambiguous one on the USSR and Eastern Europe.

The mid-1980s was an era of war-scares, on both sides of the iron curtain, and in the United States several popular films and TV series were screened on the theme of Soviet attacks and invasions. One of the most implausible – and violent – was *Red Dawn* (1984).[49] The plot is far-fetched: the perfidious Europeans – with the exception of loyal Albion – have abandoned Washington; a revolutionary regime controls Mexico; and the Soviets and their allies (the Cubans and Nicaraguans) occupy vast swathes of the central United States. Rather like the inhabitants of 1950s Mosinee, Americans are subjected to the grim propagandizing of Soviet culture, and cinema-goers have to put up with screenings of *Aleksandr Nevskii*. Nevertheless, many Americans collaborate, and the Soviets become entrenched. But there is one thing the Reds did not foresee: 'the invading armies planned for everything – except for eight kids called "The Wolverines"'. The Wolverines, most of whom are members of a small-town high-school football team in Calumet, Colorado, wage a guerrilla war against the occupying forces in the name of freedom, and become a serious threat to the Soviets. They are eventually defeated, but when America is finally liberated their names are remembered, inscribed on the 'Partisan Rock'.

The film was financed by Hollywood, not sponsored by government. But it did capture a new American self-image that became increasingly influential during the second Cold War. No longer was the United States Nixon's global policeman, maintaining order against Communist revolutionaries through a network of regional gendarmes.

It was the underdog, the partisan and the freedom fighter, struggling against the totalitarian monolith. And whilst the elderly Reagan was hardly a capitalist Che Guevara, he was determined to bring an idealism and militancy to the American cause that had hitherto been the preserve of the Communist guerrillas.

Reagan, the son of a poor shoe salesman from Illinois, was not a conventional neo-conservative. His contemporaries found him unfathomable, and he remains something of an enigma to this day. He possessed an idealistic and optimistic disposition, inherited from his Evangelical Christian mother, which was very popular amongst American voters. And yet he was also a liberal militant, determined to resist the dangers to the 'free world' posed by the Communist 'evil empire'. In his fundamental optimism he was closer to the neo-liberals. He was convinced that Communism would ultimately fall because it was economically irrational, and he had a genuine commitment to nuclear disarmament. Nevertheless, he shared much of the belligerence of the neo-conservatives, especially in the early years of his presidency. He was a passionate anti-Communist ideologue, and he presided over the largest peacetime rearmament in American history, with defence spending absorbing 30 per cent of the federal budget between 1981 and 1985. He also appointed neo-conservatives like Paul Wolfowitz to junior positions (though 'doves' were also powerful in his administration), and his Marxist-inflected language echoed theirs. As he told the British parliament in 1982:

> In an ironic sense Karl Marx was right. We are witnessing today a great revolutionary crisis, a crisis where the demands of the economic order are conflicting directly with the political order. But the crisis is happening in . . . the home of Marxism-Leninism . . . It is the Soviet Union that runs against the tide of history.[50]

In the Third World, there were strong practical reasons for Reagan to adopt a revolutionary idealism. Nixon's gendarmes had failed to stem the tide of Communist success, as had Jimmy Carter's efforts to force them to respect human rights. Reagan was determined to use military force to roll back Communism – especially in Central America. He refused to accept that Communism was a response to local injustices; guerrillas were 'military personnel', trained by the USSR.[51] However, he was still constrained by Vietnam, and there was little public support for a return to sustained all-out warfare in the Third World. Reagan could fight conventional wars where victory was easy – as in the invasion of the tiny island of Grenada in 1983 – but such cases were few. The use of guerrilla strategies, developed by Communists, was therefore an excellent solution. They allowed pro-American movements to appear indigenous; they were cheap; and they could be carried out in secret, without congressional oversight. The new policy, pursued in Nicaragua, the Philippines, Afghanistan, Angola, Ethiopia and El Salvador, was blandly dubbed 'Low Intensity Conflict', but it owed a great deal to the tactics of Maoism and the guerrilla tradition.[52] Rather than supporting military dictators, the United States would support local insurgent groups. Warfare was to be 'civilianized' – the Maoist 'people's war' – whilst 'psyops' ('agitprop' in Communist language) was central to the new strategy. Leftist and Communist regimes were to be undermined using sabotage and assassinations. But efforts were also made to win the political argument and build up 'third forces', against the Communists and the old dictators. Anti-Communists amongst the urban middle classes and conservative churches were mobilized, and sometimes old authoritarian allies, like Ferdinand Marcos of the Philippines, were abandoned. By 1985 the strategy was being justified ideologically, as the 'Reagan Doctrine', a policy of 'anti-Communist revolution' designed to bring democracy to the world.[53]

Reagan began his military counter-offensive against Communism in Central America, and Low Intensity Conflict was pursued most consistently in Nicaragua. The Americans supported a number of opposition groups, including a 'third force' of liberals and conservatives and the insurgent 'Contras'. Many of the Contras were linked with the old ruler, Somoza, but covert American trainers and advisers refashioned them into a modern guerrilla force. Some CIA officials secretly issued them a manual in 1983, *Psychological Operations in Guerrilla Warfare*, whole passages of which could have been written by Mao or Che Guevara. The pamphlet began with the sentence 'Guerrilla war is essentially a political war', and went on to explain how the Contras were to politicize their own forces, so they could wage a campaign of subversion against the regime. 'Political cadres' would organize the rank and file, making sure that they became motivated through 'self-criticism' and 'group discussions' which would 'raise the spirit and improve the unity of thought'. The guerrillas would then carry out 'armed propaganda', kidnapping and assassinating government officials as 'enemies of the people'. At the same time, they would give the peasant population 'ideological training' mixed with 'folkloric songs', impressing on them the Russo-Cuban imperialist nature of the Sandinista regime.[54]

In practice, the Contras relied much more on violence, intimidation and economic sabotage than winning hearts and minds. By 1988 the Sandinistas were defeating the Contras militarily, but the war and an American embargo had wrecked the economy, and the Sandinistas themselves alienated some. When elections were held in 1990, a majority, some sick of war and believing that it would only end when the regime fell, others antagonized by the Sandinistas' overly ambitious programmes of reform and hostility to criticism, voted for the pro-American, neoliberal candidate, Violetta Barrios de Chamorro. Extreme violence was used elsewhere in Central America to suppress Marxist insurgencies, this time unleashed by local dictators' paramilitaries and aided by Washington. In Guatemala, death squads with names like *Ojo por Ojo* ('Eye for Eye') massacred tens of thousands, mainly indigenous Indians, whilst the El Salvadorean civil war was particularly brutal.[55] By the end of the 1980s, the death toll in the Central American wars was enormous: almost 1 per cent of the Nicaraguan population died in the Contra wars.[56]

The prospects for anti-Communist guerrilla war were even rosier in other regions of 1970s Communist expansion. The United States, working closely with South Africa, continued to promote UNITA's war of attrition in Angola, in which some 800,000 died and almost a third of the population of 10 million were displaced.[57] The Mozambican regime, meanwhile, was brought to its knees by the South Africans and RENAMO, and it made peace in 1984. But the centre of the guerrilla strategy lay in the struggle against the USSR in Afghanistan. Even before the Soviet invasion, the Afghan Communists were faced with powerful, Islamist insurgents – the Mujahedin. The Carter administration had given the insurgents limited military help, supplementing Saudi and Pakistani support, but aid was substantially increased in 1983. Young men from throughout the Muslim world flocked to join the *jihad* or holy war, including the son of a wealthy Saudi businessman, Osama bin Laden; this was their Spanish Civil War. For Reagan, on the other hand, supporting the Mujahedin fitted perfectly into the strategy of anti-Communist guerrilla war. Unlike the Iranian brand of Islamism, which had a strongly socialist colouring, the Mujahedin were socially conservative. They were also an anti-imperialist movement, with genuine popular support. As CIA Director William Casey enthused, 'Here is the beauty of the Afghan operation. Usually it looks as if the big bad Americans are beating up on the natives. Afghanistan is just the reverse. The Russians are beating up on the little guys.'[58] The Americans, of course, were deeply to regret their support for the Mujahedin in the 1990s when they turned on their erstwhile patron. But according to the Kirkpatrick doctrine it mattered little that they were not liberals, so long as they opposed Communist totalitarianism.

Military force therefore severely damaged Communism in the South, but the neo-conservative hope that it would undermine the USSR itself was misplaced. Indeed, the West's new hawkishness may have been counterproductive, as it hardened Soviet attitudes and strengthened the hard-liners. Superpower relations were at their worst for years, and in November 1983 the world came closer to nuclear war than at any time since the Cuban missile crisis, when the Soviets misinterpreted a NATO exercise as an attack, and retaliation was only just avoided.[59] In Moscow, nostalgia for Stalinism was rife: the ancient Viacheslav Molotov was readmitted to the party (it was commonly joked that he was being groomed to be the next leader), and there was even talk of a return to the old-style Stalinist tactics of labour mobilization. When Leonid Brezhnev died in 1982, it was the hard-line Iurii Andropov who took the helm. In the event, he did not return to the 1940s, but his ideas still contained echoes of the past. The economy was to be revived not through market reforms and liberalization, but through renewed worker discipline and purges of corrupt officials.

When Andropov died in 1984, the poor international atmosphere boosted hard-line opinion in the Kremlin. The aged and ill conservative Konstantin Chernenko took over, and even though Gorbachev, well-known to be a reformer, became his number two, there was some opposition to him. When Chernenko himself died the following year, anxieties about Gorbachev continued, but it was clear that the Politburo could not continue electing aged, ill men, unlikely to survive for long. The worst of the East European debt crisis was over (though it was still serious in Poland), but the satellite states were stagnating, unable to attract new capital for investment. It was clear that a new generation had to take over, and Gorbachev, the youngest Politburo member, was the only remotely plausible candidate.

Within four years of Gorbachev's accession, the Berlin Wall had fallen; within six, the USSR was no more. Virtually nobody in 1985 predicted these momentous events. They are still puzzling, and historians argue fiercely over them. Some suggest that Reagan's rearmament, and especially the 'Star Wars' Strategic Defense Initiative (SDI), destroyed Communism. Reagan's policies undoubtedly put economic and psychological pressure on the USSR, and SDI was a worrying sign that the USSR was not keeping up (though several officials did not take it seriously).[60] But the military burden, whilst very heavy, was not causing economic crisis or social unrest. As one well-connected senior academic mused when interviewed in the late 1990s:

> Imagine that Brezhnev is still alive. We would still be living with the old regime; nothing would have changed. Perhaps things would have been a little worse, but the country would be under control. We would still have the same totalitarian system; we would still be going to Party meetings and demonstrations with the same red flags.[61]

The man who destroyed the Soviet Communist Party was to be found not in the White House but in the Kremlin. Gorbachev himself was motivated less by a fear of American military power than by a desire to reinvigorate the system, whilst rendering it more inclusive. Initially, like his predecessors, he had hoped that he could achieve this by transforming the Communist Party, but when that failed, he found himself trying to emasculate it. Communist rule therefore imploded, not from pressure from without but as a result of an internal non-violent revolution, staged by the elite of the Communist party itself.

VII

Repentance by the Georgian director Tengiz Abuladze must be one of the most complex and high-brow films ever to become a box-office hit. Made in the early 1980s but only released in 1986 under Gorbachev's new policy of 'openness' (*glasnost'*), it is a surrealist zombie movie. It begins with the burial of Varlam, a Stalinesque local mayor, whose corpse keeps reappearing, mysteriously disinterred, however many times it is reburied. The culprit is discovered – Keti – a driven woman determined to remind the world of Varlam's rule of terror. Keti has been traumatized by the death of her mother, who was murdered by Varlam whilst trying to prevent the destruction of a historic church. She finally succeeds in exposing the horrors of the past, despite the town's attempts to keep it hidden, and Varlam's son, stricken with remorse, finally disinters the body and throws it off a cliff. Even so, the film ends on a pessimistic note. Keti is shown at home, still living on 'Varlam Street' – a neighbourhood devoid of spiritual values.

Repentance was only shown after a political struggle. Aleksandr Iakovlev was its main champion, but he ran into resistance from his colleagues, and he only won them over by convincing them that it was too obscure for ordinary people, and promising that it would only be shown in a few cities. When he arranged for its broader distribution, several local party bosses were furious and banned it.[62] Even so, *Repentance* was a sensation, and captures much of the atmosphere at the beginning of Gorbachev's *perestroika* ('restructuring'). As in the Khrushchev era, the Stalinist is depicted as a bureaucratic, reason-driven figure who views the moral and spiritual realms with contempt, whilst the heroes are people with ideals and values. Yet the film is also concerned with the Brezhnev era, its attempts to 're-inter' Stalin, and the ensuing struggle between reformers, who want to challenge Stalinist bureaucracy and Brezhnevite conservatives, who are determined to keep the old system in place.

The film offers a powerful insight into the thinking of many of the *glasnost* period, not least Mikhail Gorbachev, who himself saw and liked the film.[63] Assessments of the attractive and intelligent Gorbachev are still not settled. Why did he behave so apparently irrationally, and end up destroying the system he had hoped to strengthen? *Repentance* provides some clues. Gorbachev certainly did not have Abuladze's religious sensibility, but, like many of the generation who came to maturity in the period of de-Stalinization, he did share his anger at the 'bureaucrats' in the party – a feeling captured by Iakovlev's reaction to the film: 'The film stunned me and all my family. Intelligent, honest, with an unusual style. Merciless and convincing. It used a sledge hammer to smash the system of lies, hypocrisy and violence with all its might.'[64]

Gorbachev was the last in the long tradition of those Communists who believed that socialism could be reinvigorated by attacking conservative, status-obsessed 'bureaucrats' – a tradition running from Stalinists in the 1920s, to Khrushchev in the early 1960s, to Mao in the

Cultural Revolution. His strategy was closest to Khrushchev's, in that he hoped to render the system less bureaucratic by opening the party up to influences from society as a whole. But unlike all of his Soviet predecessors, he came to the conclusion that the powers of the party as an institution had to be curtailed. He had also learnt lessons from Khrushchev's fall in 1964 and the end of the Prague Spring. Like Keti, he was determined not to let the bureaucrats rise again, zombie-like, from the dead. He ultimately decided to destroy their power, even though it would eventually lead to the destruction of the system itself.

Moreover, Gorbachev's animus against the bureaucrats within was ultimately greater than his mistrust of the West. In addition, just as the post-war era of class compromise in the West was entering a period of crisis, Soviet Communists were beginning to appreciate its virtues. Gorbachev became increasingly eager for the USSR to be integrated into the Western sphere as a Social Democratic state, and began to favour Western-style democratic elections and market reforms. He was encouraged in his 'revolution' by the 'counter-revolutionary' intellectuals Tsipko had found in the Central Committee in the 1980s, by the neo-liberal IMF, and by much Western opinion.

When Western leaders met Mikhail Gorbachev for the first time, they were as surprised as they were disarmed. How could such a friendly, open and charming figure be a Communist? Even the militant anti-Communist Margaret Thatcher warmed to him. But they were judging him by the standards of the dour and defensive apparatchiks of the 1960s and 1970s. In fact Gorbachev was merely a high-calibre version of a common party type. He was born in southern Russia in 1931 to peasant parents; his maternal grandfather had been a party member and collective-farm chairman who had been arrested in 1937 (as had his paternal grandfather). He became an ambitious and hard-working Komsomol member, and his academic ability, together with his party activities (he was awarded the prestigious Order of the Red Banner for his heroic work in bringing in the 1948 harvest), enabled him make the huge leap from the provinces to the law department of Moscow University. He soon discovered that he had the ideal personality to become a party official: he liked the broad brush and grand principle; indeed, he seems to have been a genuine idealist. Unlike Brezhnev, he did not have the technical, nuts-and-bolts approach of the ministerial economic administrator. In fact he had a particularly poor understanding of economics, which frustrated some of his advisers.[65] He was a people person, with energy and enthusiasm, and an unshakeable belief in his own persuasive abilities. Anatolii Cherniaev, later to become one of his chief advisers, recalled how when travelling with him in Western Europe in the 1970s, 'he grabbed me by the elbows and "proved", "proved", "proved" how important it was to do this or that in Stavropol'.[66] This was very Khrushchevian behaviour, and he shared his ebullient predecessor's enthusiasm and optimism. He was, however, better educated, more politically astute and, as a consequence, much more confident – justifiably so, for he was an expert politician skilled at getting people to do things for him. It is no surprise that 'Gorbymania' swept the West and Soviet Eastern Europe.

However, those undoubtedly positive characteristics had their drawbacks. He was supremely confident, but was not always aware of the difficulties associated with his plans. And it was this, combined with an ability to convince and/or outmanoeuvre opponents, that explains how he was able to push through his ambitious but incoherent programme.

In 1985, few, if anybody, in the elite believed that the Communist system was in crisis and needed radical change. As Gorbachev himself remembered, 'neither I, nor my colleagues, evaluated the general situation at that time as one of a crisis of the system,'[67] and when Aleksandr Iakovlev presented him with an extremely radical paper, proposing that the Communist Party be split in two and each part compete against the other, he decided it was 'premature'.[68] In the first two years of his General Secretaryship Gorbachev did not depart far from the disciplinarian economic policies followed by Andropov. But abroad things were different. His main objective was to reduce tensions with the West so that he could save precious resources for domestic economic reforms. As the international oil price collapsed from August 1985 onwards, this became even more necessary. Yet he and his liberal advisers – especially Iakovlev – were also convinced that the old stand-off between the blocs both could and should end. This conflict, they argued, was in essence a continuation of the old Stalinist doctrine of international class struggle, and was now outmoded.

Gorbachev therefore badgered the Americans with arms-control proposals, but initially Reagan and the neo-conservative hawks were predictably suspicious. On their first meeting in Geneva, Gorbachev could not believe what a primitive Cold War 'caveman' Reagan was. The Third World was a particular area of disagreement. For Reagan,

Communism was always the result of Soviet conspiracy and interference; for Gorbachev, it was fuelled by anti-imperialism and reactionary elites, and he was determined to win the war in Afghanistan and defend other Soviet allies.

Despite these differences, the Reagan administration's approach to the USSR had changed since 1984. The war scare of November 1983 seems to have seriously shaken the President, and it was becoming clear that hawkishness had achieved little but risk Armageddon. European unease, together with electoral considerations, also contributed to a fundamental change in Washington's position, culminating in Reagan's suggestion at Reykjavik in 1986 that all nuclear weapons be decommissioned.[69] Ultimately the idea of total denuclearization came to nothing because the two sides could not agree on the future of 'Star Wars', but from then on Gorbachev realized that disarmament was a real possibility. He now had the confidence to press ahead with domestic reform. Reagan's rearmament had certainly put pressure on the Soviet leadership; however, it was his willingness to do deals with the USSR (often in the teeth of neo-conservative opposition) that contributed most to Gorbachev's reform programme – and thus to Soviet Communism's ultimate collapse.

In the course of 1986 Gorbachev's views had become more radical, as he brainstormed with Iakovlev and other his liberal Central Committee advisers. Meetings with Western leaders – including Mrs Thatcher, who lectured him on democracy in 1987 – also had their effect.[70] Gorbachev eventually came to think of himself as a Western Social Democrat, and he and his advisers became admirers of West European welfare states. But the West European Social Democratic order had been founded in the 1940s on a compromise between free markets and interventionist states. The problem was how to reach that goal. For the party lay at the heart of the Soviet state, and any attempt to undermine its power risked destroying Moscow's ability to control the country.

Gorbachev's worldview for the first few years of his rule was not, at root, a liberal one. The Soviet people, he believed, had made a 'socialist choice' in 1917 and was fundamentally unified, collectivist, and committed to socialism. So why, then, was the system not working? Gorbachev concluded that the problem lay in the fact that the masses' innate creativity was being stifled. Deploying rhetoric that was one part young Marx and one part almost liberal idealism, he explained that bureaucrats and the 'authoritarian-bureaucratic system' 'suppress the initiative of the people, alienate them in all spheres of vital activity and belittle the dignity of the individual'. The solution to this problem lay in a new form of 'democracy' that involved open discussion but not Western-style pluralism. This 'democracy' would change people's psychology, motivating them to become enthusiastic workers and citizens, or 'activating the human factor' in the jargon of the time; it would also undermine (and hopefully topple) the 'bureaucrats' who were suppressing popular energies.[71] Such a Romantic vision may seem like a inadequate basis for a practical programme of reform, but it made sense within the Marxist tradition, much as it had to Khrushchev. Indeed, the reformers saw their policies in that context. As Iakovlev explained to a sceptical Western interviewer, 'On the theoretical plane, we have never asserted that the revolution in our country, which began in 1917, has ended . . . *Perestroika* is the continuation of the revolution.'[72]

However, from the beginning of 1987 it had become clear that discipline and tinkering with the economy had achieved little, and Gorbachev embarked on a more radical programme of economic liberalization and political democratization. Imitating the liberalizing reforms that had taken place in Hungary and Yugoslavia, he gave factory directors more independence from the centre. Inevitably, the planners dragged their feet, and Gorbachev's response was to launch an attack on the 'bureaucrats', who, he declared, were a fundamentally conservative force, a 'braking mechanism' on change.

Initially – like Khrushchev before him – Gorbachev had hoped that the party would lead society towards reform, but he rapidly lost faith in it, as party officials resisted his measures. Instead he looked for new alliances among the disenchanted middle classes, relaxing censorship to some degree and permitting the organization of 'informal' discussion groups outside the party. More serious, though, was the abolition of the powerful party secretariat in 1988, and the decision to create a new, popularly elected Congress of People's Deputies. Elections were held in 1989, and whilst many Communist bosses did win seats, several high-profile leaders were defeated. The party had been humiliated. Gorbachev was essentially shifting the centre of power from the party to a popularly elected state authority.

There were limits to Gorbachev's liberalism, and he always insisted that democracy had to be controlled. The Communist Party was given a guaranteed 100 seats in the Congress of People's Deputies of 1989;

'pluralism of opinions' was fine, but the opinions all had to be 'social-ist'; and criticism had to be 'principled', not 'irresponsible'. However, Gorbachev found it very difficult to preserve these red lines, especially as the party was subjected to an unprecedented ideological assault, encouraged by the Kremlin itself. Gorbachev reopened the Stalin ques-tion, appointing a commission to investigate Stalinist repressions in September 1987, and the 'blank pages' of Soviet history were discussed much more freely than in the 1950s. If for Khrushchev, socialism had started to decay in 1934, *after* industrialization and collectivization, Gorbachev argued that the rot had set in with Stalin's victory over Bukharin in 1928, whilst the supposedly liberal Marxist Lenin of the NEP was held up as the authentic voice of socialism. As early as 1986 Gorbachev's ideology adviser, Georgii Smirnov, explained his views in a conversation with Tsipko:

> Don't think that Gorbachev doesn't recognize the gravity of the situation. Sixty years have gone down the drain. Turning away from NEP, the Party lost its only chance. People suffered in vain. The country was sacrificed in the name of scholastic conceptions of Communism that had nothing to do with real life.[73]

Gorbachev hoped he could preserve the reputation of 1917 and relaunch the Soviet project in the name of 'Leninism'. But it was inevitably diffi-cult to draw a clear line between Lenin and Stalin, and the party intel-lectuals themselves began to lose faith in the whole Marxist project. Tsipko recalls that as early as 1986, Iakovlev commissioned a 'probe into the fundamental flaws of Soviet socialism' which included Marxism itself, and at the end of 1988 Tsipko published the first major article to argue that the roots of Stalinist 'barracks-type socialism' lay in Marxism-Leninism.[74] The following year, Solzhenitsyn's *Gulag Archi-pelago*, which denounced Lenin as a founder of the prison system, was published legally in the Soviet Union for the first time. By then the lib-eral sections of the Soviet press had become remarkably anti-Soviet and pro-Western, full of criticisms of the past and the murderous system the Bolsheviks had created.

Gorbachev and Iakovlev, as long-established party apparatchiks, well understood the power of ideology, and believed that revisions of history were an essential part of their revolution. They saw *perestroika* as a moral and cultural campaign to transform old 'Stalinist' and 'bureaucratic' mentalities. But this was a very risky strategy indeed. The Communist Party based its legitimacy on moral arguments: living standards might be lower than in the West, and there might be some injustice and illegitimate privilege, but fundamentally the system was just and superior to capitalism. If leaders and intellectuals were now saying that the party had led the people along the wrong path for sixty years, exploiting their self-sacrifice for nothing, how could the regime expect to retain their loyalty? A letter to the weekly magazine *Argumenty i fakty* from a certain N. R. Zarafshan shows how the re-examination of history could reinforce a vague sense of injustice and lead to a traumatic ideological – and emotional – crisis:

> I am a party member with a good record and everyone says that I was a conscientious worker who did social work enthusiastically. But I became older and my fire disappeared, and I have seen much injustice in my life. On learning the truth about our past I was devastated.
>
> . . . I take it all very much to heart: if I remain in the party I will be dishonest, if I leave I will be disgraced. Because I am a disciplined person I cannot miss party meetings or ignore my duties.[75]

Gorbachev was inadvertently destroying the ideological foundations of the Soviet system, and opinion changed very rapidly between 1987 and 1991. More became hostile to the party and positive towards the West. This even happened in Soviet satellites, where people had had a good knowledge of the West for some time; in Hungary, the number of those believing that 'opportunities for educational and cultural growth' were fully realized in the West leapt from 22.8 per cent in 1985 to 51.1 per cent in 1989.[76] Even so, this is not to say that a majority of Soviet bloc citizens wanted a Western-style market economy. When asked what should be done to escape from the increasingly serious economic crisis, only 18 per cent of Soviet citizens wanted more private enterprise; 50 per cent wanted more discipline and order.[77] Similarly, in 1989 73 per cent of Czechoslovaks opposed the privatization of industry and 83 per cent were hostile to the end of collective farms.[78]

The real beneficiary of the ideological crisis was nationalism and some of the earliest signs of political collapse came in the Baltic States, where nationalist hostility to Soviet rule had been widespread for some time. Popular Fronts in Support of *Perestroika*, created by the KGB to channel democracy in approved directions, soon escaped central control.

Demonstrators began demanding complete independence, calling for a return to private property and the end of the Soviet system.

Gorbachev was soon faced with chaos. By attacking the old political system and ideology, he was cutting the sinews of power before an alternative power structure had been built. Much the same was true of the economy: the power of the state was undermined, before the ground had been prepared for the market to replace it. Gorbachev was faced with two coherent alternatives. There was the Chinese model, which assumed a gradual move to the market, led by a powerful party and reliant on continuing repression of dissent; or there was a neo-liberal 'shock therapy', counselled by many Western economists and the IMF. Understandably, Gorbachev resolutely set his face against the former: it contradicted his plans for political democracy, and, he believed, would only entrench the power of the bureaucrats he hated so much. However, Gorbachev also rejected shock therapy – equally predictably. It would have destroyed the economic bureaucracy at a stroke, and replaced it with markets, privatization and tough anti-inflation measures. Yet the result would also have been wild price swings, deep recession and mass unemployment. Even had this been a good idea, Gorbachev would never have pursued it because he was determined to have democracy and markets at the same time, whilst retaining his own power. The introduction of the market would inevitably have hurt many people, and democracy would have given the millions of 'losers' a powerful weapon against the government. Gorbachev himself responded to popular pressure by cushioning living standards with borrowing from the West. The consequence was ballooning foreign debt.

In place of neo-liberal shock therapy and Chinese-style state-led reform, Gorbachev settled on a deeply flawed compromise. The attack on the bureaucracy destroyed the old system that delivered supplies from one factory to another, whilst enterprise directors were given new autonomy: they were now free of any pressure – market or political – to produce efficiently and cheaply. Inevitably prices rose, shelves emptied and queues lengthened. Whilst the peace-maker 'Gorby' was being hailed in the West, his popularity at home plummeted.

Some at the time urged that Gorbachev copy the more statist Chinese model, and the debate over alternative paths continues.[79] Chinese conditions were certainly very different from Russia's. In the Soviet Union, agriculture had been more damaged by collectivization, and the old industrial apparatchiks were much more powerful and able to block economic reforms. Nevertheless, some argue that had the right incentives been put in place, some version of Deng's Four Modernizations might have produced a better economic result.

It is perhaps pointless to speculate about possible alternatives. Given the democratic, anti-bureaucratic worldview of Gorbachev and the reformers, and the liberal intellectual environment in the West, the Chinese model had little chance. And even had a version of the Chinese model secured an improved economic result, it would have been at the expense of political freedom, and probably world peace. The Communists would have remained in power, and an old guard would have been more likely to resist the retreats of 1989 in Eastern Europe.

However, the course Gorbachev chose, whatever its political advantages, had a damaging economic outcome: the effective collapse of the state and the 'theft' of the economy by managers and officials. When, in 1989, the dithering Gorbachev eventually did appoint the liberal Nikolai Petrakov as his economic adviser, and made it clear the following year that privatization was on the cards, they began to 'self-privatize', selling off equipment and pocketing the proceeds. Meanwhile party bosses and state officials took advantage of Gorbachev's attack on the central hierarchy and took the assets of the organizations they worked for. The bureaucrats were 'stealing the state'.[80] This semi-legal larceny was the source of the wealth of many of the 'oligarchs' of the 1990s. Gorbachev, intent on destroying the 'bureaucrats', had actually helped many of them to enrich themselves, and his idealism had set in train the decade of political and economic collapse that beset Russia after Communism, in turn fuelling the anti-liberal reaction that followed it under President Vladimir Putin.

From the autumn of 1989 onwards, therefore, the effects of Gorbachev's creeping revolution against the Communist Party were becoming clear: the various spheres of Soviet power were collapsing. And it was no surprise that the first to go was the weakest link in the chain: Eastern Europe.

VIII

In the days before the seventieth anniversary of the October Revolution on 7 November 1987, the citizens of Wrocław learnt of plans for an unusual commemoration of the Soviet state's foundation:

> Comrades!!!
>
> The day of the eruption of the Great Proletarian October Revolution is a day of a Great Event . . . Comrades, it is time to break the passivity of the popular masses! . . . Let us gather on November 6, Friday at 4 p.m. on Świdnicka Street under the 'clock of history'. Comrades, dress festively, in red. Put on red shoes, a red cap or a scarf . . . As a last resort, with no red flag, paint your fingernails red.

This satirical celebration of revolutionary history was just one of the events organized by Poland's 'Orange Alternative', a surrealist protest group. They satirized the early Bolshevik political festivals like the Storming of the Winter Palace of 1920 – complete with a mock-up of the revolutionary battleship *Aurora*, a 'cavalry' wearing Russian civil-war (Budionnyi) caps, and banners bearing slogans such as 'Red Borscht'. One of the organizers described the scene: 'Shouts of "RE-VO-LU-TION". The Proletariat [i.e. workers from local factories] emerged from the bus; on their shirts are signs reading "I will work more" and "Tomorrow will be better".' The police were ready in large numbers, but were put in the humiliating position of arresting anybody dressed in red or provocatively drinking strawberry juice.[81]

The Orange Alternative, whilst unusual in many ways, captured much of the character of East European dissent in the late 1980s, at least in the area of the former Austro-Hungarian Empire (including the Western Ukraine). A new younger generation of dissidents was emerging, who were less interested in grand protests and demonstrations against the regime than in creating an alternative, counter-cultural 'civil society', free of the control of the state. The new style was 'carnivalesque', as Padraic Kenney has called it, rather than militantly confrontational, and owed much to the Situationists and Western youth culture of the 1960s. Indeed, the spirit of 1989 was a non-violent adaptation of the spirit of 1968. As the Wrocław display showed, their approach could not have been more different from the old Communist model of mass mobilization. But the goals of many groups (in contrast with the Orange Alternative) were often very specific and ostensibly non-political – campaigning for environmental causes or peace, for example.[82] This was perhaps to be expected after the suppression of the Solidarity movement. The regimes had lost even more prestige, but it was clear that open opposition would only be met by force, and outside Poland it was difficult for intellectuals to mobilize workers. A new, less confrontational style was therefore required.

Whilst social activism – and ridicule – played its part in the end of Communism, more important was Moscow and the signals it was sending to the East European Communist parties. Gorbachev had told the leaders in private as early as 1985 that they could not depend on the Red Army for help, though he expected them to remain in the Soviet bloc. Ever the optimist, he believed that more popular leaders would restore Communist legitimacy. But just as Khrushchev's Secret Speech of 1956 had undermined the 'little Stalins' by encouraging reformers and splitting the parties, so *perestroika* in the USSR shook the foundations of the East European regimes. The supporters of liberal reform within the parties were strengthened, and in some cases leaders now realized they could no longer rely on repression but would have to expand the base of their social support. Opponents of the regimes also realized that they now had less to fear; when, in the winter of 1987–8, the Polish historian Wacław Felczak went to lecture in Budapest, his audience asked him what the lessons of Solidarity were for them. 'Found a party,' he replied. 'They will probably lock you up for it, but all the signs suggest that you won't be in jail for long.'[83]

Hungary was the first to respond to the signals from Moscow. Having subjected itself to multi-candidate elections where the old guard performed less well than expected, a younger, reformist group of Communist leaders, including the effectively Social Democratic Imre Pozsgay, succeeded in March 1988 in forcing the ageing János Kádár to retire. The party split; a democratic opposition now formed outside the party, and by February 1989 reformers within the regime had accepted multi-party elections. Moscow's willingness to accept this fundamental change made it crystal-clear to all that the Soviet Union would no longer underwrite the old order in Eastern Europe.

In Poland, as in Hungary, the signals from Moscow were heeded from an early stage. General Jaruzelski, one of the leaders closest to

Gorbachev, began liberal reforms in September 1986, but in August 1988 worker unrest against austerity measures again shook Communist rule. By February 1989 the government, under pressure from Gorbachev, had accepted round-table discussions with the opposition, and elections were held in June 1989, in which Solidarity swept the board. In August 1989 Tadeuz Mazowiecki became the first non-Communist head of a coalition government for over forty years.

The more hard-line regimes showed a greater determination to hold on, but soon they too were forced to heed the writing on the Wall – in East Germany. The beginning of the end was in May 1989, when the Hungarian authorities reduced controls for Hungarians at the Austrian border. East Germans then began to organize 'holidays' to Hungary to take advantage of the breach in the iron curtain, even though the border was supposed to be open for Hungarians only. On 19 August at the border town of Sopron, the Hungarian opposition, with the support of an odd duo – Imre Poszgay and Otto von Habsburg, the heir to the Austro-Hungarian empire – organized a 'Pan-European picnic' during which they planned to open a disused border crossing and allow the East Germans to cross. The Germans forced their way through the border, and three weeks later the Hungarians removed all restrictions. The GDR responded by closing its border with Hungary, and this renewed repression invigorated the opposition in East Germany. Demonstrations erupted throughout the GDR, and the party began to lose control. Honecker's rigid regime was further dented when Gorbachev visited to celebrate the fortieth anniversary of the founding of the GDR. Welcomed by enthusiastic crowds, he distinctly failed to support its leader. 'Life itself punishes those who delay', he is reported to have declared.[84] Shortly afterwards (in a palace coup on 17–18 October) Honecker was replaced by Egon Krenz.

Krenz soon realized he needed to make some concessions to retain control. Following a demonstration of half a million people in East Berlin on 4 November, he decided on a limited lifting of travel restrictions, but the order was garbled at the press conference, and confused guards simply opened the gate to the west of the city and allowed the crowds through.[85] This was to prove to be one of the most momentous 'mis-speaks' in history. That night some 50,000 Germans flooded out of the East and in to West Berlin, crying 'we are one people'. This was a massive party as much as a revolution, the culmination of the 'carnivalesque', non-violent demonstrations and 'picnics' pursued by the East European oppositions in the 1980s. The breaching of the Berlin Wall justifiably became the symbol of 1989. The opposition's vision of revolution – non-violent, joyful, even hedonistic – seemed so much more attractive and modern than the Communists' antiquated ideal of the mobilized worker, struggling against enemies. As the Wall crumbled, so did the East German Communist Party's will to govern.

The house of cards continued to fold and events in East Germany inspired resistance to other hard-line regimes. Demonstrations in early November helped party reformers to force Bulgaria's Todor Zhivkov from power, and precipitated a challenge to the party itself from a group of opposition forces. In Czechoslovakia the regime, under Husák's conservative successor Miloš Jakeš, had been facing unrest and demonstrations since the previous year, but had resolutely set its face against reform; it even put the portrait of the old Stalinist leader Klement Gottwald on the new hundred-crown banknote, an enormously provocative act. However events in the GDR – the regime ideologically closest to the Czechoslovak – emboldened the opposition. The anniversary of the student opposition to the Nazi takeover in 1939 fell on 17 November, and demonstrations were normal. This time, though, the numbers were enormous, and the police panicked. Police brutality in turn sparked off mass strikes and demonstrations and forced the party to begin negotiations with the opposition.

Despite some violence (in Czechoslovakia and elsewhere) the revolutions in Central and Eastern Europe were remarkably swift and peaceful. In part, this was because the new opposition movements embraced non-violence, but it also reflected the weaknesses of the regimes once the USSR changed its attitude towards repression. Communist parties were divided, to varying degrees, and there were normally reformists waiting in the wings, prepared to negotiate with the opposition. These were relatively peaceful, 'velvet' revolutions, as the Czechoslovak transition was described.

As might be expected, given their autonomy from the USSR and their repressiveness, the Romanian and Albanian regimes were the last to collapse. The extraordinarily harsh austerity imposed by the Romanian leader in the 1980s put Nicolae Ceauşescu under pressure; serious industrial unrest broke out in Braşov in 1987, and Ion Iliescu, a former Central Committee member sacked in 1984, levelled veiled criticism. But Romania could not insulate itself from the events in the

Soviet bloc proper. In December 1989 unrest amongst the Hungarian minority in Timişoara led to police repression, and this in turn promoted further unrest in Bucharest. Ceauşescu organized a demonstration in support of the regime and spoke from the Central Committee building balcony, hoping for a repeat of the adulation he had received in 1968. He had, however, catastrophically misjudged the mood of the truculent crowd: rather than cheering, people began to jeer the dictator in a shocking display of *lèse majesté*. The disorder was broadcast on TV, after which the army joined the opposition and the regime soon lost control. The Ceauşescus fled from Bucharest but were later captured and executed. Power was then seized by Iliescu, in charge of a new 'National Salvation Front'.

Albania was the last of the East European dominoes to fall. Ramez Alia, Hoxha's successor in 1985, had begun to make piecemeal liberal reforms, but by 1990 student demonstrations had forced him into holding multi-party elections, and although the Communists took the largest number of votes they were now part of a coalition government. The following year the coalition collapsed, and the Communists were voted out of power.

The year 1989 clearly ranks with the revolutionary years of 1848, 1917–19 and 1968, but how similar was it to those earlier upheavals? Some of the transitions from Communism were clearly more revolutionary than others. Throughout Europe, Gorbachev's willingness to abandon the Soviet empire was crucial, but the different nature of the regimes led to wide divergences. In Hungary and Poland, well-established reformist traditions within the Communist parties led to peaceful, negotiated transitions, whilst in Czechoslovakia and the GDR more unified conservative leaderships only fell after short periods of mass popular mobilization. Events in Romania were the most violent and 'revolutionary', although the effects of the regime change – the victory of the semi-authoritarian apparatchik Iliescu – was one of the least radical. If we look at popular participation in the revolutions, we see a slightly different pattern. Poland and Czechoslovakia, both unified against past Soviet oppression, and to some extent Romania, were closer to the 1917 pattern, in that they involved all classes, including workers. In Hungary and the GDR, where Communists had bought off working-class discontent more effectively, the transitions were much more intelligentsia and white-collar affairs.[86]

Similar differences can be found in the end of Communist rule in the Soviet informal empire outside Europe. Gorbachev, once determined to compete with the United States outside Europe, increasingly saw his Third World allies as a liability. His advisers had indeed been losing faith in the possibility of Communism in the developing world for some time. They were convinced that Communist ambitions were just too radical, given the level of development of their societies. But with the Reagan revolution and the economic crises of the early 1980s, the USSR found itself in an even more difficult situation. There were now significant numbers of Marxist regimes, and they all demanded subsidies at a time when Soviet citizens were themselves suffering hardship. Moreover, as they came under mounting economic pressure, regimes split between moderate liberalizers and radicals, and – in contrast with the situation in Europe – radicals often had a good deal of support; their victories increased disillusionment in a Moscow that had lost faith in fundamental social transformation. In Grenada, Maurice Bishop, who had been seeking rapprochement with the United States, was toppled by the radical Bernard Coard (a former student at Sussex University and teacher for the left-wing Inner London Education Authority), precipitating the American invasion in 1983. Similarly in South Yemen, three years later, the reformist Soviet-trained Ali Nasir Muhammed was removed by the more doctrinaire Marxist 'Abd al-Fattah Isma'il, in a bloody coup. Gorbachev would have agreed entirely with Honecker's comment: 'just like in Grenada, the events in Yemen show what left-wing childishness can lead to'.[87]

Equally unpopular in Moscow was Ethiopia's Mengistu. The Ethiopian famine had damaged the reputation of Third World Marxism, especially amongst Eurocommunists, and Gorbachev had little love for the regime. In 1988 he told Mengistu that aid would be dependent on liberalization and the peaceful settlement of wars in Eritrea and Tigray, and soon afterwards the Ethiopian party split between reformers and hard-liners. The now ex-Marxist Eritrean and Tigray separatists joined together and advanced against the Mengistu regime. In 1990 Mengistu formally renounced Marxism-Leninism, and in 1991 was forced to flee the country for exile in Zimbabwe. On his departure the huge bronze statue of Lenin in Addis Ababa was unceremoniously destroyed.

Nevertheless, Gorbachev was reluctant to cut off aid to his allies, partly because he still believed in some of them, and partly because the

Americans were continuing to support anti-Marxist forces. In Afghanistan, the Soviets removed the hard-line Babrak Karmal, and replaced him with the more pragmatic Najibullah, who then tried to forge a broad alliance against the Islamists. The Soviets were desperate to withdraw their troops, but Reagan was implacable and refused to make a deal. As the war became increasingly unpopular in the USSR, Gorbachev announced that the Soviets would leave in February 1989. Najibullah's remained one of the most long-lasting Communist regimes, surviving until 1992. With his demise, the way was open for a succession of Islamist regimes, culminating in the victory of the radically puritan Taliban.

The civil war in Angola also continued until the fall of the USSR. The Cubans and South Africans withdrew in 1988, and the MPLA abandoned Marxism-Leninism in 1990, but the Americans continued to fund Jonas Savimbi's UNITA group. Only in 1992, once the MPLA had won elections, did the United States switch sides and support the former Marxists. The civil war, however, lasted until 2002, when Savimbi was killed.

In 1985, Gorbachev had not wanted to divest the USSR of its Third World allies, or of its East European satellites. Yet by 1989, he stood by passively as the Soviet bloc disintegrated. But even had he wanted to intervene, he could have done very little. He was embroiled in the drama of Soviet reform and presided over an empty treasury. However, he could not ignore the forces pulling Eastern Europe to the West for they were also acting on the USSR itself. Nationalist forces were now corroding the Union. The Communist Party had been the main force holding the Union together, and once it began to decay and freer elections were allowed to state parliaments, separatists were given a powerful political platform. In March 1990 the Lithuanian parliament voted to secede from the USSR, whilst Latvia and Estonia also announced they would eventually seek independence. In June the Russian Republic declared its sovereignty and now claimed that its own laws took precedence over the USSR's. Other republics rapidly sought independence. It says much for Gorbachev's extraordinary radicalism that he responded not by moderating his course but by loosening the reins even further. He proposed that a new, more liberal Union Treaty be signed to replace that of 1922, and endorsed Petrakov's neo-liberal shock-therapy plan – a plan for complete marketization and privatization within 500 days, one of whose effects would have been to destroy the USSR's tax-raising powers.[88]

By September 1990 Gorbachev had second thoughts, and began try-ing to recentralize power. The following year saw him vacillate, alter-nately cracking down and then loosening control. He was desperate to preserve the USSR, but was reluctant to use violence, and he was also being outflanked by pro-market radicals in the person of the impulsive former Moscow party boss, Boris Yeltsin. Yeltsin used the Russian Republic as a base from which to challenge the USSR's President Gorbachev; in June 1991 Yeltsin was elected President of Russia. Gorbachev, severely weakened politically, was forced to agree to a new Union Treaty that gave most powers to the republics. But two days before it was due to be signed, the forces of reaction Gorbachev had been warning against finally acted. A group of conservative leaders, including the KGB boss Vladimir Kriuchkov, made a last-ditch attempt to save the Union – and the Communist Party. They confronted Gor-bachev in his Crimean *dacha* and demanded that either he impose mar-tial law or hand over power to Vice-President Ianaev. He refused, and they imprisoned him. The USSR was now ruled by a 'State Emergency Committee' whilst Gorbachev recovered from an 'illness'.

On 19 August 1991 Muscovites woke up to see tanks rumbling into Moscow, leaving deep track marks on the warm tarmac. Was this a repeat of the removal of Khrushchev, or the crushing of the Prague Spring? It looked like the former but it was a sorry excuse for a coup. Rejected by Gorbachev, the coup-leaders' confidence seemed to collapse. At their TV press conference Ianaev stumbled over his words, seemingly drunk. They failed to attract support from the mass of police and KGB, and could not prevent Yeltsin reaching the headquarters of the Russian government, the White House, where he stood on a tank in flamboyant defiance of the putschists. The coup leaders decided they had to use force against a White House full of civilian defenders, and in the early hours of 21 August they ordered an attack. The military commanders, how-ever, refused to obey, and the leaders lost the will to continue. Later that day, they ended the coup, and Gorbachev was released. The putsch of 1991 had strong echoes of the Kornilov coup of 1917. As before, the conspirators failed to secure the support of middle-ranking officers, and a coup designed to save the old order simply hastened its end.[89]

Gorbachev tried to pick up where he had left off, but everything had changed. Both the USSR and the Communist Party had been discred-ited. Yeltsin rapidly moved to take advantage of the situation, banning the Communist Party in Russia, and taking all of the USSR's Russian assets into the hands of his Russian government. In 1990 few, not even Yeltsin, had wanted to destroy the USSR; by 1991 the old Soviet elites saw that it had disintegrated, and scrambled to restore their power on new foundations – the USSR's former republics. The USSR's defenders – Gorbachev and the coup leaders – had lacked the ruthlessness to hold the Union together. On 25 December 1991 Gorbachev gave up the presidency of the USSR. The red flag with hammer and sickle flying over the Kremlin was lowered for the last time. After seventy-four years the Communist experiment in the USSR was over.

In 1985 the Soviet bloc had confronted a hostile West, each side armed with enough nuclear weapons to destroy the world. Six years later the Soviet imperial system had collapsed with barely a skirmish. Its break-up caused sporadic violence throughout much of the 1990s, and tensions continue to this day – most recently in Georgia. But few, if any, powerful multi-ethnic empires have ended so peacefully. Gorbachev himself deserves much of the credit for this outcome, just as he deserves some of the blame for the economic and political collapse of the 1990s. However, even though he can seem like an extraordinary figure, he was in truth the embodiment of broader trends: the continuing appeal of Romantic Marxism in the Soviet party and the attraction of neo-liberalism and the West. Gorbachev's main contribution was his extra-ordinary confidence and his political skill. He was prepared to press ahead with a deeply contradictory programme, even though it was destroying the system he was trying so hard to save.

IX

It could, though, have been so much worse, and in the other European country ruled by an indigenous Communist regime – Yugoslavia – it was. Yugoslavia suffered from many of the same problems of the USSR: a weak central state lacking the will or the power to reform the economy; a congeries of ethnic groups at odds with the centre; and the pressure of the neo-liberal IMF. But in Yugoslavia all were present to an extreme degree: Belgrade had been weaker for longer, nationalists had been organizing for years, and the IMF had a much greater hold over the economy. Throughout the 1980s, the IMF had persuaded an already weakened Belgrade to impose austerity on a fragmented country, and this had only intensified the resentments and rivalries dividing the republics. Communist politicians continued to use nationalist appeals to attract support; nationalisms were strong in Slovenia, Croatia and Serbia, but it was Serbia's Slobodan Milošević who excelled in the art of populist rabble-rousing.

Even so, as late as the spring of 1990 there was still widespread support for a united Yugoslavia, and the Prime Minister of Yugoslavia, the Communist Ante Marković, was the most popular politician in the state – more so than Milošević and the Croat nationalist Franjo Tudjman. This did not last for long, as this was the high point of the neo-liberal revolution. Marković, encouraged by the IMF, decided to embark on a programme of 'shock therapy', coinciding with the first multi-party elections. Inevitably, the only force for Yugoslav political unity was now linked with a deeply unpopular economic programme.[90] Marković's party was wiped out, and nationalist parties opposing shock therapy, elected in Croatia and Slovenia, began to plan for independence from Yugoslavia.

The sudden break-up of Yugoslavia, without protection for any ethnic minorities within each republic, was bound to bring war. With the exception of Slovenia, the republics were ethnically mixed, and minorities felt increasingly threatened. In Croatia 12.2 per cent of the population were ethnically Serb, and they feared Tudjman – a revisionist historian with a nostalgia for the violent Nazi collaborators, the Croat Ustaša. All of this played into Milošević's hands, and at the end of 1990 he won elections in Serbia, promising to defend Serbs throughout Yugoslavia. Even so, the Slovenes and the Croats continued the march towards independence, encouraged by international support and recognition from Germany, Austria and others.

When Croatia and Slovenia finally did declare independence in June 1991, the Yugoslav army, directed by Milošević, marched in. Both sides drew back in Slovenia, but in Croatia the fighting was vicious and bloody as civil war broke out between the Croats and the Serb minority supported by the Yugoslav army. The war ended in January 1992, but by then Yugoslavia as a state was effectively dead. Milošević's ambition was now to create an ethnically pure Greater Serbia, and he encouraged a Serb rebellion in the ethnically mixed republic of Bosnia-Herzegovina. The brutal Bosnian war began in April 1992 and lasted for over two years. The West was reluctant to intervene, but eventually horrific pictures of ethnic cleansing and concentration camps forced it to act and Milošević, crippled economically, was compelled to negotiate. The result was the unstable Dayton peace agreement of 1995. Three years later, the process of fragmentation restarted, as the Albanian Kosovars rebelled against a weakened Milošević. In 1999 NATO bombing forced Milošević to accept United Nations administration in Kosovo, which damaged his political position irreparably. The following year popular demonstrations – in which students played a major role – finally brought his resignation in October 2000. However, now that the West has recognized Kosovo as an independent state, the issue continues to fuel resentful nationalism in Serbia.

Yugoslavia's was the one transition from Communism where Western governments and the IMF were involved from the very beginning, and they did not acquit themselves with much credit. Radical neo-liberal reforms destabilized Yugoslavia, whilst foreign-policy interventions were at first ignorantly destructive, and then inadequate. The problem lay in the perceptions of Communism and its aftermath. In the late 1980s, the West was still in its militantly neo-liberal and neo-conservative phase, fighting the righteous war against Communism. It was determined to impose markets and defeat Communists like Marković, with little regard for the likely consequences. But by the 1990s, Western politicians believed that the old ideological struggle was over, and were frustrated that the Yugoslavs were still fighting. The Yugoslavs' conflict was now implausibly cast as the result of 'ancient tribal hatreds', artificially suppressed by Communism, and thus something the West could do little about. In reality, the conflicts in Yugoslavia were a more extreme form of those that affected all multi-ethnic Communist states. Understanding, political engagement and careful management might have avoided some of the worst violence in Europe since World War II.

Yet perhaps that is too optimistic. There was one place where Communists explicitly rejected the advice of the West and ignored the moralism of the twin revolutions – China. But there, too, violence ensued.

X

On 15 May 1989, Gorbachev arrived at Beijing airport. The Chinese Communist Party, like its East European counterparts, was rightly apprehensive. Welcoming Gorbachev in 1989 was rather like encountering the Grim Reaper on the doorstep, complete with cloak, hood and sickle – a warning of imminent political death. His timing could not have been worse for the CCP. Since mid-April, students had been demonstrating throughout China, and on the seventieth anniversary of the May 4th movement, Beijing University students broke through police cordons and marched to Tian'anmen Square. The Chinese Communist leadership was divided over what to do. The reformer Zhao Ziyang wanted talks; the hard-liner Li Peng favoured repression. The imminent arrival of Gorbachev – whom the students hoped would be an ally – seemed to effectively scupper Zhao's strategy.[91] Protesters decided to escalate the conflict by occupying the square and staging a hunger strike to coincide with the Soviet leader's visit. On 13 May more than 1,000 students began a hunger strike in the square, singing the 'Internationale' and anti-Japanese war songs, whilst raising banners declaring 'The country will have no peace so long as dictatorship lives' and 'Corruption is the cause of turmoil'.[92] By the evening of the 14th, 100,000 onlookers had joined them.

Deng was furious. The international press had flocked to Beijing to cover the visit. 'When Gorbachev's here,' Deng told his colleagues, 'we have to have order at Tian'anmen. Our international image depends on it. What do we look like if the Square's a mess?'[93] By 17 May, Deng had thrown in his lot with the hard-liners, and approved the use of force in principle. Embarrassingly, Gorbachev's welcome had had to be moved to the airport and his motorcade rerouted. He did not intervene on the students' side, and his visit went off without incident. Indeed, oddly, his memoirs suggest that he had more sympathy with his hosts than the protesters.[94] Yet his presence did threaten to spread his brand of revolution to China; as the intellectual Yan Jiaqi told the French newspaper *Libération*, the winds of democratization blowing from Moscow could not be resisted.[95]

Gorbachev received such an enthusiastic reception because Chinese intellectuals had been germinating their own reformist ideas, rather similar to his, from the mid-1980s – often in dialogue with East European reformers. Dissatisfaction with Deng's market authoritarianism was widespread. Economic liberalization was leading to sharp inequalities. Whilst entrepreneurial party bosses and peasants flourished, poorly paid students and urban workers suffered. Corruption flourished and demonstrations and strikes soon became commonplace. The student protesters, though, did not seek solace in a return to the Maoist past. Nor were they Western-style liberal democrats, demanding free pluralistic elections and constitutions. They were instead closer in their sentiments to the Romantic *perestroika* Communism of Gorbachev: they demanded a democracy that would energize the united, patriotic 'people'; they called for the removal of corrupt and repressive bureaucrats; and, like Gorbachev (and his successor Yeltsin), they embraced the West as a dynamic, modern society. They even supported the market, although many of them were suffering from it. They saw Deng's Communist Party much as Gorbachev saw Brezhnev's – as old-fashioned, repressive and xenophobic.

Their worldview was captured in a poetic but highly polemical TV documentary series of 1988, *River Elegy*. The films – a carefully selected set of powerful images with didactic voiceover – were a head-on assault on three enemies, each represented by a well-known emblem of Chinese identity: Chinese traditional culture, symbolized by the Yellow River; political authoritarianism, symbolized by the Chinese dragon; and isolation from the West, symbolized by the Great Wall. As the voiceover solemnly intoned at the end of the first film:

> Oh, you heirs of the dragon . . . The Yellow River cannot bring forth again the civilization that our ancestors once created. What we need to create is a brand new civilization. It cannot emerge from the Yellow River again. The dregs of the old civilization are like the sand and mud accumulated in the Yellow River; they have built up in the blood vessels of our people. We need a great tidal wave to flush them away. This great tidal wave has already arrived. It is industrial civilization. It is summoning us!

The tidal wave, it was made clear, was coming from the West. Unlike China, the West was a wide blue ocean – a Romantic place of grand emotions, open thinking and dynamism. In the final episode, the voiceover predicted the ultimate merging of China and the West: 'The Yellow River is fated to traverse the yellow soil plateau. The Yellow River will ultimately empty into the blue sea.'[96]

The documentary series was screened twice on Chinese TV before it was banned, and was one of the most watched documentaries in the history of world television. The climax of this pro-Western idealism came in Tian'anmen Square on 30 May 1989, when the students con-structed a thirty-foot-high polystyrene statue, the 'Goddess of Democ-racy', resembling the the American Statue of Liberty – challenging the giant portrait of Mao.

During the previous few days, it looked as if the demonstrations might lose momentum and violence could be avoided. But the statue was a sign of the students' determination to continue. Now with work-ers protesting, too, and party members defecting to the rebels, Deng and the leadership began to fear a repeat of the Polish collapse of 1980. The apparent success of Jaruzelski's military crack-down emboldened them, and they decided to act. On 3 June, troops were sent in to clear the square. Confronting the protesters blocking their way, they fired into the crowds. By early on 4 June, the tanks had reached Tian'anmen and crushed the Goddess of Democracy. Between 600 and 1,200 were killed and 6,000–10,000 injured.[97]

The Tian'anmen Square massacre was a serious humiliation for Deng, and its shockwaves resonate to this day. In the immediate aftermath, the violence damaged Deng's reforms. The lesson seemed to be obvious: only conservatism could save the state. It seemed that China was on the path to Brezhnevite retrenchment and stagnation. But perceptions were to change again with the failure of the putschists' coup and the collapse of the USSR in 1991; the tide of history now seemed to favour capital-ism. For the residents of Zhongnanhai – the centre of party power – the lessons of 1989–1991 pointed in one direction: China had to reject the two revolutions of the 1980s – the liberal democratic one and *per-estroika*. She would resist the attractions of the West and follow her own non-revolutionary path, one that married muscle and markets.

Epilogue

Red, Orange, Green . . . and Red?

I

In 2002, Chinese pollsters asked Beijing students to name their greatest hero, but the choice offered was oddly circumscribed: the American IT entrepreneur Bill Gates or the Bolshevik civil-war fighter Pavel Korchagin. It was a dead heat: both received 45 per cent support. But when asked whose example they would follow, 44 per cent chose Gates, 27 per cent said both and only 13 per cent mentioned Korchagin alone.[1] And even that result rather exaggerated support for the values of socialist self-sacrifice in twenty-first-century China, for the 'Korchagin' being discussed was far from the Soviet writer Nikolai Ostrovskii's creation. The Korchagin at the forefront of Chinese minds had recently been the subject of a phenomenally popular twenty-part TV adaptation of *How the Steel was Tempered* made in 2000. The TV series was the product of a typically post-modern fusion of cultures: a Soviet socialist realist classic, made in post-Communist Ukraine with Ukrainian actors, financed by a private Shenzhen property developer, and screened by a nominally Communist Chinese TV station. Its Korchagin was rather different from the figure of the novel of the 1930s, or of previous Soviet cinematic treatments of the 1940s and 1950s: he disapproves of the Red Army's violence, and is seen to marry his beloved Tonia, even though in the novel her bourgeois class origins lead him to break off the relationship. As the series director explained, 'We've watered down the class-consciousness and made him more of a human-rights figure that everyone can relate to.'

The neo-liberal revolutionaries, so marginal in the early 1970s, were now triumphant – ideologically, culturally and politically. When the Chinese had seen *How the Steel was Tempered* at the height of the Russophilia of the 1950s, they were in no doubt that Korchagin's self-sacrifice was superior to money-grubbing capitalism. Fifty years later, Bill Gates, the epitome of billionaire corporate values, was the figure of heroic aspiration. In internet discussions about the book there was a nostalgia for Pavel's values amongst the older generation, but amongst the middle-aged there was often a resentment that they had followed Pavel's example in vain, and amongst the young a general lack of interest.

The Romanticism of the entrepreneur did, of course, involve struggle, but it was the peaceful struggle of business competition and not the violent militancy of the Communist revolutionary. And it looked as if for much of the world, the two-century-long global 'civil war' was over. Though the neo-liberal order increased economic inequalities enormously (most notably in China, which became the second most unequal society in Asia after Nepal's Hindu monarchy), there was little pressure for social revolution. China, once the most radical opponent of the American-led order had become one of its main beneficiaries, growing wealthy by exporting its goods to the West. Within China, and indeed in much of the rest of the world, neo-liberalism offered the promise of wealth and improvement without the need for class struggle or war. Everybody, it seemed, could become Bill Gates if they were energetic enough. Francis Fukuyama's claim that history had ended looked highly plausible a decade after 1989.

The lessons learnt from the fall of Communism played a central role in the neo-liberals' intellectual victory. If Communism's role in the defeat of Nazism contributed to the widespread acceptance of mixed economies after 1945, its implosion in 1989 was commonly regarded as proof that Friedman, Reagan and Thatcher had been right and the state should withdraw from the economy. The Soviet command economy was not seen as fundamentally different from the post-war mixed economy, but as a more statist version of it. As the journalists Daniel Yergin and Joseph Stanislaw argued in their popular 1998 obituary of socialism, *The Commanding Heights*, the fall of the Berlin Wall brought with it 'a vast discrediting of central planning, state intervention, and state ownership'.[2] Unsurprisingly, the failures of Communism were regularly used by supporters of liberal globalization, flexible labour markets, free trade and sound money to condemn their critics; in 2000 the *New York Times* columnist Thomas Friedman ended an attack on the anti-globalization protesters in Seattle with a contemptuous history lesson:

too many [trade] unions and activists want the quick fix for globalization: just throw up some walls [i.e. trade barriers] and tell everyone else how to live. There was a country that tried that. It guaranteed everyone's job, maintained a protected market and told everyone how to live. It was called the Soviet Union. Didn't work out so well.[3]

The supporters of 1990s-style liberal capitalism did not only use the experience of Communism to argue that the free market was economically necessary; they also insisted that it was morally superior. Fukuyama, in *The End of History and the Last Man* (1992), made the case most forcefully. All men and women, he argued, needed individual dignity and recognition (*thymos*), and only liberal democracy could deliver that to everybody in equal measure. Communist and other totalitarian states, which put party ideology and collectivism first, were unable to do this. Fukuyama was, then, offering a liberal Romantic alternative to Marxist Romanticism. People were not happiest when involved in creative, collective labour, free of the shackles of the market, but when they were free to express themselves and secure recognition from others.[4]

Fukuyama's thesis captured the spirit of the times. Capitalism, it was now widely believed, was not only inevitable but morally good. It had inherited the revolutionary mantle from a discredited Communism, solving the problems of equality and settling the global civil war. A new, high-tech capitalism, free of the old hierarchical production line, was creating a culturally and politically 'flatter' society. It might produce economic inequalities, but they mattered little, for greater wealth would help everybody. The real enemies of equality were not bloated plutocrats but desiccated bureaucrats, who arrogantly set themselves above ordinary people.

The ideology of the new capitalism, with its love of cultural rather than economic equality, appealed to the Romantic generation of 1968 who were now taking over positions of power. The language of Tom Freston, the boss of the American music channel MTV, showed how far the new capitalism defined itself against the old Communism in a 2000 interview:

We have tried to avoid the command, cult-of-personality type of company, which you see a lot of in the entertainment business ... If you want to have a creative, cutting-edge company, there has to be ... bottom-up idea flow ... We are decentralized ... So many of the entertainment companies today, particularly with the megamedia conglomerates, have really become like factories . . . I wasn't a child of the '60s in the classic way . . . I wasn't a hippie or a political radical. But I was there . . . and the '60s in some ways were a prelude for the [pop culture] industry. In the '60s you got a sense that new things were possible. You got a sense that nonconformity was something not to be feared, but something to be revered.[5]

Freston was condemning the disciplined societies of the 1950s West as much as Communism, and the end of the Cold War saw the dissolution of the old Revolutionary Liberal alliance, the triumph of the neo-liberals and the end of the neo-conservative era – at least temporarily. In part, neo-conservatism was too expensive. Reagan's combination of military build-up and tax cuts had led to enormous state deficits, which threatened a serious crisis.[6] But electorates were also pleased to see the end of Cold War militancy and the moralistic neo-conservatives, and they welcomed a new 1960s generation.

The neo-liberal revolution, now separated from its neo-conservative twin, was therefore conducted not by the nationalistic right but by the cosmopolitan centre-left. The American Bill Clinton, the German Gerhard Schröder and the British Tony Blair, all products of the counter-cultural shifts of the 1960s, announced their discovery of a 'Third Way' – steering a path between social justice and the market. However, this turned out to be a path that veered rather more sharply in the direction of the market. Free-market capitalism now had a new and more appealing set of champions: the relaxed, jeans-wearing, 1960s left rather than the angry, be-suited right of the 1940s and 1950s. By the end of the decade, 'Second International' parties ruled virtually every West European country, but few ideological connections remained with the organization founded in 1889.

Beyond the developed world, neo-liberalism was a much more revolutionary force – its vanguard the IMF and the World Bank, and behind them their chief financiers, the United States. Former Communist Eastern Europe was especially affected, though not everybody accepted the IMF's recipe. The results of such a revolutionary onslaught were predictable: exposing inefficient Communist industry to the rigours of the market overnight brought severe recessions, high unemployment and pockets of extreme poverty and inequality. Economies contracted sharply throughout the former Soviet bloc, shrinking by an average of 17 per cent in 1992, and only beginning to recover three years later. By 1997 every East European country bar Poland still had a smaller economy than in 1990.[7]

The results, though, differed sharply. In countries where there was a reasonably strong state machine and where elites had already begun to disengage from Communism by the 1980s, such as Poland, Hungary, Slovenia and the newly split Czech Republic and Slovakia, neo-liberal 'shock therapies' were largely implemented and were successful in restoring growth, although at the cost of poverty for many. The promise of European Union membership – with its emphasis on the rule of law – also helped. By the new millennium, these economies were emerging from the slump. In much of the former Soviet bloc, however, states were already very weak and neo-liberal assaults on them merely enfeebled them further. Governments therefore lacked the power and authority to enforce market reforms and instead corrupt kleptocratic economies emerged – unhappy half-way houses between state control and the market. Businessmen and ex-officials soon 'captured' these struggling states, bribing officials to give them preferential treatment; taxes were left uncollected, foreigners refused to invest, and capital, rather than flowing in, poured out into shady offshore accounts.[8]

The greatest failure of neo-liberal experiments came in Russia itself. By 2000 Russia's economy had shrunk to less than two thirds of its 1989 level – a more devastating recession than America's Great Depression.[9] The collapse of the Soviet state and the theft of its economy had already begun under Gorbachev but the neo-liberal policies pursued by the post-Communist Yeltsin government intensified the problem.[10] Rapid privatization amounted to little more than the asset-stripping of state enterprises by government crony capitalists, and lawlessness deterred investment and encouraged capital flight. The problem lay, as before, in the weakness of the state, which could not raise taxes, impose legal norms and contracts, or prevent organized crime and bureaucratic-cum-capitalist larceny. The collapse finally came following a further fall in the oil price in 1998. Foreign investors financing the now vast government debt lost faith and foreclosed. The Russian state was forced to default on its debts, bringing with it humiliation for its key adviser, the IMF, and laying the grounds for a backlash against the West and liberal democracy in the 2000s. President Vladimir Putin – the grandson of one of Lenin's and Stalin's cooks and a former KGB officer – combined capitalist economics with an increasingly authoritarian politics, whilst rehabilitating some of the symbols of the Stalinist past; one of his earliest acts was to bring back the tune (though not the words) of the old 1944 Soviet national anthem, abandoned by Yeltsin in 1990.

If the end of Soviet Communism brought one of the great economic failures of the twentieth century, the effective end of Chinese Communism brought one of the century's – and indeed history's – great economic successes. The Chinese regime, whatever its other failings, lifted more people out of poverty more rapidly than any other government in modern history, with the help of the new globalized economy which allowed it to export to the West. After a brief freeze after the Tian'anmen massacre, Deng Xiaoping pressed ahead with market reforms from the early 1990s. And in 1993 the archetypical command economy was finally abandoned and the plan abolished. But in China, unlike the Soviet bloc, encouraging markets did not mean undermining the state; on the contrary, the Communists strengthened it. Both their own experience in the 1980s and that of Yeltsin's USSR convinced them that, paradoxically, to flourish markets needed a powerful state, controlled by a powerful party.[11] Corruption still remained embedded within the system, and inequality has increased, but the newly assertive market-state laid the foundations for the extraordinary take-off that made China the most dynamic economy in the world throughout the 2000s. At the same time the repressive machinery of the old Communist state remains, including the old penal 'reform through labour' system (*laogai*).[12]

II

The global neo-liberal revolution of the 1990s and 2000s was naturally traumatic for Communists, and they engaged in a number of diverse adaptations – some embracing the market, others battening down the hatches and resisting the forces of globalization. Where neo-liberalism was reasonably successful and political collapse avoided, Communists quietly ditched their Marxism and signed up to the market. In Central Eastern Europe they abjured red for pink and refashioned themselves as pro-capitalist Social Democrats. Though they criticized shock therapy and promised to soften the effects of economic liberalization, when they were returned to power in the mid-1990s (in Hungary, Poland and

Bulgaria) they did little to challenge the new system. The high point of the pink *revanche* came in the Polish presidential election of 1995 when former Communist Aleksandr Kwaśniewski defeated the anti-Communist hero Lech Wałęsa. The most successful Communists-turned-Social-Democrats were, predictably, the Italians; most Italian Communists joined the new Democratic Party of the Left, which dominated coalition governments in the late 1990s and in 2006. The old symbols of activism and labour – the hammer and sickle – were combined with a distinctly conservative image of rootedness: the oak tree.

In Asia, similarly, a successful capitalism reconciled Chinese, Vietnamese and Laotian Communists to the market, if not to liberal democracy, and elected Communist governments in the Indian states of Kerala and West Bengal pursued free-market policies. Mao's mummified corpse still occupies the mausoleum on Tian'anmen Square and he still stares from the banknotes, but his ideological influence has been reduced to a negligible amount. The official ideology is still Marxism-Leninism-Mao-Zedong-Thought, and a Beijing academic institute is dedicated to its study. However, this is a technocratic Marxism, stripped of any radical commitment to equality. The official line is that once China has become rich, it can then think about Communism. Nobody predicts when this might happen. Meanwhile, efforts to infuse the party with ideological commitment have failed. In 2005 President Hu Jintao launched a Mao-style campaign, demanding that all party members spend every Thursday afternoon and Saturday studying party history and engaging in self-criticism. He was disconcerted to find that they were not taking it seriously, and that commercial websites were doing a brisk trade in pre-prepared self-criticisms. A new rule was introduced requiring that they be written by hand, but the campaign was generally agreed to have been a failure.[13]

The resulting ideological vacuum has been filled with a potent nationalism and by the strange reappearance of official Confucianism. After spending decades trying to root out this ancient ideology of patriarchy, obedience and order, the party is now assiduously embedding it. In 2004 the Chinese government set up the first of a planned hundred or so Confucius Institutes to promote Chinese language and culture abroad – a far cry indeed from Mao's propagation of international Marxism in the 1960s.[14]

Even so, the Chinese Communists are apprehensive. That a Communist party presides over rampant and red-blooded capitalism is, of course, rather difficult to justify. Levels of inequality in China (largely between urban and rural households, and between different regions) exceed that of the United States. The choice made in the 1970s – to embrace market reforms with the support of the bureaucrats – avoided a Soviet-style collapse, but it left local officials with enormous economic power. Bosses and their children – the new Communist 'princelings' – have leveraged their political clout into extreme privilege. Predictably, many ordinary people are disillusioned, especially in the poorer rural areas, and most peasants have a very negative view of their local rulers.[15]

Political interference can also have a damaging impact on the economy. Local party pressure on banks to help friendly businesses means that investment decisions are often made on political, not economic grounds. The Chinese Communists' dilemma is a common one: how can a political elite, however expert, control and direct an economy when there is no independent non-party authority – democratic or legal – to curtail officials? Campaigns against corruption may work for a while, but soon run out of steam.

In the rest of the former Soviet bloc, Communist parties refused to adapt to the neo-liberal revolution, and their response combined resentment and nostalgia. East Germany's successor Communists, who attracted a great deal of support in the eastern regions of the newly reunited Germany, were highly ambivalent about the market. In much of the former USSR, a strong hostility to capitalism has also become the norm. Gennadii Ziuganov's Russian Communist Party adopted a highly nationalistic version of High Stalinism; his mixture of a yearning for the USSR as a Russian empire, social egalitarianism, and hatred of the West and resentment of the plundering oligarchs, was a heady brew. By the mid-1990s disillusionment with the West and economic collapse fuelled popular support, and in the parliamentary elections in 1995 the Communist Party won the largest number of votes. This, however, was to be the high point of Communist support. In the presidential election of 1996 Yeltsin narrowly defeated Ziuganov, though in somewhat dubious circumstances. In effect, old-style Communists had been trounced by an ex-Communist, presiding over a highly corrupt semi-democratic, semi-authoritarian regime, bankrolled by friendly businessmen.

This became the pattern throughout the former USSR, as former Communist bosses tried to rebuild their power without the old Communist parties. Many embraced a mixture of crony capitalism, nationalism and authoritarianism. But from the late 1990s to the mid-2000s, a second wave of democratization swept the region. In Bulgaria and Romania, then in Slovakia, Croatia and Serbia-Montenegro, mass protests at electoral fraud and corruption forced elections and removed ex-Communist bosses.[16] These democratic revolutions became an exportable package. Serbia's '*Otpor*' ('Resistance') pioneered a model of revolution for a postmodern, ironic and media-driven age. Using a combination of rock music, 1980s 'Orange Alternative'-style stunts and irreverent catchy slogans, such as '*Gotov je*' ('He's finished') (applied successfully to Milošević in 2000), they brought their model of revolution to the former USSR, spawning the '*Kmara*' ('Enough') movement in Georgia and '*Pora*' ('It's time') in Ukraine. Although they had a great deal of domestic support, they were also helped by a United States anxious to reduce Russian influence over the region, which funnelled funding to the protestors through various non-governmental organizations. The 'colour revolutions' – 'Rose' in Georgia in 2003, 'Orange' in Ukraine in 2004 and 'Tulip' in Kyrgyzstan in 2005 – all succeeded in toppling old orders dominated by former Communists. But they found it far less easy to replace the nexus of crony capitalists and bosses with genuinely liberal democracies; new rulers soon found themselves dependent on the power structures that had existed before.

Ex-Communists have been noticeably more resilient in former Soviet Central Asia. But in the absence of the old Communist parties, political leaders found themselves increasingly dependent on traditional clans.[17] Only Askar Akayev, the ex-Communist leader of Kyrgyzstan, seriously tried to liberalize politics in the early 1990s, but even so local notables eventually returned to power. Nursultan Nazarbayev of energy-rich Kazakhstan established an authoritarian, clan-based regime more rapidly, as did the eccentric former First Secretary of the Communist Party of Turkmenistan, Saparmurat Niiazov. Niiazov had initially supported the Russian coup leaders of 1991, but when they failed, the newly fashioned 'Turkmenbashi' (leader of the Turkmen) compensated for the weakness of his support amongst the clans by creating an extreme leadership cult. His *Ruhnama*, or the 'Book of the Soul' – a mixture of moral principles, dubious nationalist history and sufism – became compulsory reading in all schools. A giant mechanical model of the *Ruhnama* graces the capital, Ashgabat. The book opens at 8 p.m. every day and recorded readings are broadcast, rather like the Muslim call to prayer. Niiazov, in true Jacobin style, also renamed the days and months, although the new nomenclature was more narcissistic than rationalistic: September became 'Ruhnama', whilst April became 'Gurbansoltan' – his mother's name. Since Niiazov's death in 2006 his successor, formerly his personal dentist, Gurbanguly Berdimuhammedov, has continued the old regime, though he has moderated some of the more idiosyncratic manifestations of the personality cult. These ex-Communists still found the old Stalinist tools essential if they were to shore up their regimes, even though they had long abandoned Stalinist ideology.

Two particularly vulnerable former Soviet allies have retained not only the tools but also much of the substance of Marxist-Leninist ideology: North Korea and Cuba. Both were severely hit by the collapse of the USSR. They not only lost crucial economic assistance, but were now also internationally and ideologically isolated. Even so, they have shown the willpower to survive, as both see themselves as Davids in confrontations with neighbouring Goliaths. Both have also used a mixture of repression and nationalism to stave off collapse.

In the case of North Korea, Kim Il Sung bequeathed the old guerrilla mentality to his son and successor from 1994, Kim Jong Il, and the economic crisis that came with the end of Soviet support, together with the success of South Korea, only convinced the Kims that they should make no serious concessions. In the mid-1990s bad weather and rigid agrarian policies led to famine, causing an estimated 2–3 million deaths.[18] Nevertheless, North Korea has been able to attract aid – partly through blackmail. Fear of Korea's nuclear weapons, and of the chaos caused by its economic collapse, has persuaded foreigners to open their chequebooks. The economy remains depressed, but there have been no signs that the regime is losing control.

The fall of the USSR was an even greater blow for Cuba, because it depended so much on trade with the Eastern bloc. Since 1991 the regime has been beleaguered, but it has remained resilient. Continuing American hostility and the economic embargo, extended under President Clinton in 1999, have helped the regime exploit nationalist resentment at their big neighbour's bullying tactics. Cuba's economic strategy, though, has been very different to North Korea's. By allowing private citizens to participate in the international economy – receiving money from relatives abroad or tourists at home – the Cuban regime has acquired valuable dollar earnings. It has thus stayed afloat, though at the cost of losing control over a substantial part of the economy. Inequalities, especially between blacks and whites, have increased; the state sector is losing talented people to a private, black-market sector; and cynicism has grown, as the gap between ideals and reality widens.[19]

In February 2008 Castro handed over power to his brother Raúl and economic liberalization has continued, though the economic downturn has also forced Raúl to impose new austerity measures. As Cuba celebrates the fiftieth anniversary of Castro's entry into Havana, the mood is pessimistic. But regime change in Washington may have the greatest effect on the state: if President Obama restores relations with Cuba he may well hasten the regime's collapse.

Communists and ex-Communists therefore preside over some of the world's most and least successful economies. But in both cases, the old Radical Marxism has disappeared. Only in poor, peasant societies, where economic inequalities were reinforced with the sharper inequalities of status and race, could revolutionary Marxism still appeal.

III

In April 1980, Abimael Guzmán, a philosophy professor teaching in the poor, remote Peruvian town of Huamanga, made a rousing appeal:

> Comrades. Our labour has ended, the armed struggle has begun ...
> The invincible flames of the revolution will glow, turning to lead and steel
> ...There will be a great rupture and we will be the makers of the new dawn
> ...We shall convert the black fire into red and the red into pure light.[20]

With this, Guzmán – nicknamed 'President Gonzalo' – launched the Communist Party of Peru – Shining Path (*Sendero Luminoso*). His intense, apocalyptic language was highly idiosyncratic, far from both orthodox Soviet and Maoist rhetoric, and he did indeed claim to be creating a new Marxism designed to appeal to his Peruvian Indian supporters. As the party's slogan went: 'Uphold, defend and apply Marxism-Leninism-Maoism, Gonzalo Thought, Mainly Gonzalo Thought!' However, in practice, Gonzalo Thought was pretty close to Maoism, and Guzmán had visited China at least three times during the Cultural Revolution. His one notable departure from Maoism was his attitude towards violence, which was glorified as an almost redemptive force.

One *Sendero* anthem contained the gruesome line: 'the people's blood has a rich perfume, like jasmine, daisies, geraniums and violets'.[21]

Shining Path's violence made sense to its supporters amongst the poverty-stricken indigenous peasantry of Peru's Southern Highlands, the urban poor and middle-class students. Racial discrimination against Indians had a long history, and a brutal military regime had used violence itself to defend a highly unequal agrarian system. Crude military repression in the mid-1980s, followed by a serious debt crisis, primed the pump of rebellion, and at its height in 1991 Shining Path had some 23,000 armed members and its campaign of urban and rural violence threatened to topple the government.[22] However, the guerrillas, obsessed with building up a wholly unified body of peasant militants, spent as much time terrorizing the peasants as they did attacking their enemies. Traditional peasant markets were outlawed and complete subordination to the organization was enforced. Shining Path's white, urban leadership had a very alien culture to that of their peasant supporters. Guerrillas would paint slogans such as 'Death to the Traitor Deng Xiaoping' on the walls of remote Andean villages, even though they meant nothing to the locals.[23] The Peruvian government made much of this culture gap when it released a captured video of Guzmán and his associates drunkenly dancing to Zorba the Greek at a party in a Lima hideaway.[24] When Guzmán and much of the leadership were arrested in 1992, the insurgency collapsed, though remnants survive to this day. The story of *Sendero Luminoso* became a cautionary one for Maoists, and did much to discredit the use of such extreme violence.

One group to learn the lessons of Peru were Maoists on the other side of the world – in Nepal.[25] Nepal, like Peru, was a highly stratified society – this time along lines of both ethnicity and caste. The Maoists, under Prachandra ('the Fierce One'), launched a 'people's war' in 1996, which intensified as the monarchy, encouraged by a Hindu Nationalist India and a neo-conservative United States, cracked down in 2002. By 2005 the Maoists could have made an attempt to take the country by force, but they decided not to. They perhaps felt they were not strong enough, but they had also learnt from Guzmán's failure. Having forced the King to give in, they decided that elections would give them more legitimacy than a guerrilla takeover. In 2008 they won elections and formed a government. A crucial question today is how local guerrilla leaders will adapt to the new democratic politics.

The Maoist victory in Nepal has encouraged Naxalites in neighbouring India, whose insurgency has spread in Bihar and Central India. Again, unrest arises from the discontent of poor peasants as the wealthier benefit from economic change, intensifying economic inequality and poverty. They are generally local movements, engaged in violent conflicts with the police and landlords' private armies, and their attitudes to violence differ.[26] One, reasonably sympathetic, Indian journalist who spent some time with Naxalite guerrillas in the state of Maharashtra in 1998 described one of their leaders thus:

> Vishwanath is well aware of Marxism and Maoism. But not in the wide, world-encompassing sense. His world is small, his views matching it. His fight is for a classless society, yes – but in a narrower sense of the word. He wants betterment. He wants escape from exploitation. He wants an end to the 'police repression' which he sees 'all around'.[27]

In the late 2000s, radical guerrilla Communism flourishes mainly in Nepal and India. In Latin America, in contrast, populist socialist movements – like those of Hugo Chávez of Venezuela – have been more successful than radical Marxists. The Colombian guerrillas – the FARC – have moved away from Marxism-Leninism to a more eclectic 'Bolivarian' socialism, although they continue to use violent methods. A new Latin American Marxist guerrilla movement did emerge in the mid-1990s, and it was the last to gain a significant international reputation – the Mexican Zapatistas. But their history showed how far Third World Marxism had evolved since the 1960s.

On New Year's Eve 1994, a group of masked guerrillas appeared in San Cristóbal de las Casas, the capital of the Mexican state of Chiapas. They engaged in a few skirmishes with the authorities and then melted back into the rainforest; more significant than the fighting was the torrent of words that followed. 'Subcomandante Marcos' – Rafael Sebastián Guillén Vicente – was, like Guzmán, a Marxist philosophy professor determined to defend the rights of the indigenous Indian peasantry. His Zapatista Liberation National Army (EZLN) found inspiration in an eclectic collection of figures, including Marx, the old Mexican socialist revolutionary Emiliano Zapata, and the Sandinista revolutionaries. But Che Guevara was a primary influence – indeed the 'Subcomandante' modelled himself on the 'Comandante', adopting his pipe, beard, cap, his love of *Don Quixote* and self-satirizing, mock heroic prose style.[28] But he rejected Che's warlike methods and emphasized his 'Marxist humanism'. Marcos's guerrillas were effectively isolated by the Mexican army by 1995, and Mexico's politics in the 1990s was much more liberal than much of Latin America's in the 1980s, so culture and propaganda became more important in the Zapatistas' politics than military action. One of the volumes of Marcos's works was entitled *Our Word is Our Weapon*, and he was serious in attempting to forge a non-violent Communism. As he explained, 'our army is very different from others, because its proposal is to cease being an army. A soldier is an absurd person who has to resort to arms in order to convince others, and in that sense the movement has no future if its future is military.'[29]

His approach – democratic and participatory – was indeed closer to that of the Western left of 1968 and the 'Orange' Alternative in Eastern Europe than the old Marxist left of the developing world. His style, which included writing politically committed children's stories featuring Don Durito, a stubborn Zapatista beetle, as well as mastery of the internet, was ironic and even whimsical: ideal for these more peaceable times. It is therefore not surprising that Marcos became a hero of the anti-globalization movement that emerged in the 1990s to criticize the inequalities produced by the neo-liberal order. The Che–Marcos tradition was then the only strand of Communism that retained any real appeal on the left after the wreckage of 1989, and in 1997, on the thirtieth anniversary of Che's death a new techno-version of 'Hasta Siempre, Comandante' performed by the glamorous singer Nathalie Cardone topped the French pop charts. Its extraordinary accompanying pop video showed Cardone viewing Che's corpse, before leading a revolution of the Cuban poor encumbered only by an AK-47 in one hand and a small infant in the other. Notably, however, she only practises her shooting skills on a row of bottles; no blood is spilt.

The potential for radical socialist politics remains wherever sharp social inequalities can be linked to a critique of direct foreign intervention and 'imperialism', although the end of the Cold War has undermined those resentments. Soviet and American interventions helped to intensify social and ethnic conflicts, and in much of the world the United States had filled the vacuum left by the old European empires, propping up conservative elites because it believed that there was a threat from Communism. With the end of the Cold War, the Americans have been much less willing to use force to support unpopular elites. Since the mid-2000s much of Latin America has moved to the populist left, re-acting against neo-liberal reforms, but the United States has largely tolerated such radicalism, however much it dislikes it.

By the turn of the millennium, therefore, the old conflicts that linked the international, the social and the ideological had ended in most areas of the world, except for one region: the Middle East. For the most power-ful revolutionary forces of the 1990s and 2000s did not gather beneath the red flag of Communism, but around the green banner of Islamism. They too believed that they were fighting on two fronts: Western 'imper-ialism' in the Middle East, and traditionalism, in the form of an 'impure', 'superstitious' Islam. They embraced social and gender hierarchies, unlike Communists, but like them they were mobilizers, seeking to unite their divided societies against the enemy. And when they launched the attacks of 11 September 2001 against the United States, they provoked a mili-tant neo-conservative revival – much as the Soviets had in the 1970s. The Reaganite neo-liberal and neo-conservative alliance emerged once again under George W. Bush, to dominate politics for much of the 2000s.

This era, though, was to be a brief one. In the summer and autumn of 2008 the powerful order that had prevailed since 1979–80 finally col-lapsed. The failure of Lehman Brothers Bank in September – largely caused by an extreme laissez-faire approach to economics – marked the end of the neo-liberal age. Meanwhile the defeat of the American-aided 'Rose' revolutionary President of Georgia, Mikheil Saakashvili, by Russia in the August war over the disputed Georgian province of South Ossetia, showed that neo-conservative efforts to spread liberal democracy, already weakened by failures of the 2003 Iraq invasion, had reached their limits.

IV

In a poem of 1938, 'To Those Born Later', Bertolt Brecht sought to jus-tify his life as a Communist to future sceptics. He accepted that 'hatred' 'contorts the features', but even so, asked for 'forbearance'; the times he had lived in were very different: they were 'dark' times of injustice, and there was no alternative to his harsh behaviour. Whilst he had wanted to 'prepare the ground for friendliness', he could not himself be friendly.[30]

Should we exercise forbearance? It is not the purpose of this book to grant, or to deny, Brecht's appeal. We do need to make moral judgements about historical crimes, but we also need to explain. Also, it is one thing to indulge a Brecht; another a Stalin or a Pol Pot.

Brecht's poem does, however, help us to understand the appeal of Soviet-style Communism – even to somebody as resistant to idealism and Romanticism as he. Communism sought to achieve universal 'friendliness' by unfriendly means. It was a movement whose goal was to overcome inequality and bring modernity, but it was founded on the view that this could only be achieved by radical means, ultimately through revolution.

Marxism's desire to unite modernity and equality was to prove especially appealing to the patriotic students and educated elites who perceived their societies to be 'backward': men and women who followed in the footsteps of the Jacobins, Chernyshevskii and Lu Xun in their eagerness not only to challenge old patriarchal power, but also to compete with more 'advanced' nations. Even so the turn to Communism was not the inevitable result of backwardness and inequality. Had it not been for the chaos prevailing in Russia in 1917, or the Japanese invasion of China, the two states which provided the major inspiration for the Communist movement might never have emerged. Nevertheless, Communism often made sense to a variety of different people beyond core activists, even if it was rarely supported by the majority. But it was in its least Romantic and most illiberal form, Marxism-Leninism, that it was most often triumphant. This hybrid placed peculiar emphasis on a militant, secretive disciplined minority, the vanguard party.

Lenin's 'party of a new type' emerged from the experience of Russian conspiratorial politics and civil war. It developed a peculiar mixture of quasi-religious and military culture, and became an almost sect-like organization, concerned with converting and transforming its members into adepts of the true socialist cause. And once it had consolidated its power, under Stalin its energies were harnessed to a yet another 'heroic' task: the industrialization of the country. The party saw itself as a developmental engine seeking to drag the peasantry and other 'backward' groups forward into modernity. It was this promise of dynamic but disciplined energy that gripped elites in so many developing and colonized countries. And it was this organizational élan that attracted those on the left engaged in war, placing Communists at the centre of effective resistance to lands occupied by Nazi Germany and Japanese imperialism.

And indeed Communists were often at their most confident when they were members of a revolutionary movement, opposing autocracy and imperialism, particularly in conditions of war. It was the actual practice of government that was more difficult. In the early years of Communist rule, the parties generally sought Radical transformation, designed to propel the society towards Communism, often using warlike methods. As Che Guevara admitted to the poet Pablo Neruda, 'War . . . War . . . We are always against war, but once we have fought in a war, we can't live without it. We want to go back to it all the time.'[31] Radicalism also seemed to be more necessary because of war and foreign threats. More technocratic or pragmatic Marxism seemed much less relevant in these conditions. War or threat of war often helped Radical Communists to power, as was the case with Stalin in 1928 and Mao in 1943.

The mass mobilizations, the economic 'leaps' forward, land reform and collectivization campaigns all imitated military campaigns, and often inspired self-sacrifice amongst Communists and their supporters. A quasi-military campaigning style proved especially attractive to the young; but harsh methods inevitably created victims. These Communists, convinced that they were fighting a righteous cause, often acted brutally towards traditional peasant cultures, the religious and those deemed 'bourgeois' – now seen as enemies of progress and of the people.

Of course, some Communist regimes did not resort to mass violence. However, it was in Communism's more ambitious, radical phases that most of its victims suffered – particularly when regimes were establishing themselves. The degree of the violence differed, depending on leadership and circumstances. It was most extreme in the Khmer Rouge's Kampuchea; it was more muted amongst the 'Marxist humanists' of Cuba. Preparation for war could also lead to mass killings, as during Stalin's Terror of the 1930s. Many of the victims of Communist regimes were supposed 'class enemies', but the majority of those who died under Communist regimes were killed by famine, the result of callously dogmatic agrarian policies.

Radical methods could not be used for long, as they damaged the economy and caused chaos. The experts and managers who had to run the planned system were undermined, overambitious 'leaps' created disorder, and ultra-egalitarian methods failed. Narrow, militant groups could not transform large, complex societies without broader support. Eventually the regimes realized that they had to 'retreat', and give themselves a more secure foundation. In the USSR after the war, a more technocratic approach was merged with one that stressed 'patriotic' unity, rather than sectarian division. But Stalin still sought to maintain the system's militancy, and continued to use harsh methods against 'anti-patriotic' 'enemies of the people'.

On Stalin's death many Communists would begin to challenge the pre-eminence of the old model and demand that the movement become more inclusive and 'democratic'. However, there was little agreement on how this was to be achieved. Technocratic solutions were tried by some, but they ran into opposition from leaders and people alike; others, such as Mao and Guevara, returned to a more Radical form of Communism, and inevitably economic disorder, chaos and civil war were the result. Yet another group combined a more ethical, Romantic socialism of human liberation, with pragmatic elements of the market and pluralist democracy, most notably during the Prague Spring. But the party was not ready to give up its monopoly of power, or to dilute the old planned system to such an extent. It was this that precipitated a conservative reaction in the Eastern bloc of the 1970s, under Brezhnev, which in turn strengthened the resolve of Gorbachev and his reformers to launch a peaceful 'revolution' against the party, and ultimately to destroy the old system itself.

Communist regimes had not always seemed so reactionary. Their emphasis on welfare, education and social mobility was often in sharp contrast to the priorities of the rulers who went before, and could be very popular. They also did much to modernize their societies, promoting national integration, social mobility and welfare. There were, however, severe limits to their achievements. Problems were most stark in the economy. They were wasteful and ecologically damaging. And for citizens of Eastern European Communist regimes who were aware of Western consumer societies the gap was very obvious. Communism had the feel of stagnating wartime austerity, not vibrant modernity.

But perhaps more damaging than the economic sclerosis was the gap between the ideal of Communism and the reality. By the 1970s in the USSR, few believed that the party was seriously seeking to create a new, dynamic and equal society. The party, having come to power as a militant, idealistic elite, now seemed to have lost its function, and seemed like an entity solely committed to keeping its power and privileges. Having overcome systems of entrenched inequalities, they seemed to be creating a new one. Urban, educated groups became especially disillusioned with their exclusion from power and lack of freedoms, and as the Western world – partly in response to the Communist threat after World War II – became more inclusive and equal, Communism now appeared as more elitist and less modern than its rival.

Communism was also increasingly discredited by its own legacy of violence, whether the behaviour of the new regimes in the developing world, or the memory of Stalinist and Maoist crimes. The Great Leap Forward, the Cultural Revolution, the Terror, the Cambodian and Ethiopian violence, all presented as essential for achieving Communism, called into question the whole Marxist project. Everyday repression also highlighted the link between Marxism and inhumanity. This sparked an ongoing debate about Marx's own responsibility for the apparently inherent tendency to violence his ideas provoked. Some of Marx's ideas – especially his rejection of liberal rights and his assumption of complete popular consensus in the future – were used to justify projects of total state control and mobilization, even if that was not what he envisaged. Marx's and Engels' praise of revolutionary tactics at times in their careers was also used to legitimize violence. Even so, as his defenders argued, Marx himself opposed the elitist politics pursued by Marxist-Leninist parties, and would not have approved of the regimes that Communists created.

V

In October 2008 Frau Müller, a German teacher, saw one of her Karlsruhe pupils wearing a hooded jacket sporting the letters 'USA', and told him to stand up. 'Face the class,' she ordered. 'How dare you come to school wearing a Western pullover. This is not a fashion show for the class enemy – a letter will be sent to your parents' collective.' No letter, of course, was actually sent. Teacher and pupil were both taking part in a Communist re-enactment, designed to show young Germans the evils of the Communist system. The eighteen-year-olds were given Young Pioneer neckerchiefs and told to sing Communist songs. They were also ordered to denounce a 'dissident' student, and were apparently happy to obey. As the project organizer complained, 'I deliberately create a totalitarian atmosphere and I am still always shocked how quickly and easily people are conditioned by it.'[32] More generally, she feared the nostalgia amongst students for the GDR: 'some think that it was like living in a social paradise'.

As this episode suggests, in some former Communist societies, economic crisis will probably produce increased nostalgia for Communism, with its commitment to full employment and welfare. However, there is little likelihood of a return to 'real existing socialism'; memories of its excesses and failures are too recent. It is true that current resentment at extreme inequalities of wealth has fuelled distinctly left-wing populism in some countries. But past experience suggests that while extreme economic inequalities have often been necessary, they are rarely a sufficient condition for the success of an extreme left. Empires and deeply entrenched hierarchies have also been required. Should these elements (or something resembling them) re-emerge, then a new form of extremist left-wing politics could certainly develop.

It is also possible that the Romantic, participatory tradition of Communism – last sighted on the barricades of 1968 – will assume a new relevance. Indeed the anti-globalization and ecological movements share much with this form of politics. If a crisis of globalized capitalism develops, Romantic Marxist ideals of authenticity and democratic participation may therefore become more widely appealing. But the problem that Marx raised still remains: how can decentralized communities be combined with economic prosperity? Are they only compatible with a reduction in living standards and a narrowing of horizons, as Marx himself believed? If they are, it is difficult to see how this kind of politics could secure mass support.

The history of Communism should have taught us two things. The first lesson, now drawn by many writers, is how destructive dogmatic utopian thinking can be. The second lesson, rather more neglected today, is the danger of sharp inequalities and perceived injustice – for they can make that utopian politics very appealing. Since 1989 the dominant powers have learnt neither lesson. Reacting sharply against Communist utopias, messianic dogmatic liberals have sought to export their system – sometimes by force – across the globe. Perhaps only now, chastened by the crises of 2008, will we finally learn from the history of Communism. Only if we do so will we be spared another bloody act in the tradgedy of Prometheus.

Notes

INTRODUCTION

1. F. Fukuyama, 'The End of History?', *The National Interest* 16 (1989), pp.3–18; F. Fukuyama, *The End of History and the Last Man* (London, 1992).
2. For a strong statement of this case, see N. Podhoretz, *World War IV. The Long Struggle against Islamofascism* (New York, 2007).
3. For the background to this claim, see W. Taubman, *Khrushchev. The Man and His Era* (London, 2002), p.511.
4. This view was most coherently expressed by E. H. Carr in his histories of the Soviet Union. See E. H. Carr, *The Russian Revolution: From Lenin to Stalin (1917–1929)* (London, 1979). On ideas of 'convergence', see Talcott Parsons, *The System of Modern Societies* (Englewood Cliffs, 1971), ch.6; D. Engerman, *Modernization from the Other Shore: American Intellectuals and the Romance of Economic Development* (Cambridge, Mass., 2003).
5. For the most explicit expression of this view, see S. Courtois, 'Introduction', in S. Courtois et al., *The Black Book of Communism. Crimes, Terror, Repression* (Cambridge, Mass., 1999), pp.1–31.
6. For the argument that Stalin self-consciously followed in the traditions of the tsars, see, for instance, R. Tucker, *Stalin in Power. The Revolution from Above, 1928–1941* (New York, 1990), pp.60–4.
7. Trotsky argued that Stalinism was a fundamentally conservative regime ruled by a bureaucracy corrupted by bourgeois mores. L. Trotsky, *The Revolution Betrayed. What is the Soviet Union and Where is It Going?* (New York, 1970), pp.101–4. For the Trotskyist analysis, see B. Knei-Paz, *The Social and Political Thought of Leon Trotsky* (Oxford, 1975), pp.380–410.
8. See, for instance, M. Malia, *The Soviet Tragedy* (New York, 1994).
9. See, for instance, Courtois, 'Introduction', p.16.
10. Simon Goldhill argues that Greek tragedy explored the problems inherent in the 'civic society' emerging in the Greek city states, as more 'modern', 'democratic' ideals took over from the old Homeric aristocratic ethos. S. Goldhill, *Reading Greek Tragedy* (Cambridge, 1986), pp.77–8, 155–6, chs.3–4.

11. Aeschylus, *Prometheus Bound*, trans. and ed. A. Podliecki (Oxford, 2005), ll.1041–53.

12. R. Berki points to four elements within socialism: egalitarianism, moralism, rationalism and libertarianism. He argues that Marxism included all four, but libertarianism was the weakest. R. Berki, *Socialism* (London, 1975).

13. K. Marx and F. Engels, *Collected Works* (London, 1976), vol. i, p.31. For the influence of the Prometheus myth on Marx, see L. P. Wessel, *Prometheus Bound. The Mythic Structure of Karl Marx's Scientific Thinking* (Baton Rouge, 1984).

14. These different forms of Communism, 'Romantic', 'Radical', 'Modernist' and 'Pragmatic', are of course 'ideal types'. They rarely existed in pure form, and often overlapped. The Romantic elements of Marxism, seen most strongly in the early writings of Marx, were more 'libertarian', in Berki's terms, less concerned with political power and more interested in overcoming human alienation and encouraging creativity. These themes re-emerged in the 'Western Marxisms' of the 1950s and 1960s, as is seen in Chapter Eleven.

15. For the contrast between party sectarianism and 'inclusion' in Communist regimes, see K. Jowitt, *New World Disorder. The Leninist Extinction* (Berkeley, 1992), ch.3.

PROLOGUE

1. For this festival, see M. Ozouf, *Festivals and the French Revolution*, trans. A. Sheridan (Cambridge, Mass., 1988); Warren Roberts, *Jacques Louis David, Revolutionary Artist: Art, Politics and the French Revolution* (Chapel Hill, 1989), pp.292–3.

2. Cited in L. Hunt, *Politics, Culture, and Class in the French Revolution* (London, 1986), p.99.

3. Cited ibid., p.107.

4. For the symbolism of Hercules, see Hunt, *Politics*, pp.94–103; James A. Leith, *Space and Revolution. Projects for Monuments, Squares and Public Buildings in France, 1789–1799* (Montreal, 1991), pp.130–4.

5. This is not to argue that the Bolsheviks were significantly influenced by the Jacobins, as some have postulated. See J. Talmon, *The Origins of Totalitarian Democracy* (Harmondsworth, 1986). For differences between Bolsheviks and Jacobins, see P. Higgonet, *Goodness Beyond Virtue. Jacobins during the French Revolution* (Cambridge, Mass., 1998), p.330. For comparisons between the Jacobins and Stalin's 'revolutionary patriotism', see E. Van Ree, *The Political Thought of Joseph Stalin. A Study in Twentieth-Century Revolutionary Patriotism* (London, 2002).

6. See David Bell, *The Cult of the Nation in France. Inventing Nationalism, 1680–1800,* (Cambridge, Mass., 2001), pp.146–54. See also Sièyes's condemnation of

the weak, 'oriental' bourgeoisie: W. Sewell, *A Rhetoric of Bourgeois Revolution. The Abbé Sièyes and What is the Third Estate?* (Durham, NC, 1994), p.62.

7. Cited in Bell, *The Cult of the Nation*, p.151.

8. Marat-Mauger, quoted in Hunt, *Politics*, p.27. For the concept of the 'new man', see M. Ozouf, 'La Révolution Française et l'idée de l'homme nouveau', in C. Lucas (ed.), *The French Revolution and the Creation of Modern Political Culture. Vol. 2: The Political Culture of the French Revolution* (Oxford, 1988).

9. See, for instance, the views of the Abbé Sièyes: E.-J. Sièyes, *Qu'est-ce que le tiers état?* (Paris, 1988); Sewell, *Rhetoric*, pp.103–4.

10. Cited in N. Parker, *Portrayals of Revolution. Images, Debates and Patterns of Thought on the French Revolution* (Carbondale, Ill., 1990), pp.83–7.

11. Cited in F. Hemmings, *Culture and Society in France 1789–1848* (London, 1987), p.25; Roberts, *Jacques-Louis David*, pp.16–29.

12. J.-J. Rousseau, 'Considerations on the Government of Poland and on Its Projected Reformation', in *The Social Contract and Other Later Political Writings*, trans. and ed. V. Gourevitch (Cambridge, 1997), p.227. For the 'heroism' of the 'revolutionary man', see A.-L. Saint-Just, *Oeuvres complètes*, ed. C. Vellay (Paris, 1908), vol. ii, p.327. For heroes and self-sacrifice, see Higgonet, *Goodness*, p.1.

13. J.-J. Rousseau, *The Social Contract*, trans. M Cranston (Harmondsworth, 1968), bk 2.

14. J. Shklar, *Men and Citizens: a Study of Rousseau's Social Theory* (Cambridge, 1969), p.206.

15. J.-J. Rousseau, *Julie, ou la Nouvelle Héloïse*, trans. B. Thompson (Paris, 1966). For the paternalism of Wolmar, and the distinction between Rousseau's hierarchical ideas of the family and more democratic views of the state, see N. Fermon, *Domesticating Passions. Rousseau, Woman and the Nation* (Hanover, NH, 1997). See also Shklar, *Men and Citizens* pp.150–4.

16. Cited in K. Baker, *Inventing the French Revolution: Essays on French Political Culture in the Eighteenth Century* (Cambridge, 1990), p.135.

17. D. Jordan, *The Revolutionary Career of Maximilien Robespierre* (London, 1985), p.160.

18. M. Robespierre, *Oeuvres complètes*, ed. E. Hamel (10 vols.) (Paris, 1903–68), vol. i, p.211.

19. Cited in Jordan, *Revolutionary Career*, p.142.

20. S. Maréchal, 'Le jugement dernier des rois', *in* L. Moland, *Théâtre de la révolution: ou, choix de pièces de théâtre qui ont fait sensation pendant la période révolutionnaire* (Paris, 1877).

21. Cited in R. Rose, *Gracchus Babeuf: the First Revolutionary Communist* (Stanford, 1978), p.11.

22. Cited in ibid., p.140.

23. Cited in J. Lynn, 'French Opinion and the Military Resurrection of the Pike, 1792–1794', *Military Affairs* (1977), p.3.

24. K. Alder, *Engineering the Revolution. Arms and Enlightenment in France, 1763–1815* (Princeton, 1997), pp.264–5, 255.

25. Quoted in J. Lynn, *The Bayonets of the Republic: Motivation and Tactics in the Army of Revolutionary France, 1791–94* (Urbana, Ill., 1984), p.173.

26. Cited in D. Bell, *The First Total War: Napoleon's Europe and the Birth of Modern Warfare* (London, 2007), p.131.

27. Cited in A. Forrest, *The Soldiers of the French Revolution* (Durham, NC, 1990), p.160.

28. For their radicalism and the hostility they caused, see especially C. Lucas, *The Structure of the Terror: the Example of Javogues and the Loire* (Oxford, 1973).

29. Robespierre, *Oeuvres*, vol. x, p.357.

30. Cited in J. Hardman, *Robespierre* (London, 1999), p.137.

31. Ibid., p.127.

32. See Higgonet, *Goodness*, pp.118–20.

33. Hunt, *Politics*, pp.76–7.

34. K. Marx and F. Engels, *Selected Works* (Moscow, 1962), vol. i, p.247.

A GERMAN PROMETHEUS

1. H. Adhémar, 'La Liberté sur les barricades de Delacroix, étudiée d'après des documents inédits', *Gazette des Beaux Arts* 43 (1954), p.88. See also T. Clark, *The Absolute Bourgeois. Artists and Politics in France 1848–1851* (London, 1999), pp.18–20; B. Joubert, *Delacroix* (Princeton, 1998).

2. See F. Furet, *Marx and the French Revolution*, trans. D. Furet (Chicago, 1988).

3. Ibid., p.21.

4. P. Buonarotti, *Conspiration pour l'égalité dite de Babeuf: suivie du procès auquel elle donna lieu, et des pièces justicatives* (Brussels, 1828), vol. ii, pp.132–8; R. Rose, *Gracchus Babeuf: the First Revolutionary Communist* (Stanford, 1978), 213.

5. Cited in R. Hunt, *The Political Ideas of Marx and Engels* (2 vols.) (London, 1984), vol. i, pp.155–6. See also C. Lattek, *Revolutionary Refugees. German Socialism in Britain, 1840–1860* (London, 2006), ch.2.

6. For the use of this term, and the distinction between utopians and the egalitarian Communists, see G. Stedman Jones, 'Introduction', K. Marx and F. Engels, *The Communist Manifesto* (London, 2002), pp.66, 69.

7. C. Fourier, *The Theory of the Four Movements*, eds. G. Stedman Jones and I. Patterson (Cambridge, 1996).

8. P.-J. Proudhon, *What is Property?*, eds. D. Kelley and B. Smith (Cambridge, 1994), p.196.

9. R. Owen, *Selected Works, vol. 3, The Book of the New Moral World*, ed. G. Claeys (London, 1993), p.292.

10. Keith Taylor (ed.), *Henri Saint-Simon (1760–1825): Selected Writings on Science, Industry and Social Organization* (London, 1975), pp.166–8.

11. *Reminiscences of Marx and Engels* (Moscow, n.d), p.130.

12. David McLellan, *Karl Marx: a Biography* (London, 1995), p.12.

13. Cited in S. Barer, *The Doctors of Revolution* (London, 2000), pp.548–9.

14. Cited in L. P. Wessel, *Prometheus Bound. The Mythic Structure of Karl Marx's Scientific Thinking* (Baton Rouge, 1984), p.118.

15. Cited in ibid., p.119.

16. For this contrast between the two, see especially Stedman Jones, 'Introduction', Marx and Engels, *Communist Manifesto*, pp.50–71. See also McLellan, *Karl Marx*, pp.112 ff.

17. For Marx's understanding of this idea, see A. Walicki, *Marxism and the Leap to the Kingdom of Freedom* (Stanford, 1995), p.41.

18. For a discussion of these ideas, see B. Yack, *The Longing for Total Revolution. Philosophic Sources of Social Discontent from Rousseau to Marx and Nietzsche* (Berkeley, 1992), pp.256 ff.

19. K. Marx, 'On James Mill', in K. Marx, *The Early Texts*, ed. D. McLellan (Oxford, 1971), p.202.

20. K. Marx and F. Engels, *Collected Works* [MECW] (New York, 1975–), vol. v, p.47.

21. K. Marx, 'Economic and Philosophical Manuscripts of 1844', in Marx, *Early Texts*, pp.146–7.

22. Cited in Barer, *Doctors*, p.351.

23. For this analysis, see Walicki, *Marxism*, pp.82–3.

24. Marx and Engels, *Communist Manifesto*, pp.222–3.

25. Ibid., p.225.

26. Ibid., pp.243–4.

27. For a more detailed discussion of the tension between these Marxisms, see D. Priestland, *Stalinism and the Politics of Mobilization. Ideas, Power and Terror in Inter-war Russia* (Oxford, 2007), pp.21–34. Many others have commented on contradictions in Marx's thought, drawing slightly different distinctions. See A. Gouldner, *The Two Marxisms. Contradictions and Anomalies in the Development of Theory* (London, 1980), p.32; S. Hanson, *Time and Revolution. Marxism and the Design of Soviet Institutions* (Chapel Hill, 1997), pp.37–55.

28. 'Diary of Norbert Truquin', in M. Traugott (ed.), *The French Worker. Autobiographies from the Early Industrial Era* (Berkeley, 1993), p.276.

29. Ibid., p.285.

30. W. Sewell, *Work and Revolution in France: the Language of Labor from the Old Regime to 1848* (Cambridge, 1980), ch.9; for the Lyon uprising of 1831, see R. Bezucha, *The Lyon Uprising of 1834: Social and Political Conflict in the Early July Monarchy* (Cambridge, Mass., 1974), ch.2.

31. *MECW*, vol. iii, p.313.

32. Marx and Engels, *Communist Manifesto*, p.258. See also A. Gilbert, *Marx's Politics. Communists and Citizens* (Oxford, 1981), pp.197, 217–19.

33. There is an enormous debate on the 'Dictatorship of the Proletariat'. This

follows the view of D. Lovell, *From Marx to Lenin. An Evalutation of Marx's Responsibility for Soviet Authoritarianism* (Cambridge, 1984). For the view that it merely meant radical democracy, and did not involve real dictatorship over other classes, see Hunt, *Political Ideas*, pp.284–336; H. Draper, *Karl Marx's Theory of Revolution. Vol. III: The Dictatorship of the Proletariat* (New York, 1986).

34. For a detailed account, see G. Duveau, *1848. The Making of a Revolution*, trans. A. Carter (London, 1967). On labour motivations, see R. Bezucha, 'The French Revolution of 1848 and the Social History of Work', *Theory and Society* 12 (1983), pp.469–84; M. Traugott, 'The Crowd in the French Revolution of February 1848', *American Historical Review* 93 (1988), pp.638–52.

35. For artisans and the June revolution, see R. Gould, *Insurgent Identities: Class, Communities and Protest from 1848 to the Commune* (Chicago, 1995).

36. For Marx's and Engels' revolutionary Radicalism in Germany, see Gilbert, *Marx's Politics*, ch.10.

37. K. Marx and F. Engels, *The Revolution of 1848–1849. Articles from the Neue Rhenische Zeitung*, trans. S. Ryazanskaya, ed. B. Isaacs (New York, 1972), p.136.

38. For this argument, see Gilbert, *Marx's Politics*.

39. J. Sperber, *The European Revolutions, 1848–1851* (Cambridge, 1994), p.247.

40. J. Rougerie, 'Sur l'histoire de la Première Internationale', *Mouvement Social* 51 (1965), pp.23–46.

41. J. Rougerie, *Le Procès des Communards* (Paris, 1971), pp.155–6. For the power of 'associational' ideas in the Paris Commune, its defence of producers and consumers' cooperatives and direct democracy, see M. Johnson, *The Paradise of Association. Political Culture and Popular Organization in the Paris Commune of 1871* (Ann Arbor, 1996).

42. *MECW*, vol. ii, p.189.

43. Cited in Y. Kapp, *Eleanor Marx* (London, 1972), vol. i, p.88.

44. Karl Marx, *Capital* (3 vols.) (New York, 1967), vol. i, pp.330, 337.

45. Marx, *Capital*, vol. iii, p.820. See also A. Rattansi, *Marx and the Division of Labour* (London, 1982).

46. For the notion of scientific laws in history, see K. Marx, *Preface and Introduction to a Contribution to the Critique of Political Economy* (Beijing, 1976), pp.3–4.

47. Cited in W. Henderson, *A Life of Friedrich Engels* (London, 1976), vol. ii, p.569.

48. F. Engels, *Dialectics of Nature*, trans. C. Dutt (London, 1940), ch.2.

49. F. Engels, *Anti-Dühring. Herr Eugen Dühring's Revolution in Science* (Moscow, 1959), p.82.

50. See especially Engels' introduction to the 1895 edition of Marx's 'Class Struggles in France', *MECW*, vol. i, pp.187–204.

51. Marx and Engels, *Communist Manifesto*, p.234. See also D. Lovell, *Marx's Proletariat: the Making of a Myth* (London, 1988), p.177.

52. Marx and Engels, *Communist Manifesto*, p.243. Though Marx's view of the proletariat and the state was inconsistent, and in 1871 he argued that the proletariat had to smash the state machine as the Paris Commune had done.

53. K. Marx, *Critique of the Gotha Programme* (Peking, 1974), pp.15–21. For this route-map, see Walicki, *Marxism*, p.96.

54. For this charge, see D. Lovell, *From Marx to Lenin. An Evaluation of Marx's Responsibility for Soviet Authoritarianism* (Cambridge, 1984), pp.61–4.

55. K. Marx and F. Engels, *Gespräche mit Marx und Engels*, ed. H. Enzensberger (Frankfurt, 1973), vol. ii, pp.709–10.

56. McLellan, *Karl Marx*, p.371.

57. For a summary and analysis of its effect on workers, see M. Mann, *Sources of Social Power. Vol. 2: The Rise of Classes and Welfare States, 1760–1914* (Cambridge, 1993), pp.597–601.

58. For the distinction between earlier and later protest, see D. Geary, *European Labour Protest, 1848–1939* (London, 1981), pp.35–7. There is some debate on the political radicalism of workers in this period. This analysis owes a great deal to Mann, *Sources of Power*, vol. ii, pp.597–601, 680–2. Geary emphasizes continuing radicalism, see Geary, *European Labour Protest*, pp.107–26.

59. Cited in D. Baguley, 'Germinal: The Gathering Storm', in B. Nelson (ed.), *Cambridge Companion to Zola* (Cambridge, 2007), p.139.

60. E. Zola, *Germinal*, trans. P. Collier (Oxford, 1993), p.288.

61. Ibid., p.349.

62. Ibid., p.523.

63. For this analysis, see Mann, *Sources of Power*, vol. ii, chs.17–18; G. Eley, *Forging Democracy. The History of the Left in Europe, 1850–2000* (New York, 2002), pp. 64–5, 79.

64. 'The Diary of Nikolaus Osterroth', in *The German Worker. Working-Class Autobiographies from the Age of Industrialization*, trans. and ed. A. Kelly (Berkeley, 1987), pp.170–1.

65. Ibid., p.172.

66. Ibid., p.187.

67. E. Weitz, *Creating German Communism 1890–1990: From Popular Protests to Socialist State* (Princeton, 1997), p.51.

68. Cited in *The German Worker*, p.409.

69. V. Lidtke, *The Alternative Culture: Socialist Labor in Imperial Germany* (New York, 1985), pp.186–7.

70. 'The Diary of Otto Krille', in *The German Worker*, p.276.

71. For this point, see S. Berger, 'Germany', in *The Force of Labour*, eds. S. Berger and D. Broughton (Oxford, 1995), p.73.

72. Lidtke, *Alternative Culture*; B. Emig, *Die Veredelung des Arbeiters. Sozial-demokratie als Kulturbewegung* (Frankfurt am Main, 1980).

73. Lidtke, *Alternative Culture*, p.88.

74. Ibid., pp.107–8; see also A. Körner, *Das Lied von einer anderen Welt. Kulturelle Praxis im französischen und deutschen Arbeitermilieu 1840–1890* (Frankfurt am Main, 1997), p.117.

75. Weitz, *Creating German Communism*, p.50.

76. Lidtke, *Alternative Culture*, p.52.

77. 'Diary of Otto Krille', in *The German Worker*, pp.267–8.

78. Eley, *Forging Democracy*, p.79.

79. K. Kautsky, *Selected Political Writings*, trans. and ed. P. Goode (London, 1983), pp.11–12.

80. S. Hickey, *Workers in Imperial Germany: the Miners of the Ruhr* (Oxford, 1985).

81. J. Rupnik, 'The Czech Socialists and the Nation (1848–1918)', in E. Cahm and V. Fišera (eds.), *Socialism and Nationalism in Contemporary Europe (1848–1945)*, vol. ii (Nottingham, 1979).

82. R. Evans, *Proletarians and Politics. Socialism, Protest and the Working Class in Germany before the First World War* (New York, 1990), p.93.

83. August Bebel, *Die Frau und der Sozialismus*, cited in S. Berger, *Social Democracy and the Working Class in Nineteenth and Twentieth Century Germany* (Harlow, 2000), p.89.

84. The twenty comprised Austria, Belgium, Bulgaria, the Czech lands, Denmark, France, Germany, Great Britain, Hungary, Italy, the Netherlands, Norway, Poland, Romania, Russia, Serbia, Spain, Sweden, Switzerland and the United States.

85. For this episode, see James Joll, *The Second International* (London, 1968), p.33.

86. Ibid., p.45.

87. Quoted in G. Steenson, *Karl Kautsky, 1854–1938: Marxism in the Classical Years* (Pittsburgh, 1991), p.47.

88. G. Steenson, *"Not One Man! Not One Penny!" German Social Democracy, 1863–1914* (Pittsburgh, 1981), pp.120–1.

89. Cited in Steenson, *Karl Kautsky*, pp.120–1.

90. H. Goldberg, *Life of Jean Jaurès* (Madison, 1962), ch.11.

91. J. Miller, *From Elite to Mass Politics. Italian Socialism in the Giolittian Era, 1900–1914* (Kent, Ohio, 1990), pp.25–9.

92. For an older view, that conflict was well-established before 1914, see C. Schorske, *German Social Democracy. The Development of the Great Schism* (Cambridge, Mass., 1955); for a combination of this view and the argument that the war precipitated the split, see W. Kruse, *Krieg und nationale Integration. Eine Neuinterpretation des sozialdemokratischen Burgfriedensschlusses, 1914–15* (Essen, 1993).

93. Cited in P. Gay, *The Dilemma of Democratic Socialism. Eduard Bernstein's Challenge to Marx* (New York, 1952), p.296.

94. For Bernstein and revisionism, see M. Steger, *The Quest for Evolutionary Socialism. Eduard Bernstein and Social Democracy* (Cambridge, 1997).

95. For the Social Democratic right and imperialism, see R. Fletcher, *Revisionism and Empire. Socialist Imperialism in Germany, 1897–1914* (London, 1984).

96. Cited in H. Mitchell and P. Stearns, *Workers and Protest: the European Labor Movement, the Working Classes and the Origins of Social Democracy, 1890–1914* (Itasca, Ill., 1971), p.211.

97. For the 1905 revolution, see Chapter Two, pp.77–9.

98. For the SPD's acceptance of a doctrine of 'national defence', see N. Stargardt, *The German Idea of Militarism* (Cambridge, 1994), p.148.

99. Haase to Rappoport, cited in G. Haupt, *Socialism and the Great War. The Collapse of the Second International* (Oxford, 1972), p.208.

100. Cited in Joll, *The Second International*, p.178.

BRONZE HORSEMEN

1. *Konets Peterburga* (1927), dir. V. Pudovkin. For the themes in the film, see A. Sargeant, *Vsevolod Pudovkin. Classic Films of the Soviet Avant-Garde* (London, 2000), pp.94–5.

2. For the film and its reception, see V. Kepley, *The End of St Petersburg: The Film Companion* (London, 2003).

3. R. Wortman, *Scenarios of Power: Myth and Ceremony in Russian Monarchy, Vol. 2: From Alexander II to the Abdication of Nicholas II* (Princeton, 2000), pp.351–8.

4. Cited in Wortman, *Scenarios of Power*, p.354.

5. Cited in ibid., p.362. For the incident see pp.358–64.

6. S. Kanatchikov, *A Radical Worker in Tsarist Russia: the Autobiography of Semen Ivanovich Kanatchikov*, trans. and ed. R. Zelnik (Stanford, 1986), p.45.

7. G. Freeze, 'The *Soslovie* (Estate) Paradigm and Russian Social History', *American Historical Review* 91 (1986), pp.11–36.

8. For peasants' attitudes, see O. Figes, *A People's Tragedy. The Russian Revolution, 1891–1924* (London, 1996), pp.98–102.

9. Kanatchikov, *Radical Worker*, pp.9–10.

10. Cited in T. McDaniel, *Autocracy, Capitalism and Revolution in Russia* (Berkeley, 1988), p.172.

11. For the effect of *What is to be Done?* on the Russian intelligentsia, see I. Paperno, *Chernyshevsky and the Age of Realism: a Study in the Semiotics of Behavior* (Stanford, 1988), pp.30–2.

12. J. Scanlan, 'Chernyshevsky and Rousseau', in A. Mikotin (ed.), *Western*

Philosophical Systems in Russian Literature: a Collection of Critical Studies (Los Angeles, 1979), pp.103–6.

13. N. Chernyshevskii, *What is to be Done? Tales about New People*, trans. B. Tucker, expanded by C. Porter (London, 1982), pp.320–6.

14. For the argument that Chernyshevskii was actually very critical of his characters, even if his readers may not have been, see A. Drozd, *Chernyshevskii's What is to be Done?: A Reevaluation* (Evanston, 2001).

15. For the critique of *aziatchina*, see C. Ingerflom, *Le Citoyen impossible. Les Racines russes du leninisme* (Paris, 1988), pp.60–1.

16. Drozd, *Chernyshevskii's What is to be Done?*

17. Chernyshevskii, *What is to be Done?*, pp.228–60.

18. Ibid., p.242.

19. Ibid., pp.228–60.

20. See S. Morrissey, *Heralds of Revolution: Russian Students and the Mythologies of Radicalism* (New York, 1998), p.19.

21. Ibid., p.25.

22. For the debate, see F. Venturi, *Roots of Revolution. A History of the Socialist and Populist Movements in Nineteenth Century Russia*, trans. F. Haskell (New York, 1966), pp.429–68.

23. Cited in A. Gleason, *Young Russia. The Genesis of Russian Radicalism in the 1860s* (Chicago, 1980), p.356.

24. Daniel Field, 'Peasants and Propagandists in the Russian Movement to the People of 1874', *Journal of Modern History* 59 (1987), pp.415–38.

25. A. Geifman, *Thou Shalt Kill. Revolutionary Terrorism in Russia, 1894–1917* (Princeton, 1993), pp.20–1.

26. N. Valentinov, *Encounters with Lenin*, trans. Paul Rosta and Brian Pearce (Oxford, 1968), p.23.

27. A. Resis, '*Das Kapital* Comes to Russia', *Slavic Review* 29 (1970), p.121.

28. This account is taken from Morrissey, *Heralds*, pp.75–80.

29. R. Service, *Lenin. A Biography* (Basingstoke, 2005), pp.21–9; C. Read, *Lenin. A Revolutionary Life* (London, 2005), p.7.

30. Service, *Lenin*, pp.21–9; Read, *Lenin*, pp.4–9.

31. Cited in Read, *Lenin*, p.9.

32. Service, *Lenin*, pp.100–1.

33. N. Krupskaya, *Memories of Lenin*, trans. E. Verney (London, 1970), pp.264–5.

34. V. Lenin, *Selected Works* [SW] (Moscow, 1977), vol. ii, p.304.

35. Valentinov, *Encounters*, pp.67–8.

36. Service, *Lenin*, p.115.

37. Krupskaya, *Memories*, p.17.

38. Cited in R. Pipes, *Struve: Liberal on the Left* (Cambridge, Mass., 1970), p.195.

39. A. Walicki, *Marxism and the Leap to the Kingdom of Freedom* (Stanford, 1995), pp.298–9.

40. V. Lenin, *Polnoe Sobranie Sochinenii [PSS]* (Moscow, 1965–8, 5th edn), vol. vi, pp.99–100, 171.

41. Lenin, *PSS*, vol. viii, p.379.

42. For the influence of Chernyshevskii on Lenin, see Ingerflom, *Citoyen impossible*, ch.11.

43. For this point, see L. Lih, 'How a Founding Document was Found, or One Hundred Years of Lenin's *What is to be Done?*', *Kritika* 4 (2003), pp.5–49.

44. V. Lenin, *Collected Works* (47 vols.) (Moscow, 1960–70), vol. xxxiv, p.64.

45. A. Ascher, *1905. Vol. 1: Russia in Disarray* (Stanford, 1988), p.91.

46. *Tretyi s"ezd RSDRP. Protokoly* (Moscow, 1959), p.262.

47. L. Trotsky, *1905* (Moscow, n.d.).

48. N. Harding, *Lenin's Political Thought. Theory and Practice in the Democratic Revolutions* (London, 1983), bk 1, pp.213–48, though some argue that Lenin and Trotsky were rather closer than this suggests. See M. Donald, *Marxism and Revolution. Karl Kautsky and the Russian Marxists* (New Haven, 1993), pp.87–93.

49. R. Hilferding, *Finance Capital: a Study of the Latest Phase of Capitalist Development*, trans. and eds. M. Watnick and S. Gordon (London, 1981).

50. V. Lenin, *Imperialism, the Highest Stage of Capitalism* (Moscow, 1982).

51. A. Bely, *Petersburg*, trans. R. Maguire and J. Malmstad (Harmondsworth, 1983), pp.51–2.

52. Ibid., p.14.

53. Ibid., p.214.

54. For the role of the Bronze Horseman in *Petersburg*, see R. Maguire and J. Malmstad, 'Petersburg', in J. Malmstad (ed.), *Andrey Bely. Spirit of Symbolism* (Ithaca, 1987), pp.133–4.

55. Bely, *Petersburg*, p.64.

56. Ibid., p.65.

57. Cited in J. Sanborn, *Drafting the Russian Nation. Military Conscription, Total War, and Mass Politics, 1905–1925* (Dekalb, Ill., 2003), p.33.

58. L. Siegelbaum, *The Politics of Industrial Mobilization in Russia, 1914–17: a Study of the War Industries Committees* (London, 1983), ch.3.

59. P. Holquist, *Making War, Forging Revolution: Russia's Continuum of Crisis, 1914–1921* (Cambridge, Mass., 2002), pp.26–36.

60. O. Figes and B. Kolonitskii, *Interpreting the Russian Revolution: the Language and Symbols of 1917* (New Haven, 1999), p.31.

61. J. von Geldern, *Bolshevik Festivals 1917–1920* (Berkeley, 1993), p.23.

62. Figes and Kolonitskii, *Interpreting the Russian Revolution*, pp.70, 62.

63. Ibid., pp.40, 62–4.

64. For the soldiers' committees, see A. Wildman, *The End of the Russian Imperial Army* (Princeton, 1980), vol. i, pp.228–45.

65. See, for instance, the resolution of workers at the Putilov factory, St Petersburg, 9 September 1917, in V. Cherniaev et al. (eds.), *Piterskie rabochie i 'Diktatura*

proletariata', oktiabr' 1917–1929: ekonomicheskie konflikty i politicheskii protest: sbornik dokumentov (St Petersburg, 2000), p.292.

66. Resolution of workers at the Nobel plant, 4 April 1917, Cherniaev et al., *Piterskie*, p.334.

67. Resolution translated in M. D. Steinberg, *Voices of Revolution, 1917* (New Haven, 2001), pp.221–2.

68. *In the Shadow of Revolution: Life Stories of Russian Women from 1917 to the Second World War*, trans. Y. Slezkine, eds. S. Fitzpatrick and Y. Slezkine (Princeton, 2000).

69. 'Iz ofitserskikh pisem s fronta v 1917 g.', cited in Steinberg, *Voices of Revolution*, p.21.

70. Wildman, *End of the Russian Imperial Army*, vol. i., p.188.

71. 'Instruction, 18 October 1917', in Steinberg, *Voices of Revolution*, p.232.

72. For Hilferding's influence, see Harding, *Lenin's Political Thought*, bk 2, p.53.

73. Lenin, *PSS*, vol. xxxiii, p.91.

74. *Pravda*, 7 June 1917.

75. Lenin, *PSS*, vol. xxxiv, p.316.

76. This was the view of many members of the factory committees of 1917. See S. Smith, *Red Petrograd. Revolution in the Factories, 1917–18* (Cambridge, 1983), p.198.

77. 'A Letter', in *The Complete Works of Isaac Babel*, trans. P. Constantine, ed. N. Babel (New York, 2002), pp.208–12.

78. For this point, see Patricia Carden, *The Art of Isaac Babel* (Ithaca and London, 1972), esp. p.93.

79. Lenin, *PSS*, vol. xxxv, pp.195–202.

80. For popular involvement in the persecutions, see Figes, *People's Tragedy*, pp.520–36.

81. Anna Litveiko, in *In the Shadow of Revolution*.

82. Sofia Volkonskaia, 'The Way of Bitterness', in *In the Shadow of Revolution*, p.156.

83. R. Fuelop-Miller, *The Mind and Face of Bolshevism* (New York, 1965), pp.142–4; von Geldern, *Bolshevik Festivals*, pp.156–60; R. Stites, *Revolutionary Dreams. Utopian Vision and Experimental Life in the Russian Revolution* (New York, 1989), pp.94–5.

84. B. Taylor, *Art and Literature under the Bolsheviks, Volume I: The Crisis of Renewal, 1917–1924* (London, 1991), pp.56–60.

85. Stites, *Revolutionary Dreams*, pp.88–90.

86. Lenin, *PSS*, vol. xxxvi, pp.189–200.

87. K. Bailes, *Technology and Society under Lenin and Stalin. Origins of the Soviet Technical Intelligentsia, 1917–1941* (Princeton, 1978), p.49.

88. For the debate over Taylorism, see K. Bailes, 'Alexei Gastev and the Soviet Controversy over Taylorism, 1918–1924', *Soviet Studies* 29 (1977), pp.373–94; S. Smith, 'Taylorism Rules OK?', *Radical Science Journal* 13 (1983), pp.3–27.

89. Lenin, *PSS*, vol. xxxvi, p.293.

90. Although in the spring of 1918, Lenin only called for 'state capitalism' rather than state control over the economy. Nationalization occurred only gradually.

91. Lenin, *PSS*, vol. xlii, p.157.

92. N. Bukharin and E. Preobrzhensky, *The ABC of Communism* (Harmondsworth, 1969), p.444.

93. A. Gastev, *Poeziia rabochego udara* (Moscow, 1971), p.19.

94. Stites, *Revolutionary Dreams*, pp.156–7.

95. A. Gastev, *O tendentsiiakh proletarskoi kul'tury*, cited in Bailes, 'Alexei Gastev and the Soviet Controversy over Taylorism', pp.377–8.

96. E. Zamiatin, *We*, trans. C. Brown (London, 1993).

97. For these developments, see M. von Hagen, *Soldiers in the Proletarian Dictatorship: the Red Army and the Soviet Socialist State, 1917–1930* (Ithaca, 1990), ch.1.

98. Holquist, *Making War*, pp.232–40.

99. L. Trotsky, *Terrorism and Communism* (Ann Arbor, 1971), p.170.

100. Von Hagen, *Soldiers*, pp.89–114.

101. Ibid., p.107.

102. Sanborn, *Drafting the Russian Nation*, p.178.

103. O. Figes, 'Village and Volost Soviet Elections of 1919', *Soviet Studies* 40 (1988), p.43.

104. Lenin, *PSS*, vol. xlv, p.389.

105. See, for instance, D. Raleigh, *Experiencing Russia's Civil War: Politics, Society and Revolutionary Culture in Saratov, 1917–1922* (Princeton, 2002), pp.248–51.

106. Figes, *People's Tragedy*, p.649.

107. O. Figes, *Peasant Russia, Civil War: The Volga Countryside in Revolution, 1917–1921* (Oxford, 1989), pp.91 ff.

108. For this argument, see ibid., p.314.

109. 'Belaia armiia, chernyi baron' (1920), lyrics P. Grigoriev. The 'black baron' was Baron Wrangel, the White commander.

110. Cited in S. Smith, *The Russian Revolution. A Very Short Introduction* (Oxford, 2002), p.95.

111. Cited in I. Deutscher, *The Prophet Armed. Trotsky 1879–1940* (New York, 1965), p.495.

112. For Bogdanov's ideas, see Z. Sochor, *Revolution and Culture. The Bogdanov-Lenin Controversy* (Ithaca, 1988), pp.28–35.

113. T. Sapronov, *Deviataia konferentsiia RKP(b), sentiabr' 1920 goda. Protokoly* (Moscow, 1972), p.161.

114. Figes, *Peasant Russia*, pp.329–31, 334, 339, 344.

115. P. Avrich, *Kronstadt, 1921* (Princeton, 1970), ch.5.

116. I. Getzler, *Kronstadt, 1917–1921. The Fate of a Soviet Democracy* (Cambridge, 1983), pp.233–4.

117. Lenin, *PSS*, vol. xliv, pp.157–8.

118. E. H. Carr, *The Bolshevik Revolution, 1917–1923* (3 vols.) (London, 1966–71), vol. ii, pp.302–9.

119. For Lenin's views of 'cultural revolution', see C. Claudin Urondo, *Lenin and the Cultural Revolution*, trans. B. Dean (Brighton, 1977), pp.79–83.

120. R. Williams, *Artists in Revolution. Portraits of the Russian Avant-Garde, 1905–1925* (London, 1978), pp.158–9.

121. Taylor, *Art and Literature*, p.69.

UNDER WESTERN EYES

1. B. Brecht, 'Drums in the Night', in *Collected Plays*, trans. and ed. J. Willett and R. Mannheim (London, 1970), vol. i, pp.63–115.

2. L. Trotsky, *Moia zhizn'. Opyt avtobiografii* (Berlin, 1930), vol. i, p.285.

3. Hans Arp, *On My Way. Poetry and Essays, 1912–1947* (New York, 1948), p.39.

4. Grosz's self-critical account of his conversion to Communism can be found in G. Grosz, *The Autobiography of George Grosz: A Small Yes and a Big No*, trans. Arnold J. Pomerans (London, 1982), pp.91–2.

5. For these developments, see G. Eley, *Forging Democracy. A History of the Left in Europe, 1850–2000* (Oxford, 2002), pp.132–4.

6. G. Feldman, 'Socio-Economic Structures in the Industrial Sector and Revolutionary Potentialities, 1917–1922', in C. Bertrand (ed.), *Revolutionary Situations in Europe, 1917–1922: Germany, Italy, Austria-Hungary* (Montreal, 1977).

7. See, for instance, H. Lagrange, 'Strikes and the War', in L. Haimson and C. Tilly (eds.), *Strikes, Wars and Revolutions in an International Perspective. Strike Waves in the Late Nineteenth and Early Twentieth Centuries* (Cambridge, 1989); B. Bezza, 'Social Characteristics, Attitudes and Patterns of the Metalworkers in Italy during the First World War', in Haimson and Tilly, *Strikes*; E. Tobin, 'War and the Working Class: The Case of Düsseldorf, 1914–1918', *Central European History* 13 (1985), pp.257–98.

8. For these figures, see D. Blackbourn, *History of Germany, 1780–1918. The Long Nineteenth Century* (Oxford, 1997), p.366.

9. D. Kirby, *War, Peace and Revolution. International Socialism at the Crossroads 1914–1918* (New York, 1986), p.57.

10. U. Schneede (ed.), *George Grosz: His Life and Work*, trans. Susanne Flatauer (London, 1979), p.160.

11. See P. von Oertzen, *Betriebsräte in der Novemberrevolution* (Bonn, 1976); E. Kolb, *Die Arbeiterräte in der deutschen Innenpolitik 1918 bis 1919* (Düsseldorf, 1962).

12. For this argument, see S. Berger, *Social Democracy and the Working Class in Nineteenth and Twentieth Century Germany* (Harlow, 2000), p.96.

13. J. Riddell (ed.), *Workers of the World and Oppressed Peoples, Unite! Proceedings and Documents of the Second Congress, 1920* (New York, 1991) vol. i, p.8.

14. K. McDermott and J. Agnew, *The Comintern. A History of International Communism from Lenin to Stalin* (Basingstoke, 1996), pp.20–1.

15. C. Epstein, *The Last Revolutionaries. The German Communists and their Century* (Cambridge, Mass., 2003), pp.20–2.

16. H. Mann, *Man of Straw* (Harmondsworth, 1984).

17. Karl Kraus in *Die Fackel*, November 1920, cited in J. Nettl, *Rosa Luxemburg* (London, 1966), vol. i, p.xviii.

18. For 'Romantic anti-capitalism' amongst Marxists and the nationalist right, see Z. Sternhell, *The Birth of Fascist Ideology. From Cultural Rebellion to Political Revolution* (Princeton, 1994), esp. ch.1 on Georges Sorel. For the influence of Sorel and 'syndicalism' on Marxists, see R. Williams, *The Other Bolsheviks. Lenin and his Critics, 1904–1914* (Bloomington, 1986). For the influence of Nietzsche on Marxism, see B. Rosenthal, *New Myth, New World. From Nietzsche to Stalinism* (University Park, Pa, 2002), pp.68–93.

19. See M. Kane, *Weimar Germany and the Limits of Political Art: a Study of the Work of George Grosz and Ernst Toller* (Tayport, 1987).

20. M. Löwy, *Georg Lukács: From Romanticism to Bolshevism*, trans. P. Camiller (London, 1979), p.93. See also A. Arato and P. Breines, *The Young Lukács and the Origins of Western Marxism* (New York, 1979); M. Gluck, *Georg Lukács and his Generation, 1900–1918* (Cambridge, Mass., 1985).

21. Cited in Löwy, *Lukács*, p.123.

22. According to an autobiographical novel by József Lengyel, quoted in Löwy, *Lukács*, p.152.

23. B. Kovrig, *Communism in Hungary. From Kun to Kádár* (Stanford, 1979), p.77.

24. See G. Lukács, *History and Class Consciousness*, trans. R. Livingstone (London, 1971), pp.173, 313.

25. T. Mann, *The Magic Mountain*, trans. H. Lowe-Porter (Harmondsworth, 1960), p.478.

26. Cited in J. Cammett, *Antonio Gramsci and the Origins of Italian Communism* (Stanford, 1967), p.7.

27. *Avanti*, 18 December 1917, cited in A. Gramsci, *Selections from Cultural Writings*, eds. D. Forgacs and G. Nowell-Smith (London, 1985), pp.20–3.

28. A. Gramsci, 'Workers' Democracy', in *L'Ordine Nuovo*, 21 June 1919, in Gramsci, *Selections from Political Writings, 1910–1920*, trans. J. Mathews, ed. Q. Hoare (London, 1977), pp.65–8.

29. M. Jay, *The Dialectical Imagination: a History of the Frankfurt School and the Institute of Social Research, 1923–1950* (London, 1973).

30. Nettl, *Rosa Luxemburg*, vol. i, pp.512–13.

31. Cited in ibid., pp.792–3.

32. J. Riddell (ed.), *Founding the Communist International: Proceedings and Documents of the First Congress, March 1919* (New York, 1987), pp.19–20.

33. 'Manifesto of the Communist International', in ibid., pp.222–32.

34. These are broadly the conclusions of Stefano Bartolini, in Bartolini, *The Political Mobilization of the European Left, 1860–1980: the Class Cleavage* (Cambridge, 2000), pp.537–45.

35. Lajos Kassák, cited in R. Tökés, *Béla Kun and the Hungarian Soviet Republic: the Origins and Role of the Communist Party of Hungary in the Revolutions of 1918–1919* (New York, 1967).

36. G. Peteri, *Effects of World War I: War Communism in Hungary* (New York, 1984), ch.1.

37. T. Hajdu, *The Hungarian Soviet Republic*, trans. E. De Láczay and R. Fischer (Budapest, 1979).

38. Tökés, *Béla Kun*, p.185.

39. A. Gramsci, 'Unions and Councils', *L'Ordine Nuovo*, 25 October 1919, in Gramsci, *Selections*, pp.98–108.

40. See R. Bellamy and D. Schecter, *Gramsci and the Italian State* (Manchester, 1993), p.24.

41. E. Weitz, *Creating German Communism, 1890–1990: From Popular Protests to Socialist State* (Princeton, 1997), pp.179–80.

42. W. Preston, *Aliens and Dissenters. Federal Suppression of Radicals, 1903–1933* (Cambridge, Mass., 1963), pp.118–50.

43. B. Brecht, 'The Decision', in *Collected Plays*, trans. and ed. John Willett (London, 1997), vol. iii, pp.61–91.

44. R. Fischer, *Stalin and German Communism: a Study in the Origins of the State Party* (Cambridge, Mass., 1948), p.615.

45. M. Molnár, *From Béla Kun to János Kádár. Seventy Years of Hungarian Communism*, trans. A. J. Pomerans (New York, 1990), pp.20–1.

46. V. Lenin, *Selected Works* [*SW*] (Moscow, 1977), vol. iii, p.293.

47. Riddell, *Workers of the World*, vol. i, pp.299–300.

48. See Bartolini, *Political Mobilization*, pp.107, 112–13.

49. Cited in F. Claudin, *The Communist Movement. From Comintern to Cominform* (Harmondsworth, 1975), p.63.

50. For Moscow's role, see L. Babichenko, 'Komintern i sobytiia v Germanii v 1923 g. Novye arkhivnye materialy', *Novaia i noveishaia istoriia* 2 (1994), pp.125–57.

51. J. Degras (ed.), *The Communist International, 1919–1943. Documents, Vol. 2* (London, 1971), p.154.

52. I. Stalin, *Sochineniia* (Moscow, 1946–1951), vol. x, p.51.

53. The literature is enormous. For views, based on archival sources, that stress central control, see for instance, A. Vatlin, *Komintern: Pervye desiat' let: istoricheskie ocherki* (Moscow, 1993); for those that emphasize local politics

rather than Moscow, see A. Thorpe, *The British Communist Party and Moscow between the Wars* (Manchester, 2000). For a useful survey of the historiography, see *Labour History Review* 61 (2003).

54. This is argued in K.-M. Mallmann, *Kommunisten in der Weimarer Republik. Sozialgeschichte einer revolutionären Bewegung* (Darmstadt, 1996).

55. For these subventions, see H. Klehr, J. Haynes and F. Firsov (eds.), *The Secret World of American Communism* (New Haven, 1995), pp.23–5; K. McDermott, 'The View from the Centre', in T. Rees and A. Thorpe (eds.), *International Communism and the Communist International, 1919–1943* (Manchester, 1998), p.33. It has been estimated that the British Communist Party received an initial grant of £55,000 (or £1 million in 1995 money), F. Becket, *Enemy Within. The Rise and Fall of the British Communist Party* (London, 1995), p.12.

56. For the argument that some European Communists welcomed Soviet control, see McDermott and Agnew, *The Comintern*, pp.24–5.

57. For this institution, see R. von Mayenburg, *Hotel Lux* (Munich, 1978).

58. V. Dedijer, *Tito* (New York, 1972), p.98.

59. B. Lazitch, 'Les Écoles de Cadres du Comintern', in J. Freymond, *Contributions à l'historie du Comintern* (Geneva, 1965), pp.237–41, 246–51; Weitz, *Creating German Communism*, pp.234–5. See also L. Babischenko, 'Die Kaderschulung der Komintern', in H. Weber (ed.), *Jahrbuch für historische Kommunismusforschung* (Berlin, 1993).

60. Cited in J. McIlroy, A. Campbell, B. McLoughlin and J. Halstead, 'Forging the Faithful. The British at the International Lenin School', *Labour History Review* 68 (2003), p.110. See also L. Babischenko. 'Die Kaderschulung der Komintern'.

61. W. Leonhard, *Child of the Revolution*, trans. C. M. Woodhouse (London, 1979), p.185.

62. Ibid., pp.194–5.

63. Ibid.

64. McIlroy et al., 'Forging the Faithful', pp.112–16.

65. McDermott and Agnew, *The Comintern*, pp.73–4.

66. A. Thorpe, 'Comintern "Control" of the Communist Party of Great Britain, 1920–43', *English Historical Review* 113 (1998), p.652.

67. Weitz argues for the influence of the old Luxemburgist radicalism in *Creating German Communism*. For puritanism in Britain, see K. Morgan, G. Cohen and A. Flinn, *Communists and British Society 1920–1991*(London, 2003), pp.123–9.

68. Ibid., p.235.

69. A. Kriegel, *The French Communists: Profile of a People*, trans. E. Halperin (Chicago, 1972), p.107.

70. For this phenomenon, see S. Macintyre, *Little Moscows. Communism and Working-Class Militancy in Inter-War Britain* (London, 1980). E. Rosenhaft, 'Communists and Communities: Britain and Germany between the Wars', *Historical Journal* 26 (1983), pp.221–36. On culture, see A. Howkins, '"Class

against Class". The Political Culture of the Communist Party of Great Britain, 1930–1935', in F. Gloversmith (ed.), *Class, Culture and Social Change. A New View of the 1930s* (Brighton, 1980).

71. Report on factory groups, 1925, cited in Morgan et al., *Communists and British Society*, p.63.

72. S. Berger, *Social Democracy and the Working Class in Nineteenth and Twentieth Century Germany* (Harlow, 2000), pp.104–5; K. Schönhoven, *Reformismus und Radikalismus. Gespaltene Arbeiterbewegung im Weimarer Sozialstaat* (Munich, 1989).

73. Weitz, *Creating German Communism*, pp.270–1.

74. E. Weitz, *Popular Communism: Political Strategies and Social Histories in the Formation of the German, French, and Italian Communist Parties, 1919–1948* (Ithaca, 1992), p.11.

75. For these themes, see Weitz, *Creating German Communism*, ch.6.

76. Ibid., p.249. For another view that emphasizes the overlap between Communist and Nazi messages, see Conan Fischer, *The German Communists and the Rise of Nazism* (New York, 1991).

77. E. Rosenhaft, 'Working-Class Life and Working-Class Politics: Communists, Nazis and the State in the Battle for the Streets, Berlin, 1928–1932', in R. Bessel and E. Feuchtwanger (eds.), *Social Change and Political Development in Weimar Germany* (London, 1981); E. Rosenhaft, *Beating the Fascists? The German Communists and Political Violence* (Cambridge, 1983).

78. 'America's "New" Civilization', *New York Times*, 13 May 1928.

79. D. Aldcroft, *From Versailles to Wall Street, 1919–1929* (London, 1977), p.263.

MEN OF STEEL

1. *Oktiabr* (1928), dir. S. Eisenstein.

2. S. Eisenstein, 'Perspectives', 1929, in *Film Essays*, ed. Jay Leyda (London, 1968), p.44.

3. Quoted in Y. Barna, *Eisenstein* (London, 1973), p.119.

4. R. Bergman, *Sergei Eisenstein. A Life in Conflict* (London, 1997), p.131.

5. D. Bordwell, *The Cinema of Eisenstein* (Cambridge, Mass., 1993), pp.79–96.

6. A. Rieber, 'Stalin as Georgian', in S. Davies and J. Harris (eds.), *Stalin. A New History* (Cambridge, 2005), pp.25–6. For the Prometheus legend in Georgia, see D. M. Lang and G. M. Meredith-Owens, 'Amiran-Darejaniani: A Georgian Romance and its English Rendering', *Bulletin of the School of Oriental and African Studies* 22 (1959), pp.463–4.

7. R. Suny, 'Stalin and the Making of the Soviet Union', unpublished manuscript, ch.1, p.16. My thanks to Ron Suny for showing me this draft.

8. I. Stalin, *Sochineniia* (Moscow, 1946–51), vol. xiii, pp.113–14.

9. P. Makharadze, quoted in S. Jones, *Socialism in Georgian Colours. The European Road to Social Democracy, 1883–1917* (Cambridge, Mass., 2005), p.51.

10. Jones, *Socialism*, pp.22–8.

11. Suny, 'Stalin', pp.11–13.

12. R. Tucker, *Stalin as Revolutionary, 1879–1929: a Study in History and Personality* (London, 1974), pp.80–1

13. For this point, see Suny, 'Stalin', pp.22–3.

14. Jones, *Socialism*, ch.2.

15. M. Kun, *Stalin. An Unknown Portrait* (New York, 2003), pp.31–2.

16. A. Rieber, 'Stalin, Man of the Borderlands', *American Historical Review* 106 (2001), pp.1674–6.

17. E. Van Ree, 'Stalin's Bolshevism: the First Decade', *International Review of Social History* 39 (1994), pp.361–81.

18. R. Service, *Stalin. A Biography* (London, 2004), p.112.

19. See, for instance, R. Pipes (ed.), *The Unknown Lenin. From the Secret Archive* (New Haven, 1998). For the argument that Lenin was a quasi-liberal, see M. Lewin, *Political Undercurrents in Soviet Economic Debates* (London, 1975), pp.46–7, 96.

20. For Lenin's emphasis on organization, see A. Walicki, *Marxism and the Leap to the Kingdom of Freedom* (Stanford, 1995), p.300. Lenin did compare the party with an army, though again it was the army's organization he admired. See V. Lenin, *Collected Works* (47 vols.) (Moscow, 1960–70), vol. xxi, pp.252–3.

21. For Stalin and nationalism, see E. Van Ree, *The Political Thought of Joseph Stalin. A Study in Twentieth Century Revolutionary Patriotism* (London, 2002).

22. For organic metaphors, see ibid., ch.10.

23. Stalin, *Sochineniia*, vol. i, pp.64–7.

24. Ibid., vol. v, p.71.

25. For Stalin's geopolitical attitudes, see Rieber, 'Stalin', pp.1651–91. See also Stalin, *Sochineniia*, vol. iv, pp.286–7.

26. Service, *Stalin*, p.167.

27. For similarities between the methods of the two, see A. Graziosi, 'At the Roots of Soviet Industrial Relations and Practice. Piatakov's Donbass in 1921', *Cahiers du monde russe et soviétique* 36 (1995), pp.130–2.

28. F. Gladkov, *Cement* (London, 1929), p.55.

29. Ibid., pp.98–9.

30. Ibid., p.302.

31. For notions of the party and the state in the period, see D. Priestland, *Stalinism and the Politics of Mobilization. Ideas, Power and Terror in Inter-war Russia* (Oxford, 2007), pp.226–8.

32. G. Vinokur, cited in I. Halfin, *Terror in My Soul: Communist Autobiographies on Trial* (Cambridge, Mass., 2003), p.237.

33. I. Kallistov, quoted in E. Naiman, *Sex in Public. The Incarnation of Early Soviet Ideology* (Princeton, 1997), p.183.

34. For a discussion, see S. Morrissey, *Heralds of Revolution: Russian Students and the Mythologies of Radicalism* (New York, 1998), pp.3–8.

35. Cited in Halfin, *Terror in My Soul*, p.57. For a discussion of this theme in autobiographies, see ch.2.

36. M. David-Fox, *Revolution of the Mind: Higher Learning among the Bolsheviks, 1918–1929* (Ithaca, 1997), p.127.

37. Ibid., p.177; Jane Price, *Cadres, Commanders and Commissars: The Training of the Chinese Communist Leadership, 1920–1945* (Boulder, Colo., 1976), p.36.

38. J. Cassiday, *The Enemy on Trial: Early Soviet Courts on Stage and Screen* (DeKalb, Ill., 2000).

39. Halfin, *Terror in My Soul*, pp.260, 283–315.

40. Ibid., p.32; Van Ree, *Political Thought*, p.131.

41. Stalin, *Sochineniia*, vol. viii, p.121.

42. V. Kravchenko, *I Chose Freedom. The Personal and Political Life of a Soviet Official* (London, 1947), p.51.

43. Stalin, *Sochineniia*, vol. xi, p.58.

44. Ibid., vol. xiii, pp.29–42.

45. Paul Gregory, *The Political Economy of Stalinism. Evidence from the Soviet Archives* (Cambridge, 2004), pp.111–22.

46. See, for instance, S. Strumilin, *Na Planovom Fronte, 1920–1930 gg.* (Moscow, 1958), pp.395–405. For the Marxist 'teleological' school in economics, see E. H. Carr and R. W. Davies, *Foundations of the Planned Economy 1926–1929* (London, 1971), vol. i. pt ii, ch.32.

47. L. Siegelbaum, 'Production Collectives and Communes and the "Imperatives" of Soviet Industrialization', *Slavic Review* 45 (1986), pp.65–84; H. Kuromiya, *Stalin's Industrial Revolution. Politics and Workers, 1928–1932* (Cambridge, 1988), pp.115–35.

48. For this theme, see S. Fitzpatrick, *Education and Social Mobility in the Soviet Union, 1921–1934* (Cambridge, 1979).

49. Stalin, *Sochineniia*, vol. xi, p.37. For the meaning of 'democracy' in this context, see Priestland, *Stalinism*, pp.200–10.

50. Kravchenko, *I Chose Freedom*, p.56.

51. J. Scott, *Behind the Urals. An American Worker in Russia's City of Steel* (Bloomington, 1973), pp.5–6.

52. For workers' attitudes, see J. Rossman, *Worker Resistance under Stalin: Class and Revolution on the Shop Floor* (Cambridge, Mass., 2005), pp.127–33.

53. N. Jasny, *The Soviet 1956 Statistical Handbook. A Commentary* (East Lansing, Mich., 1957), p.41.

54. L. Kopelev, *The Education of a True Believer*, trans. Gary Kern (London, 1981), p.226.

55. D. Peris, *Storming the Heavens: The Soviet League of the Militant Godless* (Ithaca, 1998).

56. Cited in L. Viola, *Peasant Rebels under Stalin. Collectivization and the Culture of Peasant Resistance* (New York, 1996), p.59.

57. For the role of women in rebellions, see Viola, *Peasant Rebels*, ch.6.

58. Kravchenko, *I Chose Freedom*, pp.99–100.

59. A. P. Nikishin to VTsIK, 1932. In L. Siegelbaum and A. Sokolov (eds.), *Stalinism as a Way of Life* (New Haven, 2000), p.67.

60. N. Ivnitskii, *Kollektivizatsiia i Raskulachivanie: Nachalo 30-kh godov* (Moscow, 1996), pp.203–25.

61. This story is told in *An American Engineer in Stalin's Russia. The Memoirs of Zara Witkin, 1932–1934*, ed. Michael Gelb (Berkeley, 1991), pp.211–12.

62. For an analysis that stresses these problems in Soviet-type economies, see J. Kornai, *The Economics of Shortage* (Amsterdam, 1980).

63. Kuromiya, *Stalin's Industrial Revolution*, p.180.

64. Gregory, *Political Economy*, p.118.

65. Stalin, *Sochineniia*, vol. xiii, p.57.

66. S. Davies, *Popular Opinion in Stalin's Russia. Terror, Propaganda and Dissent, 1934–1941* (Cambridge, 1997), p.24.

67. For the change in policy, see S. Fitzpatrick, *Stalin's Peasants. Resistance and Survival in the Russian Village after Collectivization* (Oxford, 1994), pp.121–2.

68. *Aleksandr Nevskii* (1938), dir. S. Eisenstein.

69. Though these issues remained controversial, and were opposed within the party. See Fitzpatrick, *Stalin's Peasants*, pp.240–1.

70. E. Van Ree, 'Heroes and Merchants. Stalin's Understanding of National Character', *Kritika* 8 (2007), pp.41–65.

71. S. Fitzpatrick, *Everyday Stalinism: Ordinary Life in Extraordinary Times: Soviet Russia in the 1930s* (Oxford, 1999), pp.106–9.

72. J. Brooks, *Thank You, Comrade Stalin! Soviet Public Culture from Revolution to Cold War* (Princeton, 2000), pp.126–7.

73. This is the argument of T. Martin, *The Affirmative Action Empire: Nations and Nationalism in the Soviet Union, 1923–1939* (Ithaca, 2001).

74. P. Kenez, *Cinema and Soviet Society, 1917–1953* (Cambridge, 1992), pp.202–4.

75. For this term, see D. Brandenberger, *National Bolshevism: Stalinist Mass Culture and the Formation of Modern Russian National Identity, 1931–1956* (Cambridge, Mass., 2002).

76. Cited in ibid., p.24.

77. Cited in ibid., pp.101–3.

78. L. Siegelbaum, *Stakhanovism and the Politics of Productivity in the USSR, 1935–1941* (Cambridge, 1988), p.228.

79. *Pravda*, 15 November 1935.

80. Rossiiskii Gosudarstvennyi Arkhiv Sotsial'no-Politicheskoi Istorii [RGASPI], 558/11/1121, 27 (17 March 1938).

81. Siegelbaum, *Stakhanovism*, pp.230–1.

82. For these arguments, see S. Fitzpatrick, 'Ascribing Class: the Construction of Social Identity in Soviet Russia', in Fitzpatrick, *Stalinism. New Directions* (London, 2000), pp.20–46; T. Martin, 'Modernization or Neo-traditionalism? Ascribed Nationality and Soviet Primordialism', in Fitzpatrick, *Stalinism*, pp.348–67.

83. Nicholas Ostrovsky, *The Making of a Hero*, trans. A. Brown (London, 1937).

84. J. Baberowski, *Der rote Terror: die Geschichte des Stalinismus* (Munich, 2003), p.162.

85. Cited in Davies, *Popular Opinion*, p.169.

86. Kravchenko, *I Chose Freedom*, p.101.

87. 'Diary of L. Potemkin', in V. Garros, N. Korenevskaya and T. Lahusen (eds.), *Intimacy and Terror. Soviet Diaries of the 1930s*, trans. C. Flath (New York, 1995), pp.274–5. For this diary, see J. Hellbeck, *Revolution on My Mind: Writing a Diary under Stalin* (Cambridge, Mass., 2006), ch.6.

88. 'Diary of L. Potemkin', p.277.

89. See, for instance, Stepan Podliubnyi, in Hellbeck, *Revolution*, ch.5.

90. A. Inkeles and R. Bauer, *The Soviet Citizen. Daily Life in a Totalitarian Society* (Cambridge, Mass., 1959).

91. A. Rossi, *Generational Differences in the Soviet Union* (New York, 1980), pp.295–7. See also D. Bahry, 'Society Transformed? Rethinking the Social Roots of Perestroika', *Slavic Review* 52 (1993), pp.512–15.

92. Scott, *Behind the Urals*, p.43.

93. For Magnitogorsk workers' integration into the system, see S. Kotkin, *Magnetic Mountain. Stalinism as a Civilization* (Berkeley, 1995), ch.5.

94. Scott, *Behind the Urals*, pp.47, 46.

95. Davies, *Popular Opinion*, p.139.

96. Fitzpatrick, *Everyday Stalinism*.

97. Fitzpatrick, *Stalin's Peasants*, p.288.

98. The famous song from the film *Circus* (1936).

99. 'The Diary of Arzhilovsky', in Garros et al., *Intimacy and Terror*, p.131.

100. Fitzpatrick, *Stalin's Peasants*, p.323.

101. O. Khlevniuk, *The History of the Gulag. From Collectivization to the Great Terror* (New Haven, 2004), p.328.

102. Complaint from a special settler to the Political Red Cross, before 8 August 1930. Cited in Khlevniuk, *History of the Gulag*, pp.15–16.

103. Sarah Davies stresses the discourse of 'us' and 'them'. Davies, *Popular Opinion*, ch.8.

104. RGASPI 558/11/1118, 101–2.

105. J. Harris, *The Great Urals. Regionalism and the Evolution of the Soviet System* (Ithaca, 1999), ch.5.

106. Stalin, *Sochineniia*, vol. xiii, p.232.

107. *Partiinyi billet* (1936), dir. I. Py'rev.

108. Kenez, *Cinema and Soviet* Society, p.145.

109. L. Kaganovsky, 'Visual Pleasure in Stalinist Cinema. Ivan Pyr'ev's *Party Card*', in C. Klaier and E. Naiman, *Everyday Life in Early Soviet Russia. Taking the Revolution Inside* (Bloomington, 2006), pp. 35–6, 53–4.

110. For two very different interpretations, see J. Getty and O. Naumov, *The Road to Terror: Stalin and the Self-destruction of the Bolsheviks, 1932–1939* (New Haven, 1999); O. Khlevniuk, *Master of the House. Stalin and his Inner Circle* (New Haven, 2009). For an elaboration of the approach here, see Priestland, *Stalinism*, ch.5.

111. For Ezhov's role, see J. Getty and O. Naumov, *Yezhov, The Rise of Stalin's 'Iron Fist'* (New Haven, 2008), ch.8.

112. Cited in Van Ree, *Political Thought*, p.134.

113. For this point, see Kotkin, *Magnetic Mountain*.

114. Kravchenko, *I Chose Freedom*, p.107.

115. E. Ginzburg, *Into the Whirlwind*, trans. P. Stevenson and M. Harari (London, 1967), p.44.

116. Hellbeck, *Revolution*, pp.318–19.

117. Scott, *Behind the Urals*, p.195.

118. Historians disagree over Stalin's plans, and we still lack evidence. Khlevniuk argues that Stalin was planning to destroy the regional bosses from at least mid-1936. See O. Khlevniuk, 'The First Generation of Stalinist "Party Generals"', in E. Rees (ed.), *Centre–Local Relations in the Stalinist State, 1928–1941* (Basingstoke, 2001), pp.59–60; Getty and Naumov argue he did not plan it. See Getty and Naumov, *The Road to Terror*. For economic issues, see Harris, *The Great Urals*, pp.182–5.

119. Molotov, among others, argued this. *Sto sorok besed s Molotvym. Iz dnevnika F Chueva* (Moscow, 1991), p.390.

120. For a discussion of these figures, see Getty and Naumov, *The Road to Terror*, pp.587–94.

121. *Ivan Groznyi,* parts I and II (1944 and 1946), dir. S. Eisenstein.

122. For these films, see Bordwell, *The Cinema of Eisenstein*, pp.223–53; M. Perrie, *The Cult of Ivan the Terrible in Stalin's Russia* (Basingstoke, 2001), ch.7.

POPULAR FRONTS

1. Golomstock, *Totalitarian Art in the Soviet Union, the Third Reich, Fascist Italy and the People's Republic of China*, trans. R. Chandler (London, 1990).

2. For contrasts, see C. Lindey, *Art in the Cold War. From Vladivostok to Kalamazoo, 1945–62* (London, 1990), p.25.

3. See D. Ades, 'Paris 1937. Art and the Power of Nations', in D. Ades et al. (eds.),

Art and Power. Europe under the Dictators, 1930–45 (London, 1995), pp.58–62; K. Fiss, 'In Hitler's Salon. The German Pavilion at the 1937 Paris Exposition Internationale', in R. Etlin (ed.), *Art, Culture, and Media under the Third Reich* (Chicago, 2002), pp.316–42; S. Wilson, 'The Soviet Pavilion in Paris', in M. Cullerne Bown and B. Taylor (eds.), *Art of the Soviets. Painting, Sculpture and Architecture in a One-party State, 1917–1992* (Manchester, 1993), pp.106–20.

4. Cited in James Herbert, *Paris 1937. Worlds on Exhibition* (Ithaca, 1998), p.36.

5. See M. Daniel, 'Spain: Culture at War', in Ades et al., *Art and Power*, pp.64–7.

6. Herbert, *Paris 1937*, ch.3.

7. T. Draper, *American Communism and Soviet Russia. The Formative Period* (New York, 1986), p.419.

8. K. McDermott and J. Agnew, *The Comintern. A History of International Communism from Lenin to Stalin* (Basingstoke, 1996), p.105.

9. C. Epstein, *The Last Revolutionaries. The German Communists and their Century* (Cambridge, Mass., 2003), pp.40–1.

10. Cited in R. Boyce, *British Capitalism at the Crossroads. 1919–1932: A Study in Politics, Economics and International Relations* (Cambridge, 1987), pp.115–16.

11. For this point, see R. Evans, *The Coming of the Third Reich* (London, 2008), p.286.

12. *Tsirk* (1936), dir. G. Aleksandrov.

13. McDermott and Agnew, *The Comintern*, pp.125–6.

14. See Dimitrov to Stalin, 1 July 1934, in A. Dallin and F. Firsov (eds.), *Dimitrov and Stalin 1934–1943. Letters from the Soviet Archives* (New Haven, 2000), pp.13–14.

15. I. Stalin, *Sochineniia* (Moscow, 1946–51), vol. xii, p.255.

16. Ibid.

17. Ibid., vol. x, p.169. For the comparison, see E. Van Ree, *The Political Thought of Joseph Stalin. A Study in Twentieth Century Revolutionary Patriotism* (London, 2002), pp.18–24.

18. For an exploration of this theme, see S. Pons, *Stalin and the Inevitable War 1936–1941* (London, 2002).

19. Stalin, *Sochineniia*, vol. vii, pp.26–7.

20. K. Denchev and M. Meshcheriakov, 'Dnevnikovye zapisi G. Dimitrova', *Novaia i noveishaia istoriia* 4 (1991), pp.67–8.

21. For the debate and decisions, see McDermott and Agnew, *The Comintern*, pp.121–30. For socialist thinking, see G. R. Horn, *European Socialists Respond to Fascism. Ideology, Activism and Contingency in the 1930s* (New York, 1996), ch.6.

22. J. Degras (ed.), *The Communist International, 1919–1943. Vol. iii*, (London, 1971), pp.361–5.

23. M. Denning, *The Cultural Front. The Labouring of American Culture in the Twentieth Century* (London, 1996), pp.7–11; I. Katznelson, 'Was the Great

Society a Lost Opportunity?', in S. Fraser and G. Gerstle, *The Rise and Fall of the New Deal Order, 1930–1980* (Princeton, 1989), p.186.

24. Maurice Thorez, *Fils du peuple* (Paris, 1949), pp.27–8.

25. J. Jackson, *The Popular Front in France: Defending Democracy, 1934–38* (Cambridge, 1988), p.120.

26. M. Torigian, *Every Factory a Fortress. The French Labor Movement in the Age of Ford and Hitler* (Athens, Ohio, 1999), p.86.

27. S. Bartolini, *The Political Mobilization of the European Left, 1860–1980: the Class Cleavage* (Cambridge, 2000), pp.429–31.

28. C. Pennetier and B. Pudal, 'Du parti bolchevik au parti stalinien', in M. Dreyfus et al., *Le Siècle des communismes* (Paris, 2000), pp.338–9.

29. On autobiographies, see C. Pennetier and B. Pudal (eds.), *Autobiographies, autocritiques, aveux dans le monde communiste* (Paris, 2002).

30. J. Haslam, *The Soviet Union and the Struggle for Collective Security in Europe, 1933–1938* (London, 1984), pp.107–15.

31. For support for the Communists, see H. Graham, *The Spanish Republic at War, 1936–1939* (Cambridge, 2002), pp.182–5.

32. E. Hobsbawm, *Interesting Times. A Twentieth-Century Life* (London, 2002), p.133.

33. L. Stern, *Western Intellectuals and the Soviet Union, 1920–40: From Red Square to the Left Bank* (London, 2007), p.17.

34. Ibid.

35. B. Webb and S. Webb, *Soviet Communism: A New Civilization* (London, 1937), p.429.

36. The trip is recounted by Ludmila Stern on the basis of the VOKS archive. See Stern, *Western Intellectuals*, pp.146–9.

37. S. Taylor, *Stalin's Apologist: Walter Duranty, the New York Times's Man in Moscow* (Oxford, 1990).

38. Stern, *Western Intellectuals*, pp.31, 24–5.

39. Cited in D. Caute, *Fellow Travellers. A Postscript to the Enlightenment* (London, 1973), p.165.

40. P. Neruda, *Memoirs*, trans. H. St Martin (London, 2004), p.132.

41. P. Drake, 'Chile', in M. Falcoff and F. Pike (eds.), *The Spanish Civil War, 1936–39. American Hemispheric Perspectives* (Lincoln, Nebr., 1982).

42. I. Deutscher, *The Prophet Outcast: Trotsky, 1929–1940* (London, 1963), p.434.

43. Stern, *Western Intellectuals*, p.32.

44. Jackson, *Popular Front in France*, pp.239–43.

45. Graham, *Spanish Republic*, pp.264–5.

46. S. Payne, *The Spanish Civil War, the Soviet Union, and Communism* (New Haven, 2004), pp.228–9.

47. G. Orwell, *Homage to Catalonia* (London, 1986), p.213.

48. For a view that blames the Communists and the USSR, see R. Radosh,

M. Habeck and G. Sevostianov (eds.), *Spain Betrayed: the Soviet Union in the Spanish Civil War* (New Haven, 2001). For an interpretation more sympathetic to the Communists, see Graham, *Spanish Republic*.

49. For this view, see Payne, *Spanish Civil War*, pp.240, 275–8.

50. On the ideology of the Trotskyist movement, see especially Robert Alexander, *International Trotskyism, 1929–1985. A Documented Analysis of the Movement* (Durham, NC, 1991), pp.1–20; A. Callinicos, *Trotskyism* (Milton Keynes, 1990), pp.6–16.

51. A. M. Wald, *The New York Intellectuals* (Chapel Hill, 1987), chs.6–9.

52. Soviet foreign policy in this period has been the subject of a good deal of controversy. For those who argue that Stalin positively welcomed a Nazi alliance, see R. Tucker, *Stalin in Power: the Revolution from Above, 1928–1941* (New York, 1990), chs.10, 21. For a very different view, see T. Uldricks, 'Soviet Security Policy in the 1930s', in G. Gorodestsky (ed.), *Soviet Foreign Policy, 1917–1991. A Retrospective* (London, 1994). This account agrees with Pons, *Stalin*; Van Ree, *Political Thought*, ch.15.

53. F. Firsov, 'Arkhivy Kominterna i vneshnaia politika SSSR v 1939–1941 gg.', *Novaia i noveishaia istoriia* 6 (1992), pp.18–19.

54. Ibid.

55. M. Johnstone, 'Introduction', in F. King and G. Matthews, *About Turn. The British Communist Party and the Second World War, the Verbatim Record of the Central Committee meetings of 25 September and 2–3 October 1939* (London, 1990), pp.13–49.

56. Cited in E. Mawdsley, *Thunder in the East: the Nazi–Soviet War 1941–1945* (London, 2005), p.49.

57. G. Gorodetsky, *Grand Delusion. Stalin and the German Invasion of Russia* (New Haven, 1999), esp. pp.279–80, 296–7.

58. Mawdsley, *Thunder*, p.229.

59. M. Harrison, 'The Soviet Union: the Defeated Victor', in M. Harrison (ed.), *The Economics of World War II. Six Great Powers in Comparison* (Cambridge, 1998), p.271; Mawdsley, *Thunder*, pp.26–7.

60. Mawdsley, *Thunder*, p.215.

61. I. Ehrenburg and K. Simonov, *In One Newspaper. A Chronicle of Unforgettable Years*, trans. A. Kagan (New York, 1987), p.70.

62. G. Hosking, *Rulers and Victims. The Russians in the Soviet Union* (Cambridge, Mass., 2006), p.201.

63. R. Stites, 'Frontline Entertainment', in R. Stites (ed.), *Culture and Entertainment in Wartime Russia* (Bloomington, 1995), pp.133–4.

64. McDermott and Agnew, *The Comintern*, p.207.

65. *Literaturnaia Gazeta*, 12 September 1990.

66. See A. Weiner, *Making Sense of War* (Princeton, 2001), pp.138–54.

67. W. Lower, *Nazi Empire-Building and the Holocaust in the Ukraine* (Chapel Hill, 2005), p.24.

68. A. Agosti, *PalmiroTogliatti* (Turin, 1996), pp.15–26.

69. S. Gundle, 'The Legacy of the Prison Notebooks: Gramsci, the PCI and Italian Culture in the Cold War Period', in C. Duggan and C. Wagstaff (eds.), *Italy in the Cold War. Politics, Culture and Society 1948–58* (Oxford, 1995), pp.131–47.

70. S. Gundle, *I Comunisti italiani tra Hollywood e Mosca : la sfida della cultura di massa (1943–1991)* (Florence, 1995), pp.19–28.

71. M. Harrison, *Accounting for War: Soviet Production, Employment, and the Defence Burden, 1940–1945* (Cambridge, 1996), p.163.

72. Elena Zubkova, *Russia after the War. Hopes, Illusions, and Disappointments, 1945–1957* (New York, 1998), pp.16–18.

73. G. Dimitrov, *Dnevnik (9 mart 1933–6 fevruari 1949)* (Sofia, 1997), p.464.

74. Cited in Van Ree, *Political Thought*, p.244.

75. G. Eisler, quoted by his widow. Cited in Epstein, *The Last Revolutionaries*, p.123.

76. N. Naimark, *The Russians in Germany: a History of the Soviet Zone of Occupation, 1945–1949* (Cambridge, Mass., 1995), p.180.

77. T. Toranska, *Oni: Stalin's Polish Puppets*, trans. A. Kolakowska (London, 1987), p.246.

78. M. Djilas, *Conversations with Stalin*, trans. M. Petrovich (London, 1962), p.84.

79. K. Kersten, *The Establishment of Communist Rule in Poland, 1943–1948* (Berkeley, 1991), pp.111–13.

80. A. Rieber, 'The Crack in the Plaster: Crisis in Romania and the Origins of the Cold War', *Journal of Modern History* 76 (2004), pp.62–106.

81. B. Abrams, *The Struggle for the Soul of the Nation. Czech Culture and the Rise of Communism* (Lanham, 2004), p.164.

82. M. Gorbachev and Z. Mlynář, *On Perestroika, the Prague Spring, and the Crossroads of Socialism* (New York, 2002), pp.13–14.

83. M. Pittaway, *Eastern Europe 1939–2000* (London, 2000), pp.46–7.

84. For these arguments, see M. Conway, 'Democracy in Postwar Western Europe: The Triumph of a Political Model', *European History Quarterly* 32 (2002), pp.70–6.

85. V. Dimitrov, 'Communism in Bulgaria', in M. Leffler and D. Painter, *The Origins of the Cold War: an International History* (London, 2005), pp.191–204.

86. M. Djilas, *Tito. The Story from Inside* (London, 1981), p.16.

87. V. Dedijer, *Tito Speaks. His Self-Portrait and Struggle with Stalin* (London, 1953), pp.4–7.

88. Djilas, *Tito*, p.7.

89. Ibid., p.46.

90. Ibid., p.20.

91. Djilas, *Conversations*, pp.50–1.

92. Ibid., p.76.

93. Dedijer *Tito Speaks*, p.343.

94. Djilas, *Tito*, p.31.

95. This, of course, is not the place to try to resolve this complex issue, and the literature on the debate is enormous. For a traditionalist view that emphasizes the role of ideology, see H. Feis, *From Trust to Terror: the Onset of the Cold War, 1945–1950* (New York, 1970). For one that stresses Russian national interests, see H. Morgenthau, *In Defense of National Interest. A Critical Examination of American Foreign Policy* (New York, 1951). For one of the classic early revisionist works, see G. Kolko, *The Politics of War. Allied Diplomacy and the World Crisis of 1943–1945* (London, 1969). For an account of the state of the debate, see O. Westad (ed.), *Reviewing the Cold War* (London, 2000).

96. This is argued convincingly by Van Ree, *Political Thought*, chs.15–16.

97. V. Pechatnov, 'The Soviet Union and the Outside World', p.2, forthcoming in *Cambridge History of the Cold War*, vol. i.

98. Cited in ibid., p.3.

99. This is the argument of Leffler, see M. Leffler, *A Preponderance of Power: National Security, the Truman Administration, and the Cold War* (Stanford, 1992).

100. Cited in M. Leffler, *For the Soul of All Mankind. The United States, the Soviet Union and the Cold War* (New York, 2007), p.43.

101. See especially N. Naimark, 'Stalin and Europe in the Post-war Period, 1945–1953. Issues and Problems', *Journal of Modern History* 2 (2004), pp.28–56.

102. Pechatnov, 'Soviet Union', pp.8–9.

103. G. Kennan, *Memoirs 1925–1950* (Boston, 1967), pp.549–51, 557, 555.

104. H. Truman, *1946–1952. Years of Trial and Hope* (New York, 1965), vol. ii, p.125.

105. Cited in Leffler, *Preponderance*, p.190.

106. Pechatnov, 'Soviet Union', p.13.

107. Truman, *Years of Trial*, vol. ii, p.129.

108. P. Ginsborg, *A History of Contemporary Italy: Society and Politics, 1943–1988* (Harmondsworth, 1990), p.116.

109. Kennan, *Memoirs*, p.559.

110. M. Hogan, *The Marshall Plan. America, Britain, and the Reconstruction of Western Europe, 1947–1952* (Cambridge, 1987), pp.427–30.

111. For this term, see M. Hogan, *A Cross of Iron. Harry S. Truman and the Origins of the National Security State, 1945–1954* (Cambridge, 1998), pp.312–14.

112. V. Pechatnov, *Ot soiuza – k kholodnoi voine. Sovetsko-amerikanskie otnosheniia v 1945–1947 gg.* (Moscow, 2006), pp.158–9.

113. V. Zubok and C. Pleshakov, *Inside the Kremlin's Cold War: from Stalin to Khrushchev* (Cambridge, Mass., 1996), pp.50–3.

114. Toranska, *Oni*, p.257.

115. See L. Gibianskii, 'Kak voznik Kominform. Po novym arkhivnym materialam', *Novaia i noveishaia istoriia* 4 (1993), pp.131–52; Zubok and Pleshakov, *Inside the Kremlin*, pp.125–33.

116. P. Spriano, *Stalin and the European Communists* (London, 1985), pp.292 ff.

117. Van Ree, *Political Thought*, pp.252–3.

118. S. Pons, 'Stalin and the Italian Communists', in Leffler and Painter (eds.), *Origins*, p.213.

119. *New York Times*, 2 May 1950; for a full account of these 'occupations', see Richard Fried, *The Russians are Coming! The Russians are Coming! Pageantry and Patriotism in Cold-War America* (Oxford, 1998), ch.3.

120. *Zagovor obrechennykh* (1950), dir. M. Kalatozov.

121. For the Soviet side, see Chapter Seven. For American mobilization and the Cold War, see L. McEnaney, 'Cold War Mobilization and Domestic Politics', forthcoming, in *Cambridge History of the Cold War*, vol. i; L. McEnaney, *Civil Defense Begins at Home: Militarization Meets Everyday Life in the Fifties* (Princeton, 2000).

122. Ginsborg, *History of Contemporary Italy*, p.187.

123. Several hundred were also imprisoned and two, the Rosenbergs, were executed. See E. Schrecker, *Many are the Crimes: McCarthyism in America* (Boston, 1998), p.xiii.

124. For the various groups which took part in the anti-Communist campaigns, see ibid., pp.x ff.

125. Though it was never entirely dominant. See R. Fried, 'Voting against the Hammer and Sickle: Communism as an Issue in American Politics', in W. Chafe (ed.), *The Achievement of American Liberalism: The New Deal and Its Legacies* (New York, 2003), pp.99–127.

126. G. Gerstle, *American Crucible. Race and Nation in the Twentieth Century* (Princeton, 2001), pp.245–6.

127. D. Caute, *The Dancer Defects: The Struggle for Cultural Supremacy during the Cold War* (Oxford, 2003), pp.26–7.

128. Gerstle, *American Crucible*, pp.249–56.

129. For the breach between Jews and Communism, see Y. Slezkine, *The Jewish Century* (Princeton, 2004), pp.313–15.

130. G. Lundestad, 'Empire by Invitation? The United States and Western Europe, 1945–1952', *Journal of Peace Research* 3 (1986), pp.263–77.

131. NSC 51, US Policy towards Southeast Asia, 1 July 1949. Declassified Documents Reference System.

132. Djilas, *Conversations*, p.141.

THE EAST IS RED

1. Ho Chi Minh, *On Revolution. Selected Writings 1920–1966* (London, 1967), p.5.

2. For this episode, see W. Duiker, *Ho Chi Minh: a Life* (New York, 2000), pp.57–62.

3. Brocheux is sceptical of this. See P. Brocheux, *Ho Chi Minh. A Biography*, trans. C. Duiker (New York, 2007), p.26.

4. E. Manela, *The Wilsonian Moment: Self-determination and the International Origins of Anticolonial Nationalism* (Oxford, 2007), p.107.

5. Mao Zedong, 'Study the Extremist Party', 14 July 1919, in *Mao's Road to Power. Revolutionary Writings, 1912–1949* [*MRPRW*], ed. S. Schram (Armonk, NY, 1992), vol. i, p.332.

6. Manela, *Wilsonian Moment*, pp.23–30.

7. Duiker, *Ho*, pp.46–55.

8. Cited in Brocheux, *Ho*, p.21.

9. Cited in Duiker, *Ho*, p.82.

10. Ho, *On Revolution*, p.5.

11. Ho Chi Minh, *Textes, 1914–1969*, ed. A. Ruscio (Paris, 1990), p.21, translation from Brocheux, *Ho*, p.12.

12. *Pervyi s"ezd narodov vostoka. Stenograficheskie otchety* (Petrograd, 1920), p.5.

13. M. Roy, *Memoirs* (Bombay, 1964), p.225.

14. Ibid., p.306.

15. Ibid.

16. Ibid., p.379.

17. Lu Xun, 'A Madman's Diary', in Lu Hsun, *Selected Stories* (New York, 2003), pp.8, 18.

18. L. Ou-Fan Lee, 'Literary Trends: The Quest for Modernity, 1895–1927', in M. Goldman and L. Ou-Fan Lee, *An Intellectual History of Modern China* (Cambridge, 2002), p.188.

19. Cited in V. Schwarcz, *The Chinese Enlightenment: Intellectuals and the Legacy of the May Fourth Movement of 1919* (Berkeley, 1986), p.110.

20. Cited in ibid., p.109.

21. L. Feigon, *Chen Duxiu: Founder of the Chinese Communist Party* (Princeton, 1983), p.104.

22. M. Meisner, *Li Ta-Chao and the Origins of Chinese Marxism* (New York, 1970), p.34.

23. For this point, see Feigon, *Chen*, p.145.

24. D.-S. Suh, *The Korean Communist Movement, 1918–1948* (Princeton, 1967), p.132.

25. *Thanh nien*, 20 February 1927, cited in Huỳnh Kim Khánh, *Vietnamese Communism, 1925–1945* (Ithaca, 1982), p.80.

26. W. Duiker, *The Communist Road to Power in Vietnam* (Boulder, 1996), pp.27–8.

27. S. Wilson, 'The Comintern and the Japanese Communist Party', in T. Rees and A. Thorpe (eds.), *International Communism and the Communist International, 1919–1943* (Manchester, 1998), pp.285–307.

28. Schwarcz, *Chinese Enlightenment*, pp.128–36.

29. 'The True Story of Ah Q', in Lu Hsun, *Selected Stories*, pp.65–112.

30. P. Short, *Mao: a Life* (London, 1999), p.86.

31. Cited in Feigon, *Chen*, pp.152–3.

32. This account is from S. Smith, *A Road is Made: Communism in Shanghai 1920–1927* (Honolulu, 2000), pp.59–60.

33. Zhang Guotao, *The Rise of the Chinese Communist Party. The Autobiography of Chang Kuo-t'ao* (Lawrence, Kans., 1971), vol. i, p.139.

34. J. Price, *Cadres, Commanders and Commissars. The Training of the Chinese Communist Leadership* (Folkestone, 1976), pp.31–8.

35. Ibid., pp.90–3.

36. Yu Miin-Ling 'Chiang Kaishek and the Policy of Alliance', in R. Felber, M. Titarenko and A. Grigoriev, *The Chinese Revolution in the 1920s. Between Triumph and Disaster* (London, 2002), pp.98–124.

37. S. Schram, *Mao Tse-tung* (Harmondsworth, 1966), p.48.

38. E. Snow, *Red Star over China* (Harmondsworth, 1972), pp.153–6.

39. A. Smedley, *China Correspondent* (London, 1984), pp.121–2.

40. Mao Zedong, 1 April 1917, *MRPRW*, vol. i, p.113.

41. Ibid., p.124.

42. S. Schram, *The Thought of Mao Tse-Tung* (Cambridge, 1989), p.27.

43. H. Van de Ven, *From Friend to Comrade: the Founding of the Chinese Communist Party, 1920–1927* (Berkeley, 1991), p.45.

44. Schram, *Thought of Mao*, p.46.

45. Li Zhisui, *The Private Life of Chairman Mao: the Memoirs of Mao's Personal Physician*, trans. Tai Hung-chao (London, 1996), pp.77, 103.

46. Snow, *Red Star*, pp.112–13.

47. N. Knight, *Rethinking Mao. Explorations in Mao Zedong's Thought* (Lanham, 2007), ch.4.

48. Schram, *Thought of Mao*, p.39.

49. For this episode, see J. Chang and J. Halliday, *Mao: the Unknown Story* (London, 2006), p.125.

50. H. Van de Ven, 'New States of War. Communist and Nationalist Warfare and State Building, 1928–1934', in Van de Ven (ed.), *Warfare in Chinese History* (Leiden, 2000), p.335.

51. Ibid., p.361.

52. For the contrast between the two military models, see ibid., p.323.

53. Mao Zedong, May 1930, *MRPRW*, vol. iii, pp.296–418. See also Short, *Mao*, pp.304–6.

54. Mao Zedong, June 1930, *MRPRW*, vol. iii, p.445.

55. Short, *Mao*, p.286.

56. For the myth of the Long March, see D. Apter and T. Saich, *Revolutionary Discourse in Mao's Republic* (Cambridge, Mass., 1994), p.85 and *passim*.

57. This is argued in Chang and Halliday, *Mao*, pp.254–5.

58. Snow, *Red Star*, p.64.

59. For Mao's definition of 'Sinification', see *Selected Works of Mao Tse-tung* [*SWMT*] (Beijing, 1961), vol. ii, p.209.

60. Smedley, *China Correspondent*, p.122.

61. For this point, see Schram, *Thought of Mao*, p.92. For the use of *datong* see *SWMT*, vol. ii, pp.148–9.

62. Knight, *Rethinking Mao*, pp.129–30.

63. Though this could be exaggerated. Mao first entered the realm of Marxist philosophy with a set of lectures on Dialectical Materialism in Yenan that were very reliant on Soviet sources: *MRPRW*, vol. iv, pp.573–670.

64. See, for instance, his notes on *A Course in Dialectical Materialism* by M. Shirokov and others, November 1936–April 1937, *MRPRW*, vol. iv, pp.674–5.

65. For the complexity of the relationship between Marxism and Chinese ideas in Mao's thinking, see Knight, *Rethinking Mao*, chs.5, 7.

66. Mao's attitude to this issue is controversial. Schram emphasizes the 'voluntarism' of Mao – his emphasis on will rather than economics, in S. Schram, 'The Marxist', in D. Wilson (ed.), *Mao Tse-tung in the Scales of History* (Cambridge, 1977), pp.35–69. For Mao's Marxist orthodoxy, see A. Walder, 'Marxism, Maoism and Social Change', *Modern China* 1 (1977), pp.101–18. Nick Knight argues that Mao is firmly within an ambiguous Marxist tradition. Knight, *Rethinking Mao*, ch.6, esp. p.189.

67. Knight, *Rethinking Mao*, p.141.

68. M. Selden, *China in Revolution. The Yenan Way Revisited* (Armonk, NY, 1995), p.121.

69. G. Benton, 'The Yenan "Literary Opposition"', *New Left Review* 92 (1975), pp.102–5; Dai Qing, *Wang Shiwei and 'Wild Lilies'. Rectification and Purges in the Chinese Communist Party, 1942–1944*, eds. D. Apter and T. Cheek (Armonk, NY, 1994).

70. Selden, *China*; Apter and Saich, *Revolutionary Discourse*, pp.211–13.

71. For rectification, see Apter and Saich, *Revolutionary Discourse*, pp.279–88.

72. Ibid., p.285.

73. Chang and Halliday, *Mao*, p.300.

74. Chen Yung-fa, 'Suspect History and the Mass Line. Another "Yan'an Way"', in G. Hershatter et al. (eds.), *Remapping China. Fissures in Historical Terrain* (Stanford, 1996), pp.242–60.

75. J. Byron and R. Pack, *The Claws of the Dragon. Kang Sheng – The Evil Genius behind Mao – and his Legacy of Terror in People's China* (New York, 1992), p.139.

76. F. Teiwes and W. Sun, 'From a Leninist to a Charismatic Party; The CCP's Changing Leadership, 1937–1945', in T. Saich and H. Van de Ven (eds.), *New Perspectives on the Chinese Communist Revolution* (Armonk, NY, 1995), p.378.

77. Cited in Short, *Mao*, p.392.

78. G. Benton, *Mountain Fires. The Red Army's Three-Year War in South China, 1934–1938* (Berkeley, 1994); G. Benton, 'Under Arms and Umbrellas. Perspectives on Chinese Communism in Defeat', in Saich and Van de Ven (eds.), *New Perspectives*, pp.116–43.

79. Although self-defence against the Japanese could involve opposition to all outsiders, including the Communists.

80. For this argument, see H. Van de Ven, *War and Nationalism in China, 1925–1945* (London, 2003).

81. For this argument, see Chen Yung-fa, *Making Revolution. The Communist Movement in East and Central China, 1937–1945* (Berkeley, 1986), esp. ch.3. For a summary of the literature on this debate, see L. Bianco, 'Responses to CCP Mobilization Policies', in Saich and Van de Ven, *New Perspectives*, ch.7.

82. W. Hinton, *Fanshen. A Documentary of Revolution in a Chinese Village* (New York, 1966), pp.137–8.

83. Chen, *Making Revolution*, pp.187–8.

84. O. Westad, *Decisive Encounters: the Chinese Civil War, 1946–1950* (Stanford, 2003), pp.115–18.

85. R. Thaxton, *Salt of the Earth. The Political Origins of Peasant Protest and Communist Revolution in China* (Berkeley, 1997), ch.9.

86. K. Hartford, 'Repression and Communist Success: The Case of Jin-Cha-Ji, 1938–1943', in K. Hartford and S. Goldstein (eds.), *Single Sparks. China's Rural Revolutions* (Armonk, NY, 1989), p.27.

87. Bianco, 'Responses', pp.181–2.

88. The Malay Communist Party and Mao's CCP are not directly comparable, as the Chinese in Malaya were a disadvantaged minority within a British colony, unlike the mainland Chinese. Even so, like the Chinese Communists, they were Communist guerrillas from a Chinese Confucian culture who fought against the Japanese and then against anti-Communist forces. Pye's interviewees were Communist guerrillas who had surrendered to the British and then agreed to cooperate in exchange for good treatment, not those (presumably more committed) Communists who refused and went on trial. Yet his material is revealing. See L. Pye, *Guerrilla Communism in Malaya. Its Social and Political Meaning* (Princeton, 1956). For a discussion of the research, see N. Gilman, *Mandarins of the Future. Modernization Theory in Postwar America* (Baltimore, 2003), pp.167–71.

89. Pye, *Guerrilla Communism*, p.124.

90. Ibid., p.211.

91. Though Pye argues this was a less important motivator.

92. Pye, *Guerrilla Communism*, pp.228, 229.

93. Ibid., pp.248, 296.

94. Ibid., 297, 301.

95. Westad, *Decisive Encounters*, ch.4. For the issue of corruption and the Guomindang's legitimacy, see S. Pepper, *Civil War in China. The Political Struggle, 1944–1949* (Lanham, 1999), pp.155–60.

96. For this argument, see Westad, *Decisive Encounters*, p.10.

97. Ibid., p.259.

98. Chang-lai Hung, 'Mao's Parades. State Spectacles in China in the 1950s', *China Quarterly* 190 (2007), p.415.

99. Yong-ho Ch'oe, 'Christian Background in the Early Life of Kim Il-Song', *Asian Survey* 26 (1986), pp.1082–91.

100. A. Lankov, *From Stalin to Kim Il Sung: the Formation of North Korea, 1945–1960* (London, 2002), pp.17–19.

101. O Yŏng-jin, quoted in R. Scalapino and C.-S. Lee, *Communism in Korea. Part I: The Movement* (Berkeley, 1972), pp.324–5.

102. C. Armstrong, *The North Korean Revolution, 1945–1950* (Ithaca, 2003), pp.68–70.

103. Lankov, *From Stalin to Kim*, ch.3.

104. Duiker, *Communist Road*, p.105.

105. Duiker, *Ho*, p.69.

106. D. Marr, *Vietnam 1945. The Quest for Power* (Berkeley, 1995), p.106.

107. *Ho Chi Minh Selected Writings* (Hanoi, 1977), pp.55–6.

108. B. Kerkvliet, *The Huk Rebellion. A Study of Peasant Revolt in the Philippines* (Berkeley, 1977).

109. Chin Peng, *My Side of History* (Singapore, 2003), pp.47–8.

110. Cheah Boon Kheng, *The Masked Comrades: a Study of the Communist United Front in Malaya, 1945–48* (Singapore, 1979).

111. R. Stubbs, *Hearts and Minds in Guerrilla Warfare: the Malayan Emergency, 1948–1960* (London, 1989).

EMPIRE

1. A. Åman, *Architecture and Ideology in Eastern Europe during the Stalin Era* (New York, 1992), pp.90–3.

2. W. Brumfield, *A History of Russian Architecture* (Cambridge, 1993), p.490.

3. K. Tyszka, *Nacjonalizm w Komunizmie. Ideologia Narodowa w Związku Radzieckim i Polsce Ludowej* (Warsaw, 2004), pp.115–41; Martin Mevius, *Agents of Moscow: the Hungarian Communist Party and the Origins of Socialist Patriotism, 1941–1953* (Oxford, 2004), pp.249–62.

4. N. Khrushchev, *Khrushchev Remembers. The Last Testament*, trans. and ed. S. Talbott (London, 1974), p.98.

5. Åman, *Architecture*, pp.88–9.

6. Cited in K. Boterbloem, *Life and Death under Stalin. Kalinin Province, 1945–1953* (Montreal, 1999), p.188.

7. M. Harrison, *Accounting for War. Soviet Production, Employment, and the Defence Burden, 1940–1945* (Cambridge, 1996), pp.160–2.

8. M. Edele, '"More than just Stalinists". The Political Sentiments of Victors 1945–1953', in J. Fürst (ed.), *Late Stalinist Russia. Society between Reconstruction and Reinvention* (London, 2006), p.176.

9. D. Filtzer, *Soviet Workers and Late Stalinism: Labour and the Restoration of the Stalinist System after World War II* (Cambridge, 2002), pp.34–9.

10. Ibid., pp.22–5; G. Ivanova, *Labor Camp Socialism. The Gulag in the Soviet Totalitarian System*, trans. C. Flath (Armonk, NY, 2000), p.116; A. Applebaum, *Gulag. A History* (London, 2004), p.518.

11. E. Ginzburg, *Within the Whirlwind* (London, 1989), pp.71–2.

12. O. Pohl, *The Stalinist Penal System* (Jefferson, NC, 1997), p.131.

13. Filtzer, *Soviet Workers*, p.242.

14. C. Hooper, 'A Darker "Big Deal"', in Fürst, *Late Stalinist Russia*, p.147.

15. Cited in Y. Gorlizki and O. Khlevniuk, *Cold Peace: Stalin and the Soviet Ruling Circle, 1945–1953* (New York, 2004), pp.32–3.

16. Rossiiskii Gosudarstvennyi Arkhiv Sotsial'no-Politicheskoi Istorii [RGASPI] 558/11/732/19.

17. N. Krementsov, *Stalinist Science* (Princeton, 1997), p.181; D. Joravsky, *The Lysenko Affair* (Cambridge, Mass., 1970).

18. Khrushchev, *Khrushchev Remembers*, p.263.

19. I. Stalin, *Sochineniia* (Moscow, 1946–51), vol. xiii, p.28.

20. A. Weiner, *Making Sense of War* (Princeton, 2001), ch.4.

21. Cited in Gorlizki and Khlevniuk, *Cold Peace*, p.156.

22. V. Dunham, *In Stalin's Time: Middleclass Values in Soviet Fiction* (Cambridge, 1976), p.92.

23. M. Kundera, *The Joke* (London, 1992), p.71.

24. Ibid., p.32.

25. M. Pittaway, *Eastern Europe 1939–2000* (London, 2004), p.57.

26. J. Mark, 'Discrimination, Opportunity, and Middle-Class Success in Early Communist Hungary', *Historical Journal* 48, 2 (2005), pp.502–7.

27. C. Miłosz, *The Captive Mind*, trans. J. Zielomko (New York, 1990), pp.98–9.

28. D. Crowley, 'Warsaw's Shops, Stalinism and the Thaw', in S. Reid and D. Crowley (eds.), *Style and Socialism* (Oxford, 2000), p.36.

29. Pittaway, *Eastern Europe*, pp.110–11.

30. A. Janos, *East Central Europe in the Modern World. The Politics of the Borderlands from pre- to post-Communism* (Stanford, 2000), pp.247–8.

31. T. Toranska, *Oni: Stalin's Polish Puppets*, trans. A. Kolakowska (London, 1987), p.298.

32. Janos, *East Central Europe*, p.247.

33. Miłosz, *The Captive Mind*, pp.61–2.

34. W. Leonhard, *Die Revolution entlässt ihre Kinder* (Cologne, 1957), pp.487, 493–7.

35. G. Hodos, *Show Trials. Stalinist Trials in Eastern Europe, 1948–1954* (London, 1987), ch.7.

36. C. Epstein, *The Last Revolutionaries. The German Communists and their Century* (Cambridge, Mass., 2003), pp.136–7, 144.

37. Cited in C. Jones, *Soviet Influence in Eastern Europe: Political Autonomy and the Warsaw Pact* (New York, 1981), p.7.

38. Toranska, *Oni*, pp.335–6.

39. S. Beria, *Beria My Father: Inside Stalin's Kremlin* (London, 2001), p.141.

40. W. Taubman, *Khrushchev. The Man and his Era* (London, 2003), p.214.

41. Toranksa, *Oni*, pp.235–6.

42. H. Margolius Kovaly, *Prague Farewell* (London, 1988), pp.118–19.

43. S. Bartolini, *The Political Mobilization of the European Left, 1860–1980: the Class Cleavage* (Cambridge, 2000), pp.542–3.

44. I. Wall, *French Communism in the Era of Stalin: the Quest for Unity and Integration, 1945–1962* (Westport, Conn., 1983), p.125.

45. D. Desanti, *Les Staliniens, 1944–1956: une expérience politique* (Paris, 1975).

46. For this point, see T. Judt, *Postwar. A History of Europe since 1945* (London, 2007), pp.212–13.

47. M. Adereth, 'Sartre and Communism', *Journal of European Studies* 17 (1987), p.10.

48. F. Fanon, *The Wretched of the Earth*, preface Jean-Paul Sartre, trans. C. Farrington (Harmondsworth, 1967).

49. For the case, see G. Kern, *The Kravchenko Case: One Man's War on Stalin* (New York, 2007).

50. M. Hyvarinen and J. Paastela, 'Failed Attempts at Modernization. The Finnish Communist Party', in M. Waller, *Communist Parties in Western Europe: Decline or Adaptation?* (Oxford, 1988), p.115.

51. S. Gundle, 'The Legacy of the Prison Notebooks: Gramsci, the PCI and Italian Culture in the Cold War Period', in C. Duggan and C. Wagstaff (eds.), *Italy in the Cold War. Politics, Culture and Society 1948–58* (Oxford, 1995), p.139.

52. D. Kertzer, *Comrades and Christians. Religion and Political Struggle in Communist Italy* (Cambridge, 1980), p.106; C. Duggan, 'Italy in the Cold War Years and the Legacy of Fascism', in Duggan and Wagstaff, *Italy in the Cold War*, p.20.

53. For these themes, see Duggan, 'Italy in the Cold War Years', pp.1–24.

54. For this account of the visit, see D. Heinzig, *The Soviet Union and Communist China, 1945–1950. The Arduous Road to the Alliance* (Armonk, NY, 2004), pp.263–384.

55. Shi Zhe, cited in J. Chang and J. Halliday, *Mao: the Unknown Story* (London, 2006), p.431.

56. Hua-Yu Li, 'Stalin's *Short Course* and Mao's Socialist Transformation in the Early 1950s', *Russian History/Histoire Russe* 29 (2002), p.363.

57. For their role, see O. Westad, *Decisive Encounters: the Chinese Civil War, 1946–1950* (Stanford, 2003), pp.260–1, 267–9.

58. See D. Kaple, *The Dream of a Red Factory. The Legacy of High Stalinism in Russia* (New York, 1994).

59. W. Stueck, *Rethinking the Korean War. A New Diplomatic and Strategic History* (Princeton, 2002), pp.73–4.

60. J. Strauss, 'Paternalist Terror. The Campaign to Suppress Counterrevolutionaries and Regime Consolidation in the People's Republic of China, 1950–1953', *Comparative History in Society and History* 44 (2002), pp.80–105.

61. Cited in ibid., p.97.

62. Mao Zedong, 7 February 1953, in K. Fan (ed.), *Mao Tse-tung and Lin Piao: Post-revolutionary Writings* (Garden City, NY, 1972), p.102.

63. Yu Miin-Ling, 'A Soviet Hero, Pavel Korchagin, comes to China', *Russian History/Histoire Russe* 29 (2002), pp.329–56.

64. Tina Mai Chen, 'Internationalism and Cultural Experience. Soviet Films and Popular Chinese Understandings of the Future in the 1950s', *Cultural Critique* 58 (2004), p.96.

65. Wu Hung, *Remaking Beijing: Tiananmen Square and the Creation of a Political Space* (London, 2005), pp.104–5.

66. Cited in A. Finnane, *Changing Clothes in China. Fashion, History, Nation* (London, 2007), p.209.

67. Cited in ibid., p.224.

68. This is argued by Charles Armstrong, *The North Korean Revolution, 1945–1950* (Ithaca, 2003).

69. Ibid., p.167.

70. B. Cumings, *The Origins of the Korean War, Vol. 2. The Roaring of the Cataract, 1947–1950* (Princeton, 1990), p.341.

71. Armstrong, *North Korean Revolution*, pp.222–9.

72. J. Palais, 'Confucianism and the Aristocratic/Bureaucratic Balance in Korea', *Harvard Journal of Asiatic Studies* 44 (1984), pp.427–68.

73. For this argument, see Armstrong, *North Korean Revolution*, p.73.

74. Cited in K. Lebow, 'Public Works, Private Lives. Youth Brigades in Nowa Huta in the 1950s', *Contemporary European History* 10, 2 (2001), p.205.

75. Ibid., p.208.

76. This is argued in the Hungarian case in M. Pittaway, 'The Reproduction of Hierarchy: Skill, Working-Class Culture, and the State in Early Socialist Hungary', *Journal of Modern History* 74 (2002), pp.737–69. For the disillusionment of established Polish workers, see P. Kenney, *Rebuilding Poland: Workers and Communists, 1945–1950* (Ithaca, 1997), p.292.

77. G. Pritchard, *The Making of the GDR, 1945–1953. From Antifascism to Stalinism* (Manchester, 2004), p.196.

78. M. Pittaway, 'Workers in Hungary', in E Breuning, J. Lewis and G. Pritchard, *Power and the People. A Social History of Central European Politics, 1945–56* (Manchester, 2005), pp.68–9.

79. Cited in Kenney, *Rebuilding Poland*, p.234.

80. Pittaway, *Eastern Europe*, pp.92–3.

81. Pritchard, *The Making of the GDR*, p.122.

82. Hanna Świda-Ziemba, 'Stalinizm i Społeczeństwo Polskie', in J. Kurczewski (ed.), *Stalinizm* (Warsaw, 1989), p.49.

83. Mark Frazier, *The Making of the Chinese Industrial Workplace: State, Revolution, and Labour Management* (Cambridge, 2002), p.146.

84. J. Pelikan, *The Czechoslovak Political Trials, 1950–1954: The Suppressed Report of the Dubcek Government's Commission of Enquiry, 1968* (London, 1971), p.56.

85. E. Friedman, P. Pickowicz and M. Selden, *Chinese Village, Socialist State* (New Haven, 1991), p.130.

86. Ibid.

87. Ibid., p.190.

88. Ibid., pp.188, 196.

89. G. Creed, *Domesticating Revolution. From Socialist Reform to Ambivalent Transition in a Bulgarian Village* (University Park, Pa, 1998), p.61.

90. D. Kideckel, *The Solitude of Collectivism. Romanian Villagers to the Revolution and Beyond* (Ithaca, 1993), p.85.

91. M. Lampland, *The Object of Labor: Commodification in Socialist Hungary* (Chicago, 1995), p.155.

92. Creed, *Domesticating Revolution*, p.70.

93. Pritchard, *The Making of the GDR*, p.201.

94. Pittaway, *Eastern Europe*, p.60.

PARRICIDE

1. S. Reid, *Khrushchev in Wonderland. The Pioneer Palace in Moscow's Lenin Hills, 1962*. Carl Beck Papers in Russian and East European Studies, No. 1606, pp.1–5, 25–6.

2. S. Reid, 'The Exhibition *Art of Socialist Countries*, Moscow 1958–9, and the Contemporary Style of Painting', in S. Reid and D. Crowley (eds.), *Style and Socialism. Modernity and Material Culture in Post-War Eastern Europe* (Oxford, 2000), p.103.

3. Reid, *Khrushchev*, p.2.

4. N. Khrushchev, *Khrushchev Remembers. The Last Testament*, trans. and ed. S. Talbott (London, 1974), pp.98–101.

5. M. Djilas, *Memoir of a Revolutionary*, trans. D. Willen (New York, 1973), pp.220–3.

6. For these models, see S. Woodward, *Socialist Unemployment: the Political Economy of Yugoslavia, 1945–1990* (Princeton, 1995), pp.58–60.

7. C. Lilly, *Power and Persuasion: Ideology and Rhetoric in Communist Yugoslavia, 1944–1953* (Boulder, 2001), p.123.

8. M. Djilas, *Tito: The Story from Inside*, trans. V. Kojic and R. Hayes (London, 1981), pp.83–4.

9. S. Pavlowitch, *Tito. A Reassessment* (London, 1992), p.81.

10. Djilas, *Tito*, pp.95–6.

11. M. Brkljačic, 'Popular Culture and Communist Ideology', in J. Lampe and M. Mazower (eds.), *Ideologies and National Identities. The Case of Twentieth-Century Southeastern Europe* (Budapest, 2004), p.197.

12. R. Service, *Stalin. A Biography* (London, 2004), pp.581–6.

13. F. Burlatsky, *Khrushchev and the First Russian Spring* (London, 1991), p.5.

14. Y. Gorlizki and O. Khlevniuk, *Cold Peace: Stalin and the Soviet Ruling Circle, 1945–1953* (New York, 2004), pp.124–31.

15. V. Zubok and C. Pleshakov, *Inside the Kremlin's Cold War* (Cambridge, Mass., 1996), p.142.

16. Gorlizki and Khlevniuk, *Cold Peace*, pp.132–3.

17. A. Knight, *Beria. Stalin's First Lieutenant* (Princeton, 1993), p.190.

18. V. Molotov, *Molotov Remembers: Inside Kremlin Politics. Conversations with Felix Chuev*, ed. Albert Resis (Chicago, 1993), p.334.

19. A. Malenkov, *O moem otse* (Moscow, 1992), p.103; Zubok and Pleshakov, *Inside the Kremlin*, p.143.

20. W. Hayter, *The Kremlin and the Embassy* (London, 1966), pp.106–7, 37–9.

21. See *Pravda*, 13 March 1954.

22. C. Bohlen, *Witness to History, 1929–1969* (New York, 1973), p.370.

23. Cited in M. Leffler, *For the Soul of All Mankind. The United States, the Soviet Union and the Cold War* (New York, 2007), p.98.

24. For the continuing role of ideological dogmatism on both sides, see Leffler, *For the Soul*, pp.147–50.

25. Hayter, *Kremlin*, p.108.

26. W. Thompson, *Khrushchev: a Political Life* (Basingstoke, 1995), p.8.

27. N. Khrushchev, *Khrushchev Remembers: the Glasnost Tapes*, trans. and ed. J. Schecter and V. Luchkov (Boston, 1990), p.6.

28. Cited in W. Taubman, *Khrushchev. The Man and His Era* (London, 2003), p.122.

29. Burlatsky, *Khrushchev*, pp.65–6.

30. Cited in Taubman, *Khrushchev*, p.274. For this account of the speech, see ibid., ch.11.

31. For the speech, see *Rech' Khrushcheva na zakrytom zasedanii XX s"ezda KPSS: 24–25 fevralia 1956 g.* (Munich, 1956).

32. P. Jones, 'Real and Ideal Responses to Destalinization', in P. Jones (ed.), *The*

Dilemmas of Destalinization. Negotiating Cultural and Social Change in the Khrushchev Era (London, 2006), pp.41–62.

33. Mihály, interviewed by James Mark, in J. Mark, 'Society, Resistance and Revolution: The Budapest Middle Class and the Hungarian Communist State 1948–56', *English Historical Review* 488 (2005), pp.975–6.

34. Molotov, *Molotov Remembers*, p.334.

35. R. János, 'The Development of Imre Nagy as a Politician and a Thinker', in G. Péteri (ed.), *Intellectual Life and the Crisis of State Socialism in East Central Europe, 1953–1956* (Trondheim, 2001), pp.16–30.

36. S. Csoóri, 'Pamphlet', cited in G. Litván (ed.), *The Hungarian Revolution of 1956. Reform, Revolt and Repression, 1953–1963* (London, 1996), p.29.

37. F. Lewis, *The Polish Volcano. A Case History of Hope* (London, 1959), p.146.

38. Ibid., p.155.

39. For an account of this episode, see Taubman, *Khrushchev*, p.293.

40. M. Kramer, 'New Evidence on Soviet Decision-Making and the 1956 Polish and Hungarian Crises', *Cold War International History Project* [CWIHP] 8–9 (1996–7), p.53.

41. M. Molnar, *Budapest 1956* (London, 1971), p.266.

42. Cited in Litván, *Hungarian Revolution*, p.127.

43. S. Khrushchev, *Khrushchev and the Creation of a Superpower* (University Park, Pa, 2000), p.188.

44. M. Kramer, 'The "Malin Notes" on the Crises in Hungary and Poland, 1956', *CWIHP* 8–9 (1996–7), pp.392 ff.

45. V. Mićunović, *Moscow Diary*, trans. D. Floyd (Garden City, NY, 1980), pp.133–4.

46. Litván, *Hungarian Revolution*, pp.143–4.

47. E. Hobsbawm, *Interesting Times. A Twentieth-Century Life* (London, 2002), p.205.

48. Cited in D. Kertzer, *Comrades and Christians. Religion and Political Struggle in Communist Italy* (Cambridge, 1980), p.148.

49. Ibid., pp.146–57.

50. K. Middlemas, *Power and the Party. Changing Faces of Communism in Western Europe* (London, 1980), p.100.

51. S. Gundle, *I comunisti italiani tra Hollywood e Mosca: la sfida della cultura di massa (1943–1991)* (Florence, 1995), p.252.

52. Taubman, *Khrushchev*, pp.308–9.

53. D. Kozlov, 'Naming the Social Evil. The Readers of *Novyi mir* and Vladimir Dudintsev's *Not by Bread Alone*, 1956–59 and Beyond', in Jones (ed.), *The Dilemmas of Destalinization*, pp.80, 89.

54. V. Dudintsev, *Not by Bread Alone*, trans. E. Bone (London, 1957), p.246.

55. Ibid., p.438.

56. Cited in Thompson, *Khrushchev*, p.238.

57. Z. Mlynár, *Conversations with Gorbachev: On Perestroika, the Prague Spring, and the Crossroads of Socialism* (New York, 2002), p.36.

58. W. L. Hixson, *Parting the Curtain. Propaganda, Culture and the Cold War, 1945–1961* (London, 1997), pp.178–9.

59. L. Attwood, 'Housing in the Khrushchev Era', in M. Iliĉ et al. (eds.), *Women in the Khrushchev Era* (London, 2004), pp.186–8.

60. Reid, 'The Exhibition *Art of Socialist Countries*', p.103.

61. S. Reid, 'Women in the Home', in illiĉ et al. (eds.), *Women in the Khrushchev Era*, p.168.

62. D. Filtzer, *Soviet Workers and De-Stalinization* (Cambridge, 1992), pp.232–3.

63. S. Baron, *Bloody Sunday in the Soviet Union. Novocherkassk, 1962* (Stanford, 2001), pp.26–7.

64. A. Mikoian, *Tak bylo. Razmyshlennia o minuvshem* (Moscow, 1999), p.610.

65. L. Alexeyeva and P. Goldberg, *The Thaw Generation. Coming of Age in the post-Stalin Era* (Boston, 1990), pp.95–7.

66. P. McMillan, *Khrushchev and the Arts. The Politics of Soviet Culture, 1962–1964* (Cambridge, Mass., 1965), pp.101–5.

67. Reported in D. Volkogonov, *Autopsy for an Empire. The Seven Leaders Who Built the Soviet Regime* (New York, 1998), p.236.

68. Wu Hung, *Remaking Beijing: Tiananmen Square and the Creation of a Political Space* (London, 2005), pp.108–30.

69. S. Schram, *The Thought of Mao Tse-Tung* (Cambridge, 1989), p.154.

70. S. Schram (ed.), *Mao Tse-tung Unrehearsed: Talks and Letters, 1956–71* (Harmondsworth, 1974), pp.114–15.

71. S. Goncharenko, 'Sino-Soviet Military Cooperation', in O. E. Westad (ed.), *Brothers in Arms. The Rise and Fall of the Sino-Soviet Alliance 1945–63* (Stanford, 1998), p.160.

72. *Communist China. Policy Documents with Analysis* (Cambridge, Mass., 1962), pp.151–63.

73. Li Zhisui, *The Private Life of Chairman Mao* (London, 1994), p.222.

74. J. Ch'en, *Mao Papers: Anthology and Bibliography* (New York, 1970), pp.62–3.

75. D. Yang, *Calamity and Reform in China. State, Rural Society, and Institutional Change since the Great Leap Famine* (Stanford, 1996), p.34.

76. L. Zhang and C. Macleod (eds.), *China Remembers* (Oxford, 1999), p.76.

77. S. Potter and J. Potter, *China's Peasants. The Anthropology of a Revolution* (Cambridge, 1990), p.71.

78. Zhang and Macleod, *China Remembers*, p.78.

79. Li, *Private Life*, pp.277–8.

80. Ibid., p.302.

81. For the debate over the causes of the famine, see Yang, *Calamity*, pp.55–67. Yang emphasizes the wastefulness of the communal dining halls.

82. For the estimate of 30 million 'excess deaths' (including 'lost births'), see J. Banister, *China's Changing Population* (Stanford, 1987), p.85. Chang and Halliday give much higher estimates, of 38 million deaths: J. Chang and J. Halliday, *Mao: the Unknown Story* (London, 2006), p.534.

83. Cited in H. Harding, 'The Chinese State in Crisis', in R. Macfarquhar (ed.), *The Politics of China. The Eras of Mao and Deng*, 2nd edn (Cambridge, 1993), p.234.

84. *Decision of the Central Committee of the Chinese Communist Party Concerning the Great Proletarian Cultural Revolution* (Beijing, 1966), p.1.

85. Cited in Harding, 'Chinese State', p.169.

86. Gao Yuan, *Born Red: a Chronicle of the Cultural Revolution* (Stanford, 1987), pp.86, 89–90.

87. Cited in P. Clark, *The Chinese Cultural Revolution. A History* (Cambridge, 2008), p.61.

88. Ibid., p.2.

89. A. Finnane, *Changing Clothes in China. Fashion, History, Nation* (London, 2007), p.237.

90. For the concept of 'virtuocracy', see S. Shirk, 'The Decline of Virtuocracy in China', in J. Watson (ed.), *Class and Social Stratification in post-Revolution China* (Cambridge, 1984).

91. Liu Guokai, *A Brief Analysis of the Cultural Revolution*, trans. A. Chan (Armonk, NY, 1987), p.47.

92. J. Sheehan, *Chinese Workers: A New History* (London, 1998), pp.123–4.

93. R. Madsen, *Morality and Power in a Chinese Village* (Berkeley and Los Angeles, 1984), pp.180–98.

94. G. White, *The Politics of Class and Class Origin: The Case of the Cultural Revolution*, Contemporary China Papers, 9 (Canberra, 1976), p.46.

95. Cited in ibid., p.37.

96. See R. Kraus, *Class Conflict in Chinese Socialism* (New York, 1981), pp.164–6.

97. Zhang and Macleod, *China Remembers*, p.120.

98. Ibid., pp.120–1.

99. Cited in R. Macfarquhar and M. Schoenhals, *Mao's Last Revolution* (Cambridge, Mass., 2006), p.199.

100. Ibid., p.155.

101. Ibid., pp.162–3.

102. Gao Yuan, *Born Red*, pp.179 ff.

103. For these examples, see D. Leese, 'The Mao Cult as Communicative Space', *Totalitarian Movements and Political Religions* 8 (2007), pp.632–4.

104. Cited in ibid., pp.633–4.

105. Zhang and Macleod, *China Remembers*, p.140.

GUERRILLAS

1. Cited in J. L. Anderson, *Che Guevara. A Revolutionary Life* (London, 1997), p.130.

2. Ernesto 'Che' Guevara, *The Bolivian Diary of Ernesto Che Guevara*, 2nd edn (New York, 1996), p.316.

3. P. Neruda, 'La United Fruit Co.' (1950), in P. Neruda, *Canto General*, trans. J. Schmitt (Berkeley, 1991).

4. Cited in Anderson, *Che Guevara*, p.126.

5. Anderson, *Che Guevara*, pp.163, 23.

6. Cited in G. M. Kahin, *The Asian-African Conference. Bandung, Indonesia, April 1955* (Port Washington, NY, 1972), p.42.

7. The film was originally called *Potomok Chingiz-Khana* (*The Heir to Genghis Khan*).

8. C. Romulo, *The Meaning of Bandung* (Chapel Hill, 1956), p.91.

9. Ibid., p.11.

10. Kahin, *The Asian-African Conference*, p.46.

11. *The Conference of Heads of State or Government of Non-Aligned Countries* (Belgrade, 1961).

12. W. Shinn, 'The "National Democratic State": a Communist program for Less-Developed Areas', *World Politics* 15, 3 (1963), pp.177–89.

13. V. Zubok, *A Failed Empire. The Soviet Union in the Cold War from Stalin to Gorbachev* (Chapel Hill, 2007), pp.109–10.

14. Shinn, 'The "National Democratic State"'.

15. This idea was first developed by the Indonesian Dipa Adit. See C. Jian, *China and the Cold War* (Chapel Hill, 2001), p.212.

16. J. Edgar Hoover to W. Jenkins, FBI Report, 7 April 1964, 6. Declassified Documents Reference System.

17. C. Tripp, *A History of Iraq* (Cambridge, 2000), pp.156–7.

18. T. Nossiter, *Communism in Kerala. A Study in Political Adaptation* (London, 1982), ch.6.

19. H. Van der Wee, *Prosperity and Upheaval. The World Economy, 1945–1980* (Harmondsworth, 1987), pp.400–3.

20. NSC 162/2, in United States Department of State, *Foreign Relations of the United States, 1952–1954* (Washington, DC, 1979–2003), vol. ii, p.587.

21. S. G. Rabe, 'Latin America and Anticommunism', in R. Immerman (ed.), *John Foster Dulles and the Diplomacy of the Cold War* (Princeton, 1990), pp.163, 161.

22. W. Duiker, *The Communist Road to Power in Vietnam* (Boulder, 1996), pp.180–2. Though for a more sceptical view, see J. Carter, *Inventing Vietnam. The United States and State Building, 1954–1968* (Cambridge, 2008), pp.79–81.

23. E. Moise, *Land Reform in China and North Vietnam* (Chapel Hill, 1983), pp.201–6.

24. S. Schlesinger and S. Kinzer, *Bitter Fruit. The Story of the American Coup in Guatemala* (Cambridge, Mass., 2005).

25. Fidel Castro, *My Life*, ed. I. Ramet (London, 2007), p.173.

26. Ibid., p.67.

27. See J. Sweig, *Inside the Cuban Revolution. Fidel Castro and the Urban Underground* (Cambridge, Mass., 2002).

28. Castro, 1 January 1959, cited in M. Pérez-Stable, *The Cuban Revolution. Origins, Course and Legacy* (New York, 1999), p.61.

29. Che Guevara to Jean Daniel, 14 December 1957, in C. Franqui, *Diary of the Cuban Revolution* (New York, 1980), p.269.

30. Cited in H. Matthews, *Castro. A Political Biography* (London, 1969), p.141.

31. H. Thomas, *Cuba. The Pursuit of Freedom* (New York, 1971), pp.1215–18.

32. A. Kapcia, *Cuba. Island of Dreams* (Oxford, 2000), pp.103–4.

33. Castro, *My Life*, p.195.

34. Pérez-Stable, *The Cuban Revolution*, pp.7–9

35. Ibid., p.69.

36. Cited in Anderson, *Che Guevara*, pp.388–90.

37. T. Szulc, *Fidel. A Critical Portrait* (London, 1987), p.416.

38. P. Gleijeses, *Conflicting Missions. Havana, Washington and Africa, 1959–1976* (Chapel Hill, 2002), p.18.

39. A. Fursenko and T. Naftali, *'One Hell of a Gamble'. Khrushchev, Castro and Kennedy, 1958–1964* (New York, 1997), p.39.

40. Gleijeses, *Conflicting Missions*, p.18.

41. *Libre Belgique*, 14 October 1960, cited in S. Weissman, *American Foreign Policy in the Congo, 1960–1964* (Ithaca, 1974), p.116.

42. For these themes, see Michael E. Latham, *Modernization as Ideology: American Social Science and Nation Building in the Kennedy Era* (Chapel Hill, 2000).

43. *Revolucion*, 20 November 1959, in S. Balfour, *Castro* (London, 1990), p.80.

44. Interview with Jean Daniel, 25 July 1963, cited in M. Löwy, *The Marxism of Che Guevara. Philosophy, Economics and Revolutionary Warfare*, 2nd edn (Lanham, 2007), p.59.

45. J. Bunck, *Fidel Castro and the Quest for a Revolutionary Culture* (University Park, Pa, 1994), pp.23–7.

46. R. Fagen, *The Transformation of Political Culture in Cuba* (Stanford, 1969), p.53.

47. A. Kapcia, *Cuba in Revolution. A History since the Fifties* (London, 2008), ch.6.

48. Anderson, *Che Guevara*, p.453.

49. Cited in C. Brundenius, *Economic Growth, Basic Needs and Income Distribution in Revolutionary Cuba* (Lund, 1981), p.71.

50. Ricardo Rojo, quoted in Anderson, *Che Guevara*, p.565

51. Alberto Granado, quoted in ibid.

52. Che Guevara, *Guerrilla Warfare* (London, 2003), pp.10–11.

53. Cited in Fursenko and Naftali, *'One Hell of a Gamble'*, p.21.

54. Alfredo Maneiro, quoted in Gleijeses, *Conflicting Missions*, p.22.

55. Luben Perkoff, quoted in Richard Gott, *Guerrilla Movements in Latin America* (Oxford, 2008), p.111.

56. See T. Wickham-Crowley, 'Winners, Losers and Also-Rans: Toward a Comparative Sociology of Latin American Guerrilla Movements', in S. Eckstein (ed.), *Power and Popular Protest. Latin American Social Movements* (Berkeley, 2001), pp.138–41; T. Wickham-Crowley, *Guerrillas and Revolution in Latin America. A Comparative Study of Insurgents and Regimes since 1956* (Princeton, 1992).

57. A. Angell, 'The Left in Latin America since c.1920', in L. Benthall (ed.), *Latin America: Politics and Society since 1930* (Cambridge, 1998), p.110.

58. C. Johnson, *Communist China and Latin America, 1959–1967* (New York, 1970).

59. Gleijeses, *Conflicting Missions*, pp.81–4.

60. Lúcio Lara, cited in ibid., p.83.

61. Gleijeses, *Conflicting Missions*, p.84.

62. E. Guevara, *The African Dream. The Diaries of the Revolutionary War in the Congo* (London, 2001), pp.6–8.

63. Julius Nyerere, *Ujamaa – Essays on Socialism* (Dar-es-Salaam, 1968), p.11.

64. Kwame Nkrumah, *Revolutionary Path* (New York, 1973), p.30.

65. M. Radu and K. Somerville, 'The Congo', in C. Allen, M. Radu and K. Somerville (eds.), *Benin, the Congo and Burkina Faso. Politics, Economics and Society* (London, 1989), pp.159, 164–8.

66. Pepetela, *Mayombe* (London, 1983), p.ii.

67. Ibid., p.2.

68. M. Hall and T. Young, *Confronting Leviathan: Mozambique since Independence* (London, 1997), pp.5–11; D. Birmingham, *Frontline Nationalism in Angola and Mozambique* (London, 1992), pp.15–17.

69. P. Chabal, *Amilcar Cabral. Revolutionary Leadership and People's War* (Cambridge, 1983), p.41.

70. Ibid., p.87.

71. J. Marcum, *The Angolan Revolution. Exile Politics and Guerrilla Warfare (1962–1976)* (Cambridge, Mass., 1978), pp.48–51.

72. A. Drew, 'Bolshevizing Communist Parties: The Algerian and South African Experience', in *International Research in Social History* 48 (2003), p.192.

73. D. Fortescue, 'The Communist Party of South Africa and the African Class in the 1940s', *International Journal of African Historical Studies* 24 (1991), pp.481–512.

74. D. Everatt, 'Alliance Politics of a Special Type: The Roots of the ANC/SACP Alliance, 1950–54' *Journal of Southern African Studies* 18 (1992), pp.32–8.

75. A. Gresh, 'The Free Officers and the Comrades: The Sudanese Communist Party and Nimeiri Face to Face, 1969–1971', *International Journal of Middle*

Eastern Studies 21 (1989), p.395. See also G. Warburg, *Islam, Nationalism and Communism in a Traditional Society: The Case of Sudan* (London, 1978).

76. R. Mortimer, *Indonesian Communism under Sukarno. Ideology and Politics, 1959–1965* (Ithaca, 1974), pp.366–7.

77. See, for instance, Stephen M. Streeter, 'Nation Building in the Land of Eternal Counterinsurgency: Guatemala and the Contradictions of the Alliance for Progress', *Third World Quarterly* 27 (2006), pp.57–68.

78. M. Leffler, *For the Soul of All Mankind. The United States, the Soviet Union and the Cold War* (New York, 2007), p.211. For this obsession with personal humiliation, see F. Logevall, *Choosing War. The Lost Chance for Peace and the Escalation of War in Vietnam* (Berkeley, 1999), p.393.

79. Mortimer, *Indonesian Communism*, ch.7.

80. There is still disagreement over the role of the Communists in the coup. See H. Crouch, *The Army and Politics in Indonesia*, 2nd edn (Ithaca, 1988), ch.4; J. M. Van der Kroef, 'Origins of the 1965 Coup in Indonesia: Probabilities and Alternatives', *Journal of Southeast Asian Studies* 3 (1972), pp.277–98; Mortimer, *Indonesian Communism*, pp.413–41.

81. For interpretations of the causes of the violence, see R. Cribb, 'Unresolved Problems in the Indonesian Killings of 1965–1966', *Asian Survey* 42, 4 (2002), pp.550–63. For numbers, see ibid., pp.558–9.

82. Rostow to Johnson, 11 October 1967, cited in O. A. Westad, *The Global Cold War: Third World Interventions and the Making of Our Times* (Cambridge, 2005), p.178.

STASIS

1. K. Verdery, *National Ideology under Socialism: Identity and Cultural Politics in Ceausescu's Romania* (Berkeley, 1991), pp.174–6.

2. For this ideological change, see François Fejtö, *A History of the People's Democracies: Eastern Europe since Stalin*, trans. D. Weissbort (London, 1971), pp.76 ff.

3. R. Stone, *Satellites and Commissars. Strategy and Conflict in the Politics of Soviet-Bloc Trade* (Princeton, 1996), pp.30–1.

4. Vladimir Tismaneanu, *Stalinism for All Seasons: a Political History of Romanian Communism* (Berkeley, 2003), ch.1.

5. Cited in M. Fischer, *Nicolae Ceauşescu. A Study in Political Leadership* (London, 1989), p.85.

6. Fischer, *Ceauşescu*, p.151, ch.7.

7. A. Gabanyi, 'Nicolae Ceauşescu and his Personality Cult', in A. Gabanyi, *The Ceauşescu Cult: Propaganda and Power Policy in Communist Romania* (Bucharest, 2000), p.18.

8. A. Janos, *East Central Europe in the Modern World. The Politics of the Borderlands from pre- to post-Communism* (Stanford, 2000), p.302.

9. D. Deletant, *Ceauşescu and the Securitate: Coercion and Dissent in Romania, 1965–1989* (London, 1995), pp.154–6.

10. M. Vickers, *The Albanians: A Modern History* (London, 1995), p.196.

11. P. Lendvai, *Eagles in Cobwebs. Nationalism and Communism in the Balkans* (London, 1969), p.196.

12. A. Buzo, *The Guerrilla Dynasty: Politics and Leadership in North Korea* (London, 1999), p.59.

13. Kim Il Sung, *On the Three Principles of National Unification* (Pyongyang, 1972), p.3.

14. For a view that emphasizes stratification, see H.-L. Hunter, *Kim Il-Song's North Korea* (Westport, 1999), ch.1. For a view that emphasizes inclusiveness, see B. Cumings, 'The Last Hermit', *New Left Review* 6 (2000).

15. For these details of everyday life, see Hunter, *Kim Il-Song*, pp.173–4.

16. Á. Horváth and Á. Szakolczai, *The Dissolution of Communist Power: the Case of Hungary* (London, 1992), pp.62–3.

17. B. Denitch, *The Legitimation of a Revolution: the Yugoslav Case* (New Haven, 1976), p.94.

18. Deletant, *Ceauşescu and the Securitate*, pp.212–16.

19. L. Siegelbaum, 'The Faustian Bargain of the Soviet Automobile', in *PEECS* papers No. 24 (Trondheim, 2008), p.1.

20. Cited in J. Zatlin, 'The Vehicle of Desire: The Trabant, the Wartburg, and the End of the GDR', *German History* 15, 3 (1997), p.358.

21. Ibid., p.359

22. M. Burawoy and J. Lukács, *The Radiant Past: Ideology and Reality in Hungary's Road to Capitalism* (Chicago, 1992), pp.125–6.

23. This is the main argument of the Hungarian economist Janos Kornai, *Economics of Shortage* (Amsterdam, 1980).

24. S. Goodman, 'Soviet Computing and Technology Transfer: An Overview', *World Politics* 31 (1979), p.567.

25. S. Kotkin, *Armageddon Averted. The Soviet Collapse, 1970–2000* (Oxford, 2000), pp.63–4.

26. N. Shmelev, in S. Cohen and K. Van den Heuvel, *Voices of Glasnost. Interviews with Gorbachev's Reformers* (New York, 1989), p.149.

27. J. Kopstein, *The Politics of Economic Decline in East Germany, 1945–1989* (Chapel Hill, 1997), p.190.

28. P. Shelest, 'On umel vesti apparatnye igry, a stranu zabrosil. . .', in Iu Aksiutin, *Brezhnev: Materialy k Biografii* (Moscow, 1991), p.218.

29. Z. Mlynář, *Night Frost in Prague: the End of Humane Socialism*, trans. P. Wilson (London, 1980), p.86.

30. Kotkin, *Armageddon Averted*, p.50.

31. Cited in Kopstein, *Politics*, p.43.

32. See ibid., ch.2.

33. Mlynář, *Night Frost*, p.66.

34. G. Golan, *Reform Rule in Czecholovakia: the Dubček Era, 1968–1969* (Cambridge, 1973), pp.230–1.

35. Jaromír Navrátil, *The Prague Spring 1968: A National Security Archive Documents Reader*, trans. M. Kramer et al. (Budapest, 1998), pp.20–2.

36. Mlynář, *Night Frost*, pp.82–6.

37. Ibid., p.44.

38. J. Satterwhite, 'Marxist Critique and Czechoslovak Reform', in R. Taras (ed.), *The Road to Disillusion. From Critical Marxism to Postcommunism in Eastern Europe* (Armonk, NY, 1992), pp.115–34.

39. J. Piekalkiewicz, *Public Opinion Polling in Czechoslovakia, 1968–69: Results and Analysis of Surveys Conducted during the Dubcek Era* (New York, 1972).

40. A. Dubcek, *Hope Dies Last. The Autobiography of Alexander Dubcek*, trans. J. Hochman (London, 1993), p.150.

41. Navrátil, *The Prague Spring*, p.67.

42. M. Kramer, 'The Czechoslovak Crisis and the Brezhnev Doctrine', in C. Fink, P. Gassert and D. Junker (eds.), *1968: The World Transformed* (Cambridge, 1998), pp.121–45.

43. M. Kundera, 'Preface', in J. Skvorecky, *Mirakl* (Paris, 1978), p.4.

44. A. Brown, *The Gorbachev Factor* (Oxford, 1996), pp.30–1, 41.

45. Cited in R. Tőkés, *Hungary's Negotiated Revolution: Economic Reform, Social Change, and Political Succession, 1957–1990* (Cambridge, 1996), p.72.

46. Kopstein, *Politics*, p.81.

47. V. Bunce, 'The Empire Strikes Back: The Evolution of the Eastern Bloc from a Soviet Asset to a Soviet Liability', *International Organization* 39 (1985), p.20.

48. K. Poznanski, 'Economic Adjustment and Political Forces: Poland since 1970', *International Organization* 40 (1986), p.457.

49. Horváth and Szakolczai, *The Dissolution of Communist Power*.

50. Ibid., p.110.

51. K. Jarausch, 'Care and Coercion. The GDR as Welfare Dictatorship', in K. Jarausch (ed.), *Dictatorship as Experience. Towards a Socio-Cultural History of the GDR* (New York, 1999), ch.3.

52. M. Raeff, *The Well-ordered Police State: Social and Institutional Change through Law in the Germanies and Russia, 1600–1800* (New Haven, 1983). This parallel is drawn by Horváth and Szakolczai.

53. Xiaobo Lü and Elizabeth Perry, *Danwei. The Changing Chinese Workplace in Historical and Comparative Perspective* (Armonk, NY, 1997), pp.169–94.

54. Interviews by Andrew Walder in A. Walder, *Communist Neo-Traditionalism. Work and Authority in Chinese Industry* (Berkeley, 1986), p.140.

55. Ibid., pp.141–2.

56. A. Zinoviev, *The Reality of Communism* (London, 1985), p.139.

57. V. Shlapentokh, *Public and Private Life of the Soviet People: Changing Values in post-Stalin Russia* (New York, 1989), p.117.

58. Zinoviev, *Reality*, p.139

59. Shlapentokh, *Public and Private*, p.118.

60. Interview cited in A. Yurchak, *Everything was Forever, until It was No More. The Last Soviet Generation* (Princeton, 2006), pp.96–7.

61. This case is described in M. Fulbrook, *The People's State: East German Society from Hitler to Honecker* (New Haven, 2005), p.239.

62. Burawoy and Lukács, *Radiant Past*, pp.40–2.

63. M. Haraszti, *A Worker in a Worker's State: Piece-rates in Hungary*, trans. M. Wright (Harmondsworth, 1977), pp.88–9.

64. Interview in Walder, *Communist Neo-Traditionalism*, p.176.

65. D. Kideckel, *The Solitude of Collectivism: Romanian Villagers to the Revolution and Beyond* (Ithaca, 1993), p.130.

66. A. Zinoviev, *The Yawning Heights*, trans. G. Clough (London, 1979), pp.186–8.

67. Zinoviev, *Reality*, pp.127, 65.

68. Horváth and Szakolczai, *The Dissolution of Communist Power*, p.55.

69. S. Shirk, *Competitive Comrades: Career Incentives and Student Strategies in China* (Berkeley, 1982), p.150.

70. Shlapentokh, *Public and Private*, pp.165, 171; V. Shlapentokh, *Love, Marriage, and Friendship in the Soviet Union: Ideals and Practices* (New York, 1984).

71. Haraszti, *A Worker in a Worker's State*, pp.88–9.

72. Ibid.

73. Cited in A. Port, *Conflict and Stability in the German Democratic Republic* (Cambridge, 2007), p.245.

74. D. Mason, *Public Opinion and Political Change in Poland* (Cambridge, 1985), p.86.

75. D. Bahry, 'Society Transformed? Rethinking the Social Roots of Perestroika', *Slavic Review* 52 (1993), p.537.

76. Burawoy and Lukács, *Radiant Past*, p.123.

77. Cited in Kideckel, *Solitude of Collectivism*, p.183.

78. M. Lampland, *The Object of Labor: Commodification in Socialist Hungary* (Chicago, 1995), pp.335–6.

79. See survey in R. Tökés, *Murmur and Whispers: Public Opinion and Legitimacy Crisis in Hungary, 1972–1989* (Pittsburgh, 1997), p.14.

80. Mason, *Public Opinion*, p.63.

81. *Blondinka za uglom* (1983), dir. V. Bortko.

82. Shlapentokh, *Public and Private*, p.192.

83. Ibid., pp.80–1.

84. Fulbrook, *The People's State*, pp.230–1.

85. Tökés, *Hungary's Negotiated Revolution*, p.139.

86. Yurchak, *Everything was Forever*, p.201.

87. T. Ryback, *Rock around the Bloc: a History of Rock Music in Eastern Europe and the Soviet Union* (New York, 1990), p.129.

88. Ibid., p.146.

89. Yurchak, *Everything was Forever*, p.215.
90. Cited in ibid., p.234.
91. W. Burr (ed.), *The Kissinger Transcripts* (New York, 1998), pp.59–66.

HIGH TIDE

1. R. Balsvik, *Haile Selassie's Students. The Intellectual and Social Background to Revolution, 1952–1977* (Lansing, Mich., 1985), pp.213–23.
2. 'The Philosophy of the Fashion Show in the Era of Nationalism', pamphlet, March 1968, cited in Balsvik, *Students*, p.214.
3. For this episode, see Balsvik, *Students*, p.216.
4. Ibid., p.202.
5. See D. McAdam, *Freedom Summer* (Oxford, 1988).
6. Ibid., p.4.
7. Cited in M. Rothschild, *A Case of Black and White. Northern Volunteers and the Southern Freedom Summers, 1964–1965* (Westport, 1982), p.181.
8. Cited in R. Fraser, *1968: A Student Generation in Revolt* (New York, 1987), p.79.
9. A. Marwick, *The Sixties. Cultural Revolution in Britain, France, Italy and the United States, c.1958–c.1974* (Oxford, 1998), pp.486–9.
10. Cited in Fraser, *1968*, p.80.
11. T. Hecken and A. Grzenia, 'Situationism', in M. Klimke and J. Scharloth (eds.), *1968 in Europe. A History of Protest and Activism, 1956–1977* (New York, 2008), pp.23–32.
12. Dark Star (ed.), *Beneath the Paving Stones. Situationists and the Beach, May 1968* (Edinburgh, 2001), pp.23–4.
13. H. Marcuse, *One-Dimensional Man* (London, 1991), pp.21, xx.
14. *Dr Strangelove. Or How I Learned to Stop Worrying and Love the Bomb* (1964), dir. Stanley Kubrick.
15. *2001. A Space Odyssey* (1968), dir. Stanley Kubrick. HAL, with its sinister red 'eye', is reminiscent of the one-eyed monster of Homer's *Odyssey*, the Cyclops.
16. Mario Savio, in A. Bloom and W. Breines (eds.), *Takin' It to the Streets. A Sixties Reader* (New York, 1995), pp.111–12.
17. Gregory Calvert, in Bloom and Breines, *Takin' It to the Streets*, p.126.
18. Wright Mills, in Bloom and Breines, *Takin' It to the Streets*.
19. Rayna Rapp (SDS, University of Michigan), cited in Fraser, *1968*, p.88.
20. C. Wilkerson, *Flying Close to the Sun* (New York, 2007), pp.115–16.
21. Cited in K. Sale, *SDS* (New York, 1973), p.391.
22. M. Berg, '1968: A Turning Point in American Race Relations?' in C. Fink, P. Gassert and D. Junker (eds.), *1968: The World Transformed* (Cambridge, 1998), p.407.

23. S. Carmichael, *Stokely Speaks. From Black Power to Pan-Africanism* (Chicago, 2007), p.93.

24. Anthony Barnett, cited in Fraser, *1968*, p.88.

25. George Ball, cited in F. Logevall, *Choosing War: The Lost Chance for Peace and the Escalation of the War in Vietnam* (Berkeley, 1999), p.291.

26. Peter Tautfest, cited in Fraser, *1968*, p.152.

27. Cited in G. Herring, 'Tet and the Crisis of Hegemony', in Fink et al., *1968*, p.48.

28. G. R. Horn, *The Spirit of '68: Rebellion in Western Europe and North America, 1956–76* (Oxford, 2007), pp.228–31.

29. A. Glyn, *Capitalism Unleashed: Finance, Globalization and Welfare* (Oxford, 2007), p.10.

30. Cited in M. H. Little, *America's Uncivil Wars* (New York, 2006), p.254.

31. Horn, *Spirit of '68*, pp.158–60; A. Belden Fields, *Trotskyism and Maoism. Theory and Practice in France and the United States* (New York, 1988), ch.3.

32. J. Bourg, *From Revolution to Ethics. May 1968 and Contemporary Thought* (Montreal, 2007), p.51.

33. D. Singer, *Prelude to Revolution. France in May 1968* (London, 1970), p.57.

34. *Monty Python's Life of Brian* (1979), dir. Terry Jones.

35. Horn, *Spirit of '68*, pp.162–3.

36. Wilkerson, *Flying Close to the Sun*, p.257.

37. M. Klimke and J. Scharloth, 'Terrorism', in Klimke and Scharloth, *1968 in Europe*, pp.270–1.

38. S. Aust, *The Baader–Meinhof Group: The Inside Story of a Phenomenon* (London, 1987), p.38.

39. D. Hauser, 'Terrorism in Europe', in Klimke and Scharloth, *1968 in Europe*, p.272.

40. Susanna Ronconi, quoted in D. Novelli and N. Tranfaglia, *Vite Sospese: le generazioni del terrorismo* (Milan, 1988), p.114. See also A. Jamieson, 'Identity and Morality in the Italian Red Brigades', in *Terrorism and Political Violence* 2, 4 (1990), p.511.

41. A. Jamieson, 'Entry, Discipline and Exit in the Italian Red Brigades', *Terrorism and Political Violence* 2, 1 (1990), p.2.

42. B. Silver, *Forces of Labour. Workers' Movements and Globalization since 1870* (Cambridge, 2005), pp.52–3.

43. *L'Humanité*, 9 July 1968.

44. C. Marighella, *Manual of the Urban Guerrilla*, trans. G. Hanrahan (Chapel Hill, 1985), p.1.

45. See R. Gott, *Guerrilla Movements in Latin America* (Oxford, 2008), pp.494–5; D. James, *Resistance and Integration. Peronism and the Argentine Working Class, 1946–1976* (Cambridge, 1976); A. Labrousse, *The Tupamaros* (Harmondsworth, 1973).

46. S. B. Liss, *Marxist Thought in Latin America* (Berkeley, 1984), p.159.

47. *The Church in the Present Day Transformation of Latin America in the Light of the Council*, vol. 2 (Washington, DC, 1979).

48. M. Pérez-Stable, *The Cuban Revolution. Origins, Course and Legacy* (New York, 1999), pp.116–20.

49. A. Cabral, *Revolution in Guinea. An African People's Struggle* (London, 1974), p.87.

50. *First Solidarity Conference of the Peoples of Africa, Asia and Latin America. Proceedings* (Havana, 1966), p.166.

51. On links with the European Communist Parties, see D. Ottaway and M. Ottaway, *Afrocommunism* (New York, 1981), pp.30–5. On students and links with the West in Ethiopia, see R. Balsvik, 'The Ethiopian Student Movement in the 1960s: Challenges and Responses', *Proceedings of the Seventh International Conference of Ethiopian Studies* (Lund, 1982), pp.491–509.

52. Cabral, *Revolution in Guinea*, p.82.

53. P. Chabal, *Amilcar Cabral: Revolutionary Leadership and People's War* (Cambridge, 1983), pp.167–72.

54. See Ottaway and Ottaway, *Afrocommunism*, pp.25–30.

55. For their thinking, see O. A. Westad, *The Global Cold War* (Cambridge, 2005), pp.204–6; K. Brutents, *Sovremennye natsional'no-osvoboditel'nye revoliutsii (Nekotorye voprosy teorii)* (Moscow, 1974).

56. H. Cobban, *The Palestinian Liberation Organisation: People, Power and Politics* (Cambridge, 1984), ch.3.

57. C. Andrew and V. Mitrokhin, *The Mitrokhin Archive. The KGB in Europe and the West* (London, 1999), pp.143–4.

58. F. Halliday, 'The People's Democratic Republic of Yemen: The "Cuban" Path in Arabia', in G. White, R. Murray and C. White (eds.), *Revolutionary Socialist Development in the Third World* (Brighton, 1983), pp.37–42.

59. M. Ram, *Maoism in India* (New York, 1971), ch.2.

60. A. Isaacman and B. Isaacman, *Mozambique: From Colonialism to Revolution, 1900–1982* (Boulder, 1983), pp.98–9; M. Hall and T. Young, *Confronting Leviathan. Mozambique since Independence* (London, 1997), pp.62–8.

61. For similarities and differences with Maoist people's war, see T. Henriksen, 'People's War in Angola, Mozambique, and Guinea-Bissau', *Journal of Modern African Studies* 14 (1976), pp.377–99.

62. Ibid., pp.382–3.

63. On Guinea, for positive views of the PAIGC, see Lars Rudebeck, *Guinea-Bissau. A Study of Political Mobilization* (Uppsala, 1974). For negative views, see M. Dhada, *Warriors at Work. How Guinea Really was Set Free* (Niwot, Colo., 1993).

64. I. Brinkman, 'War, Witches and Traitors: Cases from the MPLA's Eastern Front in Angola (1966–1975)', *Journal of African History* 44 (2003), pp.303–25.

65. Isaacman and Isaacman, *Mozambique*, p.86.

66. M. Anne Pitcher, *Transforming Mozambique. The Politics of Privatization, 1975–2000* (New York, 2002), pp.28–37.

67. Quoted in R. Dallek, *Nixon and Kissinger. Partners in Power* (London, 2007), pp.228.

68. On party thinking, see Westad, *Global Cold War*, pp.202–3; on military and foreign ministry thinking, see V. M. Zubok, *A Failed Empire: The Soviet Union in the Cold War from Stalin to Gorbachev* (Chapel Hill, 2007), p.249.

69. P. Sigmund, *The Overthrow of Allende and the Politics of Chile, 1964–1976* (Pittsburgh, 1977), ch.13.

70. J. Haslam, *The Nixon Administration and the Death of Allende's Chile: a Case of Assisted Suicide* (London, 2005), ch.7; P. Kornbluh, *The Pinochet File: A Declassified Dossier on Atrocity and Accountability* (New York, 2003).

71. Zubok, *Failed Empire*, p.249.

72. On the army, see D. Porch, *The Portuguese Armed Forces and the Revolution* (London, 1977).

73. P. Pinto, 'Urban Social Movements and the Transition to Democracy in Portugal, 1974–1976', *Historical Journal* 51 (2008), pp.1025–46; Nancy G. Bermeo, *The Revolution within the Revolution: Workers' Control in Rural Portugal* (Princeton, 1986).

74. Pinto, 'Urban Social Movements', p.1025.

75. M. Couto, 'The Secret Love of Deolinda', in Couto, *Everyman is a Race*, trans. D. Brookshaw (Portsmouth, NH, 1994), p.112.

76. For comparisons between Soviet Marxism and African Marxism, see M. Ottaway, 'Soviet Marxism and African Socialism', *Journal of Modern African Studies* 16, 3 (1978), pp.477–85.

77. Machel, 18 November 1976, quoted in Hall and Young, *Confronting Leviathan*, pp.76, 67.

78. Hall and Young, *Confronting Leviathan*, p.102.

79. J. Coelho, 'State Resettlement Policies in post-Colonial Rural Mozambique: The Impact of the Communal Village Programme on Tete Province, 1977–1982', *Journal of Southern African Studies* 24 (1988), pp.61–91.

80. D. Birmingham, 'Angola', in P. Chabal (ed.), *A History of Lusophone Africa* (London, 2002), pp.152–3.

81. H. Tuma, *The Case of the Socialist Witchdoctor and Other Stories* (Oxford, 1993), p.8.

82. Balsvik, *Students*, p.133.

83. B. Zewde, *A History of Modern Ethiopia, 1855–1991* (Oxford, 2001), p.222.

84. Ibid., pp.149–50.

85. Balsvik, *Students*, p.294.

86. Cited in Dawit Wolde Giorgis, *Red Tears. War, Famine and Revolution in Ethiopia* (Trenton, NJ, 1989), p.11.

87. R. Lefort, *Ethiopia: An Heretical Revolution?* trans. A. Berret (London, 1983), p.276.

88. Zewde, *Modern Ethiopia*, p.249.

89. Lefort, *Ethiopia*, p.278.

90. For this view of Mengistu, see D. Donham, *Marxist Modern. An Ethnographic History of the Ethiopian Revolution* (Berkeley, 1999), pp.129–30; Dawit, *Red Tears*, pp.30–1.

91. A. Tiruneh, *The Ethiopian Revolution, 1974–1987* (Cambridge, 1993), p.79.

92. Donham, *Marxist Modern*, p.29.

93. Report to USAID mission in Ethiopia, 1976.

94. Lefort, *Ethiopia*, p.278.

95. See M. Ezra, *Ecological Degradation, Rural Poverty, and Migration in Ethiopia. A Contextual Analysis* (New York, 2001).

96. F. Bizot, *The Gate*, trans. E. Cameron (London, 2004).

97. Ibid., p.119.

98. Ibid., p.116.

99. Ibid., p.117.

100. Ibid., p.115.

101. D. P. Chandler, *Brother Number One: A Political Biography of Pol Pot*, rev. edn (Boulder, 1999), pp.8–9, 37.

102. F. Debré, *Cambodge: La Révolution de la forêt* (Paris, 1976), p.82.

103. Interview with Soth Polin, cited in Chandler, *Brother Number One*, p.52.

104. Pol Pot, 'Abbreviated History Lesson on the History of the Kampuchean Revolutionary Movement Led by the Communist Party of Kampuchea' (early 1977), in D. Chandler, B. Kiernan and C. Boua (eds.), *Pol Pot Plans the Future* (New Haven, 1988), pp.218–19.

105. See, for instance, F. Ponchaud, 'Social Change in the Vortex of Revolution', in K. Jackson (ed.), *Cambodia 1975–1978: Rendezvous with Death* (Princeton, 1989), pp.170 ff.

106. Bizot, *The Gate*, p.110.

107. B. Kiernan, 'Enver Pasha and Pol Pot: A Comparison between the Armenian and Cambodian Genocides', in *Proceedings of the International Conference on the 'Problems of Genocide'* (Cambridge, Mass., 1997), pp.56–7.

108. P. Short, *Pol Pot: The History of a Nightmare* (London, 2004), p.337.

109. J.-L. Margolin, 'Cambodia. The Country of Disconcerting Crimes', in S. Courtois et al., *The Black Book of Communism: Crimes, Terror, Repression* (Cambridge, Mass., 1999), p.626.

110. For different views, see K. Jackson, 'Introduction', in Jackson (ed.), *Cambodia*, pp.9, 11; M. Vickery, 'Democratic Kampuchea: Themes and Variations', in D. Chandler and B. Kiernan (eds.), *Revolution and Its Aftermath in Kampuchea: Eight Essays* (New Haven, 1983), p.131.

111. Cited in B. Kiernan, *The Pol Pot Regime: Race, Power and Genocide in Cambodia under the Khmer Rouge, 1975–79* (New Haven, 1996), p.62.

112. See Short, *Pol Pot*, p.287.

113. A. Hinton, 'Why Did You Kill? The Cambodian Genocide and the Dark Side of Face and Honor', *The Journal of Asian Studies* 57 (1998), p.110.

114. Chandler et al., *Pol Pot Plans the Future*, p.158.

115. S. Heder, *Kampuchean Occupation and Resistance* (Bangkok, 1980), p.6.

116. Cited in Chandler, *Brother Number One*, p.115.

117. D. Pran, *Children of Cambodia's Killing Fields. Memoirs of Survivors* (New Haven, 1997), p.131

118. Margolin, 'Cambodia', p.626.

119. Chandler et al., *Pol Pot Plans the Future*, p.183.

120. For higher estimates, see M. Sliwinsky, *Le Génocide Khmer Rouge: Une analyse démographique* (Paris, 1995). For numbers of deaths, see Margolin, 'Cambodia', pp.588–91.

121. Hinton, 'Why Did You Kill?', pp.113, 118.

122. A. Hyman, *Afghanistan under Soviet Domination, 1964–91* (London, 1992), pp.92–8.

123. For Soviet thinking, H. Bradsher, *Afghan Communism and Soviet Intervention* (Oxford, 2000), ch.3; Westad, *Global Cold War*, pp.299–326.

124. Silvio Pons, 'Meetings between the Italian Communist Party and the Communist Party of the Soviet Union, Moscow and Rome, 1978–80', *Cold War History* 3 (2002), pp.157–66.

125. *The Economist*, 20 December 1978.

TWIN REVOLUTIONS

1. D. Remnick, *Lenin's Tomb. The Last Days of the Soviet Empire* (London, 1994), p.156.

2. Cited in M. Leffler, *For the Soul of All Mankind. The United States, the Soviet Union and the Cold War* (New York, 2007), p.385.

3. Ibid., p.394.

4. D. Reynolds, *Summits. Six Meetings That Shaped the Twentieth Century* (London, 2007), p.360.

5. M. Gorbachev, *Memoirs* (London, 1997), p.489.

6. Liu Binyan, *People or Monsters? And Other Stories and Reportage from China after Mao*, ed. P. Link (Bloomington, 1983), pp.11–68.

7. R. Baum, *Burying Mao: Chinese Politics in the Age of Deng Xiaoping* (Princeton, 1994), p.8.

8. S. Shirk, *The Political Logic of Economic Reform in China* (Berkeley, 1993), ch.10.

9. W. Jenner and D. Davin (eds.), *Chinese Lives* (London, 1986), pp.8–9, 13.

10. L. Zhang and C. Macleod (eds.), *China Remembers* (Oxford, 1999), p.5.

11. *People's Daily*, 3 August 2006.

12. A. Yurchak, *Everything was Forever, until It was No More. The Last Soviet Generation* (Princeton, 2006), p.113.

13. Ibid., pp.96–7.

14. Ibid.

15. R. Tökés, *Murmur and Whispers: Public Opinion and Legitimacy Crisis in Hungary, 1972–1989* (Pittsburgh, 1997), pp.37–9.

16. Ibid., p.56.

17. D. Bahry, 'Society Transformed? Rethinking the Social Roots of Perestroika', *Slavic Review* 52 (1993), pp.516–17.

18. D. Mason, *Public Opinion and Political Change in Poland* (Cambridge, 1985), pp.63–4.

19. H. Merskey and B. Shafran, 'Political Hazards in the Diagnosis of "Sluggish Schizophrenia"', *British Journal of Psychiatry* 148 (1986), p.253.

20. M. Fulbrook, *The People's State: East German Society from Hitler to Honecker* (New Haven, 2005), pp.241–2.

21. Interviewed in B. Miller, *Narratives of Guilt and Compliance in Unified Germany: Stasi Informers and Their Impact on Society* (London, 1999), pp.67–8.

22. Cited in Miller, *Narratives of Guilt*, pp.43–4.

23. Cited in ibid., p.101.

24. See Yurchak, *Everything was Forever*, pp.107–8.

25. Bahry, 'Society Transformed?', p.539.

26. Tökés, *Murmur and Whispers*, p.56.

27. See, for instance, J. Kopstein, *The Politics of Economic Decline in East Germany, 1945–1989* (Chapel Hill, 1997), pp.122–9.

28. A. Tsipko cited in M. Ouimet, *The Rise and Fall of the Brezhnev Doctrine in Soviet Foreign Policy* (Chapel Hill, 2003), pp.252–3.

29. M. Ellman and V. Kontorovich (eds.), *The Destruction of the Soviet Economic System: an Insiders' History* (Armonk, NY, 1998), p.173.

30. For the disillusionment of this group, see O. Westad, 'How the Cold War Crumbled', in S. Pons and F. Romero (eds.), *Reinterpreting the End of the Cold War. Issues, Interpretations, Periodizations* (London, 2005), p.76. See also A. Brown, *Seven Years That Changed the World: Perestroika in Perspective* (Oxford, 2007), pp.172–3.

31. A. Iakovlev, *Sumerki* (Moscow, 2003), p.354.

32. Mason, *Public Opinion*, p.45.

33. Ibid., p.82.

34. This argument, emphasizing the importance of the Church, rather than the working class or civil society, is made by M. Osa, *Solidarity and Contention: Networks of Polish Opposition* (Minneapolis, 2003).

35. Cited in ibid., p.136.

36. A. Glyn, *Capitalism Unleashed: Finance, Globalization, and Welfare* (Oxford, 2007), p.22.

37. See P. Buhle, *Marxism in the United States: Remapping the History of the American Left* (London, 1987), pp.206–10.

38. D. Patinikin, *Essays on and in the Chicago Tradition* (Durham, NC, 1981), p.4.

39. J. Kirkpatrick, *Dictatorships and Double Standards: Rationalism and Reason in Politics* (Washington, DC, 1982).

40. R. Brenner, *The Boom and the Bubble: the US in the World Economy* (London, 2002), p.35.

41. G. Arrighi, 'The World Economy and the Cold War, 1970–1990', forthcoming in *The Cambridge History of the Cold War*, p.22.

42. Ibid., p.16.

43. I. Zloch-Christy, *Debt Problems of Eastern Europe* (Cambridge, 1987), p.38.

44. S. Woodward, *Balkan Tragedy: Chaos and Dissolution after the Cold War* (Washington, DC, 1995), ch.3.

45. See C. Andrew and V. Mitrokhin, *The Mitrokhin Archive. The KGB in Europe and the West* (London, 1999), p.686.

46. G. Ekiert, *The State against Society: Political Crises and Their Aftermath in East Central Europe* (Princeton, 1996), pp.243–4, 247.

47. Ouimet, *Rise and Fall*, pp.249–50.

48. Baibakov to Shürer, quoted in Kopstein, *Politics of Economic Decline*, pp.93–4.

49. *Red Dawn* (1984), dir. John Milius.

50. R. Reagan, Address to British Parliament, 8 June 1982. http://www.reagan. utexas.edu/search/speeches/speech_srch.html.

51. R. Reagan, Question and Answer Session with High-School Students, 25 March 1983, http://www.reagan.utexas.edu/archives/speeches/1983/32583c.html.

52. For this argument, see I. Molloy, *Rolling Back Revolution: The Emergence of Low Intensity Conflict* (London, 2001), p.20.

53. C. Krauthammer, 'The Poverty of Realism', *The New Republic*, 17 February 1986, p.15.

54. *Psychological Operations in Guerrilla Warfare* (1983), http://www.freewebs. com/moeial/CIA's%20Psychological%20Operations%20in%20Guerrilla%20 Warefare.pdf.

55. E. Wood, *Insurgent Collective Action and Civil War in El Salvador* (Cambridge, 1993).

56. T. Walker, *Nicaragua. Living in the Shadow of the Eagle* (Boulder, 2003), p.56.

57. J. Ciment, *Angola and Mozambique: Postcolonial Wars in Southern Africa* (New York, 1997), p.87.

58. Cited in J. Persico, *Casey. From the OSS to the CIA* (New York, 1990), p.226.

59. B. Fischer, 'The Soviet–American War Scare of the 1980s', *International Journal of Intelligence* (Autumn 2006), pp.480–517.

60. For different views on the importance of SDI, see Ellman and Kontorovich, *Destruction*, pp.55–64.

61. M. I. Gerasev, cited in ibid., p.65.

62. Iakovlev, *Sumerki*, pp.394–5.

63. Ibid., p.395.

64. Ibid., p.394.

65. Ellman and Kontorovich, *Destruction*, pp.269–70; V. Boldin, *Ten Years That Shook the World: The Gorbachev Era as Witnessed by His Chief of Staff*, trans. E. Rossiter (New York, 1994), p.114.

66. A. Cherniaev, *Shest' let s Gorbachevym: po dnevnikovym zapisiam* (Moscow, 1993), p.8.

67. M. Gorbachev, *Zhizn' i reformy* (Moscow, 1995), vol. i, p.208.

68. A. Iakovlev, *Gorkaia chasha* (Yaroslavl', 1994), pp.205–12.

69. B. A. Fischer, *The Reagan Reversal: Foreign Policy and the End of the Cold War* (Columbia, 1997), pp.102–43.

70. A. Brown, *The Gorbachev Factor* (Oxford, 1996), pp.115–17.

71. M. Gorbachev, 'Report to CPSU Central Committee plenum, January 6 1989', *Current Digest of the Soviet Press* 41 (1989), p.1.

72. Aleksandr Iakovlev, in S. Cohen and K. Van den Heuvel, *Voices of Glasnost. Interviews with Gorbachev's Reformers* (New York, 1989), p.39.

73. Tsipko, in Ellman and Kontorovich, *Destruction*, p.181.

74. A. Tsipko, 'Istoki stalinizma', *Nauka i zhizn'* 11–12 (1988), 1–2 (1989).

75. N. Zarafshan, in R. MaKay, *Letters to Gorbachev: Life in Russia through the Postbag of Argumenty i Fakty* (London, 1991), p.173.

76. Tökés, *Murmurs and Whispers*, p.48.

77. Ellman and Kontorovich, *Destruction*, p.38.

78. D. Slejška, J. Herzmann a kolektiv, *Sondy do veřejného mínění (Jaro 1968, Podzim 1989)* (Prague, 1990), p.54.

79. For a defence of the Chinese model, see, for instance, P. Nolan, *China's Rise, Russia's Fall* (Basingstoke, 1995).

80. S. Solnick, *Stealing the State: Control and Collapse in Soviet Institutions* (Cambridge, Mass., 1998).

81. P. Kenney, *A Carnival of Revolution: Central Europe 1989* (Princeton, 2002), pp.161–2.

82. Ibid., pp.12–13.

83. Cited in ibid., p.141.

84. C. Maier, *Dissolution. The Crisis of Communism and the End of East Germany* (Princeton, 1997), p.156.

85. M. Fulbrook, *Anatomy of a Dictatorship. Inside the GDR, 1949–1989* (Oxford, 1995), pp.259–60.

86. For the greater involvement of workers in Poland compared with the GDR, see L. Fuller, *Where was the Working Class? Revolution in East Germany* (Urbana, Ill., 1999).

87. Cited in O. A. Westad, *The Global Cold* War (Cambridge, 2005), p.382.
88. J. Hough, *The Logic of Economic Reform in Russia* (Washington, DC, 2001), p.366.
89. A. Knight, *Spies without Cloaks: The KGB's Successors* (Princeton, 1996), pp.12–37.
90. Woodward, *Balkan Tragedy*, pp.127–8.
91. A. Nathan and P. Link (eds.), *The Tiananmen Papers* (London, 2001), p.xxx-vii.
92. Ibid., p.163.
93. Ibid., p.143.
94. Gorbachev, *Memoirs*, p.490.
95. Nathan and Link, *Tiananmen Papers*, p.173.
96. Su Xiaokang and Wang Luxiang, *Deathsong of the River: a Reader's Guide to the Chinese TV Series*, trans. R. Bodman (Ithaca, 1991), p.221.
97. R. Baum, *Reform and Reaction in post-Mao China: the Road to Tiananmen* (New York, 1991), p.456.

EPILOGUE

1. Lin Jinhui, 28 September 2002, http://www.china.org.cn/english/2002/Sep/44589.htm. See also K. Louie, *Theorizing Chinese Masculinity* (Cambridge, 2002), p.58.
2. D. Yergin and J. Stanislaw, *The Commanding Heights: the New Reality of Economic Power* (New York, 1998), p.137.
3. T. Friedman, 'Senseless in Seattle II', *New York Times*, 8 December 1999. For other examples, see Frank, *One Market under God*, pp.61–8.
4. F. Fukuyama, *The End of History and the Last Man* (London, 1992), pp.166–9, 206–7.
5. *Wall Street Journal*, 26 May 2000. For these themes, see T. Frank, *One Market under God. Extreme Capitalism, Market Populism, and the End of Economic Democracy* (London, 2000), ch.1.
6. R. Brenner, *The Boom and the Bubble: the US in the World Economy* (London, 2002), p.43.
7. J. Hellman, 'Winners Take All: The Politics of Partial Reform in Postcommunist Transitions', *World Politics* 50 (1998), p.209.
8. Ibid., pp.223–4.
9. J. Stiglitz, *Globalization and Its Discontents* (London, 2002), p.157.
10. For this argument, see P. Reddaway and D. Glinski, *The Tragedy of Market Reforms. Market Bolshevism against Democracy* (Washington, DC, 2001), pp.252–5.
11. S. Shirk, *The Political Logic of Economic Reform in China* (Berkeley, 1993), ch.3.

12. H. Wu, *Laogai. The Chinese Gulag* (Boulder, 1992).

13. S. Shirk, *China. Fragile Superpower* (Oxford, 2007), p.48.

14. D. Bell, *China's New Confucianism. Politics and Everyday Life in a Changing Society* (Princeton, 2008), ch.1.

15. Minxin Pei, *China's Trapped Transition: the Limits of Developmental Autocracy* (Cambridge, Mass., 2006), pp.191–6.

16. V. Bunce and S. Wolchik, 'International Diffusion and Postcommunist Electoral Revolutions', *Communist and Postcommunist Studies* 39 (2006), pp.283–4; M. Beissinger, 'Structure and Example in Modular Political Phenomena: The Diffusion of Bulldozer/Rose/Orange/Tulip Revolutions', *Perspectives on Politics* 5 (June 2007), pp.259–76.

17. K. Collins, 'The Logic of Clan Politics. Evidence from the Central Asian Trajectories', *World Politics* 56 (2004), pp.224–61.

18. A. Buzo, *The Guerilla Dynasty: Politics and Leadership in North Korea* (London, 1999), p.206.

19. S. Eckstein, *Back from the Future: Cuba under Castro* (Princeton, 1994), pp.233–7.

20. Cited in O. Starn, 'Maoism in the Andes. The Communist Party of Peru–Shining Path, and the Refusal of History', *Journal of Latin American Studies* 27 (1991), p.399.

21. Ibid., p.409.

22. J. Nochlin, *Vanguard Revolutionaries in Latin America* (Boulder, 2003), p.63.

23. C. McClintock, 'Peru's *Sendero Luminoso* Rebellion. Origins and Trajectory', in S. Eckstein (ed.), *Power and Popular Protest. Latin American Social Movements* (Berkeley, 2001), p.83.

24. Starn, 'Maoism', p.416.

25. A. Vanaik, 'The New Himalayan Republic', *New Left Review*, 49 (2008), p.63.

26. M. Mohanty, 'Challenges of Revolutionary Violence. The Naxalite Movement in Perspective', *Economic and Political Weekly*, 22 July 2006.

27. C. Sreedharan, 'Karl and the Kalashnikov', http://www.rediff.com/news/1998/aug/25pwg.htm, 25 August 1998.

28. For this point, see N. Henck, *Subcommander Marcos. The Man and the Mask* (Durham, NC, 2007), pp.365–6.

29. Interview with G. Marquez and R. Pombo, 'The Punch Card and the Hour Glass', *New Left Review* (May–June, 2002), p.70.

30. B. Brecht, 'To Those Born Later', trans. J. Willett, R. Mannheim and E. Fried, in P. Forbes, *Scanning the Century. The Penguin Book of the Twentieth Century in Poetry* (London, 2000), pp.55–7.

31. P. Neruda, *Memoirs* (London, 1976), pp.332–3.

32. T. Paterson, 'A Harsh Lesson for Germany, Courtesy of Its Socialist Past', *Independent*, 22 October 2008.

Select Bibliography

INTRODUCTION

S. Courtois et al., *The Black Book of Communism* (Cambridge, Mass., 1999).

M. Dreyfus et al., *Le Siècle des communismes* (Paris, 2000).

F. Furet, *The Passing of an Illusion* (Chicago, 2004).

K. Jowitt, *New World Disorder. The Leninist Extinction* (Berkeley, 1992).

L. Kolakowski, *Main Currents of Marxism* (Oxford, 1978).

W. Laqueur, *The Dream That Failed* (Oxford, 1994).

G. Lichtheim, *A Short History of Socialism* (London, 1975).

M. Malia, *The Soviet Tragedy* (New York, 1994).

R. Pipes, *Communism* (London, 2002).

D. Sassoon, *One Hundred Years of Socialism: The West European Left in the Twentieth Century* (London, 1997).

R. Service, *Comrades: a World History of Communism* (London, 2007)

A. Walicki, *Marxism and the Leap to the Kingdom of Freedom* (Stanford, 1995).

PROLOGUE

K. Baker, *Inventing the French Revolution: Essays on French Political Culture in the Eighteenth Century* (Cambridge, 1990).

D. Bell, *The Cult of the Nation in France. Inventing Nationalism, 1680–1800* (Cambridge, Mass., 2001).

A. Forrest, *The Soldiers of the French Revolution* (Durham, NC, 1990).

J. Hardman, *Robespierre* (London, 1999).

P. Higgonet, *Goodness Beyond Virtue. Jacobins during the French Revolution.* (Cambridge, Mass., 1998).

L. Hunt, *Politics, Culture, and Class in the French Revolution* (London, 1986).

D. Jordan, *The Revolutionary Career of Maximilien Robespierre* (London, 1985).

C. Lucas (ed.), *The French Revolution and the Creation of Modern Political Culture. Vol 2: The Political Culture of the French Revolution* (Oxford, 1988).

J. Lynn, *The Bayonets of the Republic: Motivation and Tactics in the Army of Revolutionary France, 1791– 94* (Urbana, 1984).

M. Ozouf, *Festivals and the French Revolution*, trans. A. Sheridan (Cambridge, Mass., 1988).

R. Rose, *Gracchus Babeuf: The First Revolutionary Communist* (London, 1978).

W. Sewell, *A Rhetoric of Bourgeois Revolution. The Abbé Sièyes and What is the Third Estate?* (Durham, NC, 1994).

J. Shklar, *Men and Citizens: a Study of Rousseau's Social Theory* (Cambridge, 1969).

A GERMAN PROMETHEUS

F. Andreucci, 'The Diffusion of Marxism in Italy during the Late Nineteenth Century', in R. Samuel and G. Stedman Jones (eds.), *Culture, Ideology, and Politics: Essays for Eric Hobsbawm* (London, 1982).

J. Beecher, *Charles Fourier: The Visionary and His World* (Berkeley, 1986).

C. Cahm, *Kropotkin and the Rise of Revolutionary Anarchism, 1872–1886* (Cambridge, 1989).

L. Derfler, *Paul Lafargue and the Founding of French Marxism, 1842–1882* (Cambridge, Mass., 1991).

G. Duveau, *1848. The Making of a Revolution*, trans. A. Carter (London, 1967).

J. Ehrenberg, *Proudhon and His Age* (Atlantic Highlands, NJ, 1996).

G. Eley, *Forging Democracy. The History of the Left in Europe, 1850–2000* (New York, 2002).

R. Fletcher, *Revisionism and Empire. Socialist Imperialism in Germany, 1897–1914* (London, 1984).

F. Furet, *Marx and the French Revolution*, trans. D. Furet (Chicago, 1988).

R. G. Garnett, *Co-operation and the Owenite Socialist Communities in Britain, 1825–45* (Manchester, 1972).

D. Geary, *European Labour Protest, 1848–1939* (London, 1981).

D. Geary, *Karl Kautsky* (Manchester, 1987).

D. Geary (ed.), *Labour and Socialist Movements in Europe before 1914* (Oxford, 1989).

A. Gilbert, *Marx's Politics. Communists and Citizens* (Oxford, 1981).

H. Goldberg, *The Life of Jean Jaurès* (Madison, 1968).

R. Gould, *Insurgent Identities: Class, Communities and Protest from 1848 to the Commune* (Chicago, 1995).

L. H. Haimson and C. Tilly (eds.), *Strikes, Wars and Revolutions in an International*

Perspective: Strike Waves in the Late Nineteenth and Early Twentieth Centuries (Cambridge, 1989).

S. Hanson, *Time and Revolution. Marxism and the Design of Soviet Institutions* (Chapel Hill, 1997).

J. F. C. Harrison, *Robert Owen and the Owenites in Britain and America: The Quest for the New Moral World* (London, 1969).

E. J. Hobsbawm (ed.), *The History of Marxism* (Brighton, 1982).

R. N. Hunt, *The Political Ideas of Marx and Engels* (2 vols.) (Pittsburgh, 1974, 1984).

C. H. Johnson, *Utopian Communism in France: Cabet and the Icarians, 1839–1851* (Ithaca, 1974).

I. Katznelson and A. R. Zolberg (eds.), *Working-Class Formation: Nineteenth-Century Patterns in Western Europe and the United States* (Princeton, 1986).

V. Lidtke, *The Alternative Culture: Socialist Labor in Imperial Germany* (New York, 1985).

V. L. Lidtke, *The Outlawed Party: Social Democracy in Germany, 1878–1890* (Princeton, 1966).

D. Lovell, *From Marx to Lenin. An Evaluation of Marx's Responsibility for Soviet Authoritarianism* (Cambridge, 1984).

D. McLellan, *Karl Marx: a Biography* (London, 1995).

F. E. Manuel, *The New World of Henri Saint-Simon* (Cambridge, Mass., 1956).

F. E. Manuel, *The Prophets of Paris* (Cambridge, Mass., 1962).

F. E. Manuel and F. P. Manuel, *Utopian Thought in the Western World* (Oxford, 1979).

J. E. Miller, *From Elite to Mass Politics: Italian Socialism in the Giolittian Era, 1900–1914* (Kent, Ohio, 1990).

M. A. Miller, *Kropotkin* (Chicago, 1976).

S. Miller and H. Potthoff, *A History of German Social Democracy from 1848 to the Present*, trans. J. A. Underwood (Leamington Spa, 1986).

R. Morgan, *The German Social Democrats and the First International, 1864–1872* (Cambridge, 1965).

J. Rougerie, *Le Procès des Communards* (Paris, 1971).

M. Salvadori, *Karl Kautsky* (London, 1979).

W. Sewell, *Work and Revolution in France: the Language of Labor from the Old Regime to 1848* (Cambridge, 1980).

A. B. Spitzer, *The Revolutionary Theories of Louis Auguste Blanqui* (New York, 1957).

G. P. Steenson, *After Marx, before Lenin: Marxism and Socialist Working-Class Parties in Europe, 1884–1914* (Pittsburgh, 1991).

G. P. Steenson, *"Not One Man! Not One Penny!": German Social Democracy, 1863–1914* (Pittsburgh, 1981).

M. Steger, *The Quest for Evolutionary Socialism. Eduard Bernstein and Social Democracy* (Cambridge, 1997).

V. K. Steven, *Between Marxism and Anarchism: Benoît Malon and French Reformist Socialism* (Berkeley, 1992).

R. Stuart, *Marxism at Work: Ideology, Class and French Socialism during the Third Republic* (Cambridge, 2002).

K. Taylor (ed.), *Henri Saint-Simon (1760–1825): Selected Writings on Science, Industry and Social* Organization (London, 1975).

F. van Holthoon and M. van der Linden (eds.), *Internationalism in the Labour Movement, 1830–1940* (Leiden, 1988).

K. S. Vincent, *Pierre-Joseph Proudhon and the Rise of French Republican Socialism* (New York, 1984).

A. Walicki, *Marxism and the Leap to the Kingdom of Freedom* (Stanford, 1995).

E. Weitz, *Creating German Communism 1890–1990. From Popular Protests to Socialist State* (Princeton, 1997).

G. Woodcock, *Anarchism: A History of Libertarian Ideas and Movements* (Harmondsworth, 1975).

BRONZE HORSEMEN

A. Ascher, *The Revolution of 1905* (2 vols.) (Stanford, 1988, 1992).

S. H. Baron, *Plekhanov: The Father of Russian Marxism* (London, 1963).

V. Bonnell, *Roots of Rebellion: Workers' Politics and Organizations in St. Petersburg and Moscow, 1900–1914* (Berkeley, 1983).

K. Clark, *Petersburg: Crucible of Cultural Revolution* (Cambridge, Mass., 1995).

O. Figes, *A People's Tragedy: the Russian Revolution, 1891–1924* (London, 1996).

O. Figes, *Peasant Russia, Civil War: The Volga Countryside in Revolution, 1917–1921* (Oxford, 1989).

O. Figes and B. Kolonitskii, *Interpreting the Russian Revolution: the Language and Symbols of 1917* (New Haven, 1999).

S. Fitzpatrick and Y. Slezkine (eds.), *In the Shadow of Revolution: Life Stories of Russian Women from 1917 to the Second World War*, trans. Y. Slezkine (Princeton, 2000).

A. Geifman, *Thou Shalt Kill. Revolutionary Terrorism in Russia, 1894–1917* (Princeton, 1993).

J. von Geldern, *Bolshevik Festivals 1917–1920* (Berkeley, 1993).

A. Gleason, *Young Russia. The Genesis of Russian Radicalism in the 1860s* (Chicago, 1980).

A. Gleason, P. Kenez and R. Stites (eds.), *Bolshevik Culture: Experiment and Order in the Russian Revolution* (Bloomington, 1985).

W. Goldman, *Women, the State and Revolution: Soviet Family Policy and Social Life, 1917–1936* (Cambridge, 1993).

T. Hasegawa, *The February Revolution, Petrograd, 1917* (Seattle, Wash., 1981).

P. Holquist, *Making War, Forging Revolution: Russia's Continuum of Crisis, 1914–1921* (Cambridge, Mass., 2002).

D. Kaiser (ed.), *The Workers' Revolution in Russia, 1917: The View from Below* (Cambridge, 1987).

S. Kanatchikov, *A Radical Worker in Tsarist Russia: the Autobiography of Semen Ivanovich Kanatchikov*, trans. and ed. R. Zelnik (Stanford, 1986).

A. Kelly, *Mikhail Bakunin: A Study in the Psychology and Politics of Utopianism* (Oxford, 1982).

T. McDaniel, *Autocracy, Capitalism and Revolution in Russia* (Berkeley, 1988).

S. Malle, *The Economic Organization of War Communism, 1918–1921* (Cambridge, 1985).

S. Morrissey, *Heralds of Revolution: Russian Students and the Mythologies of Radicalism* (New York, 1998).

J. Sanborn, *Drafting the Russian Nation. Military Conscription, Total War, and Mass Politics, 1905–1925* (Dekalb, Ill., 2003).

R. Service, *Lenin. A Biography* (Basingstoke, 2005).

S. Smith, *Red Petrograd: Revolution in the Factories, 1917–18* (Cambridge, 1983).

M. Steinberg, *Voices of Revolution, 1917* (New Haven, 2001).

R. Stites, *Revolutionary Dreams: Utopian Vision and Experimental Life in the Russian Revolution* (New York, 1989).

R. Wortman, *Scenarios of Power: Myth and Ceremony in Russian Monarchy*, Vol. 2: *From Alexander II to the Abdication of Nicholas II* (Princeton, 2000).

UNDER WESTERN EYES

W. T. Angress, *Stillborn Revolution: The Communist Bid for Power in Germany, 1921–1923* (Princeton: Princeton University Press, 1963).

A. Arato and P. Breines, *The Young Lukács and the Origins of Western Marxism* (London, 1979).

I. Banac (ed.), *The Effects of World War I: The Class War after the Great War: The Rise of Communist Parties in East Central Europe, 1918–1921* (New York, 1983).

L. Boswell, *Rural Communism in France, 1920–1939* (Ithaca, 1998).

P. Broué, *Histoire de l'Internationale Communiste: 1919–1943* (Paris, 1997).

M. Caballero, *Latin America and the Comintern, 1919–1943* (Cambridge, 1986).

F. L. Carsten, *Revolution in Central Europe, 1918–1919* (Aldershot, 1988).

M. Clark, *Antonio Gramsci and the Revolution That Failed* (New Haven, 1977).

F. Claudín, *The Communist Movement: From Comintern to Cominform*, trans. B. Pearce and F. MacDonagh (Harmondsworth, 1975).

B. Fowkes, *Communism in Germany under the Weimar Republic* (London, 1984).

G. Haupt, *Socialism and the Great War: The Collapse of the Second International* (Oxford, 1972).

J. Humbert-Droz, *De Lenine à Staline: Dix ans au service de l'Internationale communiste, 1921–1931* (Neuchâtel, 1971).

D. Kirby, *War, Peace and Revolution. International Socialism at the Crossroads 1914–1918* (New York, 1986).

B. Kovrig, *Communism in Hungary. From Kun to Kádár* (Stanford, 1979).

W. Leonhard, *Child of the Revolution*, trans. C. M. Woodhouse (London, 1979).

K. McDermott and J. Agnew, *The Comintern: A History of International Communism from Lenin to Stalin* (Basingstoke, 1996).

K.-M. Mallmann, *Kommunisten in der Weimarer Republik. Sozialgeschichte einer revolutionären Bewegung* (Darmstadt, 1996).

K. Morgan, G. Cohen and A. Flinn, *Communists and British Society 1920–1991*(London, 2003).

J. P. Nettl, *Rosa Luxemburg* (London, 1966).

T. Rees and A. Thorpe (eds.), *International Communism and the Communist International, 1919–1943* (Manchester, 1998).

P. Spriano, *The Occupation of the Factories: Italy 1920*, trans. G. Williams (London, 1975).

R. L. Tökés, *Béla Kun and the Hungarian Soviet Republic: The Origins and Role of the Communist Party of Hungary in the Revolutions of 1918–1919* (New York, 1967).

H. Weber, *Die Wandlung des deutschen Kommunismus* (2 vols.) (Frankfurt am Main, 1969).

E. D. Weitz, *Creating German Communism, 1890–1990: From Popular Protests to Socialist State* (Princeton, 1997).

J. Willett, *The New Sobriety 1917–1933: Art and Politics in the Weimar Period* (London, 1978).

R. Wohl, *French Communism in the Making, 1914–1924* (Stanford, 1966).

C. Wrigley (ed.), *Challenges of Labour: Central and Western Europe, 1917–1920* (London, 1993).

MEN OF STEEL

J. Baberowski, *Der rote Terror: die Geschichte des Stalinismus* (Munich, 2003).

D. Bordwell, *The Cinema of Eisenstein* (Cambridge, Mass., 1993).

D. Brandenberger, *National Bolshevism: Stalinist Mass Culture and the Formation of Modern Russian National Identity, 1931–1956* (Cambridge, Mass., 2002).

J. Brooks, *Thank You, Comrade Stalin! Soviet Public Culture from Revolution to Cold War* (Princeton, 2000).

S. Cohen, *Bukharin and the Bolshevik Revolution: A Political Biography, 1888–1938* (Oxford, 1980).

M. David-Fox, *Revolution of the Mind: Higher Learning among the Bolsheviks, 1918–1929* (Ithaca, 1997).

S. Davies, *Popular Opinion in Stalin's Russia. Terror, Propaganda and Dissent, 1934–1941* (Cambridge, 1997).

S. Fitzpatrick, *Everyday Stalinism: Ordinary Life in Extraordinary Times: Soviet Russia in the 1930s* (Oxford, 1999).

S. Fitzpatrick, *Stalin's Peasants. Resistance and Survival in the Russian Village after Collectivization* (Oxford, 1994).

S. Fitzpatrick, A. Rabinowitch and R. Stites (eds.), *Russia in the Era of NEP: Explorations in Soviet Society and Culture* (Bloomington, 1991).

V. Garros, N. Korenevskaya and T. Lahusen (eds.), *Intimacy and Terror. Soviet Diaries of the 1930s*, trans. C. Flath (New York, 1995).

J. Getty and O. Naumov, *The Road to Terror: Stalin and the Self-destruction of the Bolsheviks, 1932–1939* (New Haven, 1999).

J. Getty and O. Naumov, *Yezhov, the Rise of Stalin's "Iron Fist"* (New Haven, 2008).

J. Hellbeck, *Revolution on My Mind: Writing a Diary under Stalin* (Cambridge, Mass., 2006).

S. Kotkin, *Magnetic Mountain. Stalinism as a Civilization* (Berkeley, 1995).

V. Kravchenko, *I Chose Freedom. The Personal and Political Life of a Soviet Official* (London, 1947).

T. Martin, *The Affirmative Action Empire: Nations and Nationalism in the Soviet Union, 1923–1939* (Ithaca, 2001).

E. Naiman, *Sex in Public: The Incarnation of Early Soviet Ideology* (Princeton, 1997).

D. Priestland, *Stalinism and the Politics of Mobilization. Ideas, Power, and Terror in Inter-war Russia* (Oxford, 2007).

R. Service, *Stalin. A Biography* (London, 2004).

L. Siegelbaum and A. Sokolov (eds.), *Stalinism as a Way of Life* (New Haven, 2000).

E. Van Ree, *The Political Thought of Joseph Stalin. A Study in Twentieth Century Revolutionary Patriotism* (London, 2002).

POPULAR FRONTS

B. Abrams, *The Struggle for the Soul of the Nation. Czech Culture and the Rise of Communism* (Lanham, 2004).

A. Agosti, *Palmiro Togliatti* (Turin, 1996).

M. S. Alexander and H. Graham (eds.), *The French and Spanish Popular Fronts: Comparative Perspectives* (Cambridge, 1989).

R. J. Alexander, *International Trotskyism, 1929–1985: A Documented Analysis of the Movement* (Durham, NC, 1991).

R. Cerdas, *The Communist International in Central America* (London, 1993).

S. Courtois and M. Lazar, *Histoire du communisme français* (Paris, 2000).

A. Dallin and F. Firsov (eds.), *Dimitrov and Stalin 1934–1943. Letters from the Soviet Archives* (New Haven, 2000).

I. Deutscher, *The Prophet Outcast: Trotsky, 1929–1940* (London, 1963)

M. Djilas, *Conversations with Stalin*, trans. M. Petrovich (Harmondsworth, 1969).

T. Draper, *American Communism and Soviet Russia: The Formative Period*, rev. edn (New York, 1986).

F. Fejtö, *A History of the People's Democracies: Eastern Europe since Stalin*, trans. D. Weissbort (Harmondsworth, 1974).

C. Fischer, *The German Communists and the Rise of Nazism* (Basingstoke, 1991).

P. Frank, *The Fourth International: The Long March of the Trotskyists*, trans. R. Schein, expanded edn (London, 1979).

J. Gaddis, *We Now Know. Rethinking Cold War History* (Oxford, 1997).

G. Gorodestsky (ed.), *Soviet Foreign Policy, 1917–1991. A Retrospective* (London, 1994).

H. Graham, *Socialism and War: the Spanish Socialist Party in Power and Crisis, 1936–1939* (Cambridge, 1991).

H. Graham and P. Preston (eds.), *The Popular Front in Europe* (Basingstoke, 1987).

J. T. Gross, *Revolution from Abroad: The Soviet Conquest of Poland's Western Ukraine and Western Belorussia* (Princeton, 1988).

H. Gruber, *Léon Blum, French Socialism, and the Popular Front: A Case of Internal Contradictions* (Ithaca, 1986).

J. Hæstrup, *Europe Ablaze: An Analysis of the History of the European Resistance Movements 1939–45* (Odense, 1978).

P. Heywood, *Marxism and the Failure of Organized Socialism in Spain, 1879–1936* (Cambridge, 1990).

J. Jackson, *The Popular Front in France: Defending Democracy, 1934–38* (Cambridge, 1988).

K. Kersten, *The Establishment of Communist Rule in Poland, 1943–1948* (Berkeley, 1991).

H. Klehr, J. Haynes and K. Anderson (eds.), *The Secret World of American Communism* (New Haven, 1998).

M. Lazar, *Maisons rouges: les partis communistes français et italiens de la Libération à nos jours* (Paris, 1992).

M. P. Leffler, *Preponderance of Power: National Security, the Truman Administration, and the Cold War* (Stanford, 1992).

W. Leonhard, *Child of the Revolution*, trans. C. M. Woodhouse (London, 1979).

V. Mastny, *Russia's Road to the Cold War: Diplomacy, Warfare, and the Politics of Communism, 1941–1945* (New York, 1979).

N. Naimark, *The Russians in Germany: a History of the Soviet Zone of Occupation, 1945–1949* (Cambridge, Mass., 1995).

N. Naimark and L. Gibianskii (eds.), *The Establishment of Communist Regimes in Eastern Europe, 1944–1949* (Boulder, 1997).

F. M. Ottanelli, *The Communist Party of the United States: From the Depression to World War II* (New Brunswick, 1991).

S. Payne, *The Spanish Civil War, the Soviet Union, and Communism* (New Haven, 2004).

C. Pennetier and B. Pudal (eds.), *Autobiographies, autocritiques, aveux dans le monde communiste* (Paris, 2002).

S. Pons, *Stalin and the Inevitable War 1936–1941* (London, 2002).

B. Pudal, *Prendre parti. Pour une sociologie historique du PCF* (Paris, 1989).

E. Rosenhaft, *Beating the Fascists? The German Communists and Political Violence, 1929–1933* (Cambridge, 1983).

P. Spriano, *Stalin and the European Communists*, trans. J. Rothschild (London, 1985).

P. J. Stavrakis, *Moscow and Greek Communism, 1944–1949* (Ithaca, 1989).

L. Stern, *Western Intellectuals and the Soviet Union, 1920–40: From Red Square to the Left Bank* (London, 2007).

P. Togliatti, *On Gramsci, and Other Writings*, trans. D. Sassoon (London, 1979).

T. Toranska, *Oni: Stalin's Polish Puppets*, trans. A. Kolakowska (London, 1987).

J. Vigreux and S. Wolikow (eds.), *Cultures communistes au XXᵉ siècle. Entre guerre et modernité* (Paris, 2003).

A. Weiner, *Making Sense of War* (Princeton, 2001).

P. Zinner (ed.), *National Communism and Popular Revolt in Eastern Europe: A Selection of Documents on Events in Poland and Hungary* (New York, 1986).

E. Zubkova, *Russia after the War. Hopes, Illusions, and Disappointments, 1945–1957* (New York, 1998).

V. Zubok and C. Pleshakov, *Inside the Kremlin's Cold War: From Stalin to Khrushchev* (Cambridge, Mass., 1996).

THE EAST IS RED

D. Apter and T. Saich, *Revolutionary Discourse in Mao's Republic* (Cambridge, Mass., 1994).

C. Armstrong, *The North Korean Revolution, 1945–1950* (Ithaca, 2003).

G. Benton, *Mountain Fires. The Red Army's Three-Year War in South China, 1934–1938* (Berkeley, 1994).

J. Chang and J. Halliday, *Mao: the Unknown Story* (London, 2006).

Chen Yung-fa, *Making Revolution. The Communist Movement in East and Central China, 1937–1945* (Berkeley, 1986).

B. Cumings, *The Origins of the Korean War* (2 vols.) (Princeton, 1981, 1990).

A. Dirlik, *The Origins of Chinese Communism* (New York, 1989).

W. Duiker, *The Communist Road to Power in Vietnam* (Boulder, 1996).

W. Duiker, *Ho Chi Minh: a Life* (New York, 2000).

L. Feigon, *Chen Duxiu: Founder of the Chinese Communist Party* (Princeton, 1983).

D. N. Jacobs, *Borodin: Stalin's Man in China* (Cambridge, Mass., 1981).

B. Kerkvliet, *The Huk Rebellion. A Study of Peasant Revolt in the Philippines* (Berkeley, 1977).

Huỳnh Kim Khánh, *Vietnamese Communism, 1925–1945* (Ithaca, 1982).

S. I. Levine, *Anvil of Victory: The Communist Revolution in Manchuria, 1945–1948* (New York, 1987).

Lin Yü-sheng, *The Crisis of Chinese Consciousness: Radical Anti-Traditionalism in the May Fourth Era* (Madison, 1979).

M. Y. L. Luk, *The Origins of Chinese Bolshevism: An Ideology in the Making, 1920–1928* (Hong Kong, 1990).

D. Marr, *Vietnam 1945. The Quest for Power* (Berkeley, 1995).

M. Meisner, *Li Ta-Chao and the Origins of Chinese Marxism* (New York, 1970).

M. Meisner, *Marxism, Maoism, and Utopianism: Eight Essays* (Madison, 1982).

S. Pepper, *Civil War in China: The Political Struggle, 1945–1949*, 2nd edn (Lanham, 1999).

T. Saich and H. van de Ven (eds.), *New Perspectives on the Chinese Communist Revolution* (Armonk, NY, 1995).

S. Schram, *The Thought of Mao Tse-Tung* (Cambridge, 1989).

V. Schwarcz, *The Chinese Enlightenment: Intellectuals and the Legacy of the May Fourth Movement of 1919* (Berkeley, 1986).

M. Selden, *China in Revolution. The Yenan Way Revisited* (Armonk, NY, 1995).

P. Short, *Mao: a Life* (London, 1999).

Shum Kui-Kwong, *The Chinese Communists' Road to Power: the Anti-Japanese National United Front, 1935–1945* (Hong Kong, 1988).

S. A. Smith, *A Road is Made: Communism in Shanghai, 1920–27* (Honolulu, 2000).

E. Snow, *Red Star over China* (London, 1937).

D.-S. Suh, *The Korean Communist Movement, 1918–1948* (Princeton, 1967).

H. J. van de Ven, *From Friend to Comrade: the Founding of the Chinese Communist Party, 1920–1927* (Berkeley, 1991).

C. M. Wilbur and J. Lien-ying How, *Missionaries of Revolution: Soviet Advisers and Nationalist China, 1920–1927* (Cambridge, Mass., 1989).

B. Yang, *From Revolution to Politics: Chinese Communists on the Long March* (Boulder, 1990).

P. Zarrow, *Anarchism and Chinese Political Culture* (New York, 1990).

EMPIRE

C. Armstrong, *The North Korean Revolution, 1945–1950* (Ithaca, 2003).

J. Bloomfield, *Passive Revolution: Politics and the Czechoslovak Working Class, 1945–1948* (London, 1979).

G. Creed, *Domesticating Revolution. From Socialist Reform to Ambivalent Transition in a Bulgarian Village* (University Park, Pa, 1998).

B. Cumings, *The Origins of the Korean War, vol. 2, The Roaring of the Cataract, 1947–1950* (Princeton, 1990).

D. Filtzer, *Soviet Workers and Late Stalinism: Labour and the Restoration of the Stalinist System after World War II* (Cambridge, 2002).

M. Frazier, *The Making of the Chinese Industrial Workplace: State, Revolution, and Labour Management* (Cambridge, 2002).

E. Friedman, P. Pickowicz and M. Selden, *Chinese Village, Socialist State* (New Haven, 1991).

J. Fürst (ed.), *Late Stalinist Russia. Society between Reconstruction and Reinvention* (London, 2006).

Y. Gorlizki and O. Khlevniuk, *Cold Peace: Stalin and the Soviet Ruling Circle, 1945–1953* (New York, 2004).

S. Gundle, *Between Hollywood and Moscow: The Italian Communists and the Challenge of Mass Culture, 1943–1991* (Durham, NC, 2000).

G. H. Hodos, *Show Trials: Stalinist Purges in Eastern Europe, 1948–54* (New York, 1987).

T. Judt, *Postwar. A History of Europe since 1945* (London, 2007).

P. Kenney, *Rebuilding Poland: Workers and Communists, 1945–1950* (Ithaca, 1997).

K. Kersten, *The Establishment of Communist Rule in Poland, 1943–1948*, trans. and eds. J. Micgiel and M. H. Bernhard (Berkeley, 1991).

D. Kertzer, *Comrades and Christians: Religion and Political Struggle in Communist Italy* (Cambridge, 1980).

S. Khilnani, *Arguing Revolution: The Intellectual Left in Post-War France* (New Haven, 1993).

D. Kideckel, *The Solitude of Collectivism. Romanian Villagers to the Revolution and Beyond* (Ithaca, 1993).

M. Lampland, *The Object of Labor: Commodification in Socialist Hungary* (Chicago, 1995).

M. Myant, *Socialism and Democracy in Czechoslovakia, 1945–1948* (Cambridge, 1981).

N. Naimark and L. Gibianskii (eds.), *The Establishment of Communist Regimes in Eastern Europe, 1944–1949* (Boulder, 1997).

G. Pritchard, *The Making of the GDR, 1945–1953. From Antifascism to Stalinism* (Manchester, 2004).

D. Sassoon, *The Strategy of the Italian Communist Party: From the Resistance to the Historic Compromise* (London, 1981).

T. Toranska, *Oni: Stalin's Polish Puppets*, trans. A. Kolakowska (London, 1987).

PARRICIDE

D. Bachman, *Bureaucracy, Economy, and Leadership in China: The Institutional Origins of the Great Leap Forward* (Cambridge, 1991).

J. Becker, *Hungry Ghosts: China's Secret Famine* (London, 1996).

G. Bennett, with K. Kieke and K. Yoffy, *Huadong: The Story of a Chinese People's Commune* (Boulder, 1978).

M. R. Beschloss, *The Crisis Years: Kennedy and Khrushchev, 1960–1963* (New York, 1991).

M. K. Bokovoy, *Peasants and Communists: Politics and Ideology in the Yugoslav Countryside, 1941–1953* (Pittsburgh, 1998).

G. W. Breslauer, *Khrushchev and Brezhnev as Leaders: Building Authority in Soviet Politics* (London, 1982).

A. Chan, *Children of Mao: Personality Development and Political Activism in the Red Guard Generation* (London, 1985).

A. Chan, R. Madsen and J. Unger, *Chen Village: The Recent History of a Peasant Community in Mao's China* (Berkeley, 1984).

P. Clark, *The Chinese Cultural Revolution. A History* (Cambridge, 2008).

M. Djilas, *Memoir of a Revolutionary*, trans. D. Willen (New York, 1973).

D. Filtzer, *Soviet Workers and De-Stalinization* (Cambridge, 1992).

E. Friedman, P. G. Pickowicz and M. Selden (eds.), *Chinese Village, Socialist State* (New Haven, 1991).

Gao Yuan, *Born Red: A Chronicle of the Cultural Revolution* (Stanford, 1987).

P. Jones (ed.), *The Dilemmas of Destalinization. Negotiating Cultural and Social Change in the Khrushchev Era* (London, 2006).

W. A. Joseph, C. P. W. Wong and D. Zweig (eds.), *New Perspectives on the Cultural Revolution* (Cambridge, Mass., 1991).

D. Kertzer, *Comrades and Christians. Religion and Political Struggle in Communist Italy* (Cambridge, 1980).

A. Knight, *Beria. Stalin's First Lieutenant* (Princeton, 1993).

G. Litvan (ed.), *The Hungarian Revolution of 1956: Reform, Revolt and Repression, 1953–1963*, trans. J. M. Bak and L. H. Legters (London, 1996).

C. S. Lilly, *Power and Persuasion: Ideology and Rhetoric in Communist Yugoslavia, 1944–1953* (Boulder, 2001).

R. MacFarquhar, *The Origins of the Cultural Revolution* (3 vols.) (London, 1974–97).

R. Macfarquhar and M. Schoenhals, *Mao's Last Revolution* (Cambridge, Mass., 2006).

R. MacFarquhar, T. Cheek and E. Wu (eds.), *The Secret Speeches of Chairman Mao: From the Hundred Flowers to the Great Leap Forward* (Cambridge, Mass., 1989).

R. Madsen, *Morality and Power in a Chinese Village* (Berkeley and Los Angeles, 1984).

Nien Cheng, *Life and Death in Shanghai* (London, 1986).

E. J. Perry and Li Xun, *Proletarian Power: Shanghai in the Cultural Revolution* (Boulder, 1997).

G. Péteri (ed), *Intellectual Life and the First Crisis of State Socialism in East Central Europe, 1953–1956* (Trondheim, 2001).

J. Sheehan, *Chinese Workers: A New History* (London, 1998).

W. Taubman, *Khrushchev. The Man and his Era* (New York, 2003).

L. T. White, *Policies of Chaos: The Organizational Causes of Violence in China's Cultural Revolution* (Princeton, 1989).

S. Woodward, *Socialist Unemployment: the Political Economy of Yugoslavia, 1945–1990* (Princeton, 1995).

GUERRILLAS

L. Aguilar (ed.), *Marxism in Latin America* (Philadelphia, 1978).

C. Allen, M. Radu and K. Somerville (eds.), *Benin, the Congo and Burkina Faso. Politics, Economics and Society* (London, 1989).

R. Allison, *The Soviet Union and the Strategy of Non-Alignment in the Third World* (Cambridge, 1988).

J. Anderson, *Che Guevara: A Revolutionary Life* (London, 1997).

J. M. Bunck, *Fidel Castro and the Quest for a Revolutionary Culture in Cuba* (University Park, Pa, 1994).

P. Chabal, *Amílcar Cabral: Revolutionary Leadership and People's War* (Cambridge, 1983).

N. J. Chander (ed.), *Dynamics of State Politics, Kerala* (New Delhi, 1986).

Chen Jian, *Mao's China and the Cold War* (Chapel Hill, 2001).

F. D. Colburn, *The Vogue for Revolution in Poor Countries* (Princeton, 1994).

R. Debray's *La Critique des armes* (Paris, 1974).

J. I. Dominguez, *Cuba: Order and Revolution* (Cambridge, Mass., 1978).

W. Duiker, *The Communist Road to Power in Vietnam* (Boulder, 1996).

S. Eckstein (ed.), *Power and Popular Protest. Latin American Social Movements* (Berkeley, 2001).

S. E. Eckstein, *Back from the Future: Cuba under Castro*, 2nd edn (New York, 2003).

L. Fuller, *Work and Democracy in Socialist Cuba* (Philadelphia, 1992).

A. Fursenko and T. Naftali, *Khrushchev's Cold War* (New York, 2006).

A. Fursenko and T. Naftali, *'One Hell of a Gamble': Khrushchev, Castro and Kennedy, 1958–1964* (New York, 1997).

R. Gillespie (ed.), *Cuba after Thirty Years: Rectification and the Revolution* (London, 1989).

P. Gleijeses, *Conflicting Missions: Havana, Washington, and Africa, 1959–1976* (Chapel Hill, 2002).

P. Gleijeses, *Shattered Hope: The Guatemalan Revolution and the United States, 1944–1954* (Princeton, 1991).

E. Gonzalez, *Cuba under Castro: The Limits of Charisma* (Boston, 1974).

R. Gott, *Guerrilla Movements in Latin America* (Oxford, 2008).

G. Grandin, *The Blood of Guatemala: A History of Race and Nation* (Durham, NC, 2000).

R. Harris, *Marxism, Socialism, and Democracy in Latin America* (Boulder, 1992).

D. James, (ed.), *The Complete Bolivian Diaries of Che Guevara and Other Captured Documents* (New York, 1968).

C. Johnson, *Communist China and Latin America, 1959–1967* (New York, 1970).

A. Kapcia, *Cuba in Revolution. A History since the Fifties* (London, 2008).

Z. Karabell, *Architects of Intervention: The United States, the Third World, and the Cold War, 1946–1962* (Baton Rouge, 1999).

Kuo-kang Shao, *Zhou Enlai and the Foundations of Chinese Foreign Policy* (New York, 1996).

S. B. Liss, *Marxist Thought in Latin America* (Berkeley, 1984).

N. Miller, *Soviet Relations with Latin America, 1959–1987* (Cambridge, 1989).

R. Mortimer, *Indonesian Communism under Sukarno: Ideology and Politics, 1959–65* (Ithaca, 1974).

T. Nossiter, *Communism in Kerala. A Study in Political Adaptation* (London, 1982).

L. A. Pérez, *Cuba: Between Reform and Revolution*, 2nd edn (New York, 1995).

M. Pérez-Stable, *The Cuban Revolution. Origins, Course and Legacy* (New York, 1999).

V. Prasad, *The Darker Nations: A People's History of the Third World* (New York, 2007).

C. G. Rosberg and T. M. Callaghy (eds.), *Socialism in Sub-Saharan Africa: A New Assessment* (Berkeley, 1979).

S. Schlesinger and S. Kinzer, *Bitter Fruit. The Story of the American Coup in Guatemala* (Cambridge, Mass., 2005).

L. Schoultz, *Beneath the United States: A History of U.S. Policy toward Latin America* (Cambridge, Mass., 1998).

L. Senghor, *On African Socialism*, trans. M. Cook (New York, 1964).

J. Smail, *Bandung in the Early Revolution, 1945–46* (Ithaca, 1964).

P. Snow, *The Star Raft: China's Encounter with Africa* (New York, 1988).

T. Szulc, *Fidel: A Critical Portrait* (New York, 1987).

H. Thomas, *The Cuban Revolution* (London, 1986).

G. Warburg, *Islam, Nationalism and Communism in a Traditional Society: The Case of Sudan* (London, 1978).

O. A. Westad, *The Global Cold War: Third World Interventions and the Making of Our Times* (New York, 2005).

T. Wickham-Crowley, *Guerrillas and Revolution in Latin America. A Comparative Study of Insurgents and Regimes since 1956* (Princeton, 1992).

V. Zubok, *A Failed Empire. The Soviet Union in the Cold War from Stalin to Gorbachev* (Chapel Hill, 2007).

STASIS

S. Bialer, *The Soviet Paradox: External Expansion, Internal Decline* (London, 1986).

G. W. Breslauer, *Khrushchev and Brezhnev as Leaders: Building Authority in Soviet Politics* (London, 1982).

M. Burawoy and J. Lukács, *The Radiant Past: Ideology and Reality in Hungary's Road to Capitalism* (Chicago, 1992).

G. W. Creed, *Domesticating Revolution: From Socialist Reform to Ambivalent Transition in a Bulgarian village* (University Park, Pa., 1998).

D. Deletant, *Ceauşescu and the Securitate: Coercion and Dissent in Romania, 1965–1989* (London, 1995).

D. Deletant, *Communist Terror in Romania: Gheorghiu-Dej and the Police State, 1948–1965* (London, 1999).

G. Ekiert, *The State against Society: Political Crises and Their Aftermath in East Central Europe* (Princeton, 1996).

M. Fischer, *Nicolae Ceauşescu. A Study in Political Leadership* (London, 1989).

M. Fulbrook, *Anatomy of a Dictatorship: Inside the GDR, 1949–1989* (New York, 1995).

M. Fulbrook, *The People's State: East German Society from Hitler to Honecker* (New Haven, 2005).

C. Gati, *Hungary and the Soviet Bloc* (Durham, NC, 1986).

G. Golan, *Reform Rule in Czechoslovakia: The Dubcek Era, 1968–1969* (Cambridge, 1973).

M. Haraszti, *A Worker in a Worker's State*, trans. M. Wright (New York, 1978).

A. Heitlinger, *Women and State Socialism: Sex Inequality in the Soviet Union and Czechoslovakia* (London, 1979).

K. H. Jarausch (ed.), *Dictatorship as Experience: Towards a Socio-Cultural History of the GDR*, trans. E. Duffy (New York, 1999).

D. Kideckel, *The Solitude of Collectivism: Romanian Villagers to the Revolution and Beyond* (Ithaca, 1993).

R. King, *A History of the Romanian Communist Party* (Stanford, 1980).

J. Kopstein, *The Politics of Economic Decline in East Germany, 1945–1989* (Chapel Hill, 1997).

M. Lampland, *The Object of Labor: Commodification in Socialist Hungary* (Chicago, 1995).

D. Lane, *The Rise and Fall of State Socialism: Industrial Society and the Socialist State* (Cambridge, 1996).

P. Lendvai, *Eagles in Cobwebs. Nationalism and Communism in the Balkans* (London, 1969).

M. Myant, *The Czechoslovak Economy 1948–1988: The Battle for Economic Reform* (Cambridge, 1989).

J. Navrátil, *The Prague Spring 1968: A National Security Archive Documents Reader*, trans. M. Kramer et al. (Budapest, 1998).

P. Pittaway, *Eastern Europe 1939–2000* (London, 2000).

T. W. Ryback, *Rock around the Bloc: A History of Rock Music in Eastern Europe and the Soviet Union* (New York, 1990).

V. Shlapentokh, *Public and Private Life of the Soviet People: Changing Values in post-Stalin Russia* (New York, 1989).

H. G. Skilling, *Charter 77 and Human Rights in Czechoslovakia* (London, 1981).

V. Tismaneanu, *Stalinism for All Seasons: a Political History of Romanian Communism* (Berkeley, 2003).

R. Tökés, *Hungary's Negotiated Revolution: Economic Reform, Social Change, and Political Succession, 1957–1990* (Cambridge, 1996).

M. Vickers, *The Albanians: A Modern History* (London, 1999).

A. Walder, *Communist Neo-Traditionalism. Work and Authority in Chinese Industry* (Berkeley, 1986).

K. Williams, *The Prague Spring and Its Aftermath: Czechoslovak Politics 1968–70* (Cambridge, 1997).

S. Wolle, *Die heile Welt der Diktatur. Alltag und Herrschaft in der DDR, 1971–1989* (Berlin, 1998).

A. Yurchak, *Everything was Forever, until It was No More. The Last Soviet Generation* (Princeton, 2006).

Xiaobo Lü and Elizabeth Perry, *Danwei. The Changing Chinese Workplace in Historical and Comparative Perspective* (Armonk, NY, 1997).

HIGH TIDE

C. Andrew and V. Mitrokhin, *The KGB and the World. The Mitrokhin Archive II* (London, 1999).

A. Arnold, *Afghanistan's Two-Party Communism: Parcham and Khalq* (Stanford, 1983).

T. Babile, *To Kill a Generation: Red Terror in Ethiopia* (Washington, DC, 1989).

R. R. Balsvik, *Haile Sellassie's Students: The Intellectual and Social Background to Revolution, 1952–1977* (East Lansing, Mich., 1985).

N. G. Bermeo, *The Revolution within the Revolution: Workers' Control in Rural Portugal* (Princeton, 1986).

D. Birmingham, *Frontline Nationalism in Angola & Mozambique* (London, 1992).

A. Bloom and W. Breines (eds.), *Takin' It to the Streets. A Sixties Reader* (New York, 1995).

H. S. Bradsher, *Afghan Communism and Soviet Intervention* (Oxford, 1999).

P. R. Brass and M. F. Franda (eds.), *Radical Politics in South Asia* (Cambridge, Mass., 2005).

P. Chabal, *Amílcar Cabral: Revolutionary Leadership and People's War* (Cambridge, 1983).

P. Chabal and D. Birmingham (eds.), *A History of post-Colonial Lusophone Africa* (London, 2002).

P. Chabal and N. Vidal, *Angola: The Weight of History* (London, 2007).

D. P. Chandler, *Brother Number One: A Political Biography of Pol Pot* (Boulder, 1992).

D. P. Chandler, *The Tragedy of Cambodian History: Politics, War and Revolution since 1945* (New Haven, 1991).

D. P. Chandler and B. Kiernan (eds.), *Revolution and Its Aftermath in Kampuchea: Eight Essays* (New Haven, 1983).

D. P. Chandler, B. Kiernan and C. Boua (eds. and trans.), *Pol Pot Plans the Future: Confidential Leadership Documents from Democratic Kampuchea, 1976–1977* (New Haven, 1988).

I. Christie, *Machel of Mozambique* (Harare, 1988).

C. Clapham (ed.), *African Guerrillas* (Oxford, 1998).

C. Clapham, *Transformation and Continuity in Revolutionary Ethiopia* (Cambridge, 1988).

H. Cobban, *The Palestinian Liberation Organisation: People, Power and Politics* (Cambridge, 1984).

B. Davidson, *In the Eye of the Storm: Angola's People* (London, 1972).

B. Davidson, *No Fist is Big Enough to Hide the Sky: The Liberation of Guinea and Cape Verde, Aspects of an African Revolution* (London, 1981).

F. Debré, *Cambodge: La Révolution de la forêt* (Paris, 1976).

M. Dhada, *Warriors at Work: How Guinea was Really Set Free* (Niwot, Col., 1993).

D. L. Donham, *Marxist Modern: an Ethnographic History of the Ethiopian Revolution* (Berkeley and Oxford, 1999).

S. Ellis and T. Sechaba, *Comrades Against Apartheid* (London, 1992).

G. Evans and K. Rowley, *Red Brotherhood at War: Vietnam, Cambodia and Laos since 1975*, rev. edn (London, 1990).

M. Ezra, *Ecological Degradation, Rural Poverty, and Migration in Ethiopia. A Contextual Analysis* (New York, 2001).

A. B. Fields, *Trotskyism and Maoism. Theory and Practice in France and the United States* (New York, 1988).

C. Fink, P. Gassert and D. Junker (eds.), *1968: The World Transformed* (Cambridge, 1998).

V. Fišera (ed.), *Writing on the Wall: May 1968: A Documentary Anthology* (London, 1978).

R. Fraser et al., *1968: A Student Generation in Revolt* (London, 1988).

E. George, *The Cuban Intervention in Angola, 1965–1991* (London, 2005).

S. Ghosh, *The Naxalite Movement: A Maoist Experiment* (Calcutta, 1974).

D. W. Giorgis, *Red Tears: War, Famine, and Revolution in Ethiopia* (Trenton, NJ, 1989).

A. Glyn, *Capitalism Unleashed: Finance, Globalization and Welfare* (Oxford, 2007).

F. A. Guimarães, *The Origins of the Angolan Civil War: Foreign Intervention and Domestic Political Conflict* (London, 1997).

T. Haile-Selassie, *The Ethiopian Revolution, 1974–91: From a Monarchical Autocracy to a Military Oligarchy* (London, 1997).

M. Hall and T. Young, *Confronting Leviathan: Mozambique since Independence* (London, 1997).

J. Haslam, *The Nixon Administration and the Death of Allende's Chile* (London, 2005).

S. R. Heder, *Kampuchean Occupation and Resistance* (Bangkok, 1980).

S. R. Heder, *Pol Pot and Khieu Samphan* (Clayton, 1991).

N. Henck, *Subcommander Marcos: The Man and the Mask* (Durham, NC, 2007).

T. H. Henriksen, 'People's War in Angola, Mozambique, and Guinea-Bissau', *Journal of Modern African Studies* 14, 3 (1976).

T. Hodges, *Angola: From Afro-Stalinism to Petro-Diamond Capitalism* (Oxford, 2001).

G. R. Horn, *The Spirit of '68: Rebellion in Western Europe and North America, 1956–76* (Oxford, 2007).

A. Hyman, *Afghanistan under Soviet Domination, 1964–91*, 3rd edn (Basingstoke, 1992).

A. Isaacman and B. Isaacman, *Mozambique: From Colonialism to Revolution, 1900–1982* (Boulder, 1983).

K. D. Jackson (ed.), *Cambodia 1975–1978: Rendezvous with Death* (Princeton, 1989).

D. James, *Resistance and Integration. Peronism and the Argentine Working Class, 1946–1976* (Cambridge, 1976).

G. Katsiaficas, *The Imagination of the New Left: A Global Analysis of 1968* (Boston, 1987).

M. N. Katz (ed.), *The USSR and Marxist Revolutions in the Third World* (Cambridge, 1990).

E. J. Keller and D. Rothschild (eds.), *Afro-Marxist Regimes: Ideology and Public Policy* (Boulder, 1987).

B. Kiernan, *How Pol Pot Came to Power: A History of Communism in Kampuchea, 1930–1975* (London, 1985).

B. Kiernan, *The Pol Pot Regime: Race, Power, and Genocide in Cambodia under the Khmer Rouge, 1975–79*, 2nd edn (New Haven, 2002).

B. Kiernan and C. Boua (eds.), *Peasants and Politics in Kampuchea, 1942–81* (London, 1982).

M. Klimke and J. Scharloth (eds.), *1968 in Europe. A History of Protest and Activism, 1956–1977* (New York, 2008).

P. Kornbluh, *The Pinochet File: A Declassified Dossier on Atrocity and Accountability* (New York, 2003).

D. J. Kotze, *Communism in South Africa* (Cape Town, 1979).

D. Kruijt, *Guerrillas* (London, 2008).

M. H. Little, *America's Uncivil Wars* (New York, 2006).

F. Logevall, *Choosing War: The Lost Chance for Peace and the Escalation of the War in Vietnam* (Berkeley, 1999).

D. McAdam, *Freedom Summer* (Oxford, 1988).

D. T. McKinley, *The ANC and the Liberation Struggle* (London, 1997).

N. Macqueen, *The Decolonization of Portuguese Africa: Metropolitan Revolution and the Dissolution of Empire* (London, 1997).

B. Male, *Revolutionary Afghanistan: A Reappraisal* (London, 1982).

J. A. Marcum, *The Angolan Revolution, Vol 1: The Anatomy of an Explosion; Vol 2: Exile Politics and Guerrilla Warfare* (Cambridge, Mass., 1969, 1978).

F. Marwat, *The Evolution and Growth of Communism in Afghanistan, 1971–79* (Karachi, 1997).

A. Marwick, *The Sixties: Cultural Revolution in Britain, France, Italy, and the United States, c.1958–c.1974* (Oxford, 1998).

A. P. Mukherjee, *Maoist 'Spring Thunder': The Naxalite movement 1967–1972* (Kolkata, 2007).

B. Munslow, *Afrocommunism?* (Liverpool, 1985).

B. Munslow (ed.), *Samora Machel: An African Revolutionary: Selected Speeches and Writings*, trans. M. Wolfers (London, 1985).

D. Ottaway and M. Ottaway, *Afrocommunism* (New York, 1981).

M. A. Pitcher, *Transforming Mozambique: The Politics of Privatization, 1975–2000* (New York, 2002).

S. Plant, *The Most Radical Gesture: The Situationist International in a Post-Modern Age* (London, 1992).

F. Ponchaud, *Cambodia Year Zero* (New York, 1978).

D. Porch, *The Portuguese Armed Forces and the Revolution* (London, 1977).

Qiang Zhai, *China and the Vietnam Wars, 1950–1975* (Chapel Hill, 2000).

M. Ram, *Maoism in India* (New York, 1971).

R. Ray, *The Naxalites and their Ideology*, 2nd edn. (New Delhi, 2002).

M. Rothschild, *A Case of Black and White. Northern Volunteers and the Southern Freedom Summers, 1964–1965* (Westport, 1982).

A. Z. Rubinstein, *Moscow's Third World Strategy* (Princeton, 1988).

J. S. Saul (ed.), *A Difficult Road: The Transition to Socialism in Mozambique* (New York, 1985).

R. J. Spalding, *Capitalists and Revolution in Nicaragua: Opposition and Accommodation, 1979–1993* (Chapel Hill, 1994).

R. J. Spalding (ed.), *The Political Economy of Revolutionary Nicaragua* (London, 1987).

A. Tiruneh, *The Ethiopian Revolution, 1974–1987: A Transformation from an Aristocratic to a Totalitarian Autocracy* (Cambridge, 1993).

J. Young, *Peasant Revolution in Ethiopia: the Tigray People's Liberation Front, 1975–1991* (Cambridge, 1997).

B. Zewde, *History of Modern Ethiopia, 1855–1991*, 2nd edn (Oxford, 2001).

V. M. Zubok, *A Failed Empire: The Soviet Union in the Cold War from Stalin to Gorbachev* (Chapel Hill, 2007).

TWIN REVOLUTIONS

R. Baum, *Burying Mao: Chinese Politics in the Age of Deng Xiaoping* (Princeton, 1994).

R. Baum, *Reform and Reaction in post-Mao China: the Road to Tiananmen* (New York, 1991).

D. S. Bell (ed.), *Western European Communists and the Collapse of Communism* (Oxford, 1993).

G. Breslauer, *Gorbachev and Yeltsin as Leaders* (Cambridge, 2002).

A. Brown, *The Gorbachev Factor* (Oxford, 1996).

A. Brown, *Seven Years that Changed the World: Perestroika in Perspective* (Oxford, 2007).

M. Burawoy and J. Lukács, *The Radiant Past: Ideology and Reality in Hungary's Road to Capitalism* (Chicago, 1992).

Chen Fong-ching and Jin Guantao, *From Youthful Manuscripts to River Elegy:*

The Chinese Popular Cultural Movement and Political Transformation 1979–1989 (Hong Kong, 1997).

Dingxin Zhao, *The Power of Tiananmen: State–Society Relations and the 1989 Beijing Student Movement* (Chicago, 2001).

G. Ekiert, *The State against Society: Political Crises and Their Aftermath in East Central Europe* (Princeton, 1996).

M. Friedman, *The Neoconservative Revolution: Jewish Intellectuals and the Shaping of Public Policy* (Cambridge, 2006).

M. Fulbrook, *Anatomy of a Dictatorship. Inside the GDR, 1949–1989* (Oxford, 1995).

T. Garton Ash, *The Polish Revolution: Solidarity, 1980–82* (London, 1983).

M. Goldman, *Sowing the Seeds of Democracy in China: Political Reform in the Deng Xiaoping Era* (Cambridge, Mass., 1994).

M. Gorbachev, *Memoirs* (London, 1997).

S. Hellman, *Italian Communism in Transition: The Rise and Fall of the Historic Compromise in Turin 1975–1980* (New York, 1988).

Jing Wang, *High Culture Fever: Politics, Aesthetics, and Ideology in Deng's China* (Berkeley, 1996).

P. Kenney, *A Carnival of Revolution: Central Europe 1989* (Princeton, 2002).

J. Kopstein, *The Politics of Economic Decline in East Germany, 1945–1989* (Chapel Hill, 1997).

S. Kotkin, *Armageddon Averted. The Soviet Collapse, 1970–2000* (Oxford, 2000).

L. Kürti, *Youth and the State in Hungary: Capitalism, Communism and Class* (London, 2002).

R. Laba, *The Roots of Solidarity: A Political Sociology of Poland's Working-Class Democratization* (Princeton, 1991).

K. J. Lepak, *Prelude to Solidarity: Poland and the Politics of the Gierek Regime* (New York, 1988).

M. Lewin, *The Gorbachev Phenomenon: A Historical Interpretation* (London, 1988).

B. Magas, *The Destruction of Yugoslavia: Tracking the Break-up 1980–92* (London, 1993).

C. S. Maier, *Dissolution: The Crisis of Communism and the End of East Germany* (Princeton, 1997).

D. Mason, *Public Opinion and Political Change in Poland* (Cambridge, 1985).

B. Miller, *Narratives of Guilt and Compliance in Unified Germany: Stasi Informers and their Impact on Society* (London, 1999).

J. R. Millar (ed.), *Politics, Work, and Daily Life in the USSR: A Survey of Former Soviet Citizens* (Cambridge, 1987).

A. Nathan and P. Link (eds.), *The Tiananmen Papers* (London, 2001).

A. J. Nathan, *Chinese Democracy* (New York, 1985).

V. Nee and D. Stark with M. Selden (eds.), *Remaking the Economic Institutions of Socialism: China and Eastern Europe* (Stanford, 1989).

J. C. Oi, *State and Peasant in Contemporary China: The Political Economy of Village Government* (Berkeley, 1989).

M. Oksenberg, L. R. Sullivan and M. Lambert (eds.), *Beijing Spring, 1989: Confrontation and Conflict: The Basic Documents*, trans. H. R. Lan and J. Dennerline (New York, 1990).

M. Osa, *Solidarity and Contention: Networks of Polish Opposition* (Minneapolis, 2003).

D. Philipsen, *We were the People: Voices from East Germany's Revolutionary Autumn of 1989* (Durham, NC, 1993).

G. Sanford (ed. and trans.), *Democratization in Poland 1988–90: Polish Voices* (Basingstoke, 1992).

S. Shirk, *The Political Logic of Economic Reform in China* (Berkeley, 1993).

V. Shue, *The Reach of the State: Sketches of the Chinese Body Politic* (Stanford, 1988).

R. G. Suny, *The Revenge of the Past: Nationalism, Revolution, and the Collapse of the Soviet Union* (Stanford, 1993).

R. L. Tökés, *Hungary's Negotiated Revolution: Economic Reform, Social Change, and Political Succession, 1957–1990* (Cambridge, 1996).

B. Wheaton and Z. Kavan, *The Velvet Revolution: Czechoslovakia, 1988–1991* (Boulder, 1992).

E. Wood, *Insurgent Collective Action and Civil War in El Salvador* (Cambridge, 1993).

S. Woodward, *Balkan Tragedy: Chaos and Dissolution after the Cold War* (Washington, DC, 1995).

EPILOGUE

G. Breslauer, *Gorbachev and Yeltsin as Leaders* (Cambridge, 2002).

C. Bukowski and B. Racz (eds.), *The Return of the Left in post-Communist States: Current Trends and Future Prospects* (Cheltenham, 1999).

M. Burawoy and K. Verdery (eds.), *Uncertain Transition: Ethnographies of Change in the post-Socialist World* (Lanham, 1999).

J. G. Castañeda, *Utopia Unarmed: The Latin American Left after the Cold War* (New York, 1993).

L. J. Cook, M. A. Orenstein and M. Rueschemeyer (eds.), *Left Parties and Social Policy in post-Communist Europe* (Boulder, 1999).

K. Dawisha and B. Parrott (eds.), *The Consolidation of Democracy in East-Central Europe* (Cambridge, 1997).

S. Eckstein (ed.), *Power and Popular Protest. Latin American Social Movements* (Berkeley, 2001).

G. Eyal, I. Szelényi and E. Townsley, *Making Capitalism without Capitalists:*

Class Formation and Elite Struggles in post-Communist Central Europe (London, 1998).

C. M. Hann (ed.), *Post-Socialism: Ideals, Ideologies and Practices in Eurasia* (London, 2002).

N. Henck, *Subcommander Marcos. The Man and the Mask* (Durham, NC, 2007).

A. Knight, *Spies without Cloaks: The KGB's Successors* (Princeton, 1996).

K. Louie, *Theorizing Chinese Masculinity* (Cambridge, 2002).

J. Nochlin, *Vanguard Revolutionaries in Latin America* (Boulder, 2003).

D. S. Palmer (ed.), *The Shining Path of Peru* (London, 1992).

P. Reddaway and D. Glinski, *The Tragedy of Russia's Reforms. Market Bolshevism against Democracy* (Washington, DC, 2001).

S. Shirk, *China. Fragile Superpower* (Oxford, 2007).

S. Stern (ed.), *Shining and Other Paths: War and Society in Peru, 1980–1995* (Durham, NC, 1998).

K. Verdery, *What was Socialism and What Comes Next?* (Princeton, 1996).

Index